Business Communication Essentials

Business Communication Essentials

FIFTH EDITION

Courtland L. Bovée

Professor of Business Communication
C. Allen Paul Distinguished Chair
Grossmont College

John V. Thill

Chairman and Chief Executive Officer
Global Communication Strategies

PEARSON

Boston   Columbus   Indianapolis   New York   San Francisco   Upper Saddle River
Amsterdam   Cape Town   Dubai   London   Madrid   Milan   Munich   Paris   Montreal   Toronto
Delhi   Mexico City   Sao Paulo   Sydney   Hong Kong   Seoul   Singapore   Taipei   Tokyo

Editorial Director: Sally Yagan
Director of Development: Stephen Deitmer
Editor in Chief: Eric Svendsen
Acquisitions Editor: James Heine
Editorial Project Manager: Karin Williams
Editorial Assistant: Jason Calcano
Director of Marketing: Patrice Jones
Marketing Manager: Nikki A. Jones
Marketing Assistant: Ian Gold
Senior Managing Editor: Judy Leale
Senior Production Project Manager:
  Karalyn Holland
Senior Operations Supervisor: Arnold Vila
Operations Specialist: Cathleen Petersen
Creative Director: Christy Mahon
Sr. Art Director/Design Supervisor: Janet Slowik

Interior Designer: Liz Harasymcuk
Cover Designer: Jodi Notowitz
Manager, Rights and Permissions: Hessa Albader
Cover Images: Matka Wariatka/Dreamstime and
  Imagebroker.net/SuperStock
Acquisitions Editor, Digital Learning & Assessment:
  Josh Keefe
Multimedia Product Manager: Cathi Profitko
Editorial Media Project Manager: Joan Waxman
Media Project Manager: Lisa Rinaldi
Full-Service Project Management: PreMediaGlobal, Inc.
Composition: PreMediaGlobal, Inc.
Printer/Binder: Courier/Kendallville
Cover Printer: Lehigh Phoenix
Text Font: Minion

Credits and acknowledgments borrowed from other sources and reproduced, with permission, in this textbook appear on pages 501–514 and 515–516.

Microsoft® and Windows® are registered trademarks of the Microsoft Corporation in the U.S.A. and other countries. Screen shots and icons reprinted with permission from the Microsoft Corporation. This book is not sponsored or endorsed by or affiliated with the Microsoft Corporation.

If you purchased this book within the United States or Canada you should be aware that it has been imported without the approval of the Publisher or the Author.

Many of the designations by manufacturers and seller to distinguish their products are claimed as trademarks. Where those designations appear in this book, and the publisher was aware of a trademark claim, the designations have been printed in initial caps or all caps.

Library of Congress Cataloging-in-Publication Data
Bovée, Courtland L.
  Business communication essentials / Courtland Bovée, John Thill.—5th ed.
    p. cm.
  Includes bibliographical references and index.
  ISBN 978-0-13-256480-9
  1. Business communication. 2. Business writing. 3. Business presentations. I. Thill, John V. II. Title.
  HF5718.B659 2012
  658.4'5—dc22

                                                                        2010040869

10 9 8 7 6 5 4 3 2

Prentice Hall
is an imprint of

www.pearsonhighered.com

ISBN-10:   0-13-256480-7
ISBN-13: 978-0-13-256480-9

Contents in Brief

Contents

Real-Time Updates—Learn More

Real-Time Updates "Learn More" is a unique feature you will see strategically located throughout the text, connecting you with dozens of carefully selected online media. These elements—categorized by the icons shown below representing podcasts, PDF files, articles/websites, videos, and PowerPoint presentations—complement the text's coverage by providing contemporary examples and valuable insights from successful professionals.

REAL-TIME UPDATES
Learn More by Reading This Article

REAL-TIME UPDATES
Learn More by Listening to This Podcast

REAL-TIME UPDATES
Learn More by Watching This Presentation

REAL-TIME UPDATES
Learn More by Reading This PDF

REAL-TIME UPDATES
Learn More by Watching This Video

Preface

MAJOR CHANGES AND IMPROVEMENTS IN THIS EDITION

Significant content additions
In addition to numerous updates throughout, the following sections are all new or substantially revised with new material:

- *Understanding Why Communication Matters (in Chapter 1)*
- *The Social Communication Model (in Chapter 1)*
- *The Advantages and Challenges of a Diverse Workforce, including Age Differences, Religious Differences, and Ability Differences (in Chapter 1)*
- *Guarding Against Information Overload (in Chapter 1)*
- *Characteristics of Effective Teams (in Chapter 2)*
- *Technologies for Collaborative Writing (in Chapter 2)*
- *Social Networks and Virtual Communities (in Chapter 2)*
- *Business Etiquette Online (in Chapter 2)*
- *Building Reader Interest with Storytelling Techniques (in Chapter 3)*
- *Designing Multimedia Documents (in Chapter 5)*
- *Using Electronic Media for Business Communication (in Chapter 6)* (new introduction to topic)
- *The Human Side of Electronic Communication (in Chapter 6)*
- *Compositional Modes for Electronic Media (in Chapter 6)*
- *Communicating on Networking, UGC, and Community Q&A Sites (in Chapter 6)*
  - *Social Networks*
    - *Business Communication Uses of Social Networks*
    - *Strategies for Business Communication on Social Networks*
  - *User-Generated Content Sites*
  - *Community Q&A Sites*
- *New two-page highlight feature: Business Communicators Innovating with Social Media (in Chapter 6)*
- *Announcing Good News (in Chapter 7)*
- *Giving Negative Performance Reviews (in Chapter 8) (substantially revised)*
- *Responding to Negative Information in a Social Media Environment (in Chapter 8)*
- *Online Monitoring Tools (in Chapter 10)*
- *Data Visualization (in Chapter 11)*
- *Ending with Clarity and Confidence (in Chapter 12)*
- *Choosing Structured or Free-Form Slides (in Chapter 12)*
- *Embracing the Backchannel (in Chapter 12)*
- *Finding the Ideal Opportunity in Today's Job Market (in Chapter 13)*
- *Writing the Story of You (in Chapter 13)*
- *Learning to Think Like an Employer (in Chapter 13)*
- *Translating Your General Potential into a Specific Solution for Each Employer (in Chapter 13)*
- *Taking the Initiative to Find Opportunities (in Chapter 13)*
- *Building Your Network (in Chapter 13) (substantially revised)*
- *Avoiding the Easily Avoidable Mistakes (in Chapter 13)*
- *Composing Your Résumé (in Chapter 13)* (revised with the latest advice on keywords)
- *Printing a Scannable Résumé (in Chapter 13)* (updated to reflect the decline of this format)
- *Creating an Online Résumé (in Chapter 13)*
- *Following Up After Submitting a Résumé (in Chapter 14)*

(continued)

Major Changes and Improvements in This Edition (continued)

The social media revolution	This edition includes up-to-date coverage of the social communication model that is redefining business communication and reshaping the relationships between companies and their stakeholders. Social media concepts and techniques are integrated throughout the book, from career planning to presentations. Here are some examples: ■ Social media questions, activities, and cases appear throughout the book, using Twitter, Facebook, and other media that have taken the business world by storm in the past couple of years. ■ More than 30 examples of business applications of social media are illustrated and annotated to explain how companies use these tools. ■ The social communication model is now covered in Chapter 1. ■ A new two-page feature in Chapter 6 highlights the innovative uses of social media by a variety of companies. ■ Social networking sites are now covered as a brief-message medium in Chapter 6. ■ The Twitter-enabled *backchannel*, which is revolutionizing electronic presentations, is covered in Chapter 12. ■ Social media tools are covered extensively in the career-planning Prologue and the two employment communication chapters (13 and 14).
Compositional modes for electronic media	For all the benefits they offer, social media and other innovations place new demands on business communicators. This edition introduces you to nine important modes of writing for electronic media.
Personal branding	As the workforce continues to evolve and with the employment likely to remain unstable for some time to come, taking control of your career is more important than ever. An important first step is clarifying and communicating your *personal brand*, a topic that is now addressed in the Prologue and carried through to the employment-message chapters.
Storytelling techniques	Storytelling might sound like an odd topic for a business communication course, but some of the most effective business messages, from advertising to proposals to personal branding, rely on storytelling techniques.
Full implementation of objective-driven learning	Every aspect of this new edition is organized by learning objectives, from the chapter content to the student activities in the textbook and online at mybcommlab.com, which makes it easier for you to study, practice, check your progress, and focus on those areas where you need a little extra work.
Deeper integration with mybcommlab	This optional online resource now offers even more ways to test your understanding of the concepts presented in every chapter, practice vital skills, and create customized study plans.
Multimedia resources	Extend your learning experience with unique *Real-Time Updates* "Learn More" media elements that connect you with dozens of handpicked videos, podcasts, and other items that complement chapter content.
New communication cases	Communication cases give you the opportunity to solve real-world communication challenges using the media skills you'll be expected to have in today's workplace; more than one-third of the cases are new in this edition.
New figures and more annotated model documents	More than 50 new figures provide examples of the latest trends in business communication. You can now learn from more than 60 annotated model documents, ranging from printed letters and reports to websites, blogs, and social networking sites. These examples feature many companies you probably recognize, including Adidas, Bigelow Tea, IBM, Patagonia, Red Bull, Segway, and Zappos.
Critique the Professionals	This new activity invites you to analyze an example of professional communication using the principles learned in each chapter.
Communication Matters	Communication skills are the single most important way you can advance your career prospects. This new chapter-opening feature offers thought-provoking ideas from successful professionals to help you grasp the essential value of business communication.

EXTEND THE VALUE OF YOUR TEXTBOOK WITH FREE MULTIMEDIA CONTENT

Business Communication Essentials's unique **Real-Time Updates** system automatically provides weekly content updates, including podcasts, PowerPoint presentations, online videos, PDF files, and articles. You can subscribe to updates chapter by chapter, so you get only the material that applies to the chapter you are studying. Access Real-Time Updates through **mybcommlab** (www.mybcommlab.com) or by visiting http://real-timeupdates.com/bce5.

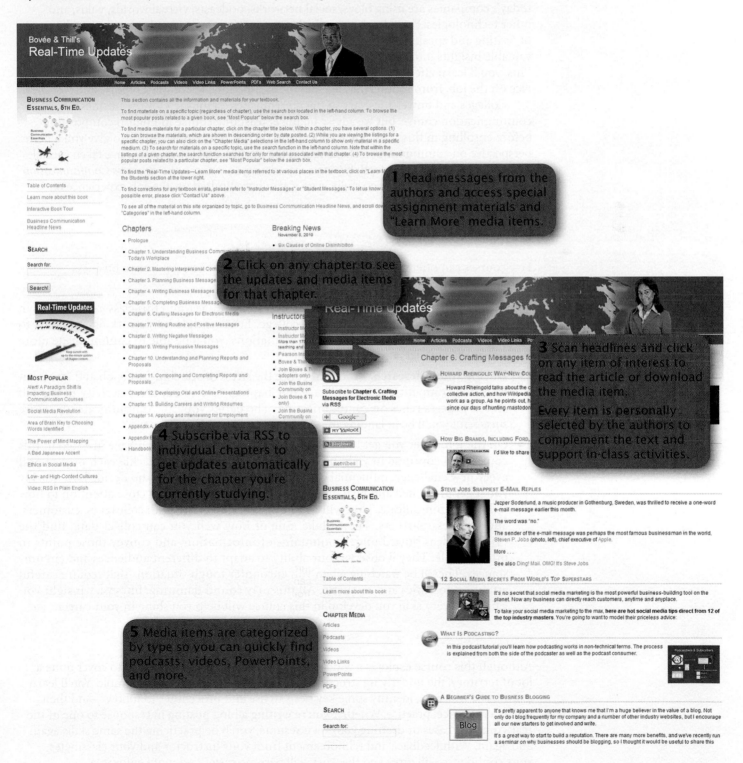

WHAT IS THE SINGLE MOST IMPORTANT STEP YOU CAN TAKE TO ENHANCE YOUR CAREER PROSPECTS?

No matter what profession you want to pursue, the ability to communicate will be an essential skill—and a skill that employers expect you to have when you enter the workforce. This course introduces you to the fundamental principles of business communication and gives you the opportunity to develop your communication skills. You'll discover how business communication differs from personal and social communication, and you'll see how today's companies are using blogs, social networks, podcasts, virtual worlds, wikis, and other technologies. You'll learn a simple three-step writing process that works for all types of writing and speaking projects, both in college and on the job. Along the way, you'll gain valuable insights into ethics, etiquette, listening, teamwork, and nonverbal communication. Plus, you'll learn effective strategies for the many types of communication challenges you'll face on the job, from routine messages about transactions to complex reports and websites.

Colleges and universities vary in the prerequisites established for the business communication course, but we advise taking at least one course in English composition before enrolling in this class. Some coursework in business studies will also give you a better perspective on communication challenges in the workplace. However, we have taken special care not to assume any in-depth business experience, so you can use *Business Communication Essentials*, Fifth Edition, successfully even if you have limited on-the-job experience or business coursework.

HOW THIS COURSE WILL HELP YOU

Few courses can offer the three-for-the-price-of-one value you get from a business communication class. Check out these benefits:

- **In your other classes.** The communication skills you learn in this class can help you in every other course you will take in college. From simple homework assignments to complicated team projects to class presentations, you'll be able to communicate more effectively with less time and effort.

- **During your job search.**   You can reduce the stress of searching for a job and stand out from the competition. As you'll see in Chapters 13 and 14, every activity in the job search process relies on communication. The better you can communicate, the more successful you'll be in landing interesting and rewarding work.

- **On the job.** After you get that great job, the time and energy you have invested in this course will continue to yield benefits year after year. As you tackle each project and every new challenge, influential company leaders—the people who decide how quickly you'll get promoted and how much you'll earn—will be paying close attention to how well you communicate. They will observe your interactions with colleagues, customers, and business partners. They'll take note of how well you can collect data, find the essential ideas buried under mountains of information, and convey those points to other people. They'll observe your ability to adapt to different audiences and circumstances. They'll be watching when you encounter tough situations that require careful attention to ethics and etiquette. All this may sound daunting, but every insight you gain and every skill you develop in this course will help you shine in your career.

HOW TO SUCCEED IN THIS COURSE

Although this course explores a wide range of message types and appears to cover quite a lot of territory, the underlying structure of the course is actually rather simple. You'll learn a few basic concepts, identify some key skills to use and procedures to follow—and then practice, practice, practice. Whether you're writing a blog posting in response to one of the real-company cases or drafting your own résumé, you'll be practicing the same skills again and again. With feedback and reinforcement from your instructor and your classmates, your confidence will grow and the work will become easier and more enjoyable.

The following sections offer advice on approaching each assignment, using your textbook, and taking advantage of some other helpful resources.

Approaching Each Assignment

In the spirit of practice and improvement, you will have a number of writing (and possibly speaking) assignments throughout this course. These suggestions will help you produce better results with less effort:

- **First, don't panic!** If the thought of writing a report or giving a speech sends a chill up your spine, you're not alone. Everybody feels that way when first learning business communication skills, and even experienced professionals can feel nervous about major projects. Keeping three points in mind will help. First, every project can be broken down into a series of small, manageable tasks. Don't let a big project overwhelm you; it's nothing more than a bunch of smaller tasks. Second, remind yourself that you have the skills you need to accomplish each task. As you move through the course, the assignments are carefully designed to match the skills you've developed up to that point. Third, if you feel panic creeping up on you, take a break and regain your perspective.

- **Focus on one task at a time.** A common mistake writers make is trying to organize and express their ideas while simultaneously worrying about audience reactions, grammar, spelling, formatting, page design, and a dozen other factors. Fight the temptation to do everything at once; otherwise, your frustration will soar and your productivity will plummet. In particular, don't worry about grammar, spelling, and word choices during your first draft. Concentrate on the organization of your ideas first, then the way you express those ideas, and then the presentation and production of your messages. Following the three-step writing process is an ideal way to focus on one task at a time in a logical sequence.

- **Give yourself plenty of time.** As with every other school project, putting things off to the last minute creates unnecessary stress. Writing and speaking projects in particular are much easier if you tackle them in small stages with breaks in between, rather than trying to get everything done in one frantic blast. Moreover, there will be instances when you simply get stuck on a project, and the best thing to do is walk away and give your mind a break. If you allow room for breaks in your schedule, you'll minimize the frustration and spend less time overall on your homework, too.

- **Step back and assess each project before you start.** The writing and speaking projects you'll have in this course cover a wide range of communication scenarios, and it's essential that you adapt your approach to each new challenge. Resist the urge to dive in and start writing without a plan. Ponder the assignment for a while, consider the various approaches you might take, and think carefully about your objectives before you start writing. Nothing is more frustrating than getting stuck halfway through because you're not sure what you're trying to say or you've wandered off track. Spend a little time planning, and you'll spend a lot less time writing.

- **Use the three-step writing process.** Those essential planning tasks are the first step in the three-step writing process, which you'll learn about in Chapter 3 and use throughout the course. This process has been developed and refined by professional writers with decades of experience and thousands of projects ranging from short blog posts to 500-page textbooks. It works, so take advantage of it.

- **Learn from the examples and model documents.** This textbook offers dozens of realistic examples of business messages, many with notes along the sides that explain strong and weak points. Study these and any other examples that your instructor provides. Learn what works and what doesn't work, then apply these lessons to your own writing.

- **Learn from experience.** Finally, learn from the feedback you get from your instructor and from other students. Don't take the criticism personally; your instructor and your classmates are commenting about the work, not about you. View every bit of feedback as an opportunity to improve.

Using This Textbook Package

This book and its accompanying online resources introduce you to the key concepts in business communication while helping you develop essential skills. As you read each chapter, start by studying the learning objectives. They will help you identify the most important concepts in the chapter and give you a feel for what you'll be learning.

Following the learning objectives, the "Communication Matters" feature offers helpful advice from a successful professional who uses the same skills you will be learning in the chapter.

As you work your way through the chapter, compare the advice given with the various examples, both the brief in-text examples and the standalone model documents. Also, keep an eye out for the "Real-Time Updates" elements in each chapter. The authors have selected these videos, podcasts, presentations, and other online media to provide informative and entertaining enhancements to the text material.

At the end of each chapter, "Learning Objectives: Check Your Progress" gives you the chance to quickly verify your grasp of important concepts. Following that, you'll see two sets of questions that help you test and apply your knowledge, and two sets of projects that help you practice and expand your skills. Chapters 6 through 14 also feature communication cases, which are more involved projects that require you to plan and complete a variety of messages and documents. All these activities are tagged by learning objective, so if you have any questions about the concepts you need to apply, just revisit that part of the chapter.

Several chapters have activities with downloadable media such as presentations and podcasts; if your instructor assigns these elements, follow the instructions in the text to locate the correct files. You can also download the two-page Quick Learning Guide to review the essential points from the chapter. And if you'd like some help on using Facebook and Twitter for business communication, we have created screencasts with helpful advice on these topics.

In addition to the 14 chapters of the text itself, here are some special features that will help you succeed in the course and on the job:

- **Prologue: Building a Career with Your Communication Skills.** This section (immediately following this Preface) helps you understand today's dynamic workplace, the steps you can take to adapt to the job market, and the importance of creating an employment portfolio and building your personal brand.

- **Handbook.** The Handbook of Grammar, Mechanics, and Usage (see page H-1) serves as a convenient reference of essential business English.

- **mybcommlab.** Take advantage of this unique resource to test your understanding of the concepts presented in every chapter. Each mybcommlab chapter offers assessment resources which include study plans, videos, mini-simulations, PowerPoints, Document Makeovers and critical thinking questions to reinforce chapter concepts.

- **Real-Time Updates.** You can use this unique newsfeed service to make sure you're always kept up to date on important topics. Plus, at strategic points in every chapter,

you will be directed to the Real-Time Updates website to get the latest information about specific subjects. To sign up via RSS, visit http://real-timeupdates.com/bce5. You can also access Real-Time Updates through mybcommlab.

- **Quick Learning Guides.** We prepared these downloadable, two-page study guides to help you study for exams or review important concepts whenever you need a quick refresher. They are available on the Real-Time Updates site at http://real-timeupdates.com.

- **Business Communication Web Search.** With our unique web search approach, you can quickly access more than 325 search engines. The tool uses a simple and intuitive interface engineered to help you find precisely what you want, whether it's PowerPoint files, Adobe Acrobat PDF files, Microsoft Word documents, Excel files, videos, or podcasts. Check it out at http://businesscommunicationblog.com/websearch.

- **Companion Website.** This text's Companion Website at www.pearsonhighered.com/bovee offers free access to ungraded Document Makeovers, an updated list of featured websites, and the "English-Spanish Audio Glossary of Business Terms."

FEEDBACK

We would appreciate hearing from you! Let us know what you think about this textbook by writing to college_marketing@prenhall.com. Please include "Feedback about Bovée/Thill BCE 5e" in the subject line. We review every comment we receive from students and use this feedback to make sure that future editions meet student needs in every way possible.

ABOUT THE AUTHORS

Courtland L. Bovée and John V. Thill have been leading textbook authors for more than two decades, introducing millions of students to the fields of business and business communication. Their award-winning texts are distinguished by proven pedagogical features, extensive selections of contemporary case studies, hundreds of real-life examples, engaging writing, thorough research, and the unique integration of print and electronic resources. Each new edition reflects the authors' commitment to continuous refinement and improvement, particularly in terms of modeling the latest practices in business and the use of technology.

Professor Bovée has 22 years of teaching experience at Grossmont College in San Diego, where he has received teaching honors and was accorded that institution's C. Allen Paul Distinguished Chair. Mr. Thill is a prominent communications consultant who has worked with organizations ranging from Fortune 500 multinationals to entrepreneurial start-ups. He formerly held positions with Pacific Bell and Texaco.

Courtland Bovée and John Thill were recently awarded proclamations from the Governor of Massachusetts for their life-long contributions to education and for their commitment to the summer youth baseball program that is sponsored by the Boston Red Sox.

ACKNOWLEDGMENTS

The fifth edition of *Business Communication Essentials* reflects the professional experience of a large team of contributors and advisors. We express our thanks to the many individuals whose valuable suggestions and constructive comments influenced the success of this book.

Reviewers of Previous Editions

Thank you to the following professors: Victoria Austin, Las Positas College; Faridah Awang, Eastern Kentucky University; Jeanette Baldridge, University of Maine at Augusta; Diana Baran, Henry Ford Community College; JoAnne Barbieri, Atlantic Cape Community College; Kristina Beckman, John Jay College; Judy Bello, Lander University; Carol Bibly, Triton College; Nancy Bizal, University of Southern Indiana; Yvonne Block, College of Lake County; Edna Boroski, Trident Technical College; Nelvia M. Brady, Trinity Christian College; Arlene Broeker, Lincoln University; David Brooks, Indiana University Southeast; Carol Brown, South Puget Sound Community College; Domenic Bruni, University of Wisconsin; Jeff Bruns, Bacone College; Gertrude L. Burge, University of Nebraska; Sharon Burton, Brookhaven College; Robert Cabral, Oxnard College; Dorothy Campbell, Brevard Community College; Linda Carr, University of West Alabama; Sharon Carson, St. Philip's College; Rick Carter, Seattle University; Dacia Charlesworth, Indiana University–Purdue University Fort Wayne; Jean Chenu, Genesee Community College; Connie Clark, Lane Community College; Jerrie Cleaver, Central Texas College; Clare Coleman, Temple University; M. Cotton, North Central Missouri College; Pat Cowherd, Campbellsville University; Pat Cuchens, University of Houston–Clear Lake; Walt Dabek, Post University; Cathy Daly, California State University–Sacramento; Linda Davis, Copiah–Lincoln Community College; Harjit Dosanjh, North Seattle Community College; Amy Drees, Defiance College; Lou Dunham, Spokane Falls Community College; Donna Everett, Morehead State University; Donna Falconer, Anoka–Ramsey Community College; Kate Ferguson Marsters, Gannon University; Darlynn Fink, Clarion University of Pennsylvania; Bobbi Fisher, University of Nebraska–Omaha; Laura Fitzwater, Community College of Philadelphia; Matthew Gainous, Ogeechee Technical College; Yolande Gardner, Lawson State Community College; Gina Genova, University of California–Santa Barbara; Lonny Gilbert, Central State University; Nancy Goehring, Monterey Peninsula College; Dawn Goellner, Bethel College; Robert Goldberg, Prince George's Community College; Jeffrey Goldberg, MassBay Community College; Helen Grattan, Des Moines Area Community College; Barbara Grayson, University of Arkansas at Pine Bluff; Deborah Griffin, University of Houston–Clear Lake; Alice Griswold, Clarke College; Bonnie Grossman, College of Charleston; Lisa Gueldenzoph, North Carolina A&T State University; Wally Guyot, Fort Hays State University; Valerie Harrison, Cuyamaca College; Tim Hartge, The University of Michigan–Dearborn; Richard Heiens, University of South Carolina–Aiken; Maureece Heinert, Sinte Gleska University; Leighanne Heisel, University of Missouri–St. Louis; Gary Helfand, University of Hawaii–West Oahu; Cynthia Herrera, Orlando Culinary Academy; Kathy Hill, Sam Houston State University; Pashia Hogan, Northeast State Tech Community College; Sarah Holmes, New England Institute of Technology; Ruth Hopkins Zajdel, Ohio University–Chillicothe; Michael Hricik, Westmoreland County Community College; Rebecca Hsiao, East Los Angeles College; Mary Ann Hurd, Sauk Valley Community College; Pat Hurley, Leeward Community College; Harold Hurry, Sam Houston State University; Marcia James, University of Wisconsin–Whitewater; Frank Jaster, Tulane University; Jonatan Jelen, Parsons The New School For Design; Irene Joanette Gallio, Western Nevada Community College; Mark Johnson, Rhodes State College; Joanne Kapp, Siena College; Jeanette A. Karjala, Winona State University; Christy L. Kinnion, Lenior Community College; Deborah Kitchin, City College of San Francisco; Lisa Kirby, North Carolina Wesleyan College; Claudia Kirkpatrick, Carnegie Mellon University; Betty Kleen, Nicholls State University; Fran Kranz, Oakland University; Jana Langemach, University of Nebraska–Lincoln; Joan Lantry, Jefferson Community College; Kim Laux, Saginaw Valley State University; Ruth Levy, Westchester Community College; Nancy Linger, Moraine Park Technical College; Jere Littlejohn, University of Mississippi; Dana Loewy, California State University–Fullerton; Jennifer Loney, Portland State University; Susan Long, Portland Community College; Sue Loomis, Maine Maritime Academy; Thomas Lowderbaugh, University of Maryland–College Park; Jayne Lowery, Jackson State Community College; Lloyd Matzner, University of Houston–Downtown; Ron McNeel, New Mexico State University at Alamogordo; Dr. Bill McPherson, Indiana University of Pennsylvania; Phyllis Mercer, Texas Woman's University; Donna Meyerholz, Trinidad State Junior College; Annie Laurie I. Meyers, Northampton Community College; Catherine "Kay" Michael, St. Edward's University; Kathleen Miller, University of Delaware; Gay Mills, Amarillo College; Julie Mullis, Wilkes Community College; Pamela Mulvey, Olney Central College; Jimidene Murphey, Clarendon College; Cindy Murphy, Southeastern Community College; Dipali Murti-Hali, California State University–Stanislaus; Shelley Myatt, University of Central Oklahoma; Cora Newcomb, Technical College of the Lowcountry; Ron Newman, Crafton Hills College; Linda Nitsch, Chadron State College; Leah Noonan, Laramie County Community College; Mabry O'Donnell, Marietta College; Diana Oltman, Central Washington University; Ranu Paik, Santa Monica College; Lauren Paisley, Genesee Community College; Patricia Palermo, Drew University; John Parrish, Tarrant County College; Diane Paul, TVI Community College; John T. Pauli, University of Alaska–Anchorage; Michael Pennell, University of Rhode Island; Melinda Phillabaum, Indiana University; Ralph Phillips, Geneva College; Laura Pohopien, Cal Poly Pomona; Diane Powell, Utah Valley State College; Christine Pye, California Lutheran University; Norma Pygon, Triton College; Dave Rambow, Wayland Baptist University; Richard David Ramsey, Southeastern Louisiana University; Charles Riley, Tarrant County College–Northwest Campus; Jim Rucker, Fort Hays State University; Dr. Suzan Russell, Lehman College; Calvin Scheidt, Tidewater Community College; Nancy Schneider, University of Maine at Augusta; Brian Sheridan, Mercyhurst College; Bob Shirilla, Colorado State University; Joyce Simmons, Florida State University; Gordon J. Simpson, SUNY Cobleskill; Jeff Smith, University of Southern California; Eunice Smith, Bismarck State College; Harvey Solganick, LeTourneau University–Dallas campus; Stephen Soucy, Santa Monica College; Linda Spargo, University of Mississippi; W. Dees Stallings, Park University; Angelique Stevens, Monroe Community College; Steven Stovall, Wilmington College; Alden Talbot, Weber State University; Michele Taylor, Ogeechee Technical College; Wilma Thomason, Mid-South Community College; Ed Thompson, Jefferson Community College; Lori Townsend, Niagara County Community College; Lani Uyeno, Leeward Community College; Wendy Van Hatten, Western Iowa Tech Community College; Jay Wagers, Richmond Community College; Jie Wang, University of Illinois at Chicago; Chris Ward, The University of Findlay; Dorothy Warren, Middle Tennessee State University; Glenda Waterman, Concordia University; Kellie Welch, Jefferson Community College; Mathew Williams, Clover Park Technical College; Beth Williams, Stark State College of Technology; Brian Wilson, College of Marin; Sandra D. Young, Orangeburg–Calhoun Technical College; Kathryn J. Lee, University of Cincinnati; Sylvia Beaver Perez, Nyack College; Ann E. Tippett, Monroe Community College; Camille Girardi-Levy, Siena College; Cynthia Drexel, Western State College of Colorado; Edgar Dunson Johnson III, Augusta State University; Danielle Scane, Orange Coast College; Lynda K. Fuller, Wilmington University; Lydia E. Anderson, Fresno City College; Anita Leffel, The University of Texas, San Antonio.

Reviewers of "Document Makeover" Feature

We sincerely thank the following reviewers for their assistance with the Document Makeover feature: Lisa Barley, Eastern Michigan University; Marcia Bordman, Gallaudet University; Jean Bush-Bacelis, Eastern Michigan University; Bobbye Davis, Southern Louisiana University; Cynthia Drexel, Western State College of Colorado; Kenneth Gibbs, Worcester State College; Ellen Leathers, Bradley University; Diana McKowen, Indiana University; Bobbie Nicholson, Mars Hill College; Andrew Smith, Holyoke Community College; Jay Stubblefield, North Carolina Wesleyan College; Dawn Wallace, Southeastern Louisiana University.

Reviewers of Model Documents

The many model documents in the text and their accompanying annotations received invaluable review from Dacia Charlesworth, Indiana University–Purdue University Fort Wayne; Diane Todd Bucci, Robert Morris University; Estelle Kochis, Suffolk County Community College; Sherry Robertson, Arizona State University; Nancy Goehring, Monterey Peninsula College; James Hatfield, Florida Community College at Jacksonville; Avon Crismore, Indiana University.

Personal Acknowledgments

We wish to extend a heartfelt thanks to our many friends, acquaintances, and business associates who provided materials or agreed to be interviewed so that we could bring the real world into the classroom.

A very special acknowledgment goes to George Dovel, whose superb writing skills, distinguished background, and wealth of business experience assured this project of clarity and completeness. Also, recognition and thanks to Jackie Estrada for her outstanding skills and excellent attention to details. Her creation of the "Peak Performance Grammar and Mechanics" material is especially noteworthy. Jill Gardner's professionalism and keen eye for quality were invaluable.

We also feel it is important to acknowledge and thank the Association for Business Communication, an organization whose meetings and publications provide a valuable forum for the exchange of ideas and for professional growth.

Additionally, we would like to thank the supplement authors who prepared material for this new edition. They include: Gina Genova, University of California, Santa Barbara; Jackie Estrada, University of California, San Diego; Lori Cerreto; Jay Stubblefield, North Carolina Wesleyan College; Myles Hassell, University of New Orleans; Gordon Laws at PreMediaGlobal; Luz Costa; and the teams at ANSRSource.

This book is dedicated to you and the many thousands of other students who have used this book in years past. We appreciate the opportunity to play a role in your education, and we wish you success and satisfaction in your studies and in your career.

Courtland L. Bovée
John V. Thill

Prologue

Building a Career with Your Communication Skills

USING THIS COURSE TO HELP LAUNCH YOUR CAREER

This course will help you develop vital communication skills that you'll use throughout your career—and those skills can help you launch an interesting and rewarding career, too. This brief prologue sets the stage by helping you understand today's dynamic workplace, the steps you can take to adapt to the job market, and the importance of creating an employment portfolio and building your personal brand. Take a few minutes to read it while you think about the career you hope to create for yourself.

UNDERSTANDING TODAY'S DYNAMIC WORKPLACE

Social, political, and financial events continue to change workplace conditions from year to year, so the job market you read about this year might not be the same market you try to enter a year or two from now. However, you can count on a few forces that are likely to affect your entry into the job market and your career success in years to come:[1]

- **Unpredictability.** Your career probably won't be as stable as careers were in your parents' generation. In today's business world, your career will likely be affected by globalization, mergers and acquisitions, short-term mentality driven by the demands of stockholders, ethical upheavals, and the relentless quest for lower costs. On the plus side, new opportunities, new companies, and even entire industries can appear almost overnight. So while your career might not be as predictable as careers used to be, it could well be more of an adventure.

- **Flexibility.** As companies try to become more agile in a globalized economy, many employees—sometimes of their choice and sometimes not—are going solo and setting up shop as independent contractors. Innovations in electronic communication and social media will continue to spur the growth of *virtual organizations* and *virtual teams*, in which independent contractors and companies of various sizes join forces for long- or short-term projects, often without formal employment arrangements.

- **Economic globalization.** Commerce across borders has been going on for thousands of years, but the volume of international business has roughly tripled in the past 30 years. One significant result is *economic globalization*, the increasing integration and interdependence of national economies around the world. Just as companies now compete across borders, as an employee or independent contractor you also compete globally. This situation can be disruptive and traumatic in some instances, but it also creates opportunities.

- **Growth of small business.** Small businesses employ about half of the private-sector workforce in this country and create somewhere between two-thirds and three-quarters of new jobs, so chances are good that you'll work for a small firm at some point.

What do all these forces mean to you? First, take charge of your career—and stay in charge of it. Understand your options, have a plan, and don't count on others to watch out for your future. Second, as you will learn throughout this course, understanding your audience is key to successful communication, so it is essential for you to understand how employers view today's job market.

How Employers View Today's Job Market

From an employer's perspective, the employment process is always a question of balance. Maintaining a stable workforce can improve practically every aspect of business performance, yet many employers want the flexibility to shrink and expand payrolls as business conditions change. Employers obviously want to attract the best talent, but the best talent is more expensive and more vulnerable to offers from competitors, so there are always financial trade-offs to consider.

Employers also struggle with the ups and downs of the economy. When unemployment is low, the balance of power shifts to employees, and employers have to compete in order to attract and keep top talent. When unemployment is high, the power shifts back to employers, who can afford to be more selective and less accommodating. In other words, pay attention to the economy; at times you can be more aggressive in your demands, but, at other times, you need to be more accommodating.

Many employers now fill some labor needs by hiring temporary workers or engaging contractors on a project-by-project basis. Many U.S. employers are now also more willing to move jobs to cheaper labor markets outside the country and to recruit globally to fill positions in the United States. Both trends have stirred controversy, especially in the technology sector, as U.S. firms recruit top engineers and scientists from other countries while shifting mid- and low-range jobs to India, China, Russia, the Philippines, and other countries with lower wage structures.[2]

In summary, companies view employment as a complex business decision with lots of variables to consider. To make the most of your potential, regardless of the career path you pursue, you need to view employment in the same way.

What Employers Look For in Job Applicants

Given the complex forces in the contemporary workplace and the unrelenting pressure of global competition, what are employers looking for in the candidates they hire? The short answer: a lot. Like all "buyers," companies want to get as much as they can for the money they spend. The better you can present yourself as the ideal candidate, the better your chances are of getting a crack at the most exciting opportunities.

Specific expectations vary by profession and position, of course, but virtually all employers look for the following general skills and attributes:[3]

- **Communication skills.** This item isn't listed first because you're reading a business communication textbook. Communication is listed first because it is far and away the most commonly mentioned skill set when employers are asked about what they look for in employees. Improving your communication skills will help in every aspect of your professional life.

- **Interpersonal and team skills.** You will have many individual responsibilities on the job, but chances are you won't work all alone very often. Learn to work with others—and help them succeed as you succeed.

- **Intercultural and international awareness and sensitivity.** Successful employers tend to be responsive to diverse workforces, markets, and communities, and they look for employees with the same outlook.

- **Data collection, analysis, and decision-making skills.** Employers want people who know how to identify information needs, find the necessary data, convert the data into useful knowledge, and make sound decisions.

- **Computer and electronic media skills.** Today's workers need to know how to use common office software and to communicate using a wide range of electronic media.

- **Time and resource management.** If you've had to juggle multiple priorities during college, consider that great training for the business world. Your ability to plan projects and manage the time and resources available to you will make a big difference on the job.

- **Flexibility and adaptability.** Stuff happens, as they say. Employees who can roll with the punches and adapt to changing business priorities and circumstances will go further (and be happier) than employees who resist change.

- **Professionalism.** Professionalism is the quality of performing at the highest possible level and conducting oneself with confidence, purpose, and pride. True professionals strive to excel, continue to hone their skills and build their knowledge, are dependable and accountable, demonstrate a sense of business etiquette, make ethical decisions, show loyalty and commitment, don't give up when things get tough, and maintain a positive outlook.

ADAPTING TO TODAY'S JOB MARKET

Adapting to the workplace is a lifelong process of seeking the best fit between what you want to do and what employers (or clients, if you work independently) are willing to pay you to do. It's important to know what you want to do, what you have to offer, and how to make yourself more attractive to employers.

What Do You Want to Do?

Economic necessities and the vagaries of the marketplace will influence much of what happens in your career, of course; nevertheless, it's wise to start your employment search by examining your values and interests. Identify what you want to do first, then see whether you can find a position that satisfies you at a personal level while also meeting your financial needs. Consider these questions:

- **What would you like to do every day?** Research occupations that interest you. Find out what people really do every day. Ask friends, relatives, alumni from your school, and contacts in your social networks. Read interviews with people in various professions to get a sense of what their careers are like.
- **How would you like to work?** Consider how much independence you want on the job, how much variety you like, and whether you prefer to work with products, machines, people, ideas, figures, or some combination thereof.
- **How do your financial goals fit with your other priorities?** For instance, many high-paying jobs involve a lot of stress, sacrifices of time with family and friends, and frequent travel or relocation. If location, lifestyle, intriguing work, or other factors are more important to you, you may well have to sacrifice some level of pay to achieve them.
- **Have you established some general career goals?** For example, do you want to pursue a career specialty such as finance or manufacturing, or do you want to gain experience in multiple areas with an eye toward upper management?
- **What sort of corporate culture are you most comfortable with?** Would you be happy in a formal hierarchy with clear reporting relationships? Or do you prefer less structure? Teamwork or individualism? Do you like a competitive environment?

Filling out the assessment in Table 1 on the next page might help you get a clearer picture of the nature of work you would like to pursue in your career.

What Do You Have to Offer?

Knowing what you want to do is one thing. Knowing what a company is willing to pay you to do is another thing entirely. You may already have a good idea of what you can offer employers. If not, some brainstorming can help you identify your skills, interests, and characteristics. Start by jotting down 10 achievements you're proud of, and think carefully about what specific skills these achievements demanded of you. For example, leadership skills, speaking ability, and artistic talent may have helped you coordinate a successful class project. As you analyze your achievements, you may well begin to recognize a pattern of skills. Which of them might be valuable to potential employers?

Next, look at your educational preparation, work experience, and extracurricular activities. What do your knowledge and experience qualify you to do? What have you learned from volunteer work or class projects that could benefit you on the job? Have you held any offices, won any awards or scholarships, mastered a second language? What skills have you developed in nonbusiness situations that could transfer to a business position?

Take stock of your personal characteristics. Are you aggressive, a born leader? Or would you rather follow? Are you outgoing, articulate, great with people? Or do you prefer working alone? Make a list of what you believe are your four or five most important qualities. Ask a relative or friend to rate your traits as well.

If you're having difficulty figuring out your interests, characteristics, or capabilities, consult your college career center. Many campuses administer a variety of tests that can help you identify interests, aptitudes, and personality traits. These tests won't reveal your "perfect" job, but they'll help you focus on the types of work best suited to your personality.

TABLE 1 Career Self-Assessment				
Activity or Situation	**Strongly Agree**	**Agree**	**Disagree**	**No Preference**
1. I want to work independently.	_____	_____	_____	_____
2. I want variety in my work.	_____	_____	_____	_____
3. I want to work with people.	_____	_____	_____	_____
4. I want to work with technology.	_____	_____	_____	_____
5. I want physical work.	_____	_____	_____	_____
6. I want mental work.	_____	_____	_____	_____
7. I want to work for a large organization.	_____	_____	_____	_____
8. I want to work for a nonprofit organization.	_____	_____	_____	_____
9. I want to work for a small business.	_____	_____	_____	_____
10. I want to work for a service business.	_____	_____	_____	_____
11. I want to start or buy a business someday.	_____	_____	_____	_____
12. I want regular, predictable work hours.	_____	_____	_____	_____
13. I want to work in a city location.	_____	_____	_____	_____
14. I want to work in a small town or suburb.	_____	_____	_____	_____
15. I want to work in another country.	_____	_____	_____	_____
16. I want to work outdoors.	_____	_____	_____	_____
17. I want to work in a structured environment.	_____	_____	_____	_____
18. I want to avoid risk as much as possible.	_____	_____	_____	_____
19. I want to enjoy my work, even if that means making less money.	_____	_____	_____	_____
20. I want to become a high-level corporate manager	_____	_____	_____	_____

How Can You Make Yourself More Valuable?

While you're figuring out what you want from a job and what you can offer an employer, you can take positive steps now toward building your career. First, look for volunteer projects, temporary jobs, freelance work, or internships that will help expand your experience base and skill set.[4] You can look for freelance projects on Craigslist (www.craigslist.org) and numerous other websites; some of these jobs have only nominal pay, but they do provide an opportunity for you to display your skills.

Also consider applying your talents to *crowdsourcing* projects, in which companies and nonprofit organizations invite the public to contribute solutions to various challenges. For example, Fellowforce (www.fellowforce.com) posts projects involving advertising, business writing, photography, graphic design, programming, strategy development, and other skills.[5] Even if your contributions aren't chosen, you still have developed solutions to real business problems that you can show to potential employers as examples of your work.

These opportunities help you gain valuable experience and relevant contacts, provide you with important references and work samples for your *employment portfolio*, and help you establish your *personal brand* (see the following sections).

Second, learn more about the industry or industries in which you want to work and stay on top of new developments. Join networks of professional colleagues and friends who can help you keep up with trends and events. Many professional societies have student chapters or offer students discounted memberships. Take courses and pursue other educational or life experiences that would be difficult while working full time.

For more ideas and advice on planning your career, check out the resources listed in Table 2.

Building an Employment Portfolio

Employers want proof that you have the skills to succeed on the job, but even if you don't have much relevant work experience, you can use your college classes to assemble that proof. Simply create and maintain an *employment portfolio*, which is a collection of projects

TABLE 2   Career Planning Resources

Resource	URL
Career Rocketeer	www.careerrocketeer.com
The Creative Career	http://thecreativecareer.com
Brazen Careerist	www.brazencareerist.com
Daily Career Connection	http://dailycareerconnection.com
The Career Key	http://careerkey.blogspot.com
Rise Smart	www.risesmart.com/risesmart/blog
Women's Leadership Blog	http://blog.futurewomenleaders.net/blog
The Career Doctor	www.careerdoctor.org/career-doctor-blog

that demonstrate your skills and knowledge. You can create a *print portfolio* and an
e-portfolio; both can help with your career effort. A print portfolio gives you something
tangible to bring to interviews, and it lets you collect project results that might not be easy
to show online, such as a handsomely bound report.

An e-portfolio is a multimedia presentation of your skills and experiences.[6] Think of it
as a website that contains your résumé, work samples, letters of recommendation, relevant
videos or podcasts you have recorded, blog posts and articles you may have written, and
other information about you and your skills. If you have set up a *life stream* (a real-time
aggregation of your content creation, online interests, and social media interactions) that is
professionally focused, consider adding that to your e-portfolio. Be creative. For example, a
student who was pursuing a degree in meteorology added a video clip of himself delivering
a weather forecast.[7] The portfolio can be burned on a CD or DVD for physical distribution
or, more commonly, it can be posted online—whether it's a personal website, your college's
site (if student pages are available), a specialized portfolio hosting site such as Behance
(www.behance.com), or a résumé hosting site such as VisualCV (www.visualcv.com) that
offers multimedia résumés. To see a selection of student e-portfolios from colleges around
the United States, go to http://real-timeupdates.com/bce5, click on "Student Assignments,"
and then click on "Prologue" to locate the link to student e-portfolios.

Throughout this course, pay close attention to the assignments marked "Portfolio
Builder" (they start in Chapter 6). These items will make particularly good samples of not
only your communication skills but also your ability to understand and solve business-
related challenges. By combining these projects with samples from your other courses, you
can create a compelling portfolio by the time you're ready to start interviewing. Your portfolio is also a great resource for writing your résumé because it reminds you of all the great
work you've done over the years. Moreover, you can continue to refine and expand your
portfolio throughout your career; many professionals use e-portfolios to advertise their services. For example, Evan Eckard, a specialist in web design, marketing, and branding, promotes his capabilities by showing a range of successful projects in his online portfolio,
which you can view at www.evaneckard.com.

As you assemble your portfolio, collect anything that shows your ability to perform,
whether it's in school, on the job, or in other venues. However, you *must* check with
employers before including any items that you created while you were an employee and
check with clients before including any *work products* (anything you wrote, designed, programmed, and so on) they purchased from you. Many business documents contain confidential information that companies don't want distributed to outside audiences.

For each item you add to your portfolio, write a brief description that helps other
people understand the meaning and significance of the project. Include such items as
these:

- **Background.** Why did you undertake this project? Was it a school project, a work
  assignment, or something you did on your own initiative?
- **Project objectives.** Explain the project's goals, if relevant.

- **Collaborators.** If you worked with others, be sure to mention that and discuss team dynamics if appropriate. For instance, if you led the team or worked with others long distance as a virtual team, point that out.

- **Constraints.** Sometimes the most impressive thing about a project is the time or budget constraints under which it was created. If such constraints apply to a project, consider mentioning them in a way that doesn't sound like an excuse for poor quality. If you had only one week to create a website, for example, you might say that "One of the intriguing challenges of this project was the deadline; I had only one week to design, compose, test, and publish this material."

- **Outcomes.** If the project's goals were measurable, what was the result? For example, if you wrote a letter soliciting donations for a charitable cause, how much money did you raise?

- **Learning experience.** If appropriate, describe what you learned during the course of the project.

Keep in mind that the portfolio itself is a communication project too, so be sure to apply everything you'll learn in this course about effective communication and good design. Assume that every potential employer will find your e-portfolio site (even if you don't tell them about it), so don't include anything that could come back to haunt you. Also, if you have anything embarrassing on Facebook, MySpace, or any other social networking site, remove it immediately.

To get started, first check with the career center at your college; many schools now offer e-portfolio systems for their students. (Some schools now require e-portfolios, so you may already be building one.) You can also find plenty of advice online; search for "e-portfolio," "student portfolio," or "professional portfolio." Finally, consider a book such as *Portfolios for Technical and Professional Communicators*, by Herb J. Smith and Kim Haimes-Korn. This book is intended for communication specialists, but it offers great advice for anyone wanting to create a compelling employment portfolio.

Building Your Personal Brand

Products and companies have brands that represent collections of certain attributes, such as the safety emphasis of Volvo cars, the performance emphasis of BMW, or the luxury emphasis of Cadillac. Similarly, when people who know you think about you, they have a particular set of qualities in mind based on your professionalism, your priorities, and the various skills and attributes you have developed over the years. Perhaps without even being conscious of it, you have created a **personal brand** for yourself.

As you plan the next stage of your career, start managing your personal brand deliberately. Branding specialist Mohammed Al-Taee defines personal branding succinctly as "a way of clarifying and communicating what makes you different and special."[8]

You can learn more about personal branding from the sources listed in Table 3, and you will have multiple opportunities to plan and refine your personal brand during this course. For example, Chapter 6 offers tips on business applications of social media, which are key

TABLE 3 Personal Branding Resources

Resource	URL
Personal Branding Blog	www.personalbrandingblog.com
Mohammed Al-Taee	http://altaeeblog.com
Brand Yourself	http://blog.brand-yourself.com
Krishna De	www.krishnade.com/blog
Cube Rules	http://cuberules.com
Jibber Jobber	www.jibberjobber.com/blog
The Engaging Brand	http://theengagingbrand.typepad.com
Brand-Yourself	http://blog.brand-yourself.com

to personal branding, and Chapters 13 and 14 guide you through the process of creating a résumé, building your network, and presenting yourself in interviews. To get you started, here are the basics of a successful personal branding strategy:[9]

- **Figure out the "story of you."** Simply put, where have you been in life, and where are you going? Every good story has dramatic tension that pulls readers in and makes them wonder what will happen next. Where is your story going next?

- **Clarify your professional theme.** Volvos, BMWs, and Cadillacs can all get you from Point A to Point B in safety, comfort, and style—but each brand emphasizes some attributes more than others to create a specific image in the minds of potential buyers. Similarly, you want to be seen as something more than just an accountant, a supervisor, a salesperson. What will your theme be? Brilliant strategist? Hard-nosed, get-it-done tactician? Technical guru? Problem solver? Creative genius? Inspirational leader?

- **Reach out and connect.** Major corporations spread the word about their brands with multimillion-dollar advertising campaigns. You can promote your brand for free or close to it. The secret is networking, which you'll learn more about in Chapter 13. You build your brand by connecting with like-minded people, sharing information, demonstrating skills and knowledge, and helping others succeed.

- **Deliver on your brand's promise—every time, all the time.** When you promote a brand, you make a promise—a promise that whoever buys that brand will get the benefits you are promoting. All of this planning and communication is of no value if you fail to deliver on the promises that your branding efforts make. Conversely, when you deliver quality results time after time, your talents and your professionalism will speak for you.

We wish you great success in this course and in your career!

Business Communication Foundations

Understanding Business Communication in Today's Workplace

LEARNING OBJECTIVES

After studying this chapter, you will be able to

1 Explain the importance of effective communication to your career and to the companies where you will work

2 Describe the communication skills employers will expect you to have and the nature of communicating in an organization using an audience-centered approach

3 Describe the communication process model and the ways that social media are changing the nature of business communication

4 Define ethics, explain the difference between an ethical dilemma and an ethical lapse, and list six guidelines for making ethical communication choices

5 Explain how cultural diversity affects business communication and describe the steps you can take to communicate more effectively across cultural boundaries

6 List four general guidelines for using communication technology effectively

PEARSON
mybcommlab   Access interactive videos, simulations, sample documents, Document Makeovers, and assessment quizzes in Chapter 1 of mybcommlab.com for mastery of this chapter's objectives.

COMMUNICATION *Matters*

" The only surprise about the stunning level of vitriol Facebook's recent changes have sparked is that, once again, Facebook is surprised. "
—Chris O'Brien, Technology columnist, *San Jose Mercury News*

Facebook, whose CEO Mark Zuckerberg is shown here, has made tremendous contributions to communication technology, but some industry observers and users criticize the company's own communication practices.

The irony is impossible to ignore. Facebook, the company whose social networking technology helps hundreds of millions of people around the world communicate more efficiently, repeatedly sparks criticism for its own communication practices. The anger Chris O'Brien writes about stems from perceptions about three aspects of communication: the way Facebook uses members' personal information, the company's failure to solicit input from users before making major changes, and its failure to explain those changes to users in a clear and timely fashion.[1] Whether or not one agrees with these criticisms, they emphasize the vital importance of communication in every business. Facebook is a business built on the very idea of communication, but companies in every industry need effective communication to connect employees, customers, and communities.

UNDERSTANDING WHY COMMUNICATION MATTERS

Communication is the process of transferring information and meaning between *senders* and *receivers*, using one or more written, oral, visual, or electronic channels. The essence of communication is sharing—providing data, information, insights, and inspiration in an exchange that benefits both you and the people with whom you are communicating.[2]

You will invest a lot of time and energy in this course to develop your communication skills, so it's fair to ask whether it will be worthwhile. This section outlines the many ways in which good communication skills are critical for your career and for any company you join.

Communication Is Important to Your Career

No matter what career path you pursue, communication skills will be essential to your success at every stage. You can have the greatest ideas in the world, but they're no good to your company or your career if you can't express them clearly and persuasively. Some jobs, such as sales and customer support, are primarily about communicating. In fields such as engineering or finance, you often need to share complex ideas with executives, customers, and colleagues, and your ability to connect with people outside your field can be as important as your technical expertise. If you have the entrepreneurial urge, you will need to communicate with a wide range of audiences, from investors, bankers, and government regulators to employees, customers, and business partners.

As you take on leadership and management roles, communication becomes even more important. The higher you rise in an organization, the less time you will spend using the technical skills of your particular profession and the more time you will spend communicating. Top executives spend most of their time communicating, and businesspeople who can't communicate well don't stand much chance of reaching the top.

In fact, improving your communication skills may be the single most important step you can take in your career. The world is full of good marketing strategists, good accountants, good engineers, and good attorneys—but it is not full of good communicators. View this as an opportunity to stand out from your competition in the job market.

Many employers express frustration at the poor communication skills of many employees—particularly recent college graduates who haven't yet learned how to adapt their communication styles to a professional business environment. If you learn to write well, speak well, listen well, and recognize the appropriate way to communicate in any situation, you'll gain a major advantage that will serve you throughout your career.[3]

This course teaches you how to send and receive information more effectively and helps you improve your communication skills through practice in an environment that provides honest, constructive criticism. You will discover how to collaborate in teams, listen effectively, master nonverbal communication, and participate in productive meetings. You'll learn about communicating across cultural boundaries. You'll learn a three-step process that helps you write effective business messages, and you'll get specific tips for crafting a variety of business messages using a wide range of media, from social networks to blogs to online presentations. Develop these skills, and you'll start your business career with a clear competitive advantage.

Communication Is Important to Your Company

Aside from the personal benefits, communication should be important to you because it is important to your company. Effective communication helps businesses in numerous ways. It provides:[4]

- Closer ties with important communities in the marketplace
- Opportunities to influence conversations, perceptions, and trends
- Ability to "humanize" otherwise impersonal business organizations
- Faster problem solving
- Stronger decision making
- Increased productivity
- Steadier work flow

- More compelling promotional messages
- Enhanced professional images and stronger brands

> ## COMMUNICATION *Matters*
>
> Good communication has clear financial advantages, too. Companies that communicate well significantly outperform those that communicate poorly.[5]

What Makes Business Communication Effective?

Effective communication strengthens the connections between a company and all of its **stakeholders**, those groups affected in some way by the company's actions: customers, employees, shareholders, suppliers, neighbors, the community, the nation, and the world as a whole.[6] Conversely, when communication breaks down, the results can range from time wasting to tragic.

To make your communication efforts as effective as possible, focus on making them practical, factual, concise, clear, and persuasive:

- **Provide practical information.** Give recipients useful information, whether it's to help them perform a desired action or understand a new company policy.
- **Give facts rather than vague impressions.** Use concrete language, specific detail, and information that is clear, convincing, accurate, and ethical. Even when an opinion is called for, present compelling evidence to support your conclusion.

Effective messages are practical, factual, concise, clear, and persuasive.

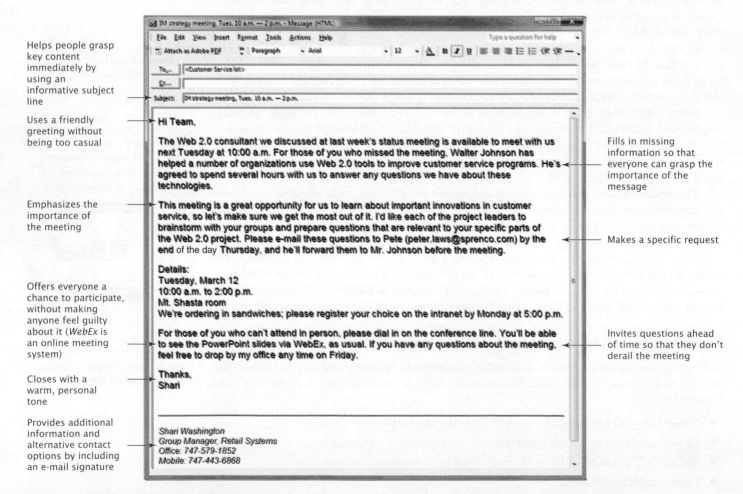

Figure 1.1 Effective Business Communication
Notice how this message is probably more formal and "professional sounding" than the messages you send to your friends and family. Except for short messages between close colleagues and team members, most businesses will expect you to communicate with a style that is more formal than the style to which you are currently accustomed.

- **Present information in a concise, efficient manner.** Concise messages show respect for people's time, and they increase the chances of a positive response.
- **Clarify expectations and responsibilities.** Craft messages to generate a specific response from a specific audience. When appropriate, clearly state what you expect from audience members or what you can do for them.
- **Offer compelling, persuasive arguments and recommendations.** Show your readers precisely how they will benefit from responding to your message the way you want them to.

Keep these five important characteristics in mind as you review Figure 1.1. You might notice that it is more formal and "professional sounding" than many of the messages you send now. Employers expect you to be able to communicate with a similar style.

COMMUNICATING IN TODAY'S GLOBAL BUSINESS ENVIRONMENT

You've been communicating your entire life, of course, but if you don't have a lot of work experience yet, meeting the expectations of a professional environment might require some adjustment. This section offers a brief look at the skills that employers will expect you to have, the nature of communication in an organizational environment, and the importance of adopting an audience-centered approach.

Understanding What Employers Expect from You

Given the importance of communication in business, employers expect you to be competent at a wide range of communication tasks:[7]

- Organizing ideas and information logically and completely
- Expressing yourself coherently and persuasively in a variety of media
- Constructing compelling narratives—telling stories, in other words—to gain acceptance for important ideas
- Evaluating data and information critically to know what you can and cannot trust
- Actively listening to others
- Communicating effectively with people from diverse backgrounds and experiences
- Using communication technologies effectively and efficiently
- Following accepted standards of grammar, spelling, and other aspects of high-quality writing and speaking
- Adapting your messages and communication styles to specific audiences and situations
- Communicating in a civilized manner that reflects contemporary expectations of business etiquette
- Communicating ethically, even when choices aren't crystal clear
- Respecting the confidentiality of private company information
- Following applicable laws and regulations
- Managing your time wisely and using resources efficiently

This is a long list, to be sure, but all these skills can be practiced and developed over time. Start by taking advantage of the opportunities you will have throughout this course, and you'll be well on your way to making a successful transition to the professional environment.

Communicating in an Organizational Context

In addition to having the proper skills, you need to learn how to apply those skills in the business environment, which can be quite different from the social and scholastic environments you are accustomed to. Every company has a unique communication system that connects people within the organization and connects the organization to the outside world. The "system" in this broad sense is a complex combination of communication channels (such as the Internet and department meetings), company policies, the organizational structure, and personal relationships.

2 **LEARNING OBJECTIVE**
Describe the communication skills employers will expect you to have and the nature of communicating in an organization using an audience-centered approach

You will need to adjust your communication habits to the more formal demands of business and the unique environment of your company.

To succeed in a job you need to figure out how your company's system operates and how to use it to gather information you need and to share information you want others to have. For example, one company might rely heavily on instant messaging, social networks, and blogs that are used in an open, conversational way by everyone in the company. In contrast, another company might use a more rigid, formal approach, in which information and instructions are passed down from top managers, and employees are expected to follow the "chain of command" when seeking or distributing information.

Adopting an Audience-Centered Approach

Focus on the needs of your audiences to make your messages more effective.

Successful business professionals take an **audience-centered approach** to their communication, meaning that they focus on understanding and meeting the needs of their audiences (see Figure 1.2). Providing the information your audiences need is obviously an important

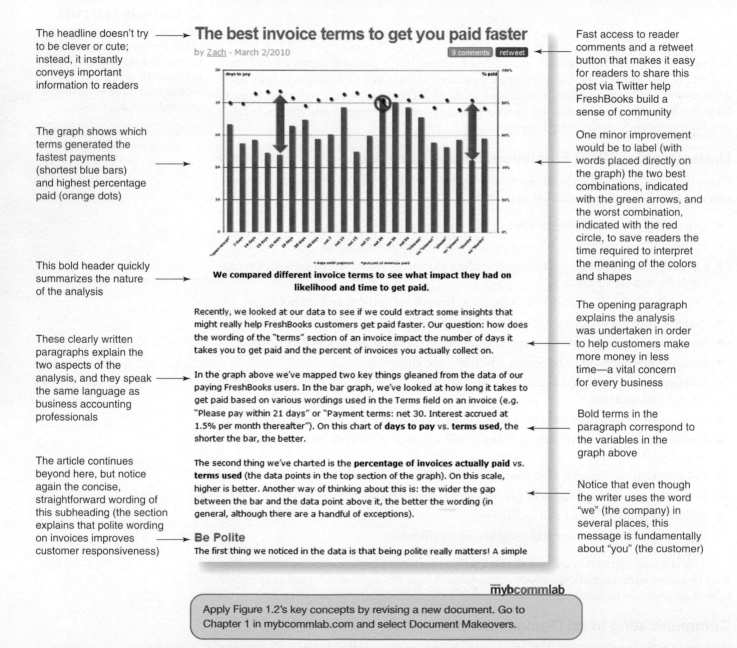

The headline doesn't try to be clever or cute; instead, it instantly conveys important information to readers

The graph shows which terms generated the fastest payments (shortest blue bars) and highest percentage paid (orange dots)

This bold header quickly summarizes the nature of the analysis

These clearly written paragraphs explain the two aspects of the analysis, and they speak the same language as business accounting professionals

The article continues beyond here, but notice again the concise, straightforward wording of this subheading (the section explains that polite wording on invoices improves customer responsiveness)

Fast access to reader comments and a retweet button that makes it easy for readers to share this post via Twitter help FreshBooks build a sense of community

One minor improvement would be to label (with words placed directly on the graph) the two best combinations, indicated with the green arrows, and the worst combination, indicated with the red circle, to save readers the time required to interpret the meaning of the colors and shapes

The opening paragraph explains the analysis was undertaken in order to help customers make more money in less time—a vital concern for every business

Bold terms in the paragraph correspond to the variables in the graph above

Notice that even though the writer uses the word "we" (the company) in several places, this message is fundamentally about "you" (the customer)

The best invoice terms to get you paid faster
by Zach - March 2/2010   9 comments   retweet

We compared different invoice terms to see what impact they had on likelihood and time to get paid.

Recently, we looked at our data to see if we could extract some insights that might really help FreshBooks customers get paid faster. Our question: how does the wording of the "terms" section of an invoice impact the number of days it takes you to get paid and the percent of invoices you actually collect on.

In the graph above we've mapped two key things gleaned from the data of our paying FreshBooks users. In the bar graph, we've looked at how long it takes to get paid based on various wordings used in the Terms field on an invoice (e.g. "Please pay within 21 days" or "Payment terms: net 30. Interest accrued at 1.5% per month thereafter"). On this chart of **days to pay** vs. **terms used**, the shorter the bar, the better.

The second thing we've charted is the **percentage of invoices actually paid** vs. **terms used** (the data points in the top section of the graph). On this scale, higher is better. Another way of thinking about this is: the wider the gap between the bar and the data point above it, the better the wording (in general, although there are a handful of exceptions).

▶ Be Polite
The first thing we noticed in the data is that being polite really matters! A simple

mybcommlab

Apply Figure 1.2's key concepts by revising a new document. Go to Chapter 1 in mybcommlab.com and select Document Makeovers.

Figure 1.2   Audience-Centered Communication
This blog post from the developers of the FreshBooks online business accounting system demonstrates audience focus in multiple ways, starting with the effort behind the message. Every business worries about how quickly customers will pay their bills, so FreshBooks analyzed the customer data it had on hand to see which payment terms and invoice messages generated the quickest responses. This alone is remarkable customer service; the audience-focused presentation of the information makes it that much better.

part of this approach, but it also involves such elements as your ability to listen, your style of writing and speaking, and your ability to maintain positive working relationships. You'll have the chance to explore all these aspects throughout this course.

An important element of audience-centered communication is **etiquette**, the expected norms of behavior in a particular situation. In today's hectic, competitive world, the notion of etiquette might seem outdated and unimportant. However, the way you conduct yourself can have a profound influence on your company's success and your career. When executives hire and promote you, they expect your behavior to protect the company's reputation. The more you understand such expectations, the better chance you have of avoiding career-damaging mistakes.

Long lists of etiquette "rules" can be overwhelming, and you'll never be able to memorize all of them. Fortunately, you can count on three principles to get you through just about any situation: respect, courtesy, and common sense. Moreover, these principles will encourage forgiveness if you do happen to make a mistake. As you encounter new situations, take a few minutes to learn the expectations of the other people involved. Don't be afraid to ask questions, either. People will respect your concern and curiosity. You'll gradually accumulate considerable knowledge, which will help you feel comfortable and be effective in a wide range of business situations. Chapter 2 offers more information about business etiquette.

> Respect, courtesy, and common sense will help you avoid etiquette mistakes.

EXPLORING THE COMMUNICATION PROCESS

3 **LEARNING OBJECTIVE**

Describe the communication process model and the ways that social media are changing the nature of business communication

As you no doubt know from your personal interactions over the years, even well-intentioned communication efforts can fail. Messages can get lost or simply ignored. The receiver of a message can interpret it in ways the sender never imagined. In fact, two people receiving the same information can reach different conclusions about what it means.

Fortunately, by understanding communication as a process with distinct steps, you can improve the odds that your messages will reach their intended audiences and produce their intended effects. This section explores the communication process in two stages: first by following a message from one sender to one receiver in the basic communication model, and then expanding on that with multiple messages and participants in the social communication model.

The Basic Communication Model

Many variations of the communication process model exist, but these eight steps provide a practical overview (see Figure 1.3):

1. **The sender has an idea.** Whether a communication effort will ultimately be effective starts right here and depends on the nature of the idea and the motivation for sending it. For example, if your motivation is to offer a solution to a problem, you have a better chance of crafting a meaningful message than if your motivation is merely to complain about a problem.

> The communication process starts with a sender having an idea and then encoding the idea into a message that can be transferred to a receiver.

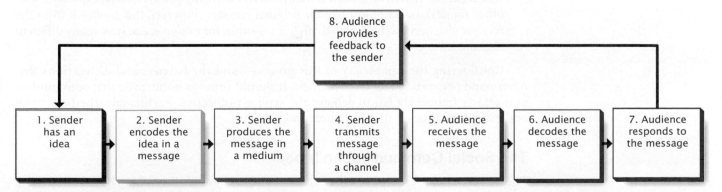

Figure 1.3 The Basic Communication Process
This eight-step model is a simplified representation of how communication works in real life, but understanding this basic model is vital to improving your communication skills. (Note that, as explained on pages 8–9, the social media revolution is changing the relationship between senders and receivers and even the nature of messages themselves.)

2. **The sender encodes the idea as a message.** When someone puts an idea into a **message**, he or she is **encoding** it, or expressing it in words or images. Much of the focus of this course is on developing the skills needed to successfully encode your ideas into effective messages.

3. **The sender produces the message in a transmittable medium.** With the appropriate message to express an idea, the sender now needs a **communication medium** to present that message to the intended audience. To update your boss on the status of a project, for instance, you might have a dozen or more media choices, from a phone call to an instant message to a slideshow presentation.

4. **The sender transmits the message through a channel.** Just as technology continues to increase the number of media options, it also continues to provide new **communication channels** senders can use to transmit their messages. The distinction between medium and channel can get a bit murky, but think of the medium as the *form* a message takes (such as a Twitter tweet) and the channel as the system used to *deliver* the message (such as the Internet).

5. **The audience receives the message.** If the channel functions properly, the message reaches its intended audience. However, mere arrival is not enough. For a message to truly be received, the recipient has to *sense* the presence of a message, *select* it from all the other messages clamoring for attention, and *perceive* it as an actual message (as opposed to random noise).[8]

Decoding is a complex process; receivers often extract different meanings from messages than the meanings senders intended.

6. **The receiver decodes the message.** After a message is received, the receiver needs to extract the idea from the message, a step known as **decoding**. Even well-crafted, well-intentioned communication efforts can fail at this stage because extracting meaning is a highly personal process that is influenced by culture, experience, learning and thinking styles, hopes, fears, and even temporary moods. Moreover, audiences tend to extract the meaning they expect to get from a message, even if it's the opposite of what the sender intended.[9] In fact, rather than extracting the sender's meaning, it's more accurate to say that receivers re-create their own meanings from the message.

7. **The receiver responds to the message.** In most instances, senders want to accomplish more than simply delivering information. They often want receivers to respond in particular ways, whether it's to invest millions of dollars in a new business venture or to accept management's explanation for why it can't afford to give employee bonuses this year. Whether a receiver responds as the sender hopes depends on the receiver (a) *remembering* the message long enough to act on it, (b) being *able* to act on it, and (c) being *motivated* to respond.

8. **The receiver provides feedback.** If a mechanism is available for them to do so, receivers can "close the loop" in the communication process by giving the sender **feedback** that helps the sender evaluate the effectiveness of the communication effort. Feedback can be verbal (using written or spoken words), nonverbal (using gestures, facial expressions, or other signals), or both. Just like the original message, however, this feedback from the receiver also needs to be decoded carefully. A smile, for example, can have many different meanings.

Considering the complexity of this process—and the barriers and distractions that often stand between sender and receiver—it should come as no surprise that communication efforts frequently fail to achieve the sender's objective. Fortunately, the better you understand the process, the more successful you'll be.

The Social Communication Model

The basic model presented in Figure 1.3 does a good job of illustrating how a single idea moves from one sender to one receiver. In a larger sense, it also helps represent the traditional nature of much business communication, which was primarily defined by a *publishing* or *broadcasting* mindset. Externally, a company issued carefully scripted messages to a mass audience that often had few options for responding to those messages or initiating messages of their own. Customers and other interested parties had few ways to connect with

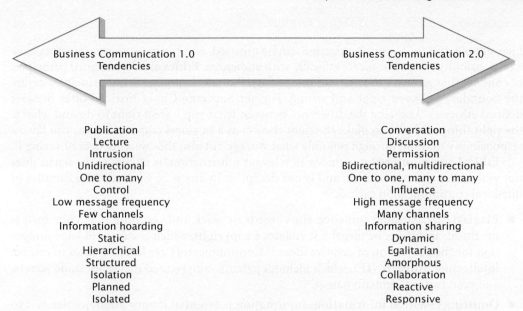

Business Communication 1.0 Tendencies	Business Communication 2.0 Tendencies
Publication	Conversation
Lecture	Discussion
Intrusion	Permission
Unidirectional	Bidirectional, multidirectional
One to many	One to one, many to many
Control	Influence
Low message frequency	High message frequency
Few channels	Many channels
Information hoarding	Information sharing
Static	Dynamic
Hierarchical	Egalitarian
Structured	Amorphous
Isolation	Collaboration
Planned	Reactive
Isolated	Responsive

Figure 1.4   Business Communication: 1.0 Versus 2.0
Business Communication 2.0 differs from conventional communication strategies and practices in a number of significant ways. You're probably already an accomplished user of many new-media tools, and this experience will help you on the job.

one another to ask questions, share information, or offer support. Internally, communication tended to follow the same "we talk, you listen" model, with upper managers issuing directives to lower-level supervisors and employees.

However, thanks to the efforts of media innovators such as Facebook, a variety of technologies have enabled and inspired a new approach to business communication. In contrast to the publishing mindset, this new **social communication model** is interactive, conversational, and usually open to all who wish to participate. Audience members are no longer passive recipients of messages but active participants in a conversation. Social media have given customers and other stakeholders a voice they did not have in the past. And businesses are listening to that voice. In a recent study, the second most common use of social media among U.S. businesses (after maintaining company profiles on social media websites) was monitoring the social media universe for discussions about the company and its brands.[10]

The social communication model is interactive, conversational, and usually open to all who wish to participate.

Instead of transmitting a fixed message, a sender in a social media environment initiates a conversation by sharing valuable information. This information is often revised and reshaped by the web of participants as they share it and comment on it. People can add to it or take pieces from it, depending on their needs and interests.

Just as **Web 2.0** signifies the second generation of World Wide Web technologies (blogs, wikis, podcasts, and other *social media* tools that you'll read about in Chapter 6), **Business Communication 2.0** is a convenient label for this new approach to business communication. Figure 1.4 lists some of the deep and profound differences between traditional business communication and this new approach.

The social communication model offers many advantages, but it has a number of disadvantages as well. Potential problems include information overload (see page 21), fragmented attention, information security risks, distractions that hurt productivity, and the blurring of the line between personal and professional lives, which can make it difficult for people to disconnect from work.[11]

Social media tools do present some potential disadvantages that managers and employees need to consider.

Of course, no company, no matter how enthusiastically it embraces the social communication model, is going to be run as a club in which everyone has a say in every business matter. Instead, a hybrid approach is emerging in which some communications (such as strategic plans and policy documents) follow the traditional approach, while others (such as project management updates and customer support messages) follow the social model.

You can learn more about business uses of social media in Chapter 6.

COMMITTING TO ETHICAL COMMUNICATION

Like all powerful tools, communication can be misused, and business communicators have a responsibility to communicate ethically with audiences. **Ethics** are the accepted principles of conduct that govern behavior within a society. Put another way, ethical principles define the boundary between right and wrong. Former Supreme Court Justice Potter Stewart defined ethics as "knowing the difference between what you have a right to do and what is the right thing to do."[12] To make the right choices as a business communicator, you have a responsibility to think through not only what you say but also the consequences of saying it.

Ethical communication avoids deception and provides the information audiences need.

Ethical communication includes all relevant information, is true in every sense, does not violate the rights of others, and is not deceptive in any way. By contrast, examples of unethical communication include[13]

- **Plagiarizing.** Stealing someone else's words or work and claiming it as your own is unethical, and it can be illegal if it violates a **copyright**, which is a form of legal protection for the expression of creative ideas.[14] Communicators are legally bound to respect **intellectual property (IP)**, which includes patents, copyrighted materials, trade secrets, and even Internet domain names.[15]

- **Omitting essential information.** Information is essential if your audience needs it to make an intelligent, objective decision.

- **Selectively misquoting.** Deliberately omitting damaging or unflattering comments to paint a better (but untruthful) picture of you or your company can be unethical.

- **Distorting statistics or visuals.** Examples include making a product look bigger or better than it really is and changing the scale of graphs and charts to exaggerate or conceal differences.

- **Failing to respect privacy or information security needs.** Failing to respect the privacy of others or failing to adequately protect information entrusted to your care can also be considered unethical (and is sometimes illegal).

Transparency involves giving audiences access to the information they need to make effective decisions.

Of course, people in a society don't always agree on what constitutes ethical behavior. A good example is **transparency**, which in this context refers to a sense of openness, of giving all participants in a conversation access to the information they need to process the messages they are receiving. Take the case of Raymond Ridder, who works in the public relations department of the Golden State Warriors professional basketball team. Using the name "Flunkster Dude," Ridder began posting positive comments about the team on its online forum. When his real identity was discovered, some people in the social media universe cried foul, saying he was deceiving people by posing as an enthusiastic fan when he was in fact a paid employee whose job it was to drum up interest in the team (which is, after all, a profit-seeking business). Ridder defended his actions, saying, "It was nothing malicious at all. I just wanted to get the conversation going in a positive direction."[16]

Some governments are taking steps to protect consumers from practices they deem unethical. The European Union, for instance, outlaws a number of online marketing tactics, including "flogs," short for "fake blogs," in which an employee or a paid agent posing as an independent consumer posts positive stories about a company's products.[17]

Stealth marketing is considered unethical by some observers because it prevents consumers from making fully informed decisions.

A major issue in business communication transparency is **stealth marketing**, which involves attempting to promote products and services to customers who don't know they're being marketed to. A common stealth marketing technique is rewarding someone to promote products to his or her friends without telling them it's a form of advertising. Critics—including the U.S. Federal Trade Commission (FTC) and the Word of Mouth Marketing Association—assert that such techniques are deceptive because they don't give their targets the opportunity to raise their instinctive defenses against the persuasive powers of marketing messages.[18] The FTC recently adopted a requirement that product-review bloggers disclose any relationship— such as receiving payments or free goods—they have with the companies whose products they discuss in their blogs.[19]

REAL-TIME UPDATES
Learn More by Reading This Article

Guidelines for trouble-free blogging

The free *Legal Guide for Bloggers* can help bloggers steer clear of legal problems, including improper use of intellectual property. Go to **http://real-timeupdates .com/bce5** and click on "Learn More." If you are using mybcommlab, you can access Real-Time Updates within each chapter or under Student Study Tools.

Aside from ethical and legal concerns, trying to fool the public is simply bad for business. As LaSalle University communication professor Michael Smith puts it, "The public backlash can be long, deep, and damaging to a company's reputation."[20]

Distinguishing Ethical Dilemmas from Ethical Lapses

Some ethical questions are easy to recognize and resolve, but others are not. Deciding what is ethical can be a considerable challenge in complex business situations. An **ethical dilemma** involves choosing among alternatives that aren't clear-cut. Perhaps two conflicting alternatives are both ethical and valid, or perhaps the alternatives lie somewhere in the gray area between clearly right and clearly wrong. Every company has responsibilities to multiple groups of people inside and outside the firm, and those various groups often have competing interests. For instance, employees generally want higher wages and more benefits, but investors who have risked their money in the company want management to keep costs low so that profits are strong enough to drive up the stock price. Both sides have a valid position; neither one is "right" or "wrong."

Unlike a dilemma, an **ethical lapse** is a clearly unethical (and frequently illegal) choice. For example, homebuyers in an Orlando, Florida, housing development were sold houses without being told that the area was once a U.S. Army firing range and that live bombs and ammunition are still buried in multiple locations around the neighborhood.[21]

Making Ethical Choices

Ensuring ethical business communication requires three elements: ethical individuals, ethical company leadership, and the appropriate policies and structures to support ethical decision making.[22] Many companies establish an explicit ethics policy by using a written **code of ethics** to help employees determine what is acceptable. Showing employees that the company is serious about ethical behavior is also vital. As Sharon Allen, chairman of the financial services firm Deloitte LLP, puts it, "Management and leadership have a huge responsibility in setting examples for their organizations and living the values they preach if they want to sustain a culture of ethics."[23]

Even the best codes and policies can't address every unique situation, however. If you find yourself in a situation in which the law or a code of ethics can't guide you, answer the following questions:[24]

- Have you defined the situation fairly and accurately?
- What is your intention in communicating this message?
- What impact will this message have on the people who receive it, or who might be affected by it?
- Will the message achieve the greatest possible good while doing the least possible harm?
- Will the assumptions you've made change over time? That is, will a decision that seems ethical now seem unethical in the future?
- Are you comfortable with your decision? Would you be embarrassed if it were printed in tomorrow's newspaper or spread across the Internet?

If you ever have doubts about the legal ramifications of a message you intend to distribute, ask for guidance from your company's legal department.

COMMUNICATING IN A WORLD OF DIVERSITY

Throughout your career, you will interact with colleagues from a variety of cultures, people who differ in race, age, gender, sexual orientation, national and regional attitudes and beliefs, family structure, religion, native language, physical and cognitive abilities, life

If you must choose between two ethical alternatives, you are facing an ethical dilemma.

If you choose an alternative that is unethical or illegal, you have committed an ethical lapse.

Responsible employers establish clear ethical guidelines for their employees to follow.

If company ethics policies don't cover a specific situation, you can ask yourself a number of questions in order to make an ethical choice.

5 LEARNING OBJECTIVE

Explain how cultural diversity affects business communication, and describe the steps you can take to communicate more effectively across cultural boundaries experience, and educational background. This section looks at the advantages and challenges of a diverse workforce from a communication perspective, examines key differences among cultures, and offers advice for communicating across cultures.

The Advantages and Challenges of a Diverse Workforce

A diverse workforce offers a broader spectrum of viewpoints and ideas, helps companies understand and identify with diverse markets, and enables companies to benefit from a wider range of employee talents. According to IBM executive Ron Glover, more diverse teams tend to be more innovative over the long term than teams composed of people from the same culture.[25]

For all their benefits, diverse workforces and markets do present some communication challenges, and understanding the effect of culture on communication is essential. **Culture** is a shared system of symbols, beliefs, attitudes, values, expectations, and norms for behavior. Culture is often viewed as a matter of race, but it is much broader in scope. You are a member of several cultures, in fact, based on your national origin, religious beliefs, age, and other factors.

Culture influences the way people perceive the world and respond to others, which naturally affects the way they communicate as both senders and receivers. These influences operate on such a fundamental level that people often don't even recognize the influence of culture on their beliefs and behaviors.[26]

This subconscious effect of culture can create friction because it leads people to assume that everybody thinks and feels they way they do. However, differences between cultures can be profound. For example, in a comparison of the 10 most important values in three cultures, people from the United States had no values in common with people from Japanese or Arab cultures.[27]

The first step to making sure cultural differences don't impede communication is recognizing key factors that distinguish one culture from another.

Key Aspects of Cultural Diversity

You don't need to become an expert in the details of every culture with which you do business, but you do need to attain a basic level of cultural proficiency to ensure successful communication.[28] You can start by recognizing and accommodating the differences described in the following sections. Be aware that this is an overview only, so some generalizations won't be accurate in every situation. Always consider the unique circumstances of each encounter when making communication decisions.

Cultural Context

Every attempt at communication occurs within a **cultural context**, the mixture of traditions, expectations, and unwritten social rules that help convey meaning between members of the same culture. Cultures vary widely in the role that context plays in communication.

In a **high-context culture** people rely less on the explicit content of the message and more on the context of nonverbal actions and environmental setting to convey meaning. Examples of high-context cultures include Japan, China, and many Middle Eastern and Southern European countries.[29] In such cultures, the rules of everyday life are rarely stated explicitly. Instead, as individuals grow up, they learn how to recognize situational cues (such as gestures and tone of voice) and how to respond as expected.[30] Also, in a high-context culture, the primary role of communication is often building relationships, not exchanging information.[31]

In a **low-context culture** people rely more on the explicit content of the message and less on circumstances and cues to convey meaning. In other words, more of the conveyed meaning is encoded into the actual message itself.[32] The United States and many Northern European countries are considered high-context cultures.[33] For example, an English speaker feels responsible for transmitting the meaning of a message and often places sentences in strict chronological sequence to establish a clear cause-and-effect pattern.[34] In a low-context culture, rules and expectations are usually spelled out through explicit statements such as "Please wait until I'm finished."[35] Exchanging information is the primary task of communication in low-context cultures.[36]

The different expectations of low- and high-context cultures can create friction and misunderstanding when people try to communicate across cultural boundaries. For example, people from a low-context culture might view the high-context emphasis on building relationships as a waste of time. Conversely, people from a high-context culture might view the low-context emphasis on information exchange and task completion as being insensitive to group harmony.[37] Discussing the differences between American and Chinese business cultures, for instance, an American executive working in China explained that "in the West, there is such a premium on getting things done quickly, but when you come to work in China, you need to work on listening and being more patient and understanding of local ways of doing business."[38]

Legal and Ethical Differences

Cultural context influences legal and ethical behavior, which in turn can affect communication. For example, because low-context cultures value the written word, they consider written agreements binding. But high-context cultures put less emphasis on the written word and consider personal pledges more important than contracts. They also tend to take a more flexible approach regarding adherence to the law, whereas low-context cultures tend to adhere to the law strictly.[39]

> Members of different cultures sometimes have different views of what is ethical or even legal.

Ethical principles are based to a large extent on cultural values, so trying to make ethical choices across cultures can be complicated. When communicating with people in other cultures, keep your messages ethical by applying four basic principles:[40]

- Actively seek mutual ground.
- Send and receive messages without judgment.
- Send messages that are honest.
- Show respect for cultural differences.

> Learn the four principles that will help you keep your intercultural messages ethical.

Social Customs

Social behavior is guided by numerous rules, some of them formal and specifically articulated (table manners are a good example) and others more informal and learned over time (such as the comfortable standing distance between two speakers in an office). The combination of formal and informal rules influences the overall behavior of everyone in a society in areas such as manners, attitudes toward time, individual versus community values, attitudes toward status and wealth, and respect for authority. Understanding the nuances of social customs takes time and effort, but most businesspeople are happy to explain the habits and expectations of their culture. Plus, they will view your curiosity as a sign of respect.

> Whether formal or informal, the rules governing social custom differ from culture to culture.

Nonverbal Communication

Nonverbal communication is a vital part of the communication process. Factors ranging from facial expressions to style of dress can influence the way receivers decode messages, and the interpretation of nonverbal signals can vary widely from culture to culture. Gestures or clothing choices that you don't think twice about, for example, might seem inappropriate or even offensive to someone from another culture. You'll learn more about nonverbal communication in Chapter 2.

> The meanings of gestures and other nonverbal signals can vary widely from culture to culture.

> Age is an important aspect of culture, both in the way different age groups are treated in a culture and in the cultural differences between age groups.

Age Differences

In some cultures, youth is associated with strength, energy, possibilities, and freedom, while age is often associated with declining powers and a loss of respect and authority. In contrast, in cultures that value age and seniority, longevity earns respect and increasing power and freedom.

Each generation can bring particular strengths to the workplace. For instance, older workers can offer broader experience, the benefits of important business relationships nurtured over many years, and high degrees of "practical intelligence"—the ability to solve complex, poorly defined problems.[41] However, getting the benefits of having multiple generations in a workplace can require some accommodation on everyone's part because of differing habits and perspectives.

REAL-TIME UPDATES
Learn More by Watching This Presentation

An in-depth look at intercultural communication

This comprehensive presentation offers a more detailed look at many of the issues in cross-cultural communication. Go to **http://real-timeupdates.com/bce5** and click on "Learn More." If you are using mybcommlab, you can access Real-Time Updates within each chapter or under Student Study Tools.

Gender

As with age, perceptions of gender roles differ among cultures.

The perception of men and women in business varies from culture to culture, and these differences can affect communication efforts. In some cultures, men hold most or all positions of authority, and women are expected by many to play a more subservient role.[42]

Whatever the culture, evidence suggests that men and women tend to have slightly different communication styles. Broadly speaking, men tend to emphasize content in their communication efforts, whereas women place a higher premium on relationship maintenance.[43] As with every element of diversity, however, remember that these generalizations do not apply to every person or every situation.

Religious Differences

As workforce diversity broadens, more companies find themselves forced to address the issue of religion in the workplace.

As one of the most personal and influential aspects of life, religion brings potential for controversy in a work setting—as evidenced by a significant rise in the number of religious discrimination lawsuits.[44] Some employees feel they should be able to express their beliefs in the workplace, but companies try to avoid situations in which openly expressed religious differences cause friction between employees or distract employees from their responsibilities. As more companies work to establish inclusive workplaces, you can expect to see this issue being discussed more often in the coming years.

Ability Differences

Assistive technologies and other adaptations can help companies support the contribution of people with varying levels of physical and cognitive impairment.

People whose hearing, vision, cognitive ability, or physical ability to operate computers is impaired can be at a significant disadvantage in today's workplace. As with other elements of diversity, success starts with respect for individuals and sensitivity to differences. Employers can also invest in a variety of *assistive technologies* that help create a vital link for thousands of employees with disabilities, giving them opportunities to pursue a greater range of career paths and giving employers access to a broader base of talent.

Advice for Improving Intercultural Communication

In any cross-cultural situation, you can communicate more effectively if you heed the following tips:[45]

Effective intercultural communication starts with efforts to avoid ethnocentrism and stereotyping.

- Avoid **ethnocentrism**, the tendency to judge all other groups according to the standards, behaviors, and customs of one's own group. When making such comparisons, people too often decide that their own group is superior.[46]
- Similarly, avoid **stereotyping**, or assigning a wide range of generalized—and often inaccurate—attributes to an individual on the basis of membership in a particular group, without considering the individual's unique characteristics.
- Don't automatically assume that others think, believe, or behave as you do.
- Accept differences in others without judging them.
- Learn how to communicate respect in various cultures.
- Tolerate ambiguity and control your frustration.
- Don't be distracted by superficial factors such as personal appearance.
- Recognize your own cultural biases.
- Be flexible and be prepared to change your habits and attitudes.
- Observe and learn; the more you learn, the more effective you'll be.

Travel guidebooks are a great source of information about norms and customs in other countries. Also, check to see whether your library has online access to the CultureGram database or review the country profiles at www.kwintessential.co.uk.

Writing for Multilingual Audiences

Ideally, businesses can communicate with employees, customers, and other stakeholders in their native languages, and many companies invest a lot of time and money in translating print and online communication to achieve this. However, translation isn't always cost effective or possible. To write effectively for people who may not be comfortable using your language, remember these tips (see Figure 1.5):[47]

- **Use plain language.** Use short, precise words that say exactly what you mean.
- **Be clear.** Rely on specific terms and concrete examples to explain your points.
- **Cite numbers carefully.** Use figures (such as 27) instead of spelling them out (twenty-seven).
- **Avoid slang and be careful with technical jargon and abbreviations.** Slang and other nonstandard usages can be difficult or impossible for your audience to translate.
- **Be brief.** Construct sentences that are short and simple.
- **Use short paragraphs.** Each paragraph should stick to one topic.
- **Use transitions generously.** Help readers follow your train of thought; you'll learn more about transitions in Chapter 4.

Important tips for improving your intercultural writing include using plain language, avoiding slang, and using short sentences and short paragraphs.

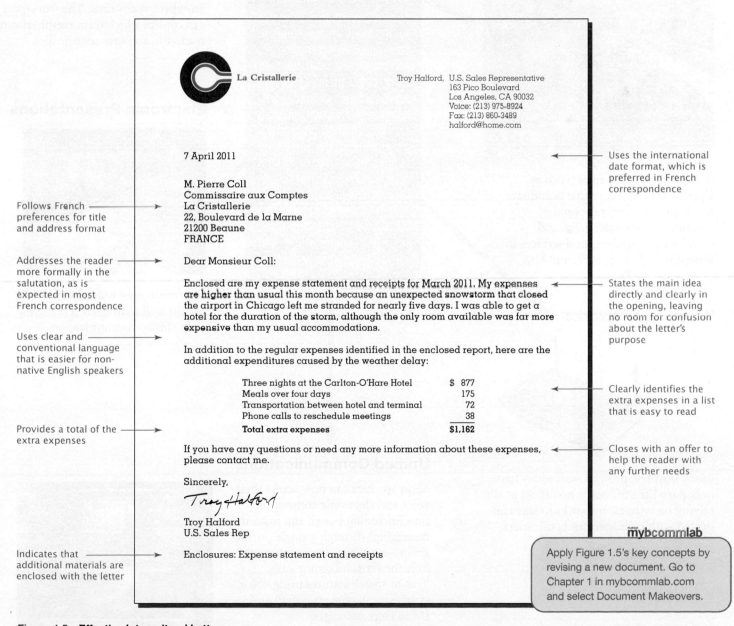

La Cristallerie

Troy Halford, U.S. Sales Representative
163 Pico Boulevard
Los Angeles, CA 90032
Voice: (213) 975-8924
Fax: (213) 860-3489
halford@home.com

7 April 2011

M. Pierre Coll
Commissaire aux Comptes
La Cristallerie
22, Boulevard de la Marne
21200 Beaune
FRANCE

Dear Monsieur Coll:

Enclosed are my expense statement and receipts for March 2011. My expenses are higher than usual this month because an unexpected snowstorm that closed the airport in Chicago left me stranded for nearly five days. I was able to get a hotel for the duration of the storm, although the only room available was far more expensive than my usual accommodations.

In addition to the regular expenses identified in the enclosed report, here are the additional expenditures caused by the weather delay:

Three nights at the Carlton-O'Hare Hotel	$ 877
Meals over four days	175
Transportation between hotel and terminal	72
Phone calls to reschedule meetings	38
Total extra expenses	**$1,162**

If you have any questions or need any more information about these expenses, please contact me.

Sincerely,

Troy Halford

Troy Halford
U.S. Sales Rep

Enclosures: Expense statement and receipts

Annotations (left):
- Follows French preferences for title and address format
- Addresses the reader more formally in the salutation, as is expected in most French correspondence
- Uses clear and conventional language that is easier for non-native English speakers
- Provides a total of the extra expenses
- Indicates that additional materials are enclosed with the letter

Annotations (right):
- Uses the international date format, which is preferred in French correspondence
- States the main idea directly and clearly in the opening, leaving no room for confusion about the letter's purpose
- Clearly identifies the extra expenses in a list that is easy to read
- Closes with an offer to help the reader with any further needs

mybcommlab

Apply Figure 1.5's key concepts by revising a new document. Go to Chapter 1 in mybcommlab.com and select Document Makeovers.

Figure 1.5   Effective Intercultural Letter
This letter from a U.S. sales representative to an accounting manager in a French company is a good example of successfully adapting to an audience in another culture. See Appendix A for tips on formatting international correspondence.

(Text continues on page 52)

Powerful Tools for Communicating Effectively

The tools of business communication evolve with every new generation of digital technology. Selecting the right tool for each situation can enhance your business communication in many ways. In today's flexible office settings, communication technology helps people keep in touch and stay productive. When co-workers in different cities or countries need to collaborate, they can meet and share ideas without costly travel. Companies use communication technology to keep track of parts, orders, and shipments—and to keep customers well-informed. Those same customers can also communicate with companies in many ways at any time of day or night. For a closer look at the latest business uses of social media tools in particular, see pages 156–162 in Chapter 6.

Virtual Meeting Spaces

A number of companies (such as Cranial Tap, whose virtual headquarters is shown here) now hold meetings, host conferences, and demonstrate products and services in virtual worlds such as Second Life.

Wireless Networks

Many business professionals today have only part-time offices or no offices at all, relying on wireless networks to stay connected with colleagues and customers.

REDEFINING THE OFFICE

Technology makes it easier for business professionals to stay connected with customers and colleagues, wherever their work takes them. Electronic presentations, shared workspaces, and virtual meeting spaces can bring professionals together at the same time or give them access to vital resources on their own schedules. Wireless networks and mobile-phone data services let workers "cut the wire" from the home office and move around as they need to.

Shared Workspaces

Online workspaces such as Documentum eRoom and SharePoint Workspace make it easy for far-flung team members to access shared files anywhere at any time. The workspace can control which team members can read, edit, and save specific files.

Electronic Presentations

Electronic presentations, both on-site and online, are a mainstay of business communication.

Unified Communications

Many workers can now access their voice and electronic communication (including e-mail and instant messaging) through a single portal. *Follow-me phone service* automatically forwards incoming calls. *Text-to-speech* features using voice synthesis can convert e-mail and IM to voice messages.

Wikis

Wikis promote collaboration by simplifying the process of creating and editing online content. Anyone with access (some wikis are private; some are public) can add and modify pages as new information becomes available.

Social Networking

Businesses use a variety of social networks as specialized networks to engage customers, find new employees, attract investors, and share ideas and challenges with peers.

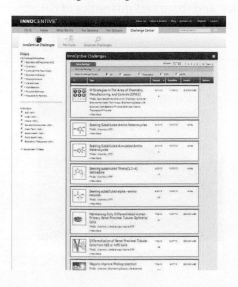

COLLABORATING

Working in teams is essential in almost every business. Teamwork can become complicated, however, when team members work in different parts of the company, in different time zones, or even for different companies. Technology helps bridge the distance by making it possible to brainstorm, attend virtual meetings, share files, meet new business partners, and collaborate with experts outside the company from widely separated locations.

Web-Based Meetings

Web-based meetings allow team members from all over the world to collaborate online. Various systems support instant messaging, video, real-time editing tools, and more.

Videoconferencing and Telepresence

Videoconferencing provides many of the benefits of in-person meetings at a fraction of the cost. Advanced systems feature *telepresence*, in which the video images are life-sized and extremely realistic.

Crowdsourcing and Collaboration Platforms

Crowdsourcing, inviting input from groups of people inside or outside the organization, can give companies access to a much wider range of ideas, solutions to problems, and insights into market trends.

RSS Newsfeeds and Aggregators

Aggregators, sometimes called *newsreaders*, automatically collect information about new blog posts, podcasts, and other content via Really Simple Syndication (RSS) newsfeeds, giving audiences more control over the content they receive.

Community Q&A

Many companies now rely heavily on communities of customers to help each other with product questions and other routine matters.

Social Tagging and Bookmarking

Audiences become part of the communication channel when they find and recommend online content through tagging and bookmarking sites such as Delicious and Digg.

Interactive Data Visualization

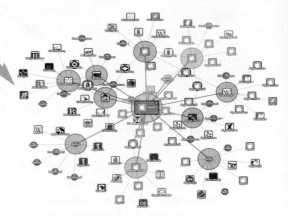

A stunning array of new tools helps business professionals analyze, display, and share vast quantities of data and nonnumeric information.

SHARING INFORMATION

Companies use a variety of communication technologies to create products and services, deliver them to customers, and support users with vital information. The ability to easily access and share the latest information improves the flow and timing of supplies, lowers operating costs, improves customer satisfaction, and boosts financial performance. Easy information access also helps companies respond to customer needs by providing them accurate information and timely product deliveries.

Supply Chain Management Software

Manufacturers, distributors, and retailers now automatically share information that used to require labor-intensive manual reporting. Improved information flow increases report accuracy and helps each company in the supply chain manage inventory.

Online Customer Support

For online shoppers who need instant help, many retail websites make it easy to connect with a live sales rep via phone or instant messaging. Alternatively, software tools known as *virtual agents* or *bots* can answer simple questions and respond to requests for electronic documents.

Podcasts

With the portability and convenience of downloadable audio and video recordings, podcasts have quickly become a popular means of delivering everything from college lectures to marketing messages. Podcasts are also used for internal communication, replacing conference calls, newsletters, and other media.

User-Generated Content

User-generated content sites let businesses host photos, videos, software programs, technical solutions, and other valuable content for their customer communities.

Blogs

Blogs let companies connect with customers and other audiences in a fast and informal way. Commenting features let readers participate in the conversation, too.

INTERACTING WITH CUSTOMERS

Maintaining an open dialog is essential to finding, engaging, and supporting customers. Today's communication technologies, particularly the ever-evolving field of social media, make it easier for customers to interact with a company whenever, wherever, and however they wish. Companies that take the lead in fostering a conversation with their markets have a big advantage over companies that don't.

Microblogs

Microblogging services (of which Twitter is by far the best known) are a great way to share ideas, solicit feedback, monitor market trends, and announce special deals and events.

Speaking with Multilingual Audiences

When speaking to people whose native language is not your own, you may find these tips helpful:

Important tips for speaking with multilingual audiences include speaking clearly and slowly, looking for feedback, and listening carefully.

- **Speak clearly, simply, and relatively slowly.** Pronounce words clearly, stop at distinct punctuation points, and make one point at a time.
- **Look for feedback, but interpret it carefully.** Nods and smiles don't necessarily mean understanding.
- **Rephrase if necessary.** If someone doesn't seem to understand you, rephrase using simpler words.
- **Clarify your meaning with repetition and examples.** Use concrete and specific examples to illustrate difficult or vague ideas.
- **Don't talk down to the other person.** Don't blame the listener for not understanding. Say, "Am I going too fast?" rather than "Is this too difficult for you?"
- **Learn important phrases in your audience's language.** Learning common greetings and a few simple phrases simplifies initial contact and shows respect.
- **Listen carefully and respectfully.** If you do not understand a comment, ask the person to repeat it.
- **Adapt your conversation style to the other person's.** For instance, if the other person appears to be direct and straightforward, follow suit.
- **Check frequently for comprehension.** After you make each point, pause to gauge the other person's comprehension before moving on.
- **Clarify what will happen next.** At the end of a conversation, be sure that you and the other person agree on what has been said and decided.

Finally, remember that oral communication can be more difficult for audiences because it happens in real time and in the presence of other people. In some situations, written communication will be more successful because it gives a reader the opportunity to translate in private and at his or her own pace.

6 **LEARNING OBJECTIVE**

List four general guidelines for using communication technology effectively

USING COMMUNICATION TECHNOLOGY EFFECTIVELY

Today's businesses rely heavily on technology to facilitate the communication process. In fact, many of the technologies you might use in your personal life, from Twitter to video games to virtual worlds, are also used in business. The four-page photo essay "Powerful Tools for Communicating Effectively" (pages 48–51) offers an overview of the technologies that connect people in offices, factories, and other business settings.

The benefits of technology are not automatic, of course. To communicate effectively, you need to keep technology in perspective, use technological tools productively, guard against information overload, and disengage from the computer frequently to communicate in person.

Keeping Technology in Perspective

Don't let technology overwhelm the communication process.

Remember that technology is an aid to communication, not a replacement for it. Technology can't think for you, make up for a lack of essential skills, or ensure that communication really happens. For example, you might have a presence on every new social media platform that comes along, but if the messages you are sending out are confused or self-serving, none of that technology will help. While this advice might sound obvious, it is easy to get caught up in the "gee whiz" factor, particularly when new and different technologies first appear. No matter how exciting or popular it may be, a technology has value only if it helps deliver the right information to the right people at the right time.

Using Tools Productively

You don't have to become an expert to use most communication technologies effectively, but you do need to be familiar with the basic features and functions of the tools your employer expects you to use. For instance, if you don't know the basic functions of your word processing or wiki software, you could spend hours trying to format a document that a skilled user could format in minutes. Whatever the tool, if you learn the basics, your work will be less frustrating and far more productive.

At the same time, don't worry about learning advanced features unless you really need to use them. Many software packages contain dozens of obscure features and functions that typical business communicators rarely need.

REAL-TIME UPDATES
Learn More by Reading This PDF

Steps you can take to help reduce information overload

Everyone needs to play a part in reducing the burden of too much data and information in the work environment; this document has plenty of helpful tips. Go to **http://real-timeupdates.com/bce5** and click on "Learn More." If you are using mybcommlab, you can access Real-Time Updates within each chapter or under Student Study Tools.

Guarding Against Information Overload

The overuse or misuse of communication technology can lead to **information overload**, in which people receive more information than they can effectively process. Information overload makes it difficult to discriminate between useful and useless information, inhibits the ability to think deeply about complex situations, lowers productivity, and amplifies employee stress both on the job and at home—even to the point of causing health and relationship problems.[48]

As a sender, make sure every message you intend to send is meaningful and important to your receivers. As a recipient, take steps to control the number and types of messages you receive. Don't activate visual alerts for incoming messages unless you absolutely need to know the instant a message arrives; each alert breaks your concentration and requires time for you to refocus.[49] Many systems have powerful filtering and tagging capabilities that can automatically sort incoming messages based on criteria you set. Use this feature to isolate high-priority messages that deserve your attention. Also, be wary of subscribing to too many blog feeds, Twitter follows, and other sources of recurring messages. Take care when expanding your social networks online so that you don't get buried with inessential posts and updates.[50] Identify the information you really need and focus on those sources.

Keep in mind that information is a means to an end, not the end itself. Collecting vast amounts of information won't get you a sweet promotion with a big, juicy raise. *Using* information creatively and intelligently will.

> Everyone has an important role to play in reducing information overload.

Reconnecting with People Frequently

Even the best technologies can hinder communication if they are overused. For instance, a common complaint among employees is that managers rely too heavily on e-mail and don't communicate face-to-face often enough.[51] Speaking with people over the phone or in person can take more time and effort, and can sometimes force you to confront unpleasant situations directly, but it is often essential for solving tough problems and maintaining productive relationships.[52] Even though she has the world's best telepresence (advanced videoconferencing) equipment at her disposal, Jill Smart of the technology consulting firm Accenture still travels frequently to meet with clients—particularly clients in other countries and cultures: "You get things from being there, over breakfast and dinner, building relationships face to face."[53]

Moreover, even the best communication technologies can't show people who you really are. You might be funny, bright, and helpful, but you're just a voice on the phone or a name on a screen until people can interact with you in person. Remember to step out from behind the technology frequently to learn more about the people you work with—and to let them learn more about you.

For the latest information on business communication technologies, visit http://real-timeupdates.com/bce5 and click on Chapter 1.

> No matter how much technology is involved, communication will always be about people connecting with people.

CHAPTER REVIEW AND ACTIVITIES

Learning Objectives: Check Your Progress

1 OBJECTIVE Explain the importance of effective communication to your career and to the companies where you will work.

The ability to communicate well will play a key role in your success as a business professional. Communication is essential to every function in business, and poor communication skills will limit your career prospects, no matter how ambitious or skilled you are in other areas. Communication skills also give you an important competitive advantage in the job market.

As an effective communicator, you will be more valuable to your company as well, because good communication skills help companies in many ways: building closer ties with important communities in the marketplace; influencing conversations, perceptions, and trends; "humanizing" otherwise impersonal business organizations; solving problems in less time; making better decisions; increasing productivity; smoothing out work flows; creating more compelling promotional messages; and enhancing professional images and company brands.

To make your communication efforts as effective as possible, focus on making them practical, factual, concise, clear, and persuasive.

2 OBJECTIVE Describe the communication skills employers will expect you to have and the nature of communicating in an organization using an audience-centered approach.

The skills employers will expect you to have include organizing ideas and information; expressing yourself coherently and persuasively in a variety of media; constructing compelling narratives to gain acceptance for important ideas; evaluating data and information critically; actively listening to others; communicating effectively with diverse audiences; using communication technologies; following accepted standards of grammar, spelling, and other aspects of high-quality writing and speaking; adapting your messages and communication styles as needed; demonstrating strong business etiquette; communicating ethically; respecting confidentiality; following applicable laws and regulations; managing your time wisely; and using resources efficiently.

Communicating in an organizational context involves adapting your skills to a professional environment and using the company's communication system (in the broadest sense of the word) to gather and distribute information. An audience-centered approach to communication means focusing on understanding and meeting the needs of all your audience members, rather than focusing on your own needs.

3 OBJECTIVE Describe the communication process model and the ways that social media are changing the nature of business communication.

Communication can be modeled as an eight-step process: (1) the sender has an idea, (2) the sender encodes that idea in a message, (3) the sender produces the message in a transmittable medium, (4) the sender transmits the message through a channel, (5) the audience receives the message, (6) the audience decodes the message, (7) the audience responds to the message, and (8) the audience provides feedback to the sender.

Social media have given customers and other stakeholders a voice they did not have in the past by giving them the tools to gather information from multiple sources, to respond to companies and other organizations, and to initiate conversations in the marketplace. Social media are also changing the nature of messages. A message initiated by one party is often revised and reshaped by the web of participants as they share it and comment on it.

4 OBJECTIVE Define ethics, explain the difference between an ethical dilemma and an ethical lapse, and list six guidelines for making ethical communication choices.

Ethics are the accepted principles of conduct that govern behavior within a society; they define the boundary between right and wrong. Ethical communication includes all relevant information, is true in every sense, does not violate the rights of others, and is not deceptive in any way.

An ethical dilemma involves choosing among alternatives that aren't clear-cut; an ethical lapse is a clearly unethical (and frequently illegal) choice. To ensure the decisions you make are ethical, follow these six guidelines: make sure you have defined the situation fairly and accurately, make sure your intentions are honest and fair, understand the impact your messages will have on others, ensure that your messages will achieve the greatest possible good while doing the least possible harm, make sure your underlying assumptions won't change over time, and make sure you are comfortable with your choices.

5 OBJECTIVE Explain how cultural diversity affects business communication, and describe the steps you can take to communicate more effectively across cultural boundaries.

Cultural diversity affects business communication because culture influences the way people create, send, and interpret messages. Moreover, the influences of culture can be profound, and they are often unrecognized by the people involved. Major aspects of culture that affect communication include cultural context, legal and ethical differences, social customs, nonverbal communication, age differences, gender, religion, and ability.

To communicate effectively across cultures, avoid ethnocentrism and stereotyping, don't make assumptions about others' beliefs and values, avoid judgment, learn to communicate respect, tolerate ambiguity, don't be distracted by superficial elements, recognize your own cultural biases, be flexible, and learn about cultures in which you do business. Also, follow the advice for writing (pages 46–47) and speaking (page 52) in multilanguage environments.

6 OBJECTIVE List four general guidelines for using communication technology effectively.

To help avoid the potential drawbacks of using communication technology, (1) keep technology in perspective so that it doesn't overwhelm the communication process, (2) learn your tools so you can use them productively, (3) guard against information overload by sending only those messages of value to your audiences and by protecting yourself from too many low-value incoming messages, and (4) disengage from the computer frequently to communicate in person.

Test Your Knowledge

To review chapter content related to each question, refer to the indicated Learning Objective.

1. Why should communicators take an audience-centered approach to communication? [LO-2]
2. What benefits does effective communication give you and your organization? [LO-1]
3. Define ethics and explain what ethical communication encompasses. [LO-4]
4. How does cultural context affect communication? [LO-5]
5. Why is it important to also connect in person when using technology to communicate? [LO-6]

Apply Your Knowledge

To review chapter content related to each question, refer to the indicated Learning Objective.

1. Why do you think communication is vital to the success of every business organization? Explain briefly. [LO-1]
2. How does the presence of a reader comments feature on a corporate blog reflect audience-centered communication? [LO-2]
3. How does your understanding of the communication process help you conduct business more effectively? [LO-3]
4. Recall one instance in which you were confused by a behavior, an attitude, or a belief you observed in another culture. (Don't limit yourself to ethnic or national definitions of culture; consider religion, age, and other factors as well.) What about this cultural difference confused you? Why do you think the culture exhibits this behavior, attitude, or belief? How might it impede communication? [LO-5]
5. You're the CEO of a company whose sales are declining, and there is a 50–50 chance you will need to lay off some of your employees sometime in the next two to three months. You have to decide whether to tell them now so they can look for new jobs as soon as possible, even though you're not yet that sure layoffs will be necessary, or wait until you are sure that layoffs will occur. Explain why this is an ethical dilemma. Be sure to consider the effect that a sudden exodus of valuable employees could have on the company's prospects. [LO-4]

Practice Your Skills

Activities

Active links for all websites in this chapter can be found on mybcommlab; see your User Guide for instructions on accessing the content for this chapter. Each activity is labeled according to the primary skill or skills you will need to use. To review relevant chapter content, you can refer to the indicated Learning Objective. In some instances, supporting information will be found in another chapter, as indicated.

1. **Writing: Compositional Modes: Summaries [LO-1], Chapter 3**   Write a paragraph introducing yourself to your instructor and your class. Address such areas as your background, interests, achievements, and goals.

Submit your paragraph using e-mail, blog, or social network, as indicated by your instructor.

2. **Media Skills: Microblogging [LO-1], Chapter 6** Write four messages of no more than 140 characters each (short enough to work as Twitter tweets, in other words) to persuade other college students to take the business communication course. Think of the first message as the "headline" of an advertisement that makes a bold promise regarding the value this course offers every aspiring business professional. The next three messages should be support points that provide evidence to back up the promise made in the first message.[54]

3. **Planning: Assessing Audience Needs [LO-2], Chapter 3** Choose a business career that sounds interesting to you and imagine that you are getting ready to apply for jobs in that field. Naturally, you want to create a compelling, audience-focused résumé that answers the key questions a hiring manager is most likely to have. Identify three personal or professional qualities you have that would be important for someone in this career field. Write a brief statement (one or two sentences) regarding each quality, describing in audience-focused terms how you can contribute to a company in this respect. Submit your statements via e-mail or class blog.

4. **Communication Etiquette: Communicating with Sensitivity and Tact [LO-2]** Potential customers often visit your production facility before making purchase decisions. You and the people who report to you in the sales department have received extensive training in etiquette issues because you frequently deal with high-profile clients. However, the rest of the workforce has not received such training, and you worry that someone might inadvertently say or do something that would offend one of these potential customers. In a two-paragraph e-mail, explain to the general manager why you think anyone who might come in contact with customers should receive basic etiquette training.

5. **Fundamentals: Evaluating Communication Effectiveness [LO-3]** Use the eight phases of the communication process to analyze a miscommunication you've recently had with a co-worker, supervisor, classmate, instructor, friend, or family member. What idea were you trying to share? How did you encode and transmit it? Did the receiver get the message? Did the receiver decode the message as you had intended? How do you know? Based on your analysis, what do you think prevented your successful communication in this instance? Summarize your conclusions in an e-mail message to your instructor.

6. **Writing: Compositional Modes: Persuasion [LO-3], Chapter 9** Social media use varies widely from company to company. Some firms enthusiastically embrace these new tools and new approaches. Others have taken a more cautious approach, either delaying the adoption of social media or restricting their use. You work for an "old school" manufacturing firm that prohibits employees from using social media during work hours. Company management believes that social media offer little or no business value and distract employees from more important duties. In a brief e-mail message to your boss, identify the ways that social media are changing the communication process and relationships between companies and their employees, customers, and communities. Provide at least one example of a real manufacturing company that uses social media.

7. **Communication Ethics: Distinguishing Ethical Dilemmas and Ethical Lapses [LO-4]** In a report of no more than one page, explain why you think each of the following is or is not ethical:

   a. Deemphasizing negative test results in a report on your product idea

   b. Taking an office computer home to finish a work-related assignment

   c. Telling an associate and close friend that she should pay more attention to her work responsibilities or management will fire her

   d. Recommending the purchase of excess equipment to use up your allocated funds before the end of the fiscal year so that your budget won't be cut next year

8. **Communication Ethics: Providing Ethical Leadership [LO-4]** Cisco is a leading manufacturer of equipment for the Internet and corporate networks and has developed a code of ethics that it expects employees to abide by. Visit the company's website at www.cisco.com and find the Code of Conduct. In a brief e-mail message or post to a class blog, describe three specific examples of things you could do that would violate these provisions; then list at least three opportunities that Cisco provides its employees to report ethics violations or ask questions regarding ethical dilemmas.

9. **Communication Ethics: Protecting Company Resources [LO-4]** Blogging has become a popular way for employees to communicate with customers and other parties outside the company. In some cases, employee blogs have been quite beneficial for both companies and their customers, providing helpful information and "putting a human face" on otherwise formal and imposing corporations. However, in some cases, employees have been fired for posting information that their employers said was inappropriate. One particular area of concern is criticism of the company or individual managers. Should employees be allowed to criticize their employers in a public forum such as a blog? In a brief e-mail message, argue for or against company policies that prohibit any critical information in employee blogs.

10. **Communication Ethics: Resolving Ethical Dilemmas [LO-4]** Knowing that you have numerous friends throughout the company, your boss relies on you for feedback concerning employee morale and other issues affecting the staff. She recently approached you and asked you to start reporting any behavior that might violate company polices, from taking office supplies home to making personal long-distance calls. List the issues you'd like to discuss with her before you respond to her request.

11. **Intercultural Communication: Writing for Multiple-Language Audiences [LO-5]** Your boss wants to send a brief e-mail message to welcome employees recently transferred to your department from your Hong Kong branch. They all speak English to some degree, but your boss asks you to review her message for clarity. What would you suggest your boss change in the following e-mail message—and why? Would you consider this message to be audience centered? Why or why not?

I wanted to welcome you ASAP to our little family here in the states. It's high time we shook hands in person and not just across the sea. I'm pleased as punch about getting to know you all, and I for one will do my level best to sell you on America.

12. **Intercultural Communication: Recognizing Cultural Variations [LO-5]** Your company represents a Canadian toy company that is negotiating to buy miniature truck wheels from a manufacturer in Osaka, Japan. In the first meeting, your boss explains that your company expects to control the design of the wheels as well as the materials that are used to make them. The manufacturer's representative looks down and says softly, "Perhaps that will be difficult." Your boss presses for agreement, and to emphasize your company's willingness to buy, he shows the prepared contract he's brought with him. However, the manufacturer seems increasingly vague and uninterested. In an e-mail message to your instructor, identify the cultural differences that may be interfering with effective communication in this situation.

13. **Intercultural Communication: Recognizing Cultural Variations; Collaboration: Solving Problems [LO-5], Chapter 2** Working with two other students, prepare a list of 10 examples of slang (in your own language) that would probably be misinterpreted or misunderstood during a business conversation with someone from another culture. Next to each example, suggest other words you might use to convey the same message. Do the alternatives mean exactly the same as the original slang or idiom? Summarize your findings in an e-mail message or post for a class blog.

14. **Intercultural Communication: Recognizing Cultural Variations [LO-5]** Choose a specific country, such as India, Portugal, Bolivia, Thailand, or Nigeria, with which you are not familiar. Research the culture and write a one-page report outlining what a U.S. businessperson would need to know about concepts of personal space and rules of social behavior in order to conduct business successfully in that country.

15. **Intercultural Communication: Recognizing Cultural Variations [LO-5]** Differences in gender, age, and physical and cognitive abilities contribute to the diversity of today's workforce. Working with a classmate, role-play a conversation in which

    a. A woman is being interviewed for a job by a male human resources manager
    b. An older person is being interviewed for a job by a younger human resources manager
    c. A person using a wheelchair is being interviewed for a job by a person who can walk

How did differences between the applicant and the interviewer shape the communication? What can you do to improve communication in such situations? Summarize your findings in an e-mail message or post for a class blog.

16. **Technology: Using Communication Tools [LO-6]** Find a free online communication service that you have no experience using as a content creator or contributor. Services to consider include blogging (such as Blogger), microblogging (such as Twitter), community Q&A sites (such as Yahoo! Answers), and user-generated content sites (such as Flickr). Perform a basic task such as opening an account or setting up a blog. Was the task easy to perform? Were the instructions clear? Could you find help online if you needed it? Is there anything about the experience that could be improved? Summarize your conclusions in a brief e-mail message to your instructor.

Expand Your Skills

Critique the Professionals

Locate an example of professional communication from a reputable online source. It can reflect any aspect of business communication, from an advertisement or a press release to a company blog or website. Evaluate this communication effort in light of any aspect of this chapter that is relevant to the sample and interesting to you. For example, is the piece effective? Audience-centered? Ethical? Using whatever medium your instructor requests, write a brief analysis of the piece (no more than one page), citing specific elements from the piece and support from the chapter.

Sharpen Your Career Skills Online

Bovée and Thill's Business Communication Web Search, at http://businesscommunicationblog.com/websearch, is a unique research tool designed specifically for business communication research. Use the Web Search function to find a website, video, PDF document, podcast, or presentation that explains at least one essential business communication skill. Write a brief e-mail message to your instructor or a post for your class blog, describing the item that you found and summarizing the career skills information you learned from it.

mybcommlab

If your course uses mybcommlab, log on to www.mybcommlab.com to access the following study and assessment aids associated with this chapter:

- Video applications
- Pre/post test
- Real-Time Updates
- Personalized study plan
- Peer review activity
- Model documents
- Quick Learning Guides
- Sample presentations

If you are not using mybcommlab, you can access Real-Time Updates and Quick Learning Guides through **http://real-time updates.com/bce5**. The Quick Learning Guide (located under "Learn More" on the website) hits all the high points of this chapter in just two pages. This guide, especially prepared by the authors, will help you study for exams or review important concepts whenever you need a quick refresher.

Improve Your Grammar, Mechanics, and Usage

You can download the text of this assignment from **http://real-timeupdates.com/bce5**; click on "Student Assignments" and then click on "Chapter 1. Improve Your Grammar, Mechanics, and Usage."

Level 1: Self-Assessment—Nouns

Use the following self-assessment exercises to improve your knowledge of and power over English grammar, mechanics, and usage. Review all of Section 1.1 in the Handbook of Grammar, Mechanics, and Usage that appears at the end of this book. Answers to these exercises appear on page AK-1.

For items 1–5, indicate which words are common nouns and which are proper nouns.

1. Give the balance sheet to Melissa.
2. After three years of declining sales, the board fired the CEO and hired a replacement from Google.
3. Tarnower Corporation donates a portion of its profits to charity every year.
4. Which aluminum bolts are packaged?
5. Please send the Joneses a dozen of each of the following: stopwatches, canteens, headbands, and wristbands.

In items 6–10, underline the subjects and circle the objects.

6. The technician has already repaired the machine for the client.
7. An attorney will talk to the group about incorporation.
8. After her vacation, the buyer prepared a third-quarter budget.
9. More than 90 percent of the research staff has contributed to the new wiki.
10. Accuracy overrides speed in importance.

For items 11–15, indicate any inappropriate noun plurals and possessives and provide the correct form.

11. Make sure that all copys include the new addresses.
12. Ask Jennings to collect all employee's donations for the Red Cross drive.
13. Charlie now has two son-in-laws to help him with his two online business's.
14. Avoid using too many parenthesises when writing your reports.
15. Follow President Nesses rules about what constitutes a weeks work.

Level 2: Workplace Applications

The following items may contain errors in grammar, capitalization, punctuation, abbreviation, number style, word division, and vocabulary. Rewrite each sentence, correcting all errors. If a sentence has no errors, write "Correct" for that number.

1. If a broken down unproductive guy like Carl can get a raise; why can't a take charge guy like me get one?
2. Visit our website and sign up for "On Your Toes", our free newsletter that keeps you informed of promotions, discounts and about Internet-only specials.
3. As of March, 2011, the Board of Directors have 9 members including: three women, one African-American, and one American of Hispanic descent.
4. As one of the nearly 3,000,000 New York Life policyholders eligible to vote, we urge you to approve the new investment advisory agreement.
5. Gerrald Higgins, vice president for marketing, told us reporters that Capital One provides financial services to one-fourth of homes in the United States.
6. Our Customer Relations associates work with people everyday to answer questions, provide assistance, and helping solve problems.
7. If anyone breaches the lease, its likely that the landlord will file legal action against them to collect on the remainder of they're lease.
8. A IRA is one of the most common plans for the self-employed because of it's ease of setting up and administering.
9. My advise to you is, to put you're mission statement on your web cite.
10. According to Karen Smiths' report small-business owners do'nt recognize the full effect that layoffs and terminations are liable to have on the motivation of surviving employees'.

11. To exacerbate the processing of your US tax return, use the mailing label and bar coded envelope that comes with your tax package.

12. The NASE have implemented a exciting array of programs that make it more easy for legislative opinions and concerns to be voiced by you.

13. Keep in mind the old saying "When we laugh the world laugh with us, when you cry you cry alone."

14. Albert Edmunds and me are Owners of the real estate firm of Edmunds & Cale, which have recently opened a new office in San Diego co.

15. The memo inferred that the economic downturn will have a greater affect on the company's bottom line then we previously assumed, this was the worse news we could of gotten.

Level 3: Document Critique

The following document may contain errors in grammar, capitalization, punctuation, abbreviation, number style, word division, and vocabulary. As your instructor indicates, photocopy this page and correct all errors using standard proofreading marks (see Appendix C) or download the document and make the corrections in your word processing software.

Memo

TO: All Employees
FROM: Roberta Smith, Personnel Director
DATE: December 28, 2011
SUBJECT: time Cards

After reviewing our Current Method of keeping track of employee hours; we have concluded that time cards leave a lot to be desired. So starting Monday, we have a new system, a time clock. You just have to punch in and punch out; when-ever you will come and go from your work area's.

The new system may take a little while to get used to, but should be helpful to those of us who are making a new years resolution to be more punctual.

Happy New Year to all!

Mastering Team Skills and Interpersonal Communication

LEARNING OBJECTIVES

After studying this chapter, you will be able to

1 List the advantages and disadvantages of working in teams and describe the characteristics of effective teams

2 Offer guidelines for collaborative communication, identify major collaboration technologies, and explain how to give constructive feedback

3 List the key steps needed to ensure productive team meetings and identify the most common meeting technologies

4 Describe the listening process and explain how good listeners overcome barriers at each stage of the process

5 Explain the importance of nonverbal communication and identify six major categories of nonverbal expression

6 Explain the importance of business etiquette and identify three key areas in which good etiquette is essential

PEARSON
mybcommlab

Access interactive videos, simulations, sample documents, Document Makeovers, and assessment quizzes in Chapter 2 of mybcommlab.com for mastery of this chapter's objectives.

COMMUNICATION
Matters

"If employees see a better way to organize or present information, they can just go ahead and do it with a wiki."
—Lee Rosen, *CEO, Rosen Law Firm*

Lee Rosen's law firm uses a wiki to manage thousands of documents while boosting teamwork and collaboration.

When communication tools function at their best, they can go beyond mere facilitation to transformation. Such was the case at Rosen Law Firm, based in Raleigh, North Carolina. Lee Rosen, the firm's owner and chief executive, wanted to replace an expensive, complicated, and inflexible computer system that employees relied on for everything from contact lists to appointment calendars to document storage. The solution he chose was a wiki, the same technology that enables tens of thousands of people around the world to contribute to Wikipedia.

The wiki certainly helped cut costs, but it also did much more. In addition to handling much of the firm's document storage and formal communication, the wiki introduced an informal social element that is helping employees bond as a community. Many employees have added personal pages with information about themselves, helping colleagues get to know each other on a more personal level.[1]

This chapter focuses on the communication skills you need in order to work well in team settings and on important interpersonal communication skills that will help you on the job: productive meetings, active listening, nonverbal communication, and business etiquette.

COMMUNICATING EFFECTIVELY IN TEAMS

A **team** is a unit of two or more people who share a mission and the responsibility for working to achieve their goal.[2] Businesses use a wide variety of teams, from short-term problem-solving teams to permanent committees that sometimes become formal parts of the organization structure. You will participate in teams throughout your career, so developing the skills to communicate successfully in team settings will give you an important advantage.

1 LEARNING OBJECTIVE

List the advantages and disadvantages of working in teams, and describe the characteristics of effective teams

Advantages and Disadvantages of Teams

When teams are successful, they can improve productivity, creativity, employee involvement, and even job security.[3] Teams are often at the core of **participative management**, the effort to involve employees in the company's decision making. Teams can play a vital role in helping an organization reach its goals, but they are not appropriate for every situation, and even when they are appropriate, companies need to weigh both the advantages and disadvantages of a team-based approach. The advantages of successful teamwork include:[4]

Team members have a shared mission and are collectively responsible for the team's performance.

- **Increased information and knowledge.** By pooling the experience of several individuals, a team has access to more information in the decision-making process.
- **Increased diversity of views.** Bringing a variety of perspectives can improve decision making—provided these diverse viewpoints are guided by a shared goal.[5]
- **Increased acceptance of a solution.** Those who participate in making a decision are more likely to support it and encourage others to accept it.
- **Higher performance levels.** Effective teams can be better than top-performing individuals at solving complex problems.[6]

Although teamwork has many advantages, teams need to be aware of and work to counter the following potential disadvantages:

- **Groupthink.** Like other social structures, business teams can generate tremendous pressures to conform. **Groupthink** occurs when peer pressures cause individual team members to withhold contrary or unpopular opinions and to go along with decisions they don't really believe in. The result can be decisions that are worse than the choices the team members might have made individually.
- **Hidden agendas.** Some team members may have a **hidden agenda**—private, counterproductive motives, such as a desire to take control of the group, to undermine someone else on the team, or to pursue an incompatible goal.
- **Cost.** Aligning schedules, arranging meetings, and coordinating individual parts of a project can eat up a lot of time and money.

Characteristics of Effective Teams

The most effective teams have a clear objective and a shared sense of purpose, communicate openly and honestly, reach decisions by consensus, think creatively, and know how to resolve conflict.[7] Learning these team skills takes time and practice, so U.S. companies now teach teamwork more frequently than any other aspect of business.[8]

Unsuccessful teamwork, in contrast, can waste time and money, generate lower-quality work, and frustrate both managers and employees. A lack of trust is cited as the most common reason for the failure of teams. This lack of trust can result from team members being suspicious of one another's motives or ability to contribute.[9] Another common reason for team failure is poor communication, particularly when teams operate across cultures, countries, and time zones.[10] Poor communication can also result from basic differences in conversational styles. For example, some people expect conversation to follow an orderly

Effective teams
- Understand their purpose
- Communicate openly and honestly
- Build consensus
- Think creatively
- Stay focused
- Resolve conflict

pattern in which team members wait their turn to speak, whereas others might view conversation as more spontaneous and are comfortable with an overlapping, interactive style.[11]

Conflict in team settings isn't necessarily bad, as long as team members can stay focused on the goal.

Many teams experience conflict in the course of their work, but conflict isn't necessarily bad. Conflict can be constructive if it forces important issues into the open, increases the involvement of team members, and generates creative ideas for solving a problem. Even teams that have some interpersonal friction can excel if they have effective leadership and team players who are committed to positive outcomes. As teamwork experts Andy Boynton and Bill Fischer put it, "Virtuoso teams are not about getting polite results."[12]

2 LEARNING OBJECTIVE
Offer guidelines for collaborative communication, identify major collaboration technologies, and explain how to give constructive feedback

COLLABORATING ON COMMUNICATION EFFORTS

When a team collaborates on reports, websites, presentations, and other communication projects, the collective energy and expertise of the various members can lead to results that transcend what each individual could do otherwise.[13] However, collaborating on team messages requires special effort; the following section offers a number of helpful guidelines.

Guidelines for Collaborative Writing

In any collaborative effort, team members coming from different backgrounds may have different work habits or priorities: A technical expert may focus on accuracy and scientific standards; an editor may be more concerned about organization and coherence; and a manager may focus on schedules, cost, and corporate goals. In addition, team members differ in writing styles, work habits, and personality traits.

To collaborate effectively, everyone involved must be flexible and open to other opinions, focusing on team objectives rather than on individual priorities.[14] Successful writers know that most ideas can be expressed in many ways, so they avoid the "my way is best" attitude. The following guidelines will help you collaborate more successfully:[15]

Successful collaboration requires a number of steps, from selecting the right partners and agreeing on project goals to establishing clear processes and avoiding writing as a group.

- **Select collaborators carefully.** Whenever possible, choose a combination of people who together have the experience, information, and talent needed for each project.
- **Agree on project goals before you start.** Starting without a clear idea of what the team hopes to accomplish inevitably leads to frustration and wasted time.
- **Give your team time to bond before diving in.** If people haven't had the opportunity to work together before, make sure they can get to know each other before being asked to collaborate.
- **Clarify individual responsibilities.** Because members will be depending on each other, make sure individual responsibilities are clear.
- **Establish clear processes.** Make sure everyone knows how the work will be managed from start to finish.
- **Avoid writing as a group.** The actual composition is the only part of developing team messages that usually does not benefit from group participation. In most cases, the best approach is to plan, research, and outline together but assign the task of writing to one person or divide larger projects among multiple writers. If you divide the writing, try to have one person do a final revision pass to ensure a consistent style.
- **Make sure tools and techniques are ready and compatible across the team.** Even minor details such as different versions of software can delay projects.
- **Check to see how things are going along the way.** Don't assume that everything is working just because you don't hear anything negative.

- Access this chapter's simulation entitled Interpersonal Communication and Teamwork, located at mybcommlab.com.

PEARSON mybcommlab

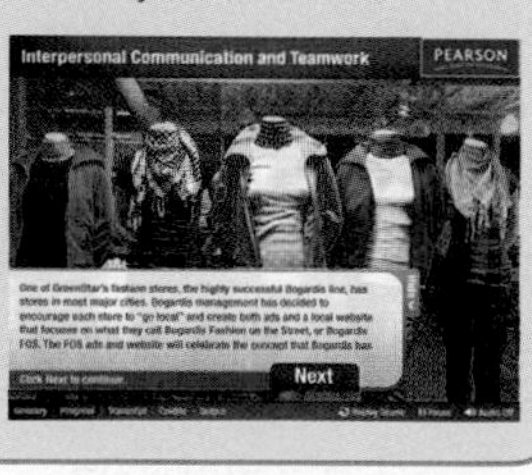

Technologies for Collaborative Writing

Collaboration tools include group review and commenting features, content management systems, and wikis.

A variety of collaboration tools exist to help teams write together, ranging from group review and editing features in word processing software and the Adobe Acrobat electronic document system (PDF files) to **content management systems** that organize and control the content for many websites (particularly larger corporate sites). A **wiki**, from the Hawaiian word for *quick,* is a website that allows anyone with access to add new material and edit existing material (see Figure 2.1). Public wikis allow any registered user to edit pages; private wikis such as the one used at Rosen Law Firm (featured at the beginning of the chapter) are accessible only with permission. Chapter 11 offers guidelines for effective wiki collaboration.

Key benefits of wikis include simple operation—writers don't need to know any of the techniques traditionally required to create web content—and the freedom to post new or revised material without prior approval. This approach is quite different from a content management system, in which both the organization of the website and the *workflow* (the rules for creating, editing, reviewing, and approving content) are tightly controlled.[16]

Wikis are part of the broader class of collaborative technologies known as **groupware**, computer-based systems that let people communicate, share files, review previous message threads, work on documents simultaneously, and connect using social networking tools. These systems help companies capture and share knowledge from multiple experts, bringing greater insights to bear on tough challenges.[17] **Shared workspaces** are online "virtual offices" that give everyone on a team access to the same set of resources and information. You may see some of these workspaces referred to as *intranets* (restricted-access websites that are open to employees only) or *extranets* (restricted sites that are available to employees and to outside parties by invitation only).

In the coming years, keep an eye out for emerging technologies that can help teams collaborate in new ways. For example, *cloud computing,* a somewhat vague term for "on-demand" software capabilities delivered over the Internet, promises to expand the ways in which geographically dispersed teams can collaborate quickly and inexpensively.[18]

 This page from the Public Relations Wiki (http://pr.wikia .com) shows the features typically used to create and edit wiki pages. Give wiki writing a try using the unique Bovée-Thill wiki simulator. Visit http:// real-timeupdates.com/bce5, click on "Student Assignments," and then click on any of the wiki exercises.

Groupware and shared workspaces give team members instant access to shared resources and information.

Figure 2.1   Collaboration Technologies
This page from the Public Relations Wiki (http://pr.wikia.com) shows the features typically used to create and edit wiki pages.

REAL-TIME UPDATES
Learn More by Reading This PDF

Social networks for professionals

See several intriguing new examples of social networks designed exclusively for members of certain professions or industries. Go to **http://real-timeupdates.com/bce5** and click on "Learn More." If you are using mybcommlab, you can access Real-Time Updates within each chapter or under Student Study Tools.

Social networking technologies are becoming vital communication linkages in many companies.

Social Networks and Virtual Communities

Chapter 1 explains how social media and the Web 2.0 approach are redefining business communication. Within that context, **social networking technologies** are redefining teamwork and team communication by helping erase the constraints of geographic and organization boundaries. In addition to enabling and enhancing teamwork, social networks have numerous other business applications and benefits; see Table 6.1 on page 157 for more information.

The two fundamental elements of any social networking technology are *profiles* (the information stored about each member of the network) and *connections* (mechanisms for finding and communicating with other members).[19] If you're familiar with Facebook, you have a basic idea of how social networks function. Thousands of companies now use Facebook, but you may also encounter networks created specifically for business use, including LinkedIn (www.linkedin.com), Ryze (www.ryze.com), Spoke (www.spoke.com), and Xing (www.xing.com).

Some companies use social networking technologies to form *virtual communities* or *communities of practice* that link employees with similar professional interests throughout the company and sometimes with customers and suppliers as well. The huge advantage that social networking brings to these team efforts is in identifying the best people to collaborate on each problem or project, no matter where they are around the world or what their official roles are in the organization. Such communities are similar to teams in many respects, but one major difference is in the responsibility for accumulating organizational knowledge over the long term. For example, the pharmaceutical company Pfizer has a number of permanent product safety communities that provide specialized advice on drug safety issues to researchers all across the company.[20]

Social networking can also help a company maintain a sense of community even as it grows beyond the size that normally permits a lot of daily interaction. At the online retailer Zappos, fostering a supportive work environment is the company's top priority. To encourage the sense of community among its expanding workforce, Zappos uses social networking tools to track employee connections and encourage workers to reach out and build relationships.[21]

TABLE 2.1 Giving Constructive Feedback	
How to Be Constructive	**Explanation**
Think through your suggested changes carefully.	Because many business documents must illustrate complex relationships between ideas and other information, isolated and superficial edits can do more harm than good.
Discuss improvements rather than flaws.	Instead of saying "this is confusing," for instance, explain how the writing can be improved to make it clearer.
Focus on controllable behavior.	The writer may not have control over every variable that affected the quality of the message, so focus on those aspects the writer can control.
Be specific.	Comments such as "I don't get this" or "Make this clearer" don't give the writer much direction.
Keep feedback impersonal.	Focus comments on the message, not on the person who created it.
Verify understanding.	If in doubt, ask for confirmation from the recipient to make sure that the person understood your feedback.
Time your feedback carefully.	Respond in a timely fashion so that the writer will have sufficient time to implement the changes you suggest.
Highlight any limitations your feedback may have.	If you didn't have time to give the document a thorough edit, or if you're not an expert in some aspect of the content, let the writer know so that he or she can handle your comments appropriately.

Giving—and Responding to—Constructive Feedback

Aside from processes and tools, collaborative communication often involves giving and receiving feedback about writing efforts. **Constructive feedback**, sometimes called *constructive criticism,* focuses on the process and outcomes of communication, not on the people involved (see Table 2.1). In contrast, **destructive feedback** delivers criticism with no effort to stimulate improvement.[22] For example, "This proposal is a confusing mess, and you failed to convince me of anything" is destructive feedback. Your goal is to be more constructive: "Your proposal could be more effective with a clearer description of the manufacturing process and a well-organized explanation of why the positives outweigh the negatives." When giving feedback, avoid personal attacks and give the person clear guidelines for improvement.

When you receive constructive feedback, resist the understandable urge to defend your work or deny the validity of the feedback. Remaining open to criticism isn't easy when you've poured your heart and soul into a project, but good feedback provides a valuable opportunity to learn and to improve the quality of your work.

> When you give writing feedback, make it constructive by focusing on how the material can be improved.

> When you receive constructive feedback on your writing, keep your emotions in check and view it as an opportunity to improve.

MAKING YOUR MEETINGS MORE PRODUCTIVE

Much of your workplace communication will occur in in-person or online meetings, so to a large degree, your ability to contribute to the company—and to be recognized for your contributions—will depend on your meeting skills. As useful as meetings can be, though, they can be a waste of time if they aren't planned and managed well. Successful meetings start with thoughtful preparation.

> **3 LEARNING OBJECTIVE**
>
> List the key steps needed to ensure productive team meetings, and identify the most common meeting technologies

Preparing for Meetings

The first step in preparing for a meeting is to make sure the meeting is really necessary. Meetings can consume hundreds or thousands of dollars of productive time and take people away from other work, so don't hold a meeting if some other form of communication (such as an e-mail message) can serve the purpose as effectively.[23] If a meeting is truly necessary, proceed with these four planning tasks:

> A single poorly planned or poorly run meeting can waste hundreds or thousands of dollars, so make sure every meeting is necessary and well managed.

- **Clarify your purpose.** Most meetings are one of two types: *Informational meetings* involve sharing information and perhaps coordinating action. *Decision-making meetings* involve analysis, problem solving, and in many cases, persuasive communication. Whatever your purpose, make sure it is clear and specific—and clearly communicated to all participants.

- **Select participants for the meeting.** The rule here is simple: Invite everyone who really needs to be involved, and don't invite anyone who doesn't. For decision-making meetings, for example, invite only those people who are in a direct position to help the meeting reach its objective.

- **Choose the venue and the time.** Online meetings are often the best way (and sometimes to the only way) to connect people in multiple locations or to reach large audiences. For onsite meetings, review the facility and the seating arrangements. Are rows of chairs suitable, or do you need a conference table or some other arrangement? Pay attention to room temperature, lighting, ventilation, acoustics, and refreshments; these details can make or break a meeting. If you have control over the timing, morning meetings are often more productive because people are generally more alert and not yet engaged with the work of the day.

- **Set and share the agenda.** People who will be presenting information need to know what is expected of them, nonpresenters need to know what will be presented so they can prepare questions, and everyone needs to know how long the meeting will last. In addition, the agenda is an important tool for guiding the progress of the meeting (see Figure 2.2 on the following page).

> To ensure a successful meeting, clarify your purpose, select the right mix of participants, choose the venue and time carefully, and set a clear agenda.

Conducting and Contributing to Efficient Meetings

Everyone in a meeting shares the responsibility for keeping the meeting productive and making it successful. If you are the designated leader of a meeting, however, you have an

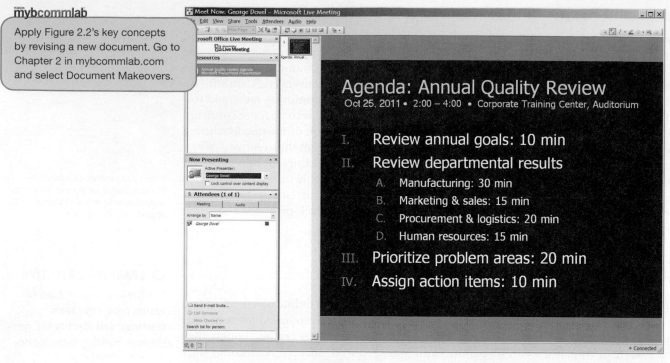

mybcommlab

Apply Figure 2.2's key concepts by revising a new document. Go to Chapter 2 in mybcommlab.com and select Document Makeovers.

Figure 2.2   Typical Meeting Agenda
Agenda formats vary widely, depending on the complexity of the meeting and the presentation technologies that will be used. For an online meeting, for instance, a good approach is to first distribute a detailed planning agenda so that presenters know what they need to prepare, then create a simpler display agenda such as this one to guide the progress of the meeting.

extra degree of responsibility and accountability. To ensure productive meetings, be sure to do the following:

Everyone shares the responsibility for successful meetings.

- **Keep the meeting on track.** A good meeting draws out the best ideas and information the group has to offer. Good leaders occasionally need to guide, mediate, probe, stimulate, summarize, and redirect discussions that have gotten off track.

- **Follow agreed-upon rules.** The larger the meeting, the more formal you'll need to be to maintain order. Formal meetings often use *parliamentary procedure,* a time-tested method for planning and running effective meetings. The best-known guide to this procedure is Robert's Rules of Order (www.robertsrules.com).

- **Encourage participation.** You may discover that some participants are too quiet and others are too talkative. Draw out nonparticipants by asking for their input. For the overly talkative, you can say that time is limited and others need to be heard.

- **Participate actively.** Try to contribute to the progress of the meeting and the smooth interaction of the participants. Use your listening skills and powers of observation to size up the interpersonal dynamics of the group, then adapt your behavior to help the group achieve its goals. Speak up if you have something useful to say, but don't talk or ask questions just to demonstrate how much you know about the subject at hand.

- **Close effectively.** At the conclusion of a meeting, verify that the objectives have been met. If they have not, arrange for follow-up work as needed. Either summarize the decisions reached or list the actions to be taken. Make sure all participants understand and agree on the outcome.

For most meetings, particularly formal meetings, it's good practice to appoint one person to record the **minutes**, a summary of the important information presented and the decisions made during a meeting. Figure 2.3 shows the type of information typically included in minutes.

Using Meeting Technologies

Expect to attend many meetings virtually, using the growing array of online meeting technologies.

A variety of meeting-related technologies have helped spur the emergence of **virtual teams,** whose members work in different locations and interact electronically through

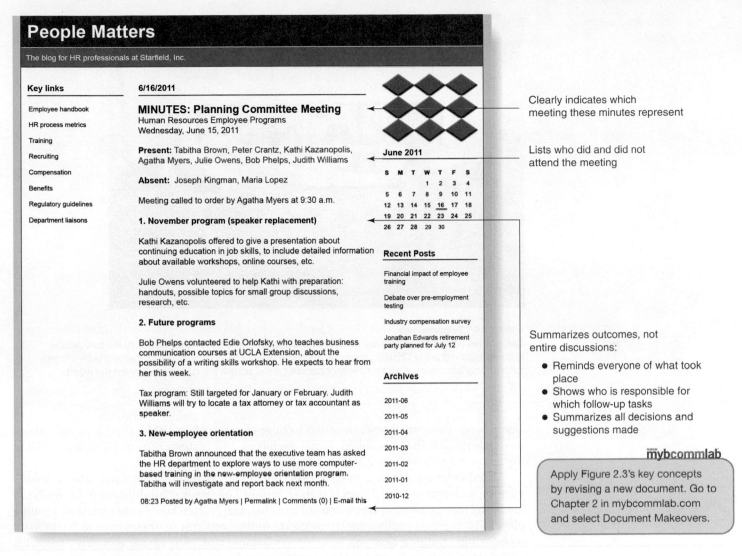

Figure 2.3   Typical Meeting Minutes
The specific format of meeting minutes is less important than making sure you record all the key information, particularly regarding responsibilities assigned during the meeting. No matter what medium is used, key elements of meeting minutes include a list of those present and a list of those who were invited but didn't attend, followed by the times the meeting started and ended, all major decisions reached at the meeting, all assignments of tasks to meeting participants, and all subjects that were deferred to a later meeting. Minutes objectively summarize important discussions, noting the names of those who contributed major points. Outlines, subheadings, and lists help organize the minutes; additional documentation is noted in the minutes and attached.

virtual meetings. Instant messaging (IM) and teleconferencing are the simplest forms of virtual meetings. Videoconferencing lets participants see and hear each other, demonstrate products, and transmit other visual information. *Telepresence* technologies (see Figure 2.4 on the following page) enable realistic conferences in which participants thousands of miles apart almost seem to be in the same room.[24] The ability to convey nonverbal subtleties such as facial expressions and hand gestures makes these systems particularly good for negotiations, collaborative problem solving, and other complex discussions.[25]

The most sophisticated web-based meeting systems combine the best of real-time communication, shared workspaces, and videoconferencing with other tools, such as *virtual whiteboards,* that let teams collaborate in real time. Such systems are used for everything from spontaneous discussions among small groups to carefully planned, formal events such as customer training seminars or press conferences.[26]

Technology continues to create intriguing opportunities for online interaction. For instance, one of the newest virtual tools is online brainstorming, in which a company can conduct "idea campaigns" to generate new ideas from people across the organization.

Figure 2.4 Telepresence
Can you tell how many people are actually in this conference room in Chicago? Only the two people in the foreground are in Chicago; the other six are in Atlanta and London. Virtual meeting technologies such as this telepresence system connect people spread across the country or around the world.

These range from small team meetings to huge events such as IBM's giant InnovationJam, in which 100,000 IBM employees, family members, and customers from 160 countries were invited to brainstorm online for three days.[27]

Companies are also beginning to experiment with virtual meetings and other communication activities in virtual worlds such as Second Life (www.secondlife.com). In much the same way that gamers can create and control characters (often known as avatars) in a multiplayer video game, professionals can create online versions of themselves to participate in meetings, training sessions, sales presentations, and even casual conversations with customers they happen to bump into (see Figure 2.5).

> Online meetings can save considerable time and money, but they can require extra planning and management steps.

Conducting successful meetings over the phone or online requires extra planning before the meeting and more diligence during the meeting. Because virtual meetings offer less visual contact and nonverbal communication than in-person meetings, leaders need to make sure everyone stays engaged and has the opportunity to contribute. Paying attention during online meetings takes greater effort as well. Participants need to stay committed to the meeting and resist the temptation to work on unrelated tasks.[28]

For the latest information on meeting technologies, visit http://real-timeupdates.com/bce5 and click on Chapter 2.

IMPROVING YOUR LISTENING SKILLS

4 **LEARNING OBJECTIVE**

Describe the listening process and explain how good listeners overcome barriers at each stage of the process

Listening is one of the most important skills in the workplace, but most people don't do it as well as they assume they do.

Your long-term career prospects are closely tied to your ability to listen effectively. In fact, some 80 percent of top executives say that listening is the most important skill needed to get things done in the workplace.[29] Plus, today's younger employees place a high premium on being heard, so listening is becoming even more vital for managers.[30]

Effective listening strengthens organizational relationships, alerts the organization to opportunities for innovation, and allows the organization to manage growing diversity both in the workforce and in the customers it serves.[31] Companies whose employees and managers listen effectively are able to stay informed, up-to-date, and out of trouble. Conversely, poor listening skills can cost companies millions of dollars per year as a result of lost opportunities, legal mistakes, and other errors. Effective listening is also vital to the process of building trust between organizations and between individuals.[32]

Figure 2.5   Meeting in a Virtual World
Cranial Tap, whose online headquarters is shown here, is one of a growing number of firms that use Second Life as a virtual meeting place.

"When you talk you merely provide information, but when you genuinely listen you show respect, create trust, and develop rapport."

—John Boe, *sales training professional*[33]

LISTENING *Matters*

Recognizing Various Types of Listening

Effective listeners adapt their listening approaches to different situations. The primary goal of **content listening** is to understand and retain the information in the speaker's message. With this type of listening, you ask questions to clarify the material but don't argue or judge. Try to overlook the speaker's style and any limitations in the presentation; just focus on the information.[34] In contrast, the goal of **critical listening** is to understand and evaluate the meaning of the speaker's message on several levels: the logic of the argument, the strength of the evidence, the validity of the conclusions, the implications of the message for you and your organization, the speaker's intentions and motives, and the omission of any important or relevant points. Be on the lookout for bias that might color the way the information is presented and be careful to separate opinions from facts.[35]

The goal of **empathic listening** is to understand the speaker's feelings, needs, and wants so that you can appreciate his or her point of view, regardless of whether you share that perspective. By listening in an empathic way, you help the individual release emotions that can prevent a calm, clear-headed approach to the subject. Don't jump in with advice unless the person asks for it, and don't judge the speaker's feelings. Instead, let the person know that you appreciate his or her feelings and understand the situation. Once you establish that connection, you can then help the speaker search for a solution.[36]

No matter what mode they are using at any given time, effective listeners try to engage in **active listening**, making a conscious effort to turn off their own filters and biases to truly

To be a good listener, adapt the way you listen to suit the situation.

hear and understand what the other party is saying. They ask questions or summarize the speaker's message to verify key points and encourage the speaker through positive body language and supportive feedback.[37]

Understanding the Listening Process

Listening seems like a simple procedure. After all, you've been doing it all your life. However, most of us aren't terribly good at it. Most people listen at or below a 25 percent efficiency rate, remember only about half of what's said during a 10-minute conversation, and forget half of that within 48 hours.[38] Furthermore, when questioned about material they've just heard, they are likely to get the facts mixed up.[39]

Why is such a seemingly simple activity so difficult? The reason is that listening is not a simple process, by any means. Listening follows the same sequence as the basic communication process model you explored in Chapter 1 (page 39), with the added difficulty that it happens in real time. To listen effectively, you need to successfully complete five steps:[40]

> *Listening involves five steps: receiving, decoding, remembering, evaluating, and responding.*

1. **Receiving.** Start by physically hearing the message and recognizing it as incoming information.

2. **Decoding.** Assign meaning to sounds, according to your own values, beliefs, ideas, expectations, roles, needs, and personal history.

3. **Remembering.** Store the information for future processing.

4. **Evaluating.** Evaluate the quality of the information.

5. **Responding.** React based on the situation and the nature of the information.

If any one of these steps breaks down, the listening process becomes less effective or even fails entirely. As both a sender and a receiver, you can reduce the failure rate by recognizing and overcoming a variety of physical and mental barriers to effective listening.

Overcoming Barriers to Effective Listening

> *Good listeners actively try to overcome the barriers to successful listening.*

Good listeners look for ways to overcome the many potential barriers to successful listening (see Table 2.2). Some factors you may not be able to control, such as conference room acoustics or poor phone reception. However, you can control other factors, such as not interrupting speakers and not creating distractions that make it difficult for others to pay attention. And don't think that you're not interrupting just because you're not talking. Such actions as texting or checking your watch can interrupt a speaker and lead to communication breakdowns.

Selective listening is one of the most common barriers to effective listening. If your mind wanders, you may stay tuned out until you hear a word or phrase that gets your attention once more. But by that time, you'll be unable to recall what the speaker actually said; instead, you'll remember what you think the speaker *probably* said.[41]

One key reason listeners' minds tend to wander is that people think faster than they speak. Most people speak at 120 to 150 words per minute. However, humans can process audio information at up to 500 words per minute or more.[42] Consequently, your brain has a lot of free time whenever you're listening, and if left unsupervised, it will find a thousand other things to think about. Make a conscious effort to focus on the speaker and use the extra time to analyze and paraphrase what you hear or to take relevant notes.

Another common barrier to successful interpretation is **prejudgment**—making up your mind before truly hearing what another person has to say. Similarly, **selective perception** leads listeners to filter incoming messages to fit what they already believe about a given subject. Listening with an open mind isn't always easy, but it's the only way to make sure you really hear what people are telling you.

Even when your intentions are the best, you can still misinterpret incoming messages if you and the speaker don't share enough language or experience. Lack of common ground is the reason misinterpretation occurs so frequently between speakers of different native languages, even when they're trying to speak the same language. When listening to a speaker

TABLE 2.2 What Makes an Effective Listener?

Effective Listeners	Ineffective Listeners
■ Listen actively	■ Listen passively
■ Take careful and complete notes, when applicable	■ Take no notes or ineffective notes
■ Make frequent eye contact with the speaker (depends on culture to some extent)	■ Make little or no eye contact—or inappropriate eye contact
■ Stay focused on the speaker and the content	■ Allow their minds to wander, are easily distracted, work on unrelated tasks
■ Mentally paraphrase key points to maintain attention level and ensure comprehension	■ Fail to paraphrase
■ Adjust listening style to the situation	■ Listen with the same style, regardless of the situation
■ Give the speaker nonverbal cues (such as nodding to show agreement or raising eyebrows to show surprise or skepticism)	■ Fail to give the speaker nonverbal feedback
■ Save questions or points of disagreement until an appropriate time	■ Interrupt whenever they disagree or don't understand
■ Overlook stylistic differences and focus on the speaker's message	■ Are distracted by or unduly influenced by stylistic differences; are judgmental
■ Make distinctions between main points and supporting details	■ Unable to distinguish main points from details
■ Look for opportunities to learn	■ Assume they already know everything that's important to know

whose native language or life experience is different from yours, try to paraphrase that person's ideas and give the speaker a chance to confirm what you think you heard.

IMPROVING YOUR NONVERBAL COMMUNICATION SKILLS

5 LEARNING OBJECTIVE

Explain the importance of nonverbal communication and identify six major categories of nonverbal expression

Nonverbal communication is the process of sending and receiving information, both intentionally and unintentionally, without using written or spoken language. Nonverbal signals play a vital role in communication because they can strengthen a verbal message (when the nonverbal signals match the spoken words), weaken a verbal message (when nonverbal signals don't match the words), or replace words entirely. For example, you might tell a client that a project is coming along nicely, but your forced smile and nervous glances will send an entirely different message.

You've been tuned in to nonverbal communication since your first contact with other human beings. Paying special attention to these signals in the workplace will enhance your ability to communicate successfully. Moreover, as you work with a diverse range of people in the global marketplace, you'll also need to grasp the different meanings of common gestures in various cultures. For instance, the thumbs-up sign and circled index finger and thumb that indicate "OK" are positive gestures in the United States but insulting gestures in some other cultures. Six types of signals are particularly important:

Nonverbal communication supplements spoken language.

- **Facial expressions.** Your face is the primary site for expressing your emotions; it reveals both the type and the intensity of your feelings.[43] Your eyes are especially effective for indicating attention and interest, influencing others, regulating interaction, and establishing dominance.[44] As with other areas of nonverbal expressions, however, facial signals can vary widely from culture to culture. For instance, maintaining eye contact is usually viewed as a sign of sincerity and openness in the United States, but it can be viewed as rude in Japan.[45]

- **Gestures and postures.** Many gestures—a wave of the hand, for example—have a specific and intentional meaning. Other types of body movement are often unintentional

Nonverbal signals include facial expression, gestures and posture, vocal characteristics, personal appearance, touch, and use of time and space.

and express more general messages. Slouching, leaning forward, fidgeting, and walking briskly are all unconscious signals that can reveal whether you feel confident or nervous, friendly or hostile, assertive or passive, powerful or powerless.

Work to make sure your nonverbal signals match the tone and content of your spoken communication.

- **Vocal characteristics.** Voice carries both intentional and unintentional messages. A speaker can intentionally control pitch, pace, and stress to convey a specific message. For instance, consider the question, "What are you doing?" with the emphasis on *what* versus the emphasis on *you* . Unintentional vocal characteristics can convey happiness, surprise, fear, and other emotions (for example, fear often increases the pitch and the pace of your speaking voice).

What signals does your personal appearance send?

- **Personal appearance.** People respond to others on the basis of their physical appearance, sometimes fairly and other times unfairly. Although an individual's body type and facial features impose limitations, most people are able to control their appearance to some degree. Grooming, clothing, accessories, piercings, tattoos, hairstyle—you can control all of these. For instance, are you talking like a serious business professional but dressing like you belong in a dance club or a frat house? If your goal is to make a good impression, adopt the style of the people you want to impress. Many employers also have guidelines concerning attire, body art, and other issues, so make sure you understand and follow them.[46]

- **Touch.** Touch is an important way to convey warmth, comfort, and reassurance—as well as control. Touch is so powerful, in fact, that it is governed by cultural customs that establish who can touch whom and how in various circumstances. In the United States and Great Britain, for instance, people usually touch less frequently than people in France or Costa Rica do. Even within each culture's norms, however, individual attitudes toward touch vary widely. A manager might be comfortable using hugs to express support or congratulations, but his or her subordinates could interpret those hugs as a show of dominance or sexual interest.[47] Touch is a complex subject. The best advice: When in doubt, don't touch.

- **Time and space.** Like touch, time and space can be used to assert authority, imply intimacy, and send other nonverbal messages. For instance, some people try to demonstrate their own importance or disregard for others by making other people wait; others show respect by being on time. Similarly, taking care not to invade private space, such as standing too close when talking, is a way to show respect for others. Keep in mind that expectations regarding both time and space vary by culture.

When you listen, be sure to pay attention to nonverbal clues. Do these signals seem to amplify the spoken words or contradict them? Is the speaker intentionally using nonverbal signals to send you a message that he or she can't put into words? Be observant but don't assume that you can "read someone like a book." Nonverbal signals are powerful, but they aren't infallible. For example, contrary to popular belief, avoiding eye contact and covering one's face while talking are not reliable clues that someone is lying. These behaviors may be influenced by culture (in some cultures, sustained eye contact can be interpreted as a sign of disrespect) or might just be ways of coping with stressful situations.[48]

6 LEARNING OBJECTIVE

Explain the importance of business etiquette, and identify three key areas in which good etiquette is essential

If you want to appear polished, professional, and confident in business settings, learn the behavioral expectations in your workplace.

DEVELOPING YOUR BUSINESS ETIQUETTE

You may have noticed a common thread running through the topics of successful teamwork, productive meetings, effective listening, and nonverbal communication: All depend on mutual respect and consideration among all participants. As Chapter 1 notes, etiquette is now considered an essential business skill. Nobody wants to work with someone who is rude to colleagues or an embarrassment to the company. Moreover, shabby treatment of others in the workplace can be a huge drain on morale and productivity.[49] Poor etiquette can drive away customers, investors, and other critical audiences—and it can limit your career potential. This section addresses some key etiquette points to remember when you're in the workplace, out in public, and online. Long lists of etiquette rules can be difficult to remember, but you can get by in most every situation by remembering to be aware of your effect on others, treating everyone with respect, and keeping in mind that the impressions you leave behind can have a lasting effect on you and your company—so make sure to leave positive impressions wherever you go.

Business Etiquette in the Workplace

Workplace etiquette includes a variety of behaviors, habits, and aspects of nonverbal communication. Although it isn't always thought of as an element of etiquette, your personal appearance in the workplace sends a strong signal to managers, colleagues, and customers. Pay attention to the style of dress where you work and adjust your style to match. Observe others and don't be afraid to ask for advice. If you're not sure, dress modestly and simply— earn a reputation for what you can *do*, not for what you can wear.

Grooming is as important as attire. Pay close attention to cleanliness and avoid using products with powerful scents, such as perfumed soaps, colognes, shampoos, and after-shave lotions. Many people are bothered by these products, and some are allergic to them.

If you work in a conventional office setting, you'll spend as much time with your officemates as you do with family and friends. Personal demeanor is therefore a vital element of workplace harmony. No one expects you to be artificially upbeat and bubbly every second of the day, but a single negative personality can make an entire office miserable and unproductive. Every person in the company has a responsibility to contribute to a positive, energetic work environment.

> Contribute to harmony and productivity in your workplace with a professional, upbeat demeanor.

Given the telephone's central role in business communication, phone skills are essential in most professions. Because phone calls lack the visual richness of face-to-face conversations, you have to rely on your attitude and tone of voice to convey confidence and professionalism. Table 2.3 summarizes helpful tips for placing and receiving phone calls in a confident, professional manner.

> Your telephone skills will be vital to your business success.

Mobile phones are a contentious point of etiquette in today's workplace. They can boost productivity if used mindfully, but they can be a productivity- and morale-draining disruption when used carelessly. Be aware that attitudes about mobile phones vary widely, and don't be surprised if you encounter policies restricting their use in offices or meeting rooms. Nearly half of U.S. companies already have such policies.[50]

> Poor mobile phone etiquette is a common source of complaints in both the workplace and social settings.

Like every other aspect of communication, your phone habits say a lot about how much respect you have for the people around you. Selecting obnoxious ring tones, talking loudly in open offices or public places, using your phone right next to someone else, making excessive or unnecessary personal calls during work hours, invading someone's privacy by using your camera phone without permission, taking or making calls in restrooms and other inappropriate places, texting while someone is talking to you, allowing incoming calls to interrupt meetings or discussions—these are all disrespectful choices that will reflect negatively on you.[51]

Business Etiquette in Social Settings

From business lunches to industry conferences, you may be asked to represent your company when you're out in public. Make sure your appearance and actions are appropriate to the situation. Get to know the customs of the culture when you meet new people. For example, in North America, a firm handshake is expected when two people meet, whereas a respectful bow of the head is more appropriate in Japan. If you are expected to shake hands, be aware that the passive "dead fish" handshake creates an extremely negative impression with most people. If you are physically able, always stand when shaking someone's hand.

> You represent your company when you're out in public—or communicating online under your own name—so etiquette continues to be important even after you leave the office.

When introducing yourself, include a brief description of your role in the company. When introducing two other people, speak their first and last names clearly and then try to offer some information (perhaps a shared professional interest) to help the two people ease into a conversation.[52] Generally speaking, the lower-ranking person is introduced to the senior-ranking person, without regard to gender.[53]

Business is often conducted over meals, and knowing the basics of dining etiquette will make you more effective and comfortable in these situations.[54] Start by choosing foods that are easy to eat. Avoid alcoholic beverages in most instances, but if drinking one is appropriate, save it for the end of the meal. Leave business documents under your chair until entrée plates have been removed; the business aspect of the meal doesn't usually begin until then.

Just as in the office, when you use your mobile phone inappropriately in public, you send the message that people around you aren't as important as your call and that you don't respect your caller's privacy.[55] If it's not a matter of life and death, or at least an urgent request from your boss or a customer, wait until you're back in the office.

TABLE 2.3 Quick Tips for Improving Your Phone Skills

General Tips	Placing Calls	Receiving Calls	Using Voice Mail
Use frequent verbal responses that show you're listening ("Oh yes," "I see," "That's right").	Be ready before you call so that you don't waste the other person's time.	Answer promptly and with a smile so that you sound friendly and positive.	When recording your own outgoing message, make it brief and professional.
Increase your volume just slightly to convey your confidence.	Minimize the noise level in your environment as much as possible to avoid distracting the other party.	Identify yourself and your company (some companies have specific instructions for what to say when you answer).	If you can, record temporary greetings on days when you are unavailable all day so that callers will know you're gone for the day.
Don't speak in a monotone; vary your pitch and inflections so people know you're interested.	Identify yourself and your organization, briefly describe why you're calling, and verify that you've called at a good time.	Establish the needs of your caller by asking, "How may I help you?" If you know the caller's name, use it.	Check your voice-mail messages regularly and return all necessary calls within 24 hours.
Slow down when conversing with people whose native language isn't the same as yours.	Don't take up too much time. Speak quickly and clearly, and get right to the point of the call.	If you can, answer questions promptly and efficiently; if you can't help, tell them what you can do for them.	Leave simple, clear messages with your name, number (don't assume the recipient has caller ID), purpose for calling, and times when you can be reached.
Stay focused on the call throughout; others can easily tell when you're not paying attention.	Close in a friendly, positive manner and double-check all vital information such as meeting times and dates.	If you must forward a call or put someone one hold, explain what you are doing first.	State your name and telephone number slowly so that the other person can easily write them down; repeat both if the other person doesn't know you.
		If you forward a call to someone else, try to speak with that person first to verify that he or she is available and to introduce the caller.	Be careful what you say; most voice-mail systems allow users to forward messages to anyone else in the system.
		If you take a message for someone else, be complete and accurate, including the caller's name, number, and organization.	Replay your message before leaving the system to make sure it is clear and complete.

Finally, always remember that business meals are a forum for business, period. Don't discuss politics, religion, or any other topic that's likely to stir up emotions. Don't complain about work, don't ask deeply personal questions, avoid profanity, and be careful with humor—a joke that entertains some people could easily offend others.

Business Etiquette Online

Electronic media seem to be a breeding ground for poor etiquette. Learn the basics of professional online behavior to avoid mistakes that could hurt your company or your career. Here are some guidelines to follow whenever you are representing your company while using electronic media:[56]

When you represent your company online, you must adhere to a high standard of etiquette and respect for others.

- **Avoid personal attacks.** The anonymous and instantaneous nature of online communication can cause even level-headed people to lose their tempers and go after others.
- **Stay focused on the original topic.** If you want to change the subject of an online conversation, start with a new message or thread.
- **Don't present opinions as facts; support facts with evidence.** This guideline applies to all communication, of course, but online venues in particular seem to tempt people into presenting their beliefs and opinions as unassailable truths.
- **Follow basic expectations of spelling, punctuation, and capitalization.** Sending careless, acronym-filled messages that look like you're texting your high school buddies makes you look like an amateur.

- **Use virus protection and keep it up to date.** Sending or posting a file that contains a computer virus is rude.
- **Ask if this is a good time for an IM chat.** Don't assume that just because a person is showing as "available" on your IM system that he or she wants to chat with you right this instant.
- **Watch your language and keep your emotions under control.** A moment of indiscretion could haunt you forever.
- **Avoid multitasking while using IM or other tools.** You might think you're saving time by doing a dozen things at once, but you're probably making the other person wait while you bounce back and forth between IM and your other tasks.
- **Never assume you have privacy.** Assume that anything you type will be stored forever, could be forwarded to other people, and might be read by your boss or the company's security staff.
- **Don't use "reply all" in e-mail unless everyone can benefit from your reply.** If one or more recipients of an e-mail message don't need the information in your reply, remove their addresses before you send.
- **Don't waste others' time with sloppy, confusing, or incomplete messages.** Doing so is disrespectful.
- **Respect boundaries of time and virtual space.** For instance, don't start using an employee's personal Facebook page for business messages unless you've discussed it beforehand, and don't assume people are available to discuss work matters around the clock, even if you do find them online in the middle of the night.

REAL-TIME UPDATES
Learn More by Watching This Presentation

Don't let etiquette blunders derail your career

Get great advice on developing professional telephone skills, making a positive impression while dining, and dressing for success in any career environment (including great tips on buying business suits). Go to **http://real-timeupdates.com/bce5** and click on "Learn More." If you are using mybcommlab, you can access Real-Time Updates within each chapter or under Student Study Tools.

Respect personal and professional boundaries when using social networking tools.

---

mybcommlab   Are you an active learner? Go to mybcommlab.com to master Chapter 2's content. Chapter 2's interactive activities include:

- Customizable Study Plan and Chapter 2 practice quizzes
- Chapter 2 Simulation (Interpersonal Communication and Teamwork), which helps you think critically and prepare to make choices in the business world
- Chapter 2 Video Exercise (Business Etiquette), which shows you how textbook concepts are put into practice every day
- Flash Cards for mastering the definition of chapter terms
- Interactive Lessons that visually review key chapter concepts
- Document Makeovers for hands-on, scored practice in revising documents

CHAPTER REVIEW AND ACTIVITIES

Learning Objectives: Check Your Progress

1 OBJECTIVE List the advantages and disadvantages of working in teams, and describe the characteristics of effective teams.

The advantages of successful teamwork include improved productivity, creativity, and employee involvement; increased information and knowledge; greater diversity of views; and increased acceptance of new solutions and ideas. The potential disadvantages of working in teams include groupthink (the tendency to let peer pressure overcome one's better judgment), the pursuit of hidden agendas, and the cost (in money and time) of planning and conducting team activities. The most effective teams have a clear objective and a shared sense of purpose, communicate openly and honestly, reach decisions by consensus, think creatively, and know how to resolve conflict.

2 OBJECTIVE Offer guidelines for collaborative communication, identify major collaboration technologies, and explain how to give constructive feedback.

To succeed with collaborative writing, (1) select team members carefully to balance talents and viewpoints; (2) agree on project goals; (3) make sure team members have time to get to know one another; (4) make sure that everyone clearly understands individual responsibilities, processes, and tools; (5) generally, avoid writing as a group (assign the writing phase to one person, or assign separate sections to individual writers and have one person edit them all); (6) make sure tools and techniques are compatible; and (7) check in with everyone periodically.

Some of the major collaboration technologies are review and commenting features in document preparation software, wikis, content management systems, groupware, and shared workspaces. Social networking technologies are redefining teamwork and team communication by helping to erase the constraints of geographic and organization boundaries. A key benefit of social networking is combining the insights of multiple experts across an organization (or even outside the organization) in order to address tough business challenges.

When you are asked to give feedback on someone's writing, focus on how the writing can be improved. Avoid personal attacks and give the person clear and specific advice.

3 OBJECTIVE List the key steps needed to ensure productive team meetings, and identify the most common meeting technologies.

Meetings are an essential business activity, but they can waste considerable time and money if conducted poorly. Help your company make better use of meetings by preparing carefully, conducting meetings efficiently, and using meeting technologies wisely. Make sure your meetings are necessary, are carefully planned, include only the necessary participants, and follow clear agendas.

A variety of meeting technologies are available to help teams and other groups communicate more successfully. The primary advantage of these tools is the ability to conduct virtual meetings that don't require everyone to be in the same place at the same time. The tools range from simple instant messaging sessions and teleconferences to videoconferencing and web-based meetings to specialized capabilities such as online brainstorming systems and virtual reality simulators.

4 OBJECTIVE Describe the listening process, and explain how good listeners overcome barriers at each stage of the process.

The listening process involves five steps: receiving, decoding, remembering, evaluating, and responding. At any stage, barriers can disrupt the process, so good listeners practice active listening, avoid disrupting the speaker or other people, work hard to see past superficial differences and distractions, and take care not to let selective perception filter out important information.

5 OBJECTIVE Explain the importance of nonverbal communication, and identify six major categories of nonverbal expression.

Nonverbal signals play a vital role in communication because they can strengthen a verbal message (when the nonverbal signals match the spoken words), weaken a verbal message (when nonverbal signals don't match the words), or replace words entirely. The six major categories of nonverbal expression are facial expressions, gestures and posture, vocal characteristics, personal appearance, touch, and use of time and personal space.

6 OBJECTIVE Explain the importance of business etiquette, and identify three key areas in which good etiquette is essential.

Etiquette is an essential business skill because the impression you make on others and your ability to help others feel comfortable will be major contributors to your career success. Poor etiquette can hinder team efforts, drain morale and productivity, drive away customers and investors, and limit your career potential.

Three key areas that require good business etiquette are the workplace, social settings in which you represent your company, and online venues. Matters of workplace etiquette include personal appearance, grooming, demeanor, and telephone habits. In social settings, make a positive impression by learning how to introduce yourself and others in a professional manner and by conducting yourself gracefully at dinners and other social gatherings. In online settings, learn and follow the standards of acceptable behavior for each system.

▎ Test Your Knowledge

To review chapter content related to each question, refer to the indicated Learning Objective.
1. What is the difference between constructive and destructive feedback? [LO-2]
2. What are five characteristics of effective teams? [LO-1]
3. How does an agenda help make a meeting more successful? [LO-3]
4. What are the six main categories of nonverbal signals? [LO-5]
5. What activities make up the listening process? [LO-4]

▎ Apply Your Knowledge

To review chapter content related to each question, refer to the indicated Learning Objective.
1. You head up the interdepartmental design review team for a manufacturer of high-performance motorcycles, and things are not going well at the moment. The design engineers and marketing strategists keep arguing about which should be a higher priority, performance or aesthetics, and the accountants say both groups are driving the cost of the

new model through the roof by adding too many new features. Everyone has valid points to make, but the team is getting bogged down in conflict. Explain how you could go about resolving the stalemate. [LO-1]

2. Whenever your boss asks for feedback, she blasts anyone who offers criticism, so people tend to agree with everything she says. You want to talk to her about it, but what should you say? List some of the points you want to make when you discuss this issue with your boss. [LO-2]

3. Considering what you've learned about nonverbal communication, what are some of the ways in which communication might break down during an online meeting in which the participants can see video images of only the person presenting at any given time—and then only his or her head? [LO-5]

4. Chester never seems to be paying attention during weekly team meetings. He has never contributed to the discussion, and you've never seen him take notes. He says he wants to support the team but that he finds it difficult to focus during routine meetings. List some ideas you could give him that might improve his listening skills. [LO-4]

5. Several members of your sales team are protesting the company's "business casual" dress code, claiming that dressing nicely makes them feel awkward and overly formal in front of customers. You have to admit that most of the company's customers dress like they've just walked in from a picnic or a motorcycle ride, but that doesn't change the fact that you want your company to be seen as conscientious and professional. How will you explain the policy to these employees in a way that will help them understand and accept it? [LO-6]

Practice Your Skills

Activities

Active links for all websites in this chapter can be found on mybcommlab; see your User Guide for instructions on accessing the content for this chapter. Each activity is labeled according to the primary skill or skills you will need to use. To review relevant chapter content, you can refer to the indicated Learning Objective. In some instances, supporting information will be found in another chapter, as indicated.

1. **Collaboration: Working in Teams [LO-1]** In teams assigned by your instructor, prepare a 10-minute presentation on the potential disadvantages of using social media for business communication. When the presentation is ready, discuss how effective the team was using the criteria of (1) having a clear objective and a shared sense of purpose, (2) communicating openly and honestly, (3) reaching decisions by consensus, (4) thinking creatively, and (5) knowing how to resolve conflict. Be prepared to discuss your findings with the rest of the class.

2. **Collaboration: Working in Teams [LO-1]** In teams of four or five classmates, role play a scenario in which the team is to decide which department at your college will receive a $1 million gift from an anonymous donor. The catch: Each member of the team will advocate for a different department (decide among yourselves who represents which departments), which means that all but one member will "lose" in the final decision. Working as a team, decide which department will receive the donation and discuss the results to help everyone on the team support the decision. Be prepared to present your choice and your justification for it to the rest of the class.

3. **Collaboration: Collaborating on Writing Projects: Media Skills: Blogging [LO-2]** In this project, you will conduct research on your own and then merge your results with those of the rest of your team. Search Twitter for messages on the subject of workplace safety. (You can use Twitter's advanced search page at http://search.twitter.com/advanced or use the "site: twitter.com" qualifier on a regular search engine.)

   Compile at least five general safety tips that apply to any office setting, and then meet with your team to select the five best tips from all those the team has collected. Collaborate on a blog post that lists the team's top five tips.

4. **Collaboration: Using Collaboration Technologies [LO-2]** In a team assigned by your instructor, use Zoho (www.zoho.com; free for personal use) or a comparable system to collaborate on a set of directions that out-of-town visitors could use to reach a specific point on your campus, such as a stadium or dorm. The team should choose the location and the mode(s) of transportation involved. Be creative—brainstorm the best ways to guide first-time visitors to the selected location using all the media at your disposal.

 Learn how to use Twitter search. Visit http://real-timeupdates .com/bce5, click on "Students Assignments," and then click on "Twitter Screencast."

---

5. **Collaboration: Planning Meetings: Media Skills: Presentations [LO-3]** A project leader has made notes about covering the following items at the quarterly budget meeting. Prepare an agenda by putting these items into a logical order and rewriting them, where necessary, to give phrases a more consistent sound. Create a presentation slide (or a blog post, as your instructor indicates).

   - Budget Committee Meeting to be held on December 12, 2011, at 9:30 a.m.
   - I will call the meeting to order.
   - Site director's report: A closer look at cost overruns on Greentree site.
   - The group will review and approve the minutes from last quarter's meeting.

- I will ask the finance director to report on actual vs. projected quarterly revenues and expenses.
- I will distribute copies of the overall divisional budget and announce the date of the next budget meeting.
- Discussion: How can we do a better job of anticipating and preventing cost overruns?
- Meeting will take place in Conference Room 3.
- What additional budget issues must be considered during this quarter?

6. **Collaboration: Participating in Meetings [LO-3]** With a classmate, attend a local community or campus meeting where you can observe group discussion. Take notes individually during the meeting and then work together to answer the following questions. Submit your conclusions in an e-mail message to your instructor.

   a. What is your evaluation of this meeting? In your answer, consider (1) the leader's ability to clearly state the meeting's goals, (2) the leader's ability to engage members in a meaningful discussion, and (3) the group's listening skills.

   b. How well did the individual participants listen? How could you tell?

   c. Compare the notes you took during the meeting with those of your classmate. What differences do you notice? How do you account for these differences?

7. **Collaboration: Leading Meetings [LO-3], Chapter 1** Every month, each employee in your department is expected to give a brief oral presentation on the status of his or her ongoing projects. However, your department has recently hired an employee who has a severe speech impediment that prevents people from understanding most of what he has to say. As assistant department manager, how will you resolve this dilemma? Explain your plan in an e-mail message to your instructor.

8. **Interpersonal Communication: Listening Actively [LO-4]** For the next several days, take notes on your listening performance during at least a half-dozen situations in class, during social activities, and at work, if applicable. Referring to the traits of effective listeners in Table 2.2 on page 71, rate yourself using *always, frequently, occasionally,* or *never* on these positive listening habits. In a report no longer than one page, summarize your analysis and identify specific areas in which you can improve your listening skills.

9. **Interpersonal Communication: Listening to Empathize [LO-4]** Think back over conversations you have had with friends, family members, co-workers, or classmates in the past week. Select a conversation in which the other person wanted to talk about something that was troubling him or her—a bad situation a work, a scary exam on the horizon, difficulties with a professor, a health problem, financial concerns, or the like. As you replay this conversation in your mind, think about how well you did in terms of empathic listening (see page 69). For example, did you find yourself being critical when the person really just needed someone to listen? Did you let the person know, by your words or actions, that you cared about his or her dilemma, even if you were not able to help in any other way? Analyze your listening performance in a brief e-mail to your instructor. Be sure not to disclose any private information; you can change the names of the people involved or the circumstances as needed to maintain privacy.

10. **Nonverbal Communication: Analyzing Nonverbal Signals [LO-5]** Select a piece of mail, from any company, that you received at work or at home. Analyze its appearance. What nonverbal messages does this piece send? Are these messages consistent with the content of the mailing? If not, what could the sender have done to make the nonverbal communication consistent with the verbal communication? Summarize your findings in a post on your class blog or in an e-mail message to your instructor.

11. **Nonverbal Communication: Analyzing Nonverbal Signals [LO-5]** Describe what the following gestures or postures suggest when they are exhibited by someone during a conversation. How did you reach your conclusions about each nonverbal signal? How do such signals influence your interpretation of spoken words? Summarize your findings in a post on your class blog or in an e-mail message to your instructor.
    a. Shifting one's body continuously while seated
    b. Twirling and playing with one's hair
    c. Sitting in a sprawled position
    d. Rolling one's eyes
    e. Extending a weak handshake

12. **Communication Etiquette: Telephone Skills; Media Skills: Scripting a Podcast [LO-6]** Late on a Friday afternoon, you learn that the facilities department is going to move you—and your computer, your desk, and all your files—to another office first thing Monday morning. However, you have an important client meeting scheduled in your office for Monday afternoon, and you need to finalize some contract details on Monday morning. You simply can't lose access to your office at that point, and you're more than a little annoyed that your boss didn't ask you before approving the move. He has already left for the day, but you know he usually checks his voice mail over the weekend, so you decide to leave a voice-mail message, asking him to cancel the move or at least call you at home as soon as possible. Using the voice-mail guidelines listed in Table 2.3, plan your message (use an imaginary phone number as your contact number and make up any other details you need for the call). As directed by your instructor, submit either a written script of the message or a podcast recording of the actual message.

13. **Communication Etiquette: Online Etiquette; Media Skills: Writing Blog Posts [LO-6]** Between the immediate nature of electronic communication and the ability for people to disguise their identity by using screen

names, online discussions sometimes get nasty. Posting rude comments or vicious product reviews might help a person release some pent-up anger, but such messages rarely help the situation. The people on the receiving end of these messages are likely to get defensive or ignore the comments entirely, rather than focusing on finding a solution. Find an online review of a product, service, or company that strikes you as rude to the point of being nasty. For your class blog (or other media as assigned by your instructor) write a summary of the situation, explain why the rude comment is ineffective, and write a new version that is more effective (as in, more likely to bring about the change the writer wanted).

Expand Your Skills

Critique the Professionals

Celebrities can learn from successful businesses when it comes to managing their careers, but businesses can learn from successful celebrities, too—particularly when it comes to building communities online using social media. For instance, social media guru Dan Schawbel cites Vin Diesel, Ashton Kutcher, Lady Gaga, Lenny Kravitz, and Michael Phelps as celebrities who have used Facebook to build their personal brands.[57] Locate three celebrities (musicians, actors, authors, or athletes) who have sizable fan bases on Facebook and analyze how they use the social network. Using whatever medium your instructor requests, write a brief analysis (no more than one page) of the lessons, positive or negative, that a business could learn from these celebrities. Be sure to cite specific elements from the Facebook pages you've chosen, and if you think any of the celebrities have made mistakes in their use of Facebook, describe those as well.

Sharpen Your Career Skills Online

Bovée and Thill's Business Communication Web Search, at http://businesscommunicationblog.com/websearch, is a unique research tool designed specifically for business communication research. Use the Web Search function to find a website, video, PDF document, podcast, or presentation that explains at least one essential skill related to teamwork, collaborative writing, listening, nonverbal communication, or business etiquette. Write a brief e-mail message to your instructor, describing the item that you found and summarizing the career skills information you learned from it.

mybcommlab

If your course uses mybcommlab, log on to www.mybcommlab.com to access the following study and assessment aids associated with this chapter:

- Video applications
- Pre/post test
- Real-Time Updates
- Personalized study plan
- Peer review activity
- Model documents
- Quick Learning Guides
- Sample presentations

If you are not using mybcommlab, you can access Real-Time Updates and Quick Learning Guides through http://real-time updates.com/bce5. The Quick Learning Guide (located under "Learn More" on the website) hits all the high points of this chapter in just two pages. This guide, especially prepared by the authors, will help you study for exams or review important concepts whenever you need a quick refresher.

Improve Your Grammar, Mechanics, and Usage

You can download the text of this assignment from http://real-timeupdates.com/bce5; click on "Student Assignments," and then click on "Chapter 2. Improve Your Grammar, Mechanics, and Usage."

Level 1: Self-Assessment—Pronouns

Review Section 1.2 in the Handbook of Grammar, Mechanics, and Usage and then complete the following 15 items. Answers to these exercises appear on page AK-1.

In items 1–5, replace the underlined nouns with the correct pronouns.

1. To which retailer will you send your merchandise?
2. Have you given John and Nancy a list of parts?
3. The main office sent the invoice to Mr. and Mrs. Litvak on December 5.
4. The company settled the company's accounts before the end of the year.
5. Which person's umbrella is this?

In items 6–15, identify which of the pronoun forms provided in parentheses is correct.

6. The sales staff is preparing guidelines for (their, its) clients.
7. Few of the sales representatives turn in (their, its) reports on time.
8. The board of directors has chosen (their, its) officers.
9. Gomez and Archer have told (his, their) clients about the new program.
10. Each manager plans to expand (his, their, his or her) sphere of control next year.
11. Has everyone supplied (his, their, his or her) Social Security number?
12. After giving every employee (his, their, a) raise, George told (them, they, all) about the increased workload.
13. Bob and Tim have opposite ideas about how to achieve company goals. (Who, Whom) do you think will win the debate?
14. City Securities has just announced (who, whom) it will hire as CEO.
15. Either of the new products would readily find (their, its) niche in the marketplace.

Level 2: Workplace Applications

The following items may contain errors in grammar, capitalization, punctuation, abbreviation, number style, word division, and vocabulary. Rewrite each sentence, correcting all errors. If a sentence has no errors, write "Correct" for that number.

1. Anita Doig from Data Providers will outline their data interpretations as it relates to industry trends, additionally Miss Doig will be asked to comment on how their data should be ulililized.

2. You're order for 2000 mylar bags has been received by us; please be advised that orders of less than 5000 bags only get a 20 percent discount.

3. Just between you and I, the new 'customer centric' philosophy seems pretty confusing.

4. Podcasting can be an effective way to distribute messages to a widespread audience, but you need to pay close attention to the demands of an audio medium.

5. Among the specialties of Product Marketers International is promotional efforts for clients, including presence on the Internet, radio, and on television.

6. An overview of a typical marketing plan will be covered in the introduction to this report, to give you an idea of what's in it.

7. Subsidiary rights sales can be a discreet source of income and compliment your overall sales.

8. Special events ranging from author breakfasts and luncheons to awards programs and reception's offers a great way to make industry contacts.

9. We will show you how not only to meet the challenges of information rich material but also the challenges of electronic distance learning.

10. To site just one problem, the reason that the market is in such a state of confusion is the appalling lack of standards whether for hardware, software or for metadata.

11. Two leading business consultants Doug Smith and Carla McNeil will share their insights on how specialty stores can effectively compete in a world of Corporate Superstores.

12. One of the big questions we need to address are "How does buying effect inventory levels"?

13. The closing of many industry digital entities have greatly affected the perception of e-books as a viable platform.

14. A competent, motivated, and enthusiastic staff can be a managers' most important asset in a competitive marketplace.

15. Come by the Technology Lounge where you can log on to computers and plug into laptops and check out demos of sponsor's websites.

Level 3: Document Critique

The following document may contain errors in grammar, capitalization, punctuation, abbreviation, number style, word division, and vocabulary. As your instructor indicates, photocopy this page and correct all errors using standard proofreading marks (see Appendix C) or download the document and make the corrections in your word processing software.

Marketing Pro's: Are You're Messages Truthful and non-Deceptive?! In the United States, the FTC (federal Trade Commission) has the authority to impose penalty against advertisers whom violate Federal Standards for truthful advertising. The FTC considers a message to be deceptive, if they include statements that are likely to mis-lead reasonable customers and the statements are an important part of the purchasing decision. A failures to include important information are also considered deceptive. Also, the FTC also looks at so-called *"implied claims,?"* Claims you don't explicitly make but that can be inferred from what you do or don't say.

The Three-Step Writing Process

Planning Business Messages

LEARNING OBJECTIVES

After studying this chapter, you will be able to

1 Describe the three-step writing process and explain why it will help you create better messages in less time

2 Explain what it means to analyze the situation when planning a message

3 Describe the techniques for gathering information for simple messages and identify three attributes of quality information

4 Compare the four major classes of media and list the factors to consider when choosing the most appropriate medium for a message

5 Explain why good organization is important to both you and your audience and explain how to organize any business message

PEARSON mybcommlab Access interactive videos, simulations, sample documents, Document Makeovers, and assessment quizzes in Chapter 3 of mybcommlab.com for mastery of this chapter's objectives.

COMMUNICATION *Matters*

" This is the role that stories play—putting knowledge into a framework that is more lifelike, more true to our day-to-day existence. "

—Chip Heath and Dan Heath, *Made to Stick: Why Some Ideas Survive and Others Die*

Stanford University's Chip Heath and Duke University's Dan Heath have identified the key factors that lead audiences to care about and act on the messages they receive.

Why do some ideas catch on and others disappear? Why do smart ideas often go unnoticed while mediocre or even bad ideas become permanently stuck in people's consciousness? Brothers Chip and Dan Heath devoted years to solving this puzzle and concluded that audiences are more likely to pay attention to and care about ideas that are *simple*, *concrete*, *credible*, *unexpected*, and *emotional*, and they are more likely to act on ideas that are presented in a compelling *story*.[1] Every business message can be improved by making it simple, concrete, and credible, and many can be improved through the careful use of surprise, emotion, and storytelling.

This chapter is the first of three that explore the three-step writing process, a time-tested method for creating more effective messages in less time. The techniques you'll learn in this chapter will help you plan and organize messages that will capture and keep your audience's attention.

UNDERSTANDING THE THREE-STEP WRITING PROCESS

No matter what kind of information you need to convey, your goal is to craft a message that has a clear purpose, meets the needs of your audience, and communicates efficiently and effectively. For every message you send, you can reduce the time and energy required to achieve this goal by following a clear and proven three-step process (see Figure 3.1):

- **Planning business messages.** To plan any message, first *analyze the situation* by defining your purpose and developing a profile of your audience. When you're sure about what you need to accomplish with your message, *gather information* that will meet your audience's needs. Next, *select the right medium* (oral, written, visual, or electronic) to deliver your message. Then *organize the information* by defining your main idea, limiting your scope, selecting the direct or indirect approach, and outlining your content. Planning messages is the focus of this chapter.

- **Writing business messages.** Once you've planned your message, *adapt your approach to your audience* with sensitivity, relationship skills, and style. Then you're ready to *compose your message* by choosing strong words, creating effective sentences, and developing coherent paragraphs. Writing business messages is discussed in Chapter 4.

- **Completing business messages.** After writing your first draft, *revise your message* to make sure it is clear, concise, and correct. Next *produce* your message, giving it an attractive, professional appearance. *Proofread* the final product for typos, spelling errors, and other mechanical problems. Finally, *distribute* your message using an appropriate combination of personal and technological tools. Completing business messages is discussed in Chapter 5.

Throughout this book, you'll see the three steps in this process applied to a wide variety of business messages: for short messages (Chapters 6 through 9), reports and proposals

1 LEARNING OBJECTIVE

Describe the three-step writing process and explain why it will help you create better messages in less time

The three-step writing process consists of *planning*, *writing*, and *completing* your messages.

Figure 3.1   The Three-Step Writing Process
This three-step process will help you create more effective messages in any medium. As you get more practice with the process, it will become easier and more automatic.

1 Plan	**2 Write**	**3 Complete**
Analyze the Situation	**Adapt to Your Audience**	**Revise the Message**
Define your purpose and develop an audience profile.	Be sensitive to audience needs by using a "you" attitude, politeness, positive emphasis, and unbiased language. Build a strong relationship with your audience by establishing your credibility and projecting your company's preferred image. Control your style with a conversational tone, plain English, and appropriate voice.	Evaluate content and review readability, edit and rewrite for conciseness and clarity.
Gather Information		**Produce the Message**
Determine audience needs and obtain the information necessary to satisfy those needs.		Use effective design elements and suitable layout for a clean, professional appearance.
Select the Right Medium		**Proofread the Message**
Select the best medium for delivering your message.		Review for errors in layout, spelling, and mechanics.
Organize the Information	**Compose the Message**	**Distribute the Message**
Define your main idea, limit your scope, select a direct or an indirect approach, and outline your content.	Choose strong words that will help you create effective sentences and coherent paragraphs.	Deliver your message using the chosen medium; make sure all documents and all relevant files are distributed successfully.

(Chapters 10 and 11), oral presentations (Chapter 12), and employment messages (Chapters 13 and 14).

As a starting point, try to allot roughly half your available time for planning, one quarter for writing, and one quarter for completing a message.

The more you use the three-step process, the easier and faster writing will become for you. You'll also get better at allotting your time for each step. As a general rule, try using roughly half your time for planning, one-quarter of your time for writing, and the remaining quarter for completing the project. Of course, you don't need to undertake an elaborate process to create simple messages, but approaching your writing projects with the three steps in mind always helps.

> **SKILLS** *Matters*
>
> An important skill in almost any business profession is being able to prepare effective messages without getting bogged down and struggling to get the words right. Practicing the three-step process will help you figure out what to say and how to say it, so you can complete each message and move on quickly.

Even for small writing projects, resist the temptation to skip the planning step. For instance, spending even just a minute or two thinking through the purpose of an e-mail message can help you write much faster because you'll know in advance what you want to say. And leave plenty of time to complete your documents, too; you don't want to compromise the quality of a good message by shortchanging the important steps of revising, producing, proofreading, and distributing.[2]

2 LEARNING OBJECTIVE

Explain what it means to analyze the situation when planning a message

ANALYZING THE SITUATION

Analyzing the situation gives you the insights necessary to meet your own needs as a communicator while also meeting the information needs of your recipients. A successful message starts with a clear purpose that connects the sender's needs with the audience's needs. Identifying your purpose and your audience is usually a straightforward task for simple, routine messages. However, this task can be more demanding in more complex situations. For instance, if you need to communicate about a shipping problem between your Beijing and Los Angeles factories, your purpose might simply be to alert upper management to the situation, or it might involve asking the two factory managers to explore and solve the problem. These two scenarios have different purposes and different audiences, so they require distinctly different messages. If you launch directly into writing without clarifying both your purpose and your audience, you'll waste time and energy, and you'll probably generate a less effective message.

Defining Your Purpose

Business messages have both a general and a specific purpose.

All business messages have a **general purpose**: to inform, to persuade, to collaborate, or to initiate a conversation. This purpose helps define the overall approach you'll need to take, from gathering information to organizing your message. Within the scope of that general purpose, each message also has a **specific purpose**, which identifies what you hope to accomplish with your message. You need to state your specific purpose as precisely as possible, even identifying which audience members should respond, how they should respond, and when.

After you have defined your specific purpose, make sure it merits the time and effort required for you to prepare and send the message. Ask these four questions:

After defining your purpose, verify that the message will be worth the time and effort required to create, send, and receive it.

- **Will anything change as a result of your message?** Make sure you don't contribute to information overload by sending messages that won't change anything. Complaining about things that you have no influence over is a good example of a message that probably shouldn't be sent.

- **Is your purpose realistic?** If your purpose involves a radical shift in action or attitude, proceed carefully. Consider proposing a first step so that your message acts as the beginning of a learning process.

- **Is the time right?** People who are busy or distracted when they receive your message are less likely to pay attention to it.

- **Is your purpose acceptable to your organization?** Your company's business objectives and policies, and even laws that apply to your particular industry, may dictate whether a given purpose is acceptable.

When you are satisfied that you have a clear and meaningful purpose and that now is a smart time to proceed, your next step is to understand the members of your audience and their needs.

Developing an Audience Profile

Before audience members will take the time to read or listen to your messages, they need to be interested in what you're saying. They need to see what's in it for them—which of their needs will be met or problems will be solved by listening to your advice or doing what you ask. The more you know about your audience members, their needs, and their expectations, the more effectively you'll be able to communicate with them. The planning sheet in Figure 3.2 shows an example of the kind of information you need to compile in an audience analysis. Conducting an audience analysis involves the following steps:

- **Identify your primary audience.** For some messages, certain audience members might be more important than others. Don't ignore the needs of less influential members, but make sure you address the concerns of the key decision makers.
- **Determine audience size and geographic distribution.** A message aimed at 10,000 people spread around the globe will likely require a different approach than one aimed at a dozen people down the hall.

Ask yourself some key questions about your audience:
- Who are they?
- How many people do you need to reach?
- How much do they already know about the subject?
- What is their probable reaction to your message?

Audience analysis notes

Project: A report recommending that we close down the on-site exercise facility and subsidize private memberships at local health clubs.

- **Primary audience:** Nicole Perazzo, vice president of operations, and her supervisory team.
- **Size and geographic distribution:** Nine managers total; Nicole and five of her staff are here on site; three other supervisors are based in Hong Kong.
- **Composition:** All have experience in operations management, but several are new to the company.
- **Level of understanding:** All will no doubt understand the financial considerations, but the newer managers may not understand the importance of the on-site exercise facility to many of our employees.
- **Expectations and preferences.** They're expecting a firm recommendation, backed up with well-thought-out financial rationale and suggestions for communicating the bad news to employees. For a decision of this magnitude, a formal report is appropriate; e-mail distribution is expected.
- **Probable reaction.** From one-on-one discussions, I know that several of the managers receiving this report are active users of the on-site facility and won't welcome the suggestion that we should shut it down. However, some nonexercisers generally think it's a luxury the company can't afford. Audience reactions will range from highly positive to highly negative; the report should focus on overcoming the highly negative reactions since they're the ones I need to convince.

Figure 3.2   Using Audience Analysis to Plan a Message
For simple, routine messages, you usually don't need to analyze your audience in depth. However, for complex messages or messages for indifferent or hostile audiences, take the time to study their information needs and potential reactions to your message.

- **Determine audience composition.** Look for similarities and differences in culture, language, age, education, organizational rank and status, attitudes, experience, motivations, and any other factors that might affect the success of your message.

- **Gauge audience members' level of understanding.** If audience members share your general background, they'll probably understand your material without difficulty. If not, your message will need an element of education.

- **Understand audience expectations and preferences.** For example, will members of your audience expect complete details or just a summary of the main points? In general, for internal communication, the higher up the organization your message goes, the fewer details people want to see.

- **Forecast probable audience reaction.** As you'll read later in this chapter, potential audience reaction affects message organization. If you expect a favorable response, you can state conclusions and recommendations up front and offer minimal supporting evidence. If you expect skepticism, you can introduce conclusions gradually and with more proof.

If audience members have different levels of understanding of the topic, aim your message at the most influential decision makers.

A gradual approach and solid evidence are required to win over a skeptical audience.

GATHERING INFORMATION

When you have a clear picture of your audience, your next step is to assemble the information that you will include in your message. For simple messages, you may already have all the information at hand, but for more complex messages, you may need to do considerable research and analysis before you're ready to begin writing. Chapter 10 explores formal techniques for finding, evaluating, and processing information, but you can often use a variety of informal techniques to gather insights and guide your research efforts:

- **Consider the audience's perspective.** Put yourself in the audience's position; what are these people thinking, feeling, or planning? What information do they need in order to move forward? If you are initiating a conversation in a social media context, what information will stimulate discussion in your target communities?

- **Listen to the community.** For almost any subject related to business these days, chances are there is a community of customers, product enthusiasts, or other people who engage in online discussions. Find them and listen to what they have to say.

- **Read reports and other company documents.** Annual reports, financial statements, news releases, blogs and microblogs by industry experts, marketing reports, and customer surveys are just a few of the many potential sources. Find out whether your company has a *knowledge-management system*, a centralized database that collects the experiences and insights of employees throughout the organization.

- **Talk with supervisors, colleagues, or customers.** Fellow workers and customers may have information you need, or they may know what your audience will be interested in.

- **Ask your audience for input.** If you're unsure what audience members need from your message, ask them if it all possible. Admitting you don't know but want to meet their needs will impress an audience more than guessing and getting it wrong.

3 LEARNING OBJECTIVE

Describe the techniques for gathering information for simple messages and identify three attributes of quality information

If you don't have time for a formal research project, you can use a variety of informal techniques to gather the information your audience needs.

Uncovering Audience Needs

In many situations, your audience's information needs are readily apparent, such as when a consumer sends an e-mail asking a specific question. In other situations, your audience might be unable to articulate exactly what is needed, or you won't have the opportunity to communicate with audience members before you need to create a message.

In some cases, you may need to do some detective work to find out what information is needed. If you're asked to suggest steps a company can take to improve employee morale, for example, you'll need to investigate the underlying reasons for low morale. By including this information in your report—even though it wasn't specifically requested—you demonstrate to your audience that you've thoroughly investigated the problem.

Audience members might not be able to describe all the information they need, or you might not have the opportunity to ask them, so you may need to engage in some detective work.

Providing Required Information

After you have defined your audience's information needs, your next step is to satisfy those needs completely. In addition to delivering the right *quantity* of required information, you are responsible for verifying the *quality* of that information. Ask yourself these three questions:

- **Is the information accurate?** Inaccuracies can cause a host of problems, from embarrassment and lost productivity to serious safety and legal issues. Be sure to review any mathematical or financial calculations. Check all dates and schedules. Examine your own assumptions and conclusions to be certain they are valid.

- **Is the information ethical?** By working hard to ensure the accuracy of the information you gather, you'll also avoid many ethical problems in your messages. However, messages can also be unethical if important information is omitted or obscured.

- **Is the information pertinent?** Some points will be more important to your audience than others. By focusing on the information that concerns your audience the most, you increase your chances of sending an effective message.

You have a responsibility to make sure the information you provide is accurate, ethical, and pertinent.

SELECTING THE RIGHT MEDIUM

Selecting the best medium for your message can make the difference between effective and ineffective communication.[3] As Chapter 1 notes, a communication medium is the form through which you choose to communicate your message. You may choose to talk with someone face-to-face, write a letter, send an e-mail message, or create a webcast. With today's ever-expanding technology, you often have a variety of media options from which to choose. Although media categories have become increasingly blurred in recent years, for the sake of discussion you can think of media as being *oral, written, visual,* or *electronic* (which often combines several media types).

4 LEARNING OBJECTIVE

Compare the four major classes of media and list the factors to consider when choosing the most appropriate medium for a message

Oral Media

Oral media include face-to-face conversations, interviews, speeches, and in-person presentations and meetings—whenever you communicate with someone who is physically in the same place. By giving communicators the ability to see, hear, and react to each other, oral media are useful for encouraging people to ask questions, make comments, and work together to reach a consensus or decision. In particular, experts recommend that managers engage in frequent "walk-arounds," chatting with employees face-to-face to get input, answer questions, and interpret important business events and trends.[4]

The disadvantages of oral media include limited reach (because it is confined to those people who are present at a particular time), the reduced control over the message (because people can question, interrupt, or take control of a conversation), and the difficulty of refining your message before transmitting it. Also, the spontaneity of oral communication can be a disadvantage if you don't want a lot of interaction in a particular situation. However, consider your audience carefully before deciding to limit interaction by choosing a different medium. As a manager, you will encounter unpleasant situations (declining an employee's request for a raise, for example) in which sending an electronic message or otherwise avoiding personal contact will seem appealing. In many such cases, though, you owe the other party the opportunity to ask questions or express concerns. Moreover, facing the tough situations in person will earn you a reputation as an honest, caring manager.

Oral communication is best when you need to encourage interaction, express emotions, or monitor emotional responses.

Oral media limit participation to those who are present, reduce your control over the message, and make it difficult to revise or edit your message.

Written Media

Written messages take many forms, from traditional memos to glossy reports that rival magazines in production quality. **Memos** are brief printed documents traditionally used for the routine, day-to-day exchange of information within an organization. In many organizations, electronic media have replaced most paper memos, but you may need to create one from time to time.

Letters are brief written messages generally sent to recipients outside the organization. In addition to conveying a particular message, they perform an important public relations

Written media increase your control, help you reach dispersed audiences, and minimize distortion.

function in fostering good working relationships with customers, suppliers, and others. Many organizations save time and money on routine communication with *form letters*, in which a standard message is personalized as needed for each recipient.

Reports and proposals are usually longer than memos and letters, although both can be created in memo or letter format. These documents come in a variety of lengths, ranging from a few pages to several hundred, and are usually fairly formal in tone. Chapters 10 and 11 discuss reports and proposals in detail.

Visual Media

In some situations, a message that is predominantly visual with text used to support the illustration can be more effective than a message that relies primarily on text.

Although you probably won't work with many messages that are purely visual (with no text), the importance of visual elements in business communication continues to grow. Traditional business messages rely primarily on text, with occasional support from graphical elements such as charts, graphs, or diagrams to help illustrate points discussed in the text. However, many business communicators are discovering the power of messages in which the visual element is dominant and supported by small amounts of text. For the purposes of this discussion, you can think of visual media as formats in which one or more visual elements play a central role in conveying the message content (see Figure 3.3).

Messages that combine powerful visuals with supporting text can be effective for a number of reasons. Today's audiences are pressed for time and bombarded with messages, so anything that communicates quickly is welcome. Visuals are also effective at describing complex ideas and processes because they can reduce the work required for an audience to identify the parts and relationships that make up the whole. Also, in a multilingual business world, diagrams, symbols, and other images can lower communication barriers by requiring less language processing. Finally, visual images can be easier to remember than purely textual descriptions or explanations.

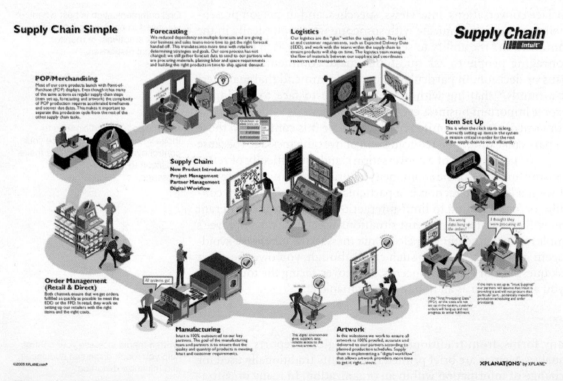

Figure 3.3   Visual Media
In traditional business messages, visual elements usually support the text. However, in some instances, the message can be presented more effectively by reversing that relationship—basing the message on a dominant visual and using text to support that image. For instance, this diagram shows the flow of material and information through a company's *supply chain*.

Electronic Media

The range of electronic media is broad and continues to grow even broader, from phone calls and podcasts to blogs and wikis to e-mail and text messaging. When you want to make a powerful impression, using electronic media can increase the excitement and visual appeal with interactivity, animation, audio, and video.

The growth of electronic communication options is both a blessing and a curse for business communicators. On the one hand, you have more tools than ever before to choose from, with more ways to deliver rational and emotional content. On the other hand, the sheer range of choices can complicate your job because you often need to choose among multiple media, and you need to know how to use each medium successfully.

To use many electronic media options successfully, a person must have at least some degree of technical skill.

You'll learn more about using electronic media in business settings throughout this book (and in Chapter 6, in particular); for now, here is a quick overview of the major electronic media used in business today:

- **Electronic versions of oral media.** These media include telephone calls, teleconferencing, voice-mail messages, audio recordings such as compact discs and podcasts (covered in Chapter 6), *voice synthesis* (creating audio signals from computer data), *voice recognition* (converting audio signals to computer data), and even animated online characters with technology borrowed from video games (see Figure 3.4). The simple telephone call is still a vital communication link for many organizations, and phone options continue to expand with *Internet telephony* services (also known by the technical term VoIP, which stands for *Voice over IP,* the Internet Protocol) such as Skype. Wi-Fi phones add a degree of mobility to VoIP as well. Although telephone calls can't convey all the nonverbal signals of an in-person conversation, they can convey quite a few, including tone of voice, pace, laughter, pauses, and so on. Using voice mail is a handy way to send brief messages when an immediate response isn't crucial, but it's a poor choice for lengthy messages because the information is difficult to retrieve.

- **Electronic versions of written media.** These options range from e-mail and IM to blogs, websites, social networks, and wikis. These media are in a state of constant change, in terms of both what is available and who tends to use which media. For example, e-mail has been a primary business medium for the past decade or two, but it is being replaced in many cases by IM, blogs, text messaging, and social networks.[5] Many reports and other documents that were once distributed on paper are now easily transferred electronically, thanks to Adobe's portable document format (PDF).

Electronic written media have largely replaced printed messages in many companies.

- **Electronic versions of visual media.** These choices can include electronic presentations (using Microsoft PowerPoint and other software), computer animation (using software such as Adobe Flash to create many of the animated sequences you see on websites, for example), and video. Businesses have made extensive use of video

Figure 3.4   Electronic Oral Media
Many websites now feature talking animated figures, sometimes called *avatars,* that offer visitors a more engaging experience. On some websites, these are the "face" of automated *bots* that attempt to answer simple questions and direct visitors to specific parts of the website.

(particularly for training, new product promotions, and executive announcements) for years—first on tape, then on DVD, and now online. Video is also incorporated in podcasting, creating *vidcasts*, and in blogging, creating *video blogs* (*vlogs*) and *mobile blogs* (*moblogs*).[6] **Multimedia** refers to the use of two or more media to craft a single message, typically some combination of audio, video, text, and visual graphics. Multimedia advances continue to create intriguing communication possibilities, such as *augmented reality*, in which computer-generated text, graphics, or sounds are superimposed onto a user's physical reality, either on a device display or directly onto the physical world itself. For example, the French company Presselite offers iPhone and iPad applications that superimpose information about businesses and other points of interest on the display as the user aims the built-in camera around his or her location.[7]

For the latest innovations in electronic media, visit **http://real-timeupdates.com/bce5** and click on Chapter 3.

Factors to Consider When Choosing Media

With so many options at your disposal, choosing the best medium for each message has become an important skill in itself (see Table 3.1). In every case, be sure to consider how your message is affected by the following factors:

Media vary widely in terms of *richness*, which encompasses the number of information cues, feedback mechanisms, and opportunities for personalization.

- **Media richness.** *Richness* is a medium's ability to (1) convey a message through more than one informational cue (visual, verbal, vocal), (2) facilitate feedback, and (3) establish personal focus. The richest medium is face-to-face communication; it's personal, it

TABLE 3.1 Media Advantages and Disadvantages

Media	Advantages	Disadvantages
Oral	■ Provide opportunity for immediate feedback ■ Allow a certain ease of interaction ■ Involve rich nonverbal cues (both physical gesture and vocal inflection) ■ Allow you to express the emotion behind your message	■ Restrict participation to those physically present ■ Unless recorded, provide no permanent, verifiable record of the communication ■ Reduce communicator's control over the message ■ Other than for messages that are prewritten and rehearsed, offer no opportunity to revise or edit your spoken words
Written	■ Allow you to plan and control your message ■ Reach geographically dispersed audiences ■ Offer a permanent, verifiable record ■ Minimize the distortion that can accompany oral messages ■ Can be used to avoid immediate interactions ■ Deemphasize any inappropriate emotional components	■ Offer limited opportunities for timely feedback ■ Lack the rich nonverbal cues provided by oral media ■ Often take more time and more resources to create and distribute ■ Can require special skills in preparation and production if document is elaborate
Visual	■ Can convey complex ideas and relationships quickly ■ Often less intimidating than long blocks of text ■ Can reduce the burden on the audience to figure out how the pieces of a message or concept fit	■ Can require artistic skills to design ■ Require some technical skills to create ■ Can require more time to create than equivalent amount of text ■ Are more difficult to transmit and store than simple textual messages
Electronic	■ Deliver messages quickly ■ Reach geographically dispersed audiences ■ Offer the persuasive power of multimedia formats ■ Can increase accessibility and openness in an organization	■ Enable audience interaction through social media features ■ Are easy to overuse (sending too many messages to too many recipients) ■ Create privacy risks and concerns (exposing confidential data; employer monitoring; accidental forwarding) ■ Entail security risks (viruses, spyware; network breaches) ■ Create productivity concerns (frequent interruptions; nonbusiness usage)

provides immediate feedback (verbal and nonverbal), and it conveys the emotion behind a message.[8] Multimedia presentations and multimedia webpages are also quite rich, with the ability to presents images, animation, text, music, sound effects, and other elements. Many electronic media are also *interactive*, in that they enable audiences to participate in the communication process. At the other extreme are the leanest media—those that communicate in the simplest ways, provide no opportunity for audience feedback, and aren't personalized. In general, use richer media to send nonroutine or complex messages, to humanize your presence throughout the organization, to communicate caring to employees, and to gain employee commitment to company goals. Use leaner media to send routine messages or to transfer information that doesn't require significant explanation.[9]

- **Message formality.** Your media choice is a nonverbal signal that affects the style and tone of your message. For example, a printed memo or letter is likely to be perceived as a more formal gesture than an e-mail message.

- **Media limitations.** Every medium has limitations. For instance, IM is perfect for communicating simple, straightforward messages, but it is ineffective for sending complex ones (unless it is incorporated into a larger collaboration system).

- **Urgency.** Some media establish a connection with the audience faster than others, so choose wisely if your message is urgent. However, be sure to respect audience members' time and workloads. If a message isn't urgent and doesn't require immediate feedback, choose a medium such as e-mail that allows people to respond at their convenience.

> Many types of media offer instantaneous delivery, but take care not to interrupt people unnecessarily (with IM or phone calls, for example) if you don't need an immediate answer.

- **Cost.** Cost is both a real financial factor and a perceived nonverbal signal. For example, depending on the context, extravagant (and expensive) video or multimedia presentations can send a nonverbal signal of sophistication and professionalism—or careless disregard for company budgets.

> Remember that media choices can also send a nonverbal signal regarding costs; make sure your choices are financially appropriate.

- **Audience preferences.** Take into account which medium or media your audience expects or prefers.[10] For instance, businesspeople in the United States, Canada, and Germany emphasize written messages, whereas in Japan professionals tend to emphasize oral messages—perhaps because Japan's high-context culture carries so much of the message in nonverbal cues and "between-the-lines" interpretation.[11]

> When choosing media, don't forget to consider your audience's expectations.

After you select the best medium for your purpose, situation, and audience, you are ready to start thinking about the organization of your message.

ORGANIZING YOUR MESSAGE

5 LEARNING OBJECTIVE
Explain why good organization is important to both you and your audience, and explain how to organize any business message

The ability to organize messages effectively is a skill that helps readers and writers alike. Good organization helps your readers in at least three ways:

- **It helps your audience understand your message.** By making your main idea clear and supporting it with logically presented evidence, you help audiences grasp the essential elements of your message.

- **It helps your audience accept your message.** Careful organization also helps you select and arrange your points in a diplomatic way that can soften the blow of unwelcome news or persuade skeptical readers to see your point of view. In contrast, a poorly organized message can trigger negative emotions that prevent people from seeing the value of what you have to say.

> Good organization benefits your audiences by helping them understand and accept your message in less time.

- **It saves your audience time.** Good organization saves readers time because they don't have to wade through irrelevant information, seek out other sources to fill in missing information, or struggle to follow your train of thought.

In addition to saving time and energy for your readers, good organization saves *you* time and consumes less of your creative energy. Writing proceeds more quickly because you don't waste time putting ideas in the wrong places or composing material that you don't need. You spend far less time rewriting and trying to extract sensible meaning from disorganized rambling. Good organizational skills are also good for your career because they help you develop a reputation as a clear thinker who cares about your readers and listeners.

> Good organization helps you by reducing the time and creative energy needed to create effective messages.

To organize any message,
  Define your main idea
  Limit the scope
  Choose the direct or indirect
  approach
  Outline your information in
  a logical sequence

The topic is the broad subject; the main idea makes a statement about the topic.

That said, what exactly is good organization? You can think of it as structuring messages in a way that helps recipients get all the information they need while requiring the least amount of time and energy for everyone involved. Good organization starts with a clear definition of your main idea.

Defining Your Main Idea

The **topic** of your message is the overall subject, such as employee insurance claims. Your **main idea** is a specific statement about the topic of your message, such as your belief that a new web-based claim filing system would reduce costs for the company and reduce reimbursement delays for employees.

In longer documents and presentations, you often need to unify a mass of material, so you'll need to define a main idea that encompasses all the individual points you want to make. Sometimes you won't even be sure what your main idea is until you sort through the information. For tough assignments like these, consider a variety of techniques to generate creative ideas:

REAL-TIME UPDATES
Learn More by Watching This Presentation

Smart advice for brainstorming sessions

Generate better ideas in less time with these helpful tips. Go to **http://real-timeupdates.com/bce5** and click on "Learn More." If you are using mybcommlab, you can access Real-Time Updates within each chapter or under Student Study Tools.

REAL-TIME UPDATES
Learn More by Watching This Presentation

Wrap your mind around mind mapping

See mind mapping in action in this colorfully illustrated presentation. Go to **http://real-timeupdates.com/bce5** and click on "Learn More." If you are using mybcommlab, you can access Real-Time Updates within each chapter or under Student Study Tools.

- **Brainstorming.** Working alone or with others, generate as many ideas and questions as you can, without stopping to criticize or organize. After you capture all these pieces, look for patterns and connections to help identify the main idea and the groups of supporting ideas.

- **Journalistic approach.** The journalistic approach asks *who, what, when, where, why,* and *how* questions to distill major thoughts from unorganized information.

- **Question-and-answer chain.** Start with a key question, from the audience's perspective, and work back toward your message. In most cases, you'll find that each answer generates new questions, until you identify the information that needs to be in your message.

- **Storyteller's tour.** Some writers find it best to talk through a communication challenge before trying to write. Record yourself as you describe what you intend to write. Then listen to the playback, identify ways to tighten and clarify the message, and repeat the process until you distill the main idea down to a single, concise message.

- **Mind mapping.** You can generate and organize ideas by using a graphic method called mind mapping. Start with a main idea and then branch out to connect every other related idea that comes to mind. You can find a number of free mind-mapping tools online, including http://bubbl.us.

Limiting Your Scope

Limit the scope of your message so that you can convey your main idea as briefly as possible.

The **scope** of your message is the range of information you present, the overall length, and the level of detail—all of which need to correspond to your main idea. Some business messages have a length limit, whether from a boss's instructions, the technology you're using, or a time frame such as individual speaker slots during a seminar. Even if you don't have a preset length, it's vital to limit yourself to the scope needed to convey your main idea—and no more.

Whatever the length of your message, keep the number of major supporting points to half a dozen or so—and if you can get your idea across with fewer points, all the better. Listing 20 or 30 supporting points might feel as though you're being thorough, but your audience is likely to view such detail as rambling and mind numbing. Instead, group your supporting points under major headings, such as finance, customers, competitors, employees, or whatever is appropriate for your subject. Look for ways to distill your supporting points so that you have a smaller number with greater impact.

The number of words, pages, or minutes you need in order to communicate and support your main idea depends on your topic, your audience members' familiarity with the material and their receptivity to your conclusions, and your credibility. You'll need fewer words to present routine information to a knowledgeable audience that already knows and respects you. You'll need more words to build a consensus about a complex and controversial subject, especially if the members of your audience are skeptical or hostile strangers.

Choosing Between Direct and Indirect Approaches

After you've defined your main idea and supporting points, you're ready to decide on the sequence you will use to present your information. You have two basic options:

- **Direct approach.** When you know your audience will be receptive to your message, use the **direct approach**: Start with the main idea (such as a recommendation, conclusion, or request) and follow that with your supporting evidence.

- **Indirect approach.** When your audience will be skeptical about or even resistant to your message, you generally want to use the **indirect approach**: Start with the evidence first and build your case before presenting the main idea. Note that taking the indirect approach does not mean avoiding tough issues or talking around in circles. It simply means building up to your main idea in a careful and logical way.

> With the direct approach, you open with the main idea of your message and support that with reasoning, evidence, and examples.

> With the indirect approach, you withhold the main idea until you have built up to it logically and persuasively with reasoning, evidence, and examples.

To choose between these two alternatives, analyze your audience's likely reaction to your purpose and message (see Figure 3.5). Bear in mind, however, that each message is unique. No simple formula will solve all your communication problems. For example, although an indirect approach may be best when you're sending bad news to outsiders, if you're writing a message to an associate, you may want to get directly to the point, even if the information is unpleasant. The direct approach might also be a good choice for long messages, regardless of your audience's attitude, because delaying the main idea could cause confusion and frustration.

The type of message also influences the choice of the direct or indirect approach. In the coming chapters, you'll get specific advice on choosing the best approach for a variety of different communication challenges.

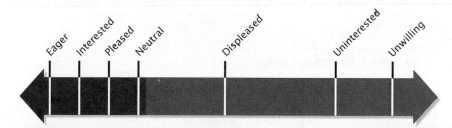

	Direct Approach	**Indirect Approach**	
Audience Reaction	Eager/interested/ pleased/neutral	Displeased	Uninterested/unwilling
Message Opening	Start with the main idea, the request, or the good news.	Start with a neutral statement that acts as a transition to the reasons for the bad news.	Start with a statement or question that captures attention.
Message Body	Provide necessary details.	Give reasons to justify a negative answer. State or imply the bad news, and make a positive suggestion.	Arouse the audience's interest in the subject. Build the audience's desire to comply.
Message Close	Close with a cordial comment, a reference to the good news, or a statement about the specific action desired.	Close cordially.	Request action.

Figure 3.5 Choosing Between the Direct and Indirect Approaches
Think about the way your audience is likely to respond before choosing your approach.

REAL-TIME UPDATES
Learn More by Watching This Presentation

Get helpful tips on creating an outline for any project

Learn these proven steps for creating robust, practical outlines. Go to **http://real-timeupdates.com/bce5** and click on "Learn More." If you are using mybcommlab, you can access Real-Time Updates within each chapter or under Student Study Tools.

Outlining takes some time and effort, but it can often save you considerable time and effort in the composing and revising stages.

Outlining Your Content

After you have chosen the right approach, it's time to figure out the most logical and effective way to present your major points and supporting details. Even if you've resisted creating outlines in your school assignments over the years, try to get into the habit of creating outlines when you're preparing most business messages. You'll save time, get better results, and do a better job of navigating through complicated business situations. Even if you're just jotting down three or four points on a notepad, making a plan and sticking to it will help you cover the important details.

You are probably familiar with the basic outline formats that identify each point with a number or letter and that indent certain points to show their relationships in hierarchy. A good outline divides a topic into at least two parts, restricts each subdivision to one category, and ensures that each subdivision is separate and distinct (see Figure 3.6). Outlining can take some work, but remember that it is much easier to rearrange your outline than it is to rearrange your first draft.

Whichever outlining or organizing scheme you use, start by stating your main idea, then list your major supporting points, and then provide examples and evidence:

- **Start with the main idea.** The main idea helps you establish the goals and general strategy of the message, and it summarizes two things: (1) *what* you want your audience members to do, think, or feel after receiving the message and (2) *why* it makes sense for them to do so. Everything in your message should either support the main idea or explain its implications. (Remember that if you choose the indirect approach, the main idea will appear toward the end of your message, after you've presented your major supporting points.)

- **State the major points.** Now it's time to support your main idea with the major points that clarify and explain your ideas in more concrete terms. If your purpose is to inform and the material is factual, your major points may be based on something physical or financial, for example—something you can visualize or measure, such as activities to be performed, functional units, spatial or chronological relationships, or parts of a whole.

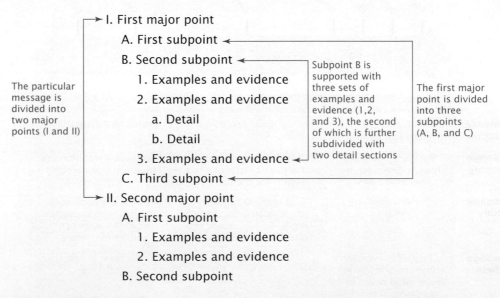

Figure 3.6   Outline Format
Outlining helps you organize the sequence and hierarchy of the blocks of information you plan to include in a message. These examples show the various ways that information can be subdivided.

When you're describing a process, the major points are usually steps in the process. When you're describing an object, the major points often correspond to the parts of the object. When you're giving a historical account, major points represent events in the chronological chain of events. If your purpose is to persuade or to collaborate, select major points that develop a line of reasoning or a logical argument that proves your central message and motivates your audience to act.

■ **Provide examples and evidence.** After you've defined the main idea and identified major supporting points, you're ready to back up those points with examples and evidence that help audience members understand, accept, and remember your message. Choose your examples and evidence carefully. Your want to be compelling and complete but also as concise as possible. One strong example or piece of evidence can be more effective than three or four weaker items.

> Choose supporting points, evidence, and examples carefully; a few strong points will make your case better than a large collection of weaker points.

Figure 3.7 on the next page illustrates several of the key themes about organizing a message: helping readers get the information they need quickly, defining and conveying the main idea, limiting the scope of the message, choosing the approach, and outlining your information.

Building Reader Interest with Storytelling Techniques

Storytelling might seem like an odd subject for a business course, but stories can be an effective way to organize messages in a surprising number of business communication scenarios, from recruiting and training employees to enticing investors and customers. In fact, you've already been on the receiving end of thousands of business stories—storytelling is one of the most common structures used in television commercials and other advertisements (see Figure 3.8 on page 97). Career-related stories, such as how someone sought and found the opportunity to work on projects he or she is passionate about, can entice skilled employees to consider joining a firm. Entrepreneurs use stories to help investors see how their new ideas have the potential to affect people's lives (and therefore generate lots of sales). Stories can be cautionary tales as well, dramatizing the consequences of career blunders, ethical mistakes, and strategic missteps.

A key reason storytelling can be so effective is that stories help readers and listeners imagine themselves living through the experience of the person in the story. As a result, people tend to remember and respond to the message in ways that can be difficult to achieve with other forms of communication. In addition, stories can demonstrate cause-and-effect relationships in a compelling fashion.[12] Imagine attending a new employee orientation and listening to the trainer read off a list of ethics rules and guidelines. Now imagine the trainer telling the story of someone who sounded a lot like you in the very near future, fresh out of college and full of energy and ambition. Desperate to hit demanding sales targets, the person in the story began entering transactions before customers had actually agreed to purchase, hoping the sales would eventually come through and no one would be the wiser. However, the scheme was exposed during a routine audit, and the rising star was booted out of the company with an ethical stain that would haunt him for years. You may not remember all the rules and guidelines, but chances are you will remember what happened to that person who sounded a lot like you.

> Storytelling is an effective way to organize many business messages because it helps readers personalize the message and understand causes and consequences.

A classic story has three basic parts. The beginning of the story presents someone with whom the audience can identify in some way, and this person has a dream to pursue or a problem to solve. (Think of how movies and novels often start by introducing a likable character who immediately gets into danger, for example.) The middle of the story shows this character taking action and making decisions as he or she pursues the goal or tries to solve the problem. The storyteller's objective here is to build the audience's interest by increasing the tension: Will the "hero" overcome the obstacles in his or her path and eventually succeed or fail? The end of the story answers that question and usually offers a lesson to be learned about the outcome as well.

> Organize stories in three parts: a beginning that introduces a sympathetic person with a dream or a challenge, a middle that shows the complications to be overcome, and an ending that resolves the situation and shows the moral or message of the story.

Consider adding an element of storytelling whenever your main idea involves the opportunity to inspire, to persuade, to teach, or to warn readers or listeners about the potential outcomes of a particular course of action.

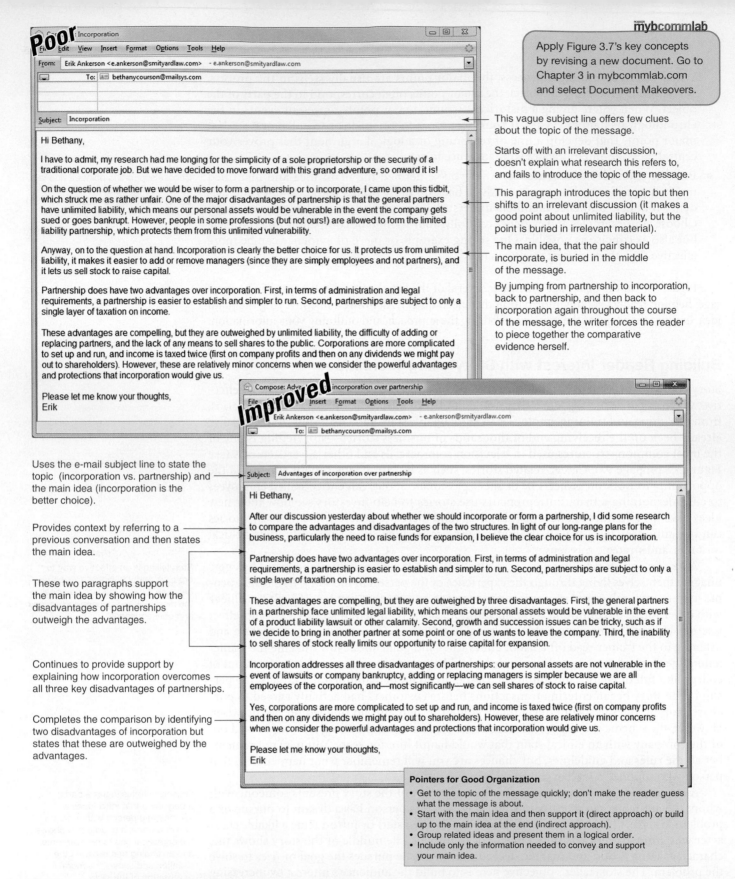

Apply Figure 3.7's key concepts by revising a new document. Go to Chapter 3 in mybcommlab.com and select Document Makeovers.

Poor

Incorporation

File   Edit   View   Insert   Format   Options   Tools   Help

From: Erik Ankerson <e.ankerson@smityardlaw.com>   - e.ankerson@smityardlaw.com

To: bethanycourson@mailsys.com

Subject: Incorporation

Hi Bethany,

I have to admit, my research had me longing for the simplicity of a sole proprietorship or the security of a traditional corporate job. But we have decided to move forward with this grand adventure, so onward it is!

On the question of whether we would be wiser to form a partnership or to incorporate, I came upon this tidbit, which struck me as rather unfair. One of the major disadvantages of partnership is that the general partners have unlimited liability, which means our personal assets would be vulnerable in the event the company gets sued or goes bankrupt. However, people in some professions (but not ours!) are allowed to form the limited liability partnership, which protects them from this unlimited vulnerability.

Anyway, on to the question at hand. Incorporation is clearly the better choice for us. It protects us from unlimited liability, it makes it easier to add or remove managers (since they are simply employees and not partners), and it lets us sell stock to raise capital.

Partnership does have two advantages over incorporation. First, in terms of administration and legal requirements, a partnership is easier to establish and simpler to run. Second, partnerships are subject to only a single layer of taxation on income.

These advantages are compelling, but they are outweighed by unlimited liability, the difficulty of adding or replacing partners, and the lack of any means to sell shares to the public. Corporations are more complicated to set up and run, and income is taxed twice (first on company profits and then on any dividends we might pay out to shareholders). However, these are relatively minor concerns when we consider the powerful advantages and protections that incorporation would give us.

Please let me know your thoughts,
Erik

This vague subject line offers few clues about the topic of the message.

Starts off with an irrelevant discussion, doesn't explain what research this refers to, and fails to introduce the topic of the message.

This paragraph introduces the topic but then shifts to an irrelevant discussion (it makes a good point about unlimited liability, but the point is buried in irrelevant material).

The main idea, that the pair should incorporate, is buried in the middle of the message.

By jumping from partnership to incorporation, back to partnership, and then back to incorporation again throughout the course of the message, the writer forces the reader to piece together the comparative evidence herself.

Uses the e-mail subject line to state the topic (incorporation vs. partnership) and the main idea (incorporation is the better choice).

Provides context by referring to a previous conversation and then states the main idea.

These two paragraphs support the main idea by showing how the disadvantages of partnerships outweigh the advantages.

Continues to provide support by explaining how incorporation overcomes all three key disadvantages of partnerships.

Completes the comparison by identifying two disadvantages of incorporation but states that these are outweighed by the advantages.

Improved

Compose: Advantages of incorporation over partnership

File   Edit   View   Insert   Format   Options   Tools   Help

Erik Ankerson <e.ankerson@smityardlaw.com>   - e.ankerson@smityardlaw.com

To: bethanycourson@mailsys.com

Subject: Advantages of incorporation over partnership

Hi Bethany,

After our discussion yesterday about whether we should incorporate or form a partnership, I did some research to compare the advantages and disadvantages of the two structures. In light of our long-range plans for the business, particularly the need to raise funds for expansion, I believe the clear choice for us is incorporation.

Partnership does have two advantages over incorporation. First, in terms of administration and legal requirements, a partnership is easier to establish and simpler to run. Second, partnerships are subject to only a single layer of taxation on income.

These advantages are compelling, but they are outweighed by three disadvantages. First, the general partners in a partnership face unlimited legal liability, which means our personal assets would be vulnerable in the event of a product liability lawsuit or other calamity. Second, growth and succession issues can be tricky, such as if we decide to bring in another partner at some point or one of us wants to leave the company. Third, the inability to sell shares of stock really limits our opportunity to raise capital for expansion.

Incorporation addresses all three disadvantages of partnerships: our personal assets are not vulnerable in the event of lawsuits or company bankruptcy, adding or replacing managers is simpler because we are all employees of the corporation, and—most significantly—we can sell shares of stock to raise capital.

Yes, corporations are more complicated to set up and run, and income is taxed twice (first on company profits and then on any dividends we might pay out to shareholders). However, these are relatively minor concerns when we consider the powerful advantages and protections that incorporation would give us.

Please let me know your thoughts,
Erik

Pointers for Good Organization

- Get to the topic of the message quickly; don't make the reader guess what the message is about.
- Start with the main idea and then support it (direct approach) or build up to the main idea at the end (indirect approach).
- Group related ideas and present them in a logical order.
- Include only the information needed to convey and support your main idea.

Figure 3.7   Improving the Organization of a Message

This writer is following up on a conversation from the previous day, in which he and the recipient discussed which of two forms of ownership, a partnership or a corporation, they should use for their new company. (*Partnership* has a specific legal meaning in this context.) That question is the topic of the message; the main idea is the recommendation that they incorporate, rather than form a partnership. Notice how the Improved version uses the direct approach to quickly get to the main idea and then supports that by comparing the advantages and disadvantages of both forms of ownership. In contrast, the Poor version contains irrelevant information, makes the comparison difficult to follow, and buries the main idea in the middle of the message.

Figure 3.8   Storytelling at Patagonia
Patagonia's Tin Shed website serves two storytelling functions. The tin shed (Patagonia's first building) plays a key role in the story of the company's founding and early years, and the online image of the shed offers gateways to a growing collection of stories on such topics as how various Patagonia's products came into being, how outdoor enthusiasts use the company's products, and how Patagonia is engaged with various causes related to the outdoors.

PEARSON mybcommlab   Are you an active learner? Go to mybcommlab.com to master Chapter 3's content. Chapter 3's interactive activities include:

- Customizable Study Plan and Chapter 3 practice quizzes
- Chapter 3 Video Exercise (Planning Business Messages: Orange Photography), which shows you how textbook concepts are put into practice every day

- Flash Cards for mastering the definition of chapter terms
- Interactive Lessons that visually review key chapter concepts
- Document Makeovers for hands-on, scored practice in revising documents

CHAPTER REVIEW AND ACTIVITIES

Learning Objectives: Check Your Progress

1 OBJECTIVE Describe the three-step writing process, and explain why it will help you create better messages in less time.

The three-step writing process is built around planning, writing, and completing business messages. Planning involves analyzing the situation, gathering the information you will need to meet audience needs, selecting the right medium or combination of media, and organizing your information. The writing step involves adapting to your audience and composing your message. Completing involves the four tasks of revising, proofreading, producing, and distributing the message. The three-step process helps you create more effective messages because it helps you focus on what your audience needs to get from a message, and it saves you time by reducing the amount of reworking that can happen when someone starts writing without clear goals or organization in mind.

2 OBJECTIVE Explain what it means to analyze the situation when planning a message.

Analyzing the situation gives you the insights necessary to meet your own needs as a communicator while also meeting the information needs of your recipients. You can accomplish this goal by looking at the communication process from both ends, by defining your purpose in sending the message and by creating a profile of your target audience. The *general purpose* of a message identifies your overall intent—to inform, to persuade, to collaborate, or to initiate a conversation. The *specific purpose* identifies what you hope to accomplish with the message. Without a clear purpose in mind, you are likely to spend more time and energy than you really need to, and chances are you won't create an effective message.

Understanding your audience is a vital aspect of planning because the more you know about your audience members, their needs, and their expectations, the more effectively you'll be able to communicate with them. To create an audience profile, identify the primary audience, its size and geographic distribution, its composition (language, education, experience, and so on), and its level of understanding, expectations and preferences, and probable reaction to your message.

3 OBJECTIVE Describe the techniques for gathering information for simple messages, and identify three attributes of quality information.

Simple messages usually don't require extensive information gathering, but to acquire useful insights, consider the audience's perspective; find and listen to online communities; read reports and other company documents; talk with supervisors, colleagues, or customers; and ask your audience for input if possible. Judge the quality of any information you include by making sure it is accurate, ethical, and pertinent.

4 OBJECTIVE Compare the four major classes of media, and list the factors to consider when choosing the most appropriate medium for a message.

The four major classes of media are oral (direct conversation between two or more people), written (printed memos, letters, and reports), visual (messages in which visual elements carry the bulk of the message), and electronic (electronic versions of the other three). To choose the most appropriate medium for every message, consider media richness, message formality, media limitations, urgency, cost, and audience preferences.

5 OBJECTIVE Explain why good organization is important to both you and your audience, and explain how to organize any business message.

Good organization helps your audience understand and accept your message with less time and effort. It also saves you time when preparing messages. With a clear path to follow when writing, you'll produce messages faster and spend far less time revising. To organize any message, define your main idea, limit the scope for maximum impact, choose the direct or indirect approach to match the situation, and outline your information in a logical sequence.

Test Your Knowledge

To review chapter content related to each question, refer to the indicated Learning Objective.

1. What are the three steps in the writing process? [LO-1]
2. What do you need to know in order to develop an audience profile? [LO-2]
3. What two types of purposes do all business messages have? [LO-2]
4. When including information in your message, what three conditions must you satisfy? [LO-3]
5. What is the difference between the topic of a message and its main idea? [LO-5]

Apply Your Knowledge

To review chapter content related to each question, refer to the indicated Learning Objective.

1. Some writers argue that planning messages wastes time because they inevitably change their plans as they go along. How would you respond to this argument? Briefly explain. [LO-1]

2. As a member of the public relations department, which medium (or media) would you recommend using to inform the local community that your toxic-waste cleanup program has been successful? Justify your choice. [LO-4]

3. Considering how fast, easy, and inexpensive they are, should electronic media messages completely replace meetings and other face-to-face communication in your company? Why or why not? [LO-4]

4. Would you use a direct or an indirect approach to ask employees to work overtime to meet an important deadline? Please explain. [LO-5]

5. A day after sending an e-mail to all 1,800 employees in your company regarding income tax implications of the company's retirement plan, you discover that one of the sources you relied on for your information plagiarized from other sources. You quickly double-check all the information in your message and confirm that it is accurate. However, you are concerned about using plagiarized information, even though you did nothing wrong. How you would handle this situation? [LO-3]

Practice Your Skills

Exercises for Perfecting Your Writing

To review chapter content related to each set of exercises, refer to the indicated Learning Objective.

Specific Purpose   For each of the following communication tasks, state a specific purpose (if you have trouble, try beginning with "I want to …"). [LO-2]

1. An e-mail message to employees about the office's high water bills

2. A blog posting to customers and the news media about your company's plans to acquire a competitor

3. A podcast to new users of the company's online content management system

4. A report to your boss, the store manager, about the outdated items in the warehouse

5. A phone call to a supplier to check on an overdue parts shipment

6. A letter to a customer who is supposed to make monthly loan payments but hasn't made a payment for three months

Audience Profile   For each communication task below, write brief answers to three questions: (1) Who is my audience? (2) What is my audience's general attitude toward my subject? (3) What does my audience need to know? [LO-2]

7. A final-notice collection letter from an appliance manufacturer to an appliance dealer, sent 10 days before initiation of legal collection procedures

8. A promotional message on your company's retailing website, announcing a temporary price reduction on high-definition television sets

9. An advertisement for peanut butter

10. A letter to the property management company responsible for maintaining your office building, complaining about persistent problems with the heating and air conditioning

11. A cover letter sent along with your résumé to a potential employer

12. A request (to the seller) for a price adjustment on a piano that incurred $150 in damage during delivery to a banquet room in the hotel you manage

Media and Purpose   List three messages you have read, viewed, or listened to lately (such as direct-mail promotions, letters, e-mail or instant messages, phone solicitations, blog posts, social network pages, podcasts, or lectures). For each message, determine the general and the specific purpose, then answer the questions listed. [LO-2] [LO-4]

Message #1:

13. General purpose:
14. Specific purpose:
15. Was the message well timed?
16. Did the sender choose an appropriate medium for the message?
17. Was the sender's purpose realistic?

Message #2:

18. General purpose:
19. Specific purpose:
20. Was the message well timed?
21. Did the sender choose an appropriate medium for the message?
22. Was the sender's purpose realistic?

Message #3:

23. General purpose:
24. Specific purpose:
25. Was the message well timed?
26. Did the sender choose an appropriate medium for the message?
27. Was the sender's purpose realistic?

Message Organization: Choosing the Approach   Indicate whether the direct or the indirect approach would be best in each of the following situations. [LO-4]

28. An internal blog post explaining that because of high air-conditioning costs, the plant temperature will be held at 78 degrees during the summer

29. A letter from a recent college graduate, requesting a letter of recommendation from a former instructor

30. A letter turning down a job applicant

31. An e-mail message to a car dealer, asking about the availability of a specific make and model of car

32. A final request to settle a delinquent debt

Message Organization: Drafting Persuasive Messages   If you were trying to persuade people to take the following actions, would you choose the direct or indirect approach? [LO-4]

33. You want your boss to approve your plan for hiring two new people.

34. You want to be granted a business loan.
35. You want to be hired for a job.
36. You want to collect a small amount from a regular customer whose account is slightly past due.
37. You want to collect a large amount from a customer whose account is seriously past due.

Activities

Active links for all websites in this chapter can be found on mybcommlab; see your User Guide for instructions on accessing the content for this chapter. Each activity is labeled according to the primary skill or skills you will need to use. To review relevant chapter content, you can refer to the indicated Learning Objective. In some instances, supporting information will be found in another chapter, as indicated.

1. **Planning: Identifying Your Purpose; Media Skills: E-Mail [LO-2]**   Identify three significant communication tasks you'll need to accomplish in the next week or two (for example, a homework assignment, a project at work, a meeting with your academic advisor, or class presentation). In an e-mail message to your instructor, list the general and specific purpose for each communication task.

2. **Planning: Analyzing the Situation; Media Skills: Electronic Presentations [LO-2]**   Go to the PepsiCo website, at www.pepsico.com, and locate the latest annual report under the Investors tab. Read the annual report's letter to shareholders. Who is the audience for this message? What is the general purpose of the message? What do you think this audience wants to know from the chairman of PepsiCo? Summarize your answers in a one-page report or five-slide presentation, as your instructor directs.

3. **Planning: Assessing Audience Needs; Media Skills: Blogging; Communication Ethics: Making Ethical Choices [LO-3], Chapter 1**   Your supervisor has asked you to withhold important information that you think should be included in a report you are preparing. Obeying him could save the company serious public embarrassment, but it would also violate your personal code of ethics. What should you do? On the basis of the discussion in Chapter 1, would you consider this situation to be an ethical dilemma or an ethical lapse? In a post on your class blog, explain your answer and describe how you would respond in this situation.

4. **Planning: Analyzing the Situation, Selecting Media; Media Skills: E-Mail [LO-4], Chapter 8**   You are the head of public relations for a cruise line that operates out of Miami. You are shocked to read a letter in a local newspaper from a disgruntled passenger, complaining about the service and entertainment on a recent cruise. You need to respond to these publicized criticisms in some way. What audiences will you need to consider in your response? What medium or media should you choose? If the letter had been published in a travel publication widely read by travel agents and cruise travelers, how might your course of action have differed? In an e-mail message to your instructor, explain how you will respond.

5. **Planning: Limiting Your Scope [LO-5]**   Suppose you are preparing to recommend that top management install a new heating system that uses the *cogeneration* process. The following information is in your files. Eliminate topics that aren't essential and then arrange the other topics so that your report will give top managers a clear understanding of the heating system and a balanced, concise justification for installing it. Submit a clear and concise outline to your instructor.

   - History of the development of the cogeneration heating process
   - Scientific credentials of the developers of the process
   - Risks assumed in using this process
   - Your plan for installing the equipment in the headquarters building
   - Stories about the successful use of cogeneration technology in comparable facilities
   - Specifications of the equipment that would be installed
   - Plans for disposing of the old heating equipment
   - Costs of installing and running the new equipment
   - Advantages and disadvantages of using the new process
   - Detailed 10-year cost projections
   - Estimates of the time needed to phase in the new system
   - Alternative systems that management might want to consider

6. **Planning: Outlining Your Content [LO-5]**   A writer is working on an insurance information brochure and is having trouble grouping the ideas logically into an outline. Prepare the outline, paying attention to appropriate subordination of ideas. If necessary, rewrite phrases to give them a more consistent sound. Submit a clear and concise outline to your instructor.

Accident Protection Insurance Plan

- Coverage is only pennies a day
- Benefit is $100,000 for accidental death on common carrier
- Benefit is $100 a day for hospitalization as result of motor vehicle or common carrier accident
- Benefit is $20,000 for accidental death in motor vehicle accident
- Individual coverage is only $17.85 per quarter; family coverage is just $26.85 per quarter
- No physical exam or health questions
- Convenient payment—billed quarterly
- Guaranteed acceptance for all applicants
- No individual rate increases
- Free, no-obligation examination period
- Cash paid in addition to any other insurance carried
- Covers accidental death when riding as fare-paying passenger on public transportation, including buses, trains, jets, ships, trolleys, subways, or any other common carrier
- Covers accidental death in motor vehicle accidents occurring while driving or riding in or on automobile, truck, camper, motor home, or nonmotorized bicycle

7. **Planning: Using Storytelling Techniques; Communication Ethics: Providing Ethical Leadership: Media Skills: Podcasting [LO-5], Chapter 1** Research recent episodes of ethical lapses by a business professional or executive in any industry. Choose one example that has a clear story "arc" from beginning to end. Outline a cautionary tale that explains the context of the ethical lapse, the choice the person made, and the consequences of the ethical lapse. Script a podcast (aim for roughly 3 to 5 minutes) that tells the story. If you instructor directs, record your podcast and post to your class blog.

▌ Expand Your Skills

Critique the Professionals

Locate an example of professional communication in any medium that you think would work equally well—or perhaps better—in another medium. Using the media selection guidelines in this chapter and your understanding of the communication process, write a brief analysis (no more than one page) of the company's media choice and explain why your choice would be at least as effective. Use whatever medium your instructor requests for your report and be sure to cite specific elements from the piece and support from the chapter.

Sharpen Your Career Skills Online

Bovée and Thill's Business Communication Web Search, at http://businesscommunicationblog.com/websearch, is a unique research tool designed specifically for business communication research. Use the Web Search function to find a website, video, PDF document, podcast, or PowerPoint presentation that offers advice on analyzing audiences, selecting media, outlining, storytelling (in a business context), or any aspect of the writing process (including models other than the three-step process covered in this text). Write a brief e-mail message to your instructor or a post for your class blog, describing the item that you found and summarizing the career skills information you learned from it.

mybcommlab

If your course uses mybcommlab, log on to www.mybcommlab.com to access the following study and assessment aids associated with this chapter:

- Video applications
- Pre/post test
- Real-Time Updates
- Personalized study plan
- Peer review activity
- Model documents
- Quick Learning Guides
- Sample presentations

If you are not using mybcommlab, you can access Real-Time Updates and Quick Learning Guides through http://real-timeupdates.com/bce5. The Quick Learning Guide (located under "Learn More" on the website) hits all the high points of this chapter in just two pages. This guide, especially prepared by the authors, will help you study for exams or review important concepts whenever you need a quick refresher.

▌ Improve Your Grammar, Mechanics, and Usage

You can download the text of this assignment from http://real-timeupdates.com/bce5; click on "Student Assignments" and then click on "Chapter 3. Improve Your Grammar, Mechanics, and Usage."

Level 1: Self-Assessment—Verbs

Review Section 1.3 in the Handbook of Grammar, Mechanics, and Usage and then complete the following 15 items.

In items 1–5, indicate the verb form called for in each sentence.

1. I (present perfect, become) the resident expert on repairing the copy machine.
2. She (past, know) how to conduct an audit when she came to work for us.
3. Since Joan was promoted, she (past perfect, move) all the files to her office.
4. Next week, call John to tell him what you (future, do) to help him set up the seminar.
5. By the time you finish the analysis, he (future perfect, return) from his vacation.

For items 6–10, rewrite the sentences so that they use active voice instead of passive.

6. The report will be written by Leslie Cartwright.
7. The failure to record the transaction was mine.
8. Have you been notified by the claims department of your rights?
9. We are dependent on their services for our operation.
10. The damaged equipment was returned by the customer before we even located a repair facility.

In items 11–15, indicate the correct verb form provided in parentheses.

11. Everyone upstairs (receive, receives) mail before we do.
12. Neither the main office nor the branches (is, are) blameless.
13. C&B Sales (is, are) listed in the directory.
14. When measuring shelves, 7 inches (is, are) significant.
15. About 90 percent of the employees (plan, plans) to come to the company picnic.

Level 2: Workplace Applications

The following items may contain errors in grammar, capitalization, punctuation, abbreviation, number style, word division, and vocabulary. Rewrite each sentence, correcting all errors. If a sentence has no errors, write "Correct" for that number.

1. Cut two inches off trunk and place in a water stand, and fill with water.
2. The newly-elected officers of the Board are: John Rogers, president, Robin Doig, vice-president, and Mary Sturhann, secretary.

3. Employees were stunned when they are notified that the trainee got promoted to Manager only after her 4th week with the company.
4. Seeking reliable data on U.S. publishers, Literary Marketplace is by far the best source.
5. Who did you wish to speak to?
6. The keynote address will be delivered by Seth Goodwin, who is the author of six popular books on marketing, has written two novels, and writes a column for "Fortune" magazine.
7. Often the reputation of an entire company depend on one employee that officially represents that company to the public.
8. The executive director, along with his staff, are working quickly to determine who should receive the Award.
9. Him and his co-workers, the top bowling team in the tournament, will represent our Company in the league finals on saturday.
10. Listening on the extension, details of the embezzlement plot were overheard by the Security Chief.
11. The acceptance of visa cards are in response to our customer's demand for a more efficient and convenient way of paying for parking here at San Diego International airport.
12. The human resources dept. interviewed dozens of people, they are seeking the better candidate for the opening.
13. Libraries' can be a challenging; yet lucrative market if you learn how to work the "system" to gain maximum visibility for you're products and services.
14. Either a supermarket or a discount art gallery are scheduled to open in the Mall.
15. I have told my supervisor that whomever shares my office with me cannot wear perfume, use spray deodorant, or other scented products.

Level 3: Document Critique

The following document may contain errors in grammar, capitalization, punctuation, abbreviation, number style, word division, and vocabulary. As your instructor indicates, photocopy this page and correct all errors using standard proofreading marks (see Appendix C) or download the document and make the corrections in your word processing software.

Memo

TO: Blockbuster mngrs.

FROM: Tom Dooley, deputy chairmen, Viacom, Inc. in care of Blockbuster Entertainment Group Corporate headquarters, Renaissance Tower 1201 Elm street; Dallas TX 75270

DATE: May 8 2011

SUB: Recent Cash Flow and consumer response—Survey

Now that our stores have been re-organized with your hard work and cooperation, we hope revenues will rise to new heights; if we reemphasize video rentals as Blockbusters core business and reduce the visibility of our sideline retail products. Just in case though, we want to be certain that these changes are having the postive affect on our cash flow that we all except and look forward to.

To help us make that determination, respond to the following survey questions and fax them back. Answer concisely; but use extra paper if necessary—for details and explanations.

When you finish the survey it will help headquarters improve service to you; but also, help us all improve service to our customers. Return your survey before before May 15 to my attention. Then blockbuster hopefully can thrive in a marketplace, that critics say we cannot conquer. Blockbuster must choose wisely and serve it's customers well in a difficult video-rental business environment.

Times are very tough but if we work hard at it its possible we might make Blockbuster 'the man on the streets' favorite 'place to go to rent videos!

mybcommlab

Apply Level 3: Document Critique's key concepts by revising a new document. Go to chapter 3 in mybcommlab.com and select Document Makeovers.

Writing Business Messages

LEARNING OBJECTIVES

After studying this chapter, you will be able to

1 Identify the four aspects of being sensitive to audience needs when writing business messages

2 Explain how establishing your credibility and projecting your company's image are vital aspects of building strong relationships with your audience

3 Explain how to achieve a tone that is conversational but businesslike, explain the value of using plain language, and define active and passive voice

4 Describe how to select words that are not only correct but also effective

5 Define the four types of sentences and explain how sentence style affects emphasis within a message

6 Define the three key elements of a paragraph and list five ways to develop coherent paragraphs

7 Identify the most common software features that help you craft messages more efficiently

mybcommlab Access interactive videos, simulations, sample documents, Document Makeovers, and assessment quizzes in Chapter 4 of mybcommlab.com for mastery of this chapter's objectives.

COMMUNICATION *Matters*

"The busier life gets, the more value there is in simplicity . . . simplicity and clarity make us more productive."
—Arkadi Kuhlmann, *Chairman, President, and CEO of ING Direct USA*

The online bank ING Direct has made simplicity one of its core business values, and that approach is reflected in everything from its uncomplicated privacy policies to its streamlined website to its succinct tagline, "Save your money."[1] Arkadi Kuhlmann knows that today's consumers are overwhelmed with information—and that even when the information is essential, it is often lost in poorly written business messages. This chapter offers practical advice on writing messages that meet audience needs efficiently and effectively. Simplicity is a competitive advantage for ING Direct, and you can make it a competitive advantage in your career, too.

ING Direct's Arkadi Kuhlmann strives for simplicity in every interaction with the online bank's customers.

1 LEARNING OBJECTIVE

Identify the four aspects of being sensitive to audience needs when writing business messages

Readers and listeners are more likely to respond positively when they believe messages address their concerns.

Adopting the "you" attitude means speaking and writing in terms of your audience's wishes, interests, hopes, and preferences.

BEING SENSITIVE TO YOUR AUDIENCE'S NEEDS

ING Direct's emphasis on simplicity reflects a desire to focus on audience needs. In any communication situation, audiences are most likely to notice, pay attention to, and respond to messages that promise to address their concerns. Delivering the information readers require is essential, of course, but being truly sensitive to audience needs also means adopting the "you" attitude, maintaining good standards of etiquette, emphasizing the positive, and using bias-free language.

Adopting the "You" Attitude

You are already becoming familiar with the audience-centered approach, trying to see a subject through your audience's eyes. Now you want to project this approach in your messages by adopting the **"you" attitude**—that is, by speaking and writing in terms of your audience's wishes, interests, hopes, and preferences.

On a simple level, you can adopt the "you" attitude by replacing terms that refer to yourself and your company with terms that refer to your audience. In other words, use *you* and *your* instead of *I, me, mine, we, us,* and *ours*:

Instead of This	Write This
Tuesday is the only day that we can promise quick response to purchase order requests; we are swamped the rest of the week.	If you need a quick response, please submit your purchase order requests on Tuesday.
We offer MP3 players with 50, 75, or 100 gigabytes of storage capacity.	You can choose an MP3 player with 50, 75, or 100 gigabytes of storage.

Of course, you will have occasions when it is entirely appropriate to write or speak from your perspective, such as when you are offering your opinions or reporting on something you have seen. However, even in those instances make sure you focus on your readers' needs.

Also, be aware that the "you" attitude is more than simply using particular pronouns; it's a matter of respecting and being genuinely interested in your recipients. You can use *you* 25 times in a single page and still offend your audience or ignore readers' true concerns. If you're writing to a retailer, try to think like a retailer; if you're dealing with a production supervisor, put yourself in that position; if you're writing to a dissatisfied customer, imagine how you would feel at the other end of the transaction.

Avoid using *you* and *your* when doing so
- Makes you sound dictatorial
- Makes someone else feel guilty
- Goes against your organization's style

Be aware that on some occasions it's better to avoid using *you*, particularly if doing so will sound overly authoritative or accusing. For instance, instead of saying, "You failed to deliver the customer's order on time," you could avoid the confrontational tone by saying, "The customer didn't receive the order on time," or "Let's figure out a system that will ensure on-time deliveries."

Maintaining Standards of Etiquette

Although you may be tempted now and then to be brutally frank, try to express the facts in a kind and thoughtful manner.

Good etiquette not only indicates respect for your audience but also helps foster a more successful environment for communication by minimizing negative emotional reaction:

Instead of This	Write This
Once again, you've managed to bring down the website through your incompetent programming.	Let's review the last website update so that we can identify potential problems before the next update.
You've been sitting on our order for two weeks, and we need it now!	Our production schedules depend on timely delivery of parts and supplies, but we have not yet received the order scheduled for delivery two weeks ago. Please respond today with a firm delivery commitment.

Use extra tact when communicating with people higher up in the organization chart or outside the company.

Of course, some situations require more diplomacy than others. If you know your audience well, a less formal approach might be more appropriate. However, when you are communicating with people who outrank you or with people outside your organization, an added measure of courtesy is usually needed.

Written communication and most forms of electronic media generally require more tact than oral communication (see Figure 4.1). When you're speaking, your words are softened by your tone of voice and facial expression. Plus, you can adjust your approach according to the feedback you get. If you inadvertently offend someone in writing or in a podcast, for example,

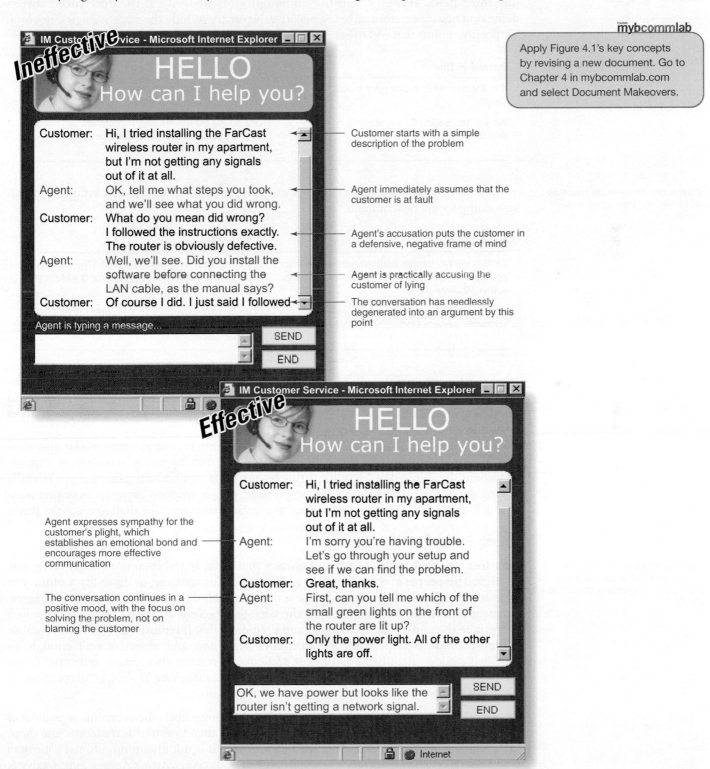

mybcommlab

Apply Figure 4.1's key concepts by revising a new document. Go to Chapter 4 in mybcommlab.com and select Document Makeovers.

Customer starts with a simple description of the problem

Agent immediately assumes that the customer is at fault

Agent's accusation puts the customer in a defensive, negative frame of mind

Agent is practically accusing the customer of lying

The conversation has needlessly degenerated into an argument by this point

Agent expresses sympathy for the customer's plight, which establishes an emotional bond and encourages more effective communication

The conversation continues in a positive mood, with the focus on solving the problem, not on blaming the customer

Figure 4.1   Fostering a Positive Relationship with an Audience
In the "poor" example, notice how the customer service agent's unfortunate word choices immediately derail this instant messaging exchange. In the "improved" example, a more sensitive approach allows both people to focus on solving the problem.

you usually don't get the immediate feedback you would need in order to resolve the situation. In fact, you may never know that you offended your audience.

Emphasizing the Positive

You can communicate negative news without being negative.

You will encounter situations throughout your career in which you need to convey unwanted news. However, sensitive communicators understand the difference between delivering negative news and being negative. Never try to hide the negative news, but look for positive points that will foster a good relationship with your audience:[2]

Instead of This	Write This
It is impossible to repair your laptop today.	Your computer can be ready by Tuesday. Would you like a loaner until then?
We wasted $300,000 advertising in that magazine.	Our $300,000 advertising investment did not pay off; let's analyze the experience and apply the insights to future campaigns.

Show audience members how they will benefit by responding to your message.

If you're trying to persuade audience members to perform a particular action, point out how doing so will benefit them:

Instead of This	Write This
We will notify all three credit reporting agencies if you do not pay your overdue bill within 10 days.	Paying your overdue bill within 10 days will prevent a negative entry on your credit record.
I am tired of seeing so many errors in the customer service blog.	Proofreading your blog postings will help avoid embarrassing mistakes that erode confidence in our brand.

Euphemisms are milder synonyms that can express an idea while triggering fewer negative connotations.

Look for appropriate opportunities to use **euphemisms**, or milder synonyms, that convey your meaning without carrying negative connotations. For example, when referring to people beyond a certain age, use "senior citizens," rather than "old people." *Senior* conveys respect in a way that *old* doesn't.

However, take care when using euphemisms; it's easy to push the idea too far and wind up sounding ridiculous—or worse yet, obscuring the truth. Speaking to your local community about the disposal of "manufacturing by-products" would be unethical if you're really talking about toxic waste. Even if it is unpleasant, people respond better to an honest message delivered with integrity than they do to a sugar-coated message that obscures the truth.

Using Bias-Free Language

Bias-free language avoids words and phrases that unfairly and even unethically categorize or stigmatize people.

Bias-free language avoids words and phrases that unfairly and even unethically categorize or stigmatize people in ways related to gender, race, ethnicity, age, or disability. Contrary to what some might think, biased language is not simply about "labels." To a significant degree, language reflects the way people think and what they believe, and biased language may well perpetuate the underlying stereotypes and prejudices that it represents.[3] Moreover, because communication is largely about perception, being fair and objective isn't enough; to establish a good relationship with your audience, you must also *appear* to be fair.[4] Good communicators make every effort to change biased language (see Table 4.1). Bias can take a variety of forms:

- **Gender bias.** Avoid sexist language by using the same labels for everyone, regardless of gender. Don't refer to a woman as *chairperson* and then to a man as *chairman*. Use *chair*, *chairperson*, or *chairman* consistently. (Note that it is not uncommon to use *chairman* when referring to a woman who heads a board of directors. Avon's Andrea Jung, Ogilvy & Mather's Shelly Lazarus, and Xerox's Ursula Burns, for example, all refer to themselves as *chairman*.[5]) Reword sentences to use *they* or to use no pronoun at all rather than refer to all individuals as *he*. Note that the preferred title for women in business is *Ms.* unless the individual asks to be addressed as *Miss* or *Mrs.* or has some other title, such as *Dr.*

TABLE 4.1   Overcoming Bias in Language

Examples	Unacceptable	Preferable
Gender Bias		
Using words containing *man*	Man-made	Artificial, synthetic, manufactured, constructed, human-made
	Mankind	Humanity, human beings, human race, people
	Manpower	Workers, workforce
	Businessman	Executive, manager, businessperson, professional
	Salesman	Sales representative, salesperson
	Foreman	Supervisor
Using female-gender words	Actress, stewardess	Actor, flight attendant
Using special designations	Woman doctor, male nurse	Doctor, nurse
Using *he* to refer to "everyone"	The average worker ... he	The average worker ... he or she
		OR
		Average workers ... they
Identifying roles with gender	The typical executive spends four hours of his day in meetings.	Most executives spend four hours a day in meetings.
	The consumer ... she	Consumers ... they
	The nurse/teacher ... she	Nurses/teachers ... they
Identifying women by marital status	Mrs. Norm Lindstrom	Maria Lindstrom
		OR
		Ms. Maria Lindstrom
	Norm Lindstrom and Ms. Drake	Norm Lindstrom and Maria Drake
		OR
		Mr. Lindstrom and Ms. Drake
Racial and Ethnic Bias		
Assigning stereotypes	Not surprisingly, Shing-Tung Yau excels in mathematics.	Shing-Tung Yau excels in mathematics.
Identifying people by race or ethnicity	Mario M. Cuomo, Italian-American politician and ex-governor of New York	Mario M. Cuomo, politician and ex-governor of New York
Age Bias		
Including age when irrelevant	Mary Kirazy, 58, has just joined our trust department.	Mary Kirazy has just joined our trust department.
Disability Bias		
Putting the disability before the person	Disabled workers face many barriers on the job.	Workers with physical disabilities face many barriers on the job.
	An epileptic, Tracy has no trouble doing her job.	Tracy's epilepsy has no effect on her job performance.

- **Racial and ethnic bias.** Avoid identifying people by race or ethnic origin unless such identification is relevant to the matter at hand—and it rarely is.

- **Age bias.** Mention the age of a person only when it is relevant. Moreover, be careful of the context in which you use words that refer to age; such words carry a variety of positive and negative connotations. For example, *young* can imply youthfulness, inexperience, or even immaturity, depending on how it's used.

- **Disability bias.** As with other labels, physical, mental, sensory, or emotional impairments should never be mentioned in business messages unless those conditions

REAL-TIME UPDATES
Learn More by Reading This PDF

Get detailed advice on using bias-free language

This in-depth guide offers practical tips for avoiding many types of cultural bias in your writing and speaking. Go to **http://real-timeupdates.com/bce5** and click on "Learn More." If you are using mybcommlab, you can access Real-Time Updates within each chapter or under Student Study Tools.

are directly relevant to the subject. If you must refer to someone's disability, put the person first and the disability second.[6] For example, by saying "employees with physical disabilities," not "handicapped employees," you focus on the whole person, not the disability. Finally, never use outdated terminology such as *crippled* or *retarded*.

BUILDING STRONG RELATIONSHIPS WITH YOUR AUDIENCE

2 LEARNING OBJECTIVE

Explain how establishing your credibility and projecting your company's image are vital aspects of building strong relationships with your audience

Whether a one-time interaction or a series of exchanges over the course of many months or years, successful communication relies on a positive relationship existing between sender and receiver. Establishing your credibility and projecting your company's image are two vital steps in building and fostering positive business relationships.

Establishing Your Credibility

People are more likely to react positively to your message when they have confidence in you.

Audience responses to your messages depend heavily on your **credibility**, a measure of your believability, based on how reliable you are and how much trust you evoke in others. With audiences that don't know you and trust you already, you need to establish credibility before they'll accept your messages (see Figure 4.2). On the other hand, when you do establish credibility, communication becomes much easier because you no longer have to spend time and energy convincing people that you are a trustworthy source of information and ideas. To build, maintain, or repair your credibility, emphasize the following characteristics:

To enhance your credibility, emphasize such factors as honesty, objectivity, and awareness of audience needs.

- **Honesty.** Demonstrating honesty and integrity will earn you the respect of your audiences, even if they don't always agree with or welcome your messages.

- **Objectivity.** Show that you can distance yourself from emotional situations and look at all sides of an issue.

- **Awareness of audience needs.** Let your audience members know that you understand what's important to them.

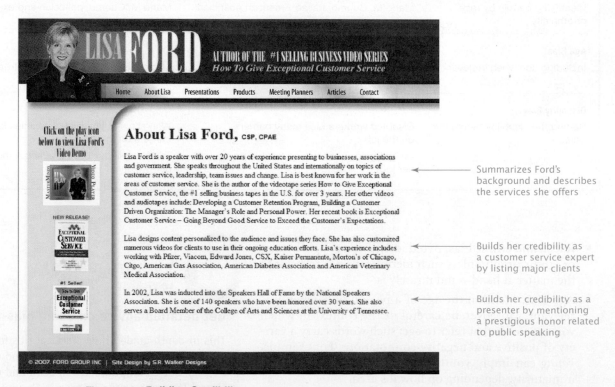

Figure 4.2 Building Credibility
Lisa Ford is a highly regarded expert in the field of customer service, but she still takes care to communicate her qualifications as a presenter so that potential audience members who aren't familiar with her work can appreciate the expertise she has to offer.

- **Credentials, knowledge, and expertise.** Audiences need to know that you have whatever it takes to back up your message, whether it's education, professional certification, special training, past successes, or simply the fact that you've done your research.
- **Endorsements.** An *endorsement* is a statement on your behalf by someone who is accepted by your audience as an expert.
- **Performance.** Demonstrating impressive communication skills is not enough; people need to know they can count on you to get the job done.
- **Confidence.** Audiences need to know that you believe in yourself and your message. If you are convinced that your message is sound, you can state your case confidently, without sounding boastful or arrogant.
- **Sincerity.** When you offer praise, don't use *hyperbole*, such as "You are the most fantastic employee I could ever imagine." Instead, point out specific qualities that warrant praise.

Credibility can take days, months, even years to establish—and it can be wiped out in an instant. An occasional mistake or letdown may be forgiven, but major lapses in honesty or integrity can destroy your reputation.

CREDIBILITY *Matters*

Projecting Your Company's Image

When you communicate with anyone outside your organization, it is more than a conversation between two individuals. You represent your company and therefore play a vital role in helping the company build and maintain positive relationships with all of its stakeholders. Most successful companies work hard to foster a specific public image, and your external communication efforts need to project that image. As part of this responsibility, the interests and preferred communication style of your company must take precedence over your own views and personal communication style.

Your company's interests and reputation take precedence over your personal views and communication style.

Many organizations have specific communication guidelines that show everything from the correct use of the company name to preferred abbreviations and other grammatical details. Specifying a desired style of communication is more difficult, however. Observe more experienced colleagues to see how they communicate and never hesitate to ask for editorial help to make sure you're conveying the appropriate tone. For instance, with clients entrusting thousands or millions of dollars to it, an investment firm communicates in a style quite different from that of a clothing retailer. And a clothing retailer specializing in high-quality business attire communicates in a different style than a store catering to the latest trends in casual wear.

CONTROLLING YOUR STYLE AND TONE

Your communication **style** involves the choices you make to express yourself: the words you select, the manner in which you use those words in sentences, and the way you build paragraphs from individual sentences. Your style creates a certain **tone**, or overall impression, in your messages. The right tone depends on the nature of your message and your relationship with the reader.

3 LEARNING OBJECTIVE
Explain how to achieve a tone that is conversational but businesslike, explain the value of using plain language, and define active and passive voice

Creating a Conversational Tone

The tone of your business messages can range from informal to conversational to formal. If you're in a large organization and you're communicating with your superiors or with customers, the right tone will usually be more formal and respectful.[7] However, that same tone might sound distant and cold in a small organization or if used with close colleagues. Part of the challenge of communicating on the job is to read each situation and figure out the appropriate tone to use.

Most business messages aim for a conversational style that is warm but businesslike.

Compare the three versions of the message in Table 4.2. The first is too formal and stuffy for today's audiences, whereas the third is too casual for any audience other than close associates or friends. The second message demonstrates the **conversational tone** used in most business communication—plain language that sounds businesslike without being stuffy at one extreme or too laid-back and informal at the other extreme. You can achieve a tone that is conversational but still businesslike following these guidelines:

- **Understand the difference between texting and writing.** The casual, acronym-filled language friends often use in text messaging, IM, and social networks is not considered professional business writing. Yes, it is an efficient way for friends to communicate—particularly taking into account the limitations of a phone keypad—but if you want to be taken seriously in business, you simply cannot write like this on the job.

- **Avoid obsolete and pompous language.** Most companies now shy away from such dated phrases as "attached please find" and "please be advised that." Similarly, avoid using obscure words, stale or clichéd expressions, and overly complicated sentences to impress others.

- **Avoid preaching and bragging.** Few things are more irritating than know-it-alls who like to preach or brag. However, if you need to remind your audience of something that should be obvious, try to work in the information casually, perhaps in the middle of a paragraph, where it will sound like a secondary comment rather than a major revelation.

- **Be careful with intimacy.** Business messages should generally avoid intimacy, such as sharing personal details or adopting a casual, unprofessional tone. However, when you have a close relationship with audience members, such as among the members of a close-knit team, a more intimate tone is sometimes appropriate and even expected.

TABLE 4.2   Formal, Conversational, and Informal Tones

Tone	Example
Stuffy: too formal for today's audiences	Dear Ms. Navarro: Enclosed please find the information that was requested during our telephone communication of May 14. As was mentioned at that time, Midville Hospital has significantly more doctors of exceptional quality than any other health facility in the state. As you were also informed, our organization has quite an impressive network of doctors and other health-care professionals with offices located throughout the state. In the event that you should need a specialist, our professionals will be able to make an appropriate recommendation. In the event that you have questions or would like additional information, you may certainly contact me during regular business hours. Most sincerely yours, Samuel G. Berenz
Conversational: just right for most business communication	Dear Ms. Navarro: Here's the information you requested during our phone conversation on Friday. As I mentioned, Midville Hospital has the highest-rated doctors and more of them than any other hospital in the state. In addition, we have a vast network of doctors and other health professionals with offices throughout the state. If you need a specialist, they can refer you to the right one. If you would like more information, please call any time between 9:00 and 5:00, Monday through Friday. Sincerely, Samuel G. Berenz
Unprofessional: too casual for business communication	Here's the 411 you requested. IMHO, we have more and better doctors than any other hospital in the state. FYI, we also have a large group of doctors and other health professionals w/offices close to U at work/home. If U need a specialist, they'll refer U to the right one Any? just ring or msg. L8R, S

- **Be careful with humor.** Humor can easily backfire and divert attention from your message. If you don't know your audience well or you're not skilled at using humor in a business setting, don't use it at all. Avoid humor in formal messages and when you're communicating across cultural boundaries.

Using Plain Language

What do you think this sentence is trying to say?

> We continually exist to synergistically supply value-added deliverables such that we may continue to proactively maintain enterprise-wide data to stay competitive in tomorrow's world.[8]

If you don't have any idea what it means, you're not alone. However, this is a real sentence from a real company. This sort of incomprehensible, buzzword-filled writing is - driving a widespread call to use *plain language* (or *plain English* specifically when English is involved).[9]

Plain language presents information in a simple, unadorned style that allows your audience to easily grasp your meaning—language that recipients "can read, understand and act upon the first time they read it."[10] You can see how this definition supports using the "you" attitude and shows respect for your audience. In addition, as ING Direct's Arkadi Kuhlmann suggested at the beginning of the chapter, plain language can make companies more productive and more profitable because people spend less time trying to figure out messages that are confusing or aren't written to meet their needs.[11]

> Audiences can understand and act on plain language without reading it over and over.

Selecting Active or Passive Voice

Your choice of active or passive voice affects the tone of your message. You are using **active voice** when the subject performs the action and the object receives the action: "Jodi sent the e-mail message." You're using **passive voice** when the subject receives the action: "The e-mail message was sent by Jodi." As you can see, the passive voice combines the helping verb *to be* with a form of the verb that is usually the past tense.

Using the active voice often makes your writing more direct, livelier, and easier to read (see Table 4.3). Passive voice is not wrong grammatically, but it can be cumbersome, lengthy, and vague. In most cases, the active voice is the better choice.[12] Nevertheless, using the passive voice can help you demonstrate the "you" attitude in some situations:

- When you want to be diplomatic about pointing out a problem or an error

> Active sentences are usually stronger than passive ones.
>
> Use passive sentences to soften bad news, to put yourself in the background, or to create an impersonal tone when needed.

TABLE 4.3   Choosing Active or Passive Voice

In general, avoid passive voice in order to make your writing lively and direct.

Dull and Indirect in Passive Voice	Lively and Direct in Active Voice
The new procedure was developed by the operations team.	The operations team developed the new procedure.
Legal problems are created by this contract.	This contract creates legal problems.
Reception preparations have been undertaken by our PR people for the new CEO's arrival.	Our PR people have begun planning a reception for the new CEO.

However, passive voice is helpful when you need to be diplomatic or want to focus attention on problems or solutions rather than on people.

Accusatory or Self-Congratulatory in Active Voice	More Diplomatic in Passive Voice
You lost the shipment.	The shipment was lost.
I recruited seven engineers last month.	Seven engineers were recruited last month.
We are investigating the high rate of failures on the final assembly line.	The high rate of failures on the final assembly line is being investigated.

- When you want to point out what's being done without taking or attributing either the credit or the blame
- When you want to avoid personal pronouns (*I* and *we*) in order to create an objective tone

The second half of Table 4.3 illustrates several situations in which the passive voice helps you focus your message on your audience.

4 LEARNING OBJECTIVE

Describe how to select words that are not only correct but also effective

COMPOSING YOUR MESSAGE: CHOOSING POWERFUL WORDS

After you have decided how to adapt to your audience, you're ready to begin composing your message. As you write your first draft, let your creativity flow. Don't try to draft and edit at the same time or worry about getting everything perfect. Make up words if you can't think of the right word, draw pictures, or talk out loud—do whatever it takes to get the ideas out of your head and onto your computer screen or a piece of paper. If you've planned carefully, you'll have time to revise and refine the material later, before showing it to anyone. In fact, many writers find it helpful to establish a personal rule of never showing a first draft to anyone. By working in this "safe zone," away from the critical eyes of others, your mind will stay free to think clearly and creatively.

You may find it helpful to hone your craft by viewing your writing at three levels: strong words, effective sentences, and coherent paragraphs. Starting at the word level, successful writers pay close attention to the correct use of words.[13] If you make errors of grammar or usage, you lose credibility with your audience—even if your message is otherwise correct. Poor grammar suggests to readers that you're uninformed, and they may choose not to trust an uninformed source. Moreover, poor grammar can imply that you don't respect your audience enough to get things right.

The "rules" of grammar and usage can be a source of worry for writers because some of these rules are complex and some evolve over time. Even professional editors and grammarians occasionally have questions about correct usage, and they sometimes disagree about the answers. For example, the word *data* is the plural form of *datum*, yet some experts now prefer to treat *data* as a singular noun when it's used in nonscientific material to refer to a body of facts or figures.

With practice, you'll become more skilled in making correct choices over time. If you have doubts about what is correct, you have many ways to find the answer. Check the "Handbook of Grammar, Mechanics, and Usage" at the end of this book, or consult the many special reference books and resources available in libraries, in bookstores, and on the Internet.

In addition to using words correctly, successful writers and speakers take care to use the most effective words and phrases. Selecting and using words effectively is often more challenging than using words correctly because it's a matter of judgment and experience. Careful writers continue to work at their craft to find words that communicate with power (see Figure 4.3).

Correctness is the first consideration when choosing words.

Effectiveness is the second consideration when choosing words.

Balancing Abstract and Concrete Words

The more abstract a word is, the more it is removed from the tangible, objective world of things that can be perceived with the senses.

Words vary dramatically in their degree of abstraction or concreteness. An **abstract word** expresses a concept, quality, or characteristic. Abstractions are usually broad, encompassing a category of ideas, and are often intellectual, academic, or philosophical. *Love, honor, progress, tradition,* and *beauty* are abstractions, as are such important business concepts as *productivity, profits, quality,* and *motivation*. In contrast, a **concrete word** stands for something you can touch, see, or visualize. Most concrete terms are anchored in the tangible, material world. *Chair, table, horse, rose, kick, kiss, red, green,* and *two* are concrete words; they are direct, clear, and exact. Incidentally, technology continues to generate new words and new meanings that describe things that don't have a physical presence but are nonetheless concrete. For example, *software, database,* and *data packet* are all concrete terms as well.

As you can imagine, abstractions tend to cause more trouble for writers and readers than concrete words.

REAL-TIME UPDATES

Learn More by Reading This Article

Grammar questions? Click here for help

This comprehensive online guide can help you out of just about any grammar dilemma. Go to **http://real-timeupdates.com/bce5** and click on "Learn More." If you are using mybcommlab, you can access Real-Time Updates within each chapter or under Student Study Tools.

Two Sides of the Story

Growing interest in the global acceptance of a single set of robust accounting standards comes from all participants in the capital markets. Many multinational companies and national regulators and users support it because they believe that the use of common standards in the preparation of public company financial statements will make it easier to compare the financial results of reporting entities from different countries. They believe it will help investors understand opportunities better. Large public companies with subsidiaries in multiple jurisdictions would be able to use one accounting language company-wide and present their financial statements in the same language as their competitors.

Another benefit some believe is that in a truly global economy, financial professionals including CPAs will be more mobile, and companies will more easily be able to respond to the human capital needs of their subsidiaries around the world.

Nevertheless, many people also believe that U.S. GAAP is the gold standard, and something will be lost with full acceptance of IFRS. However, recent SEC actions and global trends have increased awareness of the need to address possible adoption. According to a survey conducted in the first half of 2008 by Deloitte & Touche among chief financial officers and other financial professionals, U.S. companies have an interest in adopting IFRS and this interest is steadily growing. Thirty percent would consider adopting IFRS now, another 28 percent are unsure or do not have sufficient knowledge to decide, while 42 percent said they would not. Still, an AICPA survey conducted in Fall 2008 among its CPA members shows a significant and positive shift in the number of firms and companies that are starting to prepare for eventual adoption of IFRS. A 55 percent majority of CPAs at firms and companies nationwide said they are preparing in a variety of ways for IFRS adoption, an increase of 14 percentage points over the 41 percent who were preparing for change, according to an April 2008 AICPA survey.

Another concern is that worldwide, many countries that claim to be converging to international standards may never get to 100 percent compliance. Most reserve the right to carve out selectively or modify standards they do not consider in their national interest, an action that could lead to incomparability — the very issue that IFRS seek to address.

GAAP and IFRS, Still Differences

Great strides have been made by the FASB and the IASB to converge the content of IFRS and U.S. GAAP. The goal is that by the time the SEC allows or mandates the use of IFRS for U.S. publicly traded companies, most or all of the key differences will have been resolved.

Because of these ongoing convergence projects, the extent of the specific differences between IFRS and U.S. GAAP is shrinking. Yet significant differences do remain. For example:

- IFRS does not permit Last In First Out (LIFO) as an inventory costing method.

- IFRS uses a single-step method for impairment write-downs rather than the two-step method used in U.S. GAAP, making write-downs more likely.

- IFRS has a different probability threshold and measurement objective for contingencies.

- IFRS does not permit curing debt covenant violations after year-end.

- IFRS guidance regarding revenue recognition is less extensive than GAAP and contains relatively little industry-specific instruction.

5

Margin annotations (left):

In many cases, *global* is an absolute term and doesn't benefit from a modifier such as *ruly*. However, economic globalization is occurring in stages, so *truly* here suggests the point at which globalization is nearly complete.

Claim is a powerful word here because it suggests a strong element of doubt.

The diplomatic use of passive voice keeps the focus on the issue at hand, rather than on the organizations that are involved.

Margin annotations (right):

Robust goes beyond simply *strong* to suggest *resilient* and *comprehensive* as well.

Gold standard (a term borrowed from economics) refers to something against which all similar entities are compared, an unsurpassed model of excellence.

In the context of a survey *significant* means more than just *important*; it indicates a statistical observation that is large enough to be more than mere chance. *Positive* indicates the direction of the change and suggests *affirmation* and progress.

Carve out is much stronger than remove because it could suggest surgical precision if done well or perhaps violent destruction if not done with finesse. In the context, *carve out* is meant to express a concern about countries weakening the international financial standards by modifying them to meet their own needs.

Figure 4.3 Choosing Powerful Words
Notice how careful word choices help this excerpt from a report published by the American Institute of Certified Public Accountants make a number of important points. The tone is formal, which is appropriate for a report with global, public readership. (GAAP refers to accounting standards currently used in the United States; IFRS refers to international standards.)

Abstractions tend to be "fuzzy" and can be interpreted differently, depending on the audience and the circumstances. The best way to minimize such problems is to blend abstract terms with concrete ones, the general with the specific. State the concept and then pin it down with details expressed in more concrete terms. Save the abstractions for ideas that cannot be expressed any other way. In addition, abstract words such as *small, numerous, sizable, near, soon, good,* and *fine* are imprecise, so try to replace them with terms that are more accurate. Instead of referring to a *sizable loss*, give an exact number.

Finding Words that Communicate Well

When you compose business messages, look for the most powerful words for each situation (see Table 4.4 on the next page):

Try to use words that are powerful and familiar.

- **Choose strong, precise words.** Choose words that express your thoughts clearly, specifically, and strongly. If you find yourself using many adjectives and adverbs, chances are

TABLE 4.4   Finding Words That Communicate with Power

Weaker Words and Phrases (in many situations)	Stronger Alternatives (effective usage depends on the situation)
Increase (as a verb)	Accelerate, amplify, augment, enlarge, escalate, expand, extend, magnify, multiply, soar, swell
Decrease (as a verb)	Curb, cut back, depreciate, dwindle, shrink, slacken
Large, small	(Use a specific number, such as $100 million)
Good	Admirable, beneficial, desirable, flawless, pleasant, sound, superior, worthy
Bad	Abysmal, corrupt, deficient, flawed, inadequate, inferior, poor, substandard, worthless
We are committed to providing …	We provide …
It is in our best interest to …	We should …

Unfamiliar Words	Familiar Words
Ascertain	Find out, learn
Consummate	Close, bring about
Peruse	Read, study
Circumvent	Avoid
Unequivocal	Certain

Clichés and Buzzwords	Plain Language
An uphill battle	A challenge
Writing on the wall	Prediction
Call the shots	Lead
Take by storm	Attack
Costs an arm and a leg	Expensive
A new ballgame	Fresh start
Fall through the cracks	Be overlooked
Think outside the box	Be creative
Run it up the flagpole	Find out what people think about it
Eat our own dog food	Use our own products
Mission-critical	Vital
Disintermediate	Get rid of
Green light (as a verb)	Approve
Architect (as a verb)	Design
Space (as in, "we compete in the XYZ space")	Market or industry
Blocking and tackling	Basic skills
Trying to boil the ocean	Working frantically but without focus
Human capital	People, employees, workforce
Low-hanging fruit	Tasks that are easy to complete or sales that are easy to close
Pushback	Resistance

you're trying to compensate for weak nouns and verbs. Saying that *sales plummeted* is stronger and more efficient than saying *sales dropped dramatically* or *sales experienced a dramatic drop.*

- **Choose familiar words.** You'll communicate best with words that are familiar to both you and your readers. Moreover, trying to use unfamiliar words can lead to embarrassing mistakes.

Avoid clichés, be extremely careful with trendy buzzwords, and use jargon only when your audience is completely familiar with it.

- **Avoid clichés and use buzzwords carefully.** Although familiar words are generally the best choice, avoid *clichés*—terms and phrases so common that they have lost some of their power to communicate. *Buzzwords,* newly coined terms often associated with technology, business, or cultural changes, are more difficult to handle than clichés because in small doses and in the right situation, they can be useful. The careful use of a buzzword can signal that you're an insider, someone in the know.[14] However, buzzwords quickly become clichés, and using them too late in their "life cycle" can mark you as an outsider desperately trying to look like an insider.

- **Use jargon carefully.** *Jargon,* the specialized language of a particular profession or industry, has a bad reputation, but it's not always bad. Using jargon is usually an efficient way to communicate within the specific groups that understand these terms. After all, that's how jargon develops in the first place, as people with similar interests develop ways to communicate complex ideas quickly.

If you need help finding the right words, try some of the visual dictionaries and thesauruses available online. For example, Visuwords (www.visuwords.com) shows words that are similar to or different from a given word and helps you see subtle differences to find the perfect word.[15]

COMPOSING YOUR MESSAGE: CREATING EFFECTIVE SENTENCES

5 **LEARNING OBJECTIVE**
Define the four types of sentences and explain how sentence style affects emphasis within a message

Arranging your carefully chosen words in effective sentences is the next step in creating successful messages. Start by selecting the best type of sentence to communicate each point you want to make.

Choosing from the Four Types of Sentences

Sentences come in four basic varieties: simple, compound, complex, and compound-complex. A **simple sentence** has one main clause (a single subject and a single predicate), although it may be expanded by nouns and pronouns serving as objects of the action and by modifying phrases. Consider this example (with the subject underlined once and the predicate verb underlined twice):

A simple sentence has one main clause.

<u>Profits</u> <u>increased</u> 35 percent in the past year.

A **compound sentence** has two main clauses that express two or more independent but related thoughts of equal importance, usually joined by *and, but,* or *or*. In effect, a compound sentence is a merger of two or more simple sentences (independent clauses) that are related. For example:

A compound sentence has two main clauses.

<u>Wages</u> <u>declined</u> by 5 percent, and employee <u>turnover</u> <u>has</u> <u>been</u> higher than ever.

The independent clauses in a compound sentence are always separated by a comma or by a semicolon (in which case the conjunction—*and, but,* or *or*—is dropped).

A **complex sentence** expresses one main thought (the independent clause) and one or more subordinate thoughts (dependent clauses) related to it, often separated by a comma. The subordinate thought, which comes first in the following sentence, could not stand alone:

A complex sentence has one main clause and one subordinate clause.

Although you may question Gerald's conclusions, <u>you</u> <u>must</u> <u>admit</u> that his research is thorough.

A **compound-complex sentence** has two main clauses, at least one of which contains a subordinate clause:

A compound-complex sentence has two main clauses and at least one dependent clause.

<u>Profits</u> <u>increased</u> 35 percent in the past year, so although the company faces long-term challenges, <u>I</u> <u>agree</u> that its short-term prospects look quite positive.

To make your writing as effective as possible, strive for variety and balance using all four sentence types. If you use too many simple sentences, you won't be able to properly express the relationships among your ideas, and your writing will sound choppy and abrupt. At the other extreme, a long series of compound, complex, or compound-complex sentences can be tiring to read.

Maintain some variety among the four sentence types to keep your writing from getting choppy (too many short, simple sentences) or exhausting (too many long sentences).

Using Sentence Style to Emphasize Key Thoughts

Emphasize specific ideas by
- Devoting more words to them
- Putting them at the beginning or at the end of the sentence
- Making them the subject of the sentence

In every message, some ideas are more important than others. You can emphasize key ideas through your sentence style. One obvious technique is to give important points the most space. When you want to call attention to a thought, use extra words to describe it. Consider this sentence:

> The chairperson called for a vote of the shareholders.

To emphasize the importance of the chairperson, you might describe her more fully:

> Having considerable experience in corporate takeover battles, the chairperson called for a vote of the shareholders.

You can increase the emphasis even more by adding a separate, short sentence to augment the first:

> The chairperson called for a vote of the shareholders. She has considerable experience in corporate takeover battles.

You can also call attention to a thought by making it the subject of the sentence. In the following example, the emphasis is on the person:

> I can write letters much more quickly using a computer.

However, when you change the subject, the computer takes center stage:

> The computer enables me to write letters much more quickly.

Another way to emphasize an idea is to place it either at the beginning or at the end of a sentence:

> **Less emphatic:** We are cutting the price to stimulate demand.
> **More emphatic:** To stimulate demand, we are cutting the price.

The best placement of the dependent clause depends on the relationship between the ideas in the sentence.

In complex sentences, the ideal placement of the dependent clause depends on the relationship between the ideas expressed. If you want to emphasize the idea expressed in the dependent clause, put that clause at the end of the sentence (the most emphatic position) or at the beginning (the second most emphatic position). If you want to downplay the idea, position the dependent clause within the sentence.

> **Most emphatic:** The electronic parts are manufactured in Mexico, which has lower wage rates than the United States.
> **Emphatic:** Because wage rates are lower in Mexico than in the United States, the electronic parts are manufactured there.
> **Least emphatic:** Mexico, which has lower wage rates than the United States, was selected as the production site for the electronic parts.

Techniques such as these give you a great deal of control over the way your audience interprets what you have to say.

6 **LEARNING OBJECTIVE**

Define the three key elements of a paragraph, and list five ways to develop coherent paragraphs

COMPOSING YOUR MESSAGE: CRAFTING COHERENT PARAGRAPHS

Paragraphs organize sentences related to the same general topic. Readers expect every paragraph to be *unified*—focusing on a single topic—and *coherent*—presenting ideas in a logically connected way. By carefully arranging the elements of each paragraph, you help your readers grasp the main idea of your document and understand how the specific pieces of support material back up that idea.

Most paragraphs consist of
- A topic sentence that reveals the subject of the paragraph
- Related sentences that support and expand the topic
- Transitions that help readers move between sentences and paragraphs

Understanding the Elements of a Paragraph

Paragraphs vary widely in length and form, but most contain three basic elements: a topic sentence, support sentences that develop the topic, and transitional words and phrases.

Topic Sentence

An effective paragraph deals with a single topic, and the sentence that introduces that topic is called the **topic sentence.** This sentence, usually the first one in the paragraph, gives readers a summary of the general idea that will be covered in the rest of the paragraph. The following examples show how a topic sentence can introduce the subject and suggest the way the subject will be developed:

> The medical products division has been troubled for many years by public relations problems. [In the rest of the paragraph, readers will learn the details of the problems.]

> To get a refund, please supply us with the following information. [The details of the necessary information will be described in the rest of the paragraph.]

Support Sentences

In most paragraphs, the topic sentence needs to be explained, justified, or extended with one or more support sentences. These sentences must be related to the topic and provide examples, evidence, and clarification:

> The medical products division has been troubled for many years by public relations problems. Since 2006 the local newspaper has published 15 articles that portray the division in a negative light. We have been accused of everything from mistreating laboratory animals to polluting the local groundwater. Our facility has been described as a health hazard. Our scientists are referred to as "Frankensteins," and our profits are considered "obscene."

Notice how these support sentences are all more specific than the topic sentence. Each one provides another piece of evidence to demonstrate the general truth of the main thought. Also, each sentence is clearly related to the general idea being developed, which gives the paragraph its unity. A paragraph is well developed when it contains enough information to make the topic sentence convincing and interesting and doesn't contain any unneeded or unrelated sentences.

Transitions

Transitions connect ideas by showing how one thought is related to another. They also help alert the reader to what lies ahead so that shifts and changes don't cause confusion. In addition to helping readers understand the connections you're trying to make, transitions give your writing a smooth, even flow.

Depending on the specific need within a document, transitional elements can range in length from a single word to an entire paragraph or more. You can establish transitions in a variety of ways:

- **Use connecting words.** Use words such as *and, but, or, nevertheless, however,* and *in addition.*
- **Echo a word or phrase from a previous paragraph or sentence.** "A system should be established for monitoring inventory levels. This system will provide . . ."
- **Use a pronoun that refers to a noun used previously.** "Ms. Arthur is the leading candidate for the president's position. She has excellent qualifications."
- **Use words that are frequently paired.** "The machine has a *minimum* output of . . . Its *maximum* output is . . ."

Transitional elements include
- Connecting words (conjunctions)
- Repeated words or phrases
- Pronouns
- Words that are frequently paired

Some transitions serve as mood changers, alerting the reader to a change in mood from the previous material. Some announce a total contrast with what's gone on before, some announce a cause-and-effect relationship, and some signal a change in time. Here is a list of common transitions:

- **Additional detail:** moreover, furthermore, in addition, besides, first, second, third, finally
- **Cause-and-effect relationship:** therefore, because, accordingly, thus, consequently, hence, as a result, so
- **Comparison:** similarly, here again, likewise, in comparison, still
- **Contrast:** yet, conversely, whereas, nevertheless, on the other hand, however, but, nonetheless

- **Condition:** although, if
- **Illustration:** for example, in particular, in this case, for instance
- **Time sequence:** formerly, after, when, meanwhile, sometimes
- **Intensification:** indeed, in fact, in any event
- **Summary:** in brief, in short, to sum up
- **Repetition:** that is, in other words, as I mentioned earlier

Consider using a transition whenever it could help the reader understand your ideas and follow you from point to point. You can use transitions inside paragraphs to tie together related points and between paragraphs to ease the shift from one distinct thought to another. In longer reports, a transition that links major sections or chapters is often a complete paragraph that serves as a summary of the ideas presented in the section just ending or as a mini-introduction to the next section.

Figure 4.4 offers several examples of effective transitions and other features of strong paragraphs.

Developing Paragraphs

You have a variety of options for developing paragraphs, each of which can convey a specific type of idea. Five of the most common approaches are illustration, comparison or contrast, cause and effect, classification, and problem and solution (see Table 4.5).

Five ways to develop paragraphs:
- Illustration
- Comparison or contrast
- Cause and effect
- Classification
- Problem and solution

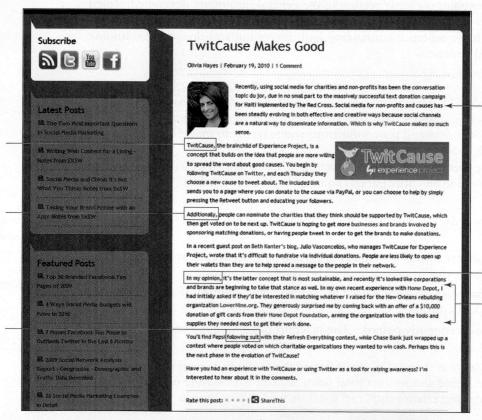

Echoing *TwitCause* at the beginning of this paragraph tells readers that this paragraph will continue on the same subject.

The transition *Additionally* signals that the topic in the previous paragraph will be expanded upon in this new paragraph.

Following suit functions as a transition from the previous paragraph by linking Pepsi back to the description of Home Depot.

The three sentences in this paragraph start with the broad topic (social media for charities and nonprofits) and narrow down the main idea, which is that TwitCause is a good tool for this purpose. (Note that the third sentence is really a fragment, but Hayes is selectively breaking the rules here to emphasize the suitability of TwitCause.)

In my opinion lets readers know she is transitioning from reporting to offering her personal thoughts on the subject at hand.

The second and third sentences in this paragraph provide an example of the observation made in the topic sentence at the beginning of the paragraph.

Apply Figure 4.4's key concepts by revising a new document. Go to Chapter 4 in mybcommlab.com and select Document Makeovers.

Figure 4.4   Crafting Unified, Coherent Paragraphs
Olivia Hayes, a copywriter with the social media marketing agency Ignite, demonstrates several aspects of effective writing in this blog post about the Twitter-based social contribution network TwitCause.

TABLE 4.5 Five Techniques for Developing Paragraphs

Technique	Description	Example
Illustration	Giving examples that demonstrate the general idea	Some of our most popular products are available through local distributors. For example, Everett & Lemmings carries our frozen soups and entrees. The J. B. Green Company carries our complete line of seasonings, as well as the frozen soups. Wilmont Foods, also a major distributor, now carries our new line of frozen desserts.
Comparison or contrast	Using similarities or differences to develop the topic	When the company was small, the recruiting function could be handled informally. The need for new employees was limited, and each manager could comfortably screen and hire her or his own staff. However, our successful bid on the Owens contract means that we will be doubling our labor force over the next six months. To hire that many people without disrupting our ongoing activities, we will create a separate recruiting group within the human resources department.
Cause and effect	Focusing on the reasons for something	The heavy-duty fabric of your Wanderer tent probably broke down for one of two reasons: (1) a sharp object punctured the fabric, and without reinforcement, the hole was enlarged by the stress of pitching the tent daily for a week or (2) the fibers gradually rotted because the tent was folded and stored while still wet.
Classification	Showing how a general idea is broken into specific categories	Successful candidates for our supervisor trainee program generally come from one of several groups. The largest group by far consists of recent graduates of accredited business management programs. The next largest group comes from within our own company, as we try to promote promising staff workers to positions of greater responsibility. Finally, we occasionally accept candidates with outstanding supervisory experience in related industries.
Problem and solution	Presenting a problem and then discussing the solution	Selling handmade toys online is a challenge because consumers are accustomed to buying heavily advertised toys from major chain stores or well-known websites such as Amazon.oom. However, if we develop an appealing website, we can compete on the basis of product novelty and quality. In addition, we can provide unusual crafts at a competitive price: a rocking horse of birch, with a hand-knit tail and mane; a music box with the child's name painted on the top; and a real teepee made by Native American artisans.

USING TECHNOLOGY TO COMPOSE AND SHAPE YOUR MESSAGES

Be sure to take advantage of the tools in your word processor or online publishing systems (for websites, blogs, and other documents) to write more efficiently and effectively. The features, functions, and names vary from system to system and version to version, but you'll encounter some combination of the following capabilities:

- **Style sheets, style sets, templates, and themes.** *Style sheets, style sets, templates,* and *themes* are various ways of ensuring consistency throughout a document and from document to document. These tools also make it easy to redesign an entire document or screen simply by redefining the various styles or selecting a different design theme. Style sheets or sets are collections of formatting choices for words, paragraphs, and other elements. Rather than manually formatting every element, you simply select one of the available styles. Templates usually set overall document parameters such as page size and provide a specific set of styles to use. Templates can be particularly handy if you create a variety of document types, such as letters, calendars, agendas, and so on. Themes tend to address the overall look and feel of the page or screen, including color palettes and background images.

- **Boilerplate and document components.** *Boilerplate* refers to a standard block of text that is reused in multiple documents. Two common examples are company descriptions and executive biographies. Some systems offer the means to store these blocks and drop them into a document as needed, which saves time and ensures consistency.

Take full advantage of your software's formatting capabilities to help produce effective, professional documents in a short time.

Moving beyond simple text blocks, some systems can store fully formatted document components such as cover pages, sidebars, and *pull quotes* (a piece of text copied from the main body of the document and formatted as a large, eye-catching visual element).

- **Autocorrection or autocompletion.** Some programs can automate text entry and correction using a feature called autocompletion, autocorrection, or something similar. In Microsoft Word, for example, the AutoCorrect feature lets you build a library of actions that automatically fill in longer entries based on the first few characters you type (such as entering a full description of the company after you type the word "boilerplate") or correct common typing errors (such as typing *teh* instead of *the*). Use these features carefully, though. First, they can make changes you might not want in every instance. Second, you may grow to rely on them to clean up your typing, but they won't be there to help when you're using other systems.

- **File merge and mail merge.** Most word processing software makes it easy to combine files, which is an especially handy feature when several members of a team write different sections of a report. Mail merge lets you personalize form letters by automatically inserting names and addresses from a database.

- **Endnotes, footnotes, indexes, and tables of contents.** Your compnuter can help you track footnotes and endnotes, renumbering them every time you add or delete references. For a report's indexes and table of contents, you can simply flag the items you want to include, and the software assembles the lists for you.

For the latest information on using technology to compose messages, visit **http://real-timeupdates.com/bce5** and click on Chapter 4.

CHAPTER REVIEW AND ACTIVITIES

Learning Objectives: Check Your Progress

1 OBJECTIVE Identify the four aspects of being sensitive to audience needs when writing business messages.

First, the "you" attitude refers to speaking and writing in terms of your audience's wishes, interests, hopes, and preferences rather than your own. Writing with this attitude is essential to effective communication because it shows your audience that you have their needs in mind, not just your own. Second, good etiquette not only indicates respect for your audience, but also helps foster a more successful environment for communication by minimizing negative emotional reaction. Third, sensitive communicators understand the difference between delivering negative news and being negative. Without hiding the negative news, they look for

ways to emphasize positive aspects. Fourth, being sensitive includes taking care to avoid biased language that unfairly and even unethically categorizes or stigmatizes people in ways related to gender, race, ethnicity, age, or disability.

2 OBJECTIVE Explain how establishing your credibility and projecting your company's image are vital aspects of building strong relationships with your audience.

Whether a one-time interaction or a series of exchanges over the course of many months or years, successful communication relies on a positive relationship existing between sender and receiver. Audience responses to your messages depend heavily on your credibility, a measure of your believability, based on how reliable you are and how much trust you evoke in others. When you have established credibility with an audience, communication becomes much easier because you no longer have to spend time and energy convincing people that you are a trustworthy source of information and ideas. Project your company's desired image when communicating with external audiences. You represent your company and therefore play a vital role in helping the company build and maintain positive relationships with all of its stakeholders.

3 OBJECTIVE Explain how to achieve a tone that is conversational but businesslike, explain the value of using plain language, and define active and passive voice.

To achieve a tone that is conversational but still businesslike, avoid obsolete and pompous language, avoid preaching and bragging, be careful with intimacy (sharing personal details or adopting an overly casual tone), and be careful with humor. Plain language is a way of presenting information in a simple, unadorned style so that your audience can easily grasp your meaning. By writing and speaking in plain terms, you demonstrate the "you" attitude and show respect for your audience. In the active voice, the subject performs the action and the object receives the action. In the passive voice, the subject receives the action. The passive voice combines the helping verb *to be* with a form of the verb that is usually in the past tense.

4 OBJECTIVE Describe how to select words that are not only correct but also effective.

Selecting words that are not only correct but also effective involves balancing abstract and concrete words, choosing powerful and familiar words, avoiding clichés, using buzzwords carefully, and using jargon carefully.

5 OBJECTIVE Define the four types of sentences, and explain how sentence style affects emphasis within a message.

The four types of sentences are *simple* (one main clause), *compound* (two main clauses that express independent but related ideas of equal importance), *complex* (one main clause and one subordinate clause of lesser importance), and *compound-complex* (two main clauses, at least one of which contains a subordinate clause). Sentence style affects emphasis by playing up or playing down specific parts of a sentence. To emphasize a certain point, you can place it at the end of the sentence or make it the subject of the sentence. To deemphasize a point, put it in the middle of the sentence.

6 OBJECTIVE Define the three key elements of a paragraph, and list five ways to develop coherent paragraphs.

The three key elements of a paragraph are a topic sentence that identifies the subject of the paragraph, support sentences that develop the topic and provide examples and evidence, and transitional words and phrases that help readers connect one thought to the next. Five ways to develop coherent paragraphs are illustration, comparison or contrast, cause and effect, classification, and problem and solution.

7 OBJECTIVE Identify the most common software features that help you craft messages more efficiently.

Common software features that help you craft messages more efficiently include style sheets, style sets, templates, and themes; features to store and use boilerplate and document components; autocorrection or autocompletion; file merge and mail merge; and endnotes, footnotes, indexes, and tables of contents.

■ Test Your Knowledge

To review chapter content related to each question, refer to the indicated Learning Objective.

1. In what three situations should you consider using passive voice? [LO-3]
2. Which writing characteristics should you avoid if you want to achieve a conversational tone? [LO-3]
3. How does an abstract word differ from a concrete word? [LO-4]
4. What functions do transitions serve? [LO-6]
5. How can you use sentence style to emphasize key thoughts? [LO-5]

■ Apply Your Knowledge

To review chapter content related to each question, refer to the indicated Learning Objective.

1. Seven million people in the United States are allergic to one or more food ingredients. Every year 30,000 of these people end up in the emergency room after suffering allergic reactions, and 200 of them die. Many of these tragic events are tied to poorly written food labels that either fail to identify dangerous allergens or use scientific terms that most consumers don't recognize.[16] Do food manufacturers have a responsibility to ensure that consumers read, understand, and follow warnings on food products? Explain your answer. [LO-1]
2. How can you demonstrate the "you" attitude if you don't know your audience personally? [LO-1]
3. When composing business messages, how can you communicate with an authentic voice and project your company's image at the same time? [LO-2]
4. What steps can you take to make abstract concepts such as *opportunity* feel more concrete in your messages? [LO-4]
5. Should you bother using transitions if the logical sequence of your message is already obvious? Why or why not? [LO-6]

■ Practice Your Skills

Exercises for Perfecting Your Writing

To review chapter content related to each set of exercises, refer to the indicated Learning Objective.

The "You" Attitude   Rewrite the following sentences to reflect your audience's viewpoint. [LO-1]

1. We request that you use the order form supplied in the back of our catalog.
2. We insist that you always bring your credit card to the store.
3. We want to get rid of all our 15-inch monitors to make room in our warehouse for the 19-inch screens. Thus we are offering a 25 percent discount on all sales this week.
4. I am applying for the position of bookkeeper in your office. I feel that my grades prove that I am bright and capable, and I think I can do a good job for you.
5. As requested, we are sending the refund for $25.

Emphasizing the Positive   Revise the following sentences to replace unflattering terms (in italics) with euphemisms. [LO-1]

6. The new boss is _____ (*stubborn*) when it comes to doing things by the book.
7. When you say we've doubled our profit level, you are _____ (*wrong*).
8. Just be careful not to make any _____ (*stupid*) choices this week.
9. Jim Riley is _____ (*incompetent*) for that kind of promotion.
10. Glen monopolizes every meeting by being _____ (*a loudmouth*).

Emphasizing the Positive   Revise these sentences to be positive rather than negative. [LO-1]

11. To avoid the loss of your credit rating, please remit payment within 10 days.
12. We don't make refunds on returned merchandise that is soiled.
13. Because we are temporarily out of Baby Cry dolls, we won't be able to ship your order for 10 days.
14. You failed to specify the color of the blouse that you ordered.
15. You should have realized that waterbeds will freeze in unheated houses during winter. Therefore, our guarantee does not cover the valve damage and you must pay the $9.50 valve-replacement fee (plus postage).

Courteous Communication   Revise the following sentences to make them more courteous. [LO-1]

16. You claim that you mailed your check last Thursday, but we have not received it.
17. It is not our policy to exchange sale items, especially after they have been worn.
18. You neglected to sign the enclosed contract.
19. I received your letter, in which you assert that our shipment was three days late.
20. You failed to enclose your instructions for your new will.

Bias-Free Language   Rewrite each of the following sentences to eliminate bias. [LO-1]

21. For an Indian, Maggie certainly is outgoing.
22. He needs a wheelchair, but he doesn't let his handicap affect his job performance.
23. A pilot must have the ability to stay calm under pressure, and then he must be trained to cope with any problem that arises.

24. Candidate Renata Parsons, married and the mother of a teenager, will attend the debate.
25. Senior citizen Sam Nugent is still an active salesman.

Message Composition: Selecting Words   In the following sentences, replace vague phrases (underlined) with concrete phrases. Make up any details you might need. [LO-4]

26. We will be opening our new facility sometime this spring.
27. You can now purchase our new Leaf-Away yard and lawn blower at a substantial savings.
28. After the reception, we were surprised that such a large number attended.
29. The new production line has been operating with increased efficiency on every run.
30. Over the holiday, we hired a crew to expand the work area.

Message Composition: Selecting Words   In the following sentences, replace weak terms (in italics) with words that are stronger: [LO-4]

31. The two reporters _____ (*ran after*) every lead enthusiastically.
32. Even large fashion houses have to match staff size to the normal _____ (*seasonal ups and downs*).
33. Health costs _____ (*suddenly rise*) when management forgets to emphasize safety issues.
34. The _____ (*bright*) colors in that ad are keeping customers from seeing what we have to sell.
35. Once we solved the zoning issue, new business construction _____ (*moved forward*), and the district has been flourishing ever since.

Message Composition: Selecting Words   Rewrite these sentences to replace the clichés with fresh, personal expressions. [LO-4]

36. Being a jack-of-all-trades, Dave worked well in his new selling job.
37. Moving Leslie into the accounting department, where she was literally a fish out of water, was like putting a square peg into a round hole, if you get my drift.
38. I knew she was at death's door, but I thought the doctor would pull her through.
39. Movies aren't really my cup of tea; as far as I am concerned, they can't hold a candle to a good book.
40. It's a dog-eat-dog world out there in the rat race of the asphalt jungle.

Message Composition: Selecting Words   In the following sentences, replace long, complicated words with short, simple ones. [LO-4]

41. Management _____ (*inaugurated*) the recycling policy six months ago.
42. You can convey the same meaning without _____ (*utilizing*) the same words.
43. You'll never be promoted unless you _____ (*endeavor*) to be more patient.
44. I have to wait until payday to _____ (*ascertain*) whether I got the raise.
45. John will send you a copy once he's inserted all the _____ (*alterations*) you've requested.

46. Grand Tree _____ (*fabricates*) office furniture that is both durable and attractive.

47. I understand from your letter that you expect a full refund; _____ (*nevertheless*), your warranty expired more than a year ago.

Message Composition: Selecting Words Rewrite the following sentences, replacing obsolete phrases with up-to-date versions. Write none if you think there is no appropriate substitute. [LO-4]

48. I have completed the form and returned it to my insurance company, as per your instructions.

49. Attached herewith is a copy of our new contract for your records.

50. Even though it will increase the price of the fence, we have decided to use the redwood in lieu of the cedar.

51. Saunders & Saunders has received your request for the Greenwood file, and in reply I wish to state that we will send you copies of Mr. Greenwood's documents only after Judge Taylor makes her ruling and orders us to do so.

52. Please be advised that your account with National Bank has been compromised, and we advise you to close it as soon as possible.

Message Composition: Creating Sentences Rewrite the following sentences so that they are active rather than passive. [LO-5]

53. The raw data are submitted to the data processing division by the sales representative each Friday.

54. High profits are publicized by management.

55. The policies announced in the directive were implemented by the staff.

56. Our computers are serviced by the Santee Company.

57. The employees were represented by Janet Hogan.

Message Organization: Transitions Add transitions to the following sentences to improve the flow of ideas. (Note: You may need to eliminate or add some words to smooth out the sentences.) [LO-6]

58. Steve Case saw infinite possibilities for the Internet. Steve Case was determined to turn his vision into reality. The techies scoffed at his strategy of building a simple Internet service for ordinary people. Case doggedly pursued his dream. He analyzed other online services. He assessed the needs of his customers. He responded to their desires for an easier way to access information over the Internet. In 1992, Steve Case named his company America Online (AOL). Critics predicted the company's demise. By the end of the century, AOL was a profitable powerhouse. AOL grew so big that it was able to merge with the giant traditional media company Time Warner. The merger was widely criticized. The merger did not live up to Case's expectations. He eventually left the company.

59. Facing some of the toughest competitors in the world, Harley-Davidson had to make some changes. The company introduced new products. Harley's management team set out to rebuild the company's production process. New products were coming to market and the company was turning a profit. Harley's quality standards were not on par with those of its foreign competitors. Harley's costs were still among the highest in the industry. Harley made a U-turn and restructured the company's organizational structure. Harley's efforts have paid off.

60. Whether you're indulging in a doughnut in New York or California, Krispy Kreme wants you to enjoy the same delicious taste with every bite. The company maintains consistent product quality by carefully controlling every step of the production process. Krispy Kreme tests all raw ingredients against established quality standards. Every delivery of wheat flour is sampled and measured for its moisture content and protein levels. Krispy Kreme blends the ingredients. Krispy Kreme tests the doughnut mix for quality. Krispy Kreme delivers the mix to its stores. Krispy Kreme knows that it takes more than a quality mix to produce perfect doughnuts all the time. The company supplies its stores with everything they need to produce premium doughnuts—mix, icings, fillings, equipment—you name it.

Activities

Active links for all websites in this chapter can be found on mybcommlab; see your User Guide for instructions on accessing the content for this chapter. Each activity is labeled according to the primary skill or skills you will need to use. To review relevant chapter content, you can refer to the indicated Learning Objective. In some instances, supporting information will be found in another chapter, as indicated.

1. Writing: Creating a Businesslike Tone; Media Skills: E-Mail [LO-3] Read the following e-mail message and then (1) analyze the strengths and weaknesses of each sentence and (2) revise the message so that it follows this chapter's guidelines. The message was written by the marketing manager of an online retailer of baby-related products in the hope of becoming a retail outlet for Inglesina strollers and high chairs. As a manufacturer of stylish, top-quality products, Inglesina (based in Italy) is extremely selective about the retail outlets through which it allows its products to be sold.[17]

Our e-tailing company, Best Baby Gear, specializes in only the very best products for parents of newborns, infants, and toddlers. We constantly scour the world looking for products that are good enough and well-built enough and classy enough—good enough that is to take their place alongside the hundreds of other carefully selected products that adorn the pages of our award-winning website, www.bestbabygear.com. We aim for the fences every time we select a product to join this portfolio; we don't want to waste our time with onesey-twosey products that might sell a half dozen units per annum—no, we want every product to be a top-drawer success, selling at least one hundred units per specific model per year in order to justify our expense and hassle factor in adding it to the abovementioned portfolio. After careful consideration, we thusly concluded that your Inglesina lines meet our needs and would therefore like to add it.

2. **Writing: Using Plain Language; Communication Ethics: Making Ethical Choices [LO-3], Chapter 1**   Your company has been a major employer in the local community for years, but shifts in the global marketplace have forced some changes in the company's long-term direction. In fact, the company plans to reduce local staffing by as much as 50 percent over the next 5 to 10 years, starting with a small layoff next month. The size and timing of future layoffs have not been decided, although there is little doubt that more layoffs will happen at some point. In the first draft of a letter aimed at community leaders, you write, "This first layoff is part of a continuing series of staff reductions anticipated over the next several years." However, your boss is concerned about the vagueness and negative tone of the language and asks you to rewrite that sentence to read "This staffing adjustment is part of the company's ongoing efforts to continually align its resources with global market conditions." Do you think this suggested wording is ethical, given the company's significant economic presence in the community? Explain your answer in an e-mail message to your instructor.

3. **Writing: Using Plain Language; Media Skills: Blogging [LO-3]**   Download the Security and Exchange Commission's (SEC's) *A Plain English Handbook*, from www.sec.gov/pdf/handbook.pdf. In one or two sentences, summarize what the SEC means by the phrase *plain English*. Now scan the SEC's introduction to mutual funds at www.sec.gov/investor/pubs/inwsmf.htm. Does this information follow the SEC's plain English guidelines? Cite several examples that support your assessment. Post your analysis on your class blog.

4. **Writing: Creating Effective Sentences; Media Skills: Social Networking [LO-4]**   If you are interested in business, chances are you've had an idea or two for starting a company. If you haven't yet, go ahead and dream up an idea now. Make it something you are passionate about, something you could really throw yourself into. Now write a four-sentence summary that could appear on the Info tab on a Facebook profile. Make sure the first sentence is a solid topic sentence, and make sure the next three sentences offer relevant evidence and examples. Feel free to make up any details you need. E-mail your summary to your instructor or post it on your class blog.

 Learn the basics of creating a company profile on Facebook. Visit http://real-timeupdates.com/bce5, click on "Student Assignments" and then click on "Facebook Screencast."

---

5. **Writing: Crafting Unified, Coherent Paragraphs; Media Skills: E-Mail [LO-5]**   Suppose that end-of-term frustrations have produced this e-mail message to Professor Anne Brewer from a student who believes he should have received a B in his accounting class. If this message were recast into three or four clear sentences, the teacher might be more receptive to the student's argument. Rewrite the message to show how you would improve it:

> I think that I was unfairly awarded a C in your accounting class this term, and I am asking you to change the grade to a B. It was a difficult term. I don't get any money from home, and I have to work mornings at the Pancake House (as a cook), so I had to rush to make your class, and those two times that I missed class were because they wouldn't let me off work because of special events at the Pancake House (unlike some other students who just take off when they choose). On the midterm examination, I originally got a 75 percent, but you said in class that there were two different ways to answer the third question and that you would change the grades of students who used the "optimal cost" method and had been counted off 6 points for doing this. I don't think that you took this into account, because I got 80 percent on the final, which is clearly a B. Anyway, whatever you decide, I just want to tell you that I really enjoyed this class, and I thank you for making accounting so interesting.

6. **Writing: Crafting Unified, Coherent Paragraphs; Collaboration: Evaluating the Work of Others [LO-6], Chapter 5**   For this exercise, work with four other students. Each of you should choose one of the following five topics and write one paragraph on it. Be sure one student writes a paragraph using the illustration technique, one using the comparison-or-contrast technique, one using a discussion of cause and effect, one using the classification technique, and one using a discussion of problem and solution. Then exchange paragraphs within the team and pick out the main idea and general purpose of the paragraph one of your teammates wrote. Was everyone able to correctly identify the main idea and purpose? If not, suggest how the paragraph might be rewritten for clarity.

   a. Types of cameras (or dogs or automobiles) available for sale

   b. Advantages and disadvantages of eating at fast-food restaurants

   c. Finding that first full-time job

   d. Good qualities of my car (or house, or apartment, or neighborhood)

   e. How to make a favorite dessert (or barbecue a steak or make coffee)

7. **Writing: Using Technology to Compose Messages [LO-7], Chapter 5**   Team up with another student and choose some form of document or presentation software that allows you to create templates or another form of "master design." (Microsoft Word, Microsoft PowerPoint, Google Docs, or their equivalents are good choices for this assignment.) Your task is to design a report template for a company that you know about first hand or whose general communication style you are able to analyze from its website and other materials. You can start your template from scratch or adapt an existing template, but if you adapt another template, make sure the final design is largely your own. Chapter 5 offers information on document design.

Expand Your Skills

Critique the Professionals

Locate an example of professional communication from a reputable online source. Choose a paragraph that has at least three sentences. Evaluate the effectiveness of this paragraph at three levels, starting with the paragraph structure. Is the paragraph unified and cohesive? Does it have a clear topic sentence and sufficient support to clarify and expand on that topic? Second, evaluate each sentence. Are the sentences easy to read and easy to understand? Did the writer vary the types and lengths of sentences used to produce a smooth flow and rhythm? Is the most important idea presented prominently in each sentence? Third, evaluate at least six word choices. Did the writer use these words correctly and effectively? Using whatever medium your instructor requests, write a brief analysis of the piece (no more than one page), citing specific elements from the piece and support from the chapter.

Sharpen Your Career Skills Online

Bovée and Thill's Business Communication Web Search, at http://businesscommunicationblog.com/websearch, is a unique research tool designed specifically for business communication research. Use the Web Search function to find a website, video, PDF document, podcast, or presentation that offers advice on adapting to your audience or composing business messages. Write a brief e-mail message to your instructor or a post for your class blog, describing the item that you found and summarizing the career skills information you learned from it.

mybcommlab

If your course uses mybcommlab, log on to www.mybcommlab.com to access the following study and assessment aids associated with this chapter:

- Video applications
- Pre/post test
- Real-Time Updates
- Personalized study plan
- Peer review activity
- Model documents
- Quick Learning Guides
- Sample presentations

If you are not using mybcommlab, you can access Real-Time Updates and Quick Learning Guides through http://real-timeupdates.com/bce5. The Quick Learning Guide (located under "Learn More" on the website) hits all the high points of this chapter in just two pages. This guide, especially prepared by the authors, will help you study for exams or review important concepts whenever you need a quick refresher.

Improve Your Grammar, Mechanics, and Usage

You can download the text of this assignment from http://real-timeupdates.com/bce5; click on "Student Assignments" and then click on "Chapter 4. Improve Your Grammar, Mechanics, and Usage."

Level 1: Self-Assessment—Adjectives

Review Section 1.4 in the Handbook of Grammar, Mechanics, and Usage and then complete the following 15 items.

In items 1–5, indicate the appropriate form of the adjective that appears in parentheses.

1. Of the two products, this one has the _____ (great) potential.
2. The _____ (perfect) solution is d.
3. Here is the _____ (interesting) of all the ideas I have heard so far.
4. Our service is _____ (good) than theirs.
5. The _____ (hard) part of my job is firing people.

In items 6–10, insert hyphens where required.

6. A highly placed source revealed Dotson's last ditch efforts to cover up the mistake.
7. Please send an extra large dust cover for my photocopier.
8. A top secret document was taken from the president's office last night.
9. A 30 year old person should know better.
10. If I write a large scale report, I want to know that it will be read by upper level management.

In items 11–15, insert required commas, where needed, between adjectives.

11. The two companies are engaged in an all-out no-holds-barred struggle for dominance.
12. A tiny metal shaving is responsible for the problem.
13. She came to the office with a bruised swollen knee.
14. A chipped cracked sheet of glass is useless to us.
15. You'll receive our usual cheerful prompt service.

Level 2: Workplace Applications

The following items may contain errors in grammar, capitalization, punctuation, abbreviation, number style, word division, and vocabulary. Rewrite each sentence, correcting all errors. If a sentence has no errors, write "Correct" for that number.

1. Its time that you learned the skills one needs to work with suppliers and vendors to get what you want and need.
2. Easy flexible wireless calling plans start for as little as $19 dollars a month.
3. There's several criteria used to select customer's to receive this offer.
4. PetFood Warehouse officially became PETsMART, Jim left the co. due to health reasons.
5. First quarter sales gains are evident in both the grocery store sector (up 1.03%) and the restaurant sector (up 3.17 per cent) according to Food Institute estimates.

6. Whatever your challenge, learning stronger "negotiating" tactics and strategies will improve the way people work and the results that comes from their efforts.

7. To meet the increasing demand for Penta bottled-drinking-water, production capacity is being expanded by Bio-Hydration Research Lab by 80 percent.

8. Seminars begin at 9 A.M. and wrap up at 4:00 P.M.

9. Temple, Texas-based McLane Co. a subsidiary of Walmart has bought a facility in Northfield, Minn that it will use to distribute products to customers such as convenience stores, stores that sell items at a discount, and mass merchants.

10. The British Retail Consortium are releasing the 3rd edition of its Technical Standards on Apr. 22, reported The New York Times.

11. The reason SkillPath is the fastest growing training company in the world is because of our commitment to providing clients with the highest-quality learning experiences possible.

12. According to professor Charles Noussair of the economics department of Purdue University, opinion surveys "Capture the respondent in the role of a voter, not in the role of a consumer".

13. The Study found that people, exposed to Purina banner ads, were almost 50 percent more likely to volunteer Purina as the first Dog Food brand that came to mind.

14. In a consent decree with the food and drug administration, E'Ola International a dietary supplement maker agreed not to sell any more products containing the drug, ephedrine.

15. Dennis Dickson is looking for a company both to make and distribute plaidberries under an exclusive license, plaidberries is blackberries that are mixed with extracts and they are used as a filling.

Level 3: Document Critique

The following document may contain errors in grammar, capitalization, punctuation, abbreviation, number style, word division, and vocabulary. You will also find errors related to topics in this chapter. Concentrate on using the "you" attitude, emphasizing the positive, being polite, and using bias-free language as you improve this message. As your instructor indicates, photocopy this page and correct all errors using standard proofreading marks (see Appendix C) or download the document and make the corrections in your word processing software.[18]

Welcome! Here is your new card for your health Savings Account (HSA)

Using your prepaid card makes HSAs: Fast + Easy + Automatic!!

Step 1: Activate and Sign Your Card(s)

- You **CANNOT** use your card until you perfom these following steps: to activate, go to the websight listed on the back of your Card(s). You can also just following the instructons written on the sticker which should be attached to the front of your card.
- Your member ID No. could be one of two things: your Social Security Number or the ID number assigned by your Health Plan
- Sign the back of your card and have the other person on the account, if any, sign the other card (you should've received two cards with this letter, by the way)

Step 2: Use Your Card as You Need

However, **DO NOT ATTEMPT** to use yoru card for anything expenses other than current year medical expenses—qualified only!—for you or your dependents if you have any

The things your Card can be used for include but are not limited to such as:

- Prescriptions, but only those covered by your health plan—obviously
- Dental
- Vision and eyewear
- OTC items if covered

Step 3: Save All Receipts!! So You can use them when you do Your Taxes

Completing Business Messages

LEARNING OBJECTIVES

After studying this chapter, you will be able to

1 Discuss the value of careful revision and describe the tasks involved in evaluating your first drafts and the work of other writers

2 List four techniques you can use to improve the readability of your messages

3 Describe the steps you can take to improve the clarity of your writing and give four tips on making your writing more concise

4 Identify four software tools that can help you revise messages and explain the risks of using them

5 List four principles of effective design and explain the role of major design elements in document readability

6 Explain the importance of proofreading and give six tips for successful proofreading

7 Discuss the most important issues to consider when distributing your messages

> " Revision can be daunting, but it doesn't have to be: it's simply reading your own work with a critical eye, and it's necessary if you want to write well. The art of writing is really the art of revision. "
>
> —Leo Babauta, *Author and blogger*

COMMUNICATION
Matters

Author and blogger Leo Babauta knows that it is in the revision stage that a message really comes alive.

As one of today's most widely read bloggers, Leo Babauta recognizes that the true power of writing often lies in rewriting—revising messages until they are as clear, concise, and effective as possible.[1] Careful revision often means the difference between a rambling, unfocused message and a lively, direct message that gets attention and spurs action. Taking the time to evaluate and improve your messages through revision can also save you from releasing the sort of poorly written messages that can hold back your career and harm your company's reputation.[2]

1 LEARNING OBJECTIVE

Discuss the value of careful revision, and describe the tasks involved in evaluating your first drafts and the work of other writers

● Access this chapter's simulation entitled The Communication Process, located at mybcommlab.com.

REVISING YOUR MESSAGE: EVALUATING THE FIRST DRAFT

This chapter covers the tasks in the third step of the three-step writing process: revising your message to achieve optimum quality and then producing, proofreading, and distributing it. After you complete your first draft, you may be tempted to breathe a sigh of relief, send the message on its way, and move on to the next project. Resist that temptation. Successful communicators recognize that the first draft is rarely as tight, clear, and compelling as it needs to be. Careful revision improves the effectiveness of your messages and sends a strong signal to your readers that you respect their time and care about their opinions.[3]

The scope of the revision task can vary somewhat, depending on the medium and the nature of your message. For informal messages to internal audiences, particularly when using short-message tools such as IM and e-mail, the revision process is often as simple as quickly looking over your message to correct any mistakes before sending or posting it. However, don't fall into the common trap of thinking that you don't need to worry about grammar, spelling, clarity, and other fundamentals of good writing when you use electronic media. These qualities can be *especially* important in electronic media, particularly if these messages are the only contact your audience has with you. First, poor-quality messages create an impression of poor-quality thinking, and even minor errors can cause confusion, frustration, and costly delays. Second, anything you write in electronic media will be stored forever and could be distributed far beyond your original audience. Don't join the business professionals who have seen ill-considered or poorly written electronic messages wind up in the news media or as evidence in lawsuits or criminal cases.

> ### QUALITY *Matters*
>
> Typing errors and other glitches might seem unimportant, but audiences often equate the quality of your writing with the quality of your thinking. Take care with proofreading to make sure your true value shines through in your writing.

If you have time, put your draft aside for a day or two before you begin the revision process.

Whenever possible—particularly with important messages—put your first draft aside for a day or two before you begin the revision process so that you can approach the material with a fresh eye. Then start with the "big picture," making sure that the document accomplishes your overall goals, before moving to finer points such as readability, clarity, and conciseness.

Evaluating Your Content, Organization, and Tone

When you begin the revision process, focus on content, organization, and tone. Today's time-pressed readers want messages that convey important content clearly and quickly.[4] To evaluate the content of your message, make sure it is accurate, relevant to audience's needs, and complete.

When you are satisfied with the basic content of your message, review its organization by asking yourself these questions:

- Are all your points covered in the most logical and convincing order?
- Do the most important ideas receive the most space and greatest emphasis?
- Are any points repeated unnecessarily?
- Are details grouped together logically, or are some still scattered through the document?

Next, consider whether you have achieved the right tone for your audience. Is your writing formal enough to meet the audience's expectations without being too formal or academic? Is it too casual for a serious subject?

The beginning and end of a message usually have the greatest impact on your readers.

Finally, spend a few extra moments on the beginning and end of your message; these sections usually have the greatest impact on the audience. Be sure that the opening of your document is relevant, interesting, and geared to the reader's probable reaction. The opening should also convey the subject and purpose of the message. For longer documents, the opening should help readers understand how the material is organized. Review the conclusion to be sure that it summarizes the main idea and leaves the audience with a positive impression.

Evaluating, Editing, and Revising the Work of Other Writers

At many points in your career, you will be asked to evaluate, edit, or revise the work of others. Whether you're suggesting improvements or actually making the improvements yourself (as you might on a wiki site, for example), you can make a contribution using all the skills you've learned in this chapter as well as in Chapters 3 and 4.

Before you dive into someone else's work, recognize the dual responsibility that doing so entails. First, unless you've specifically been asked to rewrite something in your own style, keep in mind that your job is to help the other writer succeed at his or her task, not to impose your writing style or pursue your own agenda. In other words, make sure your input focuses on making the piece more effective, not on making it more like something you would've written. Second, make sure you understand the writer's intent before you begin suggesting or making changes. If you try to edit or revise without knowing what the writer hoped to accomplish, you run the risk of making the piece less effective, not more. With those thoughts in mind, ask yourself the following questions as you evaluate someone else's writing:

> When you evaluate, edit, or revise someone else's work, your job is to help that person succeed—not to impose your own style or agenda.

- What is the purpose of this document or message?
- Who is the target audience?
- What information does the audience need?
- Does the document provide this information in a well-organized way?
- Does the writing demonstrate the "you" attitude toward the audience?
- Is the tone of the writing appropriate for the audience?
- Can the readability be improved?
- Is the writing clear? If not, how can it be improved?
- Is the writing as concise as it could be?
- Does the design support the intended message?

You can read more about using these skills in the context of wiki writing in Chapter 6.

REVISING TO IMPROVE READABILITY

After confirming the content, organization, and tone of your message, make a second pass to improve *readability*. Most professionals are inundated with more reading material than they can ever hope to consume, and they'll appreciate your efforts to make your documents easier to read—and easier to skim for the highlights when they don't have time to read in depth. You'll benefit from this effort, too: If you earn a reputation for creating well-crafted documents that respect the audience's time, people will pay more attention to your work.

> **2 LEARNING OBJECTIVE**
>
> List four techniques you can use to improve the readability of your messages

Four powerful techniques for improving readability are varying your sentence length, using shorter paragraphs, replacing narrative with lists, and adding effective headings and subheadings.

Varying Your Sentence Length

Varying sentence length is a good way to maintain reader interest and control the emphasis given to major and minor points. Look for ways to combine a mixture of sentences that are short (up to 15 words or so), medium (15–25 words), and long (more than 25 words). Each sentence length has advantages. Short sentences can be processed quickly and are easier for nonnative speakers and translators to interpret. Medium-length sentences are useful for showing the relationships among ideas. Long sentences are often the best way to convey complex ideas, to list a number of related points, or to summarize or preview information.

> To keep readers' interest, look for ways to combine a variety of short, medium, and long sentences.

Of course, each sentence length also has disadvantages. Too many short sentences in a row can make your writing choppy and disconnected. Medium sentences lack the punch of short sentences and the informative power of longer sentences. Long sentences are usually harder to understand than short sentences because they are packed with information; they are also harder to skim because readers can absorb only a few words per glance.

Keeping Your Paragraphs Short

Short paragraphs are easier to read than long ones.

Large blocks of text can be intimidating, even to the most dedicated reader. Short paragraphs (of 100 words or fewer; this paragraph has 62 words, for example) are easier to read than long ones, and they make your writing look inviting. They also help audiences read more carefully. You can also emphasize an idea by isolating it in a short, forceful paragraph.

However, don't go overboard with short paragraphs. In particular, be careful to use one-sentence paragraphs only occasionally and only for emphasis. Also, if you need to divide a subject into several pieces in order to keep paragraphs short, be sure to help your readers keep the ideas connected by guiding them with plenty of transitional elements.

Using Lists and Bullets to Clarify and Emphasize

Lists are effective tools for highlighting and simplifying material.

An effective alternative to using conventional sentences in some instances is to set off important ideas in a list. Lists can show the sequence of your ideas, heighten their impact visually, and increase the likelihood that readers will find your key points. In addition, lists simplify complex subjects, highlight the main point, enable skimming, and give readers a breather. Consider the difference between the following two approaches to the same information:

Narrative	List
Owning your own business has many advantages. One is the opportunity to build a major financial asset. Another advantage is the satisfaction of working for yourself. As a sole proprietor, you also have the advantage of privacy because you do not have to reveal your financial information or plans to anyone.	Owning your own business has three advantages: ■ The opportunity to build a major financial asset ■ The satisfaction of working for yourself ■ The freedom to keep most of your financial information private

When creating a list, you can separate items with numbers, letters, or bullets (a general term for any kind of graphical element that precedes each item). Bullets are generally preferred over numbers, unless the list is in some logical sequence or ranking, or specific list items will be referred to later on. Make your lists easy to read by making all the items parallel (see "Imposing Parallelism" on page 131) and keeping individual items as short as possible.[5] Also, be sure to introduce your lists clearly so that people know what they're about to read.

Adding Headings and Subheadings

Use headings to grab the reader's attention and organize material into short sections.

A **heading** is a brief title that tells readers about the content of the section that follows. **Subheadings** indicate subsections within a major section; complex documents may have several levels of subheadings. Headings and subheadings help in three important ways: They show readers at a glance how the material is organized, they call attention to important points, and they highlight connections and transitions between ideas.

Informative headings are generally more helpful than descriptive ones.

Descriptive headings, such as "Cost Considerations," identify a topic but do little more. **Informative headings**, such as "Redesigning Material Flow to Cut Production Costs," put your reader right into the context of your message. Well-written informative headings are self-contained, which means that readers can skim just the headings and subheadings and understand them without reading the rest of the document. Whatever types of headings you choose, keep them brief and grammatically parallel.

3 LEARNING OBJECTIVE

Describe the steps you can take to improve the clarity of your writing, and give four tips on making your writing more concise

EDITING FOR CLARITY AND CONCISENESS

After you've revised your message for readability, your next step is to make sure your message is as clear and as concise as possible.

Clarity is essential to getting your message across accurately and efficiently.

Editing for Clarity

Make sure every sentence conveys the message you intend and that readers can extract that meaning without needing to read it more than once.

Breaking Up Overly Long Sentences

If you find overly long sentences in your writing, you may be trying to make a sentence do more than it reasonably can, such as expressing two dissimilar thoughts or peppering the reader with too many pieces of supporting evidence at once. (Did you notice how difficult this long sentence was to read?)

Rewriting Hedging Sentences

Sometimes you have to *hedge* or *qualify* a statement when you aren't entirely sure of something, when you can't predict an outcome, or when you don't want to sound arrogant. However, hedging generally requires more words (and can weaken your writing if overdone), so avoid it if it isn't necessary:

> Hedging is appropriate when you can't be absolutely sure of a statement, but excessive hedging undermines your authority.

Instead of This	Write This
I believe that Mr. Johnson's employment record seems to show that he may be capable of handling the position.	Mr. Johnson's employment record shows that he is capable of handling the position.

Imposing Parallelism

Making your writing *parallel* means expressing two or more similar ideas using the same grammatical structure. Doing so helps your audience understand that the ideas are related, are of similar importance, and are on the same level of generality. Parallel patterns are also easier to read. Parallelism can be achieved by repeating a pattern in words, phrases, clauses, or entire sentences:

> When you use parallel grammatical patterns to express two or more ideas, you show that they are comparable thoughts.

Instead of This	Write This
To waste time and missing deadlines are bad habits.	Wasting time and missing deadlines are bad habits.
Interviews are a matter of acting confident and to stay relaxed.	Interviews are a matter of acting confident and staying relaxed.

Correcting Dangling Modifiers

Be careful not to leave modifying phrases "dangling," with no connection to the subject of the sentence. In the first example below, for instance, the version on the left seems to say that the *budget* was working as quickly as possible:

Instead of This	Write This
Working as quickly as possible, the budget was soon ready.	Working as quickly as possible, the committee soon had the budget ready.
After a three-week slump, we increased sales.	After a three-week slump, sales increased.

Rewording Long Noun Sequences

Stringing too many nouns together as modifiers can make a sentence difficult to read. You can often clarify such a sentence by putting some of the nouns in a modifying phrase:

Instead of This	Write This
The aluminum window sash installation company will give us an estimate on Friday.	The company that installs aluminum window sashes will give us an estimate on Friday.

Replacing Camouflaged Verbs

Watch for word endings such as *ion, tion, ing, ment, ant, ent, ence, ance,* and *ency.* Most of them "camouflage" a verb by changing it into a noun or an adjective—which requires you to add another verb in order to complete your sentence:

Instead of This	Write This
The manager undertook implementation of the rules.	The manager implemented the rules.
Verification of the shipments occurs weekly.	Shipments are verified weekly.

Clarifying Sentence Structure

Subject and predicate should be placed as close together as possible, as should modifiers and the words they modify.

Keep the subject and predicate of a sentence as close together as possible so that readers don't have to read the sentence twice to figure out who did what:

Instead of This	Write This
A 10 percent decline in market share caused by quality problems and an aggressive sales campaign by Armitage, the market leader in the Northeast, was the major problem in 2011.	The major problem in 2011 was a 10 percent loss of market share caused by quality problems and an aggressive sales campaign by Armitage, the market leader in the Northeast.

Similarly, adjectives, adverbs, and prepositional phrases usually make the most sense when placed as close as possible to the words they modify:

Instead of This	Write This
These ergonomic chairs are ideal for professionals who must spend many hours working at their computers with their adjustable sitting, kneeling, and standing positions.	With their adjustable sitting, kneeling, and standing positions, these ergonomic chairs are ideal for professionals who must spend many hours working at their computers.

Clarifying Awkward References

Be careful with directional phrases such as *the above-mentioned, as mentioned above, the aforementioned, the former, the latter,* and *respectively.* They often force readers to jump from point to point to figure out what you're saying. You're usually better off using specific references:

Instead of This	Write This
Corporate legal and North American field operations recruit the patent attorneys and the sales managers, respectively.	Corporate legal recruits the patent attorneys, and North American field operations recruits the sales managers.

Editing for Conciseness

In addition to clarity, readers appreciate conciseness—and more or less demand it in new media formats such as blogs. The following four editing steps will help you reduce the length of your documents and make them faster and easier to read.

Deleting Unnecessary Words, Phrases, and Sentences

Make your documents tighter by removing unnecessary words, phrases, and sentences.

Draft versions often contain unnecessary words, phrases, or even entire sentences. To test whether an element of text is essential, remove it and see whether your meaning is still clear. If the meaning doesn't change, leave the words out. For example, you may discover that you've said the same thing in two different ways while trying to make a point or explain a difficult concept. Also, some combinations of words have one-word equivalents that are more efficient:

Instead of This	Write This
for the sum of	for
in the event that	if
on the occasion of	on
prior to the start of	before
in the near future	soon
at this point in time	now
due to the fact that	because
in view of the fact that	because
until such time as	when
with reference to	about

In addition, avoid the clutter of unnecessary or poorly placed relative pronouns (*who, that, which*):

Instead of This	Write This
Cars that are sold after January will not have a six-month warranty.	Cars sold after January will not have a six-month warranty.
Employees who are driving to work should park in the spaces that are marked "Staff."	Employees driving to work should park in the spaces marked "Staff."

However, well-placed relative pronouns and articles prevent confusion. Notice how the meaning changes depending on where *that* is placed in these sentences:

Instead of This	Write This
The project manager told the engineers last week the specifications were changed.	The project manager told the engineers last week *that* the specifications were changed.
	The project manager told the engineers *that* last week the specifications were changed.

Shortening Long Words and Phrases

Short words are often more vivid and easier to read than long ones. The idea is to use short, simple words, not simple concepts:[6]

Instead of This	Write This
During the preceding year, the company accelerated our acquisition of social media startups, an action predicated on the assumption that the industry was poised for consolidation.	Last year, the company sped up acquisition of social media startups, based on the belief that the industry was about to consolidate.

Also, by using infinitives in place of some phrases, you can shorten your sentences and make them clearer:

Instead of This	Write This
If you want success as a writer, you must work hard.	To be a successful writer, you must work hard.
He went to the library for the purpose of studying.	He went to the library to study.
The employer increased salaries so that she could improve morale.	The employer increased salaries to improve morale.

Eliminating Redundancies

In some word combinations, the words tend to say the same thing. For instance, "visible to the eye" is redundant because *visible* is enough. Eliminate the redundant word(s):

Instead of This	Write This
absolutely complete	complete
basic fundamentals	fundamentals
follows after	follows
reduce down	reduce
refer back	refer
repeat again	repeat
collect together	collect
future plans	plans
return back	return
end result	result
actual truth	truth
final outcome	outcome
surrounded on all sides	surrounded

In addition, avoid using double modifiers that have the same meaning:

Instead of This	Write This
modern, up-to-date equipment	modern equipment

Recasting "It Is/There Are" Starters

Whenever a sentence starts with some form of *It is* or *There are*, see whether you can rewrite it to remove this phrase and thereby shorten the sentence:

Instead of This	Write This
It would be appreciated if you would sign the lease today.	Please sign the lease today.
There are five employees in this division who were late to work today.	Five employees in this division were late to work today.

Eliminating *It is* and *There are* doesn't always improve or shorten a sentence, however, so use your best judgment in each instance.

As you make all these improvements, concentrate on how each word contributes to an effective sentence and on how that sentence helps to develop a coherent paragraph. Look for opportunities to make the material more interesting through the use of strong, lively words and phrases (as discussed in Chapter 4). Sometimes you'll find that the most difficult problem in a sentence can be solved by simply removing the problem itself. When you come upon a troublesome element, ask yourself, "Do I need it at all?" Possibly not. In fact, you may find that it was giving you so much grief precisely because it was trying to do an unnecessary job.[7]

Figure 5.1 provides an example of revising for clarity and conciseness. Notice how the changes remove unnecessary words, clarify the message, and demonstrate the "you" attitude. Figure 5.2 on page 136 shows the revised document.

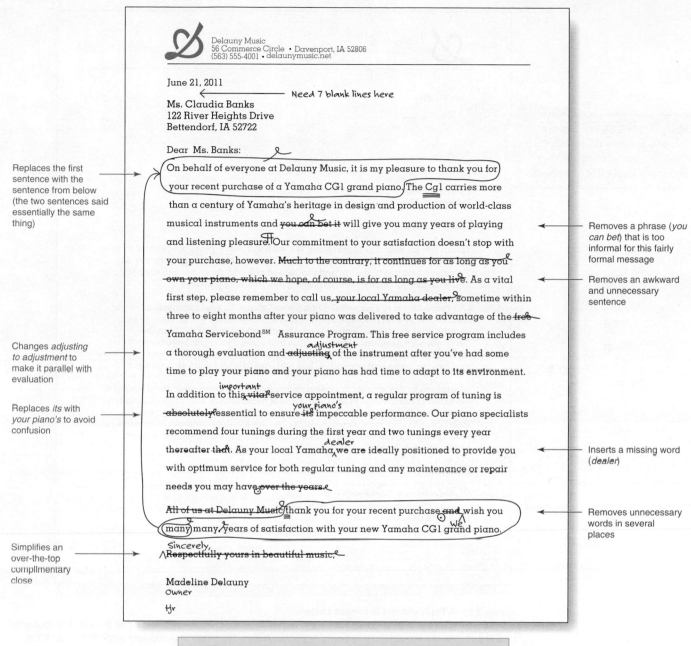

Figure 5.1   Improving a Customer Letter Through Careful Revision
Careful revision makes this draft shorter, clearer, and more focused. The proofreading symbols you see here are still widely used whenever printed documents are edited and revised; you can find a complete list of symbols in Appendix C. Note that many business documents are now "marked up" using such technological tools as *revision marks* in Microsoft Word and *comments* in Adobe Acrobat. No matter what the medium, however, careful revision is key to more effective messages.

Apply Figure 5.2's key concepts by revising a new document. Go to Chapter 5 in mybcommlab.com and select Document Makeovers.

Delauny Music
56 Commerce Circle • Davenport, IA 52806
(563) 555-4001 • delaunymusic.net

June 21, 2011

Ms. Claudia Banks
122 River Heights Drive
Bettendorf, IA 52722

Dear Ms. Banks:

Thank you for your recent purchase. We wish you many years of satisfaction with your new Yamaha CG1 grand piano. The CG1 carries more than a century of Yamaha's heritage in design and production of world-class musical instruments and will give you many years of playing and listening pleasure.

Our commitment to your satisfaction doesn't stop with your purchase, however. As a vital first step, please remember to call us sometime within three to eight months after your piano was delivered to take advantage of the Yamaha Servicebond℠ Assurance Program. This free service program includes a thorough evaluation and adjustment of the instrument after you've had some time to play your piano and your piano has had time to adapt to its environment.

In addition to this important service appointment, a regular program of tuning is essential to ensure your piano's impeccable performance. Our piano specialists recommend four tunings during the first year and two tunings every year thereafter. As your local Yamaha dealer, we are ideally positioned to provide you with optimum service for both regular tuning and any maintenance or repair needs you may have.

Sincerely,

Madeline Delauny

Madeline Delauny
Owner

tjr

Figure 5.2   A Professional Business Letter
Here is the revised and finished version of the edited letter from Figure 5.1. Note that the *block format* used here is just one of several layout options; Appendix A also describes the *modified block format* and the *simplified format*.

4 LEARNING OBJECTIVE

Identify four software tools that can help you revise messages, and explain the risks of using them

Spell checkers, thesauruses, grammar checkers, and style checkers can all help with the revision process, but they can't take the place of good writing and editing skills.

USING TECHNOLOGY TO REVISE YOUR MESSAGE

When it's time to revise and polish your message, be sure to use the revision features in your software to full advantage. For instance, *revision tracking* (look for a feature called "track changes" or something similar) and *commenting* show proposed editing changes and provide a history of a document's revisions. In Microsoft Word, for example, revisions appear in a different color, giving you a chance to review changes before accepting or rejecting them. Adobe Acrobat lets you attach comments to PDF files. Using revision marks and commenting features is also a great way to keep track of editing changes made by team members. Both Word and Acrobat let you use different colors for each reviewer, so you can keep everyone's comments separate.

Four other software tools and functions can help you find the best words and use them correctly. First, a spell checker compares your document with an electronic dictionary, highlights unrecognized words, and suggests correct spellings. Spell checkers are wonderful for finding typos, but they are no substitute for careful reviewing. For example, if you use *their* when you mean to use *there*, your spell checker won't notice because *their* is spelled correctly.

Second, a computer-based thesaurus (either within your software or on a website such as http://thesaurus.com) offers alternatives to a particular word. The best uses of a thesaurus are to find fresh, interesting words when you've been using the same word too many times and to find words that most accurately convey your intended meaning. Don't use a thesaurus simply to find impressive-sounding words, however, and don't assume that all the alternatives suggested are correct for each situation.

Third, a grammar checker tries to do for your grammar what a spell checker does for your spelling. Because the program doesn't have a clue about what you're trying to say, it can't tell whether you've said it clearly or completely. However, grammar checkers can highlight items you should consider changing, such as passive voice, long sentences, and words that tend to be misused.

Fourth, a style checker can monitor your word and sentence choices and suggest alternatives that might produce more effective writing. Style-checking options can range from basic issues, such as the spelling out of numbers and use of contractions, to more subjective matters, such as sentence structure and the use of technical terminology.

By all means, use any software tools that you find helpful when revising your documents. Just remember that it's unwise to rely on them to do all your revision work, and you're responsible for the final product.

PRODUCING YOUR MESSAGE

5 LEARNING OBJECTIVE

List four principles of effective design, and explain the role of major design elements in document readability

Now it's time to put your hard work on display. The *production quality* of your message—the total effect of page design, graphical elements, typography, screen presence, and so on—plays an important role in its effectiveness. A polished, inviting design not only makes your document easier to read but also conveys a sense of professionalism and importance.[8]

Designing for Readability

Design affects readability in two important ways. First, if used carefully, design elements can improve the effectiveness of your message. If used poorly, design elements can act as barriers, blocking your communication. Second, the visual design sends a nonverbal message to your readers, influencing their perceptions of the communication before they read a single word (see Figure 5.3).

The quality of your document design, both on paper and on screen, affects readability and audience perceptions.

Apply Figure 5.3's key concepts by revising a new document. Go to Chapter 5 in mybcommlab.com and select Document Makeovers.

Figure 5.3   Designing for Readability
This blog uses a clean, restrained design that is more than adequate for its purpose, which is sharing ideas on project management strategies and techniques.

For effective design, pay attention to
- Consistency
- Balance
- Restraint
- Detail

To achieve an effective design, pay careful attention to the following design elements:

- **Consistency.** Throughout each message, be consistent in your use of margins, typeface, type size, spacing, color, lines, and position. In most cases, you'll want to be consistent from message to message as well; that way, audiences who receive multiple messages from you recognize your documents and know what to expect.

- **Balance.** Balance is an important but sometimes subjective design issue. One document may have a formal, rigid design in which the various elements are placed in a grid pattern, whereas another may have a less formal design in which elements flow more freely across the page—and both could be in balance. Like the tone of your language, visual balance can be too formal, just right, or too informal for a given message.

- **Restraint.** Strive for simplicity. Don't clutter your message with too many design elements, too many colors, or too many decorative touches.

- **Detail.** Pay attention to details that affect your design and thus your message. For instance, extremely wide columns of text can be difficult to read; in many cases a better solution is to split the text into two narrower columns.

Even without special training in graphic design, you can make your printed and electronic messages more effective by understanding the use of white space, margins and line justification, typefaces, and type styles.

White Space

White space separates elements in a document and helps guide the reader's eye.

Any space free of text or artwork is considered **white space**. (Note that "white space" isn't necessarily white.) These unused areas provide visual contrast and important resting points for your readers. White space includes the open area surrounding headings, margins, paragraph indents, space around images, vertical space between columns, and horizontal space between paragraphs or lines of text. To increase the chance that readers will read your messages, be generous with white space; it makes pages and screens feel less intimidating and easier to read.[9]

Margins and Justification

Most business documents use a flush left margin and a ragged right margin.

Margins define the space around text and between text columns. In addition to their width, the look and feel of margins are influenced by the way you arrange lines of text, which can be set (1) *justified* (which means they are *flush*, or aligned vertically, on both the left and the right), (2) flush left with a *ragged-right* margin, (3) flush right with a *ragged-left* margin, or (4) centered. This paragraph is justified, whereas the paragraphs in Figure 5.2 on page 136 are flush left with a ragged-right margin.

Magazines, newspapers, and books often use justified type because it can accommodate more text in a given space. However, justified type needs to be used with care. First, it creates a denser look because the uniform line lengths decrease the amount of white space along the right margin. Second, it produces a more formal look that isn't appropriate for all situations. Third, unless it is formatted with skill and attention, justified type can be more difficult to read because it can produce large gaps between words and excessive hyphenation at the ends of lines. Publishing specialists have the time and skill needed to carefully adjust character and word spacing to eliminate these problems. (In some cases, sentences are even rewritten in order to improve the appearance of the printed page.) Because most business communicators don't have that time or skill, it's best to avoid justified type in most business documents.

In contrast to justified type, flush-left, ragged-right type creates a more open appearance on the page, producing a less formal and more contemporary look. Spacing between words is consistent, and only long words that fall at the ends of lines are hyphenated.

Centered type is rarely used for text paragraphs but is commonly used for headings and subheadings. Flush-right, ragged-left type is rarely used in business documents.

Typefaces

Typeface refers to the physical design of letters, numbers, and other text characters. (*Font* and *typeface* are often used interchangeably, although strictly speaking, a font is a set of characters in a given typeface.) Typeface influences the tone of your message, making it look authoritative or friendly, businesslike or casual, classic or modern, and so on (see Table 5.1). Be sure to

TABLE 5.1	Typeface Personalities: Serious to Casual to Playful	
Serif Typefaces (Best for Text)	Sans Serif Typefaces (Best for Headlines; Some Work Well for Text)	Specialty Typefaces (For Decorative Purposes Only)
Bookman Old Style	Arial	ANNA
Century Schoolbook	**Eras Bold**	Bauhaus
Courier	Franklin Gothic Book	*Edwardian*
Garamond	Frutiger	*Lucida Handwriting*
Rockwell	Gill Sans	Euclid Fraktur
Times Roman	Verdana	**STENCIL**

choose fonts that are appropriate for your message; many of the fonts on your computer are not appropriate for business use.

Serif typefaces have small crosslines (called serifs) at the ends of each letter stroke. Serif faces such as Times Roman are commonly used for body text. They can look busy and cluttered when set in large sizes for headings or other display treatments. **Sans serif typefaces**, in contrast, lack these serifs. The visual simplicity of sans serif typefaces such as Helvetica and Arial makes them ideal for the larger sizes used in headlines. Sans serif faces can be difficult to read in long blocks of text, however, unless they are formatted with generous amounts of *leading* (pronounced *ledding*), or spacing between lines.

For most documents, you shouldn't need more than two typefaces, although if you want to make captions or other text elements stand out, you can use another font.[10] If in doubt, you can't go too wrong with a sans serif typeface (such as Arial) for heads and subheads and a serif typeface (such as Times New Roman) for text and captions. Using more typefaces can clutter a document and produce an amateurish look.

Type Styles

Type style refers to any modification that lends contrast or emphasis to type, including boldface, italic, underlining, and color. For example, you can boldface individual words or phrases to draw more attention to them. Italic type has specific uses as well, such as highlighting quotations and indicating foreign words, irony, humor, book and movie titles, and unconventional usage. Use any type style in moderation. For instance, underlining or using all-uppercase letters can interfere with the reader's ability to recognize the shapes of words, improperly placed boldface or italicized type can slow down your reader, and shadowed or outlined type can seriously hinder legibility.

Avoid using any type style that inhibits your audience's ability to read your messages.

For most printed business messages, use a type size of 10 to 12 points for regular text and 12 to 18 points for headings and subheadings. (A point is approximately 1/72 inch.) Resist the temptation to reduce the type size to squeeze in text or to enlarge it to fill up space. Type that is too small is hard to read, whereas extra-large type often looks unprofessional.

Designing Multimedia Documents

A **multimedia document** contains a combination of text, graphics, photographs, audio, animation, video, and interactivity (such as hyperlinks that access webpages or software programs). Most electronic media now support multiple media formats, so you have a variety of options for creating multimedia documents. For example, you can add photos to a word processor file, audio commentary to a PDF, video clips to a blog posting, and animation to webpages.

As rich media, multimedia documents can convey large amounts of information quickly, engage people in multiple ways, express emotions, and allow recipients to personalize the communication process to meet their own needs. However, these documents are

Multimedia elements can convey large amounts of information quickly, engage audiences, express emotions, and support personalization.

more difficult to create than documents that contain only text and static images. To design and create multimedia documents, you need to consider the following factors:

Multimedia documents can be powerful communication vehicles, but they require more time, tools, and skills to create.

- **Creative and technical skills.** Depending on what you need to accomplish, creating and integrating multimedia elements can require some creative and technical skills. Fortunately, many basic tasks, such as adding photographs or video clips to a webpage, have gotten much easier in recent years.

- **Tools.** The hardware and software tools needed to create and integrate media elements are now widely available and generally affordable. For example, with simpler and less expensive consumer versions of professional photo and video editing software, you can often perform all the tasks you need for routine business multimedia (see Figure 5.4).

- **Time and cost.** Creating multimedia documents is easier than ever, but you still need to consider time and cost—and exercise good judgment when deciding whether to include multimedia and how much to include. Make sure the time and money you plan to spend will be paid back in communication effectiveness.

- **Content.** To include various media elements in a document, you obviously need to create or acquire them. Millions of graphics, photos, video clips, and other elements are available online, but you need to make sure you can legally use each item. One good option is to search Creative Commons (**www.creativecommons.org**) for multimedia elements available for use at no charge but with various restrictions (such as giving the creator credit).

- **Message structure.** Multimedia documents often lack a rigid linear structure from beginning to end, which means you need to plan for readers to take multiple, individualized paths through the material. In other words, a conventional outline is often inadequate. Chapter 11 discusses the challenge of *information architecture*, the structure and navigational flow of websites and other multimedia documents.

- **Compatibility.** Some multimedia elements require specific software to be installed on the recipient's viewing device. Another challenge is the variety of screen sizes and resolutions, from large, high-resolution computer monitors to tiny, low-resolution phone displays. Make sure you understand the demands your message will place on the audience.

Figure 5.4   Multimedia Tools
Software such as Adobe Photoshop Elements makes it easy for anyone with basic computer skills to create and modify content for multimedia documents. A simple *cropping* operation on a photo is shown here.

Using Technology to Produce Your Message

Production tools vary widely, depending on the software and systems you're using. Some systems offer limited formatting and production capabilities, whereas some word processing software now offers some capabilities that rival those of professional publishing software for many day-to-day business needs. *Desktop publishing* software, such as Adobe InDesign, goes beyond word processing, offering more advanced and precise layout capabilities that meet the technical demands of publication-quality printing. (These programs are used mainly by design professionals.)

For online content, web publishing systems make it easy to produce great-looking webpages quickly. Similarly, blogging systems now simplify the production of blog content, letting you rapidly post new material without worrying too much about design or production. Multimedia production tools such as Microsoft Producer let you combine slides, audio commentary, video clips, and other features into computer-based presentations that once cost thousands of dollars to create.

No matter what system you're using, become familiar with the basic formatting capabilities. A few hours of exploration on your own or an introductory training course can help you dramatically improve the production quality of your documents. Depending on the types of messages you're creating, you'll benefit from being proficient with the following features:

> Learn to use your communication tools effectively so that you can work productively.

- **Templates, themes, and style sheets.** As Chapter 4 notes, you can save a tremendous amount of time by using templates, themes, and style sheets.

- **Page setup.** Use page setup to control margins, orientation (*portrait* is vertical; *landscape* is horizontal), and the location of *headers* (text and graphics that repeat at the top of every page) and *footers* (similar to headers but at the bottom of the page).

- **Column formatting.** Most business documents use a single column of text, but multiple columns can be an attractive format for documents such as newsletters. Columns are also handy for formatting long lists.

- **Paragraph formatting.** Take advantage of paragraph formatting controls to enhance the look of your documents. For instance, you can offset quotations by increasing margin width around a single paragraph, subtly compress line spacing to fit a document on a single page, or use hanging indents to offset the first line of a paragraph.

> Paragraph formatting gives you greater control over the look of your documents.

- **Numbered and bulleted lists.** Let your software do the busywork of formatting numbered and bulleted lists. It can also automatically renumber lists when you add or remove items, saving you the embarrassment of misnumbering.

- **Tables.** Tables are great for displaying any information that lends itself to rows and columns, including calendars, numeric data, comparisons, and multicolumn bulleted lists. Use paragraph and font formatting thoughtfully within tables for the best look.

- **Images, text boxes, and objects.** Word processing and desktop publishing software let you insert a wide variety of images (using industry-standard formats such as JPEG and GIF). *Text boxes* are small blocks of text that stand apart from the main text and can be placed anywhere on the page; they are great for captions, callouts, margin notes, and so on. *Objects* can be anything from a spreadsheet to a sound clip to an engineering drawing. Similarly, blogging systems, wikis, and other web development tools let you insert a variety of pictures, audio and video clips, and other multimedia elements.

By improving the appearance of your documents with these tools, you'll improve your readers' impressions of you and your messages, too.

PROOFREADING YOUR MESSAGE

> **6 LEARNING OBJECTIVE**
> Explain the importance of proofreading, and give six tips for successful proofreading

Proofreading is the quality inspection stage for your documents, your last chance to make sure that your document is ready to carry your message—and your reputation—to the intended audience. Even a small mistake can doom your efforts, so take proofreading seriously.

Look for two types of problems: (1) undetected mistakes from the writing, design, and layout stages and (2) mistakes that crept in during production. For the first category, you can review format and layout guidelines in Appendix A (including standard formats for letters and memos) and brush up on writing basics with the Handbook of Grammar, Mechanics,

> Your credibility is affected by your attention to the details of mechanics and form.

REAL-TIME UPDATES
Learn More by Watching This Presentation

Practical advice for thorough proofreading

Identify and correct common problems in business writing with this handy guide. Go to **http://real-timeupdates .com/bce5** and click on "Learn More." If you are using mybcommlab, you can access Real-Time Updates within each chapter or under Student Study Tools.

and Usage that follows the appendixes. The second category can include anything from computer glitches such as incorrect typefaces or misaligned page elements to problems with the ink used in printing. Be particularly vigilant with complex documents and complex production processes that involve teams of people and multiple computers. Strange things can happen as files move from computer to computer, especially when lots of multimedia elements are involved.

Far from being a casual scan up and down the page or screen, proofreading should be a methodical procedure in which you look for specific problems. Here is some advice from the pros:

The types of details to look for when proofreading include language errors, missing material, design errors, and typographical errors.

- **Make multiple passes.** Go through the document several times, focusing on a different aspect each time. For instance, look for content errors the first time and layout errors the second time.

- **Use perceptual tricks.** To keep from missing errors that are "in plain sight," try reading pages backward, placing your finger under each word and reading it silently, covering everything but the line you're currently reading, or reading the document aloud.

- **Focus on high-priority items.** Double-check names, titles, dates, addresses, and any number that could cause grief if incorrect.

- **Get some distance.** If possible, don't proofread immediately after finishing the document; let your brain wander off to new topics and come back fresh later on.

- **Stay focused and vigilant.** Block out distractions and focus as completely as possible on your proofreading. Avoid reading large amounts of material in one sitting and try not to proofread when you're tired.

- **Take your time.** Quick proofreading is not careful proofreading.

Table 5.2 offers some handy tips to improve your proofreading efforts.

TABLE 5.2 Proofreading Tips

Look for writing and typing errors

- ☑ Typographical mistakes
- ☑ Misspelled words
- ☑ Grammatical errors
- ☑ Punctuation mistakes

Look for design and layout errors

- ☑ Violation of company standards
- ☑ Page or screen layout errors (such as incorrect margins and column formatting)
- ☑ Clumsy page breaks or line breaks
- ☑ Inconsistent font usage (such as with headings and subheadings)
- ☑ Alignment problems (columns, headers, footers, and graphics)
- ☑ Missing or incorrect page and section numbers
- ☑ Missing or incorrect page headers or footers
- ☑ Missing or incorrect URLs, e-mail addresses, or other contact information
- ☑ Missing or incorrect photos and other graphical elements
- ☑ Missing or incorrect source notes, copyright notices, or other reference items

Look for production errors

- ☑ Printing problems
- ☑ Browser compatibility problems
- ☑ Incorrect or missing tags on blog posts

DISTRIBUTING YOUR MESSAGE

With the production finished, you're ready to distribute your message. You often have several options for distribution; consider the following factors when making your choice:

- **Cost.** Cost isn't a concern for most messages, but for multiple copies of lengthy reports or multimedia productions, it might well be. Weigh the cost and the benefits before you decide. Be sure to consider the nonverbal message you send regarding cost as well. Overnight delivery of a printed report could look responsive in one instance and wasteful in another, for example.

- **Convenience.** Make sure your audience can conveniently access the material you send. For instance, sending huge files may be fine on a fast office network, but receiving such files can be a major headache for remote colleagues trying to download them over slower wireless networks.

- **Time.** How soon does the message need to reach the audience? Don't waste money on overnight delivery if the recipient won't read a report for a week.

- **Security and privacy.** The convenience offered by electronic communication needs to be weighed against security and privacy concerns. For the most sensitive messages, your company will probably restrict both the people who can receive the messages and the means you can use to distribute them. In addition, most computer users are wary of opening attachments these days. Instead of sending word processor files (which are vulnerable to macro viruses and other risks), you can convert your documents to PDF files using Adobe Acrobat or an equivalent product.

For news on the latest advances in message distribution technologies, visit http://real-timeupdates.com/bce5 and click on Chapter 5.

7 LEARNING OBJECTIVE

Discuss the most important issues to consider when distributing your messages

Consider cost, convenience, time, security, and privacy when choosing a distribution method.

PEARSON
mybcommlab™

Are you an active learner? Go to mybcommlab.com to master Chapter 5's content. Chapter 5's interactive activities include:

- Customizable Study Plan and Chapter 5 practice quizzes
- Chapter 5 Simulation (The Communication Process), which helps you think critically and prepare to make choices in the business world
- Chapter 5 Video Exercise (Completing Business Messages: Petaluma), which shows you how textbook concepts are put into practice every day

- Flash Cards for mastering the definition of chapter terms
- Interactive Lessons that visually review key chapter concepts
- Document Makeovers for hands-on, scored practice in revising documents

---

CHAPTER REVIEW AND ACTIVITIES

Learning Objectives: Check Your Progress

1 OBJECTIVE Discuss the value of careful revision, and describe the tasks involved in evaluating your first drafts and the work of other writers.

Revision is an essential aspect of completing messages because it can nearly always make your first drafts tighter, clearer, and more compelling. Revision consists of three main tasks: (1) evaluating content, organization, and tone; (2) reviewing for readability; and (3) editing for clarity and conciseness. After you revise your message, complete it by using design elements effectively, proofreading to ensure quality, and distributing it to your audience.

When asked to evaluate, edit, or revise someone else's work, recognize the dual responsibility that doing so entails: remember that your job is to help the other writer succeed at his or her task, and make sure you understand the writer's intent.

2 OBJECTIVE List four techniques you can use to improve the readability of your messages.

Four techniques that improve readability are varying sentence length, keeping paragraphs short, using lists and bullets, and adding headings and subheadings. Varying sentence length helps make your writing more dynamic while emphasizing the most important points. Paragraphs are usually best kept short to make it easier for readers to consume information in manageable chunks. Lists and bullets are effective devices for delineating sets of items, steps, or other collections of related information. Headings and subheadings organize your message, call attention to important information, and help readers make connections between related pieces of information.

3 OBJECTIVE Describe the steps you can take to improve the clarity of your writing, and give four tips on making your writing more concise.

As you work to clarify your messages, (1) break up overly long sentences, (2) rewrite hedging sentences, (3) impose parallelism, (4) correct dangling modifiers, (5) reword long noun sequences, (6) replace camouflaged verbs, (7) clarify sentence structure, and (8) clarify awkward references. To make messages more concise, include only necessary material and write uncluttered sentences by (1) deleting unnecessary words and phrases, (2) shortening overly long words and phrases, (3) eliminating redundancies, and (4) recasting sentences that begin with "It is" and "There are."

4 OBJECTIVE Identify four software tools that can help you revise messages, and explain the risks of using them.

Software tools that can help with revision include a spell checker, a thesaurus, a grammar checker, and style checker. Although these tools can be quite helpful, writers need to remember that the tools aren't foolproof, and writers shouldn't count on them without verifying their suggestions.

5 OBJECTIVE List four principles of effective design, and explain the role of major design elements in document readability.

Four key principles of effective design are consistency, balance, restraint, and detail. Major design elements for documents include white space, margins and justification, typefaces, and type styles. White space provides contrast and balance. Margins define the space around the text and contribute to the amount of white space. Typefaces influence the tone of the message. Type styles—boldface, italics, and underlining—provide contrast or emphasis. When selecting and applying design elements, be consistent throughout your document; balance text, art, and white space; show restraint in the number of elements you use; and pay attention to every detail.

6 OBJECTIVE Explain the importance of proofreading, and give six tips for successful proofreading.

When proofreading the final version of your document, always keep an eye out for errors in grammar, usage, and punctuation. In addition, watch for spelling errors and typos. Make sure that nothing is missing and no extraneous elements are included.

7 OBJECTIVE Discuss the most important issues to consider when distributing your messages.

Consider cost, convenience, time, security, and privacy when choosing the method to distribute your messages. Always consider security and privacy issues before distributing messages that contain sensitive or confidential information.

▋ Test Your Knowledge

To review chapter content related to each question, refer to the indicated Learning Objective.

1. What are your responsibilities when you review and edit the work of others? [LO-1]
2. What are the four main tasks involved in completing a business message? [LO-1]
3. What is parallel construction, and why is it important? [LO-2]
4. Why is proofreading an important part of the writing process? [LO-6]
5. What factors should you consider when choosing a method for distributing a message (other than for systems where you don't have a choice)? [LO-7]

▋ Apply Your Knowledge

To review chapter content related to each question, refer to the indicated Learning Objective.

1. Why is it essential to understand the writer's intent before suggesting or making changes to another person's document? [LO-1]
2. Why should you let a first draft "age" for a while before you begin the revision process? [LO-1]
3. What are the ethical implications of murky, complex writing in a document whose goal is to explain how customers can appeal the result of a decision made in the company's favor during a dispute? [LO-3]
4. What nonverbal signals can you send by your choice of distribution methods? [LO-7]
5. Why is it risky to rely on spell checkers and other software tools for writing and revising? [LO-4]

▋ Practice Your Skills

Exercises for Perfecting Your Writing

To review chapter content related to each set of exercises, refer to the indicated Learning Objective.

Revising Messages: Conciseness Cross out unnecessary words in the following sentences. [LO-3]

1. The board cannot act without a consensus of opinion.
2. To surpass our competitors, we need new innovations both in products and in company operations.
3. George McClannahan has wanted to be head of engineering a long period of time, and now he has finally gotten the promotion.
4. Don't pay more than you have to; you can get our new fragrance for a price of just $50.

Revising Messages: Clarity Break the following sentences into shorter ones by adding more periods and revising as necessary. [LO-3]

5. The next time you write something, check your average sentence length in a 100-word passage, and if your sentences average more than 16 to 20 words, see whether you can break up some of the sentences.
6. Unfortunately, no gadget will produce excellent writing, but using spell checkers and grammar checkers can help by catching common spelling errors and raising grammatical points that writers might want to reconsider, such as suspect sentence structure and problems with noun–verb agreement.
7. Don't do what the village blacksmith did when he instructed his apprentice as follows: "When I take the shoe out of the fire, I'll lay it on the anvil, and when I nod my head, you hit it with the hammer." The apprentice did just as he was told, and now he's the village blacksmith.
8. Know the flexibility of the written word and its power to convey an idea, and know how to make your words behave so that your readers will understand.

Revising Messages: Conciseness Revise the following sentences, using shorter, simpler words. [LO-3]

9. The antiquated calculator is ineffectual for solving sophisticated problems.
10. It is imperative that the pay increments be terminated before an inordinate deficit is accumulated.
11. There was unanimity among the executives that Ms. Jackson's idiosyncrasies were cause for a mandatory meeting with the company's personnel director.
12. The impending liquidation of the company's assets was cause for jubilation among the company's competitors.

Revising Messages: Conciseness Use infinitives as substitutes for the overly long phrases in the following sentences. [LO-3]

13. For living, I require money.
14. They did not find sufficient evidence for believing in the future.
15. Bringing about the destruction of a dream is tragic.

Revising Messages: Conciseness Condense the following sentences to as few words as possible; revise as needed to maintain clarity and sense. [LO-3]

16. We are of the conviction that writing is important.
17. In all probability, we're likely to have a price increase.

18. Our goals include making a determination about that in the near future.
19. When all is said and done at the conclusion of this experiment, I'd like to summarize the final windup.

Revising Messages: Modifiers Remove all the unnecessary modifiers from the following sentences. [LO-3]

20. Tremendously high pay increases were given to the extraordinarily skilled and extremely conscientious employees.
21. The union's proposals were highly inflationary, extremely demanding, and exceptionally bold.

Revising Messages: Hedging Rewrite the following sentences so that they no longer contain any hedging. [LO-3]

22. It would appear that someone apparently entered illegally.
23. Your report seems to suggest that we might be losing money.
24. It may be possible that sometime in the near future the situation is likely to improve.
25. I believe Nancy apparently has somewhat greater influence over employees in the word-processing department.

Revising Messages: Indefinite Starters Rewrite the following sentences to eliminate the indefinite starters. [LO-3]

26. There are several examples here to show that Elaine can't hold a position very long.
27. It would be greatly appreciated if every employee would make a generous contribution to Mildred Cook's retirement party.
28. It has been learned in Washington today from generally reliable sources that an important announcement will be made shortly by the White House.
29. There is a rule that states that we cannot work overtime without permission.

Revising Messages: Parallelism Revise the following sentences to fix the parallelism problems. [LO-3]

30. She knows not only accounting, but she also reads Latin.
31. Mr. Hill is expected to lecture three days a week, to counsel two days a week, and must write for publication in his spare time.
32. Both applicants had families, college degrees, and were in their thirties, with considerable accounting experience but few social connections.
33. This book was exciting, well written, and held my interest.

Revising Messages: Awkward References Revise the following sentences to delete the awkward references. [LO-3]

34. The vice president in charge of sales and the production manager are responsible for the keys to 34A and 35A, respectively.
35. The keys to 34A and 35A are in executive hands, with the former belonging to the vice president in charge of sales and the latter belonging to the production manager.
36. The keys to 34A and 35A have been given to the production manager, with the aforementioned keys being gold embossed.
37. A laser printer and an inkjet printer were delivered to John and Megan, respectively.

Revising Messages: Dangling Modifiers   Rewrite the following sentences to clarify the dangling modifiers. [LO-3]

38. Running down the railroad tracks in a cloud of smoke, we watched the countryside glide by.
39. Lying on the shelf, Ruby saw the seashell.
40. Based on the information, I think we should buy the property.
41. Being cluttered and filthy, Sandy took the whole afternoon to clean up her desk.

Revising Messages: Noun Sequences   Rewrite the following sentences to eliminate the long strings of nouns. [LO-3]

42. The supermarket warehouse inventory reduction plan will be implemented next month.
43. Following the government task force report recommendations, we are revising our job applicant evaluation procedures.
44. The production department quality assurance program components include employee training, supplier cooperation, and computerized detection equipment.
45. The focus of the meeting was a discussion of the bank interest rate deregulation issue.

Revising Messages: Sentence Structure   Rearrange each of the following sentences to bring the subjects closer to their verbs. [LO-3]

46. Trudy, when she first saw the bull pawing the ground, ran.
47. It was Terri who, according to Ted, who is probably the worst gossip in the office (Tom excepted), mailed the wrong order.
48. William Oberstreet, in his book *Investment Capital Reconsidered*, writes of the mistakes that bankers through the decades have made.
49. Judy Schimmel, after passing up several sensible investment opportunities, despite the warnings of her friends and family, invested her inheritance in a jojoba plantation.

Revising Messages: Camouflaged Verbs   Rewrite each of the following sentences so that the verbs are no longer camouflaged. [LO-3]

50. Adaptation to the new rules was performed easily by the employees.
51. The assessor will make a determination of the tax due.
52. Verification of the identity of the employees must be made daily.
53. The board of directors made a recommendation that Mr. Ronson be assigned to a new division.

Activities

Active links for all websites in this chapter can be found on mybcommlab; see your User Guide for instructions on accessing the content for this chapter. Each activity is labeled according to the primary skill or skills you will need to use. To review relevant chapter content, you can refer to the indicated Learning Objective. In some instances, supporting information will be found in another chapter, as indicated.

1. **Collaboration: Evaluating the Work of Other Writers [LO-1]**   Visit http://real-timeupdates.com/bce5, click on "Student Assignments," then select "Chapter 5, page 114, Activity 1." Download and open the document using word processing software that can accommodate Microsoft Word documents and offers revision tracking and commenting features. Using your knowledge of effective writing and the tips on page 129 for evaluating the work of other writers, evaluate this message. Using the revision tracking feature, make any necessary corrections. Insert comments, as needed, to explain your changes to the author.

2. **Completing: Evaluating Content, Organization, and Tone; Collaboration: Using Collaboration Technologies [LO-1]**   Chapter 2 Visit http://real-timeupdates.com/bce5, click on "Student Assignments," and then select "Chapter 5, page 114, Activity 2." Copy the text of this assignment and use it to start a document in Zoho (www.zoho.com; free for personal use) or a comparable collaboration system. In a team of three or four students, evaluate the content, organization, and tone of this message. After you reach agreement on the problems in the message, use the system's tools to rewrite and revise the text.

3. **Communication Ethics: Making Ethical Choices; Media Skills: Blogging [LO-3]**   The time and energy required for careful revision can often benefit you or your company directly, such as by increasing the probability that website visitors will buy your products. But what about situations in which the quality of your writing and revision work really doesn't stand to benefit you directly? For instance, assume that you are putting a notice on your website, informing the local community about some upcoming construction to your manufacturing plant. The work will disrupt traffic for nearly a year and generate a significant amount of noise and air pollution, but knowing the specific dates and times of various construction activities will allow people to adjust their commutes and other activities to minimize the negative impact on their daily lives. However, your company does not sell products in the local area, so the people affected by all this are not potential customers. Moreover, providing accurate information to the surrounding community and updating it as the project progresses will take time away from your other job responsibilities. Do you have an ethical obligation to keep the local community informed with accurate, up-to-date information? Why or why not? In a post on your class blog, explain your position on this question.

4. **Completing: Revising for Readability [LO-2]**   Rewrite the following paragraph using a parallel bulleted list and one introductory sentence:

Our forensic accounting services provide the insights needed to resolve disputes, recover losses, and manage risk intelligently. One of our areas of practice is insurance claims accounting and preparation services, designed to help you maximize recovery of insured value. Another practice area is dispute advisory, in which we can assist with discovery, expert witness testimony, and economic analysis. A third practice: construction consulting. This service helps our clients understand why large-scale construction projects fail to meet schedule or budget requirements. Fourth, we offer general investigative and forensic accounting services, including fraud detection and proof of loss analysis.[11]

5. **Completing: Revising for Readability [LO-2]**   Rewrite the following paragraph to vary the length of the sentences and to shorten the paragraph so it looks more inviting to readers:

Although major league baseball remains popular, more people are attending minor league baseball games because they can spend less on admission, snacks, and parking and still enjoy the excitement of America's pastime. Connecticut, for example, has three AA minor league teams, including the New Haven Ravens, who are affiliated with the St. Louis Cardinals; the Norwich Navigators, who are affiliated with the New York Yankees; and the New Britain Rock Cats, who are affiliated with the Minnesota Twins. These teams play in relatively small stadiums, so fans are close enough to see and hear everything, from the swing of the bat connecting with the ball to the thud of the ball landing in the outfielder's glove. Best of all, the cost of a family outing to see rising stars play in a local minor league game is just a fraction of what the family would spend to attend a major league game in a much larger, more crowded stadium.

6. **Completing: Designing for Readability; Media Skills: Blogging [LO-5]**   Compare the home pages of Bloomberg (www.bloomberg.com) and MarketWatch (www.marketwatch.com), two websites that cover financial markets. What are your first impressions of these two sites? How do their overall designs compare in terms of information delivery and overall user experience? Choose three pieces of information that a visitor to these sites would be likely to look for, such as a current stock price, news from international markets, and commentary from market experts. Which site makes it easier to find this information? Why? Present your analysis in a post for your class blog.

7. **Completing: Designing for Readability [LO-5]**   Visit http://real-timeupdates.com/bce5, click on "Student Assignments," and then select "Chapter 5, page 115, Activity 7." Download and open the document in word processing software capable of handling Microsoft Word documents. Using the various page, paragraph, and font formatting options available in your word processor, modify the formatting of the document so that its visual tone matches the tone of the message.

Expand Your Skills

Critique the Professionals

Identify a company website that in your opinion violates one or more of the principles of good design discussed on pages 137–139. Using whatever medium your instructor

requests, write a brief analysis of the site (no more than one page), citing specific elements from the piece and support from the chapter.

Sharpen Your Career Skills Online

Bovée and Thill's Business Communication Web Search, at http://businesscommunicationblog.com/websearch, is a unique research tool designed specifically for business communication research. Use the Web Search function to find a website, video, PDF document, podcast, or presentation that offers advice on any aspect of revising, designing, producing, or proofreading business messages. Write a brief e-mail message to your instructor or a post for your class blog, describing the item that you found and summarizing the career skills information you learned from it.

mybcommlab

If your course uses mybcommlab, log on to www.mybcommlab.com to access the following study and assessment aids associated with this chapter:

- Video applications
- Pre/post test
- Real-Time Updates
- Personalized study plan
- Peer review activity
- Model documents
- Quick Learning Guides
- Sample presentations

If you are not using mybcommlab, you can access Real-Time Updates and Quick Learning Guides through http://real-timeupdates.com/bce5. The Quick Learning Guide (located under "Learn More" on the website) hits all the high points of this chapter in just two pages. This guide, especially prepared by the authors, will help you study for exams or review important concepts whenever you need a quick refresher.

Improve Your Grammar, Mechanics, and Usage

You can download the text of this assignment from http://real-timeupdates.com/bce5; click on "Student Assignments" and then click on "Chapter 5. Improve Your Grammar, Mechanics, and Usage."

Level 1: Self-Assessment—Adverbs

Review Section 1.5 in the Handbook of Grammar, Mechanics, and Usage and then complete the following 15 items.

In items 1–5, indicate the correct adjective or adverb provided in parentheses.

1. Their performance has been (good, well).
2. I (sure, surely) do not know how to help you.

3. He feels (sick, sickly) again today.
4. Customs dogs are chosen because they smell (good, well).
5. The redecorated offices look (good, well).

In items 6–10, provide the correct form of the adverb in parentheses.

6. Which of the two programs computes _____ (fast)?
7. Kate has held five jobs over 13 years, and she was _____ (recently) employed by Graphicon.
8. Could they be _____ (happily) employed than they are now?
9. Of the two we have in stock, this model is the _____ (well) designed.
10. Of all the arguments I've ever heard, yours is the _____ (logically) reasoned.

In items 11–15, rewrite the sentences to correct double negatives.

11. He doesn't seem to have none.
12. That machine is scarcely never used.
13. They can't get no replacement parts until Thursday.
14. It wasn't no different from the first event we promoted.
15. We've looked for it, and it doesn't seem to be nowhere.

Level 2: Workplace Applications

The following items may contain errors in grammar, capitalization, punctuation, abbreviation, number style, word division, and vocabulary. Rewrite each sentence, correcting all errors. If a sentence has no errors, write "Correct" for that number.

1. All too often, whomever leaves the most out of his cost estimate is the one who wins the bid—if you can call it winning.
2. Carol Bartz CEO for fourteen years guided Autodesk; from a small company, to it's preeminent position in the computer aided design (cad) software market.
3. Shoppers were disinterested in the world-wide Web initially because many hyped services, offered no real cost or convenience advantages over offline stores.
4. Different jobs and different customers call for different pricing, estimating, and negotiating strategies.
5. Get to know the customer and their expectations, get the customer to talk about their primary use for you're product.
6. To homeowners, who feel they have found a competent contractor who has they're best interest's at heart, price will not matter nearly as much.
7. If I was you, I would of avoided investing in large conglomerates in light of the collapse of energy trader, Enron Corp., over accounting irregularities.
8. Outdoor goods retailer REI has had significant, success with in-store kiosks that let customers choose between several types of merchandise.
9. To people in some areas of cyberspace "Advertising" is a four letter word but "Marketing" is perfectly acceptable.

10. In any business effort, making money requires planning. Strategic marketing, a good product, good customer service, considerable shrewdness—and much hard work.
11. Investors must decide weather to put their capitol into bonds or CDs.
12. Running at full capacity, millions of Nike shoes are being produced by manufacturing plants every day.
13. Metropolis' stationary has a picture of the Empire state building on it.
14. Starbucks are planning to add fruit drinks to their menu in states throughout the south.
15. Credit ratings ain't what they used to be.

Level 3: Document Critique

The following document may contain errors in grammar, punctuation, capitalization, abbreviation, number style, vocabulary, and spelling. You will also find errors related to topics in this chapter. For example, look for ways to improve long words and phrases, redundancies, dangling modifiers, camouflaged verbs, and problems with parallelism as you improve this memo. As your instructor indicates, photocopy this page and correct all errors using standard proofreading marks (see Appendix C) or download the document and make the corrections in your word processing software.

Memorandum

TO: Metro power Employees

FROM: Susannah Beech, Hr Administrator

SUBJECT: Ways to improve your response to technology failures

Date: 22 September 2011

Dear Metro Employees:

There is always a chance of racing toward a deadline and suddenly having equipment fall. The following includes a few proposed suggestions to help you stave off, and cope with, technical equipment and system failures:

- Stay cool. There are many technical failures so they are commonplace in business; and it is likely that your bosses and co-workers will understand that you're having a prolbem and why.

- Practice preventive maintenance: Use cleaning cloths and sprays regularly, liquids and foods should be kept away from keyboards and printers; and you should make sure systems are shut down when you leave at night.

- It is important for faster repair asistance to promptly report computer failures to Bart Stone assistant director of information services ext. 2238, who will get to your poblem as soon as it is humanly possible for him to do so but you must keep in mind that there are many people demanding his focused attention at any given time;

- If you suspect that a problem may be developing, don't wait until the crucial last moment to call for assistance.

- When a last-minute technical failure of equipment threatens to disrupt your composure you might want to consider taking a walk to calm down.

The last suggestion is perhaps the most important to keep your career on track. Lost tempers; taking out your feelings in violent outbursts, and rude language are threatening to co-workers and could result in a reprimand or other disciplinary action. By calling technical support lines for help, your equipment can stay in good working order and your temper will stay calm.

The timely implemention of repairs is important, so ask your supervisor for a list of support numbers to keep handy. Then, the next time you experience a technology giltch in your equipment or systems, there are going to be quite a few numbers handy for you to call to help you handle it as just another aspect of your business regeem.

Sincerely,

Susannah Beech

Human Resources administrator

Brief Business Messages

Crafting Messages for Electronic Media

LEARNING OBJECTIVES

After studying this chapter, you will be able to

1 Identify the major electronic media used for brief business messages and describe the nine compositional modes needed for electronic media

2 Describe the use of social networks, user-generated content sites, and community Q&A sites in business communication

3 Describe the evolving role of e-mail in business communication and explain how to adapt the three-step writing process to e-mail messages

4 Describe the business benefits of instant messaging (IM), and identify guidelines for effective IM in the workplace

5 Describe the use of blogging and microblogging in business communication and briefly explain how to adapt the three-step process to blogging

6 Explain how to adapt the three-step writing process for podcasts

PEARSON
mybcommlab™   Access interactive videos, simulations, sample documents, Document Makeovers, and assessment quizzes in Chapter 6 of mybcommlab.com for mastery of this chapter's objectives.

COMMUNICATION *Matters*

" I blogged. You flamed. We changed. "
—Bill Owens, *Southwest Airlines employee and member of the Nuts About Southwest blogging team*

Southwest Airlines's multiauthor blog, Nuts About Southwest, features a variety of entertaining writers from around the company.

When Bill Owens posted what he thought was a routine message explaining why Southwest didn't allow customers to book reservations many months in advance, the response from readers of the company's Nuts About Southwest blog was anything but routine. Hundreds of passengers left comments on the blog, many of them disappointed, frustrated, and even angry. Customers described one scenario after another in which they had a real need to book travel further in advance than Southwest allowed, and many complained that the policy was forcing them to fly other airlines. Even some Southwest employees chimed in, too, expressing their frustration with not being able to meet customer needs at times. As Owens wrote in a follow-up post, "Talk about sticking your head in a hornet's nest!"

After bravely and patiently addressing specific customer responses over a period of several months, Owens responded with a new post titled

"I blogged. You flamed. We changed." In this message, he explained that the company had listened and was changing its scheduling policies to better accommodate customer needs.[1]

This chapter offers advice on crafting brief messages (from a few sentences to a few pages) using social networks, e-mail, IM and text messaging, blogs and microblogs, and podcasts. Wikis, another important electronic medium, are covered in Chapter 11.

USING ELECTRONIC MEDIA FOR BUSINESS COMMUNICATION

Management decisions that customers don't agree with are nothing new, of course. However, this online conversation between Southwest Airlines and its customers represents a revolutionary development in the history of business communication: the ability for customers and other audiences to quickly, easily, and publicly interact with companies. The tools that enable this interaction are **social media**, electronic media that transform passive audiences into active participants in the communication process by allowing them to share content, revise content, respond to content, or contribute new content. In addition to empowering customers and other stakeholders, media innovations help companies connect with audiences in new ways. For example, feedback from blog readers is so important that Southwest considers the blog a "customer service laboratory" that helps the company learn how to better serve its customers.[2]

Although social media have reduced the amount of control that businesses have over the content and the process of communication,[3] today's smart companies are learning how to adapt their communication efforts to this new media landscape and to welcome customers' participation. Social media are also revolutionizing internal communication, breaking down traditional barriers in the organizational hierarchy, promoting the flow of information and ideas, and enabling networks of individuals and organizations to collaborate on a global scale.[4]

Media Choices for Brief Messages

Today's business communicators have a broad range of options for sending brief messages (from one or two sentences up to several pages long):

- **Social networking and community participation websites.** Social networking sites such as Facebook and LinkedIn, user-generated content (UGC) sites such as Flickr and YouTube, and community Q&A sites provide a variety of communication tools, including status updates, user comments, and personal profiles, that support brief messages.

- **E-mail.** E-mail is a primary medium for most companies, although it is being replaced in many instances by social networks, instant messaging, blogging, wikis, and other tools that provide better support for instant communication and real-time collaboration.

- **Instant messaging (IM).** After consumers around the world began to adopt IM as a faster and simpler alternative to e-mail, businesses weren't far behind; computer-based IM usage now rivals e-mail in many companies. IM offers even greater speed than e-mail, as well as simple operation and—so far at least—fewer problems with unwanted messages or security and privacy problems.

- **Text messaging.** Phone-based text messaging has a number of applications in business communication, including order and status updates, marketing and sales messages, electronic coupons, and customer service.[5] Text messaging is also used as a *backchannel* during meetings and presentations (just as, ahem, students sometimes do doing class), giving audience members the opportunity to ask each other questions and share information (see page 370).

1 LEARNING OBJECTIVE
Identify the major electronic media used for brief business messages, and describe the nine compositional modes needed for electronic media

The range of options for short business messages continues to grow with innovations in electronic and social media.

REAL-TIME UPDATES
Learn More by Reading This Article

Integrating social media in a global corporation

IBM's Social Computing Guidelines offer practical advice for any company that wants to incorporate social media. Go to **http://real-timeupdates.com/bce5** and click on "Learn More." If you are using mybcommlab, you can access Real-Time Updates within each chapter or under Student Study Tools.

- **Blogging and microblogging.** The ability to update content quickly and easily makes blogs a natural medium when communicators need to get messages out in a hurry; bloggers can also publish information to wide audiences with relatively little effort. Microblogging systems such as Twitter are also being used widely in business, for everything from research and collaboration to customer service.

- **Podcasting.** You may be familiar with podcasts as the online equivalent of recorded radio or video broadcasts (video podcasts are often called *vidcasts* or *vodcasts*). Businesses are now using podcasts to replace or supplement conference calls, training courses, and other communication activities.

- **Online video.** Video in particular is a rich and powerful medium, and sites such as YouTube serve up videos to millions of viewers every day, including more than 100 million videos a day to mobile devices alone.[6] Creating high-quality videos (such as for formal training and marketing activities) requires some time and expertise, but even the simple video functions now widely available in cameras and mobile phones can be useful for research interviews, location surveys, product demonstrations, and other communication tasks.

Businesses continue to experiment with new media (see Figure 6.1), often adopting tools that were first intended for consumer use and applying the technologies to various forms of business communication.

Although most of your business communication is likely to be via electronic means, don't automatically dismiss the benefits of printed messages. Here are several situations in which you should use a printed message over electronic alternatives:

> Even with the widespread use of electronic media, printed memos and letters still play an important role in business communication.

- When you want to make a formal impression
- When you are legally required to provide information in printed form
- When you want to stand out from the flood of electronic messages
- When you need a permanent, unchangeable, or secure record

Obviously, if you can't reach a particular audience electronically, you'll also need to use a printed message.

Figure 6.1 Communication Innovations: Virtual Worlds
Innovative companies such as IBM are quick to experiment with new forms of electronic communication. The IBM Business Center in the virtual world Second Life offers information on a variety of topics of interest to customers, along with real-time interaction with IBM product experts.

- Meg Stivison (University of Massachusetts–Amherst) writes a blog and maintains a Flickr photo-sharing collection for the Stickley Museum at Craftsman Farms in Cary, North Carolina.
- Aga Westfall (Northern Arizona University) of The Santy Agency, an advertising firm in Phoenix, Arizona, uses Twitter for research and networking.

MEDIA
Choices Matter
Recent Grads Putting Their Communication Skills to Work

The Human Side of Electronic Communication

The benefits of electronic media are numerous, but as lean media (see page 90) they often lack the ability to convey nuances and raise the risk of miscommunication and unnecessary conflict.[7] Given the spontaneous and sometimes anonymous nature of electronic media, you will sometimes need to work hard to keep your emotions from getting the best of you when you're writing. If you're angry, walk away from your computer and calm down before firing off a message. Ask yourself two questions: First, "Would I say this to my audience face to face?" And second, "Am I comfortable with this message becoming a permanent part of my personal and professional communication history?"

Similarly, if you find yourself "stuck in a loop" with someone, sending message after message trying to resolve some point, or if you are confused or offended by a message, consider picking up the phone or arranging an in-person meeting. A brief conversation can often prevent or repair frayed nerves.

All users of electronic media also share the responsibility for information security and privacy. One careless move is all it takes to release sensitive information or expose an entire network to security risks. In fact, the problem of internal information being leaked through blogs and other public outlets is growing so acute that some companies are becoming wary of disclosing sensitive information to their own employees, and some are hiring investigating firms to track down the sources of leaks.[8]

Keep your emotions in check when you compose e-mail messages; flaming can damage relationships—and your reputation.

All users share the responsibility for network and information security.

Compositional Modes for Electronic Media

As you practice using electronic media in this course, focus on the principles of social media communication and the fundamentals of planning, writing, and completing messages, rather than on the specific details of any one medium or system.[9] Fortunately, the basic communication skills required usually transfer from one system to another. You can succeed with written communication in virtually all electronic media by using one of nine *compositional modes*:

- **Conversations.** IM is a great example of a written medium that mimics spoken conversation. And just as you wouldn't read a report to someone sitting in your office, don't use conversational modes to exchange large volumes of information.

- **Comments and critiques.** One of the most powerful aspects of social media is the opportunity for interested parties to express opinions and provide feedback, whether it's leaving comments on a blog post or reviewing products on an e-commerce site. Sharing helpful tips and insightful commentary is also a great way to build your personal brand. To be an effective commenter, focus on short chunks of information that a broad spectrum of other site visitors will find helpful. Rants, insults, jokes, and blatant self-promotion are usually of little benefit to other visitors.

- **Orientations.** The ability to help people find their way through an unfamiliar system or subject is a valuable writing skill, and a talent that readers greatly appreciate. Unlike summaries (see next list item), orientations don't give away the key points in the collection of information but rather tell readers where to find those points. Writing effective orientations can be a delicate balancing act because you need to know the material well enough to guide others through it while being able to step back and view it from the inexperienced perspective of a "newbie."

Communicating successfully with electronic media requires a wide range of writing approaches.

REAL-TIME UPDATES
Learn More by Listening to This Podcast

Violating ethical expectations in social media

Follow this discussion of how an electronics company violated the spirit of community in social commerce. Go to **http://real-timeupdates.com/bce5** and click on "Learn More." If you are using mybcommlab, you can access Real-Time Updates within each chapter or under Student Study Tools.

- **Summaries.** Summaries can serve several purposes. At the beginning of an article or webpage, a summary functions as a miniature version of the document, giving readers all the key points while skipping over details. In some instances, this is all a reader needs. In other instances, the up-front summary helps a reader decide whether to invest the time needed to read the full document. At the end of an article or webpage, a summary functions as a review, reminding readers of the key points they've just read.

- **Reference materials.** One of the greatest benefits of the Internet is the access it can provide to vast quantities of reference materials—numerical or textual information that people typically don't read in a linear sense but rather search through to find particular data points, trends, or other specific elements. One of the challenges of writing reference material is that you can't always know how readers will want to access it. Making the information accessible via search engine is an important step. However, readers don't always know which search terms will yield the best results, so include an orientation and organize the material in logical ways with clear headings that promote skimming.

- **Narratives.** The storytelling techniques covered in Chapter 3 (see page 95) can be effective in a wide variety of situations, from company histories to product reviews and demonstrations. Narratives work best when they have an intriguing beginning that piques readers' curiosity, a middle section that moves quickly through the challenges that an individual or company faced, and an inspiring or instructive ending that gives readers information they can apply in their own lives and jobs.

- **Teasers.** Teasers intentionally withhold key pieces of information as a way to pull readers or listeners into a story or other document. Teasers are widely used in marketing and sales messages, such as a bit of copy on the outside of an envelope that promises important information on the inside. In electronic media, the space limitations and URL linking capabilities of Twitter and other microblogging systems make them a natural tool for the teaser approach. Although they can certainly be effective, teasers need to be used sparingly and with respect for readers' time and intelligence. Be sure that the *payoff*, the information a teaser links to, is valuable and legitimate. You'll quickly lose credibility if readers think they are being tricked into clicking through to information they don't really want.

With Twitter and other super-short messaging systems, the ability to write a compelling *teaser* is an important skill.

- **Status updates and announcements.** If you use social media frequently, much of your writing will involve status updates and announcements. However, don't post trivial information that only you are likely to find interesting. Post only those updates that readers will find useful, and include only the information they need.

- **Tutorials.** Given the community nature of social media, the purpose of many messages is to share how-to advice. One of the biggest challenges with tutorials is gauging the level of understanding your target readers have about the subject so that you can write at the appropriate level. Are your readers beginners, experts, or somewhere in between? In addition, make your assumptions clear so readers can tell if the information is right for them. A good place to do this is in your titles, using phrases such as "getting started with" or "advanced techniques for" to alert readers about the level of the tutorial. Whatever level of information you provide, make sure your advice is clear, complete, and logically organized.

As you approach a new communication task using electronic media, ask yourself what kind of information audience members are likely to need and then choose the appropriate compositional mode. Of course, many of these modes are also used in written media, but over time you may find yourself using all of them in various electronic and social media contexts.

2 **LEARNING OBJECTIVE**

Describe the use of social networks, user-generated content sites, and community Q&A sites in business communication

COMMUNICATING ON NETWORKING, UGC, AND COMMUNITY Q&A SITES

Social networks, online services that enable individual and organizational members to form connections and share information, have become a major force in business communication in recent years. For example, Facebook is now the most-visited website on the Internet, and a number of companies, such as Adidas, Red Bull, and Starbucks, have millions of fans on their Facebook pages.[10] This section takes a look at the business communication uses of social networks and two related technologies, *user-generated content (UGC) sites* and *community Q&A sites.*

Social Networks

Most everyone is familiar with Facebook and MySpace, but these are just two of the many social networks now used for business communication. Some were created with consumers in mind but came to be used by thousands of businesses (such as Facebook and MySpace), while others were created specifically with business users in mind (LinkedIn is the largest of these).

In addition, business professionals use a variety of specialized social networks, including those that help small business owners get support and advice, those that connect entrepreneurs with investors, and those such as Segway Social and Specialized (see page 160) created by individual companies to enhance the sense of community among their customer bases. Some companies have created private social networks for internal use only. For example, the defense contractor Lockheed Martin created its Unity network, complete with a variety of social media applications, to meet the expectations of younger employees accustomed to social media use and to capture the expert knowledge of older employees nearing retirement.[11]

Business communicators make use of a wide range of social networks, in addition to the well-known Facebook.

Business Communication Uses of Social Networks

With their ability to reach virtually unlimited numbers of people through a variety of electronic formats, social networks are a great fit for many business communication needs (see Table 6.1). In the course of just a few years, in fact, social networking has become an essential business communication medium. A significant majority of consumers now want the businesses

TABLE 6.1 Business Uses of Social Networking Technology

Business Challenge	Example of Social Networking in Action
Supporting customers	Allowing customers to develop close relationships with product experts within the company
Integrating new employees	Helping new employees navigate their way through the organization, finding experts, mentors, and other important contacts
Easing the transition after reorganizations and mergers	Helping employees connect and bond after internal staff reorganizations or mergers with other organizations
Overcoming structural barriers in communication channels	Bypassing the formal communication system in order to deliver information where it is needed in a timely fashion
Assembling teams	Identifying the best people, both inside the company and in other companies, to collaborate on projects
Fostering the growth of communities	Helping people with similar—or complementary—interests and skills find each other in order to provide mutual assistance and development
Solving problems	Finding "pockets of knowledge" within the organization—the expertise and experience of individual employees
Preparing for major meetings and events	Giving participants a way to meet before an event takes place, helping to ensure that the meeting or event becomes more productive more quickly
Accelerating the evolution of teams	Accelerating the sometimes slow process of getting to know one another and identifying individual areas of expertise
Maintaining business relationships	Giving people an easy way to stay in contact after meetings and conferences
Sharing and distributing information	Making it easy for employees to share information with people who may need it and for people who need information to find employees who might have it
Finding potential customers, business partners, and employees	Identifying strong candidates by matching user profiles with current business needs and linking existing member profiles

they patronize to use social networking for distributing information and interacting with customers—and companies that aren't active in social networking risk getting left behind.[12]

In addition to the collaboration uses discussed in Chapter 2, here are some of the key business applications of social networks:

Social networks are vital tools for distributing information as well as gathering information about the business environment.

- **Gathering market intelligence.** With hundreds of millions of people expressing themselves via social media, you can be sure that smart companies are listening. For example, *sentiment analysis* is an intriguing research technique in which companies track social networks and other media with automated language-analysis software that tries to take the pulse of public opinion and identify influential opinion makers. Social media can be "an incredibly rich vein of market intelligence," says Margaret Francis of San Francisco's Scout Labs (www.scoutlabs.com).[13]

- **Recruiting and connecting.** Companies use social networks to find potential employees, short-term contractors, subject-matter experts, product and service suppliers, and business partners. A key advantage here is that these introductions are made via trusted connections in a professional network. On LinkedIn, for example, members can recommend each other based on current or past business relationships, which helps remove the uncertainty of initiating business relationships with complete strangers.

Product promotion can be done on social networks, but it needs to done in a low-key, indirect way.

- **Marketing communication.** Businesses don't invest time and money in social networking simply to gain fans, of course. The ultimate goal is profitable, sustainable relationships with customers, and attracting new customers is one of the primary reasons businesses use networks and other social media.[14] However, the traditional notions of marketing and selling need to be adapted to the social networking environment because customers and potential customers don't join a network merely to be passive recipients of advertising messages. They want to participate, to connect with fellow enthusiasts, to share knowledge about products, to communicate with company insiders, and to influence the decisions that affect the products they value. This notion of interactive participation is the driving force behind **conversation marketing**, in which companies *initiate* and *facilitate* conversations in a networked community of customers and other interested parties.

- **Fostering brand communities.** Social networking is playing an important role in the rapid spread of **brand communities**, groups of people united by their interest in and ownership or use of particular products (see Figure 6.2). These communities can be formal membership organizations, such as the Harley Owners Group, or informal networks of people with similar interests. They can be fairly independent from the company behind the brand or can have the active support and involvement of company management.[15] A strong majority of consumers now trust their peers more than any other source of product information—including conventional advertising techniques—so formal and informal brand communities are becoming an essential information source in consumer buying decisions.[16]

- **Location-based social networking.** The combination of mobile phone service, social networking, and GPS navigation has given rise to a new form of communication known as *location-based social networking* through services such as Foursquare and Loopt. Location-based networking promises to become an important business communication medium because mobile consumers are a significant economic force—through the purchases they make directly and through their ability to influence other consumers.

Strategies for Business Communication on Social Networks

Social networks offer lots of communication options, but with those opportunities comes a certain degree of complexity. Moreover, the norms and practices of business social networking continue to evolve. Follow these guidelines to make the most of social networks for both personal branding and company communication:[17]

Communicating on social networks is complicated and requires a thoughtful, well-integrated strategy.

- **Choose the best compositional mode for each message, purpose, and network.** As you visit various social networks, take some time to observe the variety of message types you see in different parts of each website. For example, the informal status update mode works well for Facebook Wall posts but would be less effective for company overviews and mission statements.

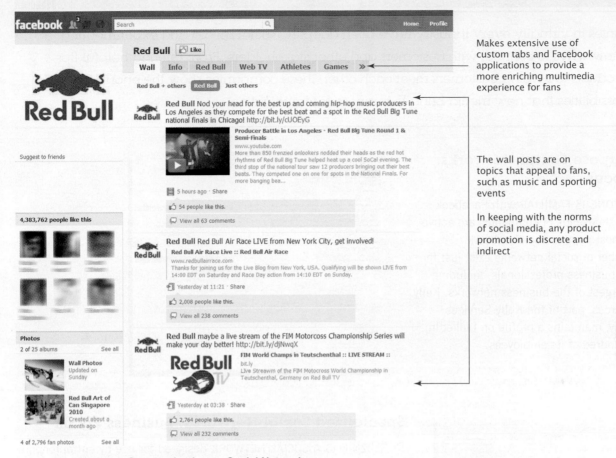

Figure 6.2   Business Communication on Social Networks
The energy drink company Red Bull has one of the largest fan bases on Facebook, giving the company the opportunity to connect with millions of enthusiastic customers.

- **Join existing conversations.** Search for online conversations that are already taking place. Answer questions, solve problems, and respond to rumors and misinformation.

- **Anchor your online presence in your hub.** Although it's important to join those conversations and be visible where your stakeholders are active, it's equally important to anchor your presence at your own central *hub*—a web presence that you own and control. This can be a combination of a conventional website, a blog, and a company-sponsored online community, for example.[18] Use the hub to connect the various pieces of your online "self" (as an individual or a company) to make it easier for people to find and follow you. For example, you can link to your blog from your LinkedIn profile, or automatically post your blog entries into the Notes tab on your Facebook page.

- **Facilitate community building.** Make it easy for customers and other audiences to connect with the company and with each other. For example, you can use the group feature on Facebook, LinkedIn, and other social networks to create and foster special-interest groups within your networks. Groups are a great way to connect people who are interested in specific topics, such as owners of a particular product.

- **Restrict conventional promotional efforts to the right time and right place.** Persuasive communication efforts are still valid for specific communication tasks, such as regular advertising and the product information pages on a website, but efforts to inject blatant "salespeak" into social networking conversations will usually be rejected by the audience.

- **Maintain a consistent personality.** Each social network is a unique environment with particular norms of communication.[19] For example, as a business-oriented network, LinkedIn has a more formal "vibe" than Facebook. However, while adapting to the expectations of each network, be sure to maintain a consistent personality across all

(*continued on page 162*)

Companies in virtually every industry have been adopting social media and experimenting with new ways to connect with customers and other stakeholders. From offering helpful tips on using products to helping customers meet each other, these companies show the enormous range of possibilities that new media bring to business communication.

General-Purpose Social Networks: Business Focus

▷ MOST EVERYONE IS FAMILIAR with Facebook these days, and thousands of companies are active on the world's most popular social network. However, a number of social networks exist just for businesses and business professionals, including LinkedIn, the largest of the business networks. Kelly Financial Resources, part of the Kelly Services staffing company, maintains a profile on LinkedIn, as do several hundred of its employees.

Specialized Social Networks: Business Focus

▷ "BIZNIK IS A SOCIAL NETWORK designed for use by entrepreneurs and small business people to aid them in connecting and collaborating with their peers and contemporaries," explains Biznik's Andrew Lippert. A great example of these groups is The Marketing Crowd. "This Biznik group consists of professionals in the marketing profession who connect with one another and discuss issues relevant to their industry. The group is an online extension of their community, which facilitates their interaction and the development of real relationships supporting and benefiting the group members' professional careers and businesses."

Specialized Social Networks: Consumer Focus

▷ A NUMBER OF COMPANIES now host their own social networking sites, where product enthusiasts interact by sharing personal stories, offering advice, and commenting on products and company news—all brief-message functions that replace more traditional media options. For example, Specialized, a major bicycle manufacturer based in Morgan Hill, California, hosts the Specialized Riders Club (www.specializedriders.com), where customers can interact with each other and the professional riders the company sponsors. Similarly, the Segway Social network connects owners of these unique personal vehicles, including helping teams organize for Segway polo matches and other events.

Community Q&A

▷ COMMUNITY Q&A SITES bring together people with questions and people with answers. The nature of these sites vary. For example, Experts Exchange is a fee-based service that lets computer users post questions on a wide range of topics and get answers from one or more technical experts. The personal finance website Mint.com and the online shoe retailer Zappos, on the other hand, team up with a company called Get Satisfaction to deliver "community powered support," providing answers to questions and solutions to customer support issues.

Value-Added Content via Blogging

▷ ONE OF THE BEST WAYS to become a valued member of a network is to provide content that is useful to others in the network. The Quizzle personal finance blog offers a steady stream of articles and advice that help people manage their finances.

Value-Added Content via Online Video

▷ LIE-NIELSEN TOOLWORKS OF WARREN, Maine, uses its YouTube channel to offer valuable information on choosing and using premium woodworking tools. By offering sought-after information for both current and potential customers free of charge, these videos help Lie-Nielsen foster relationships with the worldwide woodworking community and solidify its position as one of the leaders in this market. Animal Planet, Best Western, and Taco Bell are among the many other companies that make effective use of branded channels on YouTube.

Idea Generation Through Community Feedback

▷ STARBUCKS HAS COLLECTED TENS of thousands of ideas for new products and service enhancements through its community website, My Starbucks Idea. The company makes the clear request: "You know better than anyone else what you want from Starbucks. So tell us."

the networks in which you are active.[20] The computer giant HP, for instance, uses the same (fairly formal-sounding) company overview on LinkedIn and Facebook, while posting Wall updates on Facebook that are "chattier" and more in keeping with the tone expected by Facebook visitors.[21]

See "Writing Promotional Messages for Social Media" in Chapter 9 (pages 255–257) for more tips on writing messages for social networks and other social media.

User-Generated Content Sites

Watching entertaining video clips on YouTube is a favorite pastime for millions of web surfers. However, YouTube, Flickr, and other **user-generated content (UGC) sites**, in which users rather than website owners contribute most or all of the content, have also become serious business tools. In fact, a recent survey suggested that video company profiles on YouTube have more measurable impact than company profiles on Facebook, LinkedIn, and other prominent sites.[22]

Video is a powerful medium for product demonstrations, interviews, industry news, training, facility tours, and other uses. Moreover, the business communication value of sites such as YouTube goes beyond the mere ability to deliver content. The social aspects of these sites, including the ability to vote for, comment on, and share material, encourage enthusiasts to spread the word about the companies and products they endorse.[23]

As with other social media, the keys to effective user-generated content are making it valuable and making it easy. First, provide content that people want to see and to share with colleagues. A video clip that explains how to use a product more effectively will be more popular than a clip that talks about how amazing the company behind the product is. Also, keep videos short, generally no longer than three to five minutes if possible.[24]

Second, make material easy to find, consume, and share. For example, a *branded channel* on YouTube lets a company organize all its videos in one place, making it easy for visitors to browse the selection or subscribe in order to get automatic updates of future videos. Sharing features let fans share videos through e-mail or their accounts on Twitter, Facebook, and other platforms.

Community Q&A Sites

Community Q&A sites, on which visitors answer questions posted by other visitors, are a contemporary twist on the early ethos of computer networking, which was people helping each other. (Groups of like-minded people connected online long before the World Wide Web was even created.) Community Q&A sites include dedicated customer support communities such as those hosted on Get Satisfaction (**http://getsatisfaction.com**), public sites such as Yahoo! Answers (**http://answers.yahoo.com**), and member-only sites such as LinkedIn Answers (**www.linkedin.com/answers**).

Responding to questions on Q&A sites can be a great way to build your personal brand, to demonstrate your company's commitment to customer service, and to counter misinformation about your company and its products. Keep in mind that when you respond to an individual query on a community Q&A site, you are also "responding in advance" to every person in the future who comes to the site with the same question. In other words, you are writing a type of reference material in addition to corresponding with the original questioner, so keep the long timeframe and wider audience in mind.

3 LEARNING OBJECTIVE

Describe the evolving role of e-mail in business communication, and explain how to adapt the three-step writing process to e-mail messages

CREATING EFFECTIVE E-MAIL MESSAGES

E-mail had a long head start on other forms of electronic communication and has long been a primary medium for many companies. Over the years, e-mail began to be used (and occasionally misused) for many communication tasks, simply because it was the only widely available electronic medium for written messages and millions of users were comfortable with it. However, newer tools such as instant messaging, blogs, microblogs, social networks, and shared workspaces are taking over specialized tasks for which they are better suited.[25] For example, e-mail is usually not the best choice for brief online conversations (IM is better

[margin notes:]

YouTube is now a major resource for business communicators, hosting everything from product demonstration videos to television commercials.

Creating compelling and useful content is the key to leveraging the reach of social networks.

Community Q&A sites offer great opportunities for building your personal brand.

for this) or project management updates (blogs, wikis, and various purpose-built systems are often better for this).

In a sense, e-mail seems out of step in a world of instantaneous and open communication, where many users are accustomed to rapid-fire updates from Twitter, public forums on social networks, and never-ending streams of incoming information.[26] However, e-mail still has compelling advantages that will keep it in steady use in many companies. First, e-mail is universal. Anybody with an e-mail address can reach anybody else with an e-mail address, no matter which systems the senders and receivers are on. You don't need to join a special group or be friended by anyone in order to correspond. Second, e-mail is still the best medium for many private, short- to medium-length messages. Unlike IM, for instance, midsize messages are easy to compose and easy to read on e-mail. Third, e-mail's noninstantaneous nature is an advantage when used properly. Many business messages don't need the rapid-fire rate of IM or Twitter, for example, and the implied urgency of those systems can be a productivity-sapping interruption. E-mail allows senders to compose substantial messages in private and on their own schedule, and it allows recipients to read those messages at their leisure.

> E-mail can seem a bit "old school" in comparison to social networks and other technologies, but it is still one of the more important business communication media.

Many companies now have formal e-mail policies that specify how employees can use e-mail, including restrictions against using company e-mail service for personal messages and sending material that might be deemed objectionable. In addition, many employers now monitor e-mail, either automatically with software programmed to look for sensitive content or manually via security staff actually reading selected e-mail messages. Regardless of formal policies, though, every e-mail user has a responsibility to avoid actions that could cause trouble, from downloading virus-infected software to sending objectionable photographs. *E-mail hygiene* refers to all the efforts that companies are making to keep e-mail clean and safe—from spam blocking and virus protection to content filtering.[27]

> E-mail presents considerable legal hazards, and many companies have formal e-mail policies.

Planning E-Mail Messages

The biggest complaint about e-mail is that there is just too much of it—too many messages of little or no value. You can help with this problem during the planning step by making sure every message has a useful, business-related purpose, and when you're ready to distribute each message, don't "cc" (courtesy copy) additional recipients unless those other people really and truly need to receive the message. For instance, suppose you send a message to your boss and cc five colleagues because you want everyone to see that you're giving the boss some good information. Those five people now not only have to read your message but also might feel compelled to reply so that the boss doesn't think they're being negligent. Then everyone will start replying to those replies, and on and on. What should have been a single exchange between you and your boss quickly multiplies into a flurry of messages that wastes everybody's time.

> Do your part to stem the flood of e-mail by making sure you don't send unnecessary messages or "cc" people who don't really need to see particular messages.

Finally, be sure to respect the chain of command. In many companies, any employee can e-mail anyone else, including the president and CEO. However, take care that you don't abuse this freedom. For instance, don't send a complaint straight to the top just because it's easy to do so. Your efforts will be more effective if you follow the organizational hierarchy and give each person a chance to address the situation in turn.

> Respect the chain of command in your company when sending e-mail messages.

Writing E-Mail Messages

When you approach e-mail writing on the job, recognize that business e-mail is a more formal medium than you are probably accustomed to with e-mail for personal communication (see Figure 6.3 on the next page). The expectations of writing quality for business e-mail are higher than for personal e-mail, and the consequences of bad writing or poor judgment can be much more serious. For example, e-mail messages and other electronic documents have the same legal weight as printed documents, and they are often used as evidence in lawsuits and criminal investigations.[28]

> Business e-mail messages are more formal than the e-mail messages you send to family and friends.

The e-mail subject line might seem like a small detail, but it is actually one of the most important parts of an e-mail message because it helps recipients decide which messages to read and when to read them. To capture your audience's attention, make your subject lines informative and compelling. Go beyond simply describing or classifying your message; use the opportunity to build interest with keywords, quotations, directions, or questions.[29]

> A poorly written subject line could lead to a message being deleted or ignored.

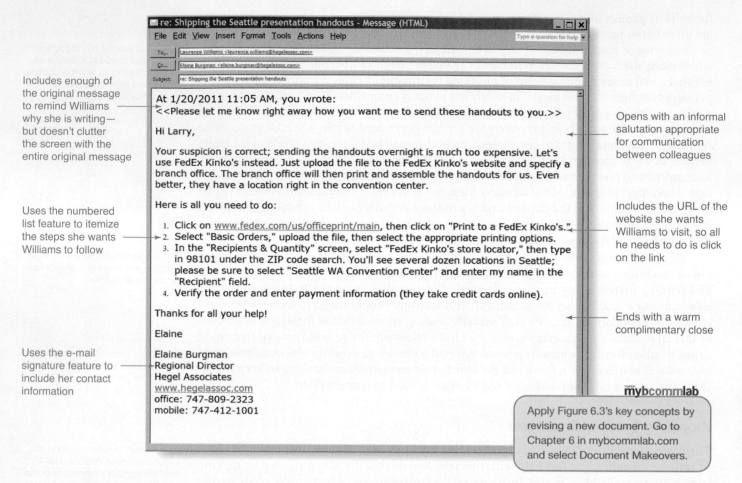

Includes enough of the original message to remind Williams why she is writing—but doesn't clutter the screen with the entire original message

Uses the numbered list feature to itemize the steps she wants Williams to follow

Uses the e-mail signature feature to include her contact information

Opens with an informal salutation appropriate for communication between colleagues

Includes the URL of the website she wants Williams to visit, so all he needs to do is click on the link

Ends with a warm complimentary close

Apply Figure 6.3's key concepts by revising a new document. Go to Chapter 6 in mybcommlab.com and select Document Makeovers.

Figure 6.3   E-Mail for Business Communication
In this response to an e-mail query from a colleague, Elaine Burgman takes advantage of her e-mail system's features to create an efficient and effective message.

For example, "July sales results" accurately describes the content of the message, but "July sales results: good news and bad news" is more intriguing. Readers will want to know why some news is good and some is bad.

In addition, many e-mail programs display the first few words or lines of incoming messages, even before the recipient opens them. In the words of social media public relations expert Steve Rubel, you can "tweetify" the opening lines of your e-mail messages to make them stand out. In other words, choose the first few words carefully to grab your reader's attention.[30] Think of the first sentence as an extension of your subject line.

Completing E-Mail Messages

Particularly for important messages, taking a few moments to revise and proofread might save you hours of headaches and damage control. Also, favor simplicity when it comes to producing your e-mail messages. A clean, easily readable font, in black on a white background, is sufficient for nearly all e-mail messages. Take advantage of your e-mail system's ability to include an **e-mail signature**, a small file that automatically includes such items as your full name, title, company, and contact information at the end of your messages.

Think twice before hitting Send; a simple mistake in your content or distribution can cause major headaches.

When you're ready to distribute your message, pause to verify what you're doing before you click Send. Make sure you've included everyone necessary—and no one else. Did you click Reply All when you meant to click only Reply? The difference could be embarrassing or even career threatening. Don't include people in the cc (courtesy copy) or bcc (blind courtesy copy) fields unless you know how these features work. (Everyone who receives the

TABLE 6.2 Tips for Effective E-mail Messages

Tip	Why It's Important
When you request information or action, make it clear what you're asking for, why it's important, and how soon you need it; don't make your reader write back for details.	People will be tempted to ignore your messages if they're not clear about what you want or how soon you want it.
When responding to a request, either paraphrase the request or include enough of the original message to remind the reader what you're replying to.	Some businesspeople get hundreds of e-mail messages a day and may need reminding what your specific response is about.
If possible, avoid sending long, complex messages via e-mail.	Long messages are easier to read as attached reports or web content.
Adjust the level of formality to the message and the audience.	Overly formal messages to colleagues can be perceived as stuffy and distant; overly informal messages to customers or top executives can be perceived as disrespectful.
Activate a signature file, which automatically pastes your contact information into every message you create.	A signature saves you the trouble of retyping vital information and ensures that recipients know how to reach you through other means.
Don't let unread messages pile up in your in-basket.	You'll miss important information and create the impression that you're ignoring other people.
Never type in all caps.	ALL CAPS ARE INTERPRETED AS SCREAMING.
Don't overformat your messages with background colors, multicolored type, unusual fonts, and so on.	Such messages can be difficult and annoying to read on screen.
Remember that messages can be forwarded anywhere and saved forever.	Don't let a moment of anger or poor judgment haunt you for the rest of your career.
Use the "return receipt requested" feature only for the most critical messages.	This feature triggers a message back to you whenever someone receives or opens your message; many consider this an invasion of privacy.
Make sure your computer has up-to-date virus protection.	One of the worst breaches of "netiquette" is infecting other computers because you haven't bothered to protect your own system.
Pay attention to grammar, spelling, and capitalization.	Some people don't think e-mail needs formal rules, but careless messages make you look unprofessional and can annoy readers.
Use acronyms sparingly.	Shorthand such as IMHO (in my humble opinion) and LOL (laughing out loud) can be useful in informal correspondence with colleagues, but avoid using them in more formal messages.

message can see who is on the cc line but not who is on the bcc line.) Also, don't set the message priority to "high" or "urgent" unless your message is truly urgent. And if you intend to include an attachment, be sure that it is indeed attached.

Table 6.2 offers a number of helpful tips for effective e-mail, and for the latest information on using e-mail in business, visit http://real-timeupdates.com/bce5 and click on Chapter 6.

CREATING EFFECTIVE INSTANT MESSAGES AND TEXT MESSAGES

4 LEARNING OBJECTIVE
Describe the business benefits of instant messaging (IM), and identify guidelines for effective IM in the workplace

Although e-mail isn't going away anytime soon, its disadvantages—including viruses, spam, and rampant overuse—are driving many people to explore alternatives. One of the most important of those alternatives is **instant messaging (IM)**. For both routine communication and exchanges during online meetings, IM is now widely used throughout

IM is taking the place of e-mail for routine communication in many companies.

the business world and is beginning to overtake and even replace e-mail for internal communication in many companies.[31] IM capabilities are also being embedded into other communication media, including social networks and online meeting systems, further extending the reach of this convenient technology.[32] Business-grade IM systems offer a range of capabilities, including basic chat, *presence awareness* (the ability to quickly see which people are at their desks and available to IM), remote display of documents, video capabilities, remote control of other computers, automated newsfeeds from blogs and websites, and automated *bot* (derived from the word *robot*) capabilities in which a computer can carry on simple conversations.[33]

Phone-based text messaging is fast and portable but not as versatile as computer-based IM.

Text messaging has a number of applications in business as well, including marketing (alerting customers about new sale prices, for example), customer service (such as airline flight status, package tracking, and appointment reminders), security (for example, authenticating mobile banking transactions), crisis management (such as updating all employees working at a disaster scene), and process monitoring (alerting computer technicians to system failures, for example).[34]

Because IM is currently more versatile and more widely used in business than text messaging, the following sections focus on IM. However, many of the benefits, risks, and guidelines that pertain to IM will pertain to text messaging as well.

Understanding the Benefits and Risks of IM

IM offers many benefits:
- Rapid response
- Low cost
- Ability to mimic conversation
- Wide availability

The benefits of IM include its capability for rapid response to urgent messages, lower cost than phone calls and e-mail, ability to mimic conversation more closely than e-mail, and availability on a wide range of devices.[35] In addition, because it more closely resembles one-on-one conversation, IM doesn't get misused as a one-to-many broadcast method as often as e-mail does.[36]

Of course, wherever technology goes, trouble seems to follow. The potential drawbacks of IM include security problems (computer viruses, network infiltration, and the possibility that sensitive messages might be intercepted by outsiders), the need for *user authentication* (making sure that online correspondents are really who they appear to be), the challenge of logging messages for later review and archiving, incompatibility between competing IM systems, and *spim* (unsolicited commercial messages, similar to e-mail spam). Fortunately, with the growth of *enterprise instant messaging (EIM)*, or IM systems designed for large-scale corporate use, many of these problems are being overcome. However, security remains a significant concern for corporate IM systems.[37]

Adapting the Three-Step Process for Successful IM

Although instant messages are often conceived, written, and sent within a matter of seconds, the principles of the three-step process still apply, particularly when communicating with customers and other important audiences:

- **Planning instant messages.** Except for simple exchanges, take a moment to plan IM "conversations" in much the same way you would plan an important oral conversation. A few seconds of planning can help you deliver information in a coherent, complete way that minimizes the number of individual messages required.

- **Writing instant messages.** As with e-mail, the appropriate writing style for business IM is more formal than the style you may be accustomed to with personal IM or text messaging (see Figure 6.4). Your company might discourage the use of IM acronyms (such as FWIW for "for what it's worth" or HTH for "hope that helps"), particularly for IM with external audiences.

- **Completing instant messages.** The only task in the completing stage is to send your message. Just quickly scan it before sending, to make sure you don't have any missing or misspelled words and verify that your message is clear and complete.

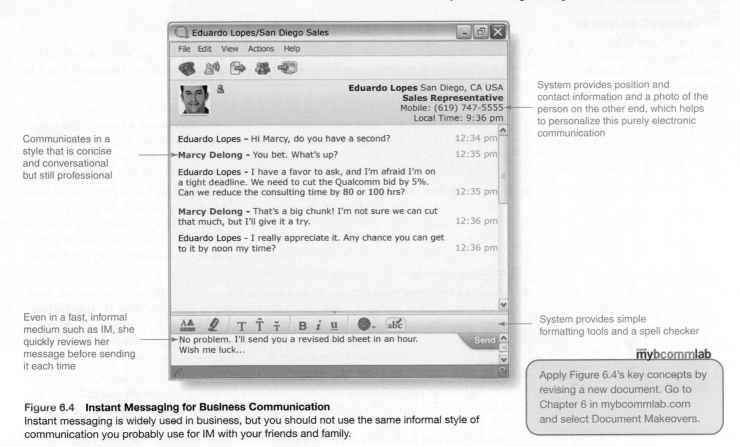

Figure 6.4   Instant Messaging for Business Communication

Instant messaging is widely used in business, but you should not use the same informal style of communication you probably use for IM with your friends and family.

To use IM effectively, keep in mind some important behavioral issues when relying on this medium: the potential for constant interruptions, the ease of accidentally mixing personal and business messages, the risk of being out of the loop (if a hot discussion or an impromptu meeting flares up when you're away from your PC or other IM device), and being at the mercy of other people's typing abilities.[38]

When using IM, be aware of the potential for constant interruptions and wasted time.

Regardless of the system you're using, you can make IM more efficient and effective by heeding these tips:[39]

Understand the guidelines for successful business IM before you begin to use it.

- Be courteous in your use of IM; if you don't need an answer instantly, you can avoid interrupting someone by sending an e-mail or other type of message instead.

- Unless a meeting is scheduled or you're expected to be available for other reasons, make yourself unavailable when you need to focus on other work.

- If you're not on a secure system, don't send confidential information using IM.

- Be extremely careful about sending personal messages—they have a tendency to pop up on other people's computers at embarrassing moments.

- Don't use IM for important but impromptu meetings if you can't verify that everyone concerned will be available.

- Don't use IM for lengthy, complex messages; e-mail is better for those.

- Try to avoid carrying on multiple IM conversations at one time, to minimize the chance of sending messages to the wrong people or making one person wait while you tend to another conversation.

- Follow all security guidelines designed to keep your company's information and systems safe from attack.

For the latest information on using IM in business, visit http://real-timeupdates.com/bce5 and click on Chapter 6.

5 LEARNING OBJECTIVE
Describe the use of blogging and
microblogging in business
communication, and briefly
explain how to adapt the three-
step process to blogging

CREATING EFFECTIVE BUSINESS BLOGS

A **blog** (short for *web log*) is an online journal that is much easier to personalize and update than a conventional website. Good business blogs and microblogs pay close attention to several important elements:

- **Communicating with personal style and an authentic voice.** Most business messages designed for large audiences are carefully scripted and written in a "corporate voice" that is impersonal and objective. In contrast, successful business blogs are written by individuals and exhibit their personal style. Audiences relate to this fresh approach and often build closer emotional bonds with the blogger's organization as a result.

- **Delivering new information quickly.** Blogging tools let you post new material as soon as you write it or film it (blogs that emphasize video content are known as *vlogs*). This feature not only allows you to respond quickly when needed—such as during a corporate crisis—but also lets your audiences know that active communication is taking place. Blogs that don't offer a continuous stream of new and interesting content are quickly ignored in today's online environment.

- **Choosing topics of peak interest to audiences.** Successful blogs cover topics that readers care about. For instance, General Motors's popular FastLane blog (http://fastlane .gmblogs.com) features top executives writing about GM cars and responding to questions and criticisms from car enthusiasts. The people who read the blog and write comments obviously care about cars and want the latest information from GM.[40]

- **Encouraging audiences to join the conversation.** Not all blogs invite comments, although most do, and many bloggers consider comments to be an essential feature. Blog comments can be a valuable source of news, information, and insights. In addition, the informal nature of blogging seems to make it easier for companies to let their guard down and converse with their audiences. To guard against comments that are not helpful or appropriate, many bloggers review all comments and post only the most helpful or interesting ones.

Most business blogs invite readers
to leave comments.

Understanding the Business Applications of Blogging

The business applications of blogs
include a wide range of internal and
external communication tasks.

Blogs are a potential solution whenever you have a continuing stream of information to share with an online audience—and particularly when you want the audience to have the opportunity to respond. Here are some of the many ways businesses are using blogs:[41]

- **Project management and team communication.** Using blogs is a good way to keep project teams up to date, particularly when team members are geographically dispersed. For instance, the trip reports that employees file after visiting customers or other external parties can be enhanced vividly with mobile blogs, or *moblogs*.

- **Company news.** Companies can use blogs to keep employees informed about general business matters, from facility news to benefit updates. Blogs also serve as online community forums, giving everyone in the company a chance to raise questions and voice concerns.

- **Customer support.** Building on the tradition of online customer support forums that have been around since the earliest days of the Internet, customer support blogs answer questions, offer tips and advice, and inform customers about new products. Also, many companies monitor the blogosphere (and Twitter), looking for complaints and responding with offers to help dissatisfied customers.[42]

- **Public relations and media relations.** Many company employees and executives now share company news with both the general public and journalists via their blogs. Walmart encourages employees to share candid opinions with the public, even when those opinions are negative comments on products the company sells.[43]

- **Recruiting.** Using a blog is a great way to let potential employees know more about your company, the people who work there, and the nature of the company culture. Conversely, companies can scan blogs and microblogs to find promising candidates. For instance, University of Oregon student Megan Soto caught the attention of the public relations and social media agency LaunchSquad after she wrote about one of the firm's clients on her Twitter account. LaunchSquad managers then studied her blog writing, which impressed them enough to invite her to interview, after which they hired her.[44]

- **Policy and issue discussions.** Executive blogs in particular provide a public forum for discussing legislation, regulations, and other broad issues of interest to an organization.

- **Crisis communication.** Using blogs is a convenient way to provide up-to-the-minute information during emergencies, correct misinformation, or respond to rumors.

- **Market research.** In addition to using their own blogs to solicit feedback, today's companies should monitor blogs that are likely to discuss them, their executives, and their products. Reputation analysts such as Evolve24 (**http://evolve24.com**) have developed ways to automatically monitor blogs and other online sources to see what people are saying about their corporate clients.[45]

- **Brainstorming.** Online brainstorming via blogs offers a way for people to toss around ideas and build on each other's contributions.

- **Employee engagement.** Blogs can enhance communication across all levels of a company. For example, as part of a program to align its corporate culture with changes in the global beverage market, Coca-Cola solicited feedback via blog comments from more than 20,000 employees.[46]

- **Viral marketing.** Bloggers often make a point of providing links to other blogs and websites that interest them, giving marketers a great opportunity to have their messages spread by enthusiasts. *Viral marketing* refers to the transmission of messages in much the same way that biological viruses are transmitted from person to person. (Although the term is used frequently, viral marketing is not really an accurate metaphor. Real viruses spread from host to host on their own, whereas these virtual "viruses" are spread *voluntarily* by their "hosts." The distinction is critical, because you need to give people a good reason—good content, in other words—to pass along your message.)

> Blogs are an ideal medium for *viral marketing*, the spread of promotional messages from one audience member to another.

- **Influencing traditional media news coverage.** According to social media consultant Tamar Weinberg, "the more prolific bloggers who provide valuable and consistent content are often considered experts in their subject matter" and are often called upon when journalists need insights into various topics.[47]

- **Community building.** Communities of readers can "grow" around a popular blog, as readers participate in the flow of ideas via comments on various posts.

The uses of blogs are limited only by your creativity, so be on the lookout for new ways you can use them to foster positive relationships with colleagues, customers, and other important audiences (see Figure 6.5 on the next page).

Adapting the Three-Step Process for Successful Blogging

The three-step writing process is easy to adapt to blogging tasks. The planning step is particularly important when you're launching a blog because you're planning an entire communication channel, not just a single message. Pay close attention to your audience, your purpose, and your scope:

- **Audience.** Except with team blogs and other efforts that have an obvious and well-defined audience, defining the target audience for a blog can be challenging. You want an audience large enough to justify the time you'll be investing but narrow enough that you can provide a clear focus for the blog. For instance, if you work for a firm that develops computer games, would you focus your blog on "hardcore" players, the types who spend thousands of dollars on super-fast PCs optimized for video games, or would you broaden the reach to include all video gamers? The decision often comes down to business strategy.

> Before you launch a blog, make sure you have a clear understanding of your target audience, the purpose of your blog, and the scope of subjects you plan to cover.

- **Purpose.** A business blog needs to have a business-related purpose that is important to your company and to your chosen audience. Moreover, the purpose has to "have legs"—that is, it needs to be something that can drive the blog's content for months or years—rather than focus on a single event or an issue of only temporary interest. For instance, if you're a technical expert, you might create a blog to give the audience tips and techniques for using your company's products more effectively—a never-ending subject that's important to both you and your audience. This would be the general purpose

Posts articles that interest her readers and encourage them to engage with her

Describes a contest conducted on her Twitter account

Posts comments from some of her Twitter followers, which helps to build the sense of community among her fans

Uses giveaways and other techniques to build her audience on various social media sites

Offers discounts to readers of her blog, which adds financial value to the sense of being part of her community

Category listing makes it easy for readers to find posts of interest

Figure 6.5   Elements of an Effective Business Blog

Amy Reed, owner of Pittsburgh's Chickdowntown clothing store, uses her blog and a variety of other social media tools to build a sense of community among her customers and to promote the store in a way that is compelling without being obtrusive.

of your blog; each posting would have a specific purpose within the context of that general purpose. Finally, if you are not writing an official company blog but rather blogging as an individual employee, make sure you understand your employer's blogging guidelines. As with e-mail and IM, more and more companies are putting policies in place to prevent employee mistakes with blogging.[48]

■ **Scope.** Defining the scope of your blog can be a bit tricky. You want to cover a subject area that is broad enough to offer discussion possibilities for months or years but narrow enough to have an identifiable focus. For instance, GM's FastLane blog is about GM cars only—not GM's stock price, financial challenges, or labor negotiations.

After you begin writing your blog, the careful planning needs to continue with each message. Unless you're posting to a restricted-access blog, such as an internal blog on a company intranet, you can never be sure who might see your posts. Other bloggers might link to them months or years later.

Write blog postings in a comfortable— but not careless—style.

Use a comfortable, personal writing style. Blog audiences don't want to hear from your company; they want to hear from *you*. Bear in mind, though, that comfortable does not mean careless. Sloppy writing damages your credibility. Successful blog content also needs to be interesting, valuable to readers, and as brief as possible.[49] In addition, although audiences expect you to be knowledgeable in the subject area your blog covers, you don't need to know everything about a topic. If you don't have all the information yourself, provide links to other blogs and websites that supply relevant information. In fact, *media curation*, selecting content to share in much the same way that museum curators decide which pieces of art to display, is one of the most valuable aspects of blogging. Just be sure that the content you share is relevant to your readers and compatible with your communication goals.

Completing messages for your blog is usually quite easy. Evaluate the content and readability of your message, proofread to correct any errors, and post using your blogging system's tools. Be sure to include one or more *newsfeed options* (often called RSS newsfeeds) so that your audience can automatically receive headlines and summaries of new blog posts. Whatever blogging system you are using can provide guidance on setting up newsfeeds. Finally, make your material easier to find by **tagging** it with descriptive words. Visitors to your blog who want to read everything you've written about recruiting just click on that word to see all your posts on that subject. Tagging can also help audiences locate your posts on blog trackers such as Technorati (http://technorati.com) or on **social bookmarking** or social news sites such as Delicious (http://delicious.com) and Digg (www.digg.com).

Table 6.3 summarizes a number of suggestions for successful blogging. For the latest information on using blogs in business, visit http://real-timeupdates.com/bce5 and click on Chapter 6.

TABLE 6.3 Tips for Effective Business Blogging

Tip	Why It's Important
Don't blog without a clear plan.	Without a clear plan, your blog is likely to wander from topic to topic and fail to build a sense of community with your audience.
Post frequently; the whole point of a blog is fresh material.	If you won't have a constant supply of new information or new links, create a traditional website instead.
Make it about your audience and the issues that are important to them.	Readers want to know how your blog will help them, entertain them, or give them a chance to communicate with others who have similar interests.
Write in an authentic voice; never create an artificial character who supposedly writes a blog.	*Flogs*, or fake blogs, violate the spirit of blogging, show disrespect for your audience, and will turn audiences against you as soon as they uncover the truth. Fake blogs used to promote products are now illegal in some countries.
Link generously—but carefully.	Providing interesting links to other blogs and websites is a fundamental aspect of blogging, but make sure the links will be of value to your readers and don't point to inappropriate material.
Keep it brief.	Most online readers don't have the patience to read lengthy reports. Rather than writing long, report-style posts, write brief posts that link to in-depth reports on your website.
Don't post anything you wouldn't want the entire world to see.	Future employers, government regulators, competitors, journalists, and community critics are just a few of the people who might eventually see what you've written.
Don't engage in blatant product promotion.	Readers who think they're being advertised to will stop reading.
Take time to write compelling, specific headlines for your postings.	Readers usually decide within a couple of seconds whether to read your postings; boring or vague headlines will turn them away instantly.
Pay attention to spelling, grammar, and mechanics.	No matter how smart or experienced you are, poor-quality writing undermines your credibility with intelligent audiences.
Respond to criticism openly and honestly.	Hiding sends the message that you don't have a valid response to the criticism. If your critics are wrong, patiently explain why you think they're wrong. If they are right, explain how you'll fix the situation.
Listen and learn.	If you don't take the time to analyze the comments people leave on your blog or the comments other bloggers make about you, you're missing out on one of the most valuable aspects of blogging.
Respect intellectual property.	Improperly using material you don't own is not only unethical but can be illegal as well.
Be scrupulously honest and careful with facts.	Honesty is an absolute requirement for every ethical business communicator, of course, but you need to be extra careful online because inaccuracies (both intentional and unintentional) are likely to be discovered quickly and shared widely.
If you review products on your blog, disclose any beneficial relationships you have with the companies that make those products.	Bloggers who receive free products or other compensation from companies whose products they write about are now required to disclose the nature of these relationships.

Microblogging

A **microblog** is a variation on blogging in which messages are sharply restricted to specific character counts. Twitter (**http://twitter.com**) is the best known of these systems, but many others exist. Some companies have private microblogging systems for internal use only; these systems are sometimes referred to as *enterprise microblogging* or *internal micromessaging*.[50]

> **DISCRETION** *Matters*   Every public tweet from every Twitter user is being archived by the Library of Congress.[51] If you plan a career in the public eye, tweet with care, because you are creating a public record.

Many of the concepts of regular blogging apply to microblogging as well, although the severe length limitations call for a different approach to composition. Microblog messages often involve short summaries or teasers that provide links to more information. In addition, microblogs tend to have a stronger social aspect that make it easier for writers and readers to forward messages and for communities to form around individual writers.[52]

Like regular blogging, microblogging quickly caught on with business users and is now a mainstream business medium. Microblogs are used for virtually all of the blog applications mentioned on pages 168–169. In addition, microblogs are frequently used for providing company updates, offering coupons and notice of sales, presenting tips on product usage, sharing relevant and interesting information from experts, serving as the backchannel in meetings and presentations, and interacting with customers individually (see Figure 6.6).

Like Facebook and YouTube, Twitter quickly became an important business communication medium.

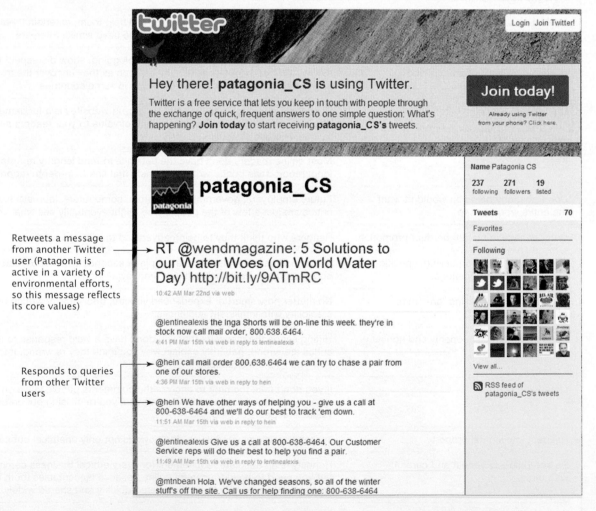

Retweets a message from another Twitter user (Patagonia is active in a variety of environmental efforts, so this message reflects its core values)

Responds to queries from other Twitter users

Figure 6.6   Business Applications of Microblogging
The outdoor clothing and equipment supplier Patagonia uses Twitter both as a general communication tool and as a way to interact with individual customers to answer questions and solve problems.

As microblogging evolves, the technology is gaining features that continue to enhance its value as a business communication medium. On Twitter, for instance, the ability to tag and search for specific words by means of a *hashtag* (the # symbol followed by a unique term) makes it easy for people to track topics of interest. For example, to establish a backchannel for a conference, you can create a unique hashtag (such as #WBSDCC, the hashtag used by Warner Brothers during the 2010 San Diego Comic-Con convention[53]) to help people follow messages on a particular subject. *Retweeting*, the practice of forwarding messages from other Twitter users, is the microblogging equivalent of sharing other content from other bloggers via media curation.

REAL-TIME UPDATES
Learn More by Reading This Article

Tweets from the boss: CEOs on Twitter

See how a number of CEOs are putting microblogging to work for their companies. Go to **http://real-timeupdates .com/bce5** and click on "Learn More." If you are using mybcommlab, you can access Real-Time Updates within each chapter or under Student Study Tools.

CREATING EFFECTIVE PODCASTS

Podcasting is the process of recording audio or video files and distributing them online. Although podcasting is not used as widely as blogging and some other electronic media, it does offer a number of interesting possibilities for business communication.

6 LEARNING OBJECTIVE

Explain how to adapt the three-step writing process for podcasts

Understanding the Business Applications of Podcasting

The most obvious use of podcasting is to replace existing audio and video messages, such as one-way teleconferences in which a speaker provides information without expecting to engage in conversation with the listeners. Training is another good use of podcasting; you may have already taken a college course via podcasts. Marketing departments can replace expensive printed brochures with video podcasts that demonstrate new products in action. Sales representatives who travel to meet with potential customers can listen to audio podcasts or view video podcasts to get the latest information on their companies' products. Human resources departments can offer video tours of their companies to entice new recruits. Podcasts are also an increasingly common feature on blogs, letting audiences listen to or watch recordings of their favorite bloggers. New services can even transcribe blogs into podcasts and vice versa.[54]

Podcasting can be used to deliver a wide range of audio and video messages.

Adapting the Three-Step Process for Successful Podcasting

Although it might not seem obvious at first, the three-step writing process adapts quite nicely to podcasting. First, focus the planning step on analyzing the situation, gathering the information you'll need, and organizing your material. One vital planning step depends on whether you intend to create podcasts for limited use and distribution (such as a weekly audio update to your virtual team) or to create a **podcasting channel** with regular recordings on a consistent theme, designed for a wider public audience. As with planning a blog, if you intend to create a podcasting channel, be sure to think through the range of topics you want to address over time to verify that you have a sustainable purpose. If you bounce from one theme to another, you risk losing your audience.[55]

The three-step process adapts quite well to podcasting.

- Melissa Popp (Millersville University), who is employed by Best Buy in Dover, Delaware, uses YouTube to educate her customers.
- Matthew Meyer (Indiana University) of Oakland, California, is an e-learning developer for Adecco who has written and produced a series of training podcasts for a major pharmaceutical client.

MEDIA
Choices Matter
Recent Grads Putting
Their Communication
Skills to Work

Steering devices such as transitions, previews, and reviews are vital in podcasts.

Plan your podcast content carefully; editing is more difficult with podcasts than with textual messages.

For basic podcasts, your computer and perhaps even your smartphone might have most of the hardware you already need, and you can download recording software.

As you organize the content for a podcast, pay close attention to previews, transitions, and reviews. These steering devices are especially vital in audio recordings because audio lacks the "street signs" (such as headings) that audiences rely on in print media. Moreover, scanning back and forth to find specific parts of an audio or video message is much more difficult than with textual messages, so you need to do everything possible to make sure your audience successfully receives and interprets your message on the first try.

One of the attractions of podcasting is the conversational, person-to-person feel of the recordings, so unless you need to capture exact wording, speaking from an outline and notes rather than a prepared script is often the best choice. However, no one wants to listen to rambling podcasts that take several minutes to get to the topic or struggle to make a point, so don't try to make up your content on the fly. Effective podcasts, like effective stories, have a clear beginning, middle, and end.

The completing step is where podcasting differs most dramatically from written communication, for the obvious reason that you are recording and distributing audio or video files. Particularly for more formal podcasts, start by revising your script or thinking through your speaking notes before you begin to record. The closer you can get to recording your podcasts in one take, the more productive you'll be.

Figure 6.7 illustrates the basic process of recording and distributing podcasts, but the process can vary depending on such factors as the production quality you need to achieve and whether you plan to record in a studio setting or on the go (using a mobile phone or digital recorder to capture your voice).

Most personal computers, smartphones, and other devices now have basic audio recording capability, including built-in microphones, and free editing software is available online (at **http://audacity.sourceforge.net**, for example). If you need higher production quality or greater flexibility, you'll need additional pieces of hardware and software, such as an audio processor (to filter out extraneous noise and otherwise improve the audio signal), a mixer (to combine multiple audio or video signals), a better microphone, more sophisticated recording and editing software, and perhaps some physical improvements in your recording location to improve the acoustics. You can find more information at Podcast Alley (**www.podcastalley.com/forum**) and Podcast Bunker (**www.podcastbunker.com**; click on "Podcasting Tips & Tools").

Podcasts can be distributed in several ways, including through media stores such as iTunes, by dedicated podcast hosting services, or on a blog with content that supports the podcast channel. If you distribute your podcast on a blog, you can provide additional information and use the commenting feature of the blog to encourage feedback from your audience.[56]

For the latest information on using podcasts in business, visit **http://real-timeupdates.com/bce5** and click on Chapter 6.

Figure 6.7   The Podcasting Process
Creating a podcast requires a few easy steps, and basic podcasts can be created using free or low-cost hardware and software.

CHAPTER REVIEW AND ACTIVITIES
Learning Objectives: Check Your Progress

1 OBJECTIVE Identify the major electronic media used for brief business messages, and describe the nine compositional modes needed for electronic media.

Electronic media for short business messages include social networking and community participation websites, e-mail, instant messaging (IM), text messaging, blogging and microblogging, podcasting, and online video. The nine compositional modes used in electronic communication are conversations, comments and critiques, orientations, summaries, reference materials, narratives, teasers, status updates and announcements, and tutorials.

2 OBJECTIVE Describe the use of social networks, user-generated content sites, and community Q&A sites in business communication.

Businesses now use a variety of social networks, including well-known public networks such as Facebook and business-oriented networks such as LinkedIn, as well as a variety of specialized networks, single-company networks for customers, and internal employee-only networks. The business communication applications of social networks are important and diverse; major uses include collaborating, gathering market intelligence, recruiting employees and connecting with business partners, marketing, and fostering brand communities. User-generated content sites such as YouTube allow companies to host media items (such as videos) that customers and other stakeholders can view, comment on, and share. Community Q&A sites give individuals the opportunity to build their personal brands by providing expertise, and they give companies the chance to address customer complaints and correct misinformation.

3 OBJECTIVE Describe the evolving role of e-mail in business communication, and explain how to adapt the three-step writing process to e-mail messages.

As the earliest widely available electronic written medium, e-mail was applied to a broad range of communication tasks—some it was well suited for and some it wasn't. Over time, newer media such as instant messaging, blogs, and social networks have been taking over some of these tasks, but e-mail remains a vital medium that is optimum for many private, short- to medium-length messages.

The three-step process adapts easily to e-mail communication. One of the most important planning decisions in crafting e-mail messages is making sure every message has a valuable purpose. Any key planning decision is to follow the chain of command in your organization; e-mailing over your boss's head is a good way to stir up resentment. When writing e-mail messages, bear in mind that the expectations of writing quality and formality are higher in business e-mail. Also, pay close attention to the wording of an e-mail message's subject line; it often determines whether and when recipients open and read the message. Effective subject lines are both informative (concisely identifying what the message is about) and compelling (giving readers a reason to read the message). Completing e-mail messages is straightforward. Proof and revise messages (particularly important ones), stick with a clean design, make use of the e-mail signature feature, and make sure you distribute the message to the right people.

4 OBJECTIVE Describe the business benefits of instant messaging (IM), and identify guidelines for effective IM in the workplace.

The benefits of IM include its capability for rapid response to urgent messages, lower cost than phone calls and e-mail, ability to mimic conversation more closely than e-mail, and availability on a wide range of devices.

As with e-mail, business IM needs to be treated as a professional medium to ensure safe and effective communication.

Be courteous in your use of IM to avoid interrupting others unnecessarily. Make yourself unavailable when you need to focus on other work, refrain from sending confidential information if you're not on a secure system, refrain from sending personal messages at work, avoid using IM for lengthy and complex messages, avoid carrying on multiple IM conversations at once, avoid IM slang with anyone other than close colleagues, and follow security guidelines.

5 OBJECTIVE Describe the use of blogging and microblogging in business communication, and briefly explain how to adapt the three-step process to blogging.

Blogs are used in numerous ways in business today, such as for project management and team communication, company news, customer support, public relations and media relations, employee recruiting, policy and issue discussions, crisis communication, market research, brainstorming, employee engagement, viral marketing, influencing traditional media news coverage, and community building. Microblogs such as Twitter are used for many of the same purposes as conventional blogging, along with electronic coupons, sale announcements, and one-on-one customer service queries. Microblogs can also serve as the backchannel during meetings and presentations.

The three-step process adapts readily to blogging. In planning, pay particular care to defining your audience, identifying the overall purpose of your blog and specific purposes of each post, and establishing a scope that is narrow enough to be focused but broad enough to afford a steady supply of topics. In writing, be sure to write in a personal, authentic style, without slipping into overly familiar or careless writing. Completing involves the usual tasks of proofing and revising, along with the particular tasks needed to distribute your posts via newsfeeds.

6 OBJECTIVE Explain how to adapt the three-step writing process for podcasts.

Although you record audio or video when creating podcasts rather than write messages, using the three-step process is an effective way to develop podcasts as well. Focus the planning step on analyzing the situation, gathering the information you'll need, and organizing your material. If you plan to create a series of podcasts on a given theme (the equivalent of starting a radio or television show), make sure you've identified a range of topics extensive enough to keep you going over time. As you organize and begin to think about the words or images you'll use as content, pay close attention to previews, transitions, and reviews so that audiences don't get lost while listening or watching. Finally, consider the necessary level of production quality; good-quality podcasts usually require some specialized hardware and software.

Test Your Knowledge

To review chapter content related to each question, refer to the indicated Learning Objective.

1. What are the situations in which a printed memo or letter might be preferable to an electronic message? [LO-1]
2. How can businesses make use of social networks such as Facebook for business communication? [LO-2]
3. How do the compositional modes of orientations, summaries, and teasers differ? [LO-2]
4. Does the three-step writing process apply to IM? Why or why not? [LO-4]
5. Why does a personal style of writing help blogs build stronger relationships with audiences? [LO-5]

Apply Your Knowledge

To review chapter content related to each question, refer to the indicated Learning Objective.

1. Given the strict limits on length, should all your microblogging messages function as teasers that link to more detailed information on a blog or website? Why or why not? [LO-1]
2. Is leveraging your connections on social networks for business purposes ethical? Why or why not? [LO-2]
3. If one of the benefits of blogging is the personal, intimate style of writing, is it a good idea to limit your creativity by adhering to conventional rules of grammar, spelling, and mechanics? Why or why not? [LO-5]
4. A former classmate reached out to you through LinkedIn and asked for a favor: Would you be willing to review her company's motorcycle accessories on your popular motorsports blog? What information would you need to make this decision, and how could you be sure you are making an ethical choice? [LO-5]
5. In your work as a video game designer, you know that eager players search the web for any scrap of information they can find about upcoming releases. In fact, to build interest, your company's public relations department carefully doles out small bits of information in the months before a new title hits the market. However, you and others in the company are also concerned about competitors getting their hands on all this "prerelease" information. If they learn too much too soon, they can use the information to improve their own products more quickly. You and several other designers and programmers maintain blogs that give players insights into game design techniques and that occasionally share tips and tricks. You have thousands of readers, and you know your blog helps build customer loyalty. The company president wants to ban blogging entirely so that bloggers don't accidentally share too much prerelease information about upcoming games. Would this be a wise move? Why or why not? [LO-5]

Practice Your Skills

Exercises for Perfecting Your Writing

To review chapter content related to each set of exercises, refer to the indicated Learning Objective.

Planning: Creating an Audience Profile, Selecting Media [LO-1], Chapter 3   You are in charge of public relations for a cruise line that operates out of Miami. You are shocked to read a letter in a local newspaper from a disgruntled passenger, complaining about the service and entertainment on a recent cruise. You will have to respond to these publicized criticisms in some way.

1. What audiences will you need to consider in your response?
2. For each of these audiences, which medium (or media) should you use to send your message?

Media Skills: Blogging [LO-5]   The members of the project team of which you are the leader have enthusiastically embraced blogging as a communication medium. Unfortunately, as emotions heat up during the project, some of the blog postings are getting too casual, too personal, and even sloppy. Because your boss and other managers around the company also read this project blog, you don't want the team to look unprofessional in anyone's eyes. Revise the following blog posting so that it communicates in a more businesslike manner while retaining the informal, conversational tone of a blog (be sure to correct any spelling and punctuation mistakes you find as well).

3. Well, to the profound surprise of absolutely nobody, we are not going to be able meet the June 1 commitment to ship 100 operating tables to Southeast Surgical Supply. (For those of you who have been living in a cave the past six month, we have been fighting to get our hands on enough high-grade chromium steel to meet our production schedule.) Sure enough, we got news, this morning that we will only get enough for 30 tables. Yes, we look lik fools for not being able to follow through on promises we made to the customer, but no, this didn't have to happpen. Six month's ago, purchasing warned us about shrinking supplies and suggested we advance-buy as much as we would need for the next 12 months, or so. We naturally tried to followed their advice, but just as naturally were shot down by the bean counters at corporate who trotted out the policy about never buying more than three months worth of materials in advance. Of course, it'll be us–not the bean counters who'll take the flak when everybody starts asking why revenues are down next quarter and why Southeast is talking to our friends at Crighton Manuf!!! Maybe, some day this company will get its head out of the sand and realize that we need to have some financial flexibility in order to compete.

Collaboration: Working in Teams; Planning: Selecting Media [Chapter 2; LO-1]   Working with at least two other students, identify the best medium to use for each of the following messages. For each of these message needs, choose a medium that you think would work effectively and explain your choice. (More than one medium could work in some cases; just be able to support your particular choice.)

4. A technical support service for people trying to use their digital music players
5. A message of condolence to the family of an employee who passed away recently
6. A message from the CEO of a small company, explaining that she is leaving the company to join a competitor
7. A series of observations on the state of the industry
8. A series of messages, questions, and answers surrounding the work of a project team

Media Skills: Writing E-Mail Subject Lines [LO-3]   Using your imagination to make up whatever details you need, revise the following e-mail subject lines to make them more informative:

9. New budget figures
10. Marketing brochure—your opinion
11. Production schedule

Activities

Active links for all websites in this chapter can be found on mybcommlab; see your User Guide for instructions on accessing the content for this chapter. Each activity is labeled according to the primary skill or skills you will need to use. To review relevant chapter content, you can refer to the indicated Learning Objective. In some instances, supporting information will be found in another chapter, as indicated.

1. **Media Skills: E-Mail [LO-3]**   The following e-mail message contains numerous errors related to what you've learned about planning and writing business messages. First, list the flaws you find in this version. Then use the following steps to plan and write a better memo.

TO: Felicia August <b_august@evertrust.com>
SUBJECT: Compliance with new break procedure

Some of you may not like the rules about break times; however, we determined that keeping track of employees while they took breaks at times they determined rather than regular breaks at prescribed times was not working as well as we would have liked it to work. The new rules are not going to be an option. If you do not follow the new rules, you could be docked from your pay for hours when you turned up missing, since your direct supervisor will not be able to tell whether you were on a "break" or not and will assume that you have walked away from your job. We cannot be responsible for any errors that result from your inattentiveness to the new rules. I have already heard complaints from some of you and I hope this memo will end this issue once and for all. The decision has already been made.

Starting Monday, January 1, you will all be required to take a regular 15-minute break in the morning and again in the afternoon, and a regular thirty-minute lunch at the times specified by your supervisor, NOT when you think you need a break or when you "get around to it."

There will be no exceptions to this new rule!

Felicia August

Manager

Billing and accounting

a. Describe the flaws you discovered in this e-mail message.

b. Develop a plan for rewriting the message. Use the following steps to organize your efforts before you begin writing:

1. Determine the purpose.
2. Identify and analyze your audience.
3. Define the main idea.
4. Outline the major supporting points.
5. Choose between a direct and an indirect approach.

c. Now rewrite the e-mail message. Don't forget to leave ample time for revision of your own work before you turn it in.

2. **Media Skills: Instant Messaging [LO-4]**   Review the following IM exchange and explain how the customer service agent could have handled the situation more effectively.

AGENT:	Thanks for contacting Home Exercise Equipment. What's up?
CUSTOMER:	I'm having trouble assembling my home gym.
AGENT:	I hear that a lot! LOL
CUSTOMER:	So is it me or the gym?
AGENT:	Well, let's see <g>. Where are you stuck?
CUSTOMER:	The crossbar that connects the vertical pillars doesn't fit.
AGENT:	What do you mean doesn't fit?
CUSTOMER:	It doesn't fit. It's not long enough to reach across the pillars.
AGENT:	Maybe you assembled the pillars in the wrong place. Or maybe we sent the wrong crossbar.
CUSTOMER:	How do I tell?
AGENT:	The parts aren't labeled so could be tough. Do you have a measuring tape? Tell me how long your crossbar is.

3. **Media Skills: Blogging [LO-5]**   Read the following blog post and (a) analyze the strengths and weaknesses of each sentence and (b) revise it so that it follows the guidelines in this chapter.

[headline]

We're DOOMED!!!!!

[post]

I was at the Sikorsky plant in Stratford yesterday, just checking to see how things were going with the assembly line retrofit we did for them last year. I think I saw the future, and it ain't pretty. They were demo'ing a prototype robot from Motoman that absolutely blows our stuff out of the water. They wouldn't let me really see it, but based on the 10-second glimpse I got, it's smaller, faster, and more maneuverable than any of our units. And when I asked about the price, the guy just grinned. And it wasn't the sort of grin designed to make me feel good.

I've been saying for years that we need to pay more attention to size, speed, and maneuverability instead of just relying on our historical strengths of accuracy and payload capacity, and you'd have to be blind not to agree that this experience proves me right. If we can't at least show a design for a better unit within two or three months, Motoman is going to lock up the market and leave us utterly in the dust.

Believe me, being able to say "I told you so" right now is not nearly as satisfying as you might think!!

4. **Media Skills: Blogging [LO-5]**   From what you've learned about planning and writing business messages, you should be able to identify numerous errors made by the writer of the following blog posting. List them below and then plan and write a better post, following the guidelines given.

[headline]

Get Ready!

[post]

We are hoping to be back at work soon, with everything running smoothly, same production schedule and no late projects or missed deadlines. So you need to clean out your desk, put your stuff in boxes, and clean off the walls. You can put the items you had up on your walls in boxes, also.

   We have provided boxes. The move will happen this weekend. We'll be in our new offices when you arrive on Monday.

   We will not be responsible for personal belongings during the move.

a. Describe the flaws you discovered in this blog post.

b. Develop a plan for rewriting the post. Use the following steps to organize your efforts before you begin writing:

1. Determine the purpose.
2. Identify and analyze your audience.
3. Define the main idea.
4. Outline the major supporting points.
5. Choose between direct and indirect approaches.

c. Now rewrite the post. Don't forget to leave ample time for revision of your own work before you turn it in.

 Learn how to set up a Twitter account and begin tweeting. Visit http://real-timeupdates.com/bce5, click on "Student Assignments" and then click on "Twitter Screencast."

5. **Media Skills: Microblogging [LO-5]**   Busy knitters can go through a lot of yarn in a hurry, so most keep a sharp eye out for sales. You're on the marketing staff of Knitting-Warehouse, and you like to keep your loyal shoppers up to date with the latest deals. Visit the "Sale Items!" section of the Knitting-Warehouse website at **www.knitting-warehouse.com**, select any product that catches your eye, and write a Twitter update that describes the product and the sale. Be sure to include a link back to the website so your Twitter followers can learn more.

6. **Media Skills: Podcasting [LO-6]**   You've recently begun recording a weekly podcast to share information with your large and far-flung staff. After a month, you ask for feedback from several of your subordinates, and you're disappointed to learn that some people stopped listening to the podcast after the first couple weeks. Someone eventually admits that many

staffers feel the recordings are too long and rambling, and the information they contain isn't valuable enough to justify the time it takes to listen. You aren't pleased, but you want to improve. An assistant transcribes the introduction to last week's podcast so you can review it. You immediately see two problems. Revise the introduction based on what you've learned in this chapter.

So there I am, having lunch with Selma Gill, who just joined and took over the Northeast sales region from Jackson Stroud. In walks our beloved CEO with Selma's old boss at Uni-Plex; turns out they were finalizing a deal to co-brand our products and theirs and to set up a joint distribution program in all four domestic regions. Pretty funny, huh? Selma left Uni-Plex because she wanted sell our products instead, and now she's back selling her old stuff, too. Anyway, try to chat with her when you can; she knows the biz inside and out and probably can offer insight into just about any sales challenge you might be running up against. We'll post more info on the co-brand deal next week; should be a boost for all of us. Other than those two news items, the other big news this week is the change in commission reporting. I'll go into the details in minute, but when you log onto the intranet, you'll now see your sales results split out by product line and industry sector. Hope this helps you see where you're doing well and where you might beef things up a bit. Oh yeah, I almost forgot the most important bit. Speaking of our beloved CEO, Thomas is going to be our guest of honor, so to speak, at the quarterly sales meeting next week and wants an update on how petroleum prices are affecting customer behavior. Each district manager should be ready with a brief report. After I go through the commission reporting scheme, I'll outline what you need to prepare.

7. **Media Skills: Podcasting [LO-6]**   To access this podcast exercise, visit http://real-timeupdates.com/bce5, click on "Student Assignments," and select "Chapter 6, page 147, Activity 7" and listen to this podcast. Identify at least three ways in which the podcast could be improved and draft a brief e-mail message that you could send to the podcaster with your suggestions for improvement.

▌ Expand Your Skills

Critique the Professionals

Locate the YouTube channel page of any company you find interesting and assess its social networking presence using the criteria for effective communication discussed in this chapter and your own experience using social media. What does this company do well with its YouTube channel? How might it improve? Using whatever medium your instructor requests, write a brief analysis of the company's YouTube presence (no more than one page), citing specific elements from the piece and support from the chapter.

Sharpen Your Career Skills Online

Bovée and Thill's Business Communication Web Search, at http://businesscommunicationblog.com/websearch, is a unique research tool designed specifically for business communication research. Use the Web Search function to find a website, video, PDF document, podcast, or PowerPoint presentation that offers advice on using social media in business. Write a brief e-mail message to your instructor or a post for your class blog, describing the item that you found and summarizing the career skills information you learned from it.

mybcommlab

If your course uses mybcommlab, log on to www.mybcommlab.com to access the following study and assessment aids associated with this chapter:

- Video applications
- Pre/post test
- Real-Time Updates
- Personalized study plan
- Peer review activity
- Model documents
- Quick Learning Guides
- Sample presentations

If you are not using mybcommlab, you can access Real-Time Updates and Quick Learning Guides through http://real-timeupdates.com/bce5. The Quick Learning Guide (located under "Learn More" on the website) hits all the high points of this chapter in just two pages. This guide, especially prepared by the authors, will help you study for exams or review important concepts whenever you need a quick refresher.

CASES

▼ *Apply the three-step writing process to the following cases, as assigned by your instructor.*

 Learn how to get started on Facebook. Visit http://real-timeupdates .com/bce5, click on "Student Assignments" and then click on "Facebook Screencast."

SOCIAL NETWORKING SKILLS

1. Media Skills: Social Networking [LO-2] Consumers looking for beauty, health, and lifestyle magazines have an almost endless array of choices, but even in this crowded field, Logan Olson found her own niche. Olson, who was born with congenital heart disease, suffered a heart attack at age 16 that left her in a coma and caused serious brain damage. The active and outgoing teen had to relearn everything from sitting up to feeding herself. As she recovered, she looked for help and advice in conquering such daily challenges as finding fashionable clothes that were easier to put on and makeup that was easier to apply. Mainstream beauty magazines didn't seem to offer any information for young women with disabilities, so she started her own magazine. *Logan* gives young women with disabilities tips on buying and using a variety of products and lets readers know there are others out there like them, facing and meeting the same challenges.

Your task Write a Wall post for your Facebook page that briefly tells Olson's story and promotes the magazine. Include a link to the Logan website (**www.loganmagazine.com**) and mention that annual subscriptions (four issues) cost only $14. The "Stories" section of the website offers more information, including a video, about Olson and her efforts to launch the magazine.[57]

SOCIAL NETWORKING SKILLS

2. Media Skills: Social Networking [LO-2] Business networking websites such as **www.linkedin.com, www.ryze.com**, and **www .spoke.com** have become popular places for professionals to make connections that would be difficult or impossible to make without the Internet. An important aspect of business networking is being able to provide a clear description of your professional background and interests. For example, a manufacturing consultant can list the industries in which she has experience, the types of projects she has worked on, and the nature of work she'd like to pursue in the future (such as a full-time position for a company or additional independent projects).

Your task Write a brief statement to introduce yourself, including your educational background, your job history, and the types of connections you'd like to make. Feel free to "fast forward" to your graduation and list your degree, the business specialty you plan to pursue, and any relevant experience. If you have business experience already, feel free to use that information instead. Make sure your statement is clear, concise (no

more than two sentences), and compelling so that anyone looking for someone like you would want to get in touch with you after reading your introduction.

E-MAIL SKILLS   PORTFOLIO BUILDER

3. Media Skills: E-Mail [LO-3] One-quarter of all motor vehicle accidents that involve children under age 12 are side-impact crashes—and these crashes result in higher rates of injuries and fatalities than those with front or rear impacts.

Your task You work in the consumer information department at Britax, a leading manufacturer of car seats. Your manager has asked you to prepare an e-mail message that can be sent out whenever parents request information about side-impact crashes and the safety features of Britax seats. Start by researching side-impact crashes at **www.britaxusa.com** (click on "Safety Center" and then "Side Impact Protection Revealed"). Write a three-paragraph message that explains the seriousness of side-impact crashes, describes how injuries and fatalities can be minimized in these crashes, and describes how Britax's car seats are designed to help protect children in side-impact crashes.[58]

E-MAIL SKILLS

4. Media Skills: E-Mail [LO-3] Many companies operate on the principle that the customer is always right, even when the customer *isn't* right. They take any steps necessary to ensure happy customers, lots of repeat sales, and a positive reputation among potential buyers. Overall, this is a smart and successful approach to business.

However, most companies eventually encounter a nightmare customer who drains so much time, energy, and profits that the only sensible option is to refuse the customer's business. For example, the nightmare customer might be someone who constantly berates you and your employees, repeatedly makes outlandish demands for refunds and discounts, or simply requires so much help that you not only lose money on this person but also no longer have enough time to help your other customers. "Firing" a customer is an unpleasant step that should be taken only in the most extreme cases and only after other remedies have been attempted (such as talking with the customer about the problem), but it is sometimes necessary for the well-being of your employees and your company.

Your task If you are currently working or have held a job in the recent past, imagine that you've encountered just such a customer. If you don't have job experience to call on, imagine that you work in a retail location somewhere around campus or in your neighborhood. Identify the type of behavior this imaginary customer exhibits and the reasons the behavior can no longer be accepted. Making up any details you need, write a brief e-mail message to the customer to explain that you will no longer be able to accommodate him or her as a customer. Calmly explain why you have had to reach this difficult decision. Maintain a professional tone and keep your emotions in check.

E-MAIL SKILLS

5. Media Skills: E-Mail [LO-3] The physical difference between the women who model clothes and women who buy them has long been a point of contention for shoppers—and a point of concern for health advocates who say that many fashion models are thin to the point of being unhealthy. The super-thin look not only is unhealthy for the models, but also, critics say, encourages eating disorders among girls and women who aspire to look like them.

Some industry insiders admit that the images portrayed in fashion advertising are often unrealistic. Designer and television host Tim Gunn says the problem starts with an unrealistic assumption in the illustration stage, when designers are sketching new clothes. "The way in which we illustrate [a model's body] is seven heads high, which isn't normal. We're always striving to have the same look of the illustration on the runway, and it's impossible. You have a few—forgive me—freaky people who can approximate that size and shape, but this look is not part of the real world."

Models weren't always much thinner than the general population, and the pendulum seems to be swinging back toward more normal body types—at least slightly. La Maison Simons, a Canadian retailer, recently pulled its back-to-school catalog following complaints that its models were too thin; the company replaced the catalog and issued an apology. Ken Downing, fashion director at the upscale American retailer Neiman-Marcus, explains, "Any retailer has to consider [its] customer and who [it's] trying to appeal to. There are models of all shapes and sizes, and the people who do the advertising and marketing really have to be conscious that they're portraying healthy, beautiful women of many ages and many colors from many backgrounds."[59]

Your task Imagine that you're the director of catalog operations at La Maison Simons, and you want to make sure that the embarrassing episode with the catalog isn't repeated. Write a brief e-mail to the catalog staff, outlining the company's new policy of using only models with healthy body mass indexes. (Make up any information you need to draft the message.) You can visit the company's website, at **www.simons.ca**, to learn more about its products, and you can research body mass index at a variety of health-related websites.

E-MAIL SKILLS   TEAM SKILLS   PORTFOLIO BUILDER

6. Media Skills: E-Mail [LO-3] For the first time in history, aside from special situations such as major wars, more than half of all U.S. adult women now live without a spouse. (In other words, they live alone, with roommates, or as part of an unmarried couple.) Twenty-five percent have never married, and 26 percent are divorced, widowed, or married but living apart from their spouses. In the 1950s and into the 1960s, only 40 percent of women lived without a spouse, but every decade since, the percentage has increased. In your work as a consumer trend specialist

for Seymour Powell (www.seymourpowell.com), a product design firm based in London that specializes in the home, personal, leisure, and transportation sectors, it's your business to recognize and respond to demographic shifts such as this.

Your task With a small team of classmates, brainstorm possible product opportunities that respond to this trend. In an e-mail message to be sent to the management team at Seymour Powell, list your ideas for new or modified products that might sell well in a society in which more than half of all adult women live without a spouse. For each idea, provide a one-sentence explanation of why you think the product has potential.[60]

IM SKILLS

7. Media Skills: Instant Messaging [LO-4] High-definition television can be a joy to watch—but, oh, what a pain to buy. The field is littered with competing technologies and arcane terminology that is meaningless to most consumers. Moreover, it's nearly impossible to define one technical term without invoking two or three others, leaving consumers swimming in an alphanumeric soup of confusion. The manufacturers themselves can't even agree on which of the many different digital TV formats truly qualify as "high definition." As a sales support manager for Crutchfield (www.crutchfield.com), a leading online retailer of audio and video systems, you understand the frustration buyers feel; your staff is deluged daily by their questions.

Your task To help your staff respond quickly to consumers who ask questions via Crutchfield's online IM chat service, you are developing a set of "canned" responses to common questions. When a consumer asks one of these questions, a sales advisor can simply click on the ready-made answer. Start by writing concise, consumer-friendly definitions of the following terms: *resolution, HDTV, 1080p,* and *HDMI*. (On the Crutchfield website, click on "Learn," "TVs, Blu-ray & Gaming," and then "Televisions" to learn more about these terms. Look for the video "Choosing an HDTV" and the article "HDTV: An Introduction.")[61]

BLOGGING SKILLS

8. Media Skills: Blogging [LO-5] You work for PreVisor, one of many companies that offer employee screening and testing services. PreVisor's offerings include a variety of online products and consulting services, all designed to help employers find and develop the best possible employees.

To help explain the value of its products and services, PreVisor publishes a variety of customer *case studies* on its website. Each case study describes the staffing challenges a particular company faces, the solution PreVisor was able to provide, and the results the company experienced after using PreVisor products or services.

Your task Select one of the customer case studies on the PreVisor website (www.previsor.com/results/clients). Write a post that could appear on PreVisor's blog, summarizing the challenges, solution, and results in no more than 100 words. Include a link to the complete case study on the PreVisor website.

BLOGGING SKILLS   TEAM SKILLS
PORTFOLIO BUILDER

9. Media Skills: Blogging [LO-5] U.S. automakers haven't had much good news to share lately. GM, in particular, has been going through a rough time, entering bankruptcy, shedding assets, and relying on bailouts from the U.S. and Canadian governments to stay in business. The news isn't entirely bleak, however. Chevrolet, one of the brands in the GM automotive stable, is about to introduce the Volt, a gas/electric hybrid that might finally give drivers a viable alternative to the wildly popular Toyota Prius.

Your task Working with a team assigned by your instructor, write a post for GM's dealer-only blog that describes the new Volt and the benefits it offers car owners. Include at least one photo and one link to the Volt section of GM's website. You can learn more about the Volt at Chevy's website, www.chevrolet.com.

BLOGGING SKILLS   TEAM SKILLS

10. Media Skills: Blogging [LO-5] The fact that 97 percent of American youth ages 12 to 17 play video games is not much of a surprise. However, more than a few adults might be surprised to learn that playing video games might not be quite the social and civic catastrophe it is sometimes made out to be. A recent study by the Pew Internet & American Life Project calls into question the stereotyped image of gamers being loners who live out violent fantasies while learning few if any skills that could make them positive members of society.[62]

Your task Working with a team assigned by your instructor, imagine that you're on the public relations staff at the Entertainment Software Association (ESA), an industry group that represents the interests of video game companies. You'd like to share the results of the Pew survey with parents to help ease their concerns. Visit http://real-timeupdates.com/bce5, click on "Student Assignments" and then "Chapter 6, page 150, Case 10." Download this PDF file, which is a summary of the Pew results. Find at least three positive aspects of video game playing and write a post that could be posted on an ESA public affairs blog.

 Learn how to set up a Twitter account and begin tweeting. Visit http://real-timeupdates.com/bce5, click on "Student Assignments" and then click on "Twitter Screencast."

MICROBLOGGING SKILLS

11. Media Skills: Microblogging [LO-5] JetBlue is known for its innovations in customer service and customer communication, including its pioneering use of the Twitter microblogging system. Thousands of JetBlue fans and customers follow the company on Twitter to get updates on flight status during weather disruptions, facility upgrades, and other news.[63]

Your task Write a Twitter update that announces the limited-time availability of flights and travel packages (flights plus hotel rooms, for example) at JetBlue's store on eBay. The key selling point is that travelers may be able to purchase flights they want at steep discounts. Include the URL http://jetblue .com/ebay. The URL takes up 24 characters, so you have a maximum of 116 characters for the rest of your message, including spaces.

BLOGGING SKILLS

12. Media Skills: Blogging [LO-5] Comic-Con International is an annual convention that highlights a wide variety of pop culture and entertainment media, from comic books and collectibles to video games and movies. From its early start as a comic book convention that attracted several hundred fans and publishing industry insiders, Comic-Con has become a major international event, with more than 125,000 attendees.

Your task Several readers of your pop culture blog have been asking for your recommendation about visiting Comic-Con in San Diego next summer. Write a two- or three-paragraph posting for your blog that explains what Comic-Con is and what visitors can expect to experience at the convention. Be sure to address your posting to fans, not industry insiders. You can learn more at www.comic-con.org.[64]

PODCASTING SKILLS   PORTFOLIO BUILDER

13. Media Skills: Podcasting [LO-6] With any purchase decision, from a restaurant meal to a college education, recommendations from satisfied customers are often the strongest promotional messages.

Your task Write a script for a one- to two-minute podcast (roughly 150 to 250 words) explaining why your college or university is a good place to get an education. Your audience is high school juniors and seniors. You can choose to craft a general message, something that would be useful to all prospective students, or you can focus on a specific academic discipline, the athletic program, or some other important aspect of your college experience. Either way, make sure your introductory comments clarify whether you are offering a general recommendation or a specific recommendation. If your instructor asks you to do so, record the podcast and submit the file electronically.

PODCASTING SKILLS   PORTFOLIO BUILDER

14. Media Skills: Podcasting [LO-6] What product do you own (or use regularly) that you can't live without? It could be something as seemingly minor as a favorite pen or something as significant as a medical device that you literally can't live without. Now imagine that you're a salesperson for this product; think about how you would sell it to potential buyers. How would you describe it, and how would you explain the benefits of owning it? After you've thought about how you would present the product to others, imagine that you've been promoted to a sales manager position, and it is your job to train other people to sell the product.

Your task Write the script for a brief podcast (200 to 300 words) that summarizes for your sales staff the most important points to convey about the product. Imagine that they'll listen to your podcast while driving to a customer's location or preparing for the day's activity in a retail store (depending on the nature of the product). Be sure to give your staffers a concise overview message about the product and several key support points. If your instructor asks you to do so, record the podcast and submit the file electronically.

PODCASTING SKILLS   PORTFOLIO BUILDER

15. Media Skills: Podcasting [LO-6] While writing the many letters and electronic messages that are part of the job search process, you find yourself wishing that you could just talk to some of these companies so your personality could shine through. Well, you've just gotten that opportunity. One of the companies that you've applied to has e-mailed you back, asking you to submit a two-minute podcast introducing yourself and explaining why you would be a good person to hire.

Your task Identify a company that you'd like to work for after graduation and select a job that would be a good match for your skills and interests. Write a script for a two-minute podcast (two minutes represents roughly 250 words for most speakers). Introduce yourself and the position you're applying for, describe your background, and explain why you think you're a good candidate for the job. Make up any details you need. If your instructor asks you to do so, record the podcast and submit the file electronically.

Improve Your Grammar, Mechanics, and Usage

You can download the text of this assignment from **http://real-timeupdates.com/bce5**; click on "Student Assignments" and then click on "Chapter 6. Improve Your Grammar, Mechanics, and Usage."

Level 1: Self-Assessment—Prepositions and Conjunctions

Review Sections 1.6.1 and 1.6.2 in the Handbook of Grammar, Mechanics, and Usage and then complete the following 15 items.

Rewrite items 1–5, deleting unnecessary words and prepositions and adding required prepositions:

1. Where was your argument leading to?
2. I wish he would get off of the phone.
3. This is a project into which you can sink your teeth.
4. U.S. Mercantile must become aware and sensitive to its customers' concerns.
5. We are responsible for aircraft safety in the air, the hangars, and the runways.

In items 6–10, provide the missing preposition:

6. Dr. Namaguchi will be talking _____ the marketing class, but she has no time for questions.
7. Matters like this are decided after thorough discussion _____ all seven department managers.
8. We can't wait _____ their decision much longer.
9. Their computer is similar _____ ours.
10. This model is different _____ the one we ordered.

In items 11–15, rewrite the sentences to make phrases parallel.

11. She is active in not only a civic group but also in an athletic organization.
12. That is either a mistake or was an intentional omission.
13. The question is whether to set up a booth at the convention or be hosting a hospitality suite.
14. We are doing better in both overall sales and in profits.
15. She had neither the preferred educational background, nor did she have suitable experience.

Level 2: Workplace Applications

The following items may contain errors in grammar, capitalization, punctuation, abbreviation, number style, word division, and vocabulary. Rewrite each sentence, correcting all errors. If a sentence has no errors, write "Correct" for that number.

1. Peabody Energys commitment to environmental excellence is driven by the companies' mission statement which states that when mining is complete, the company will leave the land in a condition equal or better than it was before mining.
2. In 1998, Blockbuster opened a state of the art distribution center in McKinney, Texas, just North of the company's Dallas Headquarters.
3. Miss Tucci was responsible for developing Terraspring's business plan, establishing the brand, and for launching the company.
4. The principle goals of the new venture will be to offer tailored financial products and meeting the needs of the community.
5. Nestle Waters North America are the number one bottled water company in the U.S. and Canada.
6. The reason egg prices dropped sharply is because of a Post Easter reduction in demand.
7. Joining bank officials during the announcement of the program were U.S. congressman Luis V. Guitierrez, Carlos Manuel Sada Solana, General Consul of Mexico in the Midwest, and "Don Francisco", the leading hispanic entertainment figure in the United States and Latin America.
8. The summer advertising campaign is the most unique in 7-Eleven's history.
9. Upon introducing it's new Quadruple Fudge flavor, consumers are expected to flock to Baskin-Robbins ice cream parlors.
10. The signing of a Trade Pact between the european union and Chile, is being delayed by european negotiators who insist the deal includes an agreement requiring Chile to stop using the names Cognac, Champagne, and Burgundy.
11. Federal Trade commissioner, Mrs. Sheila F. Anthony called on the dietary supplement industry to institute better self regulation, and called on the media to refuse ads containing claims that are obviously false.
12. Founded in 1971, GSD&M has grown to become a nationally-acclaimed advertising agency with more than 500 employees and having billings of over $1 billion dollars.

13. Although marketing may seem to be the easier place to cut costs during a downturn its actually the last place you should look to make strategic cuts.

14. After closing their plant in Mecosta county, Green Mountain will have less than 200 employees.

15. The purchasing needs of professional's differ from blue collar workers.

Level 3: Document Critique

The following document may contain errors in grammar, capitalization, punctuation, abbreviation, number style, word division, and vocabulary. As your instructor indicates, photocopy this page and correct all errors using standard proofreading marks (see Appendix C) or download the document and make the corrections in your word processing software.

TO: George Kimball <g.kimball@sprenco.com>

SUBJECT: My trip back East

Dear George:

I went back to New York for apresentation the 15th of this month and I found it very informative. The sponsor of my visat was Vern Grouper. Vern is the Manager of IS at headquarters; that is, their centralized information systems operation. They've got quite a bit of power out there. And they do encourage us to utilize their capibilities, there services, and experiences to whatever extent will be beneficial to us. However, you could say it would be my observation that although they have a tremendous amount of computing capability that capability is directed toward a business dimension very different than ours and unlike anything we have. However, their are certain services that might be performed in our behalf by headquarters. For example, we could utilize people such as Vern to come and address our IS advisory group since I am planning on convening that group on a monthly basis.

By the way, I need to talk to you about the IS advicory group when you get a chance. I have 1 or 2 thoughts about some new approaches we can take with it I'd like to run by you if you don't mind. Its not too complicated just some simple ideas.

Let me know what you think of this idea about Vern coming here. If you like it than I will go ahead and set things in motion with Vern.

Sincerely,

John

Writing Routine and Positive Messages

LEARNING OBJECTIVES

After studying this chapter, you will be able to

1 Outline an effective strategy for writing routine business requests

2 Describe three common types of routine requests

3 Outline an effective strategy for writing routine replies and positive messages

4 Describe six common types of routine replies and positive messages

---

PEARSON mybcommlab Access interactive videos, simulations, sample documents, Document Makeovers, and assessment quizzes in Chapter 7 of mybcommlab.com for mastery of this chapter's objectives.

> **"** To succeed, I don't need to be Shakespeare; I must, though, have a sincere desire to inform. **"**
>
> —Warren Buffett, *Legendary investor and chairman of Berkshire Hathaway*

COMMUNICATION *Matters*

Warren Buffett's financial acumen has made him and many of his shareholders wealthy, but he is recognized almost as widely for his communication skills. His letters, essays, and annual reports communicate complex financial topics in simple language that his readers can easily understand. His approach is simple: Even for a document that will be read by thousands of people, he visualizes a single person (often one of his sisters) as his audience. He treats this audience member as an intelligent human being, but someone who doesn't have the same level of experience with the subject matter he has. From there, he proceeds to organize and write his messages in a way that clarifies all the essential information and doesn't try to impress or obscure with complicated language.[1]

Whether you're posting a status update on a team blog or producing a report for an audience of thousands, Buffett's approach is a great example to follow. This chapter addresses routine and positive messages, including routine requests for information or action, replies on routine business matters, and positive messages such as good-news announcements and goodwill messages.

Warren Buffett often deals with complex financial issues in his line of business, but he has cultivated the ability to express even complicated subjects in clear, simple language that seeks to inform rather than to impress.

● Access this chapter's simulation entitled Routine Messages, located at mybcommlab.com.

Figure 7.1 Routine Messages
Routine and positive messages are best conveyed using a direct approach. Google uses this blog to keep users of its AdWords search engine advertising system up to date on maintenance interruptions and other important news.

---

1 LEARNING OBJECTIVE

Outline an effective strategy for writing routine business requests

For routine requests and positive messages

- State the request or main idea
- Give necessary details
- Close with a cordial request for specific action

Take care that your direct approach doesn't come across as abrupt or tactless.

STRATEGY FOR ROUTINE REQUESTS

Making requests—for information, action, products, adjustments, or other matters—is a routine part of business (see Figure 7.1). In most cases, your audience will be prepared to comply, as long as you're not being unreasonable or asking people to do work they would expect you to do yourself. By applying a clear strategy and tailoring your approach to each situation, you'll be able to generate effective requests quickly.

Like all other business messages, routine requests have three parts: an opening, a body, and a close. Using the direct approach, open with your main idea, which is a clear statement of your request. Use the body to give details and justify your request, then close by requesting specific action.

Stating Your Request Up Front

Begin routine requests by placing your initial request first; up front is where it stands out and gets the most attention. Of course, getting right to the point should not be interpreted as license to be abrupt or tactless:

- **Pay attention to tone.** Instead of demanding action ("Send me the latest version of the budget spreadsheet"), soften your request with words such as *please* and *I would appreciate*.
- **Assume that your audience will comply.** You can generally make the assumption that your audience members will comply when they clearly understand the reason for your request.
- **Be specific.** State precisely what you want. For example, if you request the latest market data from your research department, be sure to say whether you want a 1-page summary or 100 pages of raw data.

Explaining and Justifying Your Request

Use the body of your message to explain your request. Make the explanation a smooth and logical outgrowth of your opening remarks. If complying with the request could benefit the reader, be sure to mention that. You can also use the body to ask questions that will help you organize the message and help your audience identify the information you need. When asking such questions, consider these tips:

- **Ask the most important questions first.** If cost is your main concern, you might begin with a question such as "How much will it cost to have our new website created by an outside firm?" Then you may want to ask more specific but related questions, such as whether discounts are available for paying early.

- **Ask only relevant questions.** To help expedite the response to your request, ask only questions that are central to your main request.

- **Deal with only one topic per question.** If you have an unusual or complex request, break it down into specific, individual questions so that the reader can address each one separately. This consideration not only shows respect for your audience's time but also gets you a more accurate answer in less time.

If you have multiple requests or questions, start with the most important one.

Requesting Specific Action in a Courteous Close

Close your message with three important elements: (1) a specific request that includes any relevant deadlines, (2) information about how you can be reached (if it isn't obvious), and (3) an expression of appreciation or goodwill. For example: "Please send the figures by April 5 so that I can return first-quarter results to you before the April 15 board meeting. I appreciate your help." Concluding your note with "Thank you" or "Thanks for your help" is fine, although "Thank you in advance" is considered a bit stuffy and presumptuous.

Close request messages with
- *A request for some specific action*
- *Information about how you can be reached*
- *An expression of appreciation*

COMMON EXAMPLES OF ROUTINE REQUESTS

The most common types of routine messages are asking for information or action, asking for recommendations, and making claims and requesting adjustments.

2 LEARNING OBJECTIVE
Describe three common types of routine requests

Asking for Information or Action

When you need to know about something, elicit an opinion from someone, or request a simple action, you usually need only ask. In essence, simple requests say

- What you want to know or what you want readers to do
- Why you're making the request
- Why it may be in your readers' interest to help you (if applicable)

For simple requests, a straightforward request gets the job done with a minimum of fuss. In more complex situations, you may need to provide more extensive reasons and justification for your request. Naturally, be sure to adapt your request to your audience and the situation (see Figure 7.2 on the next page).

Routine requests can be handled with simple, straightforward messages, but more complicated requests can require additional justification and explanation.

Asking for Recommendations

The need to inquire about people arises often in business. For example, before extending credit or awarding contracts, jobs, promotions, or scholarships, companies often ask applicants to supply references. Companies ask applicants to list references who can vouch for their ability, skills, integrity, character, and fitness for the job. Before you volunteer someone's name as a reference, ask permission to do so. Some people don't want you to use their names, perhaps because they don't know enough about you to feel comfortable writing a letter or because they or their employers have a policy of not providing recommendations.

Always ask for permission before using someone as a reference.

Requests for recommendations and references are routine, so you can organize your inquiry using the direct approach. Open your message by clearly stating why the recommendation is required (if it's not for a job, be sure to explain what it is for) and that you would like your reader to write the letter. If you haven't had contact with the person for some time, use the opening to trigger the reader's memory of the relationship you had, the dates of association, and any special events that might bring a clear and favorable picture of you to mind.

Refresh the memory of any potential reference you haven't been in touch with for a while.

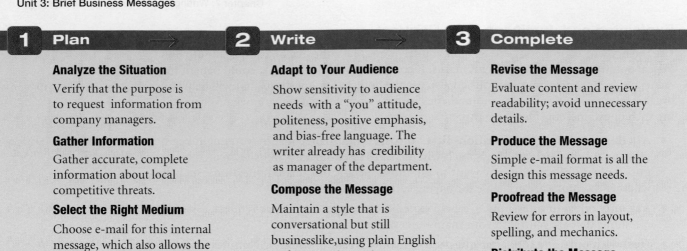

1 Plan → 2 Write → 3 Complete

Analyze the Situation
Verify that the purpose is to request information from company managers.

Gather Information
Gather accurate, complete information about local competitive threats.

Select the Right Medium
Choose e-mail for this internal message, which also allows the attachment of a Word document to collect the information.

Organize the Information
Clarify that the main idea is collecting information that will lead to a better competitive strategy, which will in turn help the various district managers.

Adapt to Your Audience
Show sensitivity to audience needs with a "you" attitude, politeness, positive emphasis, and bias-free language. The writer already has credibility as manager of the department.

Compose the Message
Maintain a style that is conversational but still businesslike, using plain English and appropriate voice.

Revise the Message
Evaluate content and review readability; avoid unnecessary details.

Produce the Message
Simple e-mail format is all the design this message needs.

Proofread the Message
Review for errors in layout, spelling, and mechanics.

Distribute the Message
Deliver the message via the company's e-mail system.

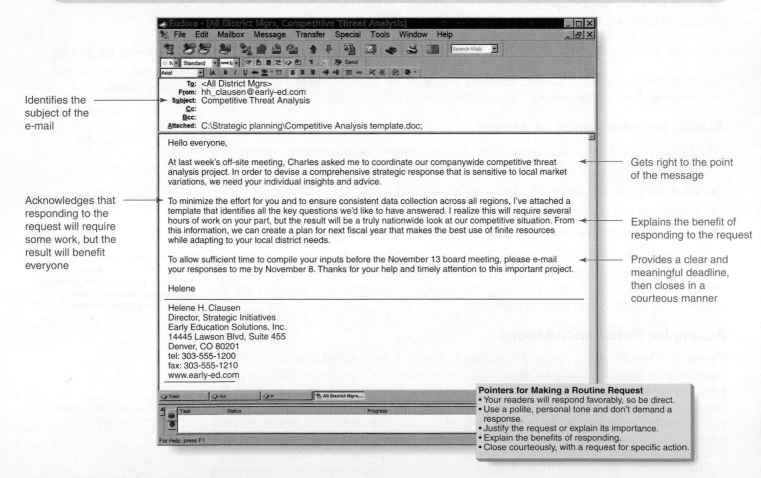

Identifies the subject of the e-mail

Acknowledges that responding to the request will require some work, but the result will benefit everyone

Gets right to the point of the message

Explains the benefit of responding to the request

Provides a clear and meaningful deadline, then closes in a courteous manner

Pointers for Making a Routine Request
- Your readers will respond favorably, so be direct.
- Use a polite, personal tone and don't demand a response.
- Justify the request or explain its importance.
- Explain the benefits of responding.
- Close courteously, with a request for specific action.

Figure 7.2   Effective Message Requesting Action
In this e-mail request to district managers across the country, Helene Clausen asks them to fill out an attached information collection form. Although the request is not unusual and responding to it is part of the managers' responsibility, Clausen asks for their help in a courteous manner and points out the benefits of responding.

Use the body of the request to list all the information the recipient would need in order to write the recommendation, including the full name and address of the person to whom the letter should be sent. Consider including an updated résumé if you've had significant career advancement since your last contact.

Close your message with an expression of appreciation. When asking for an immediate recommendation, you should also mention the deadline. Always be sure to enclose a stamped, preaddressed envelope as a convenience to the other party. Figure 7.3 on the next page provides an example of a request that follows these guidelines.

Making Claims and Requesting Adjustments

If you're dissatisfied with a company's product or service, you can opt to make a **claim** (a formal complaint) or request an **adjustment** (a settlement of a claim). In either case, it's important to maintain a professional tone in all your communication, no matter how angry or frustrated you are. Keeping your cool will help you get the situation resolved sooner.

In most cases, and especially in your first message, assume that a fair adjustment will be made and use a direct request. Open with a straightforward statement of the problem. In the body, give a complete, specific explanation of the details; provide any information an adjuster would need to verify your complaint. In your close, politely request specific action or convey a sincere desire to find a solution. And, if appropriate, suggest that the business relationship will continue if the problem is solved satisfactorily. Be prepared to back up your claim with invoices, sales receipts, canceled checks, dated correspondence, and any other relevant documents. Send copies and keep the originals for your files.

> In a claim letter
> - Explain the problem and give details
> - Provide backup information
> - Request specific action
>
> Be prepared to document any claims you make with a company. Send copies and keep the original documents.

If the remedy is obvious, tell your reader exactly what you expect from the company, such as exchanging incorrectly shipped merchandise for the right item or issuing a refund if the item is out of stock. In some cases, you might ask the recipient to resolve a problem. However, if you're uncertain about the precise nature of the trouble, you could ask the company to make an assessment and then advise you on how the situation could be fixed. Supply your contact information so that the company can discuss the situation with you, if necessary. Compare the ineffective and effective versions in Figure 7.4 on page 191 for an example of making a claim.

STRATEGY FOR ROUTINE REPLIES AND POSITIVE MESSAGES

> **3 LEARNING OBJECTIVE**
> Outline an effective strategy for writing routine replies and positive messages

Just as you'll make numerous requests for information and action throughout your career, you'll also respond to similar requests from other people. When you are responding positively to a request, sending routine announcements, or sending a positive or goodwill message, you have several goals: to communicate the information or the good news, answer all questions, provide all required details, and leave your reader with a good impression of you and your firm.

Readers receiving routine replies and positive messages will generally be interested in what you have to say, so you'll usually use the direct approach. Place your main idea (the positive reply or the good news) in the opening. Use the body to explain all the relevant details, and close cordially, perhaps highlighting a benefit to your reader.

> Use a direct approach for positive messages.

Starting with the Main Idea

By opening with the main idea or good news, you prepare your audience for the details that follow. Make your opening clear and concise. Although the following introductory statements make the same point, one is cluttered with unnecessary information that buries the purpose, whereas the other is brief and to the point:

> With the direct approach, open with a clear and concise expression of the main idea or good news.

Instead of This	Write This
I am pleased to inform you that after careful consideration of a diverse and talented pool of applicants, each of whom did a thorough job of analyzing Trask Horton Pharmaceuticals's training needs, we have selected your bid.	Trask Horton Pharmaceuticals has accepted your bid to provide public speaking and presentation training to the sales staff.

Analyze the Situation

Verify that the purpose is to request a recommendation letter from a college professor.

Gather Information

Gather information on classes and dates to help the reader recall you and to clarify the position you seek.

Select the Right Medium

The letter format gives this message an appropriate level of formality, although many professors prefer to be contacted by e-mail.

Organize the Information

Messages like this are common and expected, so a direct approach is fine.

Adapt to Your Audience

Show sensitivity to audience needs with a "you" attitude, politeness, positive emphasis, and bias-free language.

Compose the Message

The style is respectful and businesslike, while still using plain English and appropriate voice.

Revise the Message

Evaluate content and review readability; avoid unnecessary details.

Produce the Message

Simple memo format is all the design this message needs.

Proofread the Message

Review for errors in layout, spelling, and mechanics.

Distribute the Message

Deliver the message via postal mail or e-mail if you have the professor's e-mail address.

1181 Ashport Drive
Tate Springs, TN 38101
March 14, 2011

Professor Lyndon Kenton
School of Business
University of Tennessee, Knoxville
Knoxville, TN 37916

Dear Professor Kenton:

I recently interviewed for a position in the analyst training program at Strategic Investments and have been called for a second interview for their Analyst Training Program (ATP). They have requested at least one recommendation from a professor, and I immediately thought of you. May I have a letter of recommendation from you?

[Opens by stating the purpose of the letter and making the request, assuming the reader will want to comply with the request]

As you may recall, I took BUS 485, Financial Analysis, from you in the fall of 2009. I enjoyed the class and finished the term with an "A." Professor Kenton, your comments on assertiveness and cold-calling impressed me beyond the scope of the actual course material. In fact, taking your course helped me decide on a future as a financial analyst.

[Includes information near the opening to refresh the reader's memory about this former student]

My enclosed résumé includes all my relevant work experience and volunteer activities. I would also like to add that I've handled the financial planning for our family since my father passed away several years ago. Although I initially learned by trial and error, I have increasingly applied my business training in deciding what stocks or bonds to trade. This, I believe, has given me a practical edge over others who may be applying for the same job.

[Refers to résumé in the body and mentions experience that could set applicant apart from other candidates]

If possible, Ms. Blackmon in Human Resources needs to receive your letter by March 30. For your convenience, I've enclosed a preaddressed, stamped envelope.

[Gives a deadline for response and includes information about the person expecting the recommendation]

[Mentions the preaddressed, stamped envelope to encourage a timely response]

I appreciate your time and effort in writing this letter of recommendation for me. It will be great to put my education to work, and I'll keep you informed of my progress. Thank you for your consideration in this matter.

Sincerely,

Joanne Tucker

Joanne Tucker

Enclosure

Figure 7.3 Effective Request for a Recommendation

This writer uses a direct approach when asking for a recommendation from a former professor. Note how she takes care to refresh the professor's memory, since the class was taken a year and a half ago. She also indicates the date by which the letter is needed and points to the enclosure of a stamped, preaddressed envelope.

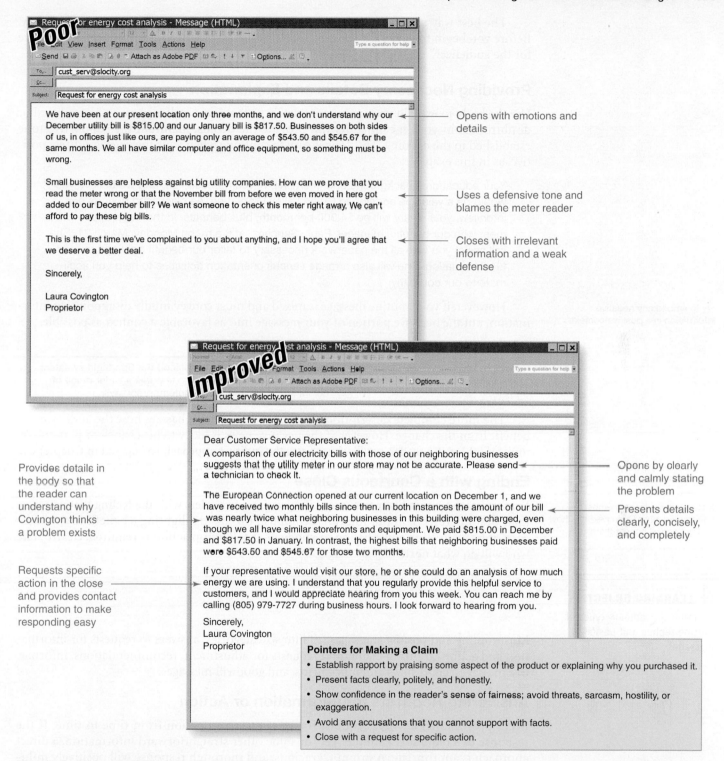

Poor

Request for energy cost analysis - Message (HTML)

File Edit View Insert Format Tools Actions Help   Type a question for help

Send   Attach as Adobe PDF   Options...

To...   cust_serv@slocity.org

Cc...

Subject: Request for energy cost analysis

We have been at our present location only three months, and we don't understand why our December utility bill is $815.00 and our January bill is $817.50. Businesses on both sides of us, in offices just like ours, are paying only an average of $543.50 and $545.67 for the same months. We all have similar computer and office equipment, so something must be wrong.

Small businesses are helpless against big utility companies. How can we prove that you read the meter wrong or that the November bill from before we even moved in here got added to our December bill? We want someone to check this meter right away. We can't afford to pay these big bills.

This is the first time we've complained to you about anything, and I hope you'll agree that we deserve a better deal.

Sincerely,

Laura Covington
Proprietor

— Opens with emotions and details

— Uses a defensive tone and blames the meter reader

— Closes with irrelevant information and a weak defense

Improved

Request for energy cost analysis - Message (HTML)

File Edit [...] Format Tools Actions Help   Type a question for help

Attach as Adobe PDF   Options...

cust_serv@slocity.org

Cc...

Subject: Request for energy cost analysis

Dear Customer Service Representative:
A comparison of our electricity bills with those of our neighboring businesses suggests that the utility meter in our store may not be accurate. Please send a technician to check it.

The European Connection opened at our current location on December 1, and we have received two monthly bills since then. In both instances the amount of our bill was nearly twice what neighboring businesses in this building were charged, even though we all have similar storefronts and equipment. We paid $815.00 in December and $817.50 in January. In contrast, the highest bills that neighboring businesses paid were $543.50 and $545.67 for those two months.

If your representative would visit our store, he or she could do an analysis of how much energy we are using. I understand that you regularly provide this helpful service to customers, and I would appreciate hearing from you this week. You can reach me by calling (805) 979-7727 during business hours. I look forward to hearing from you.

Sincerely,
Laura Covington
Proprietor

Provides details in the body so that the reader can understand why Covington thinks a problem exists

Requests specific action in the close and provides contact information to make responding easy

Opens by clearly and calmly stating the problem

Presents details clearly, concisely, and completely

Pointers for Making a Claim
- Establish rapport by praising some aspect of the product or explaining why you purchased it.
- Present facts clearly, politely, and honestly.
- Show confidence in the reader's sense of fairness; avoid threats, sarcasm, hostility, or exaggeration.
- Avoid any accusations that you cannot support with facts.
- Close with a request for specific action.

Figure 7.4 Poor and Improved Versions of a Claim
Note the difference in both tone and information content in these two versions. The poor version is emotional and unprofessional, whereas the improved version communicates calmly and clearly.

PEARSON **mybcommlab**

Apply Figure 7.4's key concepts by revising a new document. Go to Chapter 7 in mybcommlab.com and select Document Makeovers.

The best way to write a clear opening is to have a clear idea of what you want to say. Before you begin to write, ask yourself, "What is the single most important message I have for the audience?"

Providing Necessary Details and Explanation

Use the body to explain your point completely so that your audience won't be confused or doubtful about your meaning. As you provide the details, maintain the supportive tone established in the opening. This tone is easy to continue when your message is entirely positive, as in this example:

> Your educational background and internship have impressed us, and we believe you would be a valuable addition to Green Valley Properties. As discussed during your interview, your salary will be $4,300 per month, plus benefits. In that regard, you will meet with our benefits manager, Paula Sanchez, at 8 a.m. on Monday, March 21. She will assist you with all the paperwork necessary to tailor our benefit package to your family situation. She will also arrange various orientation activities to help you acclimate to our company.

Try to embed any negative information in a positive context.

However, if your routine message is mixed and must convey mildly disappointing information, put the negative portion of your message into as favorable a context as possible:

Instead of This	Write This
No, we no longer carry the Sportsgirl line of sweaters.	The new Olympic line has replaced the Sportsgirl sweaters that you asked about. Olympic features a wider range of colors and sizes and more contemporary styling.

The more complete description is less negative and emphasizes how the audience can benefit from the change. However, if the negative news is likely to be a shock or particularly unpleasant for the reader, you'll want to use the indirect approach (discussed in Chapter 8).

Ending with a Courteous Close

Make sure audience members understand what to do next and how that action will benefit them.

Your message is more likely to succeed if it leaves your readers with the feeling that you have their best interests in mind. You can accomplish this by highlighting a benefit to the audience or by expressing appreciation or goodwill. If follow-up action is required, clearly state who will do what next.

4 LEARNING OBJECTIVE

Describe six common types of routine replies and positive messages

COMMON EXAMPLES OF ROUTINE REPLIES AND POSITIVE MESSAGES

Most routine and positive messages fall into six categories: answers to requests for information and action, grants of claims and requests for adjustment, recommendations, informative messages, good-news announcements, and goodwill messages.

Answering Requests for Information or Action

Every professional answers requests for information or action from time to time. If the response to a request is a simple "yes" or some other straightforward information, a direct approach is appropriate. A prompt, gracious, and thorough response will positively influence how people think about you and the organization you represent (see Figure 7.5).

To handle repetitive queries quickly and consistently, companies usually develop form responses that can be customized as needed (see Figure 7.6 on page 194). These ready-made message templates can be printed forms, word-processor documents, e-mail templates, or blocks of instant messaging (IM) text that can be dropped into a messaging window with the click of a mouse.

Granting Claims and Requests for Adjustment

Even the best-run companies make mistakes, from billing customers incorrectly to delivering products that fail to perform properly. In other cases, the customer or a third party might be responsible for the mistake, such as misusing a product or damaging it in shipment. Each of these events represents a turning point in your relationship with your

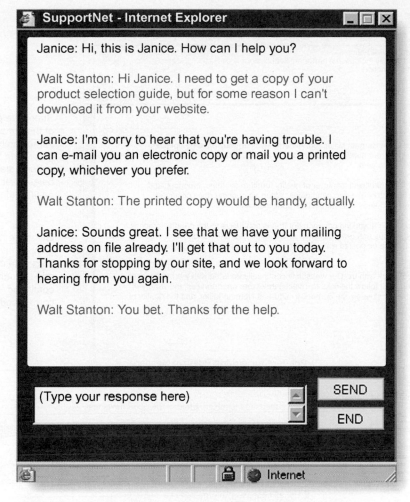

Figure 7.5 Effective IM Response to Information Request
This quick and courteous exchange is typical of IM communication in such areas
as customer service and technical support. The agent (Janice) solves the problem
quickly and leaves the customer with a positive impression of the company.

customer. If you handle the situation well, your customer will likely be even more loyal than before because you've proven that you're serious about customer satisfaction. However, if a customer believes that you mishandled a complaint, you'll make the situation even worse. Dissatisfied customers often take their business elsewhere and are likely to tell numerous friends and colleagues about the negative experience. A transaction that might be worth only a few dollars by itself could cost you many times that amount in lost business.

Consequently, view every mistake as an opportunity to improve a relationship. Unless you have strong reason to believe otherwise, start from the assumption that the information the customer provided is correct. From there, your response to the complaint depends on both your company's policies for resolving such issues and your assessment of whether the company, the customer, or some third party is at fault.

Responding to a Claim When Your Company Is at Fault

Before you respond when your firm is at fault, make sure you know your company's policies in such cases, which might include specific legal and financial steps to be taken. Most routine responses should take your company's specific policies into account and address the following points:

- Acknowledge receipt of the customer's claim or complaint.
- Sympathize with the customer's inconvenience or frustration.
- Take (or assign) personal responsibility for setting matters straight.
- Explain precisely how you have resolved, or plan to resolve, the situation.
- Take steps to repair the relationship.
- Follow up to verify that your response was correct.

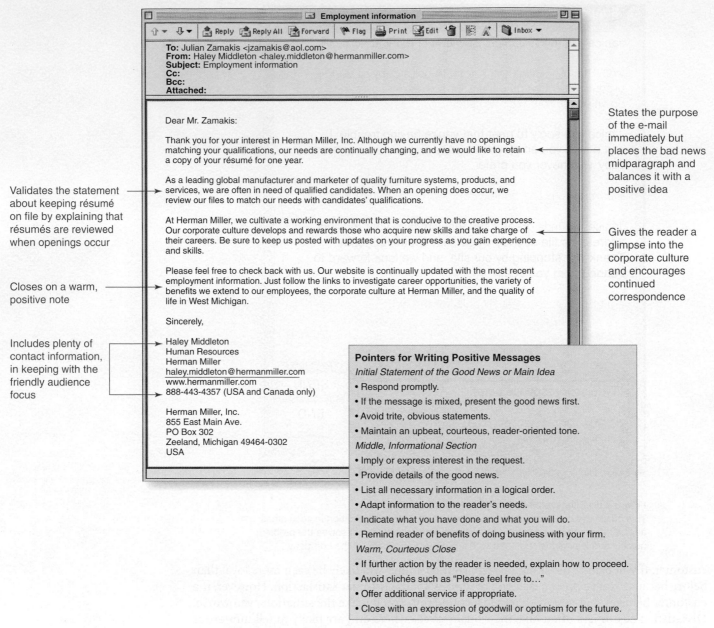

Validates the statement about keeping résumé on file by explaining that résumés are reviewed when openings occur

Closes on a warm, positive note

Includes plenty of contact information, in keeping with the friendly audience focus

States the purpose of the e-mail immediately but places the bad news midparagraph and balances it with a positive idea

Gives the reader a glimpse into the corporate culture and encourages continued correspondence

Employment information

To: Julian Zamakis <jzamakis@aol.com>
From: Haley Middleton <haley.middleton@hermanmiller.com>
Subject: Employment information
Cc:
Bcc:
Attached:

Dear Mr. Zamakis:

Thank you for your interest in Herman Miller, Inc. Although we currently have no openings matching your qualifications, our needs are continually changing, and we would like to retain a copy of your résumé for one year.

As a leading global manufacturer and marketer of quality furniture systems, products, and services, we are often in need of qualified candidates. When an opening does occur, we review our files to match our needs with candidates' qualifications.

At Herman Miller, we cultivate a working environment that is conducive to the creative process. Our corporate culture develops and rewards those who acquire new skills and take charge of their careers. Be sure to keep us posted with updates on your progress as you gain experience and skills.

Please feel free to check back with us. Our website is continually updated with the most recent employment information. Just follow the links to investigate career opportunities, the variety of benefits we extend to our employees, the corporate culture at Herman Miller, and the quality of life in West Michigan.

Sincerely,

Haley Middleton
Human Resources
Herman Miller
haley.middleton@hermanmiller.com
www.hermanmiller.com
888-443-4357 (USA and Canada only)

Herman Miller, Inc.
855 East Main Ave.
PO Box 302
Zeeland, Michigan 49464-0302
USA

Pointers for Writing Positive Messages
Initial Statement of the Good News or Main Idea
• Respond promptly.
• If the message is mixed, present the good news first.
• Avoid trite, obvious statements.
• Maintain an upbeat, courteous, reader-oriented tone.
Middle, Informational Section
• Imply or express interest in the request.
• Provide details of the good news.
• List all necessary information in a logical order.
• Adapt information to the reader's needs.
• Indicate what you have done and what you will do.
• Remind reader of benefits of doing business with your firm.
Warm, Courteous Close
• If further action by the reader is needed, explain how to proceed.
• Avoid clichés such as "Please feel free to…"
• Offer additional service if appropriate.
• Close with an expression of goodwill or optimism for the future.

Figure 7.6   Personalized Reply to a Request
This e-mail message personalizes a standardized response by including the recipient's name in the greeting.

In addition to these positive steps, maintain professional demeanor by avoiding some key negative steps as well: Don't blame anyone in your organization by name, don't make exaggerated apologies that sound insincere, don't imply that the customer is at fault, and don't promise more than you can deliver.

Responding to a Claim When the Customer Is at Fault

Communication about a claim is a delicate matter when the customer is clearly at fault. If you refuse the claim, you may lose your customer—as well as many of the customer's friends and colleagues, who will hear only one side of the dispute. You must weigh the cost of making the adjustment against the cost of losing future business from one or more customers. Some companies have strict guidelines for responding to such claims, whereas others give individual employees and managers some leeway in making case-by-case decisions.

If you choose to grant the claim, simply open with that good news. However, the body needs special attention because you need to discourage repeated mistakes without insulting the customer (see Figure 7.7). Close in a courteous manner that expresses your appreciation for the customer's business.

To grant a claim when the customer is at fault, try to discourage future mistakes without insulting the customer.

1 Plan → **2 Write** → **3 Complete**

Analyze the Situation
Verify that the purpose is to grant the customer's claim, tactfully educate him, and encourage further business.

Gather Information
Gather information on product care, warranties, and resale information.

Select the Right Medium
An e-mail message is appropriate in this case because the customer contacted the company via e-mail.

Organize the Information
You're responding with a positive answer, so a direct approach is fine.

Adapt to Your Audience
Show sensitivity to audience needs with a "you" attitude, politeness, positive emphasis, and bias-free language.

Compose the Message
Style is respectful while still managing to educate the customer on product usage and maintenance.

Revise the Message
Evaluate content and review readability; avoid unnecessary details.

Produce the Message
Emphasize a clean, professional appearance.

Proofread the Message
Review for errors in layout, spelling, and mechanics.

Distribute the Message
E-mail the reply.

re: Warranty repair? (HTML)

To: SteveC955@verizon.net
Cc:
Subject: re: Warranty repair?
Attach: Rock & Roll.pdf (248 KB)

Dear Mr. Cox:

Thank you for contacting us about your in-line skates. Even though your six-month warranty has expired, Skates Alive! is mailing you a complete wheel assembly replacement free of charge. The enclosed instructions will explain how to remove the damaged wheel line and install the new one.

The "Fastrax" (model NL 562) you purchased is our best-selling and most reliable skate. However, wheel jams may occur when fine particles of sand block the smooth rotating action of the wheels. These skates perform best when used on roadways and tracks that are relatively free of sand. We suggest that you remove and clean the wheel assemblies once a month and have them checked by your dealer every six months.

Because of your Florida location, you may want to consider our more advanced "Glisto" (model NL 988) when you decide to purchase new skates. Although more expensive than the Fastrax, the Glisto design helps shed sand and dirt quite efficiently and should provide years of carefree skating.

Enjoy the attached PDF copy of "Rock & Roll," our free skating newsletter.

We love hearing from our skaters, so keep in touch. All of us at Skates Alive! wish you good times and miles of healthy skating.

Sincerely,
Candace Parker
Customer Service Representative

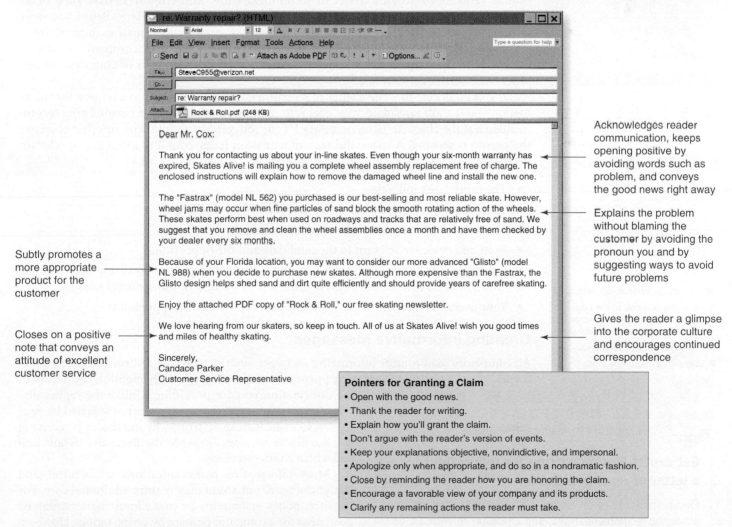

Acknowledges reader communication, keeps opening positive by avoiding words such as problem, and conveys the good news right away

Explains the problem without blaming the customer by avoiding the pronoun you and by suggesting ways to avoid future problems

Subtly promotes a more appropriate product for the customer

Gives the reader a glimpse into the corporate culture and encourages continued correspondence

Closes on a positive note that conveys an attitude of excellent customer service

Pointers for Granting a Claim
- Open with the good news.
- Thank the reader for writing.
- Explain how you'll grant the claim.
- Don't argue with the reader's version of events.
- Keep your explanations objective, nonvindictive, and impersonal.
- Apologize only when appropriate, and do so in a nondramatic fashion.
- Close by reminding the reader how you are honoring the claim.
- Encourage a favorable view of your company and its products.
- Clarify any remaining actions the reader must take.

Figure 7.7 Responding to a Claim When the Buyer Is at Fault
In the interest of positive customer relationships, this company agreed to provide replacement parts for a customer's in-line skates, even though the product is outside its warranty period. (For the sake of clarity, the content of the customer's original e-mail message is not reproduced here.)

Responding to a Claim When a Third Party Is at Fault

Sometimes neither your company nor your customer is at fault. For example, ordering a book from Amazon involves not only Amazon but also a delivery service such as UPS or the U.S. Postal Service, the publisher and possibly a distributor of the book, a credit card issuer, and a company that processes credit card transactions. If something goes wrong, any one of these other partners might be at fault, but the customer is likely to blame Amazon because that is the entity that receives the customer's payment.

Evaluate each situation carefully and know your company's policies before responding. For instance, an online retailer and the companies that manufacture its merchandise might have an agreement specifying that the manufacturers automatically handle all complaints about product quality. However, regardless of who eventually resolves the problem, if customers contact you, you need to respond with messages that explain how the problem will be solved. Pointing fingers is both unproductive and unprofessional. Resolving the situation is the only issue customers care about.

Providing Recommendations and References

Job seekers and others who need endorsements from employers or colleagues often request letters of recommendation. These messages used to be a fairly routine matter, but employment recommendations and references have become a complex legal issue in recent years. Employees have sued employers and individual managers for providing negative information or refusing to provide letters of recommendation, and employers have sued other employers for failing to disclose negative information about job candidates. Before you write a letter of recommendation for a former employee or provide information in response to another employer's background check, be sure to consult with your company's legal staff first. Your company may refuse to provide anything more than dates of employment and other basic details, for example.[2]

If you do decide to write a letter of recommendation or respond to a request for information about a job candidate, your goal is to convince readers that the person being recommended has the characteristics necessary for the job, project assignment, or other objective the person is seeking. A successful recommendation letter contains a number of relevant details (see Figure 7.8):

- The candidate's full name
- The position or other objective the candidate is seeking
- The nature of your relationship with the candidate
- Facts and evidence relevant to the candidate and the opportunity
- A comparison of this candidate's potential with that of peers, if available (for example, "Ms. Jonasson consistently ranked in the top 10 percent of our national sales force.")
- Your overall evaluation of the candidate's suitability for the opportunity

Creating Informative Messages

All companies send routine informative messages, such as reminder notices and policy statements. Use the opening to state the purpose (to inform) and briefly mention the nature of the information you are providing. Unlike the replies discussed earlier, informative messages are not solicited by your reader, so make it clear up front why the reader is receiving this particular message. Provide the necessary details and end with a courteous close.

Most informative communications are neutral and straightforward, but some may require additional care. For instance, policy statements or procedural changes may be good news for a company, perhaps by saving money. However, it may not be obvious to employees that such savings may make available additional employee resources or even pay raises. In instances in which the reader may not initially view the information positively, use the body of the message to highlight the potential benefits from the reader's perspective.

REAL-TIME UPDATES
Learn More by Reading This Article

Get expert tips on writing (or requesting) a letter of recommendation

Find helpful advice on employment recommendations, academic recommendations, and character references. Go to http://real-timeupdates.com/bce5 and click on "Learn More." If you are using mybcommlab, you can access Real-Time Updates within each chapter or under Student Study Tools.

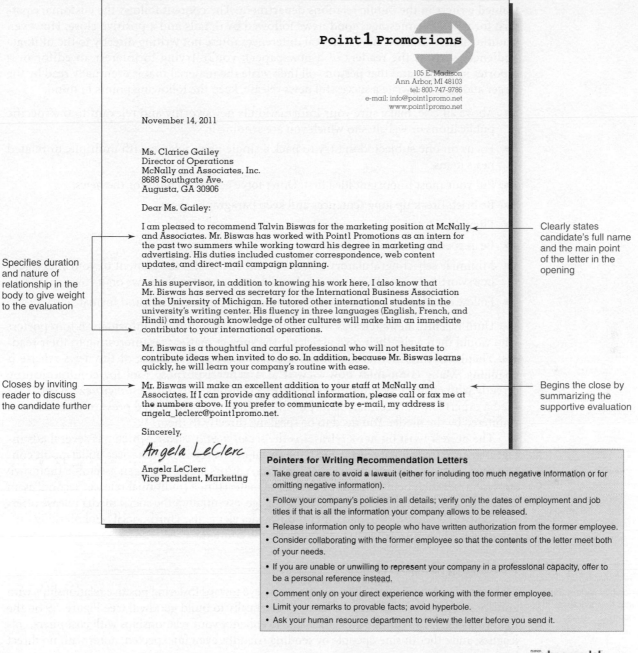

Point1 Promotions

105 E. Madison
Ann Arbor, MI 48103
tel: 800-747-9786
e-mail: info@point1promo.net
www.point1promo.net

November 14, 2011

Ms. Clarice Gailey
Director of Operations
McNally and Associates, Inc.
8688 Southgate Ave.
Augusta, GA 30906

Dear Ms. Gailey:

I am pleased to recommend Talvin Biswas for the marketing position at McNally and Associates. Mr. Biswas has worked with Point1 Promotions as an intern for the past two summers while working toward his degree in marketing and advertising. His duties included customer correspondence, web content updates, and direct-mail campaign planning.

As his supervisor, in addition to knowing his work here, I also know that Mr. Biswas has served as secretary for the International Business Association at the University of Michigan. He tutored other international students in the university's writing center. His fluency in three languages (English, French, and Hindi) and thorough knowledge of other cultures will make him an immediate contributor to your international operations.

Mr. Biswas is a thoughtful and carful professional who will not hesitate to contribute ideas when invited to do so. In addition, because Mr. Biswas learns quickly, he will learn your company's routine with ease.

Mr. Biswas will make an excellent addition to your staff at McNally and Associates. If I can provide any additional information, please call or fax me at the numbers above. If you prefer to communicate by e-mail, my address is angela_leclerc@point1promo.net.

Sincerely,

Angela LeClerc

Angela LeClerc
Vice President, Marketing

Clearly states candidate's full name and the main point of the letter in the opening *(annotation)*

Specifies duration and nature of relationship in the body to give weight to the evaluation *(annotation)*

Begins the close by summarizing the supportive evaluation *(annotation)*

Closes by inviting reader to discuss the candidate further *(annotation)*

Pointers for Writing Recommendation Letters

- Take great care to avoid a lawsuit (either for including too much negative information or for omitting negative information).

- Follow your company's policies in all details; verify only the dates of employment and job titles if that is all the information your company allows to be released.

- Release information only to people who have written authorization from the former employee.

- Consider collaborating with the former employee so that the contents of the letter meet both of your needs.

- If you are unable or unwilling to represent your company in a professional capacity, offer to be a personal reference instead.

- Comment only on your direct experience working with the former employee.

- Limit your remarks to provable facts; avoid hyperbole.

- Ask your human resource department to review the letter before you send it.

mybcommlab

Apply Figure 7.8's key concepts by revising a new document. Go to Chapter 7 in mybcommlab.com and select Document Makeovers.

Figure 7.8 Effective Recommendation Letter
This letter clearly states the nature of the writer's relationship to the candidate and provides specific examples to support the writer's endorsements.

Announcing Good News

To develop and maintain good relationships, smart companies recognize that it's good business to spread the word about positive developments. These messages can include opening new facilities, hiring a new executive, introducing new products or services, or sponsoring community events. Because good news is always welcome, use the direct approach.

Good-news announcements are often communicated in a **news release**, also known as a *press release*, a specialized document used to share relevant information with the news media. (News releases are also used to announce negative news, such as plant closings.) In most companies, news releases are usually prepared or at least supervised by specially trained writers in the public relations department. The content follows the customary pattern for a positive message: good news followed by details and a positive close. However, traditional news releases have a critical difference: You're not writing directly to the ultimate audience (such as the readers of a newspaper); you're trying to interest an editor or a reporter in a story, and that person will then write the material that is eventually read by the larger audience. To write a successful news release, keep the following points in mind:[3]

- Above all else, make sure your information is newsworthy and relevant to the specific publications or websites to which you are sending it.

- Focus on one subject; don't try to pack a single news release with multiple, unrelated news items.

- Put your most important idea first. Don't force editors to hunt for the news.

- Be brief: Break up long sentences and keep paragraphs short.

- Eliminate clutter, such as redundancy and extraneous facts.

- Be as specific as possible.

- Minimize self-congratulatory adjectives and adverbs; if the content of your message is newsworthy, the media professionals will be interested in the news on its own merits.

- Follow established industry conventions for style, punctuation, and format.

Until recently, news releases were crafted in a way to provide information to reporters who would then write their own articles if the subject matter was interesting to their readers. Thanks to the Internet and social media, however, the nature of the news release is changing. Many companies now view it as a general-purpose tool for communicating directly with customers and other audiences, creating *direct-to-consumer news releases*. As media expert David Meerman Scott puts it, "Millions of people read press releases directly, unfiltered by the media. You need to be speaking directly to them."[4]

The newest twist on news releases is the *social media release*, which has several advantages over the traditional release. First, the social media release emphasizes bullet-point content over narrative paragraphs so that bloggers, editors, and others can assemble their own stories, rather than being forced to rewrite the material in a traditional release. Second, as an electronic-only document (a specialized webpage, essentially), the social media release offers the ability to include videos and other multimedia elements. Third, social bookmarking buttons make it easy for people to help publicize the content.[5]

Fostering Goodwill

Goodwill is the positive feeling that encourages people to maintain a business relationship.

All business messages should be written with an eye toward fostering positive relationships with audiences, but some messages are written specifically to build goodwill (see Figure 7.9 on the following page). You can use these messages to enhance your relationships with customers, colleagues, and other businesspeople by sending friendly, even unexpected, notes with no direct business purpose.

> **COMMUNICATION** *Matters*
>
> Whether you're thanking an employee for a job well done or congratulating a colleague for a personal or professional achievement, the small effort to send a goodwill message can have a positive and lasting effect on the people around you.

Make sure your compliments are both sincere and honest

Effective goodwill messages must be sincere and honest. Otherwise, you'll appear to be interested in personal gain rather than in benefiting customers, fellow workers, or your organization. To come across as sincere, avoid exaggerating and support compliments with specific evidence. In addition, readers often regard more restrained praise as being more sincere:

Instead of This	Write This
Words cannot express my appreciation for the great job you did. Thanks. No one could have done it better. You're terrific! You've made the whole firm sit up and take notice, and we are ecstatic to have you working here.	Thanks again for taking charge of the meeting in my absence and doing such an excellent job. With just an hour's notice, you pulled the legal and public relations departments together to present a united front in the negotiations. Your dedication and communication abilities have been noted and are truly appreciated.

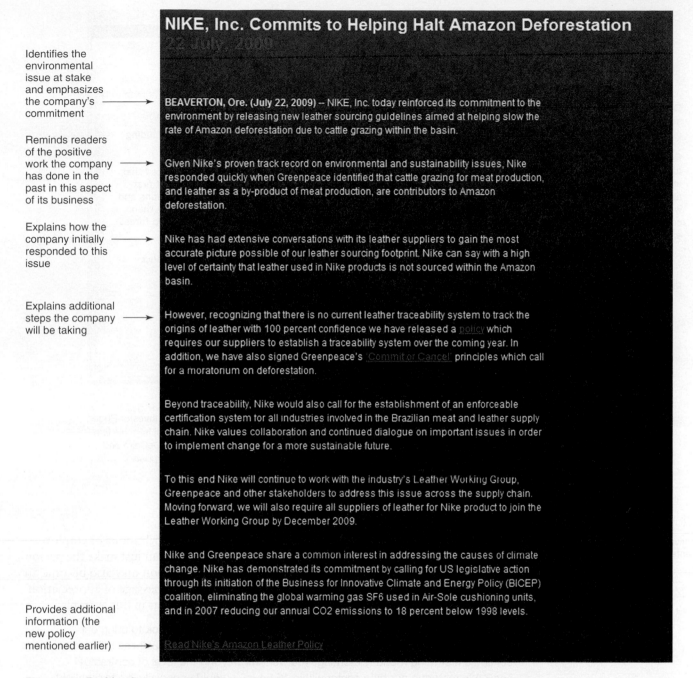

Identifies the environmental issue at stake and emphasizes the company's commitment ———▶

Reminds readers of the positive work the company has done in the past in this aspect of its business ———▶

Explains how the company initially responded to this issue ———▶

Explains additional steps the company will be taking ———▶

Provides additional information (the new policy mentioned earlier) ———▶

NIKE, Inc. Commits to Helping Halt Amazon Deforestation
22 July, 2009

BEAVERTON, Ore. (July 22, 2009) -- NIKE, Inc. today reinforced its commitment to the environment by releasing new leather sourcing guidelines aimed at helping slow the rate of Amazon deforestation due to cattle grazing within the basin.

Given Nike's proven track record on environmental and sustainability issues, Nike responded quickly when Greenpeace identified that cattle grazing for meat production, and leather as a by-product of meat production, are contributors to Amazon deforestation.

Nike has had extensive conversations with its leather suppliers to gain the most accurate picture possible of our leather sourcing footprint. Nike can say with a high level of certainty that leather used in Nike products is not sourced within the Amazon basin.

However, recognizing that there is no current leather traceability system to track the origins of leather with 100 percent confidence we have released a policy which requires our suppliers to establish a traceability system over the coming year. In addition, we have also signed Greenpeace's 'Commit or Cancel' principles which call for a moratorium on deforestation.

Beyond traceability, Nike would also call for the establishment of an enforceable certification system for all industries involved in the Brazilian meat and leather supply chain. Nike values collaboration and continued dialogue on important issues in order to implement change for a more sustainable future.

To this end Nike will continue to work with the industry's Leather Working Group, Greenpeace and other stakeholders to address this issue across the supply chain. Moving forward, we will also require all suppliers of leather for Nike product to join the Leather Working Group by December 2009.

Nike and Greenpeace share a common interest in addressing the causes of climate change. Nike has demonstrated its commitment by calling for US legislative action through its initiation of the Business for Innovative Climate and Energy Policy (BICEP) coalition, eliminating the global warming gas SF6 used in Air-Sole cushioning units, and in 2007 reducing our annual CO_2 emissions to 18 percent below 1998 levels.

Read Nike's Amazon Leather Policy

Figure 7.9   Positive Announcements
In this news release, Nike announces new policies aimed at reducing the deforestation effects of cattle ranching in the Amazon region.

Sending Congratulations

One prime opportunity for sending goodwill messages is to congratulate individuals or companies for significant business achievements—perhaps for being promoted or for attaining product sales milestones (see Figure 7.10 on the following page). Other reasons for sending congratulations include the highlights in people's personal lives, such as weddings, births, graduations, and success in nonbusiness competitions. You may congratulate business acquaintances on their own achievements or on the accomplishments of a spouse or child. You may also take note of personal events, even if you don't know the reader well. If you're already friendly with the reader, a more personal tone is appropriate.

Taking note of significant events in someone's personal life helps foster the business relationship.

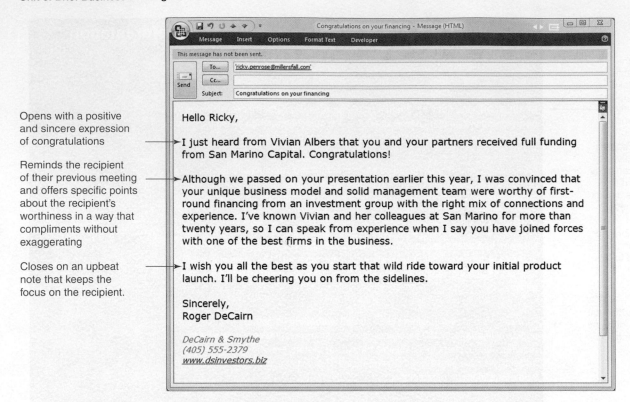

Opens with a positive and sincere expression of congratulations

Reminds the recipient of their previous meeting and offers specific points about the recipient's worthiness in a way that compliments without exaggerating

Closes on an upbeat note that keeps the focus on the recipient.

Figure 7.10   Goodwill Messages
Goodwill messages serve a variety of business functions. In this e-mail message, investor Roger DeCairn congratulates an entrepreneur who had previously sought start-up capital from his firm but later secured funding from another firm. The message may ultimately benefit DeCairn and his company by building goodwill, but it doesn't serve an immediate business purpose.

Sending Messages of Appreciation

An effective message of appreciation documents a person's contributions.

An important leadership quality is the ability to recognize the contributions of employees, colleagues, suppliers, and other associates. Your praise does more than just make the person feel good; it encourages further excellence. A message of appreciation may also become an important part of someone's personnel file. So when you write a message of appreciation, try to specifically mention the person or people you want to praise, as in this example:

> Thank you and everyone on your team for the heroic efforts you took to bring our servers back up after last Friday's flood. We were able to restore business right on schedule first thing Monday morning. You went far beyond the level of contractual service in restoring our data center within 16 hours. I would especially like to highlight the contribution of networking specialist Julienne Marks, who worked for 12 straight hours to reconnect our Internet service. If I can serve as a reference in your future sales activities, please do not hesitate to ask.

Hearing a sincere thank you can do wonders for morale.[6] Moreover, in today's electronic media environment, a handwritten thank-you note can be a particularly welcome acknowledgment.[7]

Offering Condolences

In times of serious trouble and deep sadness, well-written condolences and expressions of sympathy can mean a great deal to people who've experienced loss. This type of message is difficult to write, but don't let the difficulty of the task keep you from responding promptly.

REAL-TIME UPDATES
Learn More by Reading This Article

Simple rules for writing effective thank-you notes

These tips are easy to adapt to any business or social occasions in which you need to express appreciation. Go to http://real-timeupdates.com/bce5 and click on "Learn More." If you are using mybcommlab, you can access Real-Time Updates within each chapter or under Student Study Tools.

Open a condolence message with a brief statement of sympathy, such as "I was deeply sorry to hear of your loss" in the event of a death, for example. In the body, mention the good qualities or the positive contributions made by the deceased. State what the person meant to you or your colleagues. In closing, you can offer your condolences and your best wishes. Here are a few general suggestions for writing condolence messages:

The primary purpose of condolence messages is to let the audience know that you and the organization you represent care about the person's loss.

- **Keep reminiscences brief.** Recount a memory or an anecdote (even a humorous one) but don't dwell on the details of the loss, lest you add to the reader's anguish.

- **Write in your own words.** Write as if you were speaking privately to the person. Don't quote "poetic" passages or use stilted or formal phrases. If the loss is a death, refer to it as such rather than as "passing away" or "departing."

- **Be tactful.** Mention your shock and dismay but remember that bereaved and distressed loved ones take little comfort in lines such as "Richard was too young to die."

- **Take special care.** Be sure to spell names correctly and to be accurate in your review of facts. Try to be prompt.

- **Write about special qualities of the deceased.** You may have to rely on reputation to do this, but let the grieving person know you valued his or her loved one.

- **Consider mentioning special attributes or resources of the bereaved person.** If you know that the bereaved person has attributes or resources that will be a comfort in the time of loss, such as personal resilience, religious faith, or a circle of close friends, mentioning these can make the reader feel more confident about handling the challenges he or she faces.[8]

Supervisor George Bigalow sent the following condolence letter to his administrative assistant, Janice Case, after learning of the death of Janice's husband:

> My sympathy to you and your children. All your friends at Carter Electric were so very sorry to learn of John's death. Although I never had the opportunity to meet him, I do know how very special he was to you. Your tales of your family's camping trips and his rafting expeditions were always memorable.

For the latest information on writing routine and positive messages, visit http://real-timeupdates.com/bce5 and click on Chapter 7.

PEARSON mybcommlab™

Are you an active learner? Go to mybcommlab.com to master Chapter 7's content. Chapter 7's interactive activities include:

- Customizable Study Plan and Chapter 7 practice quizzes
- Chapter 7 Simulation (Routine Messages), which helps you think critically and prepare to make choices in the business world
- Chapter 7 Video Exercise (Routine and Positive Messages: Orange Photography), which shows you how textbook concepts are put into practice every day

- Flash Cards for mastering the definition of chapter terms
- Interactive Lessons that visually review key chapter concepts
- Document Makeovers for hands-on, scored practice in revising documents

CHAPTER REVIEW AND ACTIVITIES

Learning Objectives: Check Your Progress

1 OBJECTIVE Outline an effective strategy for writing routine business requests.

When writing a routine request, open by stating your specific request. Use the body to justify your request and explain its importance. Close routine requests by asking for specific action (including a deadline, if appropriate) and expressing goodwill. A courteous close contains three important elements: (1) a specific request, (2) information about how you can be reached (if it isn't obvious), and (3) an expression of appreciation or goodwill.

2 OBJECTIVE Describe three common types of routine requests.

The most common types of routine requests are asking for information or action, asking for recommendations, and making claims and requesting adjustments. Requests for information or action should explain what you want to know or what you want readers to do, why you're making the request, and why it may be in your readers' interest to help you (if applicable). Requests for recommendations should open by stating what it is you are requesting and asking the recipient to write the message. The body should list all the information the recipient would need to write the recommendation (refer to an attached résumé, if applicable). The close should contain an expression of appreciation and a deadline, if applicable. To make a claim (a formal complaint about a product or service) or request an adjustment (a settlement of a claim), open with a straightforward statement of the problem, use the body to give a complete explanation of the situation, and close with a polite request to resolve the situation.

3 OBJECTIVE Outline an effective strategy for writing routine replies and positive messages.

The direct approach works well for routine replies and positive messages because recipients will generally be interested in what you have to say. Place your main idea (the positive reply or the good news) in the opening. Use the body to explain all the relevant details, and close cordially, perhaps highlighting a benefit to your reader.

4 OBJECTIVE Describe six common types of routine replies and positive messages.

Most routine and positive messages fall into six categories: answers to requests for information and action, grants of claims and requests for adjustment, recommendations, informative messages, good-news announcements, and goodwill messages. Answering requests for information or action is a simple task, often assisted with form responses that can be customized as needed. Granting claims and requests for adjustments is more complicated, and the right response depends on whether the company, the customer, or a third party was at fault. Recommendations also require a careful approach to avoid legal complications; some companies prohibit managers from writing recommendation letters or providing anything beyond basic employment history. Informative messages are often simple and straightforward, but some require extra care if the information affects recipients in a significant way. Good-news announcements are often handled by news releases, which used to be sent exclusively to members of the news media but are now usually made available to the public as well. Finally, goodwill messages, meant to foster positive business relationships, include congratulations, thank-you messages, and messages of condolence. To make goodwill messages effective, make them honest, sincere, and factual.

Test Your Knowledge

To review chapter content related to each question, refer to the indicated Learning Objective.

1. Should you use the direct or indirect approach for most routine messages? Why? [LO-1]

2. What are three guidelines for asking a series of questions in a routine request? [LO-1]

3. If a message contains both positive and negative information, what is the best way to present the negative information? [LO-3]

4. What are six guidelines for writing condolence messages? [LO-4]

5. How can you avoid sounding insincere when writing a goodwill message? [LO-4]

Apply Your Knowledge

To review chapter content related to each question, refer to the indicated Learning Objective.

1. Why is it good practice to explain, when applicable, that replying to a request could benefit the reader? [LO-1]

2. Every time you send a routine request to Ted Jackson, he fails to comply. His lack of response is beginning to affect your job performance. Should you send Jackson an e-mail message to ask what's wrong? Complain to your supervisor about Jackson's uncooperative attitude? Arrange a face-to-face meeting with Jackson? Bring up the problem at the next staff meeting? Explain. [LO-2]

3. You have a complaint against one of your suppliers, but you have no documentation to back it up. Should you request an adjustment anyway? Why or why not? [LO-2]

4. You've been asked to write a letter of recommendation for an employee who worked for you some years ago. You recall that the employee did an admirable job, but you can't remember any specific information at this point. Should you write the letter anyway? Explain. [LO-4]

5. Your company's error cost an important business customer a new client; you know it, and your customer knows it. Do you apologize, or do you refer to the incident in a positive light without admitting any responsibility? Briefly explain. [LO-4]

Practice Your Skills

Exercises for Perfecting Your Writing

To review chapter content related to each set of exercises, refer to the indicated Learning Objective.

Revising Messages: Direct Approach   Revise the following short e-mail messages so that they are more direct and concise; develop a subject line for each revised message.

1. I'm contacting you about your recent order for a High Country backpack. You didn't tell us which backpack you wanted, and you know we make a lot of different ones. We have the canvas models with the plastic frames and vinyl trim, and we have the canvas models with leather trim, and we have the ones that have more pockets than the other ones. Plus they come in lots of different colors. Also they make the ones that are large for a big-boned person and the smaller versions for little women or kids.

2. Sorry it took us so long to get back to you. We were flooded with résumés. Anyway, your résumé made the final ten, and after meeting three hours yesterday, we've decided we'd like to meet with you. What is your schedule like for next week? Can you come in for an interview on June 15 at 3:00 p.m.? Please get back to us by the end of this work week and let us know if you will be able to attend. As you can imagine, this is our busy season.

3. Thank you for contacting us about the difficulty you had collecting your luggage at the Denver airport. We are very sorry for the inconvenience this has caused you. Traveling can create problems of this sort regardless of how careful the airline personnel might be. To receive compensation, please send us a detailed list of the items that you lost and complete the following questionnaire. You can e-mail it back to us.

Revising Messages: Direct Approach   Rewrite the following sentences so that they are direct and concise.

4. We wanted to invite you to our special 40 percent off by-invitation-only sale. The sale is taking place on November 9.

5. We wanted to let you know that we are giving an MP3 player with every $100 donation you make to our radio station.

6. The director planned to go to the meeting that will be held on Monday at a little before 11:00 a.m.

7. In today's meeting, we were happy to have the opportunity to welcome Paul Eccelson. He reviewed some of the newest types of order forms. If you have any questions about these new forms, feel free to call him at his office.

Teamwork   With another student, conduct an audience analysis of the following message topic: A notice to all employees announcing that to avoid layoffs, the company will institute a 10 percent salary reduction for the next six months.

8. If the company is large and employees work in a variety of locations around the world, which medium would you recommend for communicating this message?

9. If the company is small and all employees work in the same location, which medium would you recommend for communicating this message?

10. How is the audience likely to respond to this message?

11. Based on this audience analysis, would you use the direct or the indirect approach for this message? Explain your reasoning.

Revising Messages: Closing Paragraphs   Rewrite each of the following closing paragraphs to be concise, courteous, and specific.

12. I need your response sometime soon so I can order the parts in time for your service appointment. Otherwise your air-conditioning system may not be in tip-top condition for the start of the summer season.

13. Thank you in advance for sending me as much information as you can about your products. I look forward to receiving your package in the very near future.

14. To schedule an appointment with one of our knowledgeable mortgage specialists in your area, you can always call our hotline at 1-800-555-8765. This is also the number to call if you have more questions about mortgage rates, closing procedures, or any other aspect of the mortgage process. Remember, we're here to make the home-buying experience as painless as possible.

Activities

Active links for all websites in this chapter can be found on mybcommlab; see your User Guide for instructions on accessing the content for this chapter. Each activity is labeled according to the primary skill or skills you will need to use. To review relevant chapter content, you can refer to the indicated Learning Objective. In some instances, supporting information will be found in another chapter, as indicated.

1. **Message Strategies: Making Routine Requests; Completing: Evaluating Content, Organization, and Tone [LO-2], Chapter 5**   Analyze the strengths and weaknesses of this message and then revise it so that it follows this chapter's guidelines for routine requests for information:

   I'm fed up with the mistakes that our current accounting firm makes. I run a small construction company, and I don't have time to double-check every bookkeeping entry and call the accountants a dozen times when they won't return my messages. Please explain how your firm would do a better job than my current accountants. You have a good reputation among homebuilders, but before I consider hiring you to take over my accounting, I need to know that you care about quality work and good customer service.

2. **Message Strategies: Making Routine Requests; Completing: Evaluating Content, Organization, and Tone [LO-2], Chapter 5**   Analyze the strengths and weaknesses of this message and then revise it so that it follows this chapter's guidelines for routine requests for information:

I'm contacting you about your recent e-mail request for technical support on your cable Internet service. Part of the problem we have in tech support is trying to figure out exactly what each customer's specific problem is so that we can troubleshoot quickly and get you back in business as quickly as possible. You may have noticed that in the online support request form, there are a number of fields to enter your type of computer, operating system, memory, and so on. While you did tell us you were experiencing slow download speeds during certain times of the day, you didn't tell us which times specifically, nor did you complete all the fields telling us about your computer. Please return to our support website and resubmit your request, being sure to provide all the necessary information; then we'll be able to help you.

3. **Message Strategies: Making Routine Requests; Completing: Evaluating Content, Organization, and Tone [LO-2], Chapter 5**   Analyze the strengths and weaknesses of this message and then revise it so that it follows this chapter's guidelines for routine requests for adjustments:

At a local business-supply store, I recently purchased your *Negotiator Pro* for my computer. I bought the CD because I saw your ad for it in *Macworld* magazine, and it looked as if it might be an effective tool for use in my corporate seminar on negotiation.

Unfortunately, when I inserted it in my office computer, it wouldn't work. I returned it to the store, but because I had already opened it, they refused to exchange it for a CD that would work or give me a refund. They told me to contact you and that you might be able to send me a version that would work with my computer.

You can send the information to me at the letterhead address. If you cannot send me the correct disc, please refund my $79.95. Thanks in advance for any help you can give me in this matter.

4. **Message Strategies: Writing Routine Replies; Completing: Evaluating Content, Organization, and Tone [LO-4], Chapter 5**   Analyze the strengths and weaknesses of this message and then revise it so that it follows this chapter's guidelines for responding to requests for recommendations:

Your letter to Kunitake Ando, President of Sony, was forwarded to me because I am the human resources director. In my job as head of HR, I have access to performance reviews for all of the Sony employees in the United States. This means, of course, that I would be the person best qualified to answer your request for information on Nick Oshinski.

In your letter of the 15th, you asked about Nick Oshinski's employment record with us because he has applied to work for your company. Mr. Oshinski was employed with us from January 5, 1998, until March 1, 2008. During that time, Mr. Oshinski received ratings ranging from 2.5 up to 9.6, with 10 being the top score. As you can see, he must have done better reporting to some managers than to others. In addition, he took all vacation days, which is a bit unusual. Although I did not know Mr. Oshinski personally, I know that our best workers seldom use all the vacation time they earn. I do not know if that applies in this case.

In summary, Nick Oshinski performed his tasks well depending on who managed him.

5. **Message Strategies: Writing Routine Replies; Completing: Evaluating Content, Organization, and Tone [LO-4], Chapter 5**   Analyze the strengths and weaknesses of this message and then revise it so that it follows this chapter's guidelines for responding to requests for adjustments:

We read your letter, requesting your deposit refund. We couldn't figure out why you hadn't received it, so we talked to our maintenance engineer, as you suggested. He said you had left one of the doors off the hinges in your apartment in order to get a large sofa through the door. He also confirmed that you had paid him $5.00 to replace the door since you had to turn in the U-Haul trailer and were in a big hurry.

This entire situation really was caused by a lack of communication between our housekeeping inspector and the maintenance engineer. All we knew was that the door was off the hinges when it was inspected by Sally Tarnley. You know that our policy states that if anything is wrong with the apartment, we keep the deposit. We had no way of knowing that George just hadn't gotten around to replacing the door.

But we have good news. We approved the deposit refund, which will be mailed to you from our home office in Teaneck, New Jersey. I'm not sure how long that will take, however. If you don't receive the check by the end of next month, give me a call.

Next time, it's really a good idea to stay with your apartment until it's inspected, as stipulated in your lease agreement. That way, you'll be sure to receive your refund when you expect it. Hope you have a good summer.

 Learn how to set up a Twitter account and begin tweeting. Visit http://real-timeupdates.com/bce5, click on "Student Assignments" and then click on "Twitter Screencast."

6. **Message Strategies: Writing Positive Messages; Media Skills: Microblogging [LO-4], Chapter 6**   Locate an online announcement for a new product that you find interesting or useful. Read enough about the product to be able to describe it to someone else in your own words and then write four Twitter tweets: one to introduce the product to your followers and three follow-on tweets that describe three particularly compelling features or benefits of the product.

7. **Message Strategies: Writing Positive Messages; Intercultural Communication: Adapting to Cultural Differences [LO-4], Chapter 1**   You've been working two years as administrative assistant to Ron Glover, vice president of global workforce diversity at IBM's Learning Center in Armonk, New York. After listening to many of his speeches on maintaining multicultural sensitivity in the workplace, you know you're facing a sensitive situation right now.

The husband of your co-worker Chana Panichpapiboon was killed in a bus accident yesterday, along with 19 others. The bus skidded on icy pavement into a deep ravine, tipping over and crushing the occupants before rescue workers could get to them.

You met her husband, Surin, last year at a company banquet. You can still picture his warm smile and the easy way he joked with you and others over chicken Florentine, even though you were complete strangers to him. He was only 32 years old, and he left Chana with two children, a 12-year-old boy, Arsa, and a 10-year-old girl, Veera. His death is a terrible tragedy.

You know you should write a condolence letter, but you are unsure of some vital details. Chana Panichpapiboon is a native of Thailand, and so was Surin, but you are not familiar with Thai culture. Is Chana Buddhist or Catholic? Is there anything about the typical Western practice of expressing sympathy that might be inappropriate? Offensive?

After making some discreet inquiries among Chana's closest friends at work, you learn that she is Theravada Buddhist, as are most people in Thailand. In a reference book your boss lends you about doing business around the world, you read that in Thailand, "the person takes precedence over rule or law" and "people gain their social position as a result of karma, not personal achievement," which means Chana may believe in reincarnation. But the book also says that Theravada Buddhists are free to choose which precepts of their religion, if any, they will follow. So Chana's beliefs are still a mystery.

You do know that her husband was very important to her and much loved by all their family. That, at least, is universal. And you're considering using a poetic line you remember, "The hand of time lightly lays, softly soothing sorrow's wound." Is it appropriate?

You've decided to handwrite the condolence note on a blank greeting card you've found that bears a peaceful, "Eastern-flavor" image. You know you're risking a cultural gaffe, but you don't want to commit the offense of not writing at all. Use the following questions to help you think through your choices before you begin writing:[9]

   a. If you had to choose among these sentences, which one would make the best opening?

     1. I was so sorry to hear the news about your husband.

     2. What a terrible tragedy you have suffered.

     3. If there's anything I can do for you, Chana, please let me know.

     4. You and your children must be so upset, and who could blame you?

   b. In the body of the letter, you want to express something meaningful, but you're concerned about Chana's beliefs and you're not sure what's safe. Choose the best idea from the following:

     1. You could quote the poem about "the hand of time" mentioned in the case.

     2. You could express your sorrow for Chana's children.

     3. You could mention something nice about Surin you learned during your brief meeting.

   c. For your closing paragraph, which of these ideas is best?

     1. Take a moment to express your thoughts about death and the hereafter.

     2. Say something positive and encouraging about Chana.

     3. Explain that you don't understand her religious beliefs and aren't sure what's appropriate to say at this time.

     4. All of the above.

   d. In the following list, identify all the words you should avoid as you write:

     1. Death

     2. Departure

     3. Karma

     4. Unbearable

Now write the condolence letter in your own words. Remember that sincerity is the most important tool in overcoming differences of custom or tradition.

Expand Your Skills

Critique the Professionals

Locate an online example of a news release in which a company announces good news, such as a new product, a notable executive hire, an expansion, strong financial results, or an industry award. Analyze the release using the bullet list on page 198 as a guide. In what ways did the writer excel? What aspects of the release could be improved? Using whatever medium your instructor requests, write a brief analysis of the piece (no more than one page), citing specific elements from the piece and support from the chapter.

Sharpen Your Career Skills Online

Bovée and Thill's Business Communication Web Search, at http://businesscommunicationblog.com/websearch, is a unique research tool designed specifically for business communication research. Use the Web Search function to find a website, video, PDF document, podcast, or presentation that offers advice on writing goodwill messages such as thank-you notes or congratulatory letters. Write a brief e-mail message to your instructor or a post for your class blog, describing the item that you found and summarizing the career skills information you learned from it.

mybcommlab

If your course uses mybcommlab, log on to www .mybcommlab.com to access the following study and assessment aids associated with this chapter:

- Video applications
- Pre/post test
- Real-Time Updates
- Personalized study plan

- Peer review activity
- Model documents
- Quick Learning Guides
- Sample presentations

If you are not using mybcommlab, you can access Real-Time Updates and Quick Learning Guides through http://real-time updates.com/bce5. The Quick Learning Guide (located under "Learn More" on the website) hits all the high points of this chapter in just two pages. This guide, especially prepared by the authors, will help you study for exams or review important concepts whenever you need a quick refresher.

CASES

▼ *Apply the three-step writing process to the following cases, as assigned by your instructor.*

E-MAIL SKILLS

1. Message Strategies: Making Routine Requests [LO-2]   After five years of work in the human resources department at Cell Genesys (a company that is developing cancer treatment drugs), you were laid off in a round of cost-cutting moves that rippled through the biotech industry in recent years. The good news is that you found stable employment in the grocery distribution industry. The bad news is that in the three years since you left Cell Genesys, you have truly missed working in the exciting biotechnology field and having the opportunity to be a part of something as important as helping people recover from life-threatening diseases. You know that careers in biotech are uncertain, but you have a few dollars in the bank now, so you're more willing to accept the risk of being laid off at some point in the future.

Your task Draft an e-mail to Calvin Morris, your old boss at Cell Genesys, reminding him of the time you worked together and asking him to write a letter of recommendation for you.[10]

IM SKILLS

2. Message Strategies: Making Routine Requests; Intercultural Communication: Writing for Multiple-Language Audiences [LO-2]   Chapter 1 Production on a popular line of decorative lighting appliances produced at your Chinese manufacturing plant inexplicably came to a halt last month. As the product manager in the United States, you have many resources you could call on to help, such as new sources for faulty parts. But you can't do anything if you don't know the details. You've tried telephoning top managers in China, but they're evasive, telling you only what they think you want to hear.

Finally, your friend Kuei-chen Tsao has returned from a business trip. You met her during your trip to China last year. She doesn't speak English, but she's the line engineer responsible for

this particular product: a fiber-optic lighting display, featuring a plastic base with a rotating color wheel. As the wheel turns, light emitted from the spray of fiber-optic threads changes color in soothing patterns. Product #3347XM is one of Diagonal's most popular items, and you've got orders from novelty stores around the United States waiting to be filled. Kuei-chen should be able to explain the problem, determine whether you can help, and tell you how long before regular shipping resumes.

Your task Write the first of what you hope will be a productive instant messaging (IM) exchange with Kuei-chen. The IM system you are using offers real-time translation, so keep this factor in mind as you write.[11]

TEXT MESSAGING SKILLS

3. Message Strategies: Making Routine Requests [LO-2]   The vast Consumer Electronics Show (CES) is the premier promotional event in the electronics industry. More than 100,000 industry insiders from all over the world come to see the exciting new products on display from 2,500 companies—everything from video game gadgets to Internet-enabled refrigerators with built-in computer screens. You've just stumbled on a video game controller that has a built-in webcam to allow networked gamers to see and hear each other while they play. Your company also makes game controllers, and you're worried that your customers will flock to this new controller-cam. You need to know how much "buzz" is circulating around the show: Have people seen it? What are they saying about it? Are they excited about it?

Your task Compose a text message to your colleagues at the show, alerting them to the new controller-cam and asking them to listen for any buzz that it might be generating among the attendees at the Las Vegas Convention Center and the several surrounding hotels where the show takes place. Your text messaging service limits messages to 160 characters, including spaces and punctuation, so your message can't be any longer than this.[12]

E-MAIL SKILLS

4. Message Strategies: Making Routine Requests [LO-2]   Love at first listen is the only way to describe the way you felt when you discovered SongThrong.com. You enjoy dozens of styles of music, from Afrobeat and Tropicalia to mainstream pop and the occasional blast of industrial metal, and SongThrong.com has them all for only $9.99 a month. You can explore every genre imaginable, listening to as many tracks as you like for a fixed monthly fee. The service sounded too good to be true—and sadly, it was. The service was so unreliable that you began keeping note of when it was unavailable. Last month, it was down for all or part of 12 days—well over a third of the month. As much as you like it, you've had enough.

Your task   Write an e-mail to support@songthrong.com, requesting a full refund. To get the special $9.99 monthly rate, you prepaid for an entire year ($119.88), and you've been a subscriber for two months now. You know the service was out for at least part of the time on 12 separate days last month, and while you didn't track outages during the first month, you believe it was about the same number of days.

E-MAIL SKILLS

5. Message Strategies: Making Routine Requests [LO-2]   You head up the corporate marketing department for a nationwide chain of clothing stores. The company has decided to launch a new store-within-a-store concept, in which a small section of each store will showcase "business casual" clothing. To ensure a successful launch of this new strategy, you want to get input from the best retailing minds in the company. You also know it's important to get regional insights from around the country, because a merchandising strategy that works in one area might not succeed in another.

Your task   Write an e-mail message to all 87 store managers, asking them to each nominate one person to serve on an advisory team (managers can nominate themselves if they are local market experts). Explain that you want to find people with at least five years of retailing experience, a good understanding of the local business climate, and thorough knowledge of the local retail competition. In addition, the best candidates will be good team players who are comfortable collaborating long distance, using virtual meeting technologies. Also, explain that while you are asking each of the 87 stores to nominate someone, the team will be limited to no more than eight people. You've met many of the store managers, but not all of them, so be sure to introduce yourself at the beginning of the message.

LETTER WRITING SKILLS

6. Message Strategies: Making Routine Requests [LO-2]   As a consumer, you've probably bought something that didn't work right or paid for a service that didn't turn out the way you expected. Maybe it was a pair of jeans with a rip in a seam that you didn't find until you got home or a watch that broke a week after you bought it. Or maybe your family hired a lawn service to do some yard work, and no one from the company showed up on the day promised. When a man finally appeared, he did not do what he'd been hired for but did other things that wound up damaging valuable plants.

You'd be wise to write a claim letter asking for a refund, repair, replacement, or other adjustment. You'll need to include all the details of the transaction, plus your contact address and phone number.

Your task   To practice writing claim letters, choose an experience like this from your own background or make up details for these imaginary situations. If your experience is real, you might want to mail the letter. The reply you receive will provide a good test of your claim-writing skills.

PODCASTING SKILLS

7. Message Strategies: Writing Routine Messages [LO-4], Chapter 6   As a training specialist in the human resources department at Winnebago Industries, you're always on the lookout for new ways to help employees learn vital job skills. While watching a production worker page through a training manual, learning how to assemble a new recreational vehicle, you get what seems to be a great idea: Record the assembly instructions as audio files that workers can listen to while performing the necessary steps. With audio instructions, they wouldn't need to keep shifting their eyes between the product and the manual—and constantly losing their place. They could focus on the product and listen for each instruction. Plus, the new system wouldn't cost much at all; any computer can record the audio files, and you'd simply make them available on an intranet site for download onto iPods or other digital music players.

Your task   You immediately run your new idea past your boss, who has heard about podcasting but isn't sure it is appropriate for business training. He asks you to prove the viability of the idea by recording a demonstration. Choose a process that you engage in yourself—anything from replacing the strings on a guitar to sewing a quilt to changing the oil in a car—and write a brief (one page or less) description of the process that could be recorded as an audio file. Think carefully about the limitations of the audio format as a replacement for printed text (for instance, do you need to tell people to pause the audio while they perform each task?). If your instructor directs, record your podcast and submit the audio file.

E-MAIL SKILLS   TEAM SKILLS

8. Message Strategies: Writing Routine Replies; Collaboration: Team Projects [LO-4], Chapter 2   You are director of customer services at Highway Bytes, which markets a series of small, handlebar-mounted computers for bicyclists. These Cycle Computers do everything, from computing speed and distance traveled to displaying street maps with voice-controlled GPS navigation. Serious cyclists love them, but your company is growing so fast that you can't keep up with all the customer service requests you receive every day. Your boss wants not only to speed up response time but also to reduce staffing costs and allow your technical experts the time they need to focus on the most difficult and important questions.

You've just been reading about automated response systems, and you quickly review a few articles before discussing the options with your boss. Artificial intelligence researchers have been working for decades to design systems that can actually converse with customers, ask questions, and respond to requests. Some of today's systems have vocabularies of thousands of words and the ability to understand simple sentences. For example, *chatterbots* are automated bots that can mimic human conversation, to a degree.

Unfortunately, even though chatterbots hold a lot of promise, human communication is so complex that a truly automated customer service agent could take years to perfect (and may even prove to be impossible). However, the simplest automated systems, called *autoresponders*, are fast and extremely inexpensive. They have no built-in intelligence, so they do nothing more than send back the same reply to every message they receive.

You explain to your boss that although some of the messages you receive require the attention of your product specialists, many are simply requests for straightforward information. In fact, the customer service staff already answers some 70 percent of e-mail queries with three ready-made attachments:

- **Installing Your Cycle Computer.** Gives customers advice on installing the cycle computer the first time or reinstalling it on a new bike. In most cases, the computer and wheel sensor bolt directly to the bike without modification, but certain bikes require extra work.

- **Troubleshooting Your Cycle Computer.** Provides a step-by-step guide to figuring out what might be wrong with a malfunctioning cycle computer. Most problems are simple, such as dead batteries or loose wires, but others are beyond the capabilities of your typical customer.

- **Upgrading the Software in Your Cycle Computer.** Tells customers how to attach the cycle computer to their home or office PC and download new software from Highway Bytes.

Your boss is enthusiastic when you explain that you can program your current e-mail system to look for specific words in incoming messages and then respond, based on what it finds. For example, if a customer message contains the word *installation*, you can program the system to reply with the *Installing Your Cycle Computer* attachment. This reconfigured system should be able to handle a sizeable portion of the hundreds of e-mails your customer service group gets every week.

Your task With a team assigned by your instructor, first compile a list of key words that you'll want your e-mail system to look for. You'll need to be creative and spend some time with a thesaurus. Identify all the words and word combinations that could identify a message pertaining to one of the three subject areas. For instance, the word *attach* would probably indicate a need for the installation material, whereas *new software* would most likely suggest a need for the upgrade attachment. Second, draft three short e-mail messages to accompany each ready-made attachment, explaining that the attached document answers the most common questions on a particular

subject (installation, troubleshooting, or upgrading). Your messages should invite recipients to write back if the attached document doesn't solve the problem, and don't forget to provide the e-mail address: support2@highwaybytes.com.

Third, draft a fourth message to be sent out whenever your new system is unable to figure out what the customer is asking for. Simply thank the customer for writing and explain that the query will be passed on to a customer service specialist who will respond shortly.

BLOGGING SKILLS

9. Message Strategies: Writing Positive Messages [LO-4] You are normally an easygoing manager who gives your employees a lot of leeway in using their own personal communication styles. However, the weekly staff meeting this morning pushed you over the edge. People were interrupting one another, asking questions that had already been answered, sending text messages during presentations, and exhibiting just about every other poor listening habit imaginable.

Your task Review the advice in Chapter 2 on good listening skills, then write a post for the internal company blog. Emphasize the importance of effective listening and list at least five steps your employees can take to become better listeners.

BLOGGING SKILLS

10. Message Strategies: Writing Positive Messages [LO-4] You and your staff in the public relations (PR) department at Epson of America were delighted when the communication campaign you created for the new PictureMate Personal Photo Lab (www.epson.com/picturemate) was awarded the prestigious Silver Anvil award by the Public Relations Society of America. Now you'd like to give your team a pat on the back by sharing the news with the rest of the company.

Your task Write a one-paragraph message for the PR department blog (which is read by people throughout the company but is not accessible outside the company), announcing the award. Take care not to focus the attention on yourself as the manager of the PR department and use the opportunity to compliment the rest of the company for designing and producing such an innovative product.[13]

LETTER WRITING SKILLS

11. Message Strategies: Writing Positive Messages [LO-4] As chief administrator for the underwriting department of Aetna Health Plans in Walnut Creek, California, you're facing a difficult task. One of your best underwriters, Hector Almeida, recently lost his wife in an automobile accident (he and his teenage daughter weren't with her at the time). Because you're the boss, everyone in the close-knit department is looking to you to communicate the group's sympathy and concern.

Someone suggested a simple greeting card that everyone could sign, but that seems too impersonal for someone you've worked with every day for nearly five years. So you decided to write a personal note on behalf of the whole department. You met Hector's wife, Rosalia, at a few company functions, although you knew her mostly through Hector's frequent references to her. Although you didn't know her well, you do know important things about her life, which you can celebrate in the letter.

Right now he's devastated by the loss. But if anyone can overcome this tragedy, Hector can. He's always determined to get a job done no matter what obstacles present themselves, and he does it with an upbeat attitude. That's why everyone in the office likes him so much.

You also plan to suggest that when he returns to work, he might like to move his schedule up an hour so that he'll have more time to spend with his daughter, Lisa, after school. It's your way of helping make things a little easier for them during this period of adjustment.

Your task Write the letter to Hector Almeida, who lives at 47 West Ave., #10, Walnut Creek, CA 94596. Feel free to make up any details you need.[14]

BLOGGING SKILLS

12. Message Strategies: Writing Positive Messages [LO-4] Advertising agency GSD&M Idea City, of Austin, Texas, brainstorms new advertising ideas using a process it calls dynamic collaboration. A hand-picked team of insiders and outsiders are briefed on the project and given a key question or two to answer. The team members then sit down at computers and anonymously submit as many responses as they can within five minutes. The project moderators then pore over these responses, looking for any sparks that can ignite new ways of understanding and reaching out to consumers.

Your task For these brainstorming sessions, GSD&M recruits an eclectic mix of participants from inside and outside the agency—figures as diverse as economists and professional video gamers. To make sure everyone understands the brainstorming guidelines, prepare a message to be posted on the project blog. In your own words, convey the following four points as clearly and succinctly as you can:

- **Be yourself.** We want input from as many perspectives as possible, which is why we recruit such a diverse array of participants. Don't try to get into what you believe is the mindset of an advertising specialist; we want you to approach the given challenge using whatever analytical and creative skills you normally employ in your daily work.
- **Create, don't edit.** Don't edit, refine, or self-censor while you're typing during the initial five-minute session. We don't care if your ideas are formatted beautifully, phrased poetically, or even spelled correctly. Just crank 'em out as quickly as you can.
- **It's about the ideas, not the participants.** Just so you know up front, all ideas are collected anonymously. We can't tell who submitted the brilliant ideas, the boring ideas, or the already-tried-that ideas. So while you won't get personal credit, you can also be crazy and fearless. Go for it!
- **The winning ideas will be subjected to the toughest of tests.** Just in case you're worried about submitting ideas

that could be risky, expensive, or difficult to implement—don't fret. As we narrow down the possibilities, the few that remain will be judged, poked, prodded, and assessed from every angle. In other words, let us worry about containing the fire; you come up with the sparks.[15]

E-MAIL SKILLS   PORTFOLIO BUILDER

13. Message Strategies: Writing Routine Replies [LO-4] Walmart has grown to international success because it rarely fails to capitalize on a marketing scheme, and its website is no exception. To make sure the website remains effective and relevant, the webmaster asks various people to check out the site and give their feedback. As administrative assistant to Walmart's director of marketing, you have just received a request from the webmaster to visit Walmart's website and give your feedback.

Your task Visit www.walmart.com and do some online "window shopping." As you browse through the site, consider the language, layout, graphics, and overall ease of use. In particular, look for aspects of the site that might be confusing or frustrating—annoyances that could prompt shoppers to abandon their quests and head to a competitor such as Target or Amazon. Summarize your findings and recommendations in an e-mail message to the webmaster.

LETTER WRITING SKILLS   TEAM SKILLS

14. Message Strategies: Writing Positive Messages; Collaboration: Team Projects [LO-4], Chapter 2 As a project manager at Orbitz, one of the largest online travel services in the world, you've seen plenty of college interns in action. However, few have impressed you as much as Maxine "Max" Chenault. For one thing, she learned how to navigate the company's content management system virtually overnight and always used it properly, whereas other interns sometimes left things in a hopeless mess. She asked lots of intelligent questions about the business. You've been teaching her blogging and website design principles, and she's picked them up rapidly. Moreover, she has always been on time, professional, and eager to assist. Also, she hasn't minded doing mundane tasks.

On the down side, Chenault is a popular student. Early on, you often found her busy on the phone planning her many social activities when you needed her help. However, after you had a brief talk with her, this problem vanished.

You'll be sorry to see Chenault leave when she returns to school in the fall, but you're pleased to respond when she asks you for a letter of recommendation. She's not sure where she'll apply for work after graduation or what career path she'll choose, so she asks you to keep the letter fairly general.

Your task Working with a team assigned by your instructor, discuss what should and should not be in the letter. Prepare an outline based on your discussion and then draft the letter.

SOCIAL NETWORKING SKILLS

15. Message Strategies: Writing Positive Messages; Composition Modes: Summarizing [LO-4] As energy costs trend ever upward and more people become attuned to the environmental and geopolitical complexities of petroleum-based energy, interest in solar, wind, and other alternative energy sources continues to grow. In locations with high *insolation*, a measure of cumulative sunlight, solar panels can be cost-effective solutions over the long term. However, the upfront costs are still daunting for most homeowners. To help lower the entry barrier, the Foster City, California–based firm SolarCity now lets homeowners lease solar panels for monthly payments that are less than their current electricity bills.[16]

Your task   Visit www.solarcity.com, click on "Residential," and then click "SolarLease" to read about the leasing program. Next, study SolarCity's presence on Facebook (www.facebook .com/solarcity) to get a feel for how the company presents itself in a social networking environment. Now assume that you have been assigned the task of writing a brief summary of the SolarLease program that will appear on the Notes tab of SolarCity's Facebook page. In your own language and in 200 words or less, write an introduction to the SolarLease program and e-mail it to your instructor.

Improve Your Grammar, Mechanics, and Usage

You can download the text of this assignment from http://real-timeupdates.com/bce5; click on "Student Assignments" and then click on "Chapter 7. Improve Your Grammar, Mechanics, and Usage."

Level 1: Self-Assessment—Periods, Question Marks, and Exclamation Points

Review Sections 2.1, 2.2, and 2.3 in the Handbook of Grammar, Mechanics, and Usage, and then complete the following 15 items.

In items 1–15, add periods, question marks, and exclamation points wherever they are appropriate.

1. Dr Eleanor H Hutton has requested information on TaskMasters, Inc
2. That qualifies us as a rapidly growing new company, don't you think
3. Our president, Daniel Gruber, is a CPA On your behalf, I asked him why he started the company
4. In the past three years, we have experienced phenomenal growth of 800 percent
5. Contact me at 1358 N Parsons Avenue, Tulsa, OK 74204
6. Jack asked, "Why does he want to know Maybe he plans to become a competitor"
7. The debt load fluctuates with the movement of the US prime rate
8. I can't believe we could have missed such a promising opportunity
9. Is consumer loyalty extinct Yes and No.
10. Johnson and Kane, Inc, has gone out of business What a surprise

11. Will you please send us a check today so that we can settle your account
12. Mr James R Capp will be our new CEO, beginning January 20, 2009
13. The rag doll originally sold for $1098, but we have lowered the price to a mere $599
14. Will you be able to make the presentation at the conference, or should we find someone else
15. So I ask you, "When will we admit defeat" Never

Level 2: Workplace Applications

The following items may contain errors in grammar, capitalization, punctuation, abbreviation, number style, word division, and vocabulary. Rewrite each sentence, correcting all errors. If a sentence has no errors, write "Correct" for that number.

1. Attached to both the Train Station and the Marriott hotel, one doesnt even need to step outside the convention center to go from train to meeting room.
2. According to Federal statistics, 61 percent of the nations employers have less than 5 workers.
3. "The problem", said Business Owner Mike Millorn, "Was getting vendor's of raw materials to take my endeavor serious."
4. After pouring over trade journals, quizzing industry experts, and talks with other snack makers, the Harpers' decided to go in the pita chip business.
5. Some argue that a Mac with half as much RAM and a slower processor is as fast or faster than a PC.
6. The couple has done relatively little advertising, instead they give away samples in person at trade shows, cooking demonstrations, and in grocery stores.
7. CME Information Services started by videotaping doctor's conventions, and selling the recorded presentations to nonattending physicians that wanted to keep track of the latest developments.
8. For many companies, the two biggest challenges to using intranets are: getting people to use it and content freshness.
9. Company meetings including 'lunch and learn' sessions are held online often.
10. Most Children's Orchard franchisees, are men and women between the ages of 30–50; first time business owners with a wide range of computer skills.
11. Joining the company in 1993, she had watched it expand and grow from a single small office to a entire floor of a skyscraper.
12. One issue that effected practically everyone was that they needed to train interns.
13. The website includes information on subjects as mundane as the filling out of a federal express form, and as complex as researching a policy issue.

14. "Some management theories are good, but how many people actually implement them the right way?", says Jack Hartnett President of D. L. Rogers Corp.

15. Taking orders through car windows, customers are served by roller-skating carhops at Sonic restaurants.

Level 3: Document Critique

The following e-mail message (an initial inquiry to a firm that designs and builds corporate websites) may contain errors in grammar, punctuation, capitalization, abbreviation, number style, vocabulary, and spelling. You will also find errors related to topics in this chapter. For example, consider the organization and relevance of material as you improve this routine request for information. As your instructor indicates, photocopy this page and correct all errors using standard proofreading marks (see Appendix C) or download the document and make the corrections in your word processing software.

TO: info@spacewebdesign.biz
FROM: gloria_m@midwestliquidators.com
SUBJECT: New website!

To Whom it may concern.

We need a new website. One that offers all the whizzy new social media apabilities plus ful e/commerce ordering & retailing function.

I am seeing your name in the fine print of a few nice looking sights. So I wanted to get more info on you people and find out about costs, schedules, info needs from us, etc., etc., etc. What it will take to get this new thing up and running, inother words. We also need to know what you plan to do about our "visual" appearance on the website—as in—how will you design a site that screams "good values found here" without looking cheap and shoddy like some discount/retail webbsites are...

My name is Gloria MacPherson, and I am in charge of Marketing and sales department here at Midwest Liquidators. I've been with the Company since 2003; before that I was with Costco; before that I was with Sears.

Part of my analysis of outsiders like you will depend on how fast you respond to this query, just to let you know.

Sincerely.
Gloria

CHAPTER 8

Writing Negative Messages

LEARNING OBJECTIVES

After studying this chapter, you will be able to

1 Apply the three-step writing process to negative messages

2 Explain how to use the direct approach effectively when conveying negative news

3 Explain how to use the indirect approach effectively when conveying negative news and explain how to avoid ethical problems when using this approach

4 Describe successful strategies for sending negative messages on routine business matters

5 Describe successful strategies for sending negative employment-related messages

6 List the important points to consider when conveying negative organizational news

7 Describe an effective strategy for responding to negative information in a social media environment

---

PEARSON
mybcommlab

Access interactive videos, simulations, sample documents, Document Makeovers, and assessment quizzes in Chapter 8 of mybcommlab.com for mastery of this chapter's objectives.

COMMUNICATION
Matters

" Social media is a powerful crisis management tool, but only if you have been using it when you are not in crisis mode, too. It's real engagement, not campaign-based marketing. And in a crisis, it will be easy to see which is which. "

—Matt Rhodes, Client Services Director, *FreshNetworks*

Media expert Matt Rhodes advises clients to establish strong relationships with their audiences before the need to convey negative messages ever arises.

Communicating during a serious crisis is a challenge that relatively few managers will ever face, but every manager and many employees must convey negative information from time to time. Sharing unwelcome news is never pleasant, but it must be done, and learning how to do it with tact and sensitivity will make the task easier for you as a writer and easier for the recipients of your messages, too.

As Matt Rhodes of the London-based social media agency FreshNetworks suggests, your relationship with the audience is a crucial factor in the delivery of negative messages. For example, social media tools can be effective for communicating negative news and responding to crises and complaints, but they work best when you have already established a meaningful relationship with your stakeholders.[1]

USING THE THREE-STEP WRITING PROCESS FOR NEGATIVE MESSAGES

Delivering negative information is rarely easy and never enjoyable, but with some helpful guidelines, you can craft messages that minimize negative reactions. When you need to deliver bad news, you have five goals: (1) to convey the bad news, (2) to gain acceptance for it, (3) to maintain as much goodwill as possible with your audience, (4) to maintain a good image for your organization, and (5) if appropriate, to reduce or eliminate the need for future correspondence on the matter. Accomplishing all five goals requires careful attention to planning, writing, and completing your message.

Step 1: Planning Negative Messages

When planning messages that will convey negative news, you can't avoid the fact that your audience does not want to hear what you have to say. To minimize the damage to business relationships and to encourage the acceptance of your message, plan carefully. With a clear purpose and your audience's needs in mind, gather the information your audience will need in order to understand and accept your message.

Selecting the right medium is critical. For instance, experts advise that bad news for employees always be delivered in person whenever possible, both to show respect for the employees and to give them an opportunity to ask questions. Of course, delivering bad news is never easy, and an increasing number of managers appear to be using e-mail and other electronic media to convey negative messages to employees.[2]

Finally, the organization of a negative message requires particular care. One of the most critical planning decisions is choosing whether to use the direct or indirect approach (see Figure 8.1). A negative message using the **direct approach** opens with the bad news, proceeds to the reasons for the situation or the decision, and ends with a positive statement aimed at maintaining a good relationship with the audience. In contrast, the **indirect approach** opens with the reasons behind the bad news before presenting the bad news itself.

To help decide which approach to take in any situation you encounter, ask yourself the following questions:

- **Will the bad news come as a shock?** The direct approach is fine for many business situations in which people understand the possibility of receiving bad news. However, if the bad news might come as a shock to readers, use the indirect approach to help them prepare for it.

- **Does the reader prefer short messages that get right to the point?** For example, if you know that your boss always wants messages that get right to the point, even when they deliver bad news, use the direct approach.

1 LEARNING OBJECTIVE
Apply the three-step writing process to negative messages

Five goals of negative messages:
- Give the bad news.
- Ensure its acceptance.
- Maintain reader's goodwill.
- Maintain organization's good image.
- Reduce future correspondence on the matter.

Careful planning is necessary to avoid alienating your readers.

Choose the medium with care when preparing negative messages.

The appropriate organization helps readers accept your negative news.

Use the direct approach when your negative answer or information will have minimal personal impact; consider the indirect approach for more serious matters.

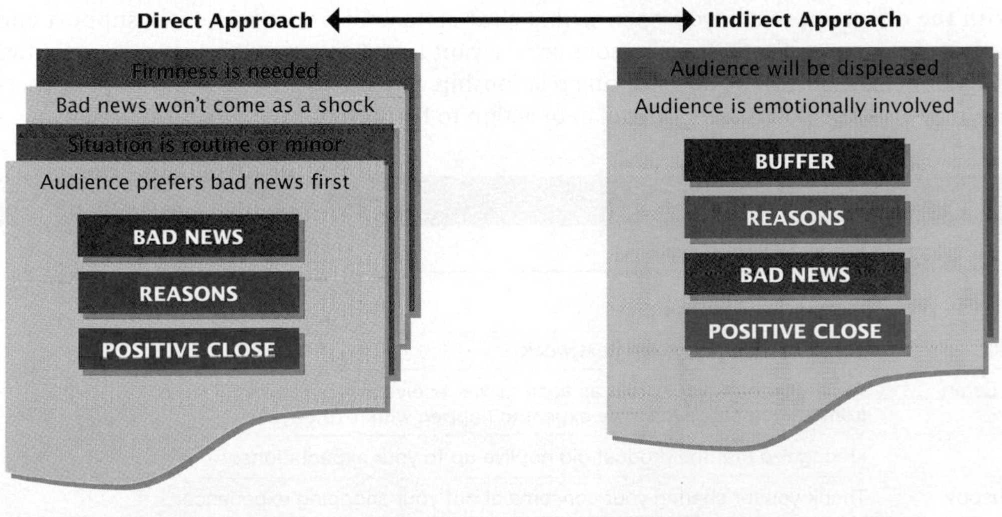

Figure 8.1   Choosing the Direct or Indirect Approach for Negative Messages
Analyze the situation carefully before choosing your approach to organizing negative messages.

- **How important is this news to the reader?** For minor or routine scenarios, the direct approach is nearly always best. However, if the reader has an emotional investment in the situation or the consequences to the reader are considerable, the indirect approach is often better.

- **Do you need to maintain a close working relationship with the reader?** The indirect approach lets you soften the blow of bad news and preserve a positive business relationship.

- **Do you need to get the reader's attention?** If someone has ignored repeated messages, the direct approach can help you get his or her attention.

- **What is your organization's preferred style?** Some companies have a distinct communication style, ranging from blunt and direct to gentle and indirect.

Step 2: Writing Negative Messages

By writing clearly and sensitively, you can take some of the sting out of bad news and help your reader accept the decision and move on. If your credibility hasn't already been established with an audience, clarify your qualifications so message recipients won't question your authority or ability.

Choose your language carefully; it is possible to deliver negative news without being negative.

When you use language that conveys respect and avoids an accusing tone, you protect your audience's pride. This kind of communication etiquette is always important, but it demands special care with negative messages. Moreover, you can ease the sense of disappointment by using positive words rather than negative, counterproductive ones (see Table 8.1).

Step 3: Completing Negative Messages

The need for careful attention to detail continues as you complete your message. Revise your content to make sure everything is clear, complete, and concise—even small flaws can be magnified in readers' minds as they react to your negative news. Produce clean, professional documents and proofread carefully to eliminate mistakes. Finally, be sure to deliver messages promptly; withholding or delaying bad news can be unethical and even illegal.

> **QUALITY** *Matters*
>
> Careless mistakes in a negative message can make a bad situation even worse by creating the impression that the sender doesn't care enough about the situation to invest the time and effort it takes to produce a professional-quality message.

2 **LEARNING OBJECTIVE**

Explain how to use the direct approach effect when conveying negative news

USING THE DIRECT APPROACH FOR NEGATIVE MESSAGES

With the direct approach, you open with a clear statement of the bad news, support and explain that news with whatever reasons are relevant to the situation, and close in a positive way that helps maintain a good working relationship with readers (see Figure 8.2). The message may also offer alternatives or a plan of action to fix the situation under discussion.

TABLE 8.1   Choosing Positive Words

Examples of Negative Phrasings	Positive Alternatives
Your request *doesn't make any sense.*	Please clarify your request.
The *damage won't be fixed* for a week.	The item will be repaired next week.
Although it wasn't *our fault*, there will be an *unavoidable delay* in your order.	We will process your order as soon as we receive an aluminum shipment from our supplier, which we expect to happen within 10 days.
You are clearly *dissatisfied*.	I recognize that the product did not live up to your expectations.
I was *shocked* to learn that you're *unhappy*.	Thank you for sharing your concerns about your shopping experience.
Unfortunately, we haven't received it.	The item hasn't arrived yet.
The enclosed statement is *wrong*.	Please verify the enclosed statement and provide a correct copy.

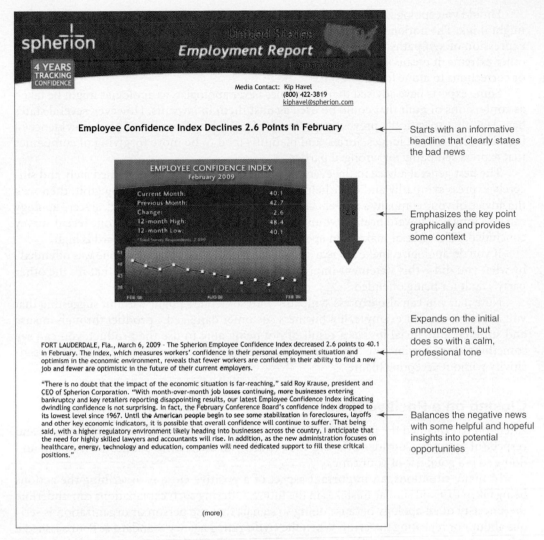

Starts with an informative headline that clearly states the bad news

Emphasizes the key point graphically and provides some context

Expands on the initial announcement, but does so with a calm, professional tone

Balances the negative news with some helpful and hopeful insights into potential opportunities

Figure 8.2 Negative Message Using the Direct Approach
Spherion Corporation, a recruiting and staffing firm based in Fort Lauderdale, Florida, conducts monthly surveys of the U.S. workforce. The company used the direct approach to announce a decline in employee confidence.

The primary advantage of the direct approach is efficiency. Direct messages take less time for you to write, and readers need less time to reach the main idea of the message.

Opening with a Clear Statement of the Bad News

If you've chosen the direct approach to convey bad news, come right out and say it. Maintain a calm, professional tone that keeps the focus on the news and not on individual failures. Also, if necessary, remind the reader why you're writing.

Providing Reasons and Additional Information

In most cases, you'll follow the direct opening with an explanation of why the news is negative. The extent of your explanation depends on the nature of the news and your relationship with the reader. For example, if you want to preserve a long-standing relationship with an important customer, a detailed explanation could well be worth the extra effort such a message would require.

The amount of detail you provide depends on your relationship with the audience.

However, you will encounter some situations in which explaining negative news is neither appropriate nor helpful, such as when the reasons are confidential, excessively complicated, or irrelevant to the reader. To maintain a cordial working relationship with the reader, you might want to explain why you can't provide the information.

The decision whether to apologize depends on a number of factors; if you do apologize, be sincere.

Should you apologize when delivering bad news? The answer isn't quite as simple as one might think. The notion of *apology* is hard to pin down. To some people, it simply means an expression of sympathy that something negative has happened to another person. At the other extreme, it means admitting fault and taking responsibility for specific compensations or corrections to atone for the mistake.

Some experts have advised that companies never apologize, as apologies might be taken as confessions of guilt that could be used against them in lawsuits. However, several states have laws that specifically prevent expressions of sympathy from being used as evidence of legal liability. In fact, judges, juries, and plaintiffs tend to be more forgiving of companies that express sympathy for wronged parties.[3]

The best general advice in the event of a mistake or accident is to immediately and sincerely express sympathy and offer help, if appropriate, without admitting guilt; then seek the advice of your company's lawyers before elaborating. A straightforward, sincere apology can go a long way toward healing wounds and rebuilding relationships. As one recent survey concluded, "The risks of making an apology are low, and the potential reward is high."[4]

If you do apologize, make it a real apology. Don't say "I'm sorry if anyone was offended" by what you did—this statement implies that you're not sorry at all and that it's the other party's fault for being offended.[5]

Note that you can also express sympathy with someone's plight without suggesting that you are to blame. For example, if a business customer damaged a product through misuse and suffered a financial loss as a result of not being able to use the product, you can say something along the lines of "I'm sorry to hear of your difficulties." This demonstrates sensitivity without accepting blame.

Closing on a Positive Note

Close your message in a positive but respectful tone.

After you've explained the negative news, close the message in a positive but still honest and respectful manner. Consider offering your readers an alternative solution if you can and doing so is a good use of your time.

In many situations, an important aspect of a positive close is describing the actions being taken to avoid similar mistakes in the future. Offering such explanations can underline the sincerity of an apology because doing so signals that the person or organization is serious about not repeating the error. When the credit rating agency Standard & Poor's issued a statement expressing regret for its role in the recent subprime mortgage meltdown that helped throw the economy into a deep recession, the company also described the changes it was making "to restore investor confidence in our ratings," as company president Deven Sharma explained.[6]

3 LEARNING OBJECTIVE

Explain how to use the indirect approach effectively when conveying negative news and explain how to avoid ethical problems when using this approach

Use the indirect approach when some preparation will help your audience accept your bad news.

USING THE INDIRECT APPROACH FOR NEGATIVE MESSAGES

As noted earlier, the indirect approach helps readers prepare for the bad news by outlining the reasons for the situation before presenting the bad news itself. However, the indirect approach is not meant to obscure bad news, delay it, or limit your responsibility. The purpose of this approach is to ease the blow and help readers accept the news. When done poorly, the indirect approach can be disrespectful and even unethical. But when done well, it is a good example of "you"-oriented communication crafted with attention to both ethics and etiquette.

Opening with a Buffer

A buffer establishes common ground with the reader.

The first step in using the indirect approach is to write a **buffer**, a neutral, noncontroversial statement that is closely related to the point of the message. A buffer establishes common ground with your reader, and if you're responding to a request, a buffer validates that request. Some critics believe that using a buffer is manipulative and unethical—or even dishonest. However, buffers are unethical only if they're insincere or deceptive. Showing consideration for the feelings of others is never dishonest.

A poorly written buffer might trivialize the reader's concerns, divert attention from the problem with insincere flattery or irrelevant material, or mislead the reader into thinking your message actually contains good news. A good buffer, on the other hand, can express your appreciation for being considered (if you're responding to a request), assure your reader of your attention to the request, or indicate your understanding of the reader's needs.

Poorly written buffers mislead or insult the reader.

Consider these possible responses to a manager of the order-fulfillment department who requested some temporary staffing help from your department (a request you won't be able to fulfill):

Our department shares your goal of processing orders quickly and efficiently.

Establishes common ground with the reader and validates the concerns that prompted the original request—without promising a positive answer

As a result of the last downsizing, every department in the company is running shorthanded.

Establishes common ground, but in a negative way that downplays the recipient's concerns

You folks are doing a great job over there, and I'd love to be able to help out.

Potentially misleads the reader into concluding that you will comply with the request

Those new state labor regulations are driving me crazy over here; how about in your department?

Trivializes the reader's concerns by opening with an irrelevant issue

Only the first of these buffers can be considered effective; the other three are likely to damage your relationship with the other manager. Table 8.2 shows several types of effective buffers you can use to tactfully open a negative message.

Providing Reasons and Additional Information

An effective buffer serves as a transition to the next part of your message, in which you build up the explanations and information that will culminate in your negative news. An ideal explanation section leads readers to your conclusion before you come right out and say it. The reader has followed your line of reasoning and is ready for the answer. By giving your reasons effectively, you help maintain focus on the issues at hand and defuse the emotions that always accompany significantly bad news.

Phrase your reasons to signal the negative news ahead.

TABLE 8.2 Types of Buffers

Buffer Type	Strategy	Example
Agreement	Find a point on which you and the reader share similar views.	We both know how hard it is to make a profit in this industry.
Appreciation	Express sincere thanks for receiving something.	Your check for $127.17 arrived yesterday. Thank you.
Cooperation	Convey your willingness to help in any way you realistically can.	Employee Services is here to assist all associates with their health insurance, retirement planning, and continuing education needs.
Fairness	Assure the reader that you've closely examined and carefully considered the problem, or mention an appropriate action that has already been taken.	For the past week, we have had our bandwidth monitoring tools running around the clock to track your actual upload and download speeds.
Good news	Start with the part of your message that is favorable.	We have credited your account in the amount of $14.95 to cover the cost of return shipping.
Praise	Find an attribute or an achievement to compliment.	The Stratford Group clearly has an impressive record of accomplishment in helping clients resolve financial reporting problems.
Resale	Favorably discuss the product or company related to the subject of the letter.	With their heavy-duty, full-suspension hardware and fine veneers, the desks and file cabinets in our Montclair line have long been popular with value-conscious professionals.
Understanding	Demonstrate that you understand the reader's goals and needs.	So that you can more easily find the printer with the features you need, we are enclosing a brochure that describes all the Epson printers currently available.

As you lay out your reasons, guide your readers' responses by starting with the most positive points first and moving forward to increasingly negative ones. Provide enough detail for the audience to understand your reasons but be concise. Your reasons need to convince your audience that your decision is justified, fair, and logical.

Whenever possible, avoid hiding behind company policy to cushion your bad news. Skilled and sympathetic communicators explain company policy (without referring to it as "policy") so that the audience can try to meet the requirements at a later time. Consider this response to a job applicant:

> Because these management positions are quite challenging, the human relations department has researched the qualifications needed to succeed in them. The findings show that the two most important qualifications are a bachelor's degree in business administration and two years' supervisory experience.

This paragraph does a good job of stating reasons for the refusal:

- It provides enough detail to logically support the refusal.
- It implies that the applicant is better off avoiding a position in which he or she might fail.
- It doesn't apologize for the decision because no one is at fault.
- It avoids negative personal statements (such as "You do not meet our requirements").

Even valid, well-thought-out reasons won't convince every reader in every situation, but if you've done a good job of laying out your reasoning, then you've done everything you can to prepare the reader for the main idea, which is the negative news itself.

Continuing with a Clear Statement of the Bad News

After you've thoughtfully and logically established your reasons and readers are prepared to receive the bad news, you can use three techniques to convey the negative information as clearly and as kindly as possible. First, deemphasize the bad news:

- Minimize the space or time devoted to the bad news—without trivializing it or withholding any important information. In other words, don't repeat it or belabor it.
- Subordinate bad news within a complex or compound sentence ("My department is already shorthanded, so I'll need all my staff for at least the next two months").
- Embed bad news in the middle of a paragraph or use parenthetical expressions ("Our profits, which are down, are only part of the picture").

However, keep in mind that it's possible to abuse this notion of deemphasizing bad news. For instance, if the primary point of your message is that profits are down, it would be inappropriate to marginalize that news by burying it in the middle of a sentence. State the negative news clearly and then make a smooth transition to any positive news that might balance the story.

Second, use a conditional (*if* or *when*) statement to imply that the audience could have received, or might someday receive, a favorable answer ("When you have more managerial experience, you are welcome to reapply"). Such a statement could motivate the audience.

Third, emphasize what you can do or have done rather than what you cannot do. Also, by implying the bad news, you may not need to actually state it, thereby making the bad news less personal ("The five positions currently open have been filled with people whose qualifications match those revealed in our research"). However, make sure your audience

Margin notes

Whenever possible, don't use "company policy" as the reason for the bad news.

Shows the reader that the decision is based on a methodical analysis of the company's needs and not on some arbitrary guideline

Establishes the criteria behind the decision and lets the reader know what to expect

Well-written reasons are
- Detailed
- Tactful
- Individualized
- Unapologetic
- As positive as possible

To handle bad news carefully
- Deemphasize the bad news visually and grammatically
- Use a conditional statement if appropriate
- Tell what you did do, not what you didn't do

Don't disguise the bad news when you emphasize the positive.

Instead of This	Write This
I *must refuse* your request.	I will be out of town on the day you need me.
We *must deny* your application.	The position has been filled.
I *am unable* to grant your request.	Contact us again when you have established . . .
We *cannot afford to* continue the program.	The program will conclude on May 1.
Much as I would like to attend...	Our budget meeting ends too late for me to attend.
We *must turn down* your extension request.	Please send in your payment by June 14.

understands the entire message—including the bad news. If an implied message might lead to uncertainty, state your decision in direct terms. Just be sure to avoid overly blunt statements that are likely to cause pain and anger (see the table on the previous page).

Closing on a Positive Note

As in the direct approach, the close in the indirect approach offers an opportunity to emphasize your respect for your audience, even though you've just delivered unpleasant news. Express best wishes without ending on a falsely upbeat note. If you can find a positive angle that's meaningful to your audience, by all means consider adding it to your conclusion. However, don't try to pretend that the negative news didn't happen or that it won't affect the reader. Suggest alternative solutions if such information is available and doing so is a good use of your time. If you've asked readers to decide between alternatives or to take some action, make sure that they know what to do, when to do it, and how to do it. Whatever type of conclusion you use, follow these guidelines:

- **Avoid an uncertain conclusion.** If the situation or decision is final, avoid statements such as "I trust our decision is satisfactory," which imply that the matter is open to discussion or negotiation.

- **Limit future correspondence.** Encourage additional communication *only* if you're willing to discuss your decision further. If you're not, avoid wording such as "If you have further questions, please write."

- **Express optimism, if appropriate.** If the situation might improve in the future, share that with your readers if it's relevant. For example, when Fran Ruderman of the electrical equipment maker Leviton announced to employees that the company needed to suspend its contributions to the employee retirement savings plan, she made it clear that the company intended to reinstate the matching program when economic conditions improved.[7]

- **Be sincere.** Steer clear of clichés that are insincere in view of the bad news. If you can't help, don't say, "If we can be of any help, please contact us."

Keep in mind that the close is the last thing audience members have to remember you by. Even though they're disappointed, leave them with the impression that they were treated with respect.

> A positive close
> - Builds goodwill
> - Offers a suggestion for action
> - Provides a look toward the future
> - Is sincere

SENDING NEGATIVE MESSAGES ON ROUTINE BUSINESS MATTERS

Professionals and companies receive a wide variety of requests and cannot respond positively to every single one. In addition, mistakes and unforeseen circumstances can lead to delays and other minor problems that occur in the course of business. Occasionally, companies must send negative messages to suppliers and other parties. Whatever the purpose, crafting routine negative responses and messages quickly and graciously is an important skill for every businessperson.

Making Negative Announcements on Routine Business Matters

Many negative messages are written in response to requests from an internal or external correspondent, but on occasion managers need to make unexpected announcements of a negative nature. For example, a company might decide to consolidate its materials purchasing with fewer suppliers and thereby need to tell several firms it will no longer be buying from them. Internally, management may need to announce the elimination of an employee benefit or other changes that employees will view negatively.

Although such announcements happen in the normal course of business, they are generally unexpected. Accordingly, except in the case of minor changes, the indirect approach is usually the better choice. Follow the steps outlined for indirect messages: Open with a buffer that establishes some mutual ground between you and the reader, advance your reasoning, announce the change, and close with as much positive information and sentiment as appropriate under the circumstances.

4 LEARNING OBJECTIVE
Describe successful strategies for sending negative messages on routine business matters

Refusing Routine Requests

When you are unable to meet a routine request, your primary communication challenge is to give a clear negative response without generating negative feelings or damaging either your personal reputation or the company's. As simple as these messages may appear to be, they can test your skills as a communicator because you often need to deliver negative information while maintaining a positive relationship with the other party.

The direct approach works best for most routine negative responses because it is simpler and more efficient. The indirect approach works best when the stakes are high for you or for the receiver, when you or your company has an established relationship with the person making the request, or when you're forced to decline a request that you might have said yes to in the past (see Figure 8.3).

Consider the following points as you develop routine negative messages:

- Manage your time carefully; focus on the most important relationships and requests.
- If the matter is closed, don't imply that it's still open by using phrases such as "Let me think about it and get back to you" as a way to delay saying no.
- Offer alternative ideas if you can, particularly if the relationship is important.
- Don't imply that other assistance or information might be available if it isn't.

Handling Bad News About Transactions

Bad news about transactions is always unwelcome and usually unexpected. When you send such messages, you have three goals: (1) modify the customer's expectations, (2) explain how you plan to resolve the situation, and (3) repair whatever damage might have been done to the business relationship.

The specific content and tone of each message can vary widely, depending on the nature of the transaction and your relationship with the customer. Telling an individual consumer that his new sweater will be arriving a week later than you promised is a much simpler task than telling Toyota that 30,000 transmission parts will be a week late, especially when you know the company will be forced to idle a multimillion-dollar production facility as a result.

If you haven't done anything specific to set the customer's expectations—such as promising delivery within 24 hours—the message simply needs to inform the customer of the situation, with little or no emphasis on apologies (see Figure 8.4 on page 222).

If you did set the customer's expectations and now find that you can't meet them, your task is more complicated. In addition to resetting those expectations and explaining how you'll resolve the problem, you may need to include an element of apology. The scope of the apology depends on the magnitude of the mistake. For the customer who ordered the sweater, a simple apology followed by a clear statement of when the sweater will arrive would probably be sufficient. For larger business-to-business transactions, the customer may want an explanation of what went wrong to determine whether you'll be able to perform as you promise in the future.

To help repair the damage to the relationship and encourage repeat business, many companies offer discounts on future purchases, free merchandise, or other considerations. Even modest efforts can go a long way to rebuilding a customer's confidence in your company.

Refusing Claims and Requests for Adjustment

Customers who make a claim or request an adjustment tend to be emotionally involved, so the indirect approach is usually the better choice. Your job as a writer is to avoid accepting responsibility for the unfortunate situation and yet avoid blaming or accusing the customer. To steer clear of these pitfalls, pay special attention to the tone of your letter. Demonstrate that you understand and have considered the complaint carefully and then rationally explain why you are refusing the request. Close on a respectful and action-oriented note (see Figure 8.5 on page 223).

If you deal with enough customers over a long-enough period, chances are you'll get a request that is particularly outrageous. You may even be convinced that the person is not telling the truth. However, you must resist the temptation to call the person dishonest or

1 Plan → **2 Write** → **3 Complete**

Analyze the Situation

Verify that the purpose is to decline a request and offer alternatives; audience is likely to be surprised by the refusal.

Gather Information

Determine audience needs and obtain the necessary information.

Select the Right Medium

For formal messages, printed letters on company letterhead are best.

Organize the Information

The main idea is to refuse the request so limit your scope to that; select the indirect approach based on the audience and the situation.

Adapt to Your Audience

Adjust the level of formality based on your degree of familiarity with the audience; maintain a positive relationship by using the "you" attitude, politeness, positive emphasis, and bias-free language.

Compose the Message

Use a conversational but professional style and keep the message brief, clear, and as helpful as possible.

Revise the Message

Evaluate content and review readability to make sure the negative information won't be misinterpreted; make sure your tone stays positive without being artificial.

Produce the Message

Maintain a clean, professional appearance on company letterhead.

Proofread the Message

Review for errors in layout, spelling, and mechanics.

Distribute the Message

Deliver your message using the chosen medium.

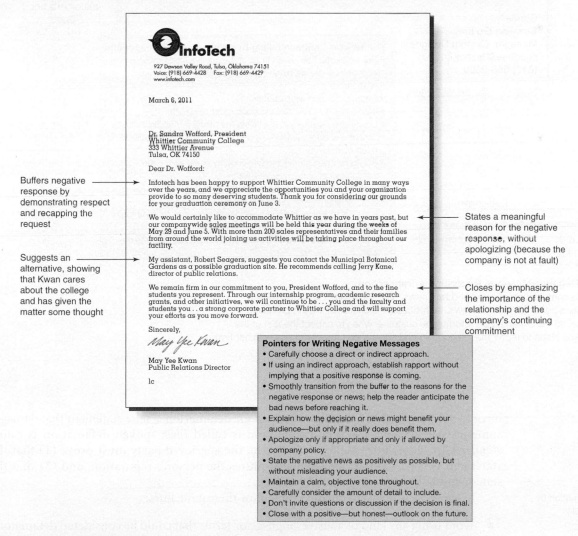

Buffers negative response by demonstrating respect and recapping the request

Suggests an alternative, showing that Kwan cares about the college and has given the matter some thought

States a meaningful reason for the negative response, without apologizing (because the company is not at fault)

Closes by emphasizing the importance of the relationship and the company's continuing commitment

InfoTech

927 Dawson Valley Road, Tulsa, Oklahoma 74151
Voice: (918) 669-4428   Fax: (918) 669-4429
www.infotech.com

March 6, 2011

Dr. Sandra Wofford, President
Whittier Community College
333 Whittier Avenue
Tulsa, OK 74150

Dear Dr. Wofford:

Infotech has been happy to support Whittier Community College in many ways over the years, and we appreciate the opportunities you and your organization provide to so many deserving students. Thank you for considering our grounds for your graduation ceremony on June 3.

We would certainly like to accommodate Whittier as we have in years past, but our companywide sales meetings will be held this year during the weeks of May 29 and June 5. With more than 200 sales representatives and their families from around the world joining us activities will be taking place throughout our facility.

My assistant, Robert Seagers, suggests you contact the Municipal Botanical Gardens as a possible graduation site. He recommends calling Jerry Kane, director of public relations.

We remain firm in our commitment to you, President Wofford, and to the fine students you represent. Through our internship program, academic research grants, and other initiatives, we will continue to be . . . you and the faculty and students you . . . a strong corporate partner to Whittier College and will support your efforts as you move forward.

Sincerely,

May Yee Kwan

May Yee Kwan
Public Relations Director

lc

Pointers for Writing Negative Messages
- Carefully choose a direct or indirect approach.
- If using an indirect approach, establish rapport without implying that a positive response is coming.
- Smoothly transition from the buffer to the reasons for the negative response or news; help the reader anticipate the bad news before reaching it.
- Explain how the decision or news might benefit your audience—but only if it really does benefit them.
- Apologize only if appropriate and only if allowed by company policy.
- State the negative news as positively as possible, but without misleading your audience.
- Maintain a calm, objective tone throughout.
- Carefully consider the amount of detail to include.
- Don't invite questions or discussion if the decision is final.
- Close with a positive—but honest—outlook on the future.

Figure 8.3   Effective Letter Declining a Routine Request

In declining a request to use her company's facilities, May Yee Kwan took note of the fact that her company has a long-standing relationship with the college and wants to maintain that positive relationship. Because the news is unexpected based on past experience, she chose an indirect approach to build up to her announcement.

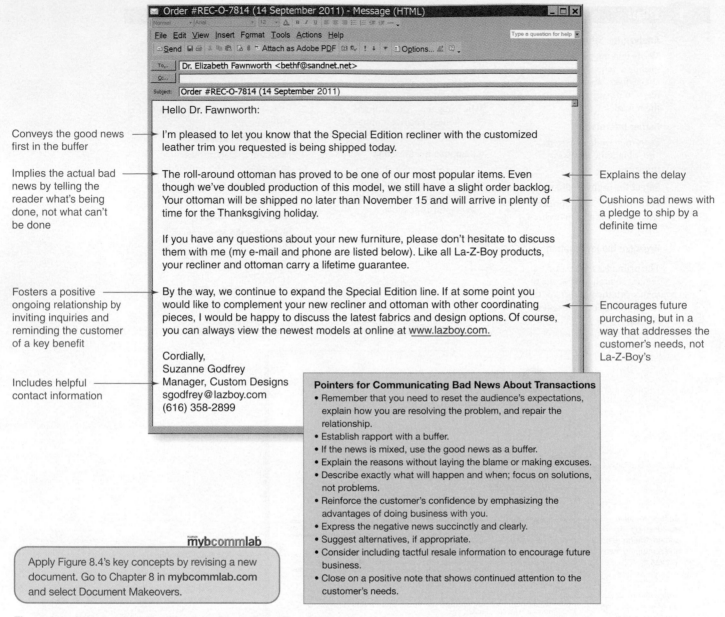

Figure 8.4   Effective Negative Message Regarding a Transaction
This message, which is a combination of good and bad news, uses the indirect approach—with
the good news serving as a buffer for the bad news. In this case, the customer wasn't promised
delivery by a certain date, so the writer simply informs the customer when to expect the rest of the
order. The writer also takes steps to repair the relationship and encourage future business with her firm.

incompetent. If you don't, you could be sued for **defamation**, a false statement that damages
someone's reputation. (Written defamation is called *libel*; spoken defamation is called
slander.) To successfully sue for defamation, the aggrieved party must prove (1) that the
statement is false, (2) that the language injures the person's reputation, and (3) that the
statement has been communicated to others.

You can help avoid defamation by not responding emotionally.

To avoid accusations of defamation, follow these guidelines:

- Avoid using any kind of abusive language or terms that could be considered defamatory.
- Provide accurate information and stick to the facts.
- Never let anger or malice motivate your messages.
- Consult your company's legal advisers whenever you think a message might have legal consequences.

1 Plan

Analyze the Situation

Verify that the purpose is to refuse a warranty claim and offer alternatives; the audience's likely reaction is disappointment and surprise.

Gather Information

Verify warranty information and research alternatives to present to the customer.

Select the Right Medium

Choose the best medium to deliver this message; the customer submitted the claim via e-mail, so a response via e-mail is appropriate.

Organize the Information

The main idea is to refuse the request so limit your scope to that; select the indirect approach based on the audience and the situation.

2 Write

Adapt to Your Audience

Adjust the level of formality based on the degree of familiarity with the audience (relatively formal is best in this case); maintain a positive relationship by using the "you" attitude, politeness, positive emphasis, and bias-free language.

Compose the Message

Use a conversational but professional style and keep the message brief, clear, and as helpful as possible.

3 Complete

Revise the Message

Evaluate content and review readability to make sure the negative information won't be misinterpreted; make sure your tone stays positive without being artificial.

Produce the Message

Emphasize a clean, professional appearance.

Proofread the Message

Review for errors in layout, spelling, and mechanics.

Distribute the Message

Deliver your message via e-mail.

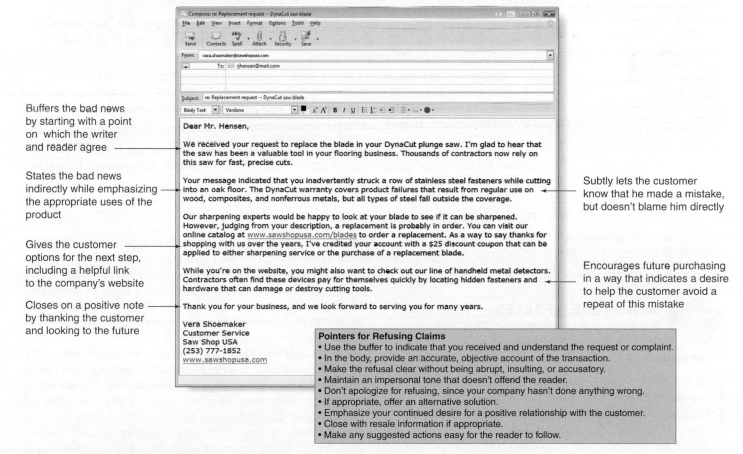

Buffers the bad news by starting with a point on which the writer and reader agree

States the bad news indirectly while emphasizing the appropriate uses of the product

Gives the customer options for the next step, including a helpful link to the company's website

Closes on a positive note by thanking the customer and looking to the future

Subtly lets the customer know that he made a mistake, but doesn't blame him directly

Encourages future purchasing in a way that indicates a desire to help the customer avoid a repeat of this mistake

Pointers for Refusing Claims
- Use the buffer to indicate that you received and understand the request or complaint.
- In the body, provide an accurate, objective account of the transaction.
- Make the refusal clear without being abrupt, insulting, or accusatory.
- Maintain an impersonal tone that doesn't offend the reader.
- Don't apologize for refusing, since your company hasn't done anything wrong.
- If appropriate, offer an alternative solution.
- Emphasize your continued desire for a positive relationship with the customer.
- Close with resale information if appropriate.
- Make any suggested actions easy for the reader to follow.

Figure 8.5 Effective Message Refusing a Claim
Vera Shoemaker diplomatically refuses this customer's request for a new saw blade. Without blaming the customer (even though the customer clearly made a mistake), she points out that the saw blade is not intended to cut steel, so the warranty doesn't cover a replacement in this instance.

- Communicate honestly and make sure that you believe what you're saying is true.
- Emphasize a desire for a good relationship in the future.

Keep in mind that nothing positive can come out of antagonizing a customer, even one who has verbally abused you or your colleagues. Reject the claim or request for adjustment in a professional manner and move on to the next challenge.

SENDING NEGATIVE EMPLOYMENT MESSAGES

5 LEARNING OBJECTIVE

Describe successful strategies for sending negative employment-related messages

Most managers must convey bad news about individual employees from time to time. Recipients have an emotional stake in your message, so taking the indirect approach is usually advised. In addition, use great care in choosing media for these messages. For instance, e-mail and other written forms let you control the message and avoid personal confrontation, but one-on-one conversations are more sensitive and facilitate questions and answers.

Refusing Requests for Recommendation Letters

When sending refusals to prospective employers who have requested information about past employees, your message can be brief and direct:

Implies that company policy prohibits the release of any more information but does provide what information is available

Ends on a positive note

> Our human resources department has authorized me to confirm that Yolanda Johnson worked for Tandy, Inc., for three years, from June 2007 to July 2010. Best of luck as you interview applicants.

This message doesn't need to say, "We cannot comply with your request." It simply gives the reader all the information that is allowable.

Refusing an applicant's direct request for a recommendation letter is another matter. Any refusal to cooperate may seem to be a personal slight and a threat to the applicant's future. Diplomacy and preparation help readers accept your refusal:

Uses the indirect approach since the other party is probably expecting a positive response

> Thank you for letting me know about your job opportunity with Coca-Cola. Your internship there and the MBA you've worked so hard to earn should place you in an excellent position to land the marketing job.

Announces that the writer cannot comply with the request, without explicitly blaming it on "policy"

Offers to fulfill as much of the request as possible and offers an alternative

Ends on a positive note

> Although we do not send out formal recommendations here at PepsiCo, I can certainly send Coca-Cola a confirmation of your employment dates. And if you haven't considered this already, be sure to ask several of your professors to write evaluations of your marketing skills. Best of luck to you in your career.

This message tactfully avoids hurting the reader's feelings because it makes positive comments about the reader's recent activities, implies the refusal, suggests an alternative, and uses a polite close.

Rejecting Job Applications

In messages informing prospective employers that you will not provide a recommendation, be direct, brief, and factual (to avoid legal pitfalls).

Traditionally, many businesses made a point of responding to all job applications, even just to acknowledge that an application was received, but the rapid growth of e-mailed résumés and online job sites such as Monster.com have flooded some companies with so many applicants that they say they can no longer reply to them all.[8] However, if you have the opportunity to respond, by all means do so. Ignoring job applications builds ill will and can harm your company's reputation.

Although rejections are routine communications, they are not always easy to write because saying no is never easy, and recipients are emotionally invested in the decision. Moreover, companies must be aware of the possibility of employment discrimination lawsuits, which have been on the rise in recent years.[9] Of course, having fair and nondiscriminatory hiring practices is essential, but rejections must also be written in a way that doesn't inadvertently suggest any hint of discrimination. Expert opinions differ on the

REAL-TIME UPDATES
Learn More by Watching This Video

Take some of the sting out of delivering bad news

No one likes to deliver bad news, but these techniques can make it easier for you and the recipient. Go to http://real-timeupdates.com/bce5 and click on "Learn More." If you are using mybcommlab, you can access Real-Time Updates within each chapter or under Student Study Tools.

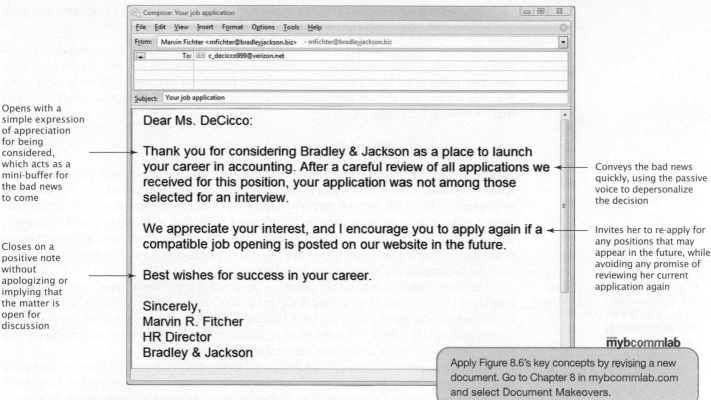

Opens with a simple expression of appreciation for being considered, which acts as a mini-buffer for the bad news to come

Closes on a positive note without apologizing or implying that the matter is open for discussion

Conveys the bad news quickly, using the passive voice to depersonalize the decision

Invites her to re-apply for any positions that may appear in the future, while avoiding any promise of reviewing her current application again

Apply Figure 8.6's key concepts by revising a new document. Go to Chapter 8 in mybcommlab.com and select Document Makeovers.

Figure 8.6 Effective Message Rejecting a Job Applicant
This message rejecting a job applicant takes care to avoid making or implying any promises about future opportunities, beyond inviting the person to apply for positions that may appear in the future. Note that this would not be appropriate if the company did not believe the applicant was a good fit for the company in general.

level of information to include in a rejection message, but the safest strategy is to avoid sharing any explanations for the company's decision and to avoid making or implying any promises of future consideration (see Figure 8.6):[10]

- **Personalize the e-mail message or letter by using the recipient's name.** For example, mail merge makes it easy to insert each recipient's name into a form letter.

- **Open with a courteous expression of appreciation for being considered.** In a sense, this is like the buffer in an indirect message because it gives you an opportunity to begin the conversation without immediately and bluntly telling the reader that his or her application has been rejected.

- **Convey the negative news politely and concisely.** The passive voice is helpful in this situation because it shifts focus away from the people involved and thereby depersonalizes the response. For example, "Your application was not among those selected for an interview," avoids putting you in a situation of saying "We have rejected your application."

- **Avoid explaining why an applicant was rejected or why other applicants were chosen instead.** Although it was once more common to offer such explanations, and some experts still advocate this approach, the simplest strategy from a legal standpoint is to avoid offering reasons for the decision. Avoiding explanations lowers the possibility that an applicant will perceive discrimination in the hiring decision or be tempted to challenge the reasons given.

- **Don't state or imply that the application will be reviewed at a later date.** Saying that "we will keep your résumé on file for future consideration" can create false hopes for the recipient and leave the company vulnerable to legal complaints if a future hiring decision is made without actually reviewing this candidate's application again. If the candidate might be a good fit for another position in the company in the future, you can suggest he or she reapply if a new job opening is posted.

Experts disagree on which elements to include in a rejection letter, but the safest strategy is a minimal approach.

- **Close with positive wishes for the applicant's career success.** A brief statement such as "We wish you success in your career" is sufficient.

Naturally, you should adjust your tactics to the circumstances. A simple and direct message is fine when someone has only submitted a job application, but rejecting a candidate who has made it at least partway through the interview process requires greater care. Personal contact has already been established through the interview process, so a phone call may be more appropriate.

Giving Negative Performance Reviews

Many companies require managers to provide written reviews of their subordinates' performance, typically once a year. The review itself is usually a combination of a standardized questionnaire in which the manager scores the employee's performance on a variety of job-related criteria, brief written assessments of broad areas such as leadership and teamwork, and a list of objectives for the upcoming year. With pay raises and promotion opportunities often depending on how employees are rated in this process, annual reviews often are a stressful occurrence for managers and workers alike.

The worst possible outcome in an annual review is a negative surprise, such as when an employee has been working toward different goals than the manager expects or has been underperforming throughout the year but didn't receive any feedback or improvement coaching along the way.[11] In some instances, failing to confront performance problems in a timely fashion can make a company vulnerable to lawsuits.[12]

By giving employees clear goals and regular feedback, you can help avoid unpleasant surprises in a performance review.

To avoid negative surprises, managers should meet with employees to agree on clear goals for the upcoming year and then provide regular feedback and coaching as needed throughout the year if an employee's performance falls below expectations. Ideally, the annual review is more of a confirmation of the past year's performance and a planning session for the next year.

Even when goals have been agreed on and employees have received feedback and coaching, managers will encounter situations in which an employee's performance has not met expectations. These situations require objective, written appraisals of the performance shortcomings. Such appraisals can help the manager and employee work on an improvement plan. They also establish documentary evidence of the employee's performance in the event that disciplinary action is needed, or the employee later disputes management decisions regarding pay or promotions.[13]

Negative evaluations should provide careful documentation of performance concerns.

When you need to write a negative review, keep the following points in mind:[14]

- **Document performance problems.** As you provide feedback throughout the year, keep a written record of performance issues. You will need this information in order to write an effective appraisal and to support any decisions that need to be made about pay, promotions, or termination.

- **Evaluate all employees consistently.** Consistency is not only fair but also helps protect the company from claims of discriminatory practices.

- **Write in a calm, objective voice.** The employee is not likely to welcome your negative assessment, but you can manage the emotions of the situation by maintaining professional reserve in your writing.

- **Focus on opportunities for improvement.** As you document performance problems, identify specific steps the employee can take to correct them. This information can serve as the foundation for an improvement plan for the coming year.

- **Keep job descriptions up to date.** Performance evaluations should be based on the criteria listed in an employee's job description. However, if a job evolves over time in response to changes in the business, the employee's current activities may no longer match an outdated job description.

Terminating Employment

If an employee's performance cannot be brought up to company standards or if other factors such as declining sales cause a reduction in the workforce, a company often has no choice but to terminate employment. As with other negative employment messages, termination is fraught with emotions and legal ramifications, so careful planning, complete documentation, and sensitive writing are essential.

Termination messages should always be written with input from the company's legal staff, but here are general writing guidelines to bear in mind:[15]

- Clearly present the reasons for this difficult action, whether it is the employee's performance or a business decision unrelated to specific employees.
- Make sure the reasons are presented in a way that cannot be construed as unfair or discriminatory.
- Follow company policy, contractual requirements, and applicable laws to the letter.
- Avoid personal attacks or insults of any kind.
- Ask another manager to review the letter before issuing it. An objective reviewer who isn't directly involved might spot troublesome wording or faulty reasoning.
- Deliver the termination letter in person if at all possible. Arrange a meeting that will ensure privacy and freedom from interruptions.

Carefully word a termination letter to avoid creating undue ill will and grounds for legal action.

Any termination is clearly a negative outcome for both employer and employee, but careful attention to content and tone in the termination message can help the employee move on gracefully and minimize the misunderstandings and anger that can lead to expensive lawsuits.

SENDING NEGATIVE ORGANIZATIONAL NEWS

As a manager or business owner, you may at times need to issue negative announcements regarding some aspect of your products, services, or operations. Unlike routine negative announcements, these messages involve significant changes that negatively affect one or more groups (such as losing a major contract or canceling a popular product), announcements of workforce reductions, and crisis communication regarding environmental incidents, workplace accidents, or other traumatic situations.

When making negative announcements, follow these guidelines:

6 LEARNING OBJECTIVE
List the important points to consider when conveying negative organizational news

- **Match your approach to the situation.** For example, in an emergency such as product tampering or a toxic spill, get to the point immediately.
- **Consider the unique needs of each group.** When a company or facility closes, for instance, employees need time to find new jobs, customers may need to find new suppliers, and community leaders may need to be prepared to help people who have lost their jobs.
- **Minimize the element of surprise whenever possible.** Give affected groups as much time as possible to prepare and respond.
- **If possible, give yourself enough time to plan and manage a response.** Make sure you're ready with answers to expected questions.
- **Look for positive angles but don't exude false optimism.** Laying off 10,000 people does not give them "an opportunity to explore new horizons." It's a traumatic event that can affect employees, their families, and their communities for years. The best you may be able to do is to thank people for their past support and to wish them well in the future.
- **Seek expert advice.** Many significant negative announcements have important technical, financial, or legal elements that require the expertise of lawyers, accountants, or other specialists.
- **Use multiple media to reach out to affected audiences.** Provide information through your normal communication network, such as your company website, Facebook page, and Twitter account, but also reach out and participate in conversations that are taking place elsewhere in the social media landscape.[16]

Negative organizational messages to external audiences often require extensive planning.

Give people as much time as possible to react to negative news.

Ask for legal help and other assistance if you're not sure how to handle a significant negative announcement.

Negative situations will test your skills as a communicator and as a business leader. Inspirational leaders try to seize such situations as opportunities to reshape or reinvigorate the organization, and they offer encouragement to those around them (see Figure 8.7 on the next page).

Opens on a complimentary note and buffers the bad news with some good news about sales

Moves readers from good news to bad news with an effective transition

Involves readers in the challenge of finding a solution

Presents the bad news along with the possible explanations

Closes by being positive, looking toward the future, and encouraging the audience

Figure 8.7   Effective Internal Message Providing Bad News About Company Operations
In this message to employees at Sybervantage, Frank Leslie shares the unpleasant news that a hoped-for licensing agreement with Warner Brothers has been rejected. Rather than dwell on the bad news, he focuses on options for the future. The upbeat close diminishes the effect of the bad news without hiding or downplaying the news itself.

7 LEARNING OBJECTIVE

Describe an effective strategy for responding to negative information in a social media environment

RESPONDING TO NEGATIVE INFORMATION IN A SOCIAL MEDIA ENVIRONMENT

For all the benefits they bring to business, social media and other communication technologies have created a major new challenge: responding to online rumors, false information, and attacks on a company's reputation. Consumers and other stakeholders can now communicate through blogs, Twitter, YouTube, social networking sites, advocacy sites such as www.walmartwatch.com, general complaint and feedback websites such as www.epinions .com, company-specific sites such as www.verizonpathetic.com, community Q&A sites such as http://getsatisfaction.com, and numerous e-commerce shopping sites that encourage product reviews.

Customers who feel they have been treated unfairly like these sites because they can use the public exposure as leverage. Many companies appreciate the feedback from these sites, too, and many actively seek out complaints to improve their products and operations. However, false rumors and unfair criticisms can spread around the world in a matter of minutes. And even when a company is being criticized fairly, it needs to respond with timely information for all affected stakeholders. For example, after a tragic accident involving its Deepwater Horizon oil well in the Gulf of Mexico in 2010, BP set up a special section on its website to provide updates on the progress toward capping the massive oil leak as well as information about how to submit a claim for economic damages that resulted from the spill.[17]

Responding to rumors and countering negative information requires an ongoing effort and case-by-case decisions about which messages require a response. Follow these four steps:[18]

1. **Engage early, engage often.** Perhaps the most important step in responding to negative information has to be done *before* the negative information appears, and that is to engage with communities of stakeholders as a long-term strategy. Companies that have active, mutually beneficial relationships with customers and other interested parties are less likely to be attacked unfairly online and more likely to survive such attacks if they do occur. In contrast, companies that ignore constituents or jump into "spin doctoring" mode when a negative situation occurs don't have the same credibility as companies that have done the long, hard work of fostering relationships within their physical and online communities. Some companies set up special websites or sections on their sites to present their perspectives on public issues, either in response to critics or to head off potential criticism.

2. **Monitor the conversation.** If people are interested in what your company does, chances are they are blogging, tweeting, podcasting, posting videos, writing on Facebook walls, and otherwise sharing their opinions. Use RSS feeds, automated reputation analysis, and other technologies to listen to what people are saying.

3. **Evaluate negative messages.** When you encounter negative messages, resist the urge to fire back immediately. Instead, evaluate the source, the tone, and the content of the message and then choose a response that fits the situation. For example, the Public Affairs Agency of the U.S. Air Force groups senders of negative messages into four categories, including "trolls" (those whose only intent is to stir up conflict), "ragers" (those who are just ranting or telling jokes), "the misguided" (those who are spreading incorrect information), and "unhappy customers" (those who have had a negative experience with the Air Force).

4. **Respond appropriately.**   After you have assessed a negative message, make the appropriate response based on an overall public relations plan. The Air Force, for instance, doesn't respond to trolls or ragers, responds to misguided messages with correct information, and responds to unhappy customers with efforts to rectify the situation and reach a reasonable solution. If appropriate, enlist the help of government agencies such as the Centers for Disease Control and Prevention (www.cdc.gov) and debunking sites such as Snopes.com (www.snopes.com).

> Responding effectively to rumors and negative information requires continual engagement with stakeholders and careful decision making about which messages should get a response.

Whatever you do, don't assume that a positive reputation doesn't need to be diligently guarded and defended. Everybody has a voice now, and some of those voices don't care to play by the rules of ethical communication.

For the latest information on writing negative messages, visit http://real-timeupdates .com/bce5 and click on Chapter 8.

PEARSON
mybcommlab™   Are you an active learner? Go to mybcommlab.com to master Chapter 8's content.
Chapter 8's interactive activities include:

- Customizable Study Plan and Chapter 8 practice quizzes
- Chapter 8 Simulation (Negative Messages) which helps you think critically and prepare to make choices in the business world
- Chapter 8 Video Exercise (Negative Messages: Orange Photography), which shows you how textbook concepts are put into practice every day

- Flash Cards for mastering the definition of chapter terms
- Interactive Lessons that visually review key chapter concepts
- Document Makeovers for hands-on, scored practice in revising documents

CHAPTER REVIEW AND ACTIVITIES

Learning Objectives: Check Your Progress

1 OBJECTIVE Apply the three-step writing process to negative messages.

Because the way you say no can be even more damaging than the fact that you're saying it, planning negative messages is crucial. Make sure your purpose is specific and use an appropriate medium to fit the message. Collect all the facts necessary to support your negative decision, adapt your tone to the situation, and choose the optimum approach. Use positive words to construct diplomatic sentences and pay close attention to quality.

2 OBJECTIVE Explain how to use the direct approach effectively when conveying negative news.

The direct approach puts the bad news up front, follows with the reasons, and closes with a positive statement. Even though it is direct, however, don't use the direct approach as a license to be rude or overly blunt.

3 OBJECTIVE Explain how to use the indirect approach effectively when conveying negative news, and explain how to avoid ethical problems when using this approach.

The indirect approach begins with a buffer, explains the reasons, clearly states the negative news, and closes with a positive statement. If the bad news is not unexpected, the direct approach is usually fine, but if the news is shocking or painful, the indirect approach is better. When using the indirect approach, pay careful attention to avoid obscuring the bad news, trivializing the audience's concerns, or even misleading your audience into thinking you're actually delivering good news. Remember that the purpose of the indirect approach is to cushion the blow, not to avoid delivering it.

4 OBJECTIVE Describe successful strategies for sending negative messages on routine business matters.

For refusing routine requests, the direct approach is usually sufficient, except when the matter at hand is significant, you or your company have an established relationship with the person making the request, or you're forced to decline a request that you might have said yes to in the past.

When conveying bad news about transactions, you need to modify the customer's expectations, explain how you plan to resolve the situation, and repair whatever damage might have been done to the business relationship. Whether or not you should apologize depends in part on the magnitude of the situation and whether you previously established specific expectations about the transaction.

When refusing a claim or a request for adjustment, the indirect approach is usually preferred because the other party is emotionally involved and expects you to respond positively. Demonstrate that you understand and have considered the complaint carefully and then rationally and calmly explain why you are refusing the request.

5 OBJECTIVE Describe successful strategies for sending negative employment-related messages.

The indirect approach is usually the better choice for negative employment messages because the recipient is always emotionally involved, and the decisions are usually significant. When refusing requests from other employers for performance-related information about past employees, your message can be brief and direct. Simply provide whatever information your company allows to be shared in these situations. Refusing a recommendation request directly from a former employee feels much more personal for the recipient, however, so the indirect approach is better.

Messages rejecting job applicants raise a number of emotional and legal issues and therefore must be approach with great care. Experts vary in their advice about how much information to include in these messages. However, the safest strategy is a brief message that opens with an expression of appreciation for being considered (which functions like a buffer in an indirect message), continues with a statement to the effect that the applicant was not chosen for the position applied for, and closes courteously without providing reasons for the rejection or making promises about future consideration.

Negative performance reviews should take care to document the performance problems, be sure that all employees are being evaluated consistently, be written in a calm and objective voice, and focus on opportunities for improvement. Moreover, they must be written with reference to accurate, current job descriptions that provide the basis for measuring employee performance.

Termination messages are the most challenging employment messages of all. They should clearly present the reasons for the decision, present the reasons in a way that cannot be construed as unfair or discriminatory, follow company policy and any relevant legal guidelines, and avoid personal attacks or insults of any kind. Asking a manager not directly involved in the situation to review your message can help you avoid troublesome wording or faulty reasoning. Lastly, try to deliver the written message in person if possible.

6 OBJECTIVE List the important points to consider when conveying negative organizational news.

When communicating negative organizational news, (1) match your approach to the situation, (2) consider the unique needs of each group, (3) minimize the element of surprise whenever possible so that affected groups have time to prepare and respond, (4) give yourself as much time as possible to plan and manage a response, (5) make sure you're ready with answers to expected questions, (6) look for positive angles but don't exude false optimism, (7) seek expert advice, and (8) use multiple media to reach out to affected audiences.

7 OBJECTIVE Describe an effective strategy for responding to negative information in a social media environment.

First, be sure you are engaged with important stakeholders before negative situations appear. Second, monitor the conversations taking place about your company and its products. Third, when you see negative messages, evaluate them before responding. Fourth, after evaluating negative messages, take the appropriate response based on an overall public relations plan. Some messages are better ignored, whereas others should be addressed immediately with corrective information.

▌ Test Your Knowledge

To review chapter content related to each question, refer to the indicated Learning Objective.
1. What questions should you ask yourself when choosing between the direct and indirect approaches? [LO-1]
2. What are the five general goals in delivering bad news? [LO-1]
3. What is the sequence of elements in a negative message organized using the direct approach? [LO-2]
4. When using the indirect approach to announce a negative decision, what is the purpose of presenting your reasons before explaining the decision itself? [LO-3]
5. What is a buffer, and why do some critics consider it unethical? [LO-3]

▌ Apply Your Knowledge

To review chapter content related to each question, refer to the indicated Learning Objective.
1. Why is attention to detail so important when producing and distributing negative messages? [LO-1]
2. Can you express sympathy with someone's negative situation without apologizing for the circumstances? Explain your answer. [LO-2]
3. Is intentionally deemphasizing bad news the same as distorting graphs and charts to deemphasize unfavorable data? Why or why not? [LO-3]
4. Why is early and frequent engagement with stakeholder communities so valuable in fending off erroneous rumors and other negative information about your company? [LO-7]
5. What new challenges do social media present to today's companies when it comes to negative information? [LO-7]

▌ Practice Your Skills

Exercises for Perfecting Your Writing

To review chapter content related to each set of exercises, refer to the indicated Learning Objective.

Message Strategies: Writing Negative Messages [LO-2] [LO-3]   Select which approach you would use (direct or indirect) for the following negative messages.
1. An e-mail message to your boss, informing her that one of your key clients is taking its business to a different accounting firm
2. An e-mail message to a customer, informing her that one of the books she ordered from your website is temporarily out of stock
3. A letter to a customer, explaining that the DVD burner he ordered for his new custom computer is on back order and that, as a consequence, the shipping of the entire order will be delayed

Message Strategies: Writing Negative Messages [LO-3]   Answer the following questions pertaining to buffers.
4. You have to tell a local restaurant owner that your plans have changed and you have to cancel the 90-person banquet scheduled for next month. Do you need to use a buffer? Why or why not?
5. Write a buffer for a letter declining an invitation to speak at the association's annual fund-raising event. Show your appreciation for being asked.
6. Write a buffer for a letter rejecting a job applicant who speaks three foreign languages fluently. Include praise for the applicant's accomplishments.

Message Strategies: Refusing Routine Requests; Collaboration: Team Projects [LO-4], Chapter 2   Working alone, revise the following statements to deemphasize the bad news without hiding it or distorting it. (Hint: Minimize the space devoted to the bad news, subordinate it, embed it, or use the passive voice.) Then team up with a classmate and read each other's revisions. Did you both use the same approach in every case? Which approach seems to be most effective for each of the revised statements?
7. The airline can't refund your money. The "Conditions" section on the back of your ticket states that there are no refunds for missed flights. Sometimes the airline makes exceptions, but only when life and death are involved. Of course, your ticket is still valid and can be used on a flight to the same destination.
8. I'm sorry to tell you, we can't supply the custom decorations you requested. We called every supplier and none of them can do what you want on such short notice. You can, however, get a standard decorative package on the same theme in time. I found a supplier that stocks these. Of course, it won't have quite the flair you originally requested.

9. We can't refund your money for the malfunctioning MP3 player. You shouldn't have immersed the unit in water while swimming; the user's manual clearly states the unit is not designed to be used in adverse environments.

Activities

Active links for all websites in this chapter can be found on mybcommlab; see your User Guide for instructions on accessing the content for this chapter. Each activity is labeled according to the primary skill or skills you will need to use. To review relevant chapter content, you can refer to the indicated Learning Objective. In some instances, supporting information will be found in another chapter, as indicated.

1. **Message Strategies: Making Negative Announcements [LO-4]**   Read the following document and (a) analyze the strengths and weaknesses of each sentence and (b) revise each document so that it follows this chapter's guidelines.

   Your spring fraternity party sounds like fun. We're glad you've again chosen us as your caterer. Unfortunately, we have changed a few of our policies, and I wanted you to know about these changes in advance so that we won't have any misunderstandings on the day of the party.

   We will arrange the delivery of tables and chairs as usual the evening before the party. However, if you want us to set up, there is now a $100 charge for that service. Of course, you might want to get some of the brothers and pledges to do it, which would save you money. We've also added a small charge for cleanup. This is only $3 per person (you can estimate because I know a lot of people come and go later in the evening).

   Other than that, all the arrangements will be the same. We'll provide the skirt for the band stage, tablecloths, bar setup, and of course, the barbecue. Will you have the tubs of ice with soft drinks again? We can do that for you as well, but there will be a fee.

   Please let me know if you have any problems with these changes and we'll try to work them out. I know it's going to be a great party.

2. **Message Strategies: Refusing Routine Requests [LO-4]**   As a customer service supervisor for a telephone company, you're in charge of responding to customers' requests for refunds. You've just received an e-mail from a customer who unwittingly ran up a $500 bill for long-distance calls after mistakenly configuring his laptop computer to dial an Internet access number that wasn't a local call. The customer says it wasn't his fault because he didn't realize he was dialing a long-distance number. However, you've dealt with this situation before; you know that the customer's Internet service provider warns its customers to choose a local access number because customers are responsible for all long-distance charges. Draft a short buffer (one or two sentences) for your e-mail reply, sympathizing with the customer's plight but preparing him for the bad news (that company policy specifically prohibits refunds in such cases).

3. **Message Strategies: Refusing Routine Requests [LO-4]**   Read the following document and (a) analyze the strengths and weaknesses of each sentence and (b) revise the message so that it follows this chapter's guidelines.

   I am responding to your letter of about six weeks ago asking for an adjustment on your wireless hub, model WM39Z. We test all our products before they leave the factory; therefore, it could not have been our fault that your hub didn't work.

   If you or someone in your office dropped the unit, it might have caused the damage. Or the damage could have been caused by the shipper if he dropped it. If so, you should file a claim with the shipper. At any rate, it wasn't our fault. The parts are already covered by warranty. However, we will provide labor for the repairs for $50, which is less than our cost, since you are a valued customer.

   We will have a booth at the upcoming trade fair there and hope to see you or someone from your office. We have many new models of computing and networking accessories that we're sure you'll want to see. I've enclosed our latest catalog. Hope to see you there.

4. **Message Strategies: Making Negative Announcements; Communication Ethics: Distinguishing Ethical Dilemmas and Ethical Lapses [LO-4], Chapter 1**   The insurance company where you work is planning to raise all premiums for health-care coverage. Your boss has asked you to read a draft of her letter to customers, announcing the new, higher rates. The first two paragraphs discuss some exciting medical advances and the expanded coverage offered by your company. Only in the final paragraph do customers learn that they will have to pay more for coverage starting next year. What are the ethical implications of this draft? What changes would you suggest?

5. **Message Strategies: Making Negative Announcements [LO-4]**   The following e-mail message about travel budget cutbacks at Black & Decker contains numerous blunders. Using what you've learned in the chapter, read the message carefully and analyze its faults. Then use the questions that follow to outline and write an improved message.

   Memo
   From: M. Juhasz, Travel & Meeting Services
             mjuhasz@blackanddecker.com
   To: [mailing list]
   Subject: Travel Budget Cuts Effective Immediately

   Dear Traveling Executives:

   We need you to start using some of the budget suggestions we are going to issue as a separate memorandum. These include using videoconference equipment instead of traveling to meetings, staying in cheaper hotels, arranging flights for cheaper times, and flying from less-convenient but also less-expensive suburban airports.

   The company needs to cut travel expenses by fifty percent, just as we've cut costs in all departments of Black & Decker.

This means you'll no longer be able to stay in fancy hotels and make last-minute, costly changes to your travel plans.

You'll also be expected to avoid hotel phone surcharges. Compose your e-mail offline when you're in the hotel. And never return a rental car with an empty tank! That causes the rental agency to charge us a premium price for the gas they sell when they fill it up upon your return.

You'll be expected to make these changes in your travel habits immediately.

M. Juhasz
Travel & Meeting Services

   a. Describe the flaws in this bad-news e-mail about company operations.

   b. Develop a plan for rewriting the e-mail to company insiders, using the direct approach. The following steps will help you organize your efforts before you begin writing:

     1. Create an opening statement of the bad news, using the "you" attitude.

     2. Decide what explanation is needed to justify the news.

     3. Determine whether you can use lists effectively.

     4. Choose some positive suggestions you can include to soften the news.

     5. Develop an upbeat closing.

   c. Now rewrite the e-mail. Don't forget to leave ample time for revision of your work before you turn it in.

6. Message Strategies: Refusing Routine Requests; Collaboration: Team Projects [LO-4], Chapter 2   The following letter rejecting a faucet manufacturer's product presentation contains many errors in judgment. Working with your classmates in a team effort, you should be able to improve its effectiveness as a negative message. First, analyze and discuss the letter's flaws. How can it be improved? Use the following questions to help guide your discussion and development of an improved version.

July 15, 2011

Pamela Wilson, Operations Manager
Sterling Manufacturing
133 Industrial Avenue
Gary, IN 46403

Dear Ms. Wilson:

We regret to inform you that your presentation at Home Depot's recent product review sessions in St. Petersburg did not meet our expert panelists' expectations. We require new products that will satisfy our customers' high standards. Yours did not match this goal.

Our primary concern is to continue our commitment to product excellence, customer knowledge, and price

competitiveness, which has helped make Home Depot a Fortune 500 company with more than a thousand stores nationwide. The panel found flaws in your design and materials. Also, your cost per unit was too high.

The product review sessions occur annually. You are allowed to try again; just apply as you did this year. Again, I'm sorry things didn't work out for you this time.

Sincerely,
Hilary Buchman, Assistant to the Vice President, Sales

HB:kl

   a. Describe the problems with this letter rejecting a product presentation.

   b. Develop a plan for rewriting the letter, using the indirect approach. Organize your thinking before you begin writing, using the following tactics:

     1. Select a buffer for the opening, using the "you" attitude.

     2. Choose the reasons you'll use to explain the rejection.

     3. Develop a way to soften or embed the bad news.

     4. Create a conditional (if/then) statement to encourage the recipient to try again.

     5. Find a way to close on a positive, encouraging note.

   c. Now rewrite the letter. Don't forget to leave ample time for revision of your work before you turn it in.

7. Message Strategies: Negative Employment Messages [LO-5]   Read the following document and (a) analyze the strengths and weaknesses of each sentence and (b) revise the message so that it follows this chapter's guidelines.

I regret to inform you that you were not selected for our summer intern program at Equifax. We had over a thousand résumés and cover letters to go through and simply could not get to them all. We have been asked to notify everyone that we have already selected students for the 25 positions based on those who applied early and were qualified.

We're sure you will be able to find a suitable position for summer work in your field and wish you the best of luck. We deeply regret any inconvenience associated with our reply.

Expand Your Skills

Critique the Professionals

Locate an example online of a negative-news message from any company. Possible examples include announcements of product recalls, poor financial results, layoffs, and fines or other legal troubles. Analyze the approach the company took; was it the most effective strategy possible? Did the company apologize, if doing so would have been appropriate under the circumstances, and does the apology seem sincere? Does the tone of the message match the seriousness of the situation? Does the message end on a positive note, as appropriate? Using whatever medium your instructor requests, write a brief analysis of the message (no more than one page), citing specific elements from the piece and support from the chapter.

Sharpen Your Career Skills Online

Bovée and Thill's Business Communication Web Search, at http://businesscommunicationblog.com/websearch, is a unique research tool designed specifically for business communication research. Use the Web Search function to find a website, video, PDF document, podcast, or presentation that offers advice on conveying negative news in business messages. Write a brief e-mail message to your instructor or a post for your class blog, describing the item that you found and summarizing the career skills information you learned from it.

mybcommlab

If your course uses mybcommlab, log on to www .mybcommlab.com to access the following study and assessment aids associated with this chapter:

- Video applications
- Pre/post test
- Real-Time Updates
- Personalized study plan
- Peer review activity
- Model documents
- Quick Learning Guides
- Sample presentations

If you are not using mybcommlab, you can access Real-Time Updates and Quick Learning Guides through http://real-timeupdates.com/bce5. The Quick Learning Guide (located under "Learn More" on the website) hits all the high points of this chapter in just two pages. This guide, especially prepared by the authors, will help you study for exams or review important concepts whenever you need a quick refresher.

CASES

▼ *Apply the three-step writing process to the following cases, as assigned by your instructor.*

LETTER WRITING SKILLS

1. Message Strategies: Making Negative Announcements [LO-4]

Your company, PolicyPlan Insurance Services, is a 120-employee insurance claims processor based in Milwaukee. PolicyPlan has engaged Midwest Sparkleen for interior and exterior cleaning for the past five years. Midwest Sparkleen did exemplary work for the first four years, but after a change of ownership last year, the level of service has plummeted. Offices are no longer cleaned thoroughly, you've had to call the company at least six times to remind them to take care of spills and other messes that they're supposed to address routinely, and they've left toxic cleaning chemicals in a public hallway on several occasions. You have spoken with the owner about your concerns twice in the past three months, but his assurances that service would improve have not resulted in any noticeable improvements. When the evening cleaning crew forgot to lock the lobby door last Thursday—leaving your entire facility vulnerable to theft from midnight until 8 a.m. Friday morning—you decided it was time for a change.

Your task Write a letter to Jason Allred, owner of Midwest Sparkleen, 4000 South Howell Avenue, Milwaukee, WI, 53207, telling him that PolicyPlan will not be renewing its annual cleaning contract with Midwest Sparkleen when the current contract expires at the end of this month. Cite the examples identified above, and keep the tone of your letter professional.

PODCASTING SKILLS

2. Message Strategies: Making Negative Announcements [LO-4]

Offering an employee concierge seemed like a great idea when you added it as an employee benefit last year. The concierge handles a wide variety of personal chores for employees, everything from dropping off their dry cleaning to ordering event tickets to sending flowers. Employees love the service, and you know that the time they save can be devoted to work or family activities. Unfortunately, profits are way down, and concierge usage is up—up so far that you'll need to add a second concierge to keep up with the demand. As painful as it will be for everyone, you decide that the company needs to stop offering the service.

Your task Script a brief podcast announcing the decision and explaining why it was necessary. Make up any details you need. If your instructor asks you to do so, record your podcast and submit the file.

E-MAIL SKILLS   PORTFOLIO BUILDER

3. Message Strategies: Making Negative Announcements [LO-4]

You can certainly sympathize with employees when they complain about having their e-mail and instant messages monitored, but you're implementing a company policy that all employees will be asked to agree to abide by when they join the company. Your firm, Webcor Builders of San Mateo, California, is one of the estimated 60 percent of U.S. companies with such monitoring systems in place. More and more companies are using these systems (which typically operate by scanning messages for key words that suggest confidential, illegal, or otherwise inappropriate content) in an attempt to avoid instances of sexual harassment and other problems.

As the chief information officer, the manager in charge of computer systems in the company, you're often the target when employees complain about being monitored. Consequently, you know you're really going to hear it when employees learn that the monitoring program will be expanded to personal blogs as well.[19]

Your task Write an e-mail to be distributed to the entire workforce, explaining that the automated monitoring program is about to be expanded to include employees' personal blogs. Explain that although you sympathize with employee concerns regarding privacy and freedom of speech, the management team's responsibility is to protect the company's intellectual property and the value of the company name. Therefore, employees' personal blogs will be added to the monitoring system to ensure that employees don't intentionally or accidentally expose company secrets or criticize management in a way that could harm the company.

E-MAIL SKILLS

4. Message Strategies: Refusing Routine Requests; Communication Ethics: Resolving Ethical Dilemmas [LO-4], Chapter 1
A not-so-secret secret is getting more attention than you'd really like after an article in *BusinessWeek* gave the world an inside look at how much money you and other electronics retailers make from extended warranties (sometimes called service contracts). The article explained that typically half of the warranty price goes to the salesperson as a commission and that only 20 percent of the total amount customers pay for warranties eventually goes to product repair.

As a sales consultant in electronics retailing, you also know why extended warranties are such a profitable business. Many electronics products follow a predictable pattern of failure: a high failure rate early in their lives, then a "midlife" period during which failures go way down, and finally an "old age" period when failure rates ramp back up again (engineers refer to the phenomenon as the *bathtub curve* because it looks like a bathtub from the side—high at both ends and low in the middle). Those early failures are usually covered by manufacturers' warranties, and the extended warranties you sell are designed to cover that middle part of the life span. In other words, many extended warranties cover the period of time during which consumers are least likely to need them and offer no coverage when consumers need them most. (Consumers can actually benefit from extended warranties in a few product categories, including laptop computers and plasma TVs. Of course, the more sense the warranty makes for the consumer, the less financial sense it makes for your company.)[20]

Your task Worried that consumers will start buying fewer extended warranties, your boss has directed you to put together a sales training program that will help cashiers sell the extended warranties even more aggressively. The more you ponder this challenge, though, the more you're convinced that your company should change its strategy so it doesn't rely so much on profits from these warranties. In addition to offering questionable value to the consumer,

they risk creating a consumer backlash that could lead to lower sales of all your products. You would prefer to voice your concerns to your boss in person, but both of you are traveling on hectic schedules for the next week. You'll have to write an e-mail instead. Draft a brief message explaining why you think the sales training specifically, and the warranties in general, are both bad ideas.

MICROBLOGGING SKILLS

5. Message Strategies: Refusing Routine Requests [LO-4]
JetBlue was one of the first companies to incorporate the Twitter microblogging service into its customer communications, and more than a million flyers and fans now follow the airline's Twittering staff members. Messages include announcements about fare sales (such as limited-time auctions on eBay or special on-site sales at shopping malls), celebrations of company milestones (such as the opening of the carrier's new terminal at New York's JFK airport in 2008), schedule updates, and even personalized responses to people who Twitter with questions or complaints about the company.[21]

Your task Write a tweet alerting JetBlue customers to the possibility that Hurricane Isaac might disrupt flight schedules from August 13 through August 15. Tell them that decisions about delays and cancellations will be made on a city-by-city basis and will be announced on Twitter and the company's website at www.jetblue.com. Your message must be no more than 140 characters (including spaces) and must include the 15-character URL.

E-MAIL SKILLS

6. Message Strategies: Refusing Routine Requests [LO-4]
Like many other software companies, the Swiss company Fookes Software (www.fookes.com) lets potential customers download free evaluation copies of its software before deciding to purchase. By using the free trial versions, people can verify that the software meets their needs and is compatible with their PCs. Because it allows potential buyers to try products for 30 days before purchasing, the company does not provide refunds except in the case of accidental duplicate orders. Here is the company's refund policy, as shown on its website:

> All of Fookes Software's products can be evaluated, **free of charge**, through a trial mode or separate trial version that can be downloaded directly from our web site. Use the trial **before you purchase** to ensure that the full product will be compatible with your computer systems and satisfy your requirements. If you do not, you accept that the product may not meet your needs and that this will not justify a refund or chargeback. If you experience an issue with our software, then please contact our *customer support* service for help in solving the problem.
>
> **All sales are final** and refunds are provided only for accidental duplicate orders. Refunds will only be made to the credit card or PayPal account through which the original purchase was made. An administration fee may apply in such cases to cover processing costs and third-party commissions.

Ordering a software license signifies your acceptance of this Refund Policy.

In addition, the ordering page on the website asks potential buyers to read the refund policy before ordering and provides a link to the policy page.

This morning you received an e-mail message from a customer who purchased a copy of Album Express, a software package that helps people organize photos in attractive online albums and slide shows. After purchasing the program, the customer discovered that his computer has only 16 MB of memory, which is not enough to run the software effectively. He is now requesting a refund of the purchase price of $24.95. The website clearly states that Album Express requires at least 32 MB of memory, but the customer's e-mail doesn't mention whether he read this.[22]

Your task Write an e-mail message, denying the customer's request for a refund.

E-MAIL SKILLS

7. Message Strategies: Refusing Routine Requests [LO-4]

Lee Valley Tools (www.leevalley.com) sells high-quality woodworking tools across Canada through its retail stores and around the world through its website and catalogs. Although weekend hobbyists can pick up a mass-produced hand plane (a tool for smoothing wood) for $20 or $30 at the local hardware store, serious woodworkers pay 5 or 10 times that much for one of Lee Valley's precision Veritas planes. For the price, they get top-quality materials, precision manufacturing, and innovative designs that help them do better work in less time.

Lee Valley sells both its own Veritas brand tools as well as 5,000 tools made by other manufacturers. One of those companies has just e-mailed you to ask if Lee Valley would like to carry a new line of midrange hand planes that would cost more than the mass-market, hardware-store models but less than Lee Valley's own Veritas models. Your job is to filter requests such as this, rejecting those that don't meet Lee Valley's criteria and forwarding those that do to the product selection committee for further analysis. After one quick read of this incoming e-mail message, you realize there is no need to send this idea to the committee. Although these planes are certainly of decent quality, they achieve their lower cost through lower-quality steel that won't hold an edge as long, and through thinner irons (the element that holds the cutting edge) that will be more prone to vibrate during use and thus produce a rougher finish. These planes have a market, to be sure, but they're not a good fit for Lee Valley's top-of-the-line product portfolio. Moreover, the planes don't offer any innovations in terms of ease of use or any other product attribute.[23]

Your task Reply to this e-mail message, explaining that the planes appear to be decent tools, but they don't fit Lee Valley's strategy of offering only the best and most innovative tools. Support your decision with the three criteria described above. Choose the direct or indirect approach carefully, taking into consideration your company's relationship with this other company.

E-MAIL SKILLS

8. Message Strategies: Negative Employment Messages [LO-5]

Tom Weiss worked in the office at Opal Pools and Patios for four months, under your supervision (you're the office manager). On the basis of what he told you he could do, you started him off as a file clerk. However, his organizational skills proved inadequate for the job, so you transferred him to logging in accounts receivable, where he performed almost adequately. Then he assured you that his "real strength" was customer relations, so you moved him to the complaint department. After he spent three weeks making angry customers even angrier, you were convinced that no place in your office was appropriate for the talents of Weiss. Five weeks ago, you encouraged him to resign before being formally fired.

Today's e-mail brings a request from Weiss, asking you to write a letter recommending him for a sales position with a florist shop. You can't assess Weiss's sales abilities, but you do know him to be an incompetent file clerk, a careless bookkeeper, and an insensitive customer service representative. Someone else is more likely to deserve the sales job, so you decide that you have done enough favors for Tom Weiss for one lifetime and plan to refuse his request.

Your task Write an e-mail reply to Weiss, indicating that you have chosen not to write a letter of recommendation for him.

MEMO WRITING SKILLS   PORTFOLIO BUILDER

9. Message Strategies: Negative Employment Messages [LO-5]

Elaine Bridgewater, the former professional golfer you hired to oversee your golf equipment company's relationship with retailers, knows the business inside and out. As a former touring pro, she has unmatched credibility. She also has seemingly boundless energy, solid technical knowledge, and an engaging personal style. Unfortunately, she hasn't been quite as attentive as she needs to be when it comes to communicating with retailers. You've been getting complaints about voice-mail messages gone unanswered for days, confusing e-mails that require two or three rounds of clarification, and reports that are haphazardly thrown together. As valuable as Bridgewater's other skills are, she's going to cost the company sales if this goes on much longer. The retail channel is vital to your company's survival, and she's the employee most involved in the channel.

Your task Draft a brief (one page maximum, in memo format) informal performance appraisal and improvement plan for Bridgewater. Be sure to compliment her on the areas in which she excels but don't shy away from highlighting the areas in which she needs to improve, too: punctual response to customer messages; clear writing; and careful revision, production, and proofreading. Use what you've learned in this course so far to supply any additional advice about the importance of these skills.

PHONE SKILLS

10. Message Strategies: Negative Organizational Messages [LO-6]   Vail Products of Toledo, Ohio, manufactured a line of

beds for use in hospitals and other institutions where there is a need to protect patients who might otherwise fall out of bed and injure themselves (including patients with cognitive impairments or patterns of spasms or seizures). These "enclosed bed systems" use a netted canopy to keep patients in bed rather than the traditional method of using physical restraints such as straps or tranquilizing drugs. The intent is humane, but the design is flawed: At least 30 patients have become trapped in the various parts of the mattress and canopy structure, and 8 of them have suffocated.

Working with the U.S. Food and Drug Administration (FDA), Vail issued a recall on the beds, as manufacturers often do in the case of unsafe products. However, the recall is not really a recall. Vail will not be replacing or modifying the beds, nor will it accept returns. Instead, the company is urging institutions to move patients to other beds if possible. Vail has also sent out revised manuals and warning labels to be placed on the beds. In addition, the company announced that it is ceasing production of enclosed beds.

Your task A flurry of phone calls from concerned patients, family members, and institutional staff is overwhelming the support staff. As a writer in Vail's corporate communications office, you've been asked to draft a short script to be recorded on the company's phone system. When people call the main number, they'll hear "Press 1 for information regarding the recall of Model 500, Model 1000, and Model 2000 enclosed beds." After they press 1, they'll hear the message you're about to write, explaining that although the action is classified as a recall, Vail will not be accepting returned beds, nor will it replace any of the affected beds. The message should also assure customers that Vail has already sent revised operating manuals and warning labels to every registered owner of the beds in question. The phone system has limited memory, and you've been directed to keep the message to 75 words or less.[24]

SOCIAL NETWORKING SKILLS

11. Message Strategies: Negative Organizational Messages [LO-6] Marketing specialists usually celebrate when target audiences forward their messages to friends and family—essentially acting as unpaid advertising and sales representatives. In fact, the practice of viral marketing (see page 256) is based on this hope. For one Starbucks regional office, however, viral marketing started to make the company just a bit sick. The office sent employees in the Southeast an e-mail coupon for a free iced drink and invited them to share the coupon with family and friends. To the surprise of virtually no one who understands the nature of online life, the e-mail coupon multiplied rapidly, to the point that Starbucks stores all around the country were quickly overwhelmed with requests for free drinks. The company decided to immediately terminate the free offer, a month ahead of the expiration date on the coupon.[25]

Your task Write a one-paragraph message that can be posted on the Starbucks Facebook page and in individual stores, apologizing for the mix-up and explaining that the offer is no longer valid.

BLOGGING SKILLS

12. Message Strategies: Negative Organizational Messages [LO-6] XtremityPlus is known for its outlandish extreme-sports products, and the Looney Launch is no exception. Fulfilling the dream of every childhood daredevil, the Looney Launch is an aluminum and fiberglass contraption that quickly unfolds to create the ultimate bicycle jump. The product has been selling as fast as you can make it, even though it comes plastered with warning labels proclaiming that its use is inherently dangerous.

As XtremityPlus's CEO, you were nervous about introducing this product, and your fears were just confirmed: You've been notified of the first lawsuit by a parent whose child broke several bones after crash-landing off a Looney Launch.

Your task Write a post for your internal blog, explaining that the Looney Launch is being removed from the market immediately. Tell your employees to expect some negative reactions from enthusiastic customers and retailers but explain that (a) the company can't afford the risk of additional lawsuits and (b) even for XtremityPlus, the Looney Launch pushes the envelope a bit too far. The product is simply too dangerous to sell in good conscience.

BLOGGING SKILLS   MICROBLOGGING SKILLS   TEAM SKILLS   PORTFOLIO BUILDER

13. Message Strategies: Negative Organizational Messages [LO-6] One of your company's worst nightmares has just come true. EQ Industrial Services (EQIS), based in Wayne, Michigan, operates a number of facilities around the country that dispose of, recycle, and transport hazardous chemical wastes. Last night, explosions and fires broke out at the company's Apex, North Carolina, facility, forcing the evacuation of 17,000 local residents.

Your task It's now Friday, the day after the fire. With a team assigned by your instructor, write a brief post for the company's blog, covering the following points. In addition, write a tweet (no more than 140 characters) summarizing the situation and including the URL www.eqonline.com.

- A fire did break out at the Apex facility at approximately 10 p.m. Thursday.
- No one was in the facility at the time.
- Because of the diverse nature of the materials stored at the plant, the cause of the fire is not yet known.
- Rumors that the facility stores extremely dangerous chlorine gas and that the fire was spreading to other nearby businesses are not true.
- Special industrial firefighters hired by EQIS have already brought the fire under control.
- Residents in the immediate area were evacuated as a precaution, and they should be able to return to their homes tomorrow, pending permission by local authorities.
- Several dozen residents were admitted to local hospitals with complaints of breathing problems, but many have been released already; about a dozen emergency responders were treated as well.

- At this point (Friday afternoon), tests conducted by the North Carolina State Department of Environment and Natural Resources "had not detected anything out of the ordinary in the air."

Conclude by thanking the local police and fire departments for their assistance and directing readers to EQIS's toll-free hot line for more information.[26]

BLOGGING SKILLS

14. Message Strategies: Negative Organizational Messages [LO-6]
As the U.S. economy continued to sag in 2009 after receiving multiple blows from the housing and financial sectors, plant closures were a common tragedy across many industries. Shaw Industries, the world's largest manufacturer of carpeting, was among those suppliers to the housing industry that suffered as fewer houses were built or remodeled.

Your task Write a brief message for Shaw's corporate blog, covering the following points:

- With more than $5 billion in annual sales, Shaw Industries is the world's number one carpet manufacturer.
- Shaw's Milledgeville, Georgia, plant makes yarn used in the manufacture of carpeting.
- The continuing struggles in the new-housing market and the inability of many current homeowners to afford remodeling projects have lowered demand for carpet. With less demand for carpet, the Milledgeville plant can no longer operate at a profit.
- Shaw is forced to close the Milledgeville plant and lay off all 150 employees at the plant.
- The plant will close in three to four weeks from the current date.
- As openings become available in other Shaw facilities, the company hopes to be able to place some of the workers in those jobs.
- Georgia Labor Commissioner Michael Thurmond promised to help the affected employees. "The layoff at Shaw Industries in Milledgeville will create a difficult situation for the workers and their families, and I want them to know they're not alone in dealing with this problem. Our staff will work closely with the laid-off workers, company officials, and local elected officials in determining how to best assist the affected employees."
- Assistance to be provided by the State of Georgia includes career counseling, unemployment benefits, and job retraining.[27]

E-MAIL SKILLS

15. Message Strategies: Negative Organizational Messages [LO-6]
People who live for an adrenaline rush can find a way to go fast from Canada's Bombardier Recreational Products. Bombardier is one of the world's top makers of snowmobiles, personal watercraft, engines for motorboats, and all-terrain vehicles (ATVs)—all designed for fast fun.

Because it sends customers hurtling across snow, water, or land at high speeds, Bombardier takes safety quite seriously. However, problems do arise from time to time, requiring a rapid response with clear communication to the company's customer base. Bombardier recently became aware of a potentially hazardous situation with the "race-ready" version of its Can-Am DS 90 X ATVs. This model is equipped with a safety device called a tether engine shutoff switch, in which a cord is connected to a special switch that turns off the engine in the event of an emergency. On the affected units, pulling the cord might not shut off the motor, which is particularly dangerous if the rider falls off—the ATV will continue on its own until the engine speed returns to idle.

Your task Write an e-mail message that will be sent to registered owners of 2008 and 2009 DS 90 X ATVs that include the potentially faulty switch. Analyze the situation carefully as you choose the direct or indirect approach for your message. Explain that the tether engine shutoff switch may not deactivate the engine when it is pulled in an emergency situation. To prevent riders from relying on a safety feature that might not work properly, Bombardier, in cooperation with transportation safety authorities in the United States and Canada, is voluntarily recalling these models to have the tether switch removed. Emphasize the serious nature of the situation by explaining that if the rider is ejected and the engine shutoff switch does not work properly, the ATV will run away on its own, potentially resulting in significant injuries or deaths. Owners should stop riding their vehicles immediately and make an appointment with an authorized dealer to have the switch removed. The service will be performed at no charge, and customers will receive a $50 credit voucher for future purchases of Bombardier accessories. Include the following contact information: www.can-am.brp.comand 1–888–638–5397.[28]

Improve Your Grammar, Mechanics, and Usage

You can download the text of this assignment from http://real-timeupdates.com/bce5; click on "Student Assignments" and then click on "Chapter 8. Improve Your Grammar, Mechanics, and Usage."

Level 1: Self-Assessment—Semicolons, Colons, and Commas

Review Sections 2.4, 2.5, and 2.6 in the Handbook of Grammar, Mechanics, and Usage, and then complete the following 15 items.

In items 1–15, insert all required semicolons, colons, and commas.

1. This letter looks good that one doesn't.

2. I want to make one thing perfectly clear neither of you will be promoted if sales figures don't improve.

3. The Zurich airport has been snowed in therefore I won't be able to meet with you before January 4.

4. His motivation was obvious to get Meg fired.

5. Only two firms have responded to our survey J. J. Perkins and Tucker & Tucker.

6. Send a copy to Mary Kent Marketing Director Robert Bache Comptroller and Dennis Mann Sales Director.

7. Please be sure to interview these employees next week Henry Gold Doris Hatch and George Iosupovich.

8. We have observed your hard work because of it we are promoting you to manager of your department.

9. You shipped three items on June 7 however we received only one of them.

10. The convention kit includes the following response cards, giveaways, brochures, and a display rack.

11. The workers wanted an immediate wage increase they had not had a raise in nearly two years.

12. This then is our goal for 2009 to increase sales 35 percent.

13. His writing skills are excellent however he still needs to polish his management style.

14. We would like to address three issues efficiency profitability and market penetration.

15. Remember this rule When in doubt leave it out.

Level 2: Workplace Applications

The following items may contain errors in grammar, capitalization, punctuation, abbreviation, number style, word division, and vocabulary. Rewrite each sentence, correcting all errors. If a sentence has no errors, write "Correct" for that number.

1. Hector's, Julie's, and Tim's report was well-received by the Committee.

2. Everyone who are interested in signing up for the training seminar must do so by 3:00 o'clock pm on friday.

3. David Stern is a management and training expert that has spent a major part of his career coaching, counseling, and giving advise both to managers and workers.

4. Be aware and comply with local "zoning ordnances" and building codes.

5. Garrett didn't seem phased when her supervisor didn't except her excuse for being late, she forgot to set her alarm.

6. Copyright laws on the Internet is not always clearly defined, be sure your research doesn't extend to "borrowing" a competitors' keywords or copy.

7. Sauder Woodworking, in Archibald, Ohio sell a line of ready to assemble computer carts, desks, file cabinets, and furniture that is modular that can be mixed and matched to meet each business owners' personal taste.

8. Spamming is the most certain way to loose you're e-mail account, Web site, and you're reputation.

9. Us programmers have always tried to help others learn the tricks of the trade, especially Roger and myself.

10. The person whom was handling Miss Martinez' account told her that an error had been made by the bank in her favor.

11. "The trouble with focus groups" says Marketing Expert Frances Knight, "Is that consumers rarely act in real life they way they do in a "laboratory" setting."

12. In a industry in which design firms tend to come and go Skyline has licensed seventy products and grown to 8 employees.

13. If youv'e ever wondered why fast food restaurants are on the left and gift shops are on the right as you walk toward the gate into a newly-constructed airport you should read Malcolm Gladwells article, 'The Science of Shopping,' in the New Yorker.

14. Anyone whose starting a business should consider using their life story, as a way to generate customer's interest.

15. Having been in business since 1993, over 1000s of sales calls has been made by Mr. Jurzang, on prospects for his minority owned company.

Level 3: Document Critique

The following document may contain errors in grammar, capitalization, punctuation, abbreviation, number style, word division, and vocabulary. As your instructor indicates, photocopy this page and correct all errors using standard proofreading marks (see Appendix C) or download the document and make the corrections in your word processing software.

TO: ALL.EMPLOYEES

SUBJECT: Health insurance—Changes

Unlike many compa nies, Bright Manufacturing has always paid a hundred % of medical car insurance for it's employees, absorbing the recent 10–20 percent annual cost increases in order to provide this important benefit. This year; Blue Cross gave us some terrible news: the cost increase for our employee's medical coverage would be a staggering fourty percent per month next year

To mange the increase and continue to offer you and your family highquality medical coverage we have negotiated several changes with Blue Cross; a new cost saving alternative is also being offered by us:

Under the Blue Cross Plus plan, copay amounts for office visits will be ten dollars next year/ $50 for emergency room visits.

80 % of employees' insurance coverage (including 10 percent of the cost increase) will be paid by Bright next year and 100 % of the prescription drug costs (including a 23 percent cost increase). The remaining twenty percent of medical coverage will be deducted by us monthly from your salary, if you choose to remain on a Blue Cross Plus plan. We realize this is alot, but its still less than many companies charge their employees.

A fully paid alternative health plan, Blue Cross HMO, will now be provided by Bright at no cost to employees. But be warned that there is a deadline. If you want to switch to this new plan you must do so during our open enrollment period, Nov. 20 to December 1, and we will not consder applications for the change after that time so don't get your forms in late.

There are forms available in the Human Resources office for changing your coverage. They must be returned between November 20 and December 1. If you wish to remain on a Blue Cross Plus policy, you do not need to notify us; payroll deductions for company employees on the plan will occur automatic beginning January first.

If you have questions, please call our new Medical Benefits Information line at ext. 3392. Our Intranet sight will also provide you easy with information about health care coverage online if you click the "Medical Benefits" icon. Since our founding in 1946, we have provided our company employees with the best medical coverage available. We all hate rising costs and although things are looking bleak for the future but we're doing all we can do to hold on to this helpful benefit for you.

Lucinda Goodman, Benefits Mangr., Human resources

Writing Persuasive Messages

LEARNING OBJECTIVES

After studying this chapter, you will be able to

1 Apply the three-step writing process to persuasive messages

2 Describe an effective strategy for developing persuasive business messages

3 Identify the three most common categories of persuasive business messages

4 Describe an effective strategy for developing marketing and sales messages

5 Explain how to modify your approach when writing promotional messages for social media

6 Identify steps you can take to avoid ethical lapses in marketing and sales messages

PEARSON
mybcommlab   Access interactive videos, simulations, sample documents, Document Makeovers, and assessment quizzes in Chapter 9 of mybcommlab.com for mastery of this chapter's objectives.

> **"**When it comes to writing engaging content, 'you' is the most powerful word in the English language, because people are ultimately interested in fulfilling their own needs.**"**
>
> —Brian Clark, *Entrepreneur and blogger*
> www.copyblogger.com

COMMUNICATION
Matters

Brian Clark, widely considered to be one of the most influential bloggers in the field of marketing communication, knows that successful persuasion starts and ends with the audience.

The "you" attitude is important in any business message, but it's absolutely vital in persuasive writing. If your audience members don't believe that you have their best interests at heart, they won't be easily persuaded by anything you write. Follow the advice of successful persuasive writers such as Brian Clark: Audiences don't really care about what you have to say until you can demonstrate that you understand and care about what's important to them.[1]

In this chapter, you'll apply what you've learned so far about writing to the unique challenges of persuasive messages. You'll explore two types of persuasive messages: *persuasive business messages* (those that try to convince audiences to approve new projects, enter into business partnerships, and so on) and *marketing and sales messages* (those that try to convince audiences to consider and then purchase products and services).

1 **LEARNING OBJECTIVE**

Apply the three-step writing process to persuasive messages

Persuasion is the attempt to change someone's attitudes, beliefs, or actions.

Having a great idea or a great product is not enough; you need to be able to convince others of its merits.

Clarifying your purpose is an essential step with persuasive messages.

Demographics include characteristics such as age, gender, occupation, income, and education.

Psychographics include characteristics such as personality, attitudes, and lifestyle.

● Access this chapter's simulation entitled Persuasive Messages, located at mybcommlab.com.

You may need to use multiple media to reach your entire audience.

USING THE THREE-STEP WRITING PROCESS FOR PERSUASIVE MESSAGES

Whether you're convincing your boss to open a new office in Europe or encouraging potential customers to try your products, you'll use many of the same techniques of **persuasion**—the attempt to change an audience's attitudes, beliefs, or actions.[2] Because persuasive messages ask audiences to give something of value (money in exchange for a product, for example) or take substantial action (such as changing a corporate policy), they are more challenging to write than routine messages. Successful professionals understand that persuasion is not about trickery or getting people to act against their own best interests; it's about letting audiences know they have choices and presenting your offering in the best possible light.[3]

Step 1: Planning Persuasive Messages

In today's information-saturated business environment, having a great idea or a great product is no longer enough. Every day, untold numbers of good ideas go unnoticed and good products go unsold simply because the messages meant to promote them aren't compelling enough to be heard above the competitive noise. Creating successful persuasive messages in these challenging situations demands careful attention to all four tasks in the planning step, starting with an insightful analysis of your purpose and your audience.

Analyzing the Situation

In defining your purpose, make sure you're clear about what you really hope to achieve. Suppose you want to persuade company executives to support a particular research project. But what does "support" mean? Do you want them to pat you on the back and wish you well? Or do you want them to give you a staff of five researchers and a $1 million annual budget?

The best persuasive messages are closely connected to your audience's desires and interests.[4] Consider these important questions: Who is my audience? What are my audience members' needs? What do I want them to do? How might they resist? Are there alternative positions I need to examine? What does the decision maker consider to be the most important issue? How might the organization's culture influence my strategy?

To understand and categorize audience needs, you can refer to specific information, such as **demographics** (the age, gender, occupation, income, education, and other quantifiable characteristics of the people you're trying to persuade) and **psychographics** (personality, attitudes, lifestyle, and other psychological characteristics). When analyzing your audiences, take into account their cultural expectations and practices so that you don't undermine your persuasive message by using an inappropriate appeal or by organizing your message in a way that seems unfamiliar or uncomfortable to your readers.

If you aim to change someone's attitudes, beliefs, or actions, it is vital to understand his or her **motivation**—the combination of forces that drive people to satisfy their needs. Table 9.1 lists some of the needs that psychologists have identified or suggested as being important in influencing human motivation. Obviously, the more closely a persuasive message aligns with a recipient's existing motivation, the more effective the message is likely to be. For example, if you try to persuade consumers to purchase a product on the basis of its fashion appeal, that message will connect with consumers who are motivated by a desire to be in fashion but probably won't connect with consumers driven more by functional or financial concerns.

Gathering Information

Once your situation analysis is complete, you need to gather the information necessary to create a compelling persuasive message. You'll learn more about the types of information to include in persuasive business messages and marketing and sales messages later in the chapter. Chapter 10 presents advice on how to find the information you need.

Selecting the Right Medium

Media choices are always important, of course, but these decisions are particularly sensitive with persuasive messages because such messages are often unexpected or even

TABLE 9.1 Human Needs That Influence Motivation

Need	Implications for Communication
Basic physiological requirements: The needs for food, water, sleep, oxygen, and other essentials	Everyone has these needs, but the degree of attention an individual gives to them often depends on whether the needs are being met; for instance, an advertisement for sleeping pills will have greater appeal to someone suffering from insomnia than to someone who has no problem sleeping.
Safety and security: The needs for protection from bodily harm, to know that loved ones are safe, and for financial security, protection of personal identity, career security, and other assurances	These needs influence both consumer and business decisions in a wide variety of ways; for instance, advertisements for life insurance often encourage parents to think about the financial security of their children and other loved ones.
Affiliation and belonging: The needs for companionship, acceptance, love, popularity, etc.	The need to feel loved, accepted, or popular drives a great deal of human behavior, from the desire to be attractive to potential mates to wearing the clothing style that a particular social group is likely to approve.
Power and control: The need to feel in control of situations or to exert authority over others	You can see many examples appealing to this need in advertisements: *Take control of your life*, *your finances*, *your future*, *your career*, and so on. Many people who lack power want to know how to get it, and people who have power often want others to know they have it.
Achievement: The need to feel a sense of accomplishment—or to be admired by others for accomplishments	This need can involve both *knowing* (when people experience a feeling of accomplishment) and *showing* (when people are able to show others that they've achieved success); advertising for luxury consumer products frequently appeals to this need.
Adventure and distraction: The need for excitement or relief from daily routine	People vary widely in their need for adventure; some crave excitement—even danger—whereas others value calmness and predictability. Some needs for adventure and distraction are met *virtually*, such as through horror movies, thriller novels, etc.
Knowledge, exploration, and understanding: The need to keep learning	For some people, learning is usually a means to an end, a way to fulfill some other need; for others, acquiring new knowledge is the goal.
Aesthetic appreciation: The desire to experience beauty, order, symmetry, etc.	Although this need may seem "noncommercial" at first glance, advertisers appeal to it frequently, from the pleasing shape of a package to the quality of the gemstones in a piece of jewelry.
Self-actualization: The need to "be all that one can be," to reach one's full potential as a human being	Psychologists Kurt Goldstein and Abraham Maslow popularized self-actualization as the desire to make the most of one's potential, and Maslow identified it as one of the higher-level needs in his classic hierarchy; even if people met most or all of their other needs, they would still feel the need to self-actualize. An often-quoted example of appealing to this need is the U.S. Army's one-time advertising slogan "Be all that you can be."
Helping others: The need to believe that one is making a difference in the lives of other people	This need is the central motivation in fundraising messages and other appeals to charity.

unwelcome. For instance, some people don't mind promotional e-mail messages for products they're interested in; others resent every piece of commercial e-mail they receive. *Permission-based marketing*, in which marketers ask permission before sending messages, can help companies avoid antagonizing their target audiences.

Social media can be particularly effective for reaching out to customers and potential customers. However, as "Writing Promotional Messages for Social Media" on page 223 explains, messages in these media require a different approach than traditional marketing and sales efforts.

Organizing Your Information

The most effective main ideas for persuasive messages have one thing in common: They are about the receiver, not the sender. For instance, if you're trying to convince others to join you in a business venture, explain how it will help them, not how it will help you.

Limiting your scope is vital. If you seem to be wrestling with more than one main idea, you haven't zeroed in on the heart of the matter. If you try to craft a persuasive message without focusing on the one central problem or opportunity your audience truly cares about, chances are you won't be able to persuade successfully.[5]

Because the nature of persuasion is to convince people to change their attitudes, beliefs, or actions, most persuasive messages use the indirect approach. That means you'll want to explain your reasons and build interest before asking for a decision or for action—or perhaps even before revealing your purpose. In contrast, when you have a close relationship with your audience and the message is welcome or at least neutral, the direct approach can be effective.

For persuasive business messages, the choice between the direct and indirect approaches is also influenced by the extent of your authority, expertise, or power in an organization. For instance, if you are a highly regarded technical expert with years of experience, you might use the direct approach in a message to top executives. In contrast, if you aren't well known and therefore need to rely more on the strength of your message than the power of your reputation, the indirect approach will probably be more successful.

Step 2: Writing Persuasive Messages

Encourage a positive response to your persuasive messages by (1) using positive and polite language, (2) understanding and respecting cultural differences, (3) being sensitive to organizational cultures, and (4) taking steps to establish your credibility.

Positive language usually happens naturally with persuasive messages because you're promoting an idea or a product you believe in. However, take care not to inadvertently insult your readers by implying that they've made poor choices in the past.

Be sure to understand cultural expectations as well. For example, a message that seems forthright and direct in a low-context culture might seem brash and intrusive in a high-context culture.

Just as social culture affects the success of a persuasive message, so too does the culture within various organizations. Some organizations handle disagreement and conflict in an indirect, behind-the-scenes way, whereas others accept and even encourage open discussion and sharing of differing viewpoints.

Finally, when trying to persuade a skeptical or hostile audience, you must convince people that you know what you're talking about and that you're not trying to mislead them. Use these techniques:

- Use simple language to avoid suspicions of fantastic claims and emotional manipulation.
- Provide objective evidence for the claims and promises you make.
- Identify your sources, especially if your audience already respects those sources.
- Establish common ground by emphasizing beliefs, attitudes, and background experiences you have in common with the audience.
- Be objective and present fair and logical arguments.
- Display your willingness to keep your audience's best interests at heart.
- Persuade with logic, evidence, and compelling narratives, rather than trying to coerce with high-pressure, "hard sell" tactics.
- Whenever possible, try to build your credibility before you present a major proposal or ask for a major decision. That way, audiences don't have to evaluate both you and your message at the same time.[6]

Margin notes:

Limit your scope to include only the information needed to help your audience take the next step toward making a favorable decision.

Most persuasive messages use the indirect approach.

The choice of approach is influenced by your position (or authority within the organization) relative to your audience's.

Persuasive messages are often unexpected or even unwelcome, so the "you" attitude is crucial.

Organizational culture can influence persuasion as much as social culture.

Audiences often respond unfavorably to over-the-top language, so keep your writing simple and straightforward.

REAL-TIME UPDATES
Learn More by Watching This Video

Persuasion skills for every business professional

Persuasion is an essential business skill, no matter what career path you follow. This video offers great tips for understanding, practicing, and applying persuasive skills. Go to **http://real-timeupdates.com/bce5** and click on "Learn More." If you are using mybcommlab, you can access Real-Time Updates within each chapter or under Student Study Tools.

Step 3: Completing Persuasive Messages

Credibility is an essential element of persuasion, so the production quality of your messages is vital. If your message shows signs of carelessness or incompetence, people might think you are careless or incompetent as well.

When you evaluate your content, try to judge your argument objectively and try not to overestimate your credibility. When revising for clarity and conciseness, carefully match the purpose and organization to audience needs. If possible, ask an experienced colleague who knows your audience well to review your draft. Your design elements must complement, not detract from, your argument. In addition, meticulous proofreading will identify any mechanical or spelling errors that would weaken your persuasive potential. Finally, make sure your distribution methods fit your audience's expectations as well as your purpose.

> Careless production undermines your credibility, so revise and proofread with care.

DEVELOPING PERSUASIVE BUSINESS MESSAGES

2 LEARNING OBJECTIVE

Describe an effective strategy for developing persuasive business messages

Your success as a businessperson is closely tied to your ability to encourage others to accept new ideas, change old habits, or act on your recommendations. Unless your career takes you into marketing and sales, most of your persuasive messages will consist of *persuasive business messages*, which are any persuasive messages designed to elicit a preferred response in a nonsales situation.

Even if you have the power to compel others to do what you want them to do, persuading them is more effective than forcing them. People who are forced into accepting a decision or plan are less motivated to support it and more likely to react negatively than if they're persuaded.[7] Within the context of the three-step process, effective persuasion involves four essential strategies: framing your arguments, balancing emotional and logical appeals, reinforcing your position, and anticipating objections.

Framing Your Arguments

Many persuasive messages follow some variation of the indirect approach. One of the most commonly used variations is called the **AIDA model**, which organizes your presentation into four phases:

- **Attention.** Your first objective is to encourage your audience to want to hear about your problem, idea, or new product—whatever your main idea is. Be sure to find some common ground on which to build your case.

- **Interest.** Provide additional details that prompt audience members to imagine how the solution might benefit them.

- **Desire.** Help audience members embrace your idea by explaining how the change will benefit them and answering potential objections.

- **Action.** Suggest the specific action you want your audience to take. Include a deadline, when applicable.

> The AIDA model is a useful approach for many persuasive messages:
> - **A**ttention
> - **I**nterest
> - **D**esire
> - **A**ction

The AIDA model is tailor-made for using the indirect approach, allowing you to save your main idea for the action phase (see Figure 9.1 on the next page). However, it can also work with the direct approach, in which case you use your main idea as an attention-getter, build interest with your argument, create desire with your evidence, and emphasize your main idea in the action phase with the specific action you want your audience to take.

> The AIDA model is ideal for the indirect approach.

When your AIDA message uses the indirect approach and is delivered by memo or e-mail, keep in mind that your subject line usually catches your reader's eye first. Your challenge is to make it interesting and relevant enough to capture reader attention without revealing your main idea. If you put your request in the subject line, you're likely to get a quick "no" before you've had a chance to present your arguments:

Instead of This	Write This
Request for development budget to add automated IM response system	Reducing the cost of customer support inquiries

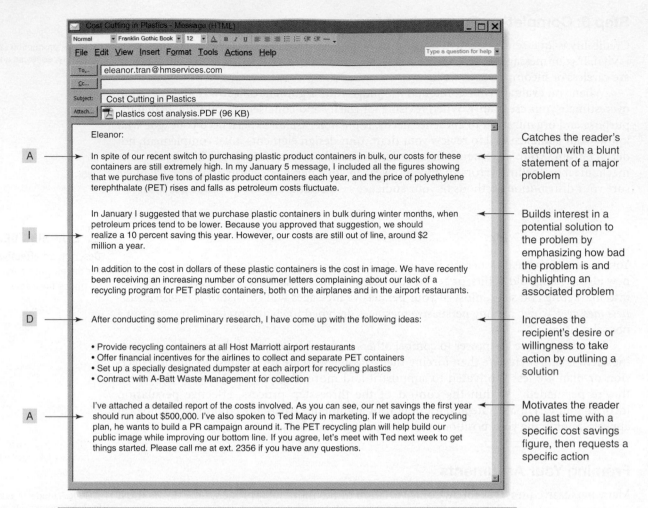

Figure 9.1   Persuasive Message Using the AIDA Model
Randy Thumwolt uses the AIDA model in a persuasive message about a program that would try to reduce Host Marriott's annual plastics costs and try to curtail consumer complaints about the company's recycling record. Note how Thumwolt "sells the problem" before attempting to sell the solution. Few people are interested in hearing about solutions to problems they don't know about or don't believe exist. His interest section introduces an additional, unforeseen problem with plastic product containers.

The AIDA approach has limitations:

■ It essentially talks *at* audiences, not *with* them

■ It focuses on one-time events not long-term relationships

With either the direct or indirect approach, AIDA and similar models do have limitations. First, AIDA is a unidirectional method that essentially talks *at* audiences, not *with* them. Second, AIDA is built around a single event, such as asking an audience for a decision, rather than on building a mutually beneficial, long-term relationship.[8] AIDA is still a valuable tool for the right purposes, but as you'll read later in the chapter, a conversational approach is more compatible with today's social media.

Balancing Emotional and Logical Appeals

Few persuasive appeals are purely logical or purely emotional, and a key skill is finding the right balance for each message. An **emotional appeal** calls on feelings or audience sympathies. For instance, you can make use of the emotion inspired by words such as *freedom*, *success*, *prestige*, *compassion*, *free*, and *comfort*. Such words put your audience in a certain frame of mind and help people accept your message.

> Emotional appeals attempt to connect with the reader's feelings or sympathies.

Many marketing and sales messages rely heavily on emotional appeals, but most persuasive business messages rely more on logic. And even if your audience reaches a conclusion based on emotions, they'll look to you to provide logical support as well. A **logical appeal** uses one of three types of reasoning:

> Logical appeals are based on the reader's notions of reason; these appeals can use analogy, induction, or deduction.

- **Analogy.** With analogy, you reason from specific evidence to specific evidence. For instance, to convince management to buy a more robust firewall to protect your company's computer network, you might use the analogy of "circling the wagons," as when covered wagons crossing the continent gathered in a circle every night to form a safe space within.

- **Induction.** With inductive reasoning, you work from specific evidence to a general conclusion. To convince your boss to change a certain production process, you could point out that every company that has adopted it has increased profits.

- **Deduction.** With deductive reasoning, you work from a generalization to a specific conclusion. To persuade your boss to hire additional customer support staff, you might point to industry surveys that show how crucial customer satisfaction is to corporate profits.

Every method of reasoning is vulnerable to misuse. To avoid faulty logic, practice the following guidelines:[9]

> Using logical appeals carries with it the ethical responsibility to avoid faulty logic.

- **Avoid hasty generalizations.** Make sure you have plenty of evidence before drawing conclusions.

- **Avoid circular reasoning.** Circular reasoning is a logical fallacy in which you try to support your claim by restating it in different words. The statement "We know temporary workers cannot handle this task because temps are unqualified for it" doesn't prove anything because the claim and the supporting evidence are essentially identical.

- **Avoid attacking an opponent.** Attack the argument your opponent is making, not your opponent's character.

- **Avoid oversimplifying a complex issue.** For example, don't reduce a complex situation to a simple "either/or" statement if the situation isn't that simple or clear-cut.

- **Avoid mistaken assumptions of cause and effect.** If you can't isolate the impact of a specific factor, you can't assume that it's the cause of whatever effect you're discussing. You lowered prices, and sales went up. Were lower prices the cause? Maybe, but the sales increase might have been caused by a better advertising campaign or some other factor.

- **Avoid faulty analogies.** Be sure that the two objects or situations being compared are similar enough for the analogy to hold.

Reinforcing Your Position

After you've worked out the basic elements of your argument, step back and look for ways to bolster the strength of your position. Are all your claims supported by believable evidence? Would a quotation from a recognized expert help make your case?

Next, examine your language. Can you find more powerful words to convey your message? For example, if your company is in serious financial trouble, talking about *fighting for survival* is a more powerful emotional appeal than talking about *ensuring continued operations*. As with any other powerful tool, though, use vivid language and abstractions carefully and honestly.

REAL-TIME UPDATES
Learn More by Reading This Article

Make sure your logic can stand on solid ground

Get sound advice on using logical appeals correctly and effectively. Go to **http://real-timeupdates.com/bce5** and click on "Learn More." If you are using mybcommlab, you can access Real-Time Updates within each chapter or under Student Study Tools.

Choose your words carefully to trigger the desired responses.

In addition to examining individual word choices, consider using metaphors and other figures of speech. If you want to describe a quality-control system as being designed to detect every possible product flaw, you might call it a "spider web" to imply that it catches everything that comes its way. Similarly, anecdotes (brief stories) can help your audience grasp the meaning and importance of your arguments. Instead of just listing the number of times the old laptop computers in your department have failed, you could describe how you lost a sale when your computer broke down during a critical sales presentation.

Beyond specific words and phrases, look for other factors that can reinforce your position. When you're asking for something, your audience members will find it easier to grant your request if they stand to benefit from it as well.

Anticipating Objections

Even powerful persuasive messages can encounter audience resistance.

Even compelling ideas and exciting projects can encounter objections, if only as a consequence of people's natural tendency to resist chance. Anticipate as many objections as you can and address them before your audience can bring them up. By doing so, you can remove these potentially negative elements from the conversation and keep the focus on positive communication. Note that you don't need to explicitly mention a particular concern. For instance, if your proposal to switch to lower-cost materials is likely to raise concerns about quality, simply emphasize that the new materials are just as good as existing materials. You'll not only get this issue out of the way sooner, but also demonstrate a broad appreciation of the issue and imply confidence in your message.[10]

If you expect to encounter strong resistance, present all sides of an issue.

If you expect a hostile audience that is biased against your plan, be sure to present all sides of the situation. As you cover each option, explain the pros and cons. You'll gain additional credibility if you present these options before presenting your recommendation or decision.[11] If you can, involve your audience in the design of the solution; people are more likely to support ideas they help create.

Avoiding Common Mistakes in Persuasive Communication

Don't let confidence or enthusiasm lead you to some common mistakes in persuasive communication.

When you believe in a concept or project you are promoting, it's easy to get caught up in your own confidence and enthusiasm and thereby fail to see things from the audience's perspective. When putting together persuasive arguments, avoid these common mistakes:[12]

- **Using a hard sell.** Don't push. No one likes being pressured into making a decision, and communicators who take this approach can come across as being more concerned with meeting their own goals than with satisfying the needs of their audiences. In contrast, a "soft sell" is more like a comfortable conversation that uses calm, rational persuasion.

- **Resisting compromise.** Successful persuasion is often a process of give-and-take, particularly in the case of persuasive business messages, where you don't always get everything you asked for in terms of budgets, investments, and other commitments.

- **Relying solely on great arguments.** Great arguments are important, but connecting with your audience on the right emotional level and communicating through vivid language are just as vital. Sometimes a well-crafted story can be even more compelling than dry logic.

- **Assuming that persuasion is a one-shot effort.** Persuasion is often a process, not a one-time event. In many cases, you need to move your audience members along one small step at a time rather than try to convince them to say "yes" in one huge step.

3 LEARNING OBJECTIVE

Identify the three most common categories of persuasive business messages

COMMON EXAMPLES OF PERSUASIVE BUSINESS MESSAGES

Throughout your career, you'll have numerous opportunities to write persuasive messages within your organization—for example, when suggesting more efficient operating procedures, asking for cooperation from other departments, pitching investors on a new business idea, or requesting adjustments that go beyond a supplier's contractual obligations. In addition, many of the routine requests you studied in Chapter 7 can become persuasive messages if you want a nonroutine result or believe that you haven't received fair treatment. Most of these messages can be divided into persuasive requests for action, persuasive presentation of ideas, and persuasive claims and requests for adjustment.

Persuasive Requests for Action

The bulk of your persuasive business messages will involve requests for action. In some cases, your request will be anticipated, so the direct approach is fine. In others, you'll need to introduce your intention indirectly, and the AIDA model or a similar approach is ideal for this purpose.

Open with an attention-getting device and show readers that you understand their concerns. Use the interest and desire sections of your message to demonstrate that you have good reason for making such a request and to cover what you know about the situation: the facts and figures, the benefits of helping, and any history or experience that will enhance your appeal. Your goals are (1) to gain credibility (for yourself and your request) and (2) to make your readers believe that helping you will indeed help solve a significant problem. Close with a request for some specific action, and make that course of action as easy to follow as possible to maximize the chances of a positive response.

Most persuasive business messages involve a request for action.

Persuasive Presentation of Ideas

You may encounter situations in which you simply want to change attitudes or beliefs about a particular topic, without asking the audience to decide or do anything—at least not yet. The goal of your first message might be nothing more than convincing your audience to reexamine long-held opinions or admit the possibility of new ways of thinking.

For instance, the World Wide Web Consortium (a global association that defines many of the guidelines and technologies behind the World Wide Web) has launched a campaign called the Web Accessibility Initiative. Although the consortium's ultimate goal is making websites more accessible to people who have disabilities or age-related limitations, a key interim goal is simply making website developers more aware of the need. As part of this effort, the consortium has developed a variety of presentations and documents that highlight the problems many web visitors face.[13]

Sometimes the objective of persuasive messages is simply to encourage people to consider a new idea.

Persuasive Claims and Requests for Adjustments

Most claims are routine messages and use the direct approach discussed in Chapter 7. However, both consumers and business professionals sometimes encounter situations in which they believe they haven't received a fair deal by following normal procedures. These situations require a more persuasive message.

The key ingredients of a good persuasive claim are a complete and specific review of the facts and a confident and positive tone. Keep in mind that you have the right to be satisfied with every transaction. Begin persuasive claims by outlining the problem and continue by reviewing what has been done about it so far, if anything. The recipient might be juggling numerous claims and other demands on his or her attention, so be clear, calm, and complete when presenting your case. Be specific about how you would like to see the situation resolved.

Next, give your reader a good reason for granting your claim. Show how the individual or organization is responsible for the problem and appeal to your reader's sense of fair play, goodwill, or moral responsibility. Explain how you feel about the problem but don't get carried away, and don't make threats. People generally respond most favorably to requests that are both calm and reasonable. Close on a positive note that reflects how a successful resolution of the situation will repair or maintain a mutually beneficial working relationship.

DEVELOPING MARKETING AND SALES MESSAGES

4 **LEARNING OBJECTIVE**

Describe an effective strategy for developing marketing and sales messages

Marketing and sales messages use the same basic techniques as other persuasive messages, with the added emphasis of encouraging someone to participate in a commercial transaction. Although the terms *marketing message* and *sales message* are often used interchangeably, they are slightly different: **Marketing messages** usher potential buyers through the purchasing process without asking them to make an immediate decision (see Figure 9.2 on the next page).

Marketing and sales messages use many of the same techniques as persuasive business messages.

Product-specific marketing messages are posted on other tabs

In the same vein as Red Bull (page 127), Adidas uses its Wall posts to promote its sponsored performances and sporting events

Figure 9.2   Marketing Versus Sales Messages
In keeping with its branding theme of "celebrating originality," Adidas uses its Adidas Originals Facebook presence to indirectly promote its brand name by linking it with cutting-edge entertainment and athletic events. Note how other than the Adidas name and logo, this page has very little to suggest that this is even a footwear company.

Sales messages take over at that point, encouraging potential buyers to make a purchase decision then and there. Marketing messages focus on such tasks as introducing new brands to the public, providing competitive comparisons, encouraging customers to visit websites for more information, and reminding buyers that a particular product or service is available. In contrast, a sales message makes a specific request for people to place an order for a particular product or service. (The text of marketing and sales messages is usually referred to as "copy," by the way.)

Most marketing and sales messages, particularly in larger companies, are created and delivered by professionals with specific training in marketing, advertising, sales, or public relations. However, you may be called on to review the work of these specialists or even to write such messages in smaller companies, and having a good understanding of how these messages work will help you be a more effective manager. The basic strategy for creating these messages includes assessing audience needs; analyzing your competition; determining key selling points and benefits; anticipating purchase objections; applying the AIDA model; adapting your writing to social media, if appropriate; and maintaining high standards of ethical and legal compliance.

Assessing Audience Needs

Understanding the purchase decision from the buyer's perspective is a vital step in framing an effective marketing or sales message.

As with every other business message, successful marketing and sales messages start with an understanding of audience needs. For some products and services, this assessment is a simple matter. For instance, customers compare only a few basic attributes when purchasing copy or printer paper, including weight, brightness, color, and finish. In contrast, they might consider dozens of features when shopping for real estate, cars, machinery, professional services, and other complex purchases. In addition, customer needs often extend beyond the basic product or service. For example, clothes do far more than simply keep you warm. What you wear makes a statement about who you are, which social groups you want to be associated with (or not), and how you view your relationship with the people around you.

Analyzing Your Competition

Marketing and sales messages nearly always compete with messages from other companies trying to reach the same audience. When Nike plans a marketing campaign to introduce a new shoe model to current customers, the company knows that its audience has also been exposed to messages from Adidas, New Balance, Reebok, and numerous other shoe companies. In crowded markets, writers sometimes have to search for words and phrases that other companies aren't already using. They might also want to avoid themes, writing styles, or creative approaches that are too similar to those of competitors' messages.

> Promotional messages have to compete for the audience's attention.

Determining Key Selling Points and Benefits

With some insight into audience needs and existing messages from the competition, you're ready to decide which benefits and features of your product or service to highlight. For all but the simplest products, you'll want to prioritize the items you plan to discuss. Some products have dozens of attributes, but you'll exhaust readers if you hit them with a long list. Focus on the few that matter the most.[14]

You'll also want to distinguish between selling points and benefits. As Table 9.2 shows, **selling points** are the most attractive features of an idea or product, whereas **benefits** are the particular advantages that purchasers can realize from those features. In other words, selling points focus on what the product does. Benefits focus on what the user experiences or gains.

> Selling points focus on the product; benefits focus on the user.

For example, the online community and social network CafeMom (**www.cafemom .com**) doesn't stress the online networking feature of its services; rather, it stresses the opportunity to connect with other moms who have similar concerns and interests—which is the benefit enabled by the networking feature. Two common ways of communicating features and benefits are showing them in a table, identifying each feature and describing the benefits it offers, and using electronic media to let readers explore the benefits of various product features (see Figure 9.3 on the next page).

Anticipating Purchase Objections

Marketing and sales messages usually encounter objections and, as with persuasive business messages, the best way to handle them is to identify these objectives up front and address as many as you can. Keep in mind that with marketing and sales messages, you often don't get a second chance to present your case. If your website for fashion jewelry aimed at college-age consumers strikes visitors as too juvenile, for instance, they'll click away to another site and never come back.

> Anticipating objections is crucial to effective marketing and sales messages.

TABLE 9.2 Features Versus Benefits	
Product or Service Feature	**Customer Benefit**
Carrier's Hybrid Heat dual-fuel system combines our Infinity 19 fuel pump with our Infinity 96 furnace.	Carrier's Hybrid Heat dual-fuel system provides the optimum balance of comfort and energy efficiency.
Our marketing communication audit accurately measures the impact of your advertising and public relations efforts.	Find out whether your message is reaching the target audience and whether you're spending your marketing budget in the best possible manner.
The spools in our fly-fishing reels are machined from solid blocks of aircraft-grade aluminum.	Go fishing with confidence: These lightweight reels will stand up to the toughest conditions.

Each of these "hotspots" highlights a particular feature of the phone; clicking a hotspot (in this case, the SureType Technology for simplifying text entry) displays a brief description

This brief description of the SureType Technology helps readers understand the benefits this feature provides

Figure 9.3 Explaining the Benefits of Product Features
This interactive webpage explains the user benefits made possible by key features of the BlackBerry Pearl smartphone. Website visitors simply click the "hotspot" associated with each feature to display an explanation of the benefits that feature provides.

Objections can range from high price or low quality to a lack of compatibility with existing products or a perceived risk involved with the product. Consumers might worry that a car won't be safe enough for a family or that a jacket will make them look unattractive. Business buyers might worry about disrupting operations or failing to realize the financial returns on a purchase.

Price can be a particularly tricky issue in any promotional message. Whether you highlight or downplay the price of your product, prepare your readers for it with words such as *luxurious* and *economical*.

If price is a major selling point, give it a position of prominence, such as in the headline or as the last item in a paragraph. If price is not a major selling point, you can handle it in several ways. You could leave the price out altogether or deemphasize it by putting the figure in the middle of a paragraph that comes well after you've presented the benefits and selling points:

Emphasizes the rarity of the edition to signal value and thus prepares the reader for the big-ticket price that follows.

Embeds the price in the middle of a sentence and ties it in with a reminder of the exclusivity of the offer.

> Only 100 prints of this exclusive, limited-edition lithograph will be created. On June 15, they will be made available to the general public, but you can reserve one now for only $350, the special advance reservation price. Simply rush the enclosed reservation card back today so that your order is in before the June 15 publication date.

Whenever price is likely to cause an objection, look for ways to increase the perceived value of the purchase and decrease the perception of high cost. For example, to help blunt the impact of the price of a home gym, you might say that it costs less than a year's worth of health club dues—plus, customers save time and transportation costs by exercising at home. Of course, any attempts to minimize perceptions of price or other potential negatives must be ethical.

Crafting a Persuasive Appeal

Conventional marketing and sales messages are often prepared using the AIDA model or some variation of it. (But compare this approach with how *conversation marketing* messages are prepared in "Writing Promotional Messages for Social Media" on page 223.) Begin with an attention-getting device, generate interest by describing some of the product's or service's unique features, increase desire by highlighting the benefits that are most appealing to your audience, and close by suggesting the action you want the audience to take.

Getting Attention

Professionals use a wide range of techniques to attract an audience's attention:

- **A strong product feature or benefit.** "Game on. And on. And on" (promoting the game-playing aspects of Apple's iPod Touch).[15]

- **A piece of genuine news.** "HealthGrades Reveals America's Best Hospitals."[16]

- **A point of common ground with the audience.** "Tough on Dirt, Gentle on the Earth" (promoting the environmentally friendly aspects of Biokleen cleaning products).[17]

- **A personal appeal to the reader's emotions and values.** "Up to 35 mpg. Unlimited Fun" (promoting the fuel efficiency and sporty driving characteristics of the Ford Focus).[18]

- **The promise of insider information.** "France may seem familiar, but nearly everything—from paying taxes to having a baby—is done quite differently. Get the practical answers to nearly 300 questions about making a life in France."[19]

- **The promise of savings.** "Summer Clearance: Nearly 10,000 Books, Savings up to 90%."[20]

- **A sample or demonstration of the product.** "These videos can provide more detail on Mint's unique and award-winning approach to personal financial management."[21]

- **A solution to a problem.** "Fees to check a bag can add $50 to the cost of a round trip. So the FlightWise Carry-On Backpack is designed to fit in all carry-on storage spaces, even underseat, saving you money with every flight."[22]

> You can use a variety of attention-getting devices in marketing and sales messages.

Of course, words aren't the only attention-getting device at your disposal. Strong, evocative images are common attention-getters (see Figure 9.4). With online messages, you have even more options, including audio, animation, and video. Even more so than in persuasive business messages, it's important to carefully balance emotion and logic in marketing and sales messages.

Without using any images of people, the solitary teacup (left), the multiple glasses of ice tea (center), and the brunch setting suggested by the tea and food (right) convey both the pleasures of a quiet time alone as well as the pleasures of sharing tea with friends and family

The red-orange color of the tea, enhanced with the glow of backlighting through the translucent liquid, speaks of warmth and comfort

Complementary colors suggest freshness and elegance, adding to the emotional appeal

The text uses the storytelling technique to explain the creation of Bigelow's signature Constant Comment tea flavor and does so in a way that highlights the emotional appeal of drinking tea

Figure 9.4   Emotional and Logical Appeals
Bigelow Tea uses an effective combination of visual and textual messages in this emotional appeal.

Building Interest

Use the interest section of your message to build on the intrigue you created with your opening. This section should also offer support for any claims or promises you made in the opening. For instance, after opening with the headline, "Game on. And on. And on," the Apple iPod touch web presentation continues with the following:[23]

> **Get your game on with friends across the room or across the globe.** Games for iPod touch are made to take advantage of its built-in technologies such as the accelerometer, Multi-Touch, Wi-Fi, and Bluetooth wireless technology. The result is truly immersive gameplay—whether you're playing alone or with others in multiplayer mode. And with an App Store that offers thousands of games ready to download and play, the fun of iPod touch never ends.

This paragraph highlights key game-related features of the iPod touch and the key benefit ("truly immersive gameplay") that those features enable. The paragraph also addresses a potential objection that some readers might have, which is the number of games available for the device. At this point, anyone interested in portable gaming devices is probably intrigued enough to keep reading, and the website continues with deeper levels of information on each of the key features.

Increasing Desire

To build desire for a product, a service, or an idea, continue to expand on and explain how using it will benefit the recipient. Think carefully about the sequence of support points and use plenty of subheadings, hyperlinks, and other devices to help people quickly find the information they need. For example, after reading this much about the iPod touch, some users might want to know more about specific technical points such as the accelerometer, the speed and quality of the graphics, or software apps available. The iPod touch product page continues with detailed discussions of various product features and benefits, and it also offers numerous links to pages with other kinds of support information. The ability to provide flexible access to information is just one of the reasons the web is such a powerful medium for marketing and sales.

Throughout the body of your message, remember to keep the focus on the audience, not on your company or your product. When you talk about product features, remember to stress the benefits and talk in terms that make sense to users. For instance, rather than going into a technical description of what an accelerometer is, the webpage offers several examples of what it does, such as how in racing games it turns the iPod into a virtual steering wheel.[24]

As you work to build reader interest, be careful not to get so enthusiastic that you lose credibility. If Apple said that the video viewing experience on the iPod touch was as "satisfying as watching a full-size TV," most people would scoff at the notion of comparing a 3.5-inch display with a full-size television.

To increase desire, as well as boost your credibility, provide support for your claims. Creative writers find many ways to provide support, including testimonials from satisfied users, articles written by industry experts, competitive comparisons, product samples and free demonstrations, independent test results, and movies or computer animations that show a product in action. YouTube in particular has been a boon to marketers because it offers an easy, inexpensive way to demonstrate products. You can also highlight guarantees that demonstrate your faith in your product and your willingness to back it up.

Motivating Action

The final step in the AIDA model is persuading the audience to take action. Whether you want people to pick up the phone to place an order or visit your website to download a free demo version of your software, try to persuade them to do it right away. Even potential buyers who want the product can get distracted or forget to respond, so the sooner you can encourage action, the better. You might offer a discount for the first 1,000 people who order, put a deadline on the offer, or simply remind audience members that the sooner they order, the sooner they'll be able to enjoy the product's benefits. Also, make the task of responding as simple as possible. If the process is confusing or time-consuming, you'll lose potential customers.

WRITING PROMOTIONAL MESSAGES FOR SOCIAL MEDIA

5 LEARNING OBJECTIVE

Explain how to modify your approach when writing promotional messages for social media

The AIDA model and similar approaches have been successful with marketing and sales messages for decades, but communicating with customers in the social media landscape requires a different approach. As earlier chapters emphasize, potential buyers in a social media environment are no longer willing to be passive recipients in a structured, one-way information delivery process or to rely solely on promotional messages from marketers. This notion of interactive participation is the driving force behind **conversation marketing**, in which companies initiate, facilitate, and participate in conversations happening in a networked community of customers, journalists, bloggers, and other interested parties (see Figure 9.5). The term **social commerce** encompasses any aspect of buying and selling products and services or supporting customers through the use of social media.

Conversation marketing promotes the interactive participation of customers and other audiences.

> **"** The bottom line is that social media marketing is about real, genuine relationships. Give of yourself, and others will give back to you because they value what you do. **"**
>
> —Tamar Weinberg, *author and social media expert.*[25]

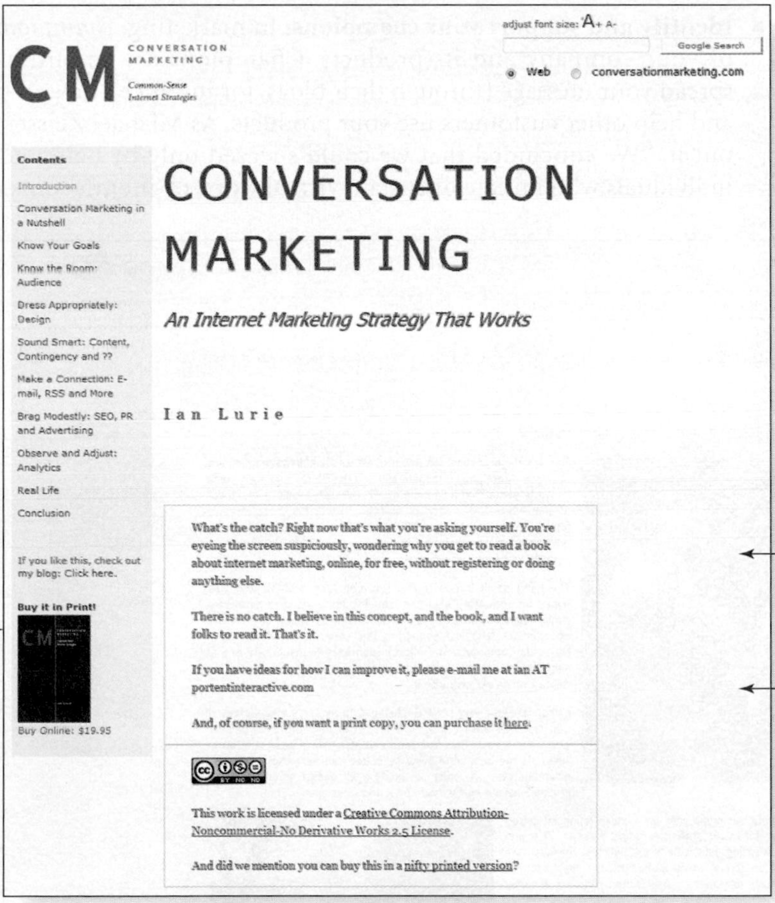

SINCERITY *Matters*

Includes a conventional sales message, but not in a way that overpowers the conversational aspect of the website

Addresses potential skepticism about his motivations for giving away access to a book

Encourages a conversation by inviting readers to suggest improvements

mybcommlab

Apply Figure 9.5's key concepts by revising a new document. Go to Chapter 9 in mybcommlab.com and select Document Makeovers.

Figure 9.5   Conversation Marketing

Talk about putting your money where your mouth is. To promote his book *Conversation Marketing*, Ian Lurie, the marketing strategist who helped popularize the concept of conversation marketing, gave everyone free access to the entire book online (a printed copy is also available for sale). By letting his blog subscribers, journalists, and potential clients of his consulting business read the book for free, Lurie stimulated multiple online conversations—some of which he discusses in brief updates inserted into the online text.

Given this shift from unidirectional speeches to multidirectional conversations, marketing and sales professionals must adapt their approach to persuasive messages. Follow these guidelines:[26]

- **Facilitate community building.** The first step is to make sure customers and other audiences can connect with your company and each other. Accomplishing this goal can be as simple as activating the commenting feature on a blog, or it may involve having a more elaborate social commerce system.

- **Listen at least as much as you talk.** Listening is just as essential for online conversations as it is for in-person conversations. Of course, trying to stay on top of a social media universe composed of millions of potential voices is no easy task. A variety of automated tools can help, from free alerts on search engines to sophisticated linguistic monitoring systems.

- **Initiate and respond to conversations within the community.** Through content on your website, blog postings, social network profiles and messages, newsletters, and other tools, make sure you provide the information customers need in order to evaluate your products and services. Use an objective, conversational style; people in social networks want useful information, not "advertising speak."

- **Provide information that people want.** Whether it's industry-insider news, in-depth technical guides to using your products, or brief answers to questions posted on community Q&A sites, fill the information gaps about your company and its products (see Figure 9.6).

- **Identify and support your champions.** In marketing, *champions* are enthusiastic fans of your company and its products. Champions are so enthusiastic that they help spread your message (through their blogs, for instance), defend you against detractors, and help other customers use your products. As Michael Zeisser of Liberty Interactive put it, "We concluded that we could succeed only by being genuinely useful to the individuals who initiate or sustain virtual word-of-mouth conversations."[27]

Figure 9.6   Providing Valuable Information Through Social Media
This article on the Bridepower blog provides information that is potentially useful for many brides. Cotton is not a fabric that many brides would instinctively consider for a wedding dress, so an article that discusses the characteristics and advantages of cotton could be quite informative. After providing information of value, the post does provide links to Bridepower's designer collections, but the promotion is discrete and doesn't hinder reading.

- **Be authentic; be transparent; be real.** Trying to fool the public through fake blogs and other tactics is not only unethical (and possibly illegal) but almost guaranteed to eventually backfire in a world where people have unprecedented access to information. Similarly, trying to tack social media onto a consumer-hostile business is likely to fail as soon as stakeholders see through the superficial attempt to "be social." In contrast, social media audiences respond positively to companies that are open and conversational about themselves, their products, and subjects of shared interest.

- **Don't rely on the news media to distribute your message.** In traditional public relations efforts, marketers have to persuade the news media to distribute their messages to consumers and other audiences by producing news stories. These media are still important, but you can also speak directly to these audiences through blogs and other electronic tools.

- **Integrate conventional marketing and sales strategies at the right time and in the right places.** AIDA and similar approaches are still valid for specific communication tasks, such as conventional advertising and the product promotion pages on your website.

For the latest information on using social media for persuasive communication, visit http://real-timeupdates.com/bce5 and click on Chapter 9.

MAINTAINING HIGH ETHICAL AND LEGAL STANDARDS

The word *persuasion* has negative connotations for some people, especially in a marketing or sales context. They associate persuasion with dishonest and unethical practices that lead unsuspecting audiences into accepting unworthy ideas or buying unneeded products. However, effective businesspeople view persuasion as a positive force, aligning their own interests with what is best for their audiences. They influence audience members by providing information and aiding understanding, which allows audiences the freedom to choose.[28] To maintain the highest standards of business ethics, always demonstrate the "you" attitude by showing honest concern for your audience's needs and interests.

As marketing and selling grow increasingly complex, so do the legal ramifications of marketing and sales messages. In the United States, the Federal Trade Commission (FTC) has the authority to impose penalties (ranging from cease-and-desist orders to multimillion-dollar fines) against advertisers that violate federal standards for truthful advertising. Other federal agencies have authority over advertising in specific industries, such as transportation and financial services. Individual states have additional laws that apply. The legal aspects of promotional communication can be quite complex, from state to state and from country to country, and most companies require marketing and sales people to get clearance from company lawyers before sending messages. In any event, pay close attention to the following legal aspects of marketing and sales communication:[29]

- **Marketing and sales messages must be truthful and nondeceptive.** The FTC considers messages to be deceptive if they include statements that are likely to mislead reasonable customers and the statements are an important part of the purchasing decision. Failing to include important information is also considered deceptive. The FTC also looks at *implied claims*—claims you don't explicitly make but that can be inferred from what you do or don't say.

- **You must back up your claims with evidence.** According to the FTC, offering a money-back guarantee or providing letters from satisfied customers is not enough; you must still be able to support your claims with objective evidence such as a survey or scientific study. If you claim that your food product lowers cholesterol, you must have scientific evidence to support that claim.

- **"Bait and switch" advertising is illegal.** Trying to attract buyers by advertising a product that you don't intend to sell—and then trying to sell them another (and usually more expensive) product—is illegal.

- **Marketing messages and websites aimed at children are subject to special rules.** For example, online marketers must obtain consent from parents before collecting personal information about children under age 13.

6 LEARNING OBJECTIVE

Identify steps you can take to avoid ethical lapses in marketing and sales messages

Marketing and sales messages are covered by a wide range of laws and regulations.

- **Marketing and sales messages are considered binding contracts in many states.** If you imply or make an offer and then can't fulfill your end of the bargain, you can be sued for breach of contract.

- **In most cases, you can't use a person's name, photograph, or other identity without permission.** Doing so is considered an invasion of privacy. You can use images of people considered to be public figures as long as you don't unfairly imply that they endorse your message.

Before you launch a marketing or sales campaign, make sure you're up to date on the latest regulations affecting spam (or *unsolicited bulk e-mail*, as it's formally known), customer privacy, and data security. The FTC website at www.ftc.gov is a good place to start.

Marketers have a responsibility to stay up to date on laws and regulations that restrict promotional messages.

PEARSON
mybcommlab™

Are you an active learner? Go to mybcommlab.com to master Chapter 9's content. Chapter 9's interactive activities include:

- Customizable Study Plan and Chapter 9 practice quizzes
- Chapter 9 Simulation (Persuasive Messages), which helps you think critically and prepare to make choices in the business world
- Chapter 9 Video Exercise (Writing Persuasive Messages: MELT), which shows you how textbook concepts are put into practice every day

- Flash Cards for mastering the definition of chapter terms
- Interactive Lessons that visually review key chapter concepts
- Document Makeovers for hands-on, scored practice in revising documents

---

CHAPTER REVIEW AND ACTIVITIES

Learning Objectives: Check Your Progress

1 OBJECTIVE Apply the three-step writing process to persuasive messages.

To plan persuasive messages, carefully clarify your purpose to make sure you focus on a single goal. Understand audience needs, which can involve research to identify relevant demographic and psychographic variables and to assess audience motivations. Persuasive messages usually ask people to give up time, money, or other resources, so gathering the right information to convince readers of the benefits of responding is essential. Media choices need to be considered carefully, particularly with marketing and sales messages in a social media landscape. For organizing persuasive messages, you will usually want to choose the indirect approach in order to establish awareness and interest before asking the audience to take action.

When writing persuasive messages, use positive and polite language, understand and respect cultural differences, be sensitive to organizational cultures when writing persuasive business messages, and take steps to establish your credibility. Seven common ways to establish credibility in persuasive messages are using simple language, supporting your claims, identifying your sources, establishing common ground, being objective, displaying good intentions, and avoiding the hard sell.

The steps for completing persuasive messages are the same as for other types of messages, but accuracy and completeness are especially important because they send signals about your credibility—a crucial element in persuasive messages.

2 OBJECTIVE Describe an effective strategy for developing persuasive business messages.

Within the context of the three-step process, effective persuasion involves four essential strategies: framing your arguments, balancing emotional and logical appeals, reinforcing your position, and anticipating objections. One of the most commonly used methods for framing a persuasive argument is the AIDA model, in which you open your message by getting the audience's attention; build interest with facts, details, and additional benefits; increase desire by providing more evidence and answering possible objections; and motivate a specific action.

Persuasive business messages combine emotional appeals (which call on feelings and sympathies) and logical appeals (which call on reason, using analogy, induction, or deduction). To reinforce your position, look for ways to add convincing evidence, quotations from experts, or other support material.

By identifying potential objections and addressing them as you craft your message, you can help prevent audience members from gravitating toward negative answers before you have the opportunity to ask them for a positive response. You can often resolve these issues before the audience has a chance to go on the defensive.

3 OBJECTIVE Identify the three most common categories of persuasive business messages.

The most common types of these messages are (1) persuasive requests for action, in which you ask the recipient to make a decision or engage in some activity; (2) persuasive presentations of ideas, in which you aren't necessarily looking for a decision or action but rather would like the audience to consider a different way of looking at a particular topic; and (3) persuasive claims and requests for adjustments, in which you believe that you have not received fair treatment under an organization's standard policies and would like the recipient to give your case fresh consideration.

4 OBJECTIVE Describe an effective strategy for developing marketing and sales messages.

Marketing and sales messages use the same basic techniques as other persuasive messages, with the added emphasis of encouraging someone to participate in a commercial transaction. Marketing messages do this indirectly, whereas sales messages do it directly. The basic strategy for creating these messages includes assessing audience needs; analyzing your competition; determining key selling points and benefits; anticipating purchase objections; applying the AIDA model; adapting your writing to social media, if appropriate; and maintaining high standards of ethical and legal compliance.

5 OBJECTIVE Explain how to modify your approach when writing promotional messages for social media.

To use social media for promotional communication, start by engaging audiences with efforts to build networked communities of potential buyers and other interested parties. Listen to conversations taking place about your company and its products. Initiate and respond to conversations within these communities, being sure to use an objective, conversational style. Provide the information that interested parties want. Identify and support the enthusiastic product champions who want to help spread your message. Be authentic and transparent in all your communication. Speak directly to customers so you don't have to rely on the news media. Finally, continue to use the AIDA model or similar approaches, but only at specific times and places.

6 OBJECTIVE Identify steps you can take to avoid ethical lapses in marketing and sales messages.

Effective and ethical persuasive communicators focus on aligning their interests with the interests of their audiences. They help audiences understand how their proposals will provide benefits to the audience, using language that is persuasive without being manipulative. They choose words that are less likely to be misinterpreted and take care not to distort the truth. Throughout, they maintain a "you" attitude with honest concern for the audience's needs and interests.

■ Test Your Knowledge

To review chapter content related to each question, refer to the indicated Learning Objective.

1. What role do demographics and psychographics play in audience analysis during the planning of a persuasive message? [LO-1]
2. What are some questions to ask when gauging the audience's needs during the planning of a persuasive message? [LO-1]
3. What three types of reasoning can you use in logical appeals? [LO-2]
4. How do emotional appeals differ from logical appeals? [LO-2]
5. What is the AIDA model, and what are its limitations? [LO-2]

■ Apply Your Knowledge

To review chapter content related to each question, refer to the indicated Learning Objective.

1. When writing persuasive messages, why is it so important to give special attention to the analysis of your purpose and audience? [LO-1]
2. Is the "hard sell" approach unethical? Why or why not? [LO-2]
3. What role do champions have in social media marketing? [LO-5]
4. How does conversation marketing differ from traditional marketing communication? [LO-5]
5. Are emotional appeals ethical? Why or why not? [LO-6]

■ Practice Your Skills

Exercises for Perfecting Your Writing

To review chapter content related to each set of exercises, refer to the indicated Learning Objective.

Message Strategies: Persuasive Business Messages; Collaboration: Team Projects [LO-2]   With another student, analyze the persuasive e-mail message at Host Marriott (Figure 9.1 on page 246) by answering the following questions.

1. What techniques are used to capture the reader's attention?
2. Does the writer use the direct or indirect organizational approach? Why?
3. Is the subject line effective? Why or why not?
4. Does the writer use an emotional appeal or a logical appeal? Why?
5. What reader benefits are included?
6. What tools does the writer use to reinforce his position?
7. How does the writer establish credibility?

Message Strategies: Persuasive Business Messages [LO-2] Compose effective subject lines for the following e-mail messages.

8. A recommendation to your branch manager to install wireless networking throughout the facility. Your primary reason is that management has encouraged more teamwork, and the teams often congregate in meeting rooms, the cafeteria, and other places that lack network access, without which they can't do much of the work they are expected to do.

9. A sales brochure to be sent to area residents, soliciting customers for your new business, "Meals à la Car," a carryout dining service that delivers from most local restaurants. Diners place orders online, and individual households can order from up to three restaurants at a time to accommodate different tastes. The price is equal to the standard menu prices plus a 10 percent delivery charge.

10. A special request to the company president to allow managers to carry over their unused vacation days to the following year. Apparently, many managers canceled their fourth-quarter vacation plans to work on the installation of a new company computer system. Under their current contract, vacation days not used by December 31 can't be carried over to the following year.

Message Strategies: Marketing and Sales Messages [LO-4] Determine whether the following sentences focus on features or benefits; rewrite them as necessary to focus on benefits.

11. With 8-millisecond response time, the Samsung LN-S4095D 40" LCD TV delivers fast video action that is smooth and crisp.[30]

12. You can call anyone and talk as long you like on Saturdays and Sundays with this new mobile phone plan.

13. All-Cook skillets are coated with a durable, patented nonstick surface.

Activities

Active links for all websites in this chapter can be found on mybcommlab; see your User Guide for instructions on accessing the content for this chapter. Each activity is labeled according to the primary skill or skills you will need to use. To review relevant chapter content, you can refer to the indicated Learning Objective. In some instances, supporting information will be found in another chapter, as indicated.

1. **Message Strategies: Persuasive Business Messages; Media Skills: Podcasting [LO-2], Chapter 6** To access this message, visit http://real-timeupdates.com/bce5, click on "Student Assignments," and click on "Chapter 9, page 228, Activity 1." Listen to this podcast and identify at least three ways in which the podcast could be more persuasive. Draft a brief e-mail message that you could send to the podcaster with your suggestions for improvement.

2. **Message Strategies: Persuasive Business Messages; Media Skills: Blogging [LO-3], Chapter 6** Download the Federal Trade Commission document "Social Networking Sites: Safety Tips for Tweens and Teens" from www.ftc.gov/bcp/edu/pubs/consumer/tech/tec14.pdf. Keeping in mind the target audience, analyze the effectiveness of this publication. Do you think it does a good job of persuading young people to surf the Internet safely? For your class blog, write a brief summary of your analysis, along with any recommendations you might have for conveying the message more persuasively.

3. **Message Strategies: Persuasive Business Messages [LO-3]** Read the following message and (a) analyze the strengths and weaknesses of each sentence and (b) revise the document so that it follows this chapter's guidelines.

Dear TechStar Computing:

I'm writing to you because of my disappointment with my new multimedia PC display. The display part works all right, but the audio volume is also set too high and the volume knob doesn't turn it down. It's driving us crazy. The volume knob doesn't seem to be connected to anything but simply spins around. I can't believe you would put out a product like this without testing it first.

I depend on my computer to run my small business and want to know what you are going to do about it. This reminds me of every time I buy electronic equipment from what seems like any company. Something is always wrong. I thought quality was supposed to be important, but I guess not.

Anyway, I need this fixed right away. Please tell me what you want me to do.

4. **Message Strategies: Persuasive Business Messages [LO-3]** The following persuasive request for adjustment contains numerous flaws. Read the message carefully and analyze its faults. Then use the following steps to outline and write an improved message.

   a. Describe the flaws in this persuasive request for adjustment.
   b. Develop a plan for rewriting the letter. The following steps will help you organize your thoughts before you begin writing:
   - Determine whether to use the direct or indirect approach.
   - Use the "you" attitude to gain attention in the opening.
   - Find a way to establish your credibility.
   - Improve the order of material presented in the body of the letter.
   - Create an appropriate closing.
   c. Now rewrite the letter. Don't forget to leave ample time for revision of your work before you turn it in.

March 22, 2011

Mr. Robert Bechtold, Manager
Kukyendahl Joint, Inc.
88 North Park Road
Houston, TX 77005

Re: Last Warning

Dear Mr. Bechtold:

Enclosed is a summary of recent ETS-related court cases in which landlords and owners were held responsible for providing toxin-free air for their tenants. In most of these cases, owners were also required to reimburse rents and pay damages for the harm done before the environmental tobacco smoke problem was remedied.

We've been plagued with this since we moved in on January 2, 2010. You haven't acted on our complaints, or responded to our explanations that secondhand smoke is making us sick, filtering in from nearby offices. You must act now or you will be hearing from our lawyers. We've told you that we were forced to hire contractors to apply weather stripping and seal openings. This cost us $3,000 (bills attached) and we expect reimbursement. But the smoke is still coming in. We also want a refund for the $9,000 we've paid you in rent since January. Call us immediately at (832) 768-3899, or our attorneys will be calling you.

Cigarette smoke from tenants on either side of us, and perhaps above and below as well, has been infiltrating our space and you have done nothing, despite our pleas, to stop it. This is unacceptable. This is a known human carcinogen. Ask the Environmental Protection Agency, which classified it as this Group A toxin. It causes lung, breast, cervical, and endocrine cancer in nonsmokers. You wouldn't want to breathe it, either.

One employee already quit who suffered from asthma. Another is threatening because he's a high risk for heart attack. Migraines, bronchitis, respiratory infections—all caused by the 4,600 chemicals in ETS, including poisons such as cyanide, arsenic, formaldehyde, carbon monoxide, and ammonia. We've had them all—the illnesses, that is.

Secondhand smoke is even more dangerous than what smokers inhale, since the inhalation process burns off some of the toxins. Sick time has already cost CMSI valuable business and lowered productivity. Plus many of us are considering finding other jobs unless our office air becomes safe to breathe again. But as the court cases prove, the responsibility for fixing this problem is yours. We expect you to live up to that responsibility immediately. Frankly, we're fed up with your lack of response.

Kathleen Thomas
Manager

5. **Message Strategies: Marketing and Sales Messages [LO-4]** Read the following message and (a) analyze the strengths and weaknesses of each sentence and (b) revise the document so that it follows this chapter's guidelines.

At Tolson Auto Repair, we have been in business for over 25 years. We stay in business by always taking into account what the customer wants. That's why we are writing. We want to know your opinions to be able to better conduct our business.

Take a moment right now and fill out the enclosed questionnaire. We know everyone is busy, but this is just one way we have of making sure our people do their job correctly. Use the enclosed envelope to return the questionnaire.

And again, we're happy you chose Tolson Auto Repair. We want to take care of all your auto needs.

6. **Message Strategies: Marketing and Sales Messages [LO-4]** Read the following message and (a) analyze the strengths and weaknesses of each sentence and (b) revise the document so that it follows this chapter's guidelines.

I am considered the country's foremost authority on employee health insurance programs. My clients offer universally positive feedback on the programs I've designed for them. They also love how much time I save them—hundreds and hundreds of hours. I am absolutely confident that I can thoroughly analyze your needs and create a portfolio that realizes every degree of savings possible. I invite you to experience the same level of service that has generated such comments as "Best advice ever!" and "Saved us an unbelievable amount of money."

7. **Message Strategies: Marketing and Sales Messages [LO-4]** Use what you know about sales messages to analyze the flaws in this promotional brochure. Then use the steps that follow to produce a better version.

11 locations in Massachusetts and Rhode Island
Bob and Dan Paisner, Owners

We are pleased to announce that ScrubaDub has added a new service, the Car Care Club.

It costs $5.95 for a lifetime membership (your car's lifetime) and features our computer automation. You'll be given a bar-coded sticker for your windshield so our computers can identify you as a club member when you pull in. If you sign up within the next 30 days, we will grant you a SuperWash for free.

The new club offers the standard ScrubaDub Touch-less systems to protect your finishes, our private formula Superglo detergent to clean your car safely and thoroughly, wheel sensors to prescribe the right treatment for whitewalls, wire, or chrome, soft, heated well water to eliminate spots, soft-cloth drying for final gloss. We also recycle our water and grant you a free wash on your birthday.

In addition, club members only will have access to a 48-hour guarantee (free rewashes) or 4 days if you purchased the premium Super Wash, Luxury Wash, Special or Works Wash. After ten washes, our computer will award you a free wash. Also available only to club members are $5 rebates for foam waxes (Turtle Wax, Simonize, or Blue Coral). Some additional specials will be granted by us to car club members, on an unplanned basis.

We can handle special requests if you inquire of our Satisfaction Supervisors. We honor our customers with refunds if they remain unsatisfied after a rewash. This is our Bumper-to-Bumper Guarantee.

a. Describe the mistakes made by the writers of this message.

b. Develop a plan for improving the message. The following questions will help you organize your thinking:

- What can you assume about the audience, which is made up of regular customers?
- How can you use this information to develop a better opening?
- Given that customers already know ScrubaDub, what can you do to improve the body of the brochure? Can you identify selling points versus benefits? What about the use of language and the tone of the text?
- Does this message make effective use of the AIDA model?
- How would you improve the "call to action," the point in the message that asks the reader to make a purchase decision?

c. Now rewrite the sales message.

8. **Message Strategies: Marketing and Sales Messages [LO-4]**   The daily mail often brings a selection of sales messages to your front door. Find a direct-mail package from your mailbox that includes a sales letter. Then answer the following questions to help you analyze and learn from the approach used by the communication professionals who prepare these glossy sales messages. Your instructor might also ask you to share the package and your observations in a class discussion.

a. Who is the intended audience?
b. What are the demographic and psychographic characteristics of the intended audience?
c. What is the purpose of the direct-mail package? Has it been designed to solicit a phone response, make a mail-order sale, obtain a charitable contribution, or do something else?
d. What, if any, technique was used to encourage you to open the envelope?
e. What kind of letter is included? Is it fully printed, printed with a computer fill-in of certain specific information, or fully computer typed? Is the letter personalized with your name or your family's name? If so, how many times?
f. Did the letter writer follow the AIDA model? If not, explain the letter's organization.
g. What needs does the letter appeal to?
h. What emotional appeals and logical arguments does the letter use?
i. What selling points and consumer benefits does the letter offer?
j. How many and what kinds of enclosures (such as brochures or CD-ROMs) are included for support?
k. Does the letter or package have an unusual format? Does it use eye-catching graphics?
l. Is the message in the letter and on the supporting pieces believable? Would the package sell the product or service to you? Why or why not?

9. **Communication Ethics: Making Ethical Choices [LO-6], Chapter 1**   Your boss has asked you to post a message on the company's internal blog, urging everyone in your department to donate money to the company's favorite charity, an organization that operates a summer camp for children with physical challenges. You wind up writing a lengthy posting packed with facts and heartwarming anecdotes about the camp and the children's experiences. When you must work that hard to persuade your audience to take an action such as donating money to a charity, aren't you being manipulative and unethical? Explain.

Expand Your Skills

Critique the Professionals

Visit the Facebook pages of six companies in several different industries. How do the companies make use of the Wall? Do any of the companies use Wall posts to promote their products? Compare the material on the Info tabs. Which company has the most compelling information here? How about the use of custom tabs; which company does the best job of using this Facebook feature? Using whatever medium your instructor requests, write a brief analysis of the message (no more than one page), citing specific elements from the piece and support from the chapter.

Sharpen Your Career Skills Online

Bovée and Thill's Business Communication Web Search, at http://businesscommunicationblog.com/websearch, is a unique research tool designed specifically for business communication research. Use the Web Search function to find a website, video, PDF document, podcast, or presentation that offers advice on writing persuasive business messages or marketing and sales messages. Write a brief e-mail message to your instructor or a post for your class blog, describing the item that you found and summarizing the career skills information you learned from it.

mybcommlab

If your course uses mybcommlab, log on to www.mybcommlab.com to access the following study and assessment aids associated with this chapter:

- Video applications
- Pre/post test
- Real-Time Updates
- Personalized study plan
- Peer review activity
- Model documents
- Quick Learning Guides
- Sample presentations

If you are not using mybcommlab, you can access Real-Time Updates and Quick Learning Guides through http://real-timeupdates.com/bce5. The Quick Learning Guide (located under "Learn More" on the website) hits all the high points of this chapter in just two pages. This guide, especially prepared by the authors, will help you study for exams or review important concepts whenever you need a quick refresher.

CASES

▼ *Apply the three-step writing process to the following cases, as assigned by your instructor.*

 Learn how to set up a Twitter account and begin tweeting. Visit http://real-timeupdates.com/bce5, click on "Student Assignments" and then click on "Twitter Screencast."

MICROBLOGGING SKILLS

1. Message Strategies: Persuasive Business Messages [LO-3]

You've been trying for months to convince your boss, company CEO Will Florence, to start using Twitter. You've told him that top executives in numerous industries now use Twitter as a way to connect with customers and other stakeholders without going through the filters and barriers of formal corporate communications, but he doesn't see the value.

Your task You come up with the brilliant plan to demonstrate Twitter's usefulness using Twitter itself. First, find three executives from three different companies who are on Twitter (choose any companies and executives you find interesting). Second, study their tweets to get a feel for the type of information they share. Third, if you don't already have a Twitter account set up for this class, set one up for the purposes of this exercise (you can deactivate later). Fourth, write four tweets to demonstrate the value of executive microblogging: one that summarizes the value of having a company CEO use Twitter and three support tweets, each one summarizing how your three real-life executive role models use Twitter.

E-MAIL SKILLS

2. Message Strategies: Persuasive Business Messages [LO-3]

As someone who came of age in the "post e-mail" world of blogs, wikis, social networks, and other Web 2.0 technologies, you were rather disappointed to find your new employer solidly stuck in the age of e-mail. You use e-mail, of course, but it is only one of the tools in your communication toolbox. From your college years, you have hands-on experience with a wide range of social media tools, having used them to collaborate on school projects, to become involved in your local community, to learn more about various industries and professions, and to research potential employers during your job search. (In fact, without social media, you might've never heard about your current employer in the first place.) Moreover, your use of social media on the job has already paid several important dividends, including finding potential sales contacts at several large companies, connecting with peers in other companies to share ideas for working more efficiently, and learning about some upcoming legislative matters in your state that could profoundly hamper your company's current way of doing business.

You hoped that by setting an example through your own use of social media at work, your new colleagues and company management would quickly adopt these tools as well. However,

just the opposite has happened. Waiting in your e-mail in-box this morning was a message from the CEO, announcing that the company is now cutting off access to social networking websites and banning the use of any social media at work. The message says that using company time and company computers for socializing is highly inappropriate and might be considered grounds for dismissal in the future if the problem gets out of hand.

Your task You are stunned by the message. You fight the urge to fire off a hotly worded reply to straighten out the CEO's misperceptions. Instead, you wisely decide to send a message to your immediate superior first, explaining why you believe the new policy should be reversed. Using your boss's favorite medium (e-mail, of course!), write a persuasive message, explaining why Facebook, Twitter, and other social networking technologies are valid—and valuable—business tools. Bolster your argument with examples from other companies and advice from communication experts. (To access a list of links to get your research started, visit http://real-timeupdates.com/bce5, click on "Student Assignments," and select "Chapter 9, page 231, Case 2.")

BLOGGING SKILLS   TEAM SKILLS

3. Message Strategies: Persuasive Business Messages [LO-3]

As a strong advocate for the use of social media in business, you are pleased by how quickly people in your company have taken up blogging, wiki writing, and other new-media activities. You are considerably less excited by the style and quality of what you see in the writing of your colleagues. Many seem to have interpreted "authentic and conversational" to mean "anything goes." Several of the Twitter users in the company seem to have abandoned any pretense of grammar and spelling. A few managers have dragged internal disagreements about company strategy out into public view, arguing with each other through comments on various industry-related forums. Production demonstration videos have been posted to the company's YouTube channel virtually unedited, making the whole firm look unpolished and unprofessional. The company CEO has written some blog posts that bash competitors with coarse and even crude language.

You pushed long and hard for greater use of these tools, so you feel a sense of responsibility for this situation. In addition, you are viewed by many in the company as the resident expert on social media, so you have some "expertise authority" on this issue. On the other hand, you are only a first-level manager, with three levels of managers above you, so while you have some "position authority" as well, you can hardly dictate best practices to the managers above you.

Your task Working with two other students, write a post for the company's internal blog (which is not viewable outside the company), outlining your concerns about these communication practices. Use the examples mentioned above, and make up any additional details you need. Emphasize that although social media communication is often less formal and more flexible than traditional business communication, it shouldn't be unprofessional. You are thinking of proposing a social media training program for everyone in the company, but for this message you just want to bring attention to the problem.

E-MAIL SKILLS

4. Message Strategies: Persuasive Business Messages [LO-3]

Whole Foods Market has grown into a nationwide chain by catering to consumer desires for healthier foods and environmentally sensitive farming methods. Along with selling these products, the company makes a commitment "to be active participants in our local communities." Whole Foods not only donates 5 percent of after-tax profits to not-for-profit organizations but also financially supports employees who volunteer their time for community service projects. Many Whole Foods stores donate food and household supplies to food banks in their local communities.

You are the manager of the Whole Foods Market on Ponce de Leon Avenue in Atlanta. You developed a program for donating surplus food to local food banks. Because of the success of that program, top executives have asked you to help other Whole Foods stores coordinate this effort into a chainwide food donation program, "Whole Foods for Life." Ideally, by streamlining the process chainwide, the company would be able to increase the number of people it helps and to get more of its employees involved.

You have a limited budget for the program, so the emphasis has to be on using resources already available to the stores and tapping into employees' creativity to come up with locally relevant ideas.[31]

Your task Write a persuasive e-mail message to all managers at Whole Foods Market, explaining the new program and requesting that they help by pooling ideas they've gleaned from their local experience. Even if they don't have food-donation programs currently in place, you want to hear ideas from them and their employees for this charitable project. With their help, you'll choose the best ideas to develop the new Whole Foods for Life program.

E-MAIL SKILLS

5. Message Strategies: Persuasive Business Messages [LO-3]

Your new company, WorldConnect Language Services, started well and is going strong. However, to expand beyond your Memphis, Tennessee, home market, you need a one-time infusion of cash to open branch offices in other cities around the Southeast. At the Entrepreneur's Lunch Forum you attended yesterday, you learned about several angels, as they are called in the investment community—private individuals who invest money in small companies in exchange for a share of ownership. One such angel, Melinda Sparks, told the audience that she is looking for investment opportunities outside high technology, where angels often invest their money. She also indicated that she looks for entrepreneurs who know their industries and markets well, who are passionate about the value they bring to the marketplace, who are committed to growing their businesses, and who

have a solid plan for how they will spend an investor's money. Fortunately, you meet all of her criteria.

Your task Draft an e-mail message to Sparks, introducing yourself and your business and asking for a meeting at which you can present your business plan in more detail. Explain that your Memphis office was booked to capacity within two months of opening, thanks to the growing number of international business professionals looking for translators and interpreters. You've researched the entire Southeast region and identified at least 10 other cities that could support language services offices such as yours. Making up whatever other information you need, draft a four-paragraph message following the AIDA model, ending with a request for a meeting within the next four weeks.

BLOGGING SKILLS   PORTFOLIO BUILDER

6. Message Strategies: Persuasive Business Messages [LO-3]

Like most other companies today, your firm makes extensive use of the web for internal and external communication. However, after reading about the Web Accessibility Initiative (WAI), you've become concerned that your company's various websites haven't been designed to accommodate people with disabilities or age-related limitations. Fortunately, as one of the company's top managers, you have a perfect forum for letting everyone in the company know how important accessible web design is: Your internal blog is read by the vast majority of employees and managers throughout the company.

Your task Visit the WAI website at www.w3.org/wai and read the two articles "Introduction to Web Accessibility" (look in the "Introducing Accessibility" section) and "Developing a Web Accessibility Business Case for Your Organization: Overview" (in the "Managing Accessibility" section). Using the information you learn in these articles, write a post for your blog that emphasizes how important it is for your company's websites to become more accessible. You don't have direct authority over the company's web developers, so it would be inappropriate for you to request them to take any specific action. Your goal is simply to raise awareness and encourage everyone to consider the needs of the company's online audiences. Don't worry about the technical aspects of web accessibility; focus instead on the benefits of improving accessibility.[32]

PODCASTING SKILLS

7. Message Strategies: Marketing and Sales Messages [LO-4]

Your new podcast channel, School2Biz, offers advice to business students making the transition from college to career. You provide information on everything from preparing résumés to interviewing to finding a place in the business world and building a successful career. As you expand your audience, you'd eventually like to turn School2Biz into a profitable operation (perhaps by selling advertising time during your podcasts). For now, you're simply offering free advice.

Your task You've chosen Podcast Bunker (www.podcastbunker .com) as the first website on which to promote School2Biz. This site lets podcasters promote their feeds with brief text listings, such as this description of Toolmonger Tool Talk: "Chuck and Sean from the web's first tool blog, Toolmonger.com, keep you up-to-date on the newest hand and power tools, and answer your home improvement, automotive, and tool-related questions."

As your instructor directs, either write a 50-word description of your new podcast that can be posted on Podcast Bunker or record a 30-second podcast describing the new service. Make up any information you need to describe School2Biz. Be sure to mention who you are and why the information you present is worth listening to.[33]

LETTER WRITING SKILLS   PORTFOLIO BUILDER

8. Message Strategies: Marketing and Sales Messages [LO-4]

Like all other states, Kentucky works hard to attract businesses that are considering expanding into the state or relocating entirely from another state. The Kentucky Cabinet for Economic Development is responsible for reaching out to these companies and overseeing the many incentive programs the state offers to both new and established businesses.

Your task As the communication director of the Kentucky Cabinet for Economic Development, you play the lead role in reaching out to companies that want to expand or relocate to Kentucky. Visit www.thinkkentucky.com and review the material in the "Why Kentucky" section. Identify the major benefits the state uses to promote Kentucky as a great place to locate a business. Summarize these reasons in a one-page form letter that will be sent to business executives throughout the country. Be sure to introduce yourself and your purpose in the letter and close with a compelling call to action (have them reach you by telephone at 800-626-2930 or by e-mail at econdev@ky.gov). As you plan your letter, try to imagine yourself as the CEO of a company and consider what a complex choice it would be to move to another state.[34]

WEB WRITING SKILLS

9. Message Strategies: Marketing and Sales Messages [LO-4]

After a shaky start as the technology matured and advertisers tried to figure out this new medium, online advertising has finally become a significant force in both consumer and business marketing. Companies in a wide variety of industries are shifting some of the ad budgets from traditional media such as TV and magazines to the increasing selection of advertising possibilities online—and more than a few companies now advertise almost exclusively online. That's fine for companies that sell advertising time and space online, but your job involves selling advertising in print magazines that are worried about losing market share to online publishers.

Online advertising has two major advantages that you can't really compete with: interactivity and the ability to precisely target individual audience members. On the other hand, you have several advantages going for you, including the ability to produce high-color photography, the physical presence of print (such as when a magazine sits on a table in a doctor's waiting room), portability, guaranteed circulation numbers, and close reader relationships that go back years or decades.

Your task You work as an advertising sales specialist for the Time Inc. division of Time Warner, which publishes more than 100 magazines around the world. Write a brief persuasive message about the benefits of magazine advertising; the statement will be posted on the individual websites of Time Inc.'s numerous magazines, so you can't narrow in on any single publication. Also, Time Inc. coordinates its print publications with an extensive online presence (including thousands of paid online ads), so you can't bash online advertising, either.[35]

LETTER WRITING SKILLS   PORTFOLIO BUILDER

10. Message Strategies: Marketing and Sales Messages [LO-4]

Kelly Services is a large staffing company based in Troy, Michigan. Client firms turn to Kelly to strategically balance their workloads and workforces during peaks and valleys of demand, to handle special projects, and to evaluate employees prior to making a full-time hiring decision. Facing the economic pressures of global competition, many companies now rely on a dynamic combination of permanent employees and temporary contractors hired through service providers such as Kelly. In addition to these staffing services, Kelly offers project services (managing both short- and long-term projects) and outsourcing and consulting services (taking over entire business functions).

Your task Write a one-page sales letter that would be sent to human resources executives at large U.S.-based corporations describing Kelly's three groups of business services. For current information, visit the Kelly website at www.kellyservices.com and look in the "Business Services" section.[36]

MEMO WRITING SKILLS

11. Message Strategies: Marketing and Sales Messages [LO-4]

This morning as you drove to your job as food services manager at the Pechanga Casino Entertainment Center in Temecula, California, you were concerned to hear on the radio that the local Red Cross chapter put out a call for blood because national supplies have fallen dangerously low. During highly publicized disasters, people are emotional and eager to help out by donating blood. But in calmer times, only 5 percent of eligible donors think of giving blood. You're one of those few.

Not many people realize that donated blood lasts only 72 hours. Consequently, the mainstay of emergency blood supplies must be replenished in an ongoing effort. No one is more skilled, dedicated, or efficient in handling blood than the American Red Cross, which is responsible for half the nation's supply of blood and blood products.

Donated blood helps victims of accidents and disease, as well as surgery patients. Just yesterday you were reading about a girl named Melissa, who was diagnosed with multiple congenital heart defects and underwent her first open-heart surgery at 1 week old. Now 5, she's used well over 50 units of donated blood, and she wouldn't be alive without them. In a thank-you letter, her mother lauded the many strangers who had "given a piece of themselves" to save her precious daughter—and countless others. You also learned that a donor's pint of blood can benefit up to four other people.

Today, you're going to do more than just roll up your own sleeve. You know the local Red Cross chapter takes its blood donation equipment to corporations, restaurants, beauty salons—anyplace willing to host public blood drives. What if you could convince the board of directors to support a blood drive at the casino? The slot machines and gaming tables are usually full, hundreds of employees are on hand, and people who've never visited before might come down to donate blood. The positive publicity will boost Pechanga's community image, too. With materials from the Red Cross, you're confident you can organize Pechanga's hosting effort and handle the promotion. (Last year, you headed the casino's successful Toys for Tots drive.)

To give blood, one must be healthy, be at least 17 years old (with no upper age limit), and weigh at least 110 pounds. Donors can give every 56 days. You'll be urging Pechanga donors to eat well, drink water, and be thoroughly rested before donating.[37]

Your task Write a memo persuading the Pechanga board of directors to host a public Red Cross blood drive. You can learn more about what's involved in hosting a blood drive at www .redcrossblood.org (click on "Hosting a Blood Drive"). Ask the board to provide water, orange juice, and snacks for donors. You'll organize food service workers to handle the distribution, but you'll need the board's approval to let your team volunteer during work hours. Use a combination of logical and emotional appeals.

WEB WRITING SKILLS   TEAM SKILLS   PORTFOLIO BUILDER

12. Message Strategies: Marketing and Sales Messages [LO-4]
You never intended to become an inventor, but you saw a way to make something work more easily, so you set to work. You developed a model, found a way to mass-produce it, and set up a small manufacturing studio in your home. You know that other people are going to benefit from your invention. Now all you need to do is reach that market.

Your task Team up with other students assigned by your instructor and imagine a useful product that you might have invented—perhaps something related to a hobby or sporting activity. List the features and benefits of your imaginary product, and describe how it helps customers. Then write the copy for a webpage that would introduce and promote this product, using what you've learned in this chapter and making up details as you need them. As your instructor indicates, submit the copy as a word processor file or as a webpage using basic HTML formatting.

IM SKILLS

13. Message Strategies: Marketing and Sales Messages [LO-4]
At IBM, you're one of the coordinators for the annual Employee Charitable Contributions Campaign. Since 1978, the company has helped employees contribute to more than 2,000 health and human service agencies. These groups may offer child care, treat substance abuse, provide health services, or fight illiteracy,

homelessness, and hunger. Some offer disaster relief or care for the elderly. All deserve support. They're carefully screened by IBM, one of the largest corporate contributors of cash, equipment, and people to nonprofit organizations and educational institutions, both in the United States and elsewhere around the world. As your literature states, the program "has engaged our employees more fully in the important mission of corporate citizenship."

During the winter holidays, you target agencies that cater to the needs of displaced families, women, and children. It's not difficult to raise enthusiasm. The prospect of helping children enjoy the holidays—children who otherwise might have nothing—usually awakens the spirit of your most distracted workers. But some of them wait until the last minute and then forget.

Employees have until Friday, December 16, to come forth with cash contributions. To make it in time for holiday deliveries, they can also bring in toys, food, and blankets through Tuesday, December 20. They shouldn't have any trouble finding the collection bins; they're everywhere, marked with bright red banners. But some people will want to call you with questions or (you hope) to make credit card contributions: 800-658-3899, ext. 3342.[38]

Your task It's December 14. Write a 75- to 100-word instant message encouraging last-minute gifts.

BLOGGING SKILLS

14. Message Strategies: Marketing and Sales Messages [LO-4]
Other than possibly wrinkling their noses at that faint smell that wafts out of the plastic bags when they bring clothes home from the dry cleaner, many consumers probably don't pay much attention to the process that goes on behind the scenes at their neighborhood cleaner. However, traditional dry cleaning is a chemically intense process—so much so that these facilities require special environmental permits and monitoring by government agencies.

At Kansas City's Hangers Cleaners, the process is different—much different. The company's innovative machines use safe liquid carbon dioxide (CO_2) and specially developed detergents to clean clothes. The process requires no heat (making it easier on clothes) and has no need for the toxic, combustible perchloroethylene used in conventional dry cleaning (making it safer for employees and the environment). Customers can tell the difference, too. As one put it, "Since I started using Hangers, my clothes are softer, cleaner and they don't have that chemical smell."

Your task Because many consumers aren't familiar with the technical details of traditional dry cleaning, they don't immediately grasp why Hangers's method is better for clothes, employees, and the environment. Write a post for the company blog, explaining why Hangers is different. Limit yourself to 400 words. You can learn more about the company and its unique process at www .hangerskc.com.[39]

 Learn how to set up a Facebook account and use the Info tab effectively. Visit http://real-timeupdates.com/bce5, click on "Student Assignments" and then click on "Facebook Screencast."

SOCIAL NETWORKING SKILLS

15. Message Strategies: Marketing and Sales Messages; Media Skills: Social Networking [LO-5], Chapter 6   Curves is a fitness center franchise that caters to women who may not feel at home in traditional gyms. With its customer-focused and research-based approach, Curves has become a significant force in the fitness industry and one of the most successful franchise operations in history.[40]

Your task   Read the Overview and History sections at www .curves.com/about-curves. Imagine that you are adapting this material for the Info tab on the company's Facebook page. Write a "Company Overview" (95–100 words) and a "Mission" statement (45–50 words).

Improve Your Grammar, Mechanics, and Usage

You can download the text of this assignment from **http:// real-timeupdates.com/bce5**; click on "Student Assignments" and then click on "Chapter 9. Improve Your Grammar, Mechanics, and Usage."

Level 1: Self-Assessment—Commas

Review Section 2.6 in the Handbook of Grammar, Mechanics, and Usage, and then complete the following 15 items.

In items 1–15, insert required commas.

1. Please send us four cases of filters two cases of wing nuts and a bale of rags.
2. Your analysis however does not account for returns.
3. As a matter of fact she has seen the figures.
4. Before May 7 1999 they wouldn't have minded either.
5. After Martha has gone talk to me about promoting her.
6. Stoneridge Inc. will go public on September 9 2012.
7. We want the new copier not the old model.
8. "Talk to me" Sandra said "before you change a thing."
9. Because of a previous engagement Dr. Stoeve will not be able to attend.
10. The company started attracting attention during the long hard recession of the mid-1970s.
11. You can reach me at this address: 717 Darby Place Scottsdale Arizona 85251.
12. Transfer the documents from Fargo North Dakota to Boise Idaho.
13. Sam O'Neill the designated representative is gone today.
14. With your help we will soon begin.
15. She may hire two new representatives or she may postpone filling those territories until spring.

Level 2: Workplace Applications

The following items may contain errors in grammar, capitalization, punctuation, abbreviation, number style, word division, and vocabulary. Rewrite each sentence, correcting all errors. If a sentence has no errors, write "Correct" for that number.

1. A pitfall of internal promotions is, that a person may be given a job beyond their competence.
2. What makes this development possible is the technological advances in todays workplace.
3. We have up to date physical safeguards, such as secure areas in buildings, electronic safeguards, such as passwords and encryption, and we have procedural safeguards, such as customer authentication procedures.
4. When asked why BASF needs to bring in a consultant after so many years, process development quality assurance manager Merritt Sink says that experience is extremely important on these type of projects.
5. Looking at just one growth indicator imports to the United States from China "ballooned" to $102 billion in 2005; compared with 15 billion in 1994.
6. Levi Strauss was the first major manufacturer to develop and do publicity about a formal Code of Conduct for it's contract manufacturers.
7. In some other countries, while the local labor laws may be comparable or even more stringent than in the United States, law enforcement mechanisms are weak or nonexistent often.
8. Motor Co., South Koreas' largest-automotive producer are building a $1 billion assembly and manufacturing plant in Montgomery, Alabama.
9. The long term success of some Internet products rest heavily on broadbands wide acceptance.
10. Being creative, flexibility, and dynamic planning are the critical elements of any successful, manufacturing process.
11. "Starbucks expanded the Frappuccino family to satisfy customers by offering a broader array of blended beverages," said Howard Behar, Starbucks president, North American Operations.
12. Internationally-renowned interior designer, Jacques Garcia will be designing the hotel's interiors; the gardens will also be designed by him.
13. Anyone who thinks they know what a CEO does is probably wrong, according to Eric Kriss; a professional Chief Executive.
14. Doctor Ichak Adizes, who founded the Adizes institute, headquartered in Santa Barbara, Calif. has spent decade's studying the life cycle of businesses.
15. The best job-description in the world wont provide you with a trusted executive, finely-honed interviewing skills only will help one do that.

Level 3: Document Critique

The following document may contain errors in grammar, capitalization, punctuation, abbreviation, number style, word division, and vocabulary. As your instructor indicates, photocopy this page and correct all errors using standard proofreading marks (see Appendix C) or download the document and make the corrections in your word processing software.

To: Promotional Customer List2

From: Sasha Morgenstern <smorgenstern@insure.com>

Subject: Insurence Service

Dear potential buyers:

You will be able to compare prices from more than three hundredinsurance companies'. Or find the lower rates for any insurance, such as Term life Automobile; Medical. dental. "No-exam" whole life, workers' compensation, Medicare supplements; Fixed annuities

$500 Dollar Guaranttes

We'll find you the lowest U.S. rates for term life insurance, or we'll deliver $500 to you overnight. Plus, every quote will carry a $five hundred dollar guarrantee of uptotheday accurracy.

"Insure.com provides rock-bottom quotes."—Forbes

All quotes are free and accurrate; We offer Lightning-Fast Service

What their saying about us can be found at **www.insure .com**. Our speedy service is being talked about by everyone, which has received high ratings and postive reviews from every major business publication "Nation's Business" "Kiplinger's Personal Finance" Good Housekeeping, The Los Angeles Times, "Money" "U.S. News & World Report"

Expert AdviSe Will be provided with No Sales Pitch:

You will not be dealing with insurance agents to save you time and money. But if you want advise our saleried insurance experts are available at our toll-free customer service number. We hope you will take a moment to peruse our webstie, **www.insure.com** today if possible.

Very truly yours,

Sasha Morgenstern

Longer Business Messages

Understanding and Planning Reports and Proposals

LEARNING OBJECTIVES

After studying this chapter, you will be able to

1 Adapt the three-step writing process to reports and proposals

2 Describe an effective process for conducting business research, explain how to evaluate the credibility of an information source, and identify the five ways to use research results

3 Explain the role of secondary research and describe the two major categories of online research tools

4 Explain the role of primary research and identify the two most common forms of primary research for business communication purposes

5 Explain how to plan informational reports and website content

6 Identify the three most common ways to organize analytical reports

7 Explain how to plan proposals

PEARSON mybcommlab Access interactive videos, simulations, sample documents, Document Makeovers, and assessment quizzes in Chapter 10 of mybcommlab.com for mastery of this chapter's objectives.

COMMUNICATION
Matters

Many reports function best as "living documents" that are reviewed often and updated as business conditions change.

❝A great business plan is a living, breathing blueprint for your business that can help you navigate and manage your company while also helping potential investors, partners, lenders, and others understand your business strategy and your chances at success.❞

—Elizabeth Wasserman, *editor, IncTechnology.com*

Finished reports, in print or on screen, can feel like they're carved in stone or cast in concrete instead—forever fixed in time, relics of a moment in the past. However, *Inc.* magazine's Elizabeth Wasserman emphasizes that vital reports such as business plans must "stay alive" if they are to deliver their full value. In the case of business plans in particular, even more important than the written report itself is the process of research, analysis, and strategic planning that leads to the information presented in the report. That process should never stop, because business conditions never stand still.[1]

APPLYING THE THREE-STEP WRITING PROCESS TO REPORTS AND PROPOSALS

In previous chapters, you learned to use the three-step writing process when developing shorter business messages; now it's time to apply those skills to longer messages such as business plans. Reports fall into three basic categories (see Figure 10.1):

- **Informational reports** offer data, facts, feedback, and other types of information, without analysis or recommendations.

- **Analytical reports** offer both information and analysis and can also include recommendations.

- **Proposals** present persuasive recommendations to internal or external audiences, often involving investments or purchases.

Try to view every business report as an opportunity to demonstrate your understanding of your audience's challenges and your ability to contribute to your organization's success.

1 LEARNING OBJECTIVE
Adapt the three-step writing process to reports and proposals

Reports can be classified as informational reports, analytical reports, and proposals.

Reports can be a lot of work, but they also give you the opportunity to demonstrate your grasp of important business issues.

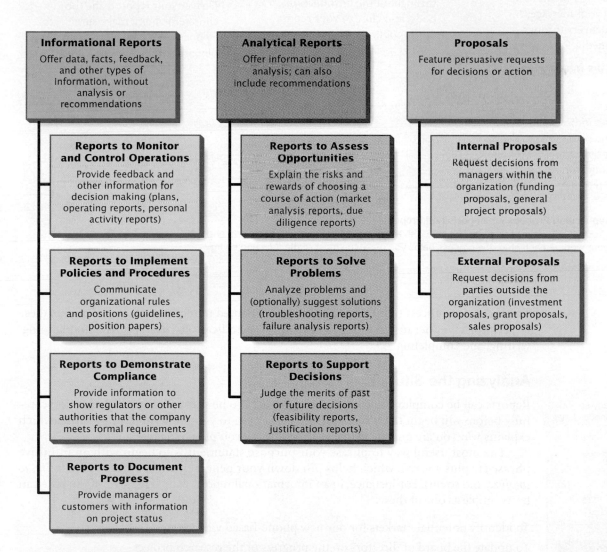

Figure 10.1   Common Business Reports and Proposals
You will have the opportunity to read and write many types of reports in your career; here are some of the most common.

1 Plan → 2 Write → 3 Complete

Analyze the Situation

Clarify the problem or opportunity at hand, define your purpose, develop an audience profile, and develop a work plan.

Gather Information

Determine audience needs and obtain the information necessary to satisfy those needs; conduct a research project if necessary.

Select the Right Medium

Choose the best medium for delivering your message; consider delivery through multiple media.

Organize the Information

Define your main idea, limit your scope, select a direct or an indirect approach, and outline your content, using an appropriate structure for an informational report, an analytical report, or a proposal.

Adapt to Your Audience

Be sensitive to audience needs with a "you" attitude, politeness, positive emphasis, and bias-free language. Build a strong relationship with your audience by establishing your credibility and projecting your company's image. Control your style with a tone and voice appropriate to the situation.

Compose the Message

Choose strong words that will help you create effective sentences and coherent paragraphs throughout the introduction, body, and close of your report or proposal.

Revise the Message

Evaluate content and review readability; edit and rewrite for conciseness and clarity.

Produce the Message

Use effective design elements and a suitable layout for a clean, professional appearance; seamlessly combine textual and graphical elements.

Proofread the Message

Review for errors in layout, spelling, and mechanics.

Distribute the Message

Deliver your report using the chosen medium; make sure all documents and all relevant files are distributed successfully.

Figure 10.2   Three-Step Writing Process for Reports and Proposals
The three-step writing process becomes even more valuable with lengthier documents such as reports and proposals. By guiding your work at each step, the process helps you make the most of the time and energy you invest.

The three-step process (see Figure 10.2) is easily adapted to reports and, in fact, makes these larger projects easier to produce by ensuring a methodical, efficient approach to planning, writing, and completing.

Analyzing the Situation

Define your purpose clearly so you don't waste time with unnecessary rework.

Reports can be complex, time-consuming projects, so be sure to analyze the situation carefully before you begin to write. Pay special attention to your **statement of purpose**, which explains *why* you are preparing the report and *what* you plan to deliver.

The most useful way to phrase your purpose statement is to begin with an infinitive phrase (*to* plus a verb), which helps pin down your general goal (*to inform, to identify, to analyze,* and so on). For instance, in an informational report, your statement of purpose can be as simple as one of these:

To identify potential markets for our new phone-based videogames

To update the board of directors on the progress of the research project

To submit required information to the Securities and Exchange Commission

The statement of purpose for an analytical report often needs to be more comprehensive. When Linda Moreno, the cost accounting manager for Electrovision, a high-tech company based in Los Gatos, California, was asked to find ways of reducing

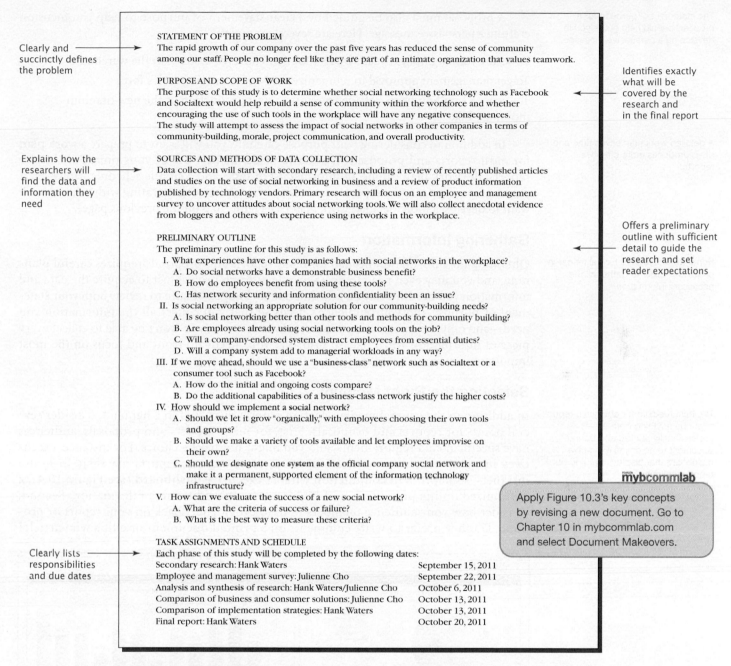

Clearly and succinctly defines the problem

STATEMENT OF THE PROBLEM
The rapid growth of our company over the past five years has reduced the sense of community among our staff. People no longer feel like they are part of an intimate organization that values teamwork.

PURPOSE AND SCOPE OF WORK
The purpose of this study is to determine whether social networking technology such as Facebook and Socialtext would help rebuild a sense of community within the workforce and whether encouraging the use of such tools in the workplace will have any negative consequences. The study will attempt to assess the impact of social networks in other companies in terms of community-building, morale, project communication, and overall productivity.

Identifies exactly what will be covered by the research and in the final report

Explains how the researchers will find the data and information they need

SOURCES AND METHODS OF DATA COLLECTION
Data collection will start with secondary research, including a review of recently published articles and studies on the use of social networking in business and a review of product information published by technology vendors. Primary research will focus on an employee and management survey to uncover attitudes about social networking tools. We will also collect anecdotal evidence from bloggers and others with experience using networks in the workplace.

PRELIMINARY OUTLINE
The preliminary outline for this study is as follows:

Offers a preliminary outline with sufficient detail to guide the research and set reader expectations

I. What experiences have other companies had with social networks in the workplace?
  A. Do social networks have a demonstrable business benefit?
  B. How do employees benefit from using these tools?
  C. Has network security and information confidentiality been an issue?
II. Is social networking an appropriate solution for our community-building needs?
  A. Is social networking better than other tools and methods for community building?
  B. Are employees already using social networking tools on the job?
  C. Will a company-endorsed system distract employees from essential duties?
  D. Will a company system add to managerial workloads in any way?
III. If we move ahead, should we use a "business-class" network such as Socialtext or a consumer tool such as Facebook?
  A. How do the initial and ongoing costs compare?
  B. Do the additional capabilities of a business-class network justify the higher costs?
IV. How should we implement a social network?
  A. Should we let it grow "organically," with employees choosing their own tools and groups?
  B. Should we make a variety of tools available and let employees improvise on their own?
  C. Should we designate one system as the official company social network and make it a permanent, supported element of the information technology infrastructure?
V. How can we evaluate the success of a new social network?
  A. What are the criteria of success or failure?
  B. What is the best way to measure these criteria?

Clearly lists responsibilities and due dates

TASK ASSIGNMENTS AND SCHEDULE
Each phase of this study will be completed by the following dates:

Secondary research: Hank Waters	September 15, 2011
Employee and management survey: Julienne Cho	September 22, 2011
Analysis and synthesis of research: Hank Waters/Julienne Cho	October 6, 2011
Comparison of business and consumer solutions: Julienne Cho	October 13, 2011
Comparison of implementation strategies: Hank Waters	October 13, 2011
Final report: Hank Waters	October 20, 2011

mybcommlab

Apply Figure 10.3's key concepts by revising a new document. Go to Chapter 10 in mybcommlab.com and select Document Makeovers.

Figure 10.3 Work Plan for a Report
A formal work plan such as this is a vital tool for planning and managing complex writing projects. The preliminary outline here helps guide the research; the report writers may well modify the outline when they begin writing the report.

employee travel and entertainment (T&E) costs, she phrased her statement of purpose accordingly:

To analyze the T&E budget, evaluate the impact of recent changes in airfares and hotel costs, and suggest ways to tighten management's control over T&E expenses

Because Moreno was assigned an analytical report rather than an informational one, she had to go beyond merely collecting data; she had to draw conclusions and make recommendations. You'll see her complete report in Chapter 11.

The statement of purpose for a proposal should help guide you in developing a persuasive message.

A proposal must also be guided by a clear statement of purpose to help you focus on crafting a persuasive message. Here are several examples:

To secure funding in next year's budget for new conveyor systems in the warehouse

To get management approval to reorganize the North American sales force

To secure $2 million from outside investors to start production of the new titanium mountain bike

A detailed work plan saves time and often produces more effective reports.

In addition to considering your purpose carefully, you will want to prepare a **work plan** for most reports and proposals in order to make the best use of your time. For simpler reports, the work plan can be an informal list of tasks and a simple schedule. However, if you're preparing a lengthy report, particularly when you're collaborating with others, you'll want to develop a more detailed work plan (see Figure 10.3 on the previous page).

Gathering Information

Some reports require formal research projects in order to gather all the necessary information.

Obtaining the information needed for many reports and proposals requires careful planning, and you may even need to do a separate research project just to acquire the data and information you need. To stay on schedule and on budget, be sure to review both your statement of purpose and your audience's needs so that you collect all the information you need—and only the information you need. In some cases, you won't be able to collect every piece of information you'd like, so prioritize your needs up front and focus on the most important questions.

Selecting the Right Medium

The best medium for any given report might be anything from a professionally printed and bound document to an online executive dashboard that displays nothing but report highlights.

In addition to the general media selection criteria discussed in Chapter 3, consider several points for reports and proposals. First, for many reports and proposals, audiences have specific media requirements, and you might not have a choice. For instance, executives in many corporations now expect to review many reports via their in-house intranets, sometimes in conjunction with an **executive dashboard** (see Figure 10.4), a customized online presentation of highly summarized business information. Second, consider how your audience members want to provide feedback on your report or proposal. Do they prefer to write comments on a printed document or edit a wiki article?

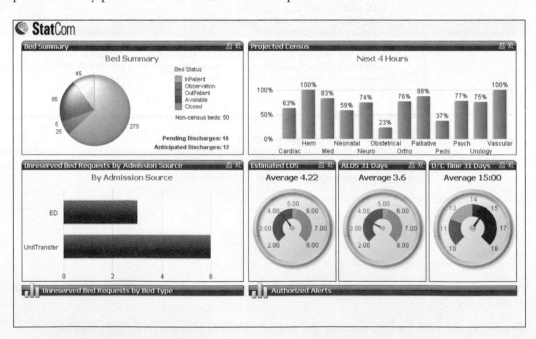

Figure 10.4   Executive Dashboards
To help managers avoid information overload, many companies now use executive dashboards to present carefully filtered highlights of key performance parameters. Dashboards are essentially super-summarized reports. The latest generation of software makes it easy to customize screens to show each manager the specific summaries he or she needs to see.

Third, will people need to search through your document electronically or update it in the future? Fourth, bear in mind that your choice of medium sends a message. For instance, a routine sales report dressed up in expensive multimedia will look like a waste of valuable company resources.

Organizing Your Information

The direct approach is by far the most popular and convenient for business reports; it saves time, makes the rest of the report easier to follow, and produces a more forceful document. However, the confidence implied by the direct approach may be misconstrued as arrogance, especially if you're a junior member of a status-conscious organization. In contrast, the indirect approach gives you a chance to prove your points and gradually overcome your audience's reservations. However, the indirect approach can become unwieldy with long reports, so carefully consider report length before deciding on the direct or indirect approach. Both approaches have merit, and businesspeople often combine them, revealing their conclusions and recommendations as they go along, rather than putting them first or last (see Figure 10.5).

The direct approach is popular with reports, but some situations call for the indirect approach.

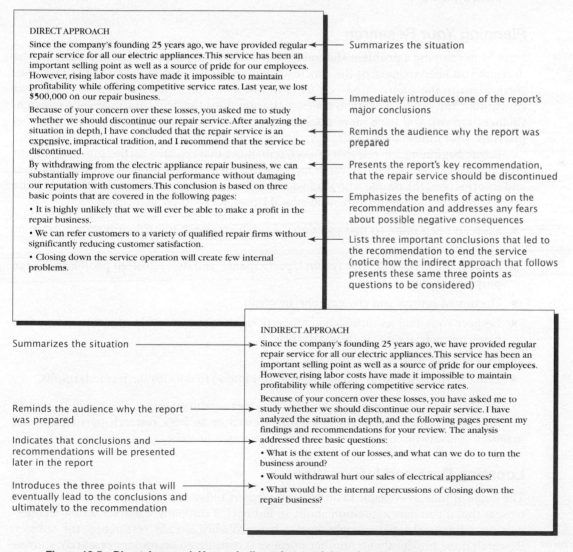

Figure 10.5   Direct Approach Versus Indirect Approach in an Introduction
In the direct version of this introduction, the writer quickly presents the report's recommendation, followed by the conclusions that led to that recommendation. In the indirect version, the same topics are introduced in the same order, but no conclusions are drawn about them; the conclusions and the ultimate recommendation appear later, in the body of the report.

Researching without a plan wastes time and usually produces unsatisfactory results.

SUPPORTING YOUR MESSAGES WITH RELIABLE INFORMATION

Effective research involves a lot more than simply typing a few terms into a search engine. Save time and get better results by using a clear process:

1. **Plan your research.** Planning is the most important step of any research project; a solid plan yields better results in less time.

2. **Locate the data and information you need.** Your next step is to figure out *where* the data and information are and *how* to access them.

3. **Process the data and information you located.** The data and information you find probably won't be in a form you can use immediately and may require statistical analysis or other processing.

4. **Apply your findings.** You can apply your research findings in three ways: summarizing information, drawing conclusions, and developing recommendations.

5. **Manage information efficiently.** Many companies are trying to maximize the return on the time and money invested in business research by collecting and sharing research results in a variety of computer-based systems, known generally as **knowledge management systems.**

Planning Your Research

The problem statement guides your research by focusing on the decision you need to make or the conclusion you need to reach.

Start by developing a **problem statement** that defines the purpose of your research—the decision you need to make or the conclusion you need to reach at the end of the process. Next, identify the information you need in order to make that decision or reach that conclusion. You can then begin to generate the questions that will constitute your research. Chances are you will have more questions than you have time or money to answer, so prioritize your information needs.

Before beginning any research project, remember that research carries some significant ethical responsibilities. Your research tactics affect the people from whom you gather data and information, the people who read your results, and the people who are affected by the way you present those results. To avoid ethical lapses, follow these guidelines:

- Keep an open mind so that you don't skew the research toward answers you want or expect to see.

- Respect the privacy of your research participants, and don't mislead people about the purposes of your research.[2]

- Document sources and give appropriate credit.

- Respect your sources' *intellectual property rights* (the ownership of unique ideas that have commercial value in the marketplace).[3]

- Don't distort information from your sources.

- Don't misrepresent who you are or what you intend to do with the research results.

In addition to ethics, research etiquette deserves careful attention. For example, respect the time of anyone who agrees to be interviewed or to be a research participant and maintain courtesy throughout the interview or research process.

Locating Data and Information

Primary research contains information that you gather specifically for a new research project; secondary research contains information that others have gathered (and published, in many cases).

The range of sources available to business researchers today can be overwhelming. The good news is that if you have a question about an industry, a company, a market, a new technology, or a financial topic, somebody else has probably already researched the subject. Research done previously for another purpose is considered **secondary research**; sources for such research information include magazines, newspapers, public websites, books, and other reports. Don't let the name *secondary* fool you, though. You want to start with secondary research because it can save you considerable time and money for many projects.

In contrast, **primary research** involves the collection of new data, through surveys, interviews, and other techniques.

Evaluating Information Sources

In every research project, you have the responsibility to verify the quality of the sources you use. This is particularly important when using information found online, because the quality and dependability of online information can vary widely. To avoid tainting your results and damaging your reputation, ask the following questions about the information you find:

- **Does the source have a reputation for honesty and reliability?** For example, try to find out how the source accepts articles and whether it has an editorial board, conducts peer reviews, or follows fact-checking procedures.

- **Is the source potentially biased?** To interpret an organization's information, you need to know its point of view.

- **What is the purpose of the material?** For instance, was the material designed to inform others of new research, to advance a political position, or to promote a product?

- **Is the author credible?** Is the author a professional journalist or merely someone with an opinion?

- **Where did the source get *its* information?** Try to find out who collected the data and the methods used.

- **Can you verify the material independently?** Verification is particularly important when the information goes beyond simple facts to include projections, interpretations, and estimates.

- **Is the material current and complete?** Make sure you are using the most current information available. Have you accessed the entire document or only a selection from it?

- **Does the information make sense?** Step back and determine whether the information stands up to logical scrutiny.

You probably won't have time to conduct a thorough background check on all your sources, so focus your efforts on the most important or most suspicious pieces of information. And if you can't verify critical facts or figures, be sure to let your readers know that.

Using Your Research Results

After you've collected your data and information, the next step is to transform this raw material into the specific content you need. This step can involve quoting, paraphrasing, or summarizing textual material; drawing conclusions; and making recommendations.

Quoting, Paraphrasing, and Summarizing Information

You can use textual information from secondary sources in three ways. *Quoting* a source means you reproduce the material exactly as you found it (giving full credit to the source, of course). Use direct quotations when the original language will enhance your argument or when rewording the passage would reduce its impact. However, be careful with direct quotes: Using too many creates a choppy patchwork of varying styles and gives the impression that all you've done is piece together the work of other people. When quoting sources, set off shorter passages with quotation marks and set off longer passages (generally, five lines or more) as separate, indented paragraphs.

You can often maximize the impact of secondary material in your own writing by *paraphrasing* it: restating it in your own words and with your own sentence structures.[4] Paraphrasing helps you maintain consistent tone while using vocabulary that's familiar to your audience. Of course, you still need to credit the originator of the information, but you don't need quotation marks or indented paragraphs.

Summarizing is similar to paraphrasing but presents the gist of the material in fewer words than the original by leaving out details, examples, and less important information (see Table 10.1 on the next page). Like quotations and paraphrases, summaries also require

Evaluate your sources carefully to avoid embarrassing and potentially damaging mistakes.

After you collect data and information, the next step is converting it into usable content.

Quoting a source means reproducing the content exactly and indicating who created the information originally.

Paraphrasing is expressing someone else's ideas in your own words.

Summarizing is similar to paraphrasing but distills the content into fewer words.

TABLE 10.1 Summarizing Effectively

Original Material (116 Words)	45-Word Summary	22-Word Summary
Our facilities costs spiraled out of control last year. The 23 percent jump was far ahead of every other cost category in the company and many times higher than the 4 percent average rise for commercial real estate in the Portland metropolitan area. The rise can be attributed to many factors, but the major factors include repairs (mostly electrical and structural problems at the downtown office), energy (most of our offices are heated by electricity, the price of which has been increasing much faster than for oil or gas), and last but not least, the loss of two sublease tenants whose rent payments made a substantial dent in our cost profile for the past five years.	Our facilities costs jumped 23 percent last year, far ahead of every other cost category in the company and many times higher than the 4 percent local average. The major factors contributing to the increase are repairs, energy, and the loss of two sublease tenants.	Our facilities costs jumped 23 percent last year, due mainly to rising repair and energy costs and the loss of sublease income.

Main idea

Major support points

Details

complete documentation of sources. Summarizing is not always a simple task, and your audience will judge your ability to separate significant issues from less significant details.

Of course, all three approaches require careful attention to ethics. When quoting directly, take care not to distort the original intent of the material by quoting selectively or out of context. And never resort to **plagiarism**—presenting someone else's words as your own, such as copying material from an online source and dropping it into a report without giving proper credit.

Drawing Conclusions

A **conclusion** is a logical interpretation of facts and other information. In addition to being logically sound, a conclusion should be based only on the information provided or at least referred to in the report. Reaching good conclusions is one of the most important skills you can develop in your business career. In fact, the ability to see patterns and possibilities that others can't see is one of the hallmarks of innovative business leaders.

Making Recommendations

Whereas a conclusion interprets information, a **recommendation** suggests what to do about the information. The following example shows the difference between a conclusion and a recommendation:

Conclusion	Recommendation
On the basis of its track record and current price, I believe that this company is an attractive buy.	I recommend that we offer to buy the company at a 10 percent premium over the current market value of its stock.

To be credible, recommendations must be practical and based on sound logical analysis. Also, when making a recommendation, be certain that you have adequately described the recommended course of action so that readers aren't left wondering what happens next.

CONDUCTING SECONDARY RESEARCH

Even if you intend to eventually conduct primary research, start with a review of any available secondary research. Inside your company, you might be able to find a variety of reports and other documents that could help. Outside the company, business researchers can choose from a wide range of print and online resources, both in libraries and online.

You'll want to start most projects by conducting secondary research first.

Finding Information at a Library

Public, corporate, and university libraries offer printed sources with information that is not available online and online sources that are available only by subscription. Libraries are also where you'll find one of your most important resources: librarians. Reference librarians are trained in research techniques and can often help you find obscure information you can't find on your own. They can also direct you to the typical library's many sources of business information:

Even in the Internet age, libraries offer information and resources you can't find anywhere else—including experienced research librarians.

- **Newspapers and periodicals.** Libraries offer access to a wide variety of popular magazines, general business magazines, *trade journals* (which provide information about specific professions and industries), and *academic journals* (which provide research-oriented articles from researchers and educators).

- **Business books.** Although less timely than newspapers, periodicals, and online sources, business books provide in-depth coverage and analysis that often can't be found anywhere else.

- **Directories.** Thousands of directories are published in print and electronic formats in the United States, and many include membership information for all kinds of professions, industries, and special-interest groups.

- **Almanacs and statistical resources.** Almanacs are handy guides to factual and statistical information about countries, politics, the labor force, and so on. One of the most extensive is the *Statistical Abstract of the United States* (available at www.census .gov).

- **Government publications.** Information on laws, court decisions, tax questions, regulatory issues, and other governmental concerns can often be found in collections of government documents.

Local, state, and federal government agencies publish a huge array of information that is helpful to business researchers.

- **Electronic databases.** Databases offer vast collections of computer-searchable information, often in specific areas such as business, law, science, technology, and education. Some of these are available only by institutional subscription, so the library can be your only way to gain access to them. Some libraries offer remote online access to some or all databases; for others, you'll need to visit in person.

Finding Information Online

The Internet can be a tremendous source of business information, provided that you know where to look and how to use the tools available. Roughly speaking, the tools fall into two categories: those you can use to actively *search* for existing information and those you can use to *monitor* selected sources for new information. (Some tools can perform both functions.)

Internet research tools fall into two basic categories: search tools and monitoring tools.

Online Search Tools

The most familiar search tools are general-purpose **search engines**, such as Google and Bing, which scan millions of websites to identify individual webpages that contain a specific word or phrase and then attempt to rank the results from most useful to least useful. (Website owners use *search engine optimization* techniques to help boost their rankings in the results, but the ranking algorithms are kept secret to prevent unfair manipulation of the results.)

General-purpose search engines are tremendously powerful tools, but they do have several shortcomings that you need to consider.

"Human-powered search engines" and web directories rely on human editors to evaluate and select content.

Online databases and specialty search engines can help you access parts of the hidden Internet.

The tools available for monitoring of new information from online sources can help you track industry trends, consumer sentiment, and other information.

Search tools work in different ways, and you can get unpredictable results if you don't know how each one operates.

For all their ease and power, conventional search engines have three primary shortcomings: (1) no human editors are involved to evaluate the quality or ranking of the search results; (2) various engines use different search techniques, so they often find different material; and (3) search engines can't reach all the content on some websites (this part of the Internet is sometimes called the *hidden Internet* or the *deep Internet*).

A variety of tools are available to overcome the three main weaknesses of general-purpose search engines, and you should consider one or more of them in your business research. First, "human-powered search engines" such as Mahalo (www.mahalo.com) offer manually compiled results for popular search queries that aim to provide more accurate and more meaningful information, although for a much narrower range of topics than a regular search engine.[5] Similarly, **web directories**, such as the Open Directory Project at www.dmoz.org use human editors to categorize and evaluate websites. A variety of other directories focus on specific media types, such as blogs or podcasts.

Second, *metacrawlers* or *metasearch engines* (such as Bovée and Thill's Web Search, at http://businesscommunicationblog.com/websearch) help overcome the differences among search engines by formatting your search request for multiple search engines, making it easy to find a broader range of results. With a few clicks, you can compare results from multiple search engines to make sure you are getting a broad view of the material.

Third, **online databases** help address the challenge of the hidden Internet by offering access to newspapers, magazines, journals, electronic copies of books, and other resources often not available with standard search engines. Some of these databases offer free access to the public, but others require a subscription (check with your library). Also, a variety of specialized search engines now exist to reach various parts of the hidden Internet.

Online Monitoring Tools

One of the most powerful aspects of online research is the ability to automatically monitor selected sources for new information. The possibilities include subscribing to newsfeeds from blogs and websites, following people on Twitter and other microblogs, setting up alerts on search engines and online databases, and using specialized monitors such as TweetBeep (http://tweetbeep.com) to track tweets that mention specific companies or other terms.

Exercise some care when setting up monitoring tools, however, because it's easy to get overwhelmed by the flood of information. Remember that you can always go back and search your information sources if you need to gather additional information.

Search Tips

Regardless of which tools you are using, search engines, web directories, and databases work in different ways, so make sure you understand how to optimize your search and interpret the results. With a *keyword search*, the engine or database attempts to find items that include all the words you enter. A *Boolean search* lets you define a query with greater precision, using such operators as AND (the search must include two terms linked by AND), OR (it can include either or both words), or NOT (the search ignores items with whatever word comes after NOT). *Natural language searches* let you ask questions in everyday English. *Forms-based searches* help you create powerful queries by simply filling out an online form.[6]

To make the best use of any search tool, keep the following points in mind:

- Read the instructions and pay attention to the details. A few minutes of learning can save hours of inefficient search time.

- Review the search and display options carefully so you don't misinterpret the results; some of these settings can make a huge difference in the results you see.

- Try variations of your terms, such as *adolescent* and *teenager* or *management* and *managerial*.

- User fewer search terms to find more results; use more search terms to find fewer results.

- Look beyond the first page of results. The algorithm used to rank the results might not reflect your priorities, so the first few hits might not be the best for your project.

Search technologies continue to evolve rapidly, so look for new ways to find the information you need. Some new tools search specific areas of information (such as Twitter) in better ways, whereas others approach search in new ways. For instance, Yolink (www.yolink .com) finds webpages like a regular search engine does but then also searches through documents and webpages that are linked to those first-level results.[7]

Other powerful search tools include *desktop search engines* that search all the files on your personal computer, *enterprise search engines* that search all the computers on a company's network, *research and content managers* such as the free Zotero browser extension (www.zotero.com), and *social tagging* or *bookmarking sites* such as Digg (http://digg.com) and Delicious (http://delicious.com).

For information on the latest online research tools and techniques, visit http: //real-timeupdates.com/bce5 and click on Chapter 10.

Documenting Your Sources

Documenting your sources serves three important functions: It properly and ethically credits the person who created the original material, it shows your audience that you have sufficient support for your message, and it helps readers explore your topic in more detail, if desired. Be sure to take advantage of the source documentation tools in your software, such as automatic endnote or footnote tracking.

Appendix B discusses the common methods of documenting sources. Whatever method you choose, documentation is necessary for books, articles, tables, charts, diagrams, song lyrics, scripted dialogue, letters, speeches—anything that you take from someone else, including ideas and information that you've re-expressed through paraphrasing or summarizing. However, you do not have to cite a source for knowledge that's generally known among your readers, such as the fact that Microsoft is a large software company or that computers are pervasive in business today.

Proper documentation of the sources you use is both ethical and an important resource for your readers.

CONDUCTING PRIMARY RESEARCH

If secondary research can't provide the information and insights you need, your next choice is to gather the information yourself with primary research. Primary research encompasses a variety of methods, from observations to experiments such as test marketing, but the two tools most commonly used for business research are surveys and interviews.

Conducting Surveys

Surveys can provide invaluable insights, but only if they are *reliable* (would produce identical results if repeated), *valid* (actually measure what they are designed to measure), and *representative* (based on information from a sample of respondents who accurately represent the entire population of interest). For important surveys, consider hiring a research

4 LEARNING OBJECTIVE
Explain the role of primary research and identify the two most common forms of primary research for business communication purposes

Surveys and interviews are the most common primary research techniques.

Surveys need to reliable, valid, and representative in order to be useful.

Provide clear instructions to prevent mistaken answers.

specialist to avoid errors in design and implementation. To develop an effective survey questionnaire, follow these tips:[8]

- Provide clear instructions to make sure people can answer every question correctly.
- Don't ask for information that people can't be expected to remember, such as how many times they went grocery shopping in the past year.
- Keep the questionnaire short and easy to answer; don't expect people to give you more than 10 or 15 minutes of their time.
- Whenever possible, formulate questions to provide answers that are easy to analyze. Numbers and facts are easier to summarize than opinions, for instance.
- Avoid *leading questions* that could bias your survey. If you ask, "Do you prefer that we stay open in the evenings for customer convenience?" you'll no doubt get a "yes." Instead, ask, "What time of day do you normally do your shopping?"
- Avoid ambiguous descriptors such as "often" or "frequently." Such terms mean different things to different people.
- Avoid compound questions such as "Do you read books and magazines?"

You have no doubt noticed simple surveys on many websites, and a number of companies offer comprehensive online survey software and services. Online surveys offer a number of advantages, including speed, cost, and the ability to adapt the question set along the way based on a respondent's answers. However, they must be designed and administered as carefully as offline surveys. For example, you can't assume that the results from a survey on your company's website reflect the attitudes, beliefs, or behaviors of the population as a whole, because chances are quite high that the visitors to your website are not an accurate sample of the entire population.

Conducting Interviews

Interviews can take place online, over the phone, or in person, and they can involve individuals or groups.

Getting in-depth information straight from an expert, customer, or other interested party can be a great method for collecting primary information. Interviews can take a variety of formats, from e-mail exchanges to group discussions. For example, the English supermarket chain Tesco invites thousands of customers to visit its stores every year for meetings known as Customer Question Time, when it asks customers how the company can serve them better.[9]

Open-ended questions, which can't be answered with a simple yes or no, can provide deeper insights, opinions, and information.

Like surveys, interviews require careful planning to get the best results. The answers you receive are influenced by the types of questions you ask and the way you ask them. Ask **open-ended questions** to invite an expert to offer opinions, insights, and information, such as "Why do you believe that South America represents a better opportunity than Europe for this product line?" Ask **closed questions** to elicit a specific answer, such as yes or no. These can be helpful for certain topics, but including too many closed questions in an interview makes the experience feel more like a simple survey and doesn't take full advantage of the interview setting.

Arrange the sequence of questions to help uncover layers of information.

Think carefully about the sequence of your questions and the potential answers so you can arrange them in an order that helps uncover layers of information. Also consider providing each subject with a list of questions at least a day or two before the interviews, especially if you'd like to quote your subjects in writing or if your questions might require people to conduct research or think extensively about the answers. If you want to record interviews, ask ahead of time; never record without permission.

5 LEARNING OBJECTIVE

Explain how to plan informational reports and website content

PLANNING INFORMATIONAL REPORTS

Informational reports provide the feedback that employees, managers, and others need in order to make decisions, take action, and respond to changes. As Figure 10.1 on page 271 indicates, informational reports can be grouped into four general categories:

- **Reports to monitor and control operations.** Managers rely on a wide range of reports to see how well their companies are functioning. *Plans* establish expectations and guidelines to direct future action. Among the most important of these are *business plans*, which summarize a proposed business venture and describe the company's goals and plans for each major functional area. *Operating reports* provide feedback on a wide variety of an organization's functions, including sales, inventories, expenses, shipments, and so on. *Personal activity* reports provide information regarding an individual's experiences during sales calls, industry conferences, and other activities.

- **Reports to implement policies and procedures.** *Policy reports* range from brief descriptions of business procedures to manuals that run dozens or hundreds of pages. *Position papers*, sometimes called *white papers* or *backgrounders*, outline an organization's official position on issues that affect the company's success.

- **Reports to demonstrate compliance.** Businesses are required to submit a variety of *compliance reports*, from tax returns to reports describing the proper handling of hazardous materials.

- **Reports to document progress.** Supervisors, investors, and customers frequently expect to be informed of the progress of projects and other activities. *Progress reports* range from simple updates in memo form to comprehensive status reports.

Informational reports are used to monitor and control operations, to implement policies and procedures, to demonstrate compliance, and to document progress.

Organizing Informational Reports

In most cases, the direct approach is the best choice for informational reports because you are simply conveying information. However, if the information is disappointing, such as a project being behind schedule or over budget, you might consider using the indirect approach to build up to the bad news. Most informational reports use a **topical organization**, arranging material in one of the following ways (see Figure 10.6 on the next page):

The messages conveyed by informational reports can range from extremely positive to extremely negative, so the approach you take warrants careful consideration.

- **Comparison.** Showing similarities and differences (or advantages and disadvantages) between two or more entities

- **Importance.** Building up from the least important item to the most important (or from most important to the least, if you don't think your audience will read the entire report)

- **Sequence.** Organizing the steps or stages in a process or procedure

- **Chronology.** Organizing a chain of events in order from oldest to newest or vice versa

- **Geography.** Organizing by region, city, state, country, or other geographic unit

- **Category.** Grouping by topical category, such as sales, profit, cost, or investment

Organizing Website Content

Most of what you've already learned about informational reports applies to website writing, but the online environment requires some special considerations:

- **Web readers are demanding.** If they can't find what they're looking for in a few minutes, most site visitors will click away to another site.[10]

- **Reading online can be difficult.** Studies show that reading speeds are about 25 percent slower on a monitor than on paper.[11] Reading from computer screens can also be exhausting and a source of physical discomfort.[12]

- **The web is a nonlinear, multidimensional medium.** Readers of online material move around in any order they please; there often is no beginning, middle, or end.

When planning online reports or other website content, remember that the online reading experience differs from offline reading in several important ways.

In addition, many websites have to perform more than one communication function and therefore have more than one purpose. Each of these individual purposes needs to be carefully defined and then integrated into an overall statement of purpose for the entire website.[13]

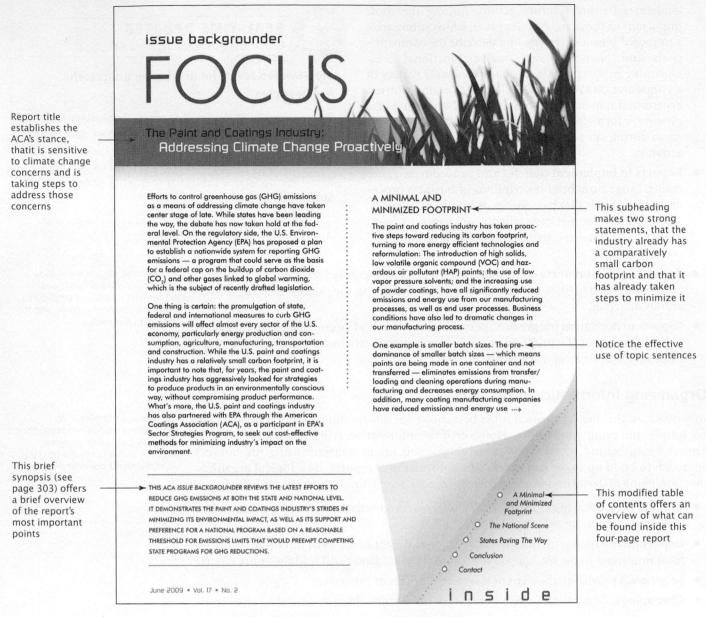

Report title establishes the ACA's stance, that it is sensitive to climate change concerns and is taking steps to address those concerns

This brief synopsis (see page 303) offers a brief overview of the report's most important points

issue backgrounder
FOCUS
The Paint and Coatings Industry:
Addressing Climate Change Proactively

Efforts to control greenhouse gas (GHG) emissions as a means of addressing climate change have taken center stage of late. While states have been leading the way, the debate has now taken hold at the federal level. On the regulatory side, the U.S. Environmental Protection Agency (EPA) has proposed a plan to establish a nationwide system for reporting GHG emissions — a program that could serve as the basis for a federal cap on the buildup of carbon dioxide (CO_2) and other gases linked to global warming, which is the subject of recently drafted legislation.

One thing is certain: the promulgation of state, federal and international measures to curb GHG emissions will affect almost every sector of the U.S. economy, particularly energy production and consumption, agriculture, manufacturing, transportation and construction. While the U.S. paint and coatings industry has a relatively small carbon footprint, it is important to note that, for years, the paint and coatings industry has aggressively looked for strategies to produce products in an environmentally conscious way, without compromising product performance. What's more, the U.S. paint and coatings industry has also partnered with EPA through the American Coatings Association (ACA), as a participant in EPA's Sector Strategies Program, to seek out cost-effective methods for minimizing industry's impact on the environment.

THIS ACA *ISSUE BACKGROUNDER* REVIEWS THE LATEST EFFORTS TO REDUCE GHG EMISSIONS AT BOTH THE STATE AND NATIONAL LEVEL. IT DEMONSTRATES THE PAINT AND COATINGS INDUSTRY'S STRIDES IN MINIMIZING ITS ENVIRONMENTAL IMPACT, AS WELL AS ITS SUPPORT AND PREFERENCE FOR A NATIONAL PROGRAM BASED ON A REASONABLE THRESHOLD FOR EMISSIONS LIMITS THAT WOULD PREEMPT COMPETING STATE PROGRAMS FOR GHG REDUCTIONS.

June 2009 • Vol. 17 • No. 2

A MINIMAL AND MINIMIZED FOOTPRINT

The paint and coatings industry has taken proactive steps toward reducing its carbon footprint, turning to more energy efficient technologies and reformulation: The introduction of high solids, low volatile organic compound (VOC) and hazardous air pollutant (HAP) paints; the use of low vapor pressure solvents; and the increasing use of powder coatings, have all significantly reduced emissions and energy use from our manufacturing processes, as well as end user processes. Business conditions have also led to dramatic changes in our manufacturing process.

One example is smaller batch sizes. The predominance of smaller batch sizes — which means paints are being made in one container and not transferred — eliminates emissions from transfer/loading and cleaning operations during manufacturing and decreases energy consumption. In addition, many coating manufacturing companies have reduced emissions and energy use ⟶

This subheading makes two strong statements, that the industry already has a comparatively small carbon footprint and that it has already taken steps to minimize it

Notice the effective use of topic sentences

This modified table of contents offers an overview of what can be found inside this four-page report

inside

Figure 10.6   Effective Informational Report (excerpt)
This background from the American Coatings Association (ACA), an organization that represents paint and coatings manufacturers, lays out the ACA's position on pending emissions legislation.

The information architecture of a website is the equivalent of the outline for a paper report, but it tends to be much more complicated than a simple linear outline.

Moreover, many websites also have multiple target audiences, such as potential employees, customers, investors, and the news media. You need to analyze each group's unique information needs and find a logical way to organize all that material. Website designers use the term **information architecture** to describe the structure and navigational flow of all the parts of a website (see Figure 10.7). As you develop the site architecture, you can begin to simulate how various audiences will enter and explore the site. Accommodating multiple entry points is one of the most difficult tasks in site design.[14]

To organize your site effectively, keep the following advice in mind:

- Plan your site structure and navigation before you write.[15]
- Let your readers be in control by creating links and pathways that let them explore on their own.
- Help online readers scan and absorb information by breaking it into self-contained, easily readable chunks that are linked together logically.

General information about the SBA is always available for access but doesn't intrude on the main screen

Always-visible tabs link to the site's four major areas

Advice is categorized by business "life stage," making it easy to find articles of interest

Figure 10.7   Information Architecture
The website of the U.S. Small Business Administration uses clearly defined and labeled navigation choices to help site visitors quickly find the information they need.

PLANNING ANALYTICAL REPORTS

The purpose of analytical reports is to analyze, to understand, or to explain—to think through a problem or an opportunity and explain how it affects an organization and how the organization should respond. As you also saw in Figure 10.1, analytical reports fall into three basic categories:

- **Reports to assess opportunities.** Every business opportunity carries some degree of risk and requires a variety of decisions and actions in order to capitalize on the opportunity. You can use analytical reports to assess both risk and required decisions and actions. For instance, *market analysis reports* are used to judge the likelihood of success for new products or sales. *Due diligence* reports examine the financial aspects of a proposed decision, such as acquiring another company.

- **Reports to solve problems.** Managers often assign *troubleshooting reports* when they need to understand why something isn't working properly and how to fix it. A variation, the *failure analysis report*, studies events that happened in the past, with the hope of learning how to avoid similar failures in the future.

- **Reports to support decisions.** *Feasibility reports* explore the potential ramifications of a decision that managers are considering, and *justification reports* explain a decision that has already been made.

Developing analytical reports presents a greater challenge than writing informational reports, for three reasons. First, you're doing more than simply delivering information—you're also analyzing a situation and presenting your conclusions. Second, when your analysis is complete, you need to present your thinking in a compelling and persuasive manner. Third, analytical reports often convince other people to make significant financial and personnel decisions, and these reports carry the added responsibility of the consequences of such decisions.

Focusing on Conclusions

When planning reports for audiences that are likely to accept your conclusions—either because they've asked you to perform an analysis or they trust your judgment—consider

6 LEARNING OBJECTIVE
Identify the three most common ways to organize analytical reports

Analytical reports are used to assess opportunities, to solve problems, and to support decisions.

Focusing on conclusions is often the best approach when you're addressing a receptive audience.

using the direct approach, focusing immediately on your conclusions. This structure communicates the main idea quickly, but it does present some risks. Even if audiences trust your judgment, they may have questions about your data or the methods you used. Moreover, starting with a conclusion may create the impression that you have oversimplified the situation. To give readers the opportunity to explore the thinking behind your conclusion, support that conclusion with solid reasoning and evidence (see Figure 10.8).

Focusing on Recommendations

A slightly different approach is useful when your readers want to know what they ought to do in a given situation (as opposed to what they ought to conclude). The actions you want your readers to take become the main subdivisions of your report.

When structuring a report around recommendations, use the direct approach, as you would for a report that focuses on conclusions. Then unfold your recommendations using a series of five steps:

1. Establish the need for action in the introduction by briefly describing the problem or opportunity.

2. Introduce the benefit(s) that can be achieved if the recommendation is adopted, along with any potential risks.

3. List the steps (recommendations) required to achieve the benefit, using action verbs for emphasis.

4. Explain each step more fully, giving details on procedures, costs, and benefits; if necessary, also explain how risks can be minimized.

5. Summarize your recommendations.

When readers want to know what you think they should do, organize your report to focus on recommendations.

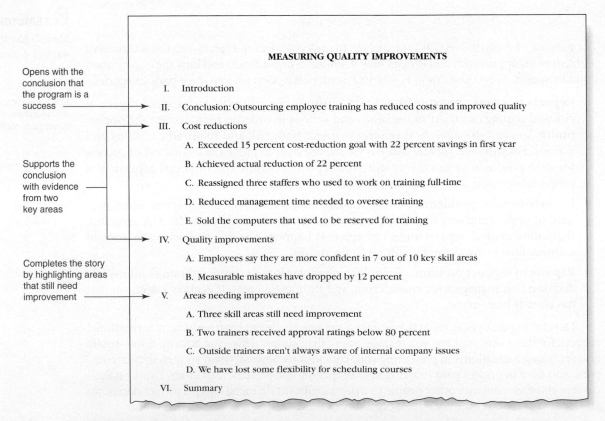

Opens with the conclusion that the program is a success

Supports the conclusion with evidence from two key areas

Completes the story by highlighting areas that still need improvement

MEASURING QUALITY IMPROVEMENTS

I.   Introduction

II. Conclusion: Outsourcing employee training has reduced costs and improved quality

III. Cost reductions

    A. Exceeded 15 percent cost-reduction goal with 22 percent savings in first year

    B. Achieved actual reduction of 22 percent

    C. Reassigned three staffers who used to work on training full-time

    D. Reduced management time needed to oversee training

    E. Sold the computers that used to be reserved for training

IV. Quality improvements

    A. Employees say they are more confident in 7 out of 10 key skill areas

    B. Measurable mistakes have dropped by 12 percent

V.   Areas needing improvement

    A. Three skill areas still need improvement

    B. Two trainers received approval ratings below 80 percent

    C. Outside trainers aren't always aware of internal company issues

    D. We have lost some flexibility for scheduling courses

VI. Summary

Figure 10.8   Preliminary Outline of a Research Report Focusing on Conclusions
Cynthia Zolonka works on the human resources staff of a bank in Houston, Texas. Her company decided to have an outside firm handle its employee training, and a year after the outsourcing arrangement was established, Zolonka was asked to evaluate the results. Her analysis shows that the outsourcing experiment was a success, and she opens with that conclusion but supports it with clear evidence. Readers who accept the conclusion can stop reading, and those who desire more information can continue.

Focusing on Logical Arguments

When readers are potentially skeptical or hostile, consider using the indirect approach to logically build toward your conclusion or recommendation. If you guide readers along a rational path toward the answer, they are more likely to accept it when they encounter it. The two most common logical approaches are known as the *2 + 2 = 4 approach*, in which you convince readers by demonstrating that everything adds up to your conclusion, and the *yardstick approach*, in which you use a number of criteria to decide which option to select from two or more possibilities (see Figure 10.9).

Logical arguments can follow two basic approaches: 2 + 2 = 4 (adding everything up) and the yardstick method (comparing ideas against a predetermined set of standards).

PLANNING PROPOSALS

7 **LEARNING OBJECTIVE**
Explain how to plan proposals

Proposals can be grouped into two general categories. *Internal proposals* (see Figure 10.10 on page 257) request decisions from managers within the organization. *External proposals* request decisions from parties outside the organization. For example, *investment proposals*

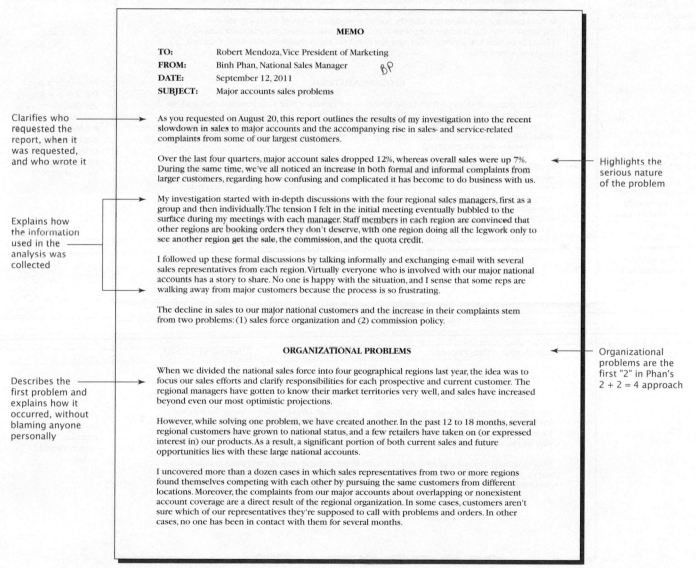

Clarifies who requested the report, when it was requested, and who wrote it

Explains how the information used in the analysis was collected

Describes the first problem and explains how it occurred, without blaming anyone personally

Highlights the serious nature of the problem

Organizational problems are the first "2" in Phan's 2 + 2 = 4 approach

(continued)

Figure 10.9   Analytical Report Focusing on Logical Arguments
As national sales manager of a New Hampshire sporting goods company, Binh Phan was concerned about his company's ability to sell to its largest customers. His boss, the vice president of marketing, shared these concerns and asked Phan to analyze the situation and recommend a solution. In this troubleshooting report, his main idea is that the company should establish separate sales teams for these major accounts, rather than continuing to service them through the company's four regional divisions. However, Phan knew his plan would be controversial because it required a big change in the company's organization and in the way sales reps are paid. His thinking had to be clear and easy to follow, so he focused on logical argumentation.

(continued)

For example, having retail outlets across the lower tier of the country, AmeriSport received pitches from reps out of our West, South, and East regions. Because our regional offices have a lot of negotiating freedom, the three were offering different prices. But all AmeriSport buying decisions were made at the Tampa headquarters, so all we did was confuse the customer. The irony of the current organization is that we're often giving our weakest selling and support efforts to the largest customers in the country.

COMMISSION PROBLEMS

The regional organization problems are compounded by the way we assign commissions and quota credit. Salespeople in one region can invest a lot of time in pursuing a sale, only to have the customer place the order in another region. So some sales rep in the second region ends up with the commission on a sale that was partly or even entirely earned by someone in the first region. Therefore, sales reps sometimes don't pursue leads in their regions, thinking that a rep in another region will get the commission.

For example, Athletic Express, with outlets in 35 states spread across all four regions, finally got so frustrated with us that the company president called our headquarters. Athletic Express has been trying to place a large order for tennis and golf accessories, but none of our local reps seem interested in paying attention. I spoke with the rep responsible for Nashville, where the company is headquartered, and asked her why she wasn't working the account more actively. Her explanation was that last time she got involved with Athletic Express, the order was actually placed from their L.A. regional office, and she didn't get any commission after more than two weeks of selling time.

RECOMMENDATIONS

Our sales organization should reflect the nature of our customer base. To accomplish that goal, we need a group of reps who are free to pursue accounts across regional borders—and who are compensated fairly for their work. The most sensible answer is to establish a national account group. Any customers whose operations place them in more than one region would automatically be assigned to the national group.

In addition to solving the problem of competing sales efforts, the new structure will also largely eliminate the commission-splitting problem because regional reps will no longer invest time in prospects assigned to the national accounts team. However, we will need to find a fair way to compensate regional reps who are losing long-term customers to the national team. Some of these reps have invested years in developing customer relationships that will continue to yield sales well into the future, and everyone I talked to agrees that reps in these cases should receive some sort of compensation. Such a "transition commission" would also motivate the regional reps to help ensure a smooth transition from one sales group to the other. The exact nature of this compensation would need to be worked out with the various sales managers.

SUMMARY

The regional sales organization is effective at the regional and local levels but not at the national level. We should establish a national accounts group to handle sales that cross regional boundaries. Then we'll have one set of reps who are focused on the local and regional levels and another set who are pursuing national accounts.

To compensate regional reps who lose accounts to the national team, we will need to devise some sort of payment to reward them for the years of work invested in such accounts. This can be discussed with the sales managers once the new structure is in place.

Figure 10.9 *(continued)*

request funding from outside investors, *grant proposals* request funds from government agencies and other sponsoring organizations, and *sales proposals* present solutions for potential customers and request purchase decisions.

The most significant factor in planning a proposal is whether the recipient has asked you to submit a proposal. *Solicited proposals* are generally prepared at the request of external parties that require a product or a service, but they may also be requested by such internal sources as management or the board of directors. Some organizations prepare a formal invitation to bid on their contracts, called a **request for proposals (RFP)**, which includes instructions that specify exactly the type of work to be performed or products to be delivered, along with budgets, deadlines, and other requirements. Other companies then respond by preparing proposals that show how they would meet those needs. In most cases,

RFPs can seem surprisingly picky, even to the point of specifying the size of paper to use, but you must follow every detail to avoid having your proposal rejected.

DETAILS *Matters*

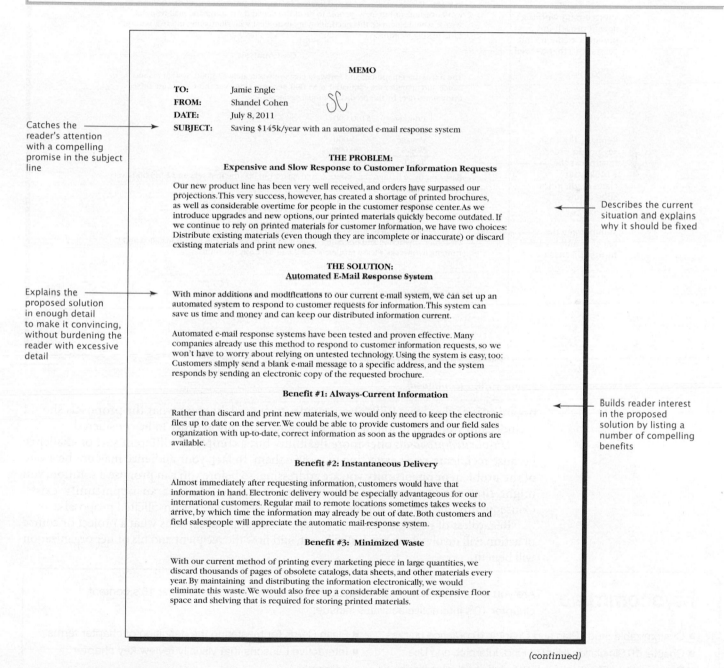

Catches the reader's attention with a compelling promise in the subject line

Describes the current situation and explains why it should be fixed

Explains the proposed solution in enough detail to make it convincing, without burdening the reader with excessive detail

Builds reader interest in the proposed solution by listing a number of compelling benefits

MEMO

TO: Jamie Engle
FROM: Shandel Cohen
DATE: July 8, 2011
SUBJECT: Saving $145k/year with an automated e-mail response system

THE PROBLEM:
Expensive and Slow Response to Customer Information Requests

Our new product line has been very well received, and orders have surpassed our projections. This very success, however, has created a shortage of printed brochures, as well as considerable overtime for people in the customer response center. As we introduce upgrades and new options, our printed materials quickly become outdated. If we continue to rely on printed materials for customer information, we have two choices: Distribute existing materials (even though they are incomplete or inaccurate) or discard existing materials and print new ones.

THE SOLUTION:
Automated E-Mail Response System

With minor additions and modifications to our current e-mail system, we can set up an automated system to respond to customer requests for information. This system can save us time and money and can keep our distributed information current.

Automated e-mail response systems have been tested and proven effective. Many companies already use this method to respond to customer information requests, so we won't have to worry about relying on untested technology. Using the system is easy, too: Customers simply send a blank e-mail message to a specific address, and the system responds by sending an electronic copy of the requested brochure.

Benefit #1: Always-Current Information

Rather than discard and print new materials, we would only need to keep the electronic files up to date on the server. We could be able to provide customers and our field sales organization with up-to-date, correct information as soon as the upgrades or options are available.

Benefit #2: Instantaneous Delivery

Almost immediately after requesting information, customers would have that information in hand. Electronic delivery would be especially advantageous for our international customers. Regular mail to remote locations sometimes takes weeks to arrive, by which time the information may already be out of date. Both customers and field salespeople will appreciate the automatic mail-response system.

Benefit #3: Minimized Waste

With our current method of printing every marketing piece in large quantities, we discard thousands of pages of obsolete catalogs, data sheets, and other materials every year. By maintaining and distributing the information electronically, we would eliminate this waste. We would also free up a considerable amount of expensive floor space and shelving that is required for storing printed materials.

(continued)

Figure 10.10   Internal Proposal
Shandel Cohen's internal proposal seeks management's approval to install an automatic mail-response system. Because the company manufactures computers, she knows that her boss won't object to a computer-based solution. Also, since profits are always a concern, her report emphasizes the financial benefits of her proposal. Her report describes the problem, her proposed solutions, the benefits to the company, and the projected costs.

(continued)

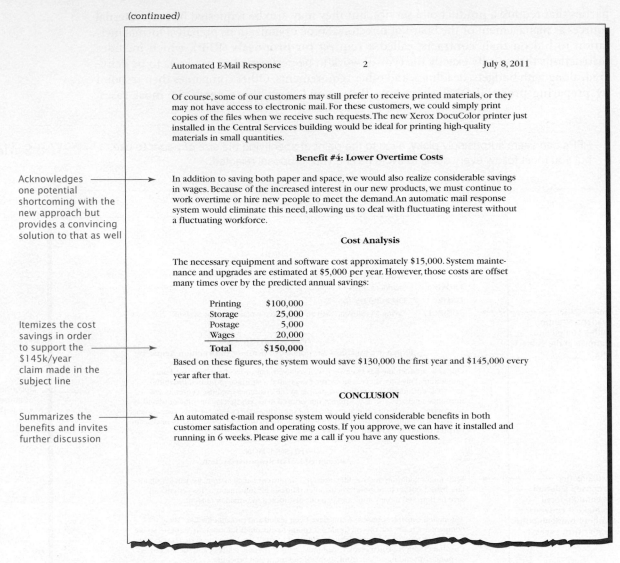

Automated E-Mail Response   2   July 8, 2011

Of course, some of our customers may still prefer to receive printed materials, or they
may not have access to electronic mail. For these customers, we could simply print
copies of the files when we receive such requests. The new Xerox DocuColor printer just
installed in the Central Services building would be ideal for printing high-quality
materials in small quantities.

Benefit #4: Lower Overtime Costs

Acknowledges one potential shortcoming with the new approach but provides a convincing solution to that as well

In addition to saving both paper and space, we would also realize considerable savings
in wages. Because of the increased interest in our new products, we must continue to
work overtime or hire new people to meet the demand. An automatic mail response
system would eliminate this need, allowing us to deal with fluctuating interest without
a fluctuating workforce.

Cost Analysis

The necessary equipment and software cost approximately $15,000. System mainte-
nance and upgrades are estimated at $5,000 per year. However, those costs are offset
many times over by the predicted annual savings:

Itemizes the cost savings in order to support the $145k/year claim made in the subject line

Printing	$100,000
Storage	25,000
Postage	5,000
Wages	20,000
Total	**$150,000**

Based on these figures, the system would save $130,000 the first year and $145,000 every
year after that.

CONCLUSION

Summarizes the benefits and invites further discussion

An automated e-mail response system would yield considerable benefits in both
customer satisfaction and operating costs. If you approve, we can have it installed and
running in 6 weeks. Please give me a call if you have any questions.

Figure 10.10   *(continued)*

organizations that issue RFPs also provide strict guidelines on what the proposals should
include, and you need to follow these guidelines carefully in order to be considered.

Unsolicited proposals offer more flexibility but a completely different sort of challenge
because recipients aren't expecting to receive them. In fact, your audience may not be aware
of the problem or opportunity you are addressing, so before you can propose a solution, you
might first need to convince your readers that a problem or an opportunity exists.
Consequently, the indirect approach is often the wise choice for unsolicited proposals.

Regardless of its format and structure, a good proposal explains what a project or course
of action will involve, how much it will cost, and how the recipient and his or her organization
will benefit.

PEARSON
mybcommlab

Are you an active learner? Go to mybcommlab.com to master Chapter 10's content.
Chapter 10's interactive activities include:

- Customizable Study Plan and Chapter 10 practice quizzes
- Chapter 10 Simulation (How to Find, Interpret, and Use Business Data Effectively), which helps you think critically and prepare to make choices in the business world
- Chapter 10 Video Exercise (Finding, Evaluating, and Processing Information: MELT), which shows you how textbook concepts are put into practice every day

- Flash Cards for mastering the definition of chapter terms
- Interactive Lessons that visually review key chapter concepts
- Document Makeovers for hands-on, scored practice in revising documents

CHAPTER REVIEW AND ACTIVITIES

Learning Objectives: Check Your Progress

1 OBJECTIVE Adapt the three-step writing process to reports and proposals.

To adapt the three-step process to reports and proposals, apply what you learned in Chapters 3 through 5, with particular emphasis on clearly identifying your purpose, preparing a work plan, determining whether a separate research project might be needed, choosing the medium, and selecting the best approach for the specific type of report.

2 OBJECTIVE Describe an effective process for conducting business research, explain how to evaluate the credibility of an information source, and identify the five ways to use research results.

Begin the research process with careful planning to make sure you focus on the most important questions. Then locate the data and information, using primary and secondary research as needed. Process the results of your research and apply your findings by summarizing information, drawing conclusions, or developing recommendations. Finally, manage information effectively so that you and others can retrieve it later and reuse it in other projects.

Evaluating the credibility of an information source can involve eight questions. (1) Does the source have a reputation for honesty and reliability? (2) Is the source potentially biased? (3) What is the purpose of the material? (4) Is the author credible? (5) Where did the source get *its* information? (6) Can you verify the material independently? (7) Is the material current and complete? (8) Does the information make sense?

Five ways to use research results are quoting, paraphrasing, or summarizing textual material; drawing conclusions; and making recommendations.

3 OBJECTIVE Explain the role of secondary research, and describe the two major categories of online research tools.

Secondary research is generally used first, both to save time in case someone else has already gathered the information needed and to offer additional insights into your research questions. The two major categories of online research tools are tools used for searching (including various types of search engines, web directories, and online databases) and tools used for automatically monitoring for new information.

4 OBJECTIVE Explain the role of primary research, and identify the two most common forms of primary research for business communication purposes.

Primary research involves the collection of new data, and it is conducted when the information required is not available through secondary research. The two most common primary research methods for business communication purposes are surveys and interviews

5 OBJECTIVE Explain how to plan informational reports and website content.

Informational reports focus on the delivery of facts, figures, and other types of information. Most informational reports use a topical organization, arranging material by comparison, importance, sequence, chronology, geography, or category.

When developing online reports and websites in general, start by planning the structure and navigation paths before writing the content. Next, make sure you let readers be in control by giving them navigational flexibility. Finally, break your information in chunks that can be scanned and absorbed quickly.

6 OBJECTIVE Identify the three most common ways to organize analytical reports.

Analytical reports assess a situation or problem and recommend a course of action in response. The three most common ways to organize analytical reports are by focusing on conclusions, focusing on recommendations, and focusing on logical arguments.

7 OBJECTIVE Explain how to plan proposals.

The most significant factor in planning a proposal is whether the proposal is solicited or unsolicited. Solicited proposals are obviously expected and welcomed by the recipient, but they often must follow a specific organization, particularly when they are submitted in response to a request for proposals (RFP). For unsolicited proposals, the writer has flexibility in choosing the most effective organization, format, and content. However, because unsolicited proposals are unexpected, the writer often needs to explain why the solution offered in the proposal is even necessary for the reader to consider. Because of this, the indirect approach is usually preferred for unsolicited proposals.

Test Your Knowledge

To review chapter content related to each question, refer to the indicated Learning Objective.

1. What are the three basic categories of reports? [LO-1]
2. What is typically covered in the work plan for a report? [LO-1]
3. How does a conclusion differ from a recommendation? [LO-2]
4. How do proposal writers use an RFP? [LO-7]
5. Should you use primary research before or after secondary research? [LO-4]

Apply Your Knowledge

To review chapter content related to each question, refer to the indicated Learning Objective.

1. Why must you be careful when using information from the Internet in a business report? [LO-2]
2. Companies occasionally make mistakes that expose confidential information, such as when employees lose laptop computers containing sensitive data files or webmasters forget to protect confidential webpages from search engine indexes. If you conducted an online search that turned up competitive information on webpages that were clearly intended to be private, what would you do? Explain your answer. [LO-3]
3. Can you use the same approach for planning website content as you use for planning printed reports? Why or why not? [LO-5]
4. Why are unsolicited proposals more challenging to write than solicited proposals? [LO-7]
5. If you were writing a recommendation report for an audience that doesn't know you, would you use the direct approach, focusing on the recommendation, or the indirect approach, focusing on logic? Why? [LO-6]

Practice Your Skills

Activities

Active links for all websites in this chapter can be found on mybcommlab; see your User Guide for instructions on accessing the content for this chapter. Each activity is labeled according to the primary skill or skills you will need to use. To review relevant chapter content, you can refer to the indicated Learning Objective. In some instances, supporting information will be found in another chapter, as indicated.

1. **Planning: Analyzing the Situation [LO-1]**   South by Southwest (SXSW) is a family of conferences and festivals in Austin, Texas, that showcase some of the world's most creative talents in music, interactive media, and film. In addition to being a major entertainment venue for a week every March, SXSW is also an increasingly important *trade show*, an opportunity for companies to present products and services to potential customers and business partners. You work for a company that makes music training equipment, such as an electronic keyboard with an integrated computer screen that guides learners through every step of learning to play the keyboard. Your manager has asked you to look into whether the company should rent an exhibition booth at SXSW next year. Prepare a work plan for an analytical report that will assess the promotional opportunities at SXSW and make a recommendation on exhibiting. Include the statement of purpose, a problem statement for any research you will conduct, a description of what will result from your investigation, the sources and methods of data collection, and a preliminary outline. Visit the SXSW website, at http://sxsw.com, for more information.[16]

2. **Research: Documenting Sources [LO-2]**   Select five business articles from a combination of print and online sources. Develop a resource list, using Appendix B as a guideline.

3. **Research: Conducting Secondary Research [LO-3]**   Using online, database, or printed sources, find the following information. Be sure to properly cite your sources, using the formats discussed in Appendix B.

   a. Contact information for the American Management Association
   b. Median weekly earnings of men and women by occupation
   c. Current market share for Perrier water
   d. Performance ratios for office supply retailers
   e. Annual stock performance for Hewlett-Packard (HP)
   f. Number of franchise outlets in the United States
   g. Composition of the U.S. workforce by profession

4. **Research: Conducting Primary Research [LO-4]**   You work for a movie studio that is producing a young director's first motion picture, the story of a group of unknown musicians finding work and making a reputation in a competitive industry. Unfortunately, some of your friends leave the screening saying that the 182-minute movie is simply too long. Others say they can't imagine any sequences to cut out. Your boss wants to test the movie on a typical audience and ask viewers to complete a questionnaire that will help the director decide whether edits are needed and, if so, where. Design a questionnaire that you can use to solicit valid answers for a report to the director about how to handle the audience's reaction to the movie.

5. **Research: Conducting Secondary Research [LO-3]**   Select any public company and find the following information.

   a. Names of the company's current officers
   b. List of the company's products or services (or, if the company has a large number of products, the product lines or divisions)
   c. Some important current issues in the company's industry
   d. The outlook for the company's industry as a whole

6. **Research: Conducting Primary Research [LO-4]** You're conducting an information interview with a manager in another division of your company. Partway through the interview, the manager shows clear signs of impatience. How should you respond? What might you do differently to prevent this from happening in the future? Explain your answers.

7. **Message Strategies: Informational Reports [LO-5]** The Securities and Exchange Commission (SEC) requires all public companies to file a comprehensive annual report (form 10-K) electronically. Many companies post links to these reports on their websites, along with links to other company reports. Visit Dell's website, at www.dell.com, and find the company's most recent annual 10-K and Year in Review reports. Compare the style and format of the two reports. For which audience(s) is the Year in Review targeted? Who besides the SEC might be interested in form 10-K? Which report do you find easier to read? More interesting? More detailed?

8. **Message Strategies: Informational Reports [LO-5]** From your college library, company websites, or an online service such as www.annualreportservice.com, find the annual reports recently released by two corporations in the same industry. Analyze each report and be prepared to discuss the following questions in class.

   a. What organizational differences, if any, do you see in the way each corporation discusses its annual performance? Are the data presented clearly so that shareholders can draw conclusions about how well the company performed?

   b. What goals, challenges, and plans do top managers emphasize in their discussion of results?

   c. How do the format and organization of each report enhance or detract from the information being presented?

9. **Message Strategies: Informational Reports [LO-5]** You're the vice president of operations for a Florida fast-food chain. In the aftermath of a major hurricane, you're drafting a report on the emergency procedures to be followed by personnel in each restaurant when storm warnings are in effect. Answer who, what, when, where, why, and how and then prepare a one-page outline of your report. Make up any details you need.

10. **Message Strategies: Informational Reports; collaboration: Team Projects [LO-5], Chapter 2** You and a classmate are helping Linda Moreno prepare her report on Electrovision's travel and entertainment costs (see pages 289–302). This time, however, the report is to be informational rather than analytical, so it will not include recommendations. Review the existing report and determine what changes would be needed to make it an informational report. Be as specific as possible. For example, if your team decides the report needs a new title, what title would you use? Draft a transmittal memo for Moreno to use in conveying this informational report to Dennis McWilliams, Electrovision's vice president of operations.

11. **Message Strategies: Informational Reports [LO-5]** Assume that your college president has received many student complaints about campus parking problems. You are appointed to chair a student committee organized to investigate the problems and recommend solutions. The president gives you a file labeled "Parking: Complaints from Students," and you jot down the essence of the complaints as you inspect the contents. Your notes look like this:

   - Inadequate student spaces at critical hours
   - Poor night lighting near the computer center
   - Inadequate attempts to keep resident neighbors from occupying spaces
   - Dim marking lines
   - Motorcycles taking up full spaces
   - Discourteous security officers
   - Spaces (usually empty) reserved for college officials
   - Relatively high parking fees
   - Full fees charged to night students even though they use the lots only during low-demand periods
   - Vandalism to cars and a sense of personal danger
   - Inadequate total space
   - Harassment of students parking on the street in front of neighboring house

Now prepare an outline for an informational report to be submitted to committee members. Use a topical organization for your report that categorizes this information.

12. **Message Strategies: Analytical Reports [LO-6]** Of the organizational approaches introduced in the chapter, which is best suited for writing a report that answers the following questions? Briefly explain why.

   a. In which market segment—energy drinks or traditional soft drinks—should Fizz Drinks, Inc., introduce a new drink to take advantage of its enlarged research and development budget?

   b. Should Major Manufacturing, Inc., close down operations of its antiquated Bellville, Arkansas, plant despite the adverse economic impact on the town that has grown up around the plant?

   c. Should you and your partner adopt a new accounting method to make your financial statements look better to potential investors?

   d. Should Grand Canyon Chemicals buy disposable test tubes to reduce labor costs associated with cleaning and sterilizing reusable test tubes?

   e. What are some reasons for the recent data loss at the college computer center, and how can we avoid similar problems in the future?

13. **Message Strategies: Proposals [LO-7]** Read the step-by-step hints and examples for writing a funding proposal at www.learnerassociates.net/proposal. Review the entire sample proposal online. What details did the writer decide to include in the appendixes? Why was this material placed in the appendixes and not the main body of the report? According to the writer's tips, when is the best time to prepare a project overview?

14. **Message Strategies: Proposals; Collaboration: Team Projects [LO-7], Chapter 2** Break into small groups

and identify an operational problem occurring at your campus—perhaps involving registration, university housing, food services, parking, or library services. Then develop a workable solution to that problem. Finally, develop a list of pertinent facts that your team will need to gather to convince readers that the problem exists and that your solution will work.

Expand Your Skills

Critique the Professionals

Company websites function as multidimensional informational reports, with numerous sections and potentially endless ways for visitors to navigate through all the various pages. Locate the website of a public corporation with a fairly complex website. Imagine that you are approaching the site as (a) a potential employee, (b) a potential investor (purchaser of stock), (c) a member of one of the local communities in which this company operators, and (d) a potential customer of the company's products and services. Analyze how easy or difficult it is to find the information that each of these four visitors would typically be looking for. Using whatever medium your instructor requests, write a brief analysis of the information architecture of the website, describing what works well and what doesn't work well.

Sharpen Your Career Skills Online

Bovée and Thill's Business Communication Web Search, at http://businesscommunicationblog.com/websearch, is a unique research tool designed specifically for business

communication research. Use the Web Search function to find a website, video, PDF document, podcast, or presentation that offers advice on conducting research for business reports. Write a brief e-mail message to your instructor or a post for your class blog, describing the item that you found and summarizing the career skills information you learned from it.

mybcommlab

If your course uses mybcommlab, log on to www.mybcommlab.com to access the following study and assessment aids associated with this chapter:

- Video applications
- Pre/post test
- Real-Time Updates
- Personalized study plan
- Peer review activity
- Model documents
- Quick Learning Guides
- Sample presentations

If you are not using mybcommlab, you can access Real-Time Updates and Quick Learning Guides through http://real-timeupdates.com/bce5. The Quick Learning Guide (located under "Learn More" on the website) hits all the high points of this chapter in just two pages. This guide, especially prepared by the authors, will help you study for exams or review important concepts whenever you need a quick refresher.

CASES

▼ Apply the three-step writing process to the following cases, as assigned by your instructor.

Informational Reports

1. Message Strategies: Informational Reports [LO-5] Success in any endeavor doesn't happen all at once. For example, success in college is built one quarter or semester at a time, and the way to succeed in the long term is to make sure you succeed in the short term. After all, even a single quarter or semester of college involves a significant investment of time, money, and energy.

Your task Imagine you work for a company that has agreed to send you to college full time, paying all your educational expenses. You are given complete freedom in choosing your courses, as long as you graduate by an agreed-upon date. All your employer asks in return is that you develop your business skills and insights as much as possible so that you can make a significant contribution to the company when you return to full-time work after graduation. To make sure that you are using your time—and your company's money—wisely, the

company requires a brief personal activity report at the end of every quarter or semester (whichever your school uses). Write a brief informational report that you can e-mail to your instructor, summarizing how you spent your quarter or semester. Itemize the classes you took, how much time you spent studying and working on class projects, whether you got involved in campus activities and organizations that help you develop leadership or communication skills, and what you learned that you can apply in a business career. (For the purposes of this assignment, your time estimates don't have to be precise.)

2. Message Strategies: Informational Reports [LO-5] You've put a lot of work into your college classes so far—make sure you don't have any glitches as you get ready to claim your certificate or degree.

Your task Prepare an interim progress report that details the steps you've taken toward completing your graduation or certification requirements. After examining the requirements listed in your college catalog, indicate a realistic schedule for completing those that remain. In addition to course requirements, include steps such as completing the residency requirement, completing all necessary forms, and paying fees. Use a memo format for your report and address it to anyone who is helping or encouraging you through school.

3. Message Strategies: Informational Reports [LO-5] Your college's administration has asked you to compare your college's tuition costs with those of a nearby college and determine which college's costs have risen more quickly. Research the trend by checking your college's annual tuition costs for each of the most recent four years. Then research the four-year tuition trends for a neighboring college. For both colleges, calculate the percentage change in tuition costs from year to year and between the first and fourth years.

Your task Prepare an informal report (using the letter format) that presents your findings and conclusions to the president of your college. Include graphics to explain and support your conclusions.

BLOGGING SKILLS   TEAM SKILLS

4. Message Strategies: Informational Reports [LO-5] If you're like many other college students, your first year was more than you expected: more difficult, more fun, more frustrating, more expensive, more exhausting, more rewarding—more of everything, positive and negative. Oh, the things you know now that you didn't know then!

Your task With several other students, identify five or six things you wish you would've realized or understood better before you started your first year of college. These can relate to your school life (such as "I didn't realize how much work I would have for my classes" or "I should've asked for help as soon as I got stuck") and your personal and social life ("I wish I would've been more open to meeting people"). Use these items as the foundation of a brief informational report that you could post on a blog that is read by high school students and their families. Your goal with this report is to help the next generation of students make a successful and rewarding transition to college.

Analytical Reports

5. Message Strategies: Analytical Reports [LO-6] Mistakes can be wonderful learning opportunities if we're honest with ourselves and receptive to learning from the mistake.

Your task Identify a mistake you've made—something significant enough to have cost you a lot of money, wasted a lot of time, harmed your health, damaged a relationship, created serious problems at work, prevented you from pursuing what could've been a rewarding opportunity, or otherwise had serious consequences. Now figure out why you made that mistake. Did you let emotions get in the way of clear thinking? Did you make a serious financial blunder because you didn't take the time to understand the consequences of a decision? Were you too cautious? Not cautious enough? Perhaps several factors led to a poor decision.

Write a brief analytical report to your instructor that describes the situation and outlines your analysis of why the failure occurred and how you can avoid making a similar mistake in the future. If you can't think of a significant mistake or failure that you're comfortable sharing with your instructor, write about a mistake that a friend or family member made (without revealing the person's identify or potentially causing him or her any embarrassment).

6. Message Strategies: Analytical Reports [LO-6] Assume that you will have time for only one course next term. Identify the criteria you will use to decide which of several courses to take. (This is the yardstick approach mentioned in the chapter.)

Your task List the pros and cons of four or five courses that interest you and use the selection criteria you identified to choose the one course that is best for you to take at this time. Write your report in memo format, addressing it to your academic adviser.

7. Message Strategies: Analytical Reports [LO-6] Visit any restaurant, possibly your school cafeteria. The workers and fellow customers will assume that you are an ordinary customer, but you are really a spy for the owner.

Your task After your visit, write a short letter to the owner explaining (a) what you did and what you observed, (b) any possible violations of policy that you observed, and (c) your recommendations for improvement. The first part of your report (what you did and what you observed) will be the longest. Include a description of the premises, inside and out. Tell how long it took for each step of ordering and receiving your meal. Describe the service and food thoroughly. You are interested in both the good and bad aspects of the establishment's décor, service, and food. For the second section (violations of policy), use some common sense: If all the servers but one have their hair covered, you may assume that policy requires hair to be covered; a dirty window or restroom obviously violates policy. The last section (recommendations for improvement) involves professional judgment. What management actions will improve the restaurant?

8. Message Strategies: Analytical Reports [LO-6] Imagine that you are a consultant hired to improve the customer service of your campus bookstore.

Your task Visit the bookstore and look critically at its operations. Then draft a letter that could be sent to the bookstore manager, offering recommendations that would help the store service customers more effectively, perhaps suggesting products it should carry, hours that it should remain open, or added services that it should make available to students. Be sure to support your recommendations.

9. Message Strategies: Analytical Reports [LO-6] When a store is open all day, every day, when's the best time to restock the shelves? That's the challenge at Store 24, a retail chain that never closes. Imagine that you're the assistant manager of a Store 24 branch that just opened near your campus. You want to set up a restocking schedule that won't conflict with prime shopping hours. Think about the number of customers you're likely to serve in the morning, afternoon, evening, and overnight hours. Consider, too, how many employees you might have during these four periods.

Your task Write a problem-solving report in letter format to the store manager (Isabel Chu) and the regional manager (Eric Angstrom), who must agree on a solution to this problem. Discuss the pros and cons of each of the four periods and include your recommendation for restocking the shelves.

10. Message Strategies: Analytical Reports [LO-6] Spurred in part by the success of numerous do-it-yourself (DIY) TV shows, homeowners across the country are redecorating, remodeling, and rebuilding. Many people are content with superficial changes, such as new paint or new accessories, but some are more ambitious. These homeowners want to move walls, add rooms, redesign kitchens, convert garages to home theaters—the big stuff.

Publishers try to create magazines that appeal to carefully identified groups of potential readers and the advertisers who'd like to reach them. The DIY market is already served by numerous magazines, but you see an opportunity in the homeowners who tackle the heavy-duty projects. Case Tables 10.1 through 10.3 summarize the results of some preliminary research you asked your company's research staff to conduct.

Your task You think the data show a real opportunity for a "big projects" DIY magazine, although you'll need more extensive research to confirm the size of the market and refine the editorial direction of the magazine. Prepare a brief analytical report that presents the data you have, identifies the opportunity or opportunities you've found (suggest your own ideas, based on the data in the tables), and requests funding from the editorial board to pursue further research.

CASE TABLE 10.1	Rooms Most Frequently Remodeled by DIYers
Room	**Percentage of Homeowners Surveyed Who Have Tackled or Plan to Tackle at Least a Partial Remodel**
Kitchen	60
Bathroom	48
Home office/study	44
Bedroom	38
Media room/home theater	31
Den/recreation room	28
Living room	27
Dining room	12
Sun room/solarium	8

CASE TABLE 10.2	Average Amount Spent on Remodeling Projects
Estimated Amount	**Percentage of Surveyed Homeowners**
Under $5k	5
$5k–$10k	21
$10k–$20k	39
$20k–$50k	22
More than $50k	13

CASE TABLE 10.3	Tasks Performed by Homeowner on a Typical Remodeling Project
Task	**Percentage of Surveyed Homeowners Who Perform or Plan to Perform Most or All of This Task Themselves**
Conceptual design	90
Technical design/architecture	34
Demolition	98
Foundation work	62
Framing	88
Plumbing	91
Electrical	55
Heating/cooling	22
Finish carpentry	85
Tile work	90
Painting	100
Interior design	52

Proposals

E-MAIL SKILLS

11. Message Strategies: Proposals [LO-7] Think of a course you would love to see added to the curriculum at your school. Conversely, if you would like to see a course offered as an elective rather than being required, write your e-mail report accordingly. Construct a sequence of logical reasons to support your choice. (This is the 2 + 2 = 4 approach mentioned in the chapter.)

Your task Plan and draft a short e-mail proposal to be submitted to the academic dean by e-mail. Be sure to include all the reasons supporting your idea.

12. Message Strategies: Proposals [LO-7] Select a product you are familiar with and imagine that you are the manufacturer, trying to get a local retail outlet to carry it. Use the Internet and other resources to gather information about the product.

Your task Write an unsolicited sales proposal in letter format to the owner (or manager) of the store, proposing that the item be stocked. Use the information you gathered to describe some of the product's features and benefits. Then make up some reasonable figures, highlighting what the item costs, what it can be sold for, and what services your company provides (return of unsold items, free replacement of unsatisfactory items, necessary repairs, and so on).

13. Message Strategies: Proposals [LO-7] You are a sales manager for Air-Trak, and one of your responsibilities is writing sales proposals for potential buyers of your company's Air-Trak tracking system. The system uses the global positioning system (GPS) to track the location of vehicles and other assets. For example, the dispatcher for a trucking company can simply click a map display on a computer screen to find out where all the company's trucks are at that instant. Air-Trak lists the following as benefits of the system:

- Making sure vehicles follow prescribed routes, with minimal loitering time
- "Geofencing," in which dispatchers are alerted if vehicles leave assigned routes or designated service areas
- Route optimization, in which fleet managers can analyze routes and destinations to find the most time- and fuel-efficient path for each vehicle
- Comparisons between scheduled and actual travel
- Enhanced security, protecting both drivers and cargos

Your task Write a brief (unsolicited) proposal to Doneta Zachs, fleet manager for Midwest Express, 338 S.W. 6th, Des Moines, Iowa, 50321. Introduce your company, explain the benefits of the Air-Trak system, and propose a trial deployment in which you would equip five Midwest Express trucks. For the purposes of this assignment, you don't need to worry about the cost or technical details of the system; focus on promoting the benefits and asking for a decision regarding the test project. (You can learn more about the Air-Trak system at www.air-trak.com.)[17]

Improve Your Grammar, Mechanics, and Usage

You can download the text of this assignment from **http://real-timeupdates.com/bce5**; click on "Student Assignments" and then click on "Chapter 10. Improve Your Grammar, Mechanics, and Usage."

Level 1: Self-Assessment—Dashes and Hyphens

Review Sections 2.7 and 2.8 in the Handbook of Grammar, Mechanics, and Usage and then complete the following 15 items.

In items 1–15, insert the required dashes (—) and hyphens (-).

1. Three qualities speed, accuracy, and reliability are desirable in any applicant to the data entry department.
2. A highly placed source explained the top secret negotiations.
3. The file on Marian Gephardt yes, we finally found it reveals a history of late payments.
4. They're selling a well designed machine.

5. A bottle green sports jacket is hard to find.
6. Argentina, Brazil, Mexico these are the countries we hope to concentrate on.
7. Only two sites maybe three offer the things we need.
8. How many owner operators are in the industry?
9. Your ever faithful assistant deserves without a doubt a substantial raise.
10. Myrna Talefiero is this organization's president elect.
11. Stealth, secrecy, and surprise those are the elements that will give us a competitive edge.
12. The charts are well placed on each page unlike the running heads and footers.
13. We got our small business loan an enormous advantage.
14. Ron Franklin do you remember him? will be in town Monday.
15. Your devil may care attitude affects everyone involved in the decision making process.

Level 2: Workplace Applications

The following items may contain errors in grammar, capitalization, punctuation, abbreviation, number style, word division, and vocabulary. Rewrite each sentence, correcting all errors. If a sentence has no errors, write "Correct" for that number.

1. Commerce One helps its customer's to more efficiently lower administrative costs, improve order times, and to manage contract negotiations.
2. The intermodal bus vehicle seats up to 35 passengers, but is equipped with a 20 feet standardized container in the rear. The same container one sees on ships, trains and on planes.
3. "The American Dream of innovation, persistence, and a refusal to except the status quo has just created, in our opinion, Americas newest and most exciting company to watch," said James Gaspard President of Neoplan USA.
4. This new, transportation paradigm may have a global affect and the barriers to entry will be extremely costly too overcome.
5. Autobytel also owns and operates Carsmart.com and Autosite.com as well as AIC Automotive Information Center] a provider of automotive marketing data and technology.
6. Mymarket.com offers a low cost high reward, entry into e-commerce not only for buyers but also suppliers.
7. Eclipse Aviation's main competitor are another start-up Safire Aircraft of west Palm Beach, Fl.
8. After identifying the factors that improve a industrial process, additional refining experiments must be conducted to confirm the results.
9. The fair labor standards Act regulates minimum wages, establishes overtime compensation, and it outlaws labor for children.
10. The Chinese government are supporting use of the Internet as a business tool because it is seen by it as necessary to enhance competitiveness.
11. At a certain point in a company's growth, the entrepreneur, who wants to control everything, can no longer

keep up so they look mistakenly for a better manager and call that person a CEO.

12. City Fresh foods is paid by City health agencies to provide Ethnic food to the homebound "elderly" in the Boston Area.

13. Being in business since 1993, Miss Rosen has boiled down her life story into a 2-minute sound bight for sales prospects.

14. Anyone that wants to gain a new perspective on their product or service must cast aside one's own biases.

15. If I was Microsoft's Steve Ballmer, I'd handle the Federal government's antitrust lawsuit much different.

Level 3: Document Critique

The following document may contain errors in grammar, capitalization, punctuation, abbreviation, number style, word division, and vocabulary. As your instructor indicates, photocopy this page and correct all errors using standard proofreading marks (see Appendix C) or download the document and make the corrections in your word processing software.

Memo
Date: March 14 2011
TO: Jeff Black and HR staff
FROM: Carrie andrews
Subject: Recruiting and hiring Seminar

As you all know the process of recruiting screening and hiring new employees might be a legal minefield. Because we don't have an inhouse lawyer to help us make every decision, its important for all of us to be aware of what actions are legally acceptible and what isn't. Last week I attended a American management Association seminar on this subject. I given enough useful information to warrant updating our online personnel handbook and perhaps developing a quick training session for all interviewing teams. First, heres a quick look at the things I learned.

Avoiding Legal Mistakes

1. How to write recruiting ads that accurately portray job openings and not discriminate.
2. Complying with the Americans with Disabilities Act
3. How to use an employment agency effectively and safe (without risk of legal entanglements)

How to Screen and Interview More Effectively

1. How to sort through résumés more efficient (including looking for telltale signs of false information)
2. We can avoid interview questions that could get us into legal trouble
3. When and how to check criminal records

Measuring Applicants

1. Which type of preemployment tests have been proven most effective?
2. Which drug-testing issues and recommendations effect us as you can see the seminar addressed alot of important information. We covering the basic guidelines for much of this already; but a number of specific recommendations and legal concepts should be emphisized and underline.

It will take me a couple of weeks to get the personel handbook updated: but we don't have any immediate hiring plans anyway so that shouldn't be too much of a problem unless you think I should ocmplete it sooner and then we can talk about that.

I'll keep the seminar handouts and my notes on my desk in case you want to peruse them.

After the handbook is updated by me, we can get together and decide whether we need to train the interviewing team members. Although we have a lot of new information, what people need to be aware of can be highlighted and the new sections can be read as schedules allow, although they might be reluctant to do this and we can also talk about that later, at a time of your conveinence that you can select later.

If you have any questions in the mean-time; don't hesitate to e-mail me or drop by for a chat.

Writing and Completing Reports and Proposals

LEARNING OBJECTIVES

After studying this chapter, you will be able to

1 List the topics commonly covered in the introduction, body, and close of informational reports, analytical reports, and proposals

2 Identify six guidelines for drafting effective website content

3 Offer guidelines for becoming a valuable wiki contributor

4 Discuss six principles of graphic design that can improve the quality of your visuals and identify the major types of business visuals

5 Summarize the four tasks involved in completing business reports and proposals

---

PEARSON mybcommlab™ Access interactive videos, simulations, sample documents, Document Makeovers, and assessment quizzes in Chapter 11 of mybcommlab.com for mastery of this chapter's objectives.

COMMUNICATION *Matters*

" The test for investor communications is shifting from technical accuracy and legal compliance to clear communication and investor understanding. "
—George Stenitzer, *Vice president of corporate communication, Tellabs*[1]

Tellabs's George Stenitzer's clear, audience-focused approach to writing annual reports stands out in a field too often known for complexity and murkiness.

Focusing on the content of your longer business documents is not only natural but necessary, because doing so helps ensure complete, correct information. However, once you have the technical content in place, you need to stand back and view the document from the perspective of your audience— the people you expect to read and act on the information. Is your message clear, compelling, and concise? Is it something a real, living, breathing person could be expected to read and understand? Follow George Stenitzer's example whenever you're writing and completing reports and proposals: Even with the most complex or technical documents, remember that another human being is at the receiving end of your communication efforts.

1 LEARNING OBJECTIVE

List the topics commonly covered in the introduction, body, and close of informational reports, analytical reports, and proposals

WRITING REPORTS AND PROPOSALS

This chapter focuses on writing and completing reports, along with creating content for websites, collaborating on wikis, and creating graphical elements to illustrate messages of all kinds.

All the writing concepts and techniques you learned in Chapter 4 apply to the longer format of business reports. However, the length and complexity of reports call for special attention to several issues, starting with adapting to your audience.

Adapting to Your Audience

> The "you" attitude is especially important with long or complex reports because they demand a lot from readers.

Reports and proposals can put heavy demands on your readers, so the "you" attitude is especially important with these long messages. Many companies have specific guidelines for communicating with public audiences, so make sure you're aware of these preferences before you start writing.

> You can adjust the formality of your writing through your word choices and writing style.

In general, try to strike a balance between overly informal (which can be perceived as trivializing important issues) and overly formal (which can put too much distance between writer and reader). If you know your readers reasonably well and your report is likely to meet with their approval, you can generally adopt an informal tone. To make your tone less formal, speak to readers in the first person, refer to them as *you*, and refer to yourself as *I* (or *we* if there are multiple report authors).

To make your tone more formal, use the impersonal journalism style: Emphasize objectivity, avoid personal opinions, and build your argument on provable facts. Eliminate all personal pronouns (including *I*, *you*, *we*, *us*, and *our*). Avoid humor, and be careful with your use of similes, metaphors, and particularly colorful adjectives or adverbs. However, don't go so far as to make the writing monotonous. For example, you can still create interest by varying the types of sentences you use to create a pleasing rhythm (see page 115).

- Access this chapter's simulation entitled Business Reports, located at mybcommlab.com.

Take into account that communicating with people in other cultures often calls for more formality in reports, both to respect cultural preferences and to reduce the risk of miscommunication. Informal elements such as humor and casual language tend to translate poorly from one culture to another.

TONE *Matters*

> " It is easy to slip into unnatural corporate-speak, particularly when under pressure to communicate a complex issue quickly. This language is an immediate turn-off. Even if you have to explain a technical issue, don't forget you are communicating to fellow human beings. "
>
> —Tania Menegatti, *human resources consultant*[2]

Composing Reports and Proposals

When you compose reports and proposals, follow the writing advice offered in Chapter 4: Select the best words, create the most effective sentences, and develop coherent paragraphs. Like other written business communications, reports and proposals have three main sections: an introduction (or opening), a body, and a close.

An effective *introduction* accomplishes at least four tasks:

> The introduction needs to put the report in context for the reader, introduce the subject, preview main ideas, and establish the tone of the document.

- It puts the report or proposal in context by tying it to a problem or an assignment.
- It introduces the subject or purpose of the report or proposal and indicates why the subject is important.
- It previews the main ideas and the order in which they'll be covered.
- It establishes the tone of the document and the writer's relationship with the audience.

> The body of your report presents, analyzes, and interprets the information you gathered during your investigation.

The *body* presents, analyzes, and interprets the information gathered during your investigation and supports your recommendations or conclusions (see Figure 11.1).

The *close* is the final section in the text of your report or proposal. It has three important functions:

- It emphasizes your main points.
- It summarizes the benefits to the reader if the document suggests a change or some other course of action.
- It brings all the action items together in one place.

The close gives you one last chance to make sure that your report says what you intended, so make sure it carries a strong, clear message.[3]

> Your close is often the last opportunity to get your message across, so make it clear and compelling.

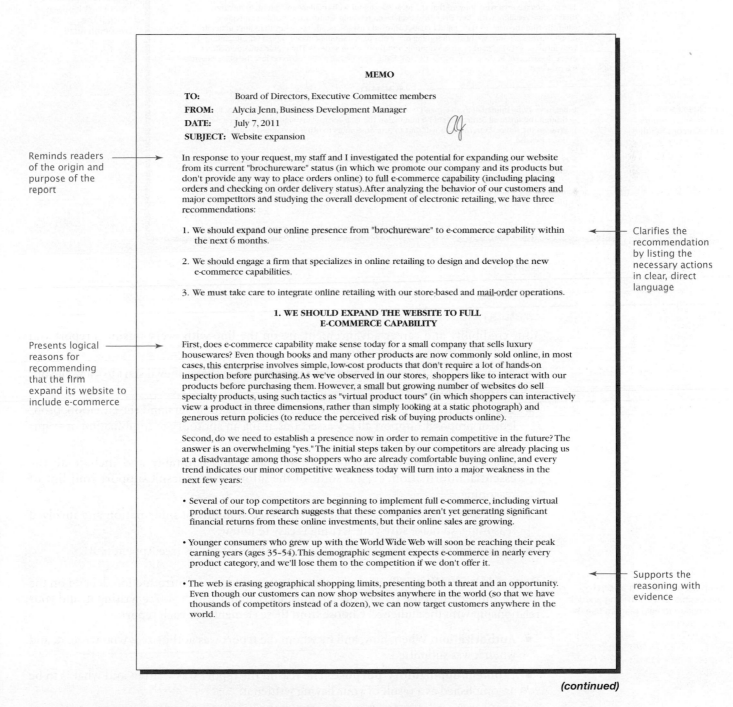

MEMO

TO: Board of Directors, Executive Committee members
FROM: Alycia Jenn, Business Development Manager
DATE: July 7, 2011
SUBJECT: Website expansion

Reminds readers of the origin and purpose of the report

In response to your request, my staff and I investigated the potential for expanding our website from its current "brochureware" status (in which we promote our company and its products but don't provide any way to place orders online) to full e-commerce capability (including placing orders and checking on order delivery status). After analyzing the behavior of our customers and major competitors and studying the overall development of electronic retailing, we have three recommendations:

1. We should expand our online presence from "brochureware" to e-commerce capability within the next 6 months.

2. We should engage a firm that specializes in online retailing to design and develop the new e-commerce capabilities.

3. We must take care to integrate online retailing with our store-based and mail-order operations.

Clarifies the recommendation by listing the necessary actions in clear, direct language

1. WE SHOULD EXPAND THE WEBSITE TO FULL E-COMMERCE CAPABILITY

Presents logical reasons for recommending that the firm expand its website to include e-commerce

First, does e-commerce capability make sense today for a small company that sells luxury housewares? Even though books and many other products are now commonly sold online, in most cases, this enterprise involves simple, low-cost products that don't require a lot of hands-on inspection before purchasing. As we've observed in our stores, shoppers like to interact with our products before purchasing them. However, a small but growing number of websites do sell specialty products, using such tactics as "virtual product tours" (in which shoppers can interactively view a product in three dimensions, rather than simply looking at a static photograph) and generous return policies (to reduce the perceived risk of buying products online).

Second, do we need to establish a presence now in order to remain competitive in the future? The answer is an overwhelming "yes." The initial steps taken by our competitors are already placing us at a disadvantage among those shoppers who are already comfortable buying online, and every trend indicates our minor competitive weakness today will turn into a major weakness in the next few years:

- Several of our top competitors are beginning to implement full e-commerce, including virtual product tours. Our research suggests that these companies aren't yet generating significant financial returns from these online investments, but their online sales are growing.

- Younger consumers who grew up with the World Wide Web will soon be reaching their peak earning years (ages 35–54). This demographic segment expects e-commerce in nearly every product category, and we'll lose them to the competition if we don't offer it.

- The web is erasing geographical shopping limits, presenting both a threat and an opportunity. Even though our customers can now shop websites anywhere in the world (so that we have thousands of competitors instead of a dozen), we can now target customers anywhere in the world.

Supports the reasoning with evidence

(continued)

Figure 11.1   Effective Problem-Solving Report Focusing on Recommendations
In this report recommending that her firm expand its website to full e-commerce capability, Alycia Jenn uses the body of her report to provide enough information to support her argument, without burdening her high-level readership with a lot of tactical details.

(continued)

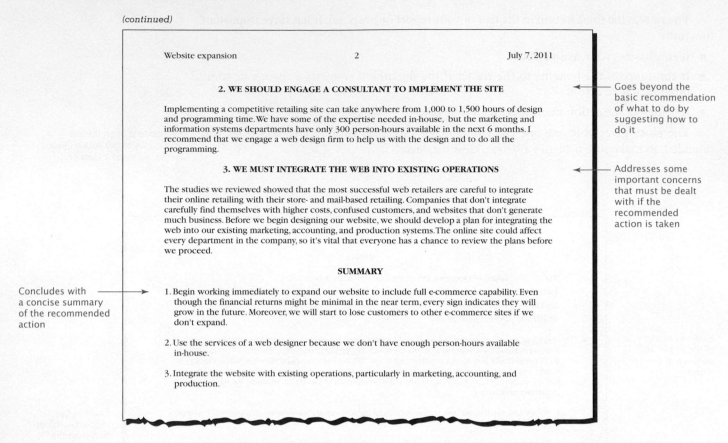

Website expansion   2   July 7, 2011

2. WE SHOULD ENGAGE A CONSULTANT TO IMPLEMENT THE SITE

Implementing a competitive retailing site can take anywhere from 1,000 to 1,500 hours of design and programming time. We have some of the expertise needed in-house, but the marketing and information systems departments have only 300 person-hours available in the next 6 months. I recommend that we engage a web design firm to help us with the design and to do all the programming.

→ Goes beyond the basic recommendation of what to do by suggesting how to do it

3. WE MUST INTEGRATE THE WEB INTO EXISTING OPERATIONS

The studies we reviewed showed that the most successful web retailers are careful to integrate their online retailing with their store- and mail-based retailing. Companies that don't integrate carefully find themselves with higher costs, confused customers, and websites that don't generate much business. Before we begin designing our website, we should develop a plan for integrating the web into our existing marketing, accounting, and production systems. The online site could affect every department in the company, so it's vital that everyone has a chance to review the plans before we proceed.

→ Addresses some important concerns that must be dealt with if the recommended action is taken

SUMMARY

Concludes with a concise summary of the recommended action →

1. Begin working immediately to expand our website to include full e-commerce capability. Even though the financial returns might be minimal in the near term, every sign indicates they will grow in the future. Moreover, we will start to lose customers to other e-commerce sites if we don't expand.

2. Use the services of a web designer because we don't have enough person-hours available in-house.

3. Integrate the website with existing operations, particularly in marketing, accounting, and production.

Figure 11.1 *(continued)*

Drafting Report Content

Your credibility and career advancement are on the line with every business report you write, so make sure your content is

- **Accurate.** If readers suspect that your information is shaky, they'll start to view all your work with skepticism.

- **Complete.** Include everything necessary for readers to understand the situation, problem, or proposal. Support all key assertions, using an appropriate combination of examples, explanations, and facts.[4]

- **Balanced.** Present all sides of the issue fairly and equitably and include all the essential information, even if some of the information doesn't support your line of reasoning.

- **Clear and logical.** Reports often contain large amounts of information and involved reasoning, so make sure your writing is easy to follow.

- **Documented properly.** Properly document all your sources (see Appendix B).

Report Introduction   The specific elements to include in an introduction depend on the nature and length of the report, the circumstances under which you're writing it, and your relationship with the audience. Choose from these elements for each report:

Keep the introduction as brief as possible while providing enough information to help readers use the report effectively.

- **Authorization.** When, how, and by whom the report was authorized; who wrote it; and when it was submitted.

- **Problem/opportunity/purpose.** The reason the report was written and what is to be accomplished as a result of your having written it.

- **Scope.** What is and what isn't covered in the report.

- **Background.** The historical conditions or factors that led up to the report.

- **Sources and methods.** A description of the primary and secondary research that provided information for the report.

- **Definitions.** A list of terms that might be unfamiliar to your audience, along with brief definitions.
- **Limitations.** Factors beyond your control that affect report quality, such as budgets, schedule constraints, or limited access to information or people. (However, don't use this section to apologize or try to explain away personal shortcomings, such as poor planning on your part.)
- **Report organization.** The organization of the report. This "road map" helps readers understand what's coming in the report and why this information is included.

Report Body   As with the introduction, the body of your report can require some tough decisions about which elements to include and how much detail to offer. Provide only enough detail in the body to support your conclusions and recommendations; you can put additional information in appendixes. The following topics are commonly covered in a report body:

> The report body should contain only enough information to convey your message in a convincing fashion; use an appendix for less important details.

- Explanations of a problem or an opportunity
- Facts, statistical evidence, and trends
- Results of studies or investigations
- Discussion and analyses of potential courses of action
- Advantages, disadvantages, costs, and benefits of a particular course of action
- Procedures or steps in a process
- Methods and approaches
- Criteria for evaluating alternatives and options
- Conclusions and recommendations
- Supporting reasons for conclusions or recommendations

For analytical reports using the direct approach, you'll generally state your conclusions or recommendations in the introduction and use the body of your report to provide your evidence and support. If you're using the indirect approach, you're likely to use the body to discuss your logic and reserve your conclusions or recommendations until the very end.

Report Close   The content and length of the close depend primarily on your choice of direct or indirect approach. If you're using the direct approach, you can end with a summary of key points, listed in the order in which they appear in the report body. If you're using the indirect approach, you can use the close to present your conclusions or recommendations (your main idea, in order words) if you didn't end the body with this information. However, don't introduce new facts in your close; your readers should have all the information they need by the time they reach this point.

> The nature of your close depends on the type of report (informational or analytical) and the approach (direct or indirect).

If your report is intended to prompt others to action, use the close to spell out exactly what should happen next. If you'll be taking all the actions yourself, make sure your readers understand this fact so that they know what to expect from you.

> If a report calls for follow-up action of any kind, clearly identify who is going to do what.

Drafting Proposal Content

With proposals, the content for each section is governed by many variables, the most important of which is the motivation behind the proposal. If a proposal is unsolicited, you have some latitude in the scope and organization of content. However, if you are responding to a request for proposals (see page 289), you need to follow the instructions in the RFP in every detail.

The general purpose of any proposal is to persuade readers to do something, so your writing approach is similar to that used for persuasive messages, perhaps including the use of the AIDA model or something similar to gain attention, build interest, create desire, and motivate action. Here are some additional strategies to strengthen your argument:[5]

> Approach proposals the same way you approach persuasive messages.

- Demonstrate your knowledge.
- Provide concrete information and examples.
- Research the competition so you know what other proposals your audience is likely to read.
- Prove that your proposal is appropriate and feasible for your audience.
- Relate your product, service, or personnel to the reader's exact needs.
- Package your proposal attractively.

> Business proposals need to provide more than just attractive ideas— readers look for evidence of practical, achievable solutions.

REAL-TIME UPDATES
Learn More by Watching This Video

Tips and techniques for writing business proposals

Get more details about the variety of business proposals and explore an effective process of planning, writing, and completing any type of business proposal. Go to **http://real-timeupdates.com/bce5** and click on "Learn More." If you are using mybcommlab, you can access Real-Time Updates within each chapter or under Student Study Tools.

Moreover, make sure your proposal is error-free, inviting, and readable. Readers will prejudge the quality of your products, services, or capabilities by the quality of the proposal you submit. Errors, omissions, and inconsistencies will work against you—and might even cost you important career and business opportunities.

Proposal Introduction   The introduction of a proposal describes the problem you intend to solve or the opportunity you want to pursue, along with your suggested solution. If your proposal is solicited, follow the RFP's instructions about indicating the specific RFP to which you're responding. If your proposal is unsolicited, mention any factors that led you to submit your proposal. The following topics are commonly covered in a proposal introduction:

> In an unsolicited proposal, your introduction needs to convince readers that a problem or an opportunity exists.

- **Background or statement of the problem.** Briefly review the reader's situation and establish a need for action. In unsolicited proposals, you may need to convince readers that a problem or an opportunity exists before you can convince them to consider and eventually accept your solution.

- **Solution.** If you are using the direct approach, briefly describe the change you propose and highlight your key selling points and their benefits to your audience. With the indirect approach, explain that you will be describing an effective solution to the reader's challenges.

- **Scope.** State the boundaries of the proposal—what you will and will not do. This section is sometimes called "Delimitations."

- **Organization.** Orient the reader to the remainder of the proposal and call attention to the major divisions of information.

In short proposals, your discussion of these topics will be brief—perhaps only a sentence or two for each one. For long, formal proposals, each of these topics may warrant separate subheadings and several paragraphs of discussion.

> Readers understand that a proposal is a persuasive message, so they're willing to accommodate a degree of promotional emphasis in your writing—as long as it is professional and focused on their needs.

Proposal Body   The proposal's body gives complete details on the proposed solution and describes the anticipated results. Because a proposal is by definition a persuasive message, your audience expects you to promote your offering in a confident but professional and objective manner.

The body of a proposal typically includes these sections:

- **Proposed solution.** Describes what you have to offer: your concept, product, or service. This section may also be titled "Technical Proposal," "Research Design," "Issues for Analysis," or something similar.

> A work plan, or statement of work, in a proposal indicates exactly how you will accomplish the solution presented in the proposal.

- **Work plan.** Explains the steps you'll take, their timing, the methods or resources you'll use, and the person(s) responsible. Specifically includes when the work will begin, how it will be divided into stages, when you will finish, and whether any follow-up is involved. The work plan, sometimes called the *statement of work*, can be contractually binding if your proposal is accepted, so don't promise more than you can deliver. (Note that *work plan* as used here is different from the work plan for your writing purposes discussed on page 274.)

- **Statement of qualifications.** Describes your organization's experience, personnel, and facilities as they relate to audience needs.

- **Costs.** Covers pricing, reimbursable expenses, discounts, and so on. If you're responding to an RFP, follow the instructions it contains.

In an informal proposal, discussion of some or all of these elements may be grouped together and presented in a letter format, as shown in the proposal in Figure 11.2. In a formal proposal, each of these elements is given its own section.

> The close is your last chance to convince the reader of the merits of your proposal, so make doubly sure it's clear, compelling, and audience-oriented.

Proposal Close   The final section of a proposal summarizes the key points, emphasizes the benefits that readers will realize from your solution, summarizes the merits of your approach, restates why you and your firm are a good choice, and asks for a decision from the reader. Keep this section brief and use a confident, optimistic tone.

Table 11.1 on page 307 summarizes the items to consider in the introduction, body, and close of a report or proposal.

Helping Readers Find Their Way

To help today's time-pressed readers find what they're looking for and stay on track as they navigate through your documents, learn to make good use of headings and links, smooth transitions, and previews and reviews:

■ **Headings or links.** Readers should be able to follow the structure of your document and pick up the key points of your message from the headings and subheadings. For online reports, make generous use of hyperlinks to help your readers navigate the reports and access additional information.

Help your readers find what they want and stay on track with headings or links, transitions, previews, and reviews.

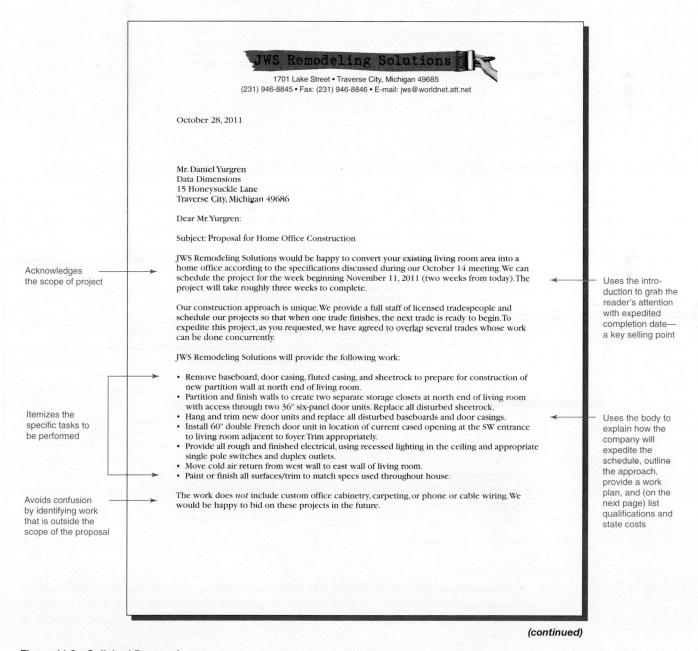

JWS Remodeling Solutions

1701 Lake Street • Traverse City, Michigan 49685
(231) 946-8845 • Fax: (231) 946-8846 • E-mail: jws@worldnet.att.net

October 28, 2011

Mr. Daniel Yurgren
Data Dimensions
15 Honeysuckle Lane
Traverse City, Michigan 49686

Dear Mr. Yurgren:

Subject: Proposal for Home Office Construction

[Acknowledges the scope of project →] JWS Remodeling Solutions would be happy to convert your existing living room area into a home office according to the specifications discussed during our October 14 meeting. We can schedule the project for the week beginning November 11, 2011 (two weeks from today). The project will take roughly three weeks to complete. **[← Uses the introduction to grab the reader's attention with expedited completion date—a key selling point]**

Our construction approach is unique. We provide a full staff of licensed tradespeople and schedule our projects so that when one trade finishes, the next trade is ready to begin. To expedite this project, as you requested, we have agreed to overlap several trades whose work can be done concurrently.

JWS Remodeling Solutions will provide the following work:

[Itemizes the specific tasks to be performed →]

- Remove baseboard, door casing, fluted casing, and sheetrock to prepare for construction of new partition wall at north end of living room.
- Partition and finish walls to create two separate storage closets at north end of living room with access through two 36" six-panel door units. Replace all disturbed sheetrock.
- Hang and trim new door units and replace all disturbed baseboards and door casings.
- Install 60" double French door unit in location of current cased opening at the SW entrance to living room adjacent to foyer. Trim appropriately.
- Provide all rough and finished electrical, using recessed lighting in the ceiling and appropriate single pole switches and duplex outlets.
- Move cold air return from west wall to east wall of living room.
- Paint or finish all surfaces/trim to match specs used throughout house.

[← Uses the body to explain how the company will expedite the schedule, outline the approach, provide a work plan, and (on the next page) list qualifications and state costs]

[Avoids confusion by identifying work that is outside the scope of the proposal →] The work does *not* include custom office cabinetry, carpeting, or phone or cable wiring. We would be happy to bid on these projects in the future.

(continued)

Figure 11.2 Solicited Proposal
This informal solicited proposal in letter format provides the information the customer needs to make a purchase. Note that by signing the proposal and returning it, the customer enters into a legal contract to pay for the services described.

(continued)

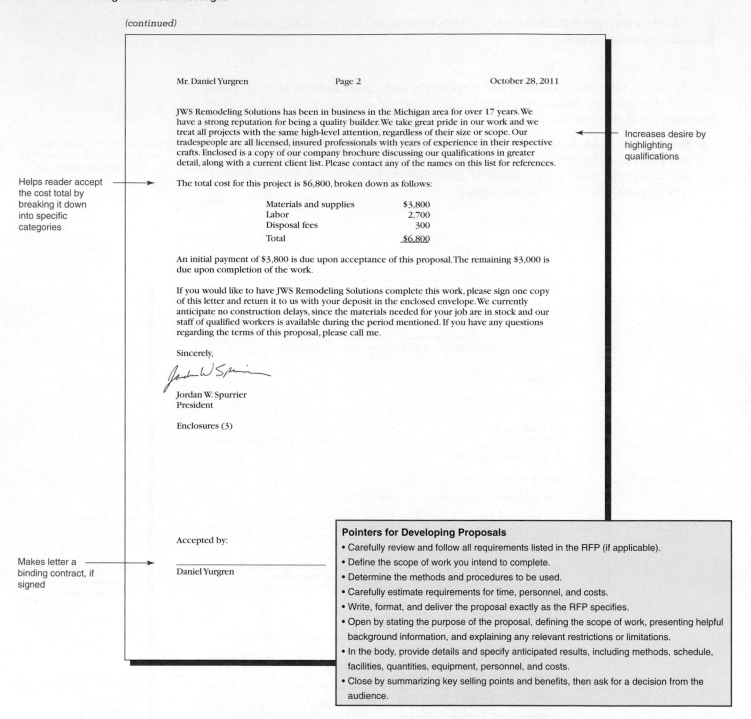

Mr. Daniel Yurgren   Page 2   October 28, 2011

JWS Remodeling Solutions has been in business in the Michigan area for over 17 years. We
have a strong reputation for being a quality builder. We take great pride in our work and we
treat all projects with the same high-level attention, regardless of their size or scope. Our
tradespeople are all licensed, insured professionals with years of experience in their respective
crafts. Enclosed is a copy of our company brochure discussing our qualifications in greater
detail, along with a current client list. Please contact any of the names on this list for references.

Increases desire by highlighting qualifications

Helps reader accept the cost total by breaking it down into specific categories

The total cost for this project is $6,800, broken down as follows:

Materials and supplies	$3,800
Labor	2,700
Disposal fees	300
Total	$6,800

An initial payment of $3,800 is due upon acceptance of this proposal. The remaining $3,000 is
due upon completion of the work.

If you would like to have JWS Remodeling Solutions complete this work, please sign one copy
of this letter and return it to us with your deposit in the enclosed envelope. We currently
anticipate no construction delays, since the materials needed for your job are in stock and our
staff of qualified workers is available during the period mentioned. If you have any questions
regarding the terms of this proposal, please call me.

Sincerely,

Jordan W. Spurrier
President

Enclosures (3)

Accepted by:

Makes letter a binding contract, if signed

_____
Daniel Yurgren

Pointers for Developing Proposals
- Carefully review and follow all requirements listed in the RFP (if applicable).
- Define the scope of work you intend to complete.
- Determine the methods and procedures to be used.
- Carefully estimate requirements for time, personnel, and costs.
- Write, format, and deliver the proposal exactly as the RFP specifies.
- Open by stating the purpose of the proposal, defining the scope of work, presenting helpful background information, and explaining any relevant restrictions or limitations.
- In the body, provide details and specify anticipated results, including methods, schedule, facilities, quantities, equipment, personnel, and costs.
- Close by summarizing key selling points and benefits, then ask for a decision from the audience.

POWERED BY mybcommlab

Apply Figure 11.2's key concepts by revising a new document. Go to Chapter 11 in mybcommlab.com and select Document Makeovers.

Figure 11.2 *(continued)*

- **Transitions.** Chapter 4 defines transitions as words or phrases that tie together ideas and show how one thought is related to another. In addition, in a long report, an entire paragraph might be used to highlight transitions from one major section to the next.

- **Previews and reviews.** *Preview sections* introduce important topics by helping readers get ready for new information. *Review sections* come after a body of material and summarize the information for your readers, helping them absorb details.

TABLE 11.1	Report and Proposal Contents

Report Contents

Introduction

- **Authorization.** Reiterate who authorized the report (when, how), who wrote it, and when it was submitted.
- **Problem/purpose.** Explain the reason for the report's existence and what the report will achieve.
- **Scope.** Describe what will and won't be covered in the report—indicating size and complexity.
- **Background.** Review historical conditions or factors that led up to the report.
- **Sources and methods.** Discuss the primary and secondary sources consulted and methods used.
- **Definitions.** List terms and their definitions, including any terms that might be misinterpreted. Terms may also be defined in the body, explanatory notes, or glossary.
- **Limitations.** Discuss factors beyond your control that affect report quality—but note that this should not be an excuse for poor research or a poorly written report.
- **Report organization.** Tell what topics are covered, in what order.

Body

- **Explanations.** Give complete details of the problem, project, or idea.
- **Facts, statistical evidence, and trends.** Lay out the results of studies or investigations.
- **Analysis of action.** Discuss potential courses of action.
- **Pros and cons.** Explain advantages, disadvantages, costs, and benefits of a particular course of action.
- **Procedures.** Outline steps for a process.
- **Methods and approaches.** Discuss how you've studied a problem (or gathered evidence) and arrived at your solution (or collected your data).
- **Criteria.** Describe the benchmarks for evaluating options and alternatives.
- **Conclusions and recommendations.** Discuss what you believe the evidence reveals and what you propose should be done about it.
- **Support.** Give the reasons behind your conclusions or recommendations.

Close

- **For direct order.** Summarize key points (except in short memos), listing them in the order in which they appear in the body. Briefly restate your conclusions or recommendations, if appropriate.
- **For indirect order.** You may use the close to present your conclusions or recommendations for the first time—just be sure not to present any new facts.
- **For motivating action.** Spell out exactly what should happen next and provide a schedule with specific task assignments.

Proposal Contents

Introduction

- **Background or statement of the problem.** Briefly review the reader's situation, establish a need for action, and explain how things could be better. In unsolicited proposals, convince readers that a problem or an opportunity exists.
- **Solution.** Briefly describe the change you propose, highlighting your key selling points and their benefits to show how your proposal will solve the reader's problem.
- **Scope.** State the boundaries of the proposal—what you will and will not do.
- **Report organization.** Orient the reader to the remainder of the proposal and call attention to the major divisions of thought.

Body

- **Facts and evidence to support your conclusions.** Give complete details of the proposed solution and anticipated results.
- **Proposed approach.** Describe your concept, product, or service. Stress reader benefits and emphasize any advantages you have over your competitors.
- **Work plan.** Describe how you'll accomplish what must be done (unless you're providing a standard, off-the-shelf item). Explain the steps you'll take, their timing, the methods or resources you'll use, and the person(s) responsible. State when work will begin, how it will be divided into stages, when you'll finish, and whether follow-up will be needed.
- **Statement of qualifications.** Describe your organization's experience, personnel, and facilities—relating it all to readers' needs. Include a list of client references.
- **Costs.** Prove that your costs are realistic—break them down so that readers can see the costs of labor, materials, transportation, travel, training, and other categories.

Close

- **Review of argument.** Briefly summarize the key points.
- **Review of reader benefits.** Briefly summarize how your proposal will help the reader.
- **Review of the merits of your approach.** Briefly summarize why your approach will be more effective than that of competitors.
- **Restatement of qualifications.** Briefly reemphasize why you and your firm should do the work.
- **Request.** Ask for a decision from the reader.

Using Technology to Craft Reports and Proposals

Creating lengthy reports and proposals can be a huge task, so take advantage of technological tools that can help throughout the process:

- **Templates, themes, and style sheets.** The size and complexity of many reports make these tools particularly helpful, even more so when you need to create a series of reports on the same subject or for the same audience (such as a monthly sales report).

Look for ways to utilize technology to reduce the mechanical work involved in writing long reports.

- **Linked and embedded documents.** In many reports and proposals, you'll include graphics, spreadsheets, databases, and other elements produced in other software programs. Make sure you know how your software handles the files. For instance, in Microsoft Office, *linking* to a file maintains a "live" connection to it, so changes in the original file will show up in the document you're working on. However, *embedding* a file "breaks the link," so to speak, so changes in the original will not automatically appear in the new document.

- **Electronic forms.** For recurring reports such as sales reports and compliance reports, consider creating a document that uses *form tools* such as text boxes (in which users can type new text) and check boxes (which can be used to select from a set of predetermined choices).

- **Electronic documents.** Portable document format (PDF) files have become a universal replacement for printed reports and proposals. Using Adobe Acrobat or similar products, you can quickly convert reports and proposals to PDF files that are easy to share electronically. Note that PDFs have long been considered safer than word processor files, but recent discoveries indicate that PDFs could also be used to transmit computer viruses.[6] For information on protecting yourself when using Adobe Reader for PDFs, visit www.adobe.com/security.

- **Multimedia documents.** Video clips, animation, presentation software slides, screencasts (recordings of on-screen activity), and other media elements can enhance the communication and persuasion powers of the written word.

- **Proposal-writing software.** Proposal-writing software can automatically personalize proposals, ensure proper structure (making sure you don't forget any sections, for instance), organize storage of all your boilerplate text, integrate contact information from sales databases, and scan RFPs to identify questions and requirements and fill in potential answers from a centralized knowledge base.[7]

2 LEARNING OBJECTIVE

Identify six guidelines for drafting effective website content

Composing effective online content requires some unique considerations.

DRAFTING ONLINE CONTENT

The basic principles of report writing apply to online content, but keep these six additional points in mind as well:

- Take special care to build trust with your intended audiences, because careful readers can be skeptical of online content. Make sure your content is accurate, current, complete, and authoritative.

- As much as possible, adapt your content for a global audience. Translating content is expensive, so some companies compromise by *localizing* the homepage while keeping the deeper, more detailed content in its original language.

- In an environment that presents many reading challenges, compelling, reader-oriented content is key to success.[8] Wherever you can, use the *inverted pyramid* style, in which you cover the most important information briefly at first and then gradually reveal successive layers of detail—letting readers choose to see those additional layers if they want to.

- Present your information in a concise, skimmable format. Most online readers won't dig for buried information. If they can't find the right information quickly, they will move on to another page or site.[9] Effective websites use a variety of means to help readers skim pages quickly, including lists, careful use of color and boldface, informative headings, and helpful summaries that give readers a choice of learning more if they want to.

- Write effective headings and links that serve for both site navigation and content skimming. Use meaningful key words at the beginning of headings and links so that readers can quickly identify items of interest.[10] Also, clearly identify where each link will take readers. Don't force them to click through and try to figure out where they're going, and don't use clever wordplay that forces people to work to get your meaning.

- Make your website a "living" document by adding fresh content and deleting content that is out of date or no longer relevant to your target audience. Over time, websites can accumulate many pages of outdated information that get in the way and send a negative message about the company's efforts to stay on top of user needs.[11]

Of course, offering audience-oriented content written with a strong "you" attitude is essential. Too many website owners fall into the trap of focusing on themselves, their companies, and their products. Make it about the reader.[12]

COLLABORATING ON WIKIS

3 **LEARNING OBJECTIVE**
Offer guidelines for becoming a valuable wiki contributor

As Chapter 2 points out, using wikis is a great way for teams and other groups to collaborate on writing projects, from brief articles to long reports and reference works. Unlike typical websites, wikis don't require contributors to have much technical expertise in order to create or edit content. Wikis also provide the opportunity to post new or revised material without prior approval. This approach is quite different from a web content management system, in which both the organization of the website and the workflow (the rules for creating, editing, reviewing, and approving content) are tightly controlled.[13]

Understanding the Wiki Philosophy

The benefits of wikis are compelling, but they do require a unique approach to writing. To be a valuable wiki contributor, keep these points in mind:[14]

Effective collaboration on wikis requires a unique approach to writing.

- Writers need to let go of traditional expectations of authorship, including individual recognition and control. The value of a wiki stems from the collective insight of all its contributors.

- Team members sometimes need to be encouraged to edit and improve each other's work.

- Using page templates and other formatting options can help ensure that your content fits the same style as the rest of the wiki.

- Many wikis provide both editing and commenting capabilities, and participants should use the appropriate tool for each. In other words, don't insert comments or questions into the main content; use the "talk page" or other commenting feature if you want to discuss the content.

- New users should take advantage of the sandbox, if available; this is a "safe," nonpublished section of the wiki where team members can practice editing and writing.

- Wikis usually have guidelines to help new contributors integrate their work into the group's ongoing effort. Be sure to read and understand these guidelines, and don't be afraid to ask for help.

Adapting the Three-Step Process for Successful Wiki Writing

You can easily adapt the three-step writing process for wikis, whether you are creating a new wiki, adding new material to an existing wiki, or revising existing material on a wiki.

If you are creating a new wiki, think through your long-term purpose carefully, just as you would with a new blog or podcast channel (see Figure 11.3 on the next page). Will the wiki be a one-time project (creating a report, for example) or an ongoing effort (such as maintaining "help" files for a software program)? Who will be allowed to add or modify content? Will you or someone else serve as editor, reviewing all additions and changes? What rules and guidelines will you establish to guide the growth of the wiki? What security measures might be required? For instance, the PlayStation development team at Sony uses a wiki to keep top managers up to date on new products, and because this information is highly confidential, access to the wiki is tightly controlled.[15]

If you are adding a page or an article to an existing wiki, figure out how this new material fits in with the existing structure of the wiki. Find out whether any similar material already exists, as it might be better to expand an existing article or add a subpage than to create a new item. Also, learn the wiki's preferred style for handling incomplete articles. For example, on the wiki that contains the user documentation for the popular WordPress blogging software, contributors are discouraged from adding new pages until the content is "fairly complete and accurate." Writers are instead encouraged to insert incomplete pages (usually called "stubs" in wiki parlance) and rough drafts under their personal pages until the material is ready to be added to the main wiki content.[16]

Before you add new pages to a wiki, figure out how the material fits with the existing content.

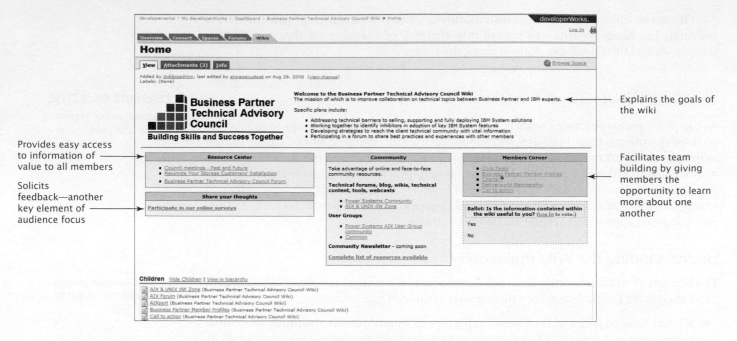

Provides easy access to information of value to all members

Solicits feedback—another key element of audience focus

Explains the goals of the wiki

Facilitates team building by giving members the opportunity to learn more about one another

Figure 11.3   IBM Business Partner Wiki
IBM created this wiki to facilitate collaboration with its external business partners.

If you are revising or updating an existing wiki article, use the checklist on page 129 in Chapter 5 to evaluate the content before you make changes. If you don't agree with published content and plan to revise it, you can use the wiki's discussion facility to share your concerns with other contributors. A well-run wiki encourages discussions and even robust disagreements, as long as everyone remains civil and respectful.

For the latest information on using wikis in business, visit **http://real-timeupdates.com/bce5** and click on Chapter 11.

4 LEARNING OBJECTIVE

Discuss six principles of graphic design that can improve the quality of your visuals, and identify the major types of business visuals

Visual literacy is the ability to create effective images and to interpret images correctly.

Pay close attention to consistency, contrast, balance, emphasis, convention, and simplicity.

ILLUSTRATING YOUR REPORTS WITH EFFECTIVE VISUALS

Well-designed visual elements can enhance the communication power of textual messages and, in some instances, even replace textual messages. Generally speaking, in a given amount of time, well-designed images can convey much more information than text.[17] Using pictures is also an effective way to communicate with multilingual audiences.

Given the importance of visuals in today's business environment, **visual literacy**—the ability (as a sender) to create effective images and (as a receiver) to correctly interpret visual messages—has become a key business skill.[18] Even without any formal training in design, being aware of the following six principles will help you be a more effective visual communicator:

- **Consistency.** Think of consistency as *visual parallelism*, similar to textual parallelism that helps audiences understand and compare a series of ideas.[19] You can achieve visual parallelism through the consistent use of color, shape, size, texture, position, scale, or typeface.
- **Contrast.** To emphasize differences, depict items in contrasting colors, such as red and blue or black and white. To emphasize similarities, make color differences more subtle.
- **Balance.** Visual balance can be either *formal*, in which the elements in the images are arranged symmetrically around a central point or axis, or *informal*, in which elements are not distributed evenly, but stronger and weaker elements are arranged in a way that achieves an overall effect of balance.[20] Generally speaking, formal balance is calming and serious, whereas informal balance tends to feel dynamic and engaging (which is why most advertising uses this approach, for example).

- **Emphasis.** Audiences usually assume that the dominant element in a design is the most important, so make sure that the visually dominant element really does represent the most important information.

- **Convention.** Just as written communication is guided by spelling, grammar, punctuation, and usage conventions, visual communication is guided by generally accepted rules or conventions that dictate virtually every aspect of design.[21] In any given culture, for example, certain colors and shapes have specific meanings.

- **Simplicity.** When you're designing graphics for your documents, limit the number of colors and design elements and take care to avoid *chartjunk*—decorative elements that clutter documents without adding any relevant information.[22] Think carefully about using some of the chart features available in your software, too. Many of these features can actually get in the way of effective visual communication.[23] For example, three-dimensional bar charts, cones, and pyramids can look appealing, but the third dimension usually adds no additional information and can be visually deceiving as well.[24]

REAL-TIME UPDATES
Learn More by Reading This PDF

See why visual design is a lot more than just "eye candy"

The visual design of a website is more than mere decoration—it is an essential, functional part of the website and a key factor in the communication process. Go to **http://real-timeupdates.com/bce5** and click on "Learn More." If you are using mybcommlab, you can access Real-Time Updates within each chapter or under Student Study Tools.

Choosing the Right Visual for the Job

After you've identified which points would benefit most from visual presentation, your next decision is to choose what types of visuals to use. As you can see in Figure 11.4 on the next page, you have many choices for business graphics. For certain types of information, the decision is usually obvious. If you want to present a large set of numeric values or detailed textual information, for example, a table is the obvious choice in most cases. Also, certain visuals are commonly used for certain applications, so, for example, your audience is likely to expect line charts and bar charts to show trends. (Note that *chart* and *graph* are used interchangeably for most of the display formats discussed here.)

You have many types of visuals to choose from, and each is best suited to particular communication tasks.

Tables

When you need to present detailed, specific information, choose a **table**, a systematic arrangement of data in columns and rows. Tables are ideal when your audience needs information that would be either difficult or tedious to handle in the main text. Most tables contain the standard parts illustrated in Figure 11.5 on page 313. Follow these guidelines to create clear, effective tables:

Printed tables can display extensive amounts of data, but tables for online display and electronic presentations need to be simpler.

- Use common, understandable units and clearly identify them: dollars, percentages, price per ton, and so on.

- Express all items in a column in the same unit and round off for simplicity.

- Label column headings clearly and use subheads if necessary.

- Separate columns or rows with lines or extra space to make the table easy to follow. Make sure the intended reading direction—down the columns or across the rows—is obvious, too.

- Don't cram so much information into a table that it becomes difficult to read.

- Keep online tables small enough to read comfortably on-screen.

- Document the source of data using the same format as a text footnote (see Appendix B).

Line Charts and Surface Charts

A **line chart** (see Figure 11.6 on page 313) illustrates trends over time or plots the relationship of two variables. In line charts that show trends, the vertical, or *y*, axis shows the amount, and the horizontal, or *x*, axis shows the time or other quantity against which the amount is being measured. You can plot just a single line or overlay multiple lines to compare different entities.

Line charts are commonly used to show trends over time or the relationship between two variables.

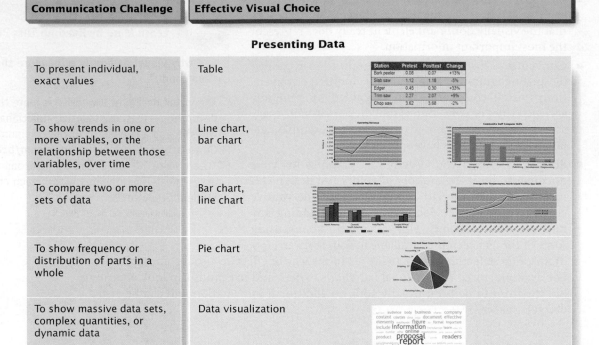

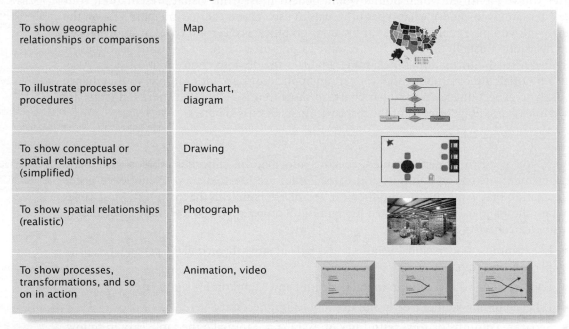

Figure 11.4 **Selecting the Best Visual**
Choose your visuals carefully for maximum communication effectiveness.

A **surface chart**, also called an **area chart**, is a form of line chart that shows a cumulative effect; all the lines add up to the top line, which represents the total (see Figure 11.7). This type of chart helps you illustrate changes in the composition of something over time. When preparing a surface chart, put the most significant line at the bottom and move up toward the least significant.

Bar Charts and Pie Charts

A **bar chart** portrays numbers with the height or length of its rectangular bars, making a series of numbers easy to grasp quickly. Bars can be oriented horizontally or vertically

Bar charts can show a variety of relationships among two or more variables.

Multicolumn Heading				
Subheading	**Subheading**	**Subheading**	**Subheading**	**Single-Column Heading**
Row heading	xxx	xxx	xxx	xxx
Row heading	xxx	xxx	xxx	xxx
Subheading	xxx	xxx	xxx	xxx
Subheading	xxx	xxx	xxx	xxx
Total	xxx	xxx	xxx	xxx

Source: (In the same format as a text footnote; see Appendix B)

*Footnote (For an explanation of elements in the table, a superscript number or small letter may be used instead of an asterisk or other symbol.)

Figure 11.5   Parts of a Table
Here are the standard parts of a table. No matter which design you choose, make sure the layout is clear and that individual rows and columns are easy to follow.

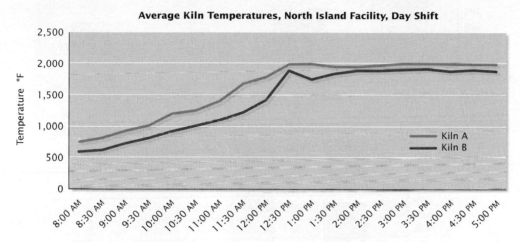

Figure 11.6   Line Chart
This two-line chart compares the temperatures measured inside two cement kilns from 8:00 A.M. to 5:00 P.M.

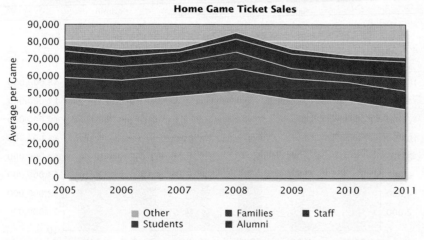

Figure 11.7   Surface Chart
Surface or area charts can show a combination of trends over time and the individual contributions of the components of a whole.

(in which case they are sometimes referred to as *column charts*). Bar charts are particularly valuable when you want to show or compare quantities over time. As the charts in Figure 11.8 on page 314 suggest, bar charts can appear in various forms. Specialized bar charts such as *timelines* and *Gantt charts* are used often in project management, for example.

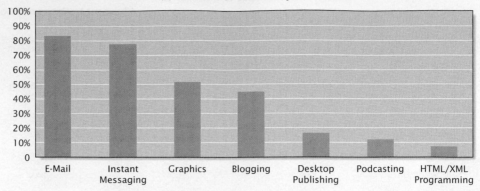

(a) CommuniCo Staff Computer Skills

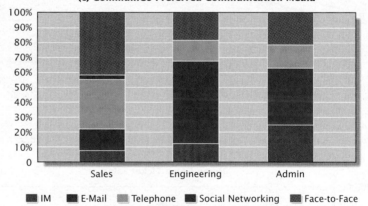

(b) Worldwide Market Share

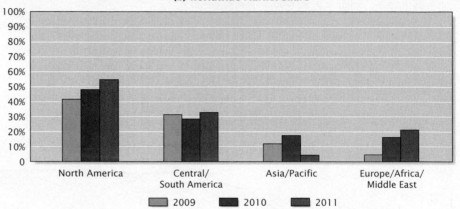

(c) CommuniCo Preferred Communication Media

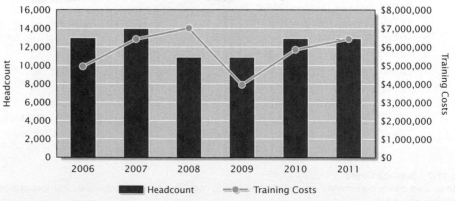

(d) CommuniCo Employee Training Costs

Figure 11.8 The Versatile Bar Chart

These charts show just four of the many variations available for bar charts: *singular* (11.8a: "CommuniCo Staff Computer Skills"), *grouped* (11.8b: "Worldwide Market Share"), *segmented* (11.8c: "CommuniCo Preferred Communication Media"), and *combination* (11.7d: "CommuniCo Employee Training Costs").

Year-End Head Count by Function

Executives, 8
Accounting, 14
Facilities, 14
Shipping, 17
Admin, 25
Engineers, 27
Sales, 28
Assemblers, 67

Year-End Head Count by Function

Function	Count
Executives	8
Accounting	14
Facilities	14
Shipping	17
Admin	25
Engineers	27
Sales	28
Assemblers	67

0 10 20 30 40 50 60 70 80

Figure 11.9   Pie Charts Versus Bar Charts
Pie charts are used frequently, but they aren't necessarily the best choice for many data presentations. This pie chart does make it easy to see that assemblers are the largest employee category, but other comparisons of slice sizes (such as Sales, Engineers, and Admin) are not as easy to make and require a numerical rather than a visual comparison. In contrast, the bar chart gives a quick visual comparison of every data point.

A **pie chart** is a commonly used tool for showing how the parts of a whole are distributed. Although pie charts are popular and can quickly highlight the dominant parts of a whole, they are often not as effective as bar charts or tables. For example, comparing percentages accurately is often difficult with a pie chart but can be fairly easy with a bar chart (see Figure 11.9). Making pie charts easier to read with accuracy can require labeling each slice with data values, in which case a table might serve the purpose more effectively.[25]

> Pie charts are used frequently in business reports, but in many instances they are not as helpful to readers as bar charts and other types of visuals would be.

Data Visualization

Conventional charts and graphs are limited in several ways: Most types can show only a limited number of data points before becoming too cluttered to interpret, they often can't show complex relationships among data points, and they can represent only numeric data. As computer technologies continue to generate massive amounts of data that can be combined and connected in endless ways, a diverse class of display capabilities known as **data visualization** works to overcome all these drawbacks.

> Data visualization tools can overcome the limitations of conventional charts and other display types.

Data visualization is less about clarifying individual data points and more about extracting broad meaning from giant masses of data or putting the data in context.[26] For instance, the Facebook "friend wheel" in Figure 11.10b offers a visual sense of this particular Facebook user's network by showing which of his friends are friends of each other and thereby indicating "clustering" within the network (work friends, social friends, and so on). The diagram doesn't attempt to show quantities but rather the overall nature of the network.

> Unlike conventional charts, data visualization tools are more about uncovering broad meaning and finding hidden connections.

In addition to displaying large data sets and linkages within data sets, other kinds of visualization tools combine data with textual information to communicate complex or dynamic data much faster than conventional presentations can. For example, a *tag cloud* shows the relative frequency of terms, or tags (user-applied content labels), in an article, a blog, a website, survey data, or another collection of text.[27] Figure 11.10 on the next page shows a few of the many data visualization tools now available.

Many of these tools are also interactive, meaning you can perform such tasks as zooming in on specific areas, changing the orientation of a display to view it from different angles, or exploring the connections of particular elements within the data set. Also, as you explore and experiment with data visualization tools, keep in mind that, like all tools, they can be used to good effect or misused to bad effect. Visualizations that might look dazzling at first can

REAL-TIME UPDATES
Learn More by Reading This Article

Data Visualization and Infographics Gateway: A comprehensive collection for business communicators

This unique web resource offers links to a vast array of data visualization and infographics techniques and examples. Go to **http://real-timeupdates.com/bce5** and click on "Learn More." If you are using mybcommlab, you can access Real-Time Updates within each chapter or under Student Study Tools.

(a) Website Linkage Map Showing the Most Active Links to and from Apple's Homepage **(www.apple.com)**

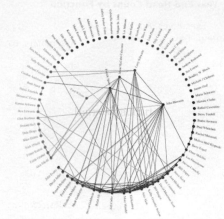

(b) Facebook "Friend Wheel" Showing How the Connections of One Facebook User Are Connected with One Another

(c) A Tag Cloud Showing the Relative Frequency of the 50 Most-Used Words in This Chapter (other than common words such as *and, or,* and *the*)

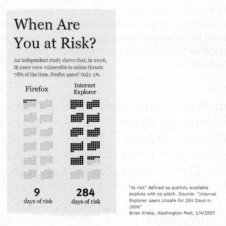

(d) Infographic That Uses a Calendar Motif to Suggest Differences in Browser Security Vulnerabilities

Figure 11.10 Data Visualization and Infographics
The range of data visualization displays is virtually endless; here are a few of the many ways to display complex sets of data.

actually have little or no practical communication value. In fact, some data visualizations are intended to be works of art more than practical tools.

Flowcharts and Organization Charts

Be aware that there is a formal symbolic "language" in flowcharting; each shape has a specific meaning.

A **flowchart** (see Figure 11.11) illustrates a sequence of events from start to finish; it is indispensable when illustrating processes, procedures, and sequential relationships. For general business purposes, you don't need to be too concerned about the specific shapes on a flowchart; just be sure to use them consistently. However, you should be aware that there is a formal flowchart "language," in which each shape has a specific meaning (diamonds are decision points, rectangles are process steps, and so on). If you're communicating with computer programmers and others who are accustomed to formal flowcharting, make sure you use the correct symbols in each case to avoid confusion.

As the name implies, an **organization chart** illustrates the positions, units, or functions in an organization and the ways they interrelate (see Figure 11.12). Organization charts can be used to portray almost any hierarchy, in fact, including the topics, subtopics, and supporting points you need to organize for a report.

Maps, Drawings, Diagrams, Infographics, and Photographs

Use maps to represent statistics by geographic area and to show spatial relationships.

Maps are useful for showing territories, routes, and locations. Simple maps are available via clip art libraries, but more powerful uses (such as automatically generating color-coded maps based on data inputs) usually require the specialized capabilities of *geographic information systems (GIS)*. You may also want to explore online resources such as Google Earth

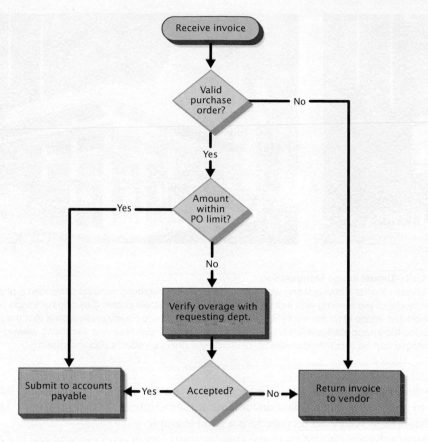

Figure 11.11   Flowchart
Flowcharts show sequences of events and are most valuable when the process or procedure has a number of decision points and variable paths.

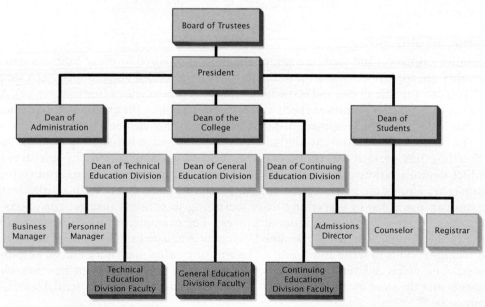

Figure 11.12   Organization Chart
An organization chart is the expected way to illustrate the hierarchy of positions in an organization.

(http://earth.google.com) and Bing maps (www.bing.com/maps), which offer a variety of mapping and aerial photography features.

Drawings can show an endless variety of business concepts, such as the network of suppliers in an industry, the flow of funds through a company, or the process for completing payroll each week. More complex diagrams can convey technical topics such as the operation

Drawings are sometimes better than photographs because they let you focus on the most important details.

Figure 11.13 Digital Image Manipulation
To show investors what a new building would look like in its environment, an artist combined a photograph of a scale model of the building with a photograph of the actual street scene. (The original image is on the left; the modified image is on the right.) Because the target audience clearly understands that the building doesn't exist, the image manipulation in this instance is not unethical. However, deceiving viewers by altering images can be considered unethical, particularly if doing so affects decision making.

of a machine or repair procedures. Diagrams that contain enough visual and textual information to function as independent documents are sometimes called **infographics**. The visual media example in Figure 3.3 on page 88 is a good example.

Use photographs for visual appeal and to show exact appearances.

Photographs offer both functional and decorative value, and nothing can top a photograph when you need to show exact appearances. However, in some situations, a photograph can show too much detail, which is one reason repair manuals frequently use drawings instead of photos, for instance. Because audiences expect photographs to show literal visual truths, you must take care when using image-processing tools such as Adobe Photoshop (see Figure 11.13).

Animation and Video

Computer animation and video are among the most specialized forms of business visuals; when they are appropriate and done well, they offer unparalleled visual impact. At a simple level, you can animate shapes and text within electronic presentations (see Chapter 12). At a more sophisticated level, software such as Adobe Flash enables the creation of multimedia files that include computer animation, digital video, and other elements.

The combination of low-cost digital video cameras and video-sharing websites such as YouTube has spurred a revolution in business video applications in recent years. Product demonstrations, company overviews, promotional presentations, and training seminars are among the most popular applications of business video. With a little creativity, you can use video in everything from recruiting to contests that get customers or employees involved in the promotional process. For example, before moving into his career in the insurance industry, Hamline University graduate Eric Binfet used his creative and technical skills to write and produce the winning video in a Dairy Queen employee contest. The video did such a great job of showcasing some important new branding elements that the store owner pitched it to corporate headquarters as a potential television commercial.[28]

Designing Effective Visuals

Computers make it easy to create visuals, but they also make it easy to create ineffective visuals. However, by following the design principles discussed on page 310, you can create basic visuals that are attractive and effective. If possible, have a professional designer set up a *template* for the various types of visuals you and your colleagues need to create. By specifying color palettes, font selections, slide layouts, and other choices, design templates have three important benefits: They help ensure better designs, they promote consistency across the organization, and they save everyone time by eliminating repetitive decision making.

Remember that the style and quality of your visuals communicate a subtle message about your relationship with the audience. A simple sketch might be fine for a working meeting but inappropriate for a formal presentation or report. On the other hand, elaborate, full-color visuals may be viewed as extravagant for an informal report but may be entirely appropriate for a message to top management or influential outsiders.

In addition to being well designed, visuals need to be well integrated with text. First, try to position your visuals so that your audience won't have to flip back and forth (in printed documents) or scroll (on-screen) between visuals and the text that discusses them. If space constraints prevent you from placing visuals close to relevant text, include pointers such as "Figure 2 (on the following page)" to help readers locate the image quickly. Second, clearly refer to visuals by number in the text of your report and help your readers understand the significance of visuals by referring to them before readers encounter them in the document or on-screen. Third, write effective *titles*, *captions*, and *legends* to complete the integration of your text and visuals. A **title** provides a short description that identifies the content and purpose of the visual. A **caption** usually offers additional discussion of the visual's content and can be several sentences long, if appropriate. A **legend** helps readers "decode" the visual by explaining what various colors, symbols, or other design choices mean.

> To tie visuals to the text, introduce them in the text and place them near the points they illustrate.

Be sure to check your visuals carefully for accuracy. Check for mistakes such as typographical errors, inconsistent color treatment, confusing or undocumented symbols, and misaligned elements. Make sure that your computer hasn't done something unexpected, such as arranging chart bars in an order you don't want or plotting line charts in unusual colors. Make sure your visuals are properly documented. Most important, make sure your visuals are honest—that they don't intentionally or unintentionally distort the truth.

> Proof visuals as carefully as you proof text.

Finally, step back and consider the ethical implications of your visuals. Visuals are easy to misuse, intentionally or unintentionally. To avoid ethical lapses in your visuals, consider all possible interpretations, provide enough background information for readers to interpret your visuals correctly, and don't hide or minimize visual information that readers need in order to make informed judgments.[29]

For more information on visual communication, including design principles, ethical matters, and the latest tools for creating and displaying visuals, visit http://real-timeupdates .com/bce5 and click on Chapter 11.

COMPLETING REPORTS AND PROPOSALS

5 LEARNING OBJECTIVE

Summarize the four tasks involved in completing business reports and proposals

As with shorter messages (Chapter 5), when you have finished your first draft, you need to perform four tasks to complete your document: revise, produce, proofread, and distribute.

Revising Reports and Proposals

The revision process is essentially the same for reports as for other business messages, although it may take considerably longer, depending on the length of your document. Evaluate your organization, style, and tone, making sure that your content is clear, logical, and reader oriented. Then work to improve the report's readability by varying sentence length, keeping paragraphs short, using lists and bullets, and adding headings and subheadings. Keep revising the content until it is clear, concise, and compelling. Remember that even minor mistakes can affect your credibility.

> The revision process for long reports can take considerable time, so be sure to plan ahead.

Tight, efficient writing that is easy to skim is always a plus, but it's especially important for impatient online audiences.[30] Review online content carefully; strip out all information that doesn't meet audience needs and condense everything else as much as possible. Audiences will gladly return to sites that deliver quality information quickly—and they'll avoid sites that don't.

> Tight, efficient writing is especially important with online content.

Producing a Formal Report

The parts included in a report depend on the type of report you are writing, the requirements of your audience, the organization you're working for, and the length of your report (see Figure 11.14 on the next page). The instructions here pertain primarily to printed reports, but you can adapt many of these elements to reports delivered electronically.

> The number and variety of parts you include in a report depend on the type of report, audience requirements, organizational expectations, and report length.

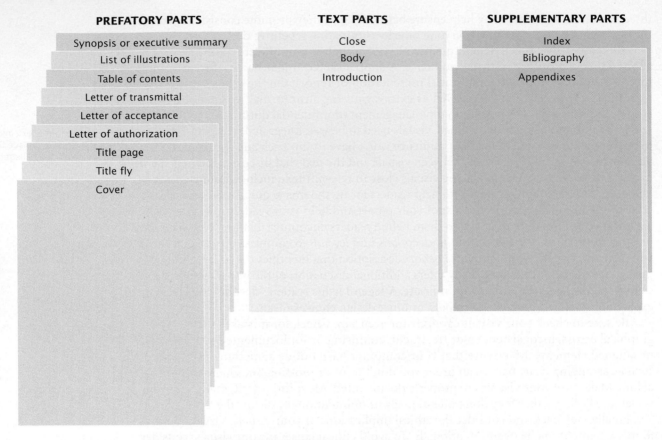

PREFATORY PARTS	TEXT PARTS	SUPPLEMENTARY PARTS
Synopsis or executive summary	Close	Index
List of illustrations	Body	Bibliography
Table of contents	Introduction	Appendixes
Letter of transmittal		
Letter of acceptance		
Letter of authorization		
Title page		
Title fly		
Cover		

Figure 11.14 Parts of a Formal Report
Formal reports can contain a variety of prefatory and supplemental parts in addition to the main text.

Most prefatory parts (such as the table of contents) should be placed on their own pages. However, the various parts in the report text are often run together. If your introduction is only a paragraph long, don't bother with a page break before moving into the body of your report. If the introduction runs longer than a page, however, a page break can signal the reader that a major shift is about to occur.

For an illustration of how the various parts fit together in a report, see Figure 11.15, beginning on the next page. This report was prepared by Linda Moreno, manager of the cost accounting department at Electrovision, a high-tech company based in Los Gatos, California. Electrovision's main product is optical character recognition equipment, which the U.S. Postal Service uses for sorting mail. Moreno's job is to help analyze the company's costs. Moreno used the direct approach and organized her report based on conclusions and recommendations.

Prefatory Parts of a Formal Report

Formal reports can contain a variety of prefatory parts; choose the elements that will make your report most successful.

Prefatory parts come before the main text of your report and help readers decide whether and how to read the report. Depending on the nature of the report, consider including some or all of the following elements:[31]

- **Cover.** The cover should start with a concise title that gives readers the information they need to grasp the purpose and scope of the report. For a formal report, choose high-quality *cover stock* (heavy, high-quality paper).

- **Title fly.** Some formal reports open with a plain sheet of paper that has only the title of the report on it, although this is certainly not necessary.

- **Title page.** The title page typically includes the report title; the name, job title, and address of the person, group, or organization that authorized the report; the name, job title, and address of the person, group, or organization that prepared the report; and the date on which the report was submitted. For many reports, including this information on the cover (as on page 321) and not using a title page is perfectly acceptable.

(continued on page 335)

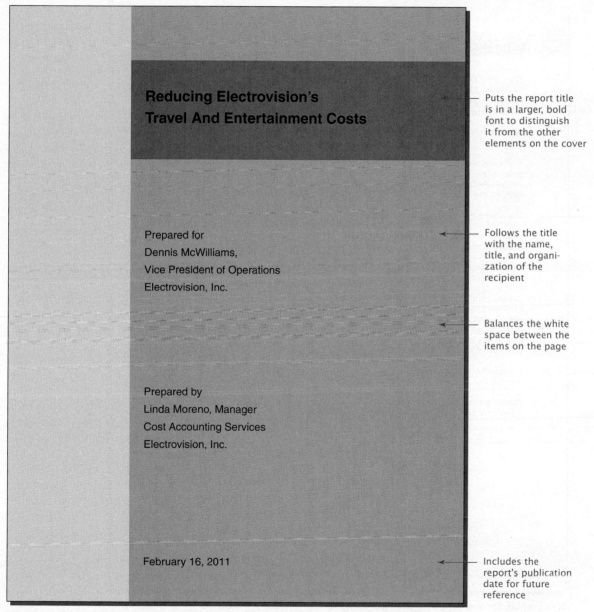

Reducing Electrovision's
Travel And Entertainment Costs

Puts the report title is in a larger, bold font to distinguish it from the other elements on the cover

Prepared for
Dennis McWilliams,
Vice President of Operations
Electrovision, Inc.

Follows the title with the name, title, and organization of the recipient

Balances the white space between the items on the page

Prepared by
Linda Moreno, Manager
Cost Accounting Services
Electrovision, Inc.

February 16, 2011

Includes the report's publication date for future reference

The "how-to" tone of Moreno's title is appropriate for an action-oriented report that emphasizes recommendations. A more neutral title, such as "An Analysis of Electrovision's Travel and Entertainment Costs," would be more suitable for an informational report.

Figure 11.15   Analyzing an Effective Formal Report *(continued)*

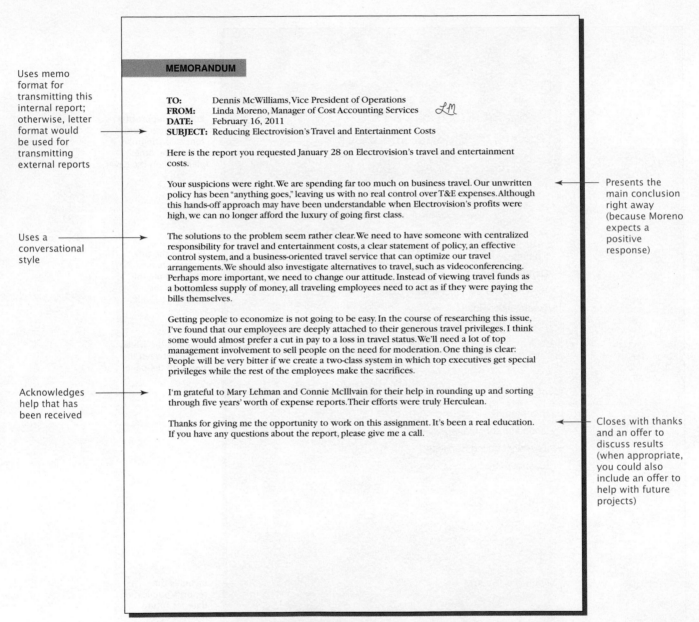

Uses memo format for transmitting this internal report; otherwise, letter format would be used for transmitting external reports

Uses a conversational style

Acknowledges help that has been received

Presents the main conclusion right away (because Moreno expects a positive response)

Closes with thanks and an offer to discuss results (when appropriate, you could also include an offer to help with future projects)

MEMORANDUM

TO: Dennis McWilliams, Vice President of Operations
FROM: Linda Moreno, Manager of Cost Accounting Services   *LM*
DATE: February 16, 2011
SUBJECT: Reducing Electrovision's Travel and Entertainment Costs

Here is the report you requested January 28 on Electrovision's travel and entertainment costs.

Your suspicions were right. We are spending far too much on business travel. Our unwritten policy has been "anything goes," leaving us with no real control over T&E expenses. Although this hands-off approach may have been understandable when Electrovision's profits were high, we can no longer afford the luxury of going first class.

The solutions to the problem seem rather clear. We need to have someone with centralized responsibility for travel and entertainment costs, a clear statement of policy, an effective control system, and a business-oriented travel service that can optimize our travel arrangements. We should also investigate alternatives to travel, such as videoconferencing. Perhaps more important, we need to change our attitude. Instead of viewing travel funds as a bottomless supply of money, all traveling employees need to act as if they were paying the bills themselves.

Getting people to economize is not going to be easy. In the course of researching this issue, I've found that our employees are deeply attached to their generous travel privileges. I think some would almost prefer a cut in pay to a loss in travel status. We'll need a lot of top management involvement to sell people on the need for moderation. One thing is clear: People will be very bitter if we create a two-class system in which top executives get special privileges while the rest of the employees make the sacrifices.

I'm grateful to Mary Lehman and Connie McIllvain for their help in rounding up and sorting through five years' worth of expense reports. Their efforts were truly Herculean.

Thanks for giving me the opportunity to work on this assignment. It's been a real education. If you have any questions about the report, please give me a call.

In this report, Moreno decided to write a brief memo of transmittal and include a separate executive summary. Short reports (fewer than 10 pages) often combine the synopsis or executive summary with the memo or letter of transmittal.

Figure 11.15   *(continued)*

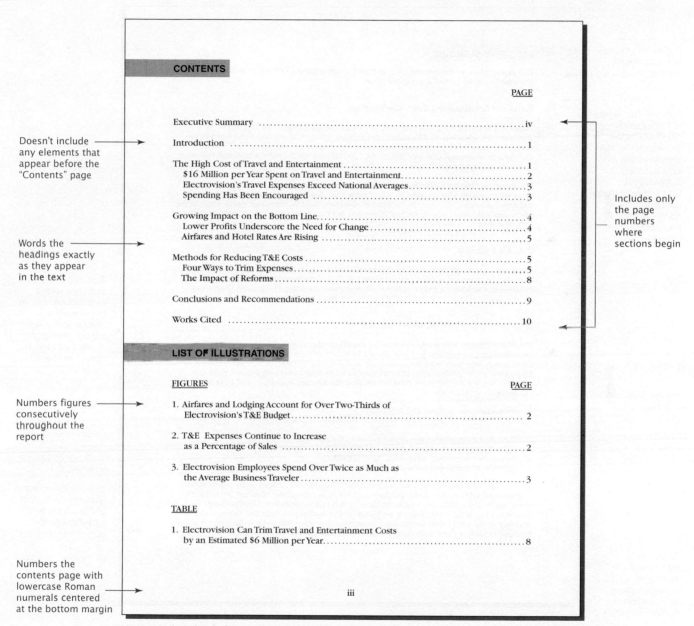

Doesn't include any elements that appear before the "Contents" page

Words the headings exactly as they appear in the text

Numbers figures consecutively throughout the report

Numbers the contents page with lowercase Roman numerals centered at the bottom margin

Includes only the page numbers where sections begin

CONTENTS

LIST OF ILLUSTRATIONS

iii

Moreno included only first- and second-level headings in her table of contents, even though the report contains third-level headings. She prefers a shorter table of contents that focuses attention on the main divisions of thought. She used informative titles, which are appropriate for a report to a receptive audience.

Figure 11.15 *(continued)*

Begins by stating the purpose of the report

Presents the points in the executive summary in the same order as they appear in the report, using subheadings that summarize the content of the main sections of the report

Continues numbering the executive summary pages with lowercase Roman numerals

EXECUTIVE SUMMARY

This report analyzes Electrovision's travel and entertainment (T&E) costs and presents recommendations for reducing those costs.

Travel and Entertainment Costs Are Too High

Travel and entertainment is a large and growing expense category for Electrovision. The company spends over $16 million per year on business travel, and these costs have been increasing by 12 percent annually. Company employees make roughly 3,390 trips each year at an average cost per trip of $4,720. Airfares are the biggest expense, followed by hotels, meals, and rental cars.

The nature of Electrovision's business does require extensive travel, but the company's costs are excessive: Our employees spend more than twice the national average on travel and entertainment. Although the location of the company's facilities may partly explain this discrepancy, the main reason for our high costs is a management style that gives employees little incentive to economize.

Cuts Are Essential

Electrovision management now recognizes the need to gain more control over this element of costs. The company is currently entering a period of declining profits, prompting management to look for every opportunity to reduce spending. At the same time, rising airfares and hotel rates are making T&E expenses more significant.

Electrovision Can Save $6 Million per Year

Fortunately, Electrovision has a number of excellent opportunities for reducing T&E costs. Savings of up to $6 million per year should be achievable, judging by the experience of other companies. A sensible travel-management program can save companies as much as 35 percent a year (Gilligan 39–40), and we should be able to save even more, since we purchase many more business-class tickets than the average. Four steps will help us cut costs:

1. Hire a director of travel and entertainment to assume overall responsibility for T&E spending, policies, and technologies, including the hiring and management of a national travel agency.
2. Educate employees on the need for cost containment, both in avoiding unnecessary travel and reducing costs when travel is necessary.
3. Negotiate preferential rates with travel providers.
4. Implement technological alternatives to travel, such as virtual meetings.

As necessary as these changes are, they will likely hurt morale, at least in the short term. Management will need to make a determined effort to explain the rationale for reduced spending. By exercising moderation in their own travel arrangements, Electrovision executives can set a good example and help other employees accept the changes. On the plus side, using travel alternatives such as web conferencing will reduce the travel burden on many employees and help them balance their business and personal lives.

Targets a receptive audience with a hard-hitting tone in the executive summary (a more neutral approach would be better for hostile or skeptical readers)

Executive summary uses the same font and paragraph treatment as the text of the report

iv

Moreno decided to include an executive summary because her report is aimed at a mixed audience, some of whom are interested in the details of her report and others who just want the "big picture." The executive summary is aimed at the second group, giving them enough information to make a decision without burdening them with the task of reading the entire report.

Her writing style matches the serious nature of the content without sounding distant or stiff. Moreno chose the formal approach because several members of her audience are considerably higher up in the organization, and she did not want to sound too familiar. In addition, her company prefers the impersonal style for formal reports.

Figure 11.15 *(continued)*

Uses a color bar to highlight the report title and the first-level headings; a variety of other design treatments are possible as well.

REDUCING ELECTROVISION'S TRAVEL AND ENTERTAINMENT COSTS

INTRODUCTION

Electrovision has always encouraged a significant amount of business travel. To compensate employees for the stress and inconvenience of frequent trips, management has authorized generous travel and entertainment (T&E) allowances. This philosophy has been good for morale, but last year Electrovision spent $16 million on travel and entertainment—$7 million more than it spent on research and development.

This year's T&E costs will affect profits even more, due to increases in airline fares and hotel rates. Also, the company anticipates that profits will be relatively weak for a variety of other reasons. Therefore, Dennis McWilliams, Vice President of Operations, has asked the accounting department to explore ways to reduce the T&E budget.

The purpose of this report is to analyze T&E expenses, evaluate the effect of recent hotel and airfare increases, and suggest ways to tighten control over T&E costs. The report outlines several steps that could reduce Electrovision's expenses, but the precise financial impact of these measures is difficult to project. The estimates presented here provide a "best guess" view of what Electrovision can expect to save.

In preparing this report, the accounting department analyzed internal expense reports for the past five years to determine how much Electrovision spends on travel and entertainment. These figures were then compared with average statistics compiled by Dow Jones (publisher of the *Wall Street Journal*) and presented as the Dow Jones Travel Index. We also analyzed trends and suggestions published in a variety of business journal articles to see how other companies are coping with the high cost of business travel.

THE HIGH COST OF TRAVEL AND ENTERTAINMENT

Although many companies view travel and entertainment as an incidental cost of doing business, the dollars add up. At Electrovision the bill for airfares, hotels, rental cars, meals, and entertainment totaled $16 million last year. Our T&E budget has increased by 12 percent per year for the past five years. Compared to the average U.S. business traveler, Electrovision's expenditures are high, largely because of management's generous policy on travel benefits.

Opens by establishing the need for action

Mentions sources and methods to increase credibility and to give readers a complete picture of the study's background

Uses a *running footer* that contains the report title and the page number

In her brief introduction, Moreno counts on topic sentences and transitions to indicate that she is discussing the purpose, scope, and limitations of the study.

Figure 11.15 *(continued)*

$16 Million per Year Spent on Travel and Entertainment

Electrovision's annual budget for travel and entertainment is only 8 percent of sales. Because this is a relatively small expense category compared with such things as salaries and commissions, it is tempting to dismiss T&E costs as insignificant. However, T&E is Electrovision's third-largest controllable expense, directly behind salaries and information systems.

Last year Electrovision personnel made about 3,390 trips at an average cost per trip of $4,720. The typical trip involved a round-trip flight of 3,000 kilometers, meals, and hotel accommodations for two or three days, and a rental car. Roughly 80 percent of trips were made by 20 percent of the staff—top management and sales personnel traveled most, averaging 18 trips per year.

Figure 1 illustrates how the T&E budget is spent. The largest categories are airfares and lodging, which together account for $7 out of $10 that employees spend on travel and entertainment. This spending breakdown has been relatively steady for the past five years and is consistent with the distribution of expenses experienced by other companies.

Figure 1
Airfares and Lodging Account for Over
Two-Thirds of Electrovision's T&E Budget

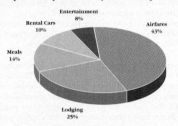

Although the composition of the T&E budget has been consistent, its size has not. As mentioned earlier, these expenditures have increased by about 12 percent per year for the past five years, roughly twice the rate of the company's sales growth (see Figure 2). This rate of growth makes T&E Electrovision's fastest-growing expense item.

Figure 2
T&E Expenses Continue to Increase as a
Percentage of Sales

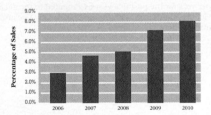

Reducing Electrovision's Travel and Entertainment Costs   P a g e   **2**

Places the visual as close as possible to the point it illustrates

Gives each visual a title that clearly indicates what it's about; titles are consistently placed to the left of each visual

Moreno opens the first main section of the body with a topic sentence that introduces an important fact about the subject of the section. Then she orients the reader to the three major points developed in the section.

Figure 11.15   *(continued)*

Numbers the visuals consecutively and refers to them in the text by their numbers

Electrovision's Travel Expenses Exceed National Averages

Much of our travel budget is justified. Two major factors contribute to Electrovision's high T&E budget:

- With our headquarters on the West Coast and our major customer on the East Coast, we naturally spend a lot of money on cross-country flights.

- A great deal of travel takes place between our headquarters here on the West Coast and the manufacturing operations in Detroit, Boston, and Dallas. Corporate managers and division personnel make frequent trips to coordinate these disparate operations.

However, even though a good portion of Electrovision's travel budget is justifiable, the company spends considerably more on T&E than the average business traveler (see Figure 3).

Introduces visuals before they appear and indicates what readers should notice about the data

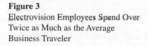

Figure 3
Electrovision Employees Spend Over
Twice as Much as the Average
Business Traveler

Source: *Wall Street Journal* and
company records

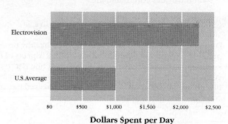

Dollars Spent per Day

The Dow Jones Travel Index calculates the average cost per day of business travel in the United States, based on average airfare, hotel rates, and rental car rates. The average fluctuates weekly as travel companies change their rates, but it has been running at about $1,000 per day for the last year or so. In contrast, Electrovision's average daily expense over the past year has been $2,250—a hefty 125 percent higher than average. This figure is based on the average trip cost of $4,720 listed earlier and an average trip length of 2.1 days.

Spending Has Been Encouraged

Although a variety of factors may contribute to this differential, Electrovision's relatively high T&E costs are at least partially attributable to the company's philosophy and management style. Since many employees do not enjoy business travel, management has tried to make the trips more pleasant by authorizing business-class airfare, luxury hotel accommodations, and full-size rental cars. The sales staff is encouraged to entertain clients at top restaurants and to invite them to cultural and sporting events.

The chart in Figure 3 is simple but effective; Moreno includes just enough data to make her point. Notice how she is as careful about the appearance of her report as she is about the quality of its content.

Figure 11.15   *(continued)*

Uses a bulleted list to make it easy for readers to identify and distinguish related points

The cost of these privileges is easy to overlook, given the weakness of Electrovision's system for keeping track of T&E expenses:

- The monthly financial records do not contain a separate category for travel and entertainment; the information is buried under Cost of Goods Sold and under Selling, General, and Administrative Expenses.

- Each department head is given authority to approve any expense report, regardless of how large it may be.

- Receipts are not required for expenditures of less than $100.

- Individuals are allowed to make their own travel arrangements.

- No one is charged with the responsibility for controlling the company's total spending on travel and entertainment.

GROWING IMPACT ON THE BOTTOM LINE

During the past three years, the company's healthy profits have resulted in relatively little pressure to push for tighter controls over all aspects of the business. However, as we all know, the situation is changing. We're projecting flat to declining profits for the next two years, a situation that has prompted all of us to search for ways to cut costs. At the same time, rising airfares and hotel rates have increased the impact of T&E expenses on the company's financial results.

Lower Profits Underscore the Need for Change

The next two years promise to be difficult for Electrovision. After several years of steady increases in spending, the Postal Service is tightening procurement policies for automated mail-handling equipment. Funding for the A-12 optical character reader has been canceled. As a consequence, the marketing department expects sales to drop by 15 percent. Although Electrovision is negotiating several other promising R&D contracts, the marketing department does not foresee any major procurements for the next two to three years.

At the same time, Electrovision is facing cost increases on several fronts. As we have known for several months, the new production facility now under construction in Salt Lake City, Utah, is behind schedule and over budget. Labor contracts in Boston and Dallas will expire within the next six months, and plant managers there anticipate that significant salary and benefits concessions may be necessary to avoid strikes.

Moreover, marketing and advertising costs are expected to increase as we attempt to strengthen these activities to better cope with competitive pressures. Given the expected decline in revenues and increase in costs, the Executive Committee's prediction that profits will fall by 12 percent in the coming fiscal year does not seem overly pessimistic.

Uses informative headings to focus reader attention on the main points (such headings are appropriate when a report uses direct order and is intended for a receptive audience; however, descriptive headings are more effective when a report is in indirect order and readers are less receptive)

Reducing Electrovision's Travel and Entertainment Costs   P a g e **4**

Moreno designed her report to include plenty of white space so even those pages that lack visuals are still attractive and easy to read.

Figure 11.15 *(continued)*

Airfares and Hotel Rates Are Rising

Business travelers have grown accustomed to frequent fare wars and discounting in the travel industry in recent years. Excess capacity and aggressive price competition, particularly in the airline business, made travel a relative bargain.

Documents the facts to add weight to Moreno's argument →

However, that situation has changed as weaker competitors have been forced out and the remaining players have grown stronger and smarter. Airlines and hotels are better at managing inventory and keeping occupancy rates high, which translates into higher costs for Electrovision. Last year saw some of the steepest rate hikes in years. Business airfares (tickets most likely to be purchased by business travelers) jumped more than 40 percent in many markets. The trend is expected to continue, with rates increasing another 5 to 10 percent overall (Phillips 331; "Travel Costs Under Pressure" 30; Dahl B6).

Given the fact that air and hotel costs account for almost 70 percent of our T&E budget, the trend toward higher prices in these two categories will have serious consequences, unless management takes action to control these costs.

METHODS FOR REDUCING T&E COSTS

Gives recommendations an objective flavor by pointing out both the benefits and the risks of taking action →

By implementing a number of reforms, management can expect to reduce Electrovision's T&E budget by as much as 40 percent. This estimate is based on the general assessment made by American Express (Gilligan 39) and on the fact that we have an opportunity to significantly reduce air travel costs by eliminating business-class travel. However, these measures are likely to be unpopular with employees. To gain acceptance for such changes, management will need to sell employees on the need for moderation in T&E allowances.

Four Ways to Trim Expenses

By researching what other companies are doing to curb T&E expenses, the accounting department has identified four prominent opportunities that should enable Electrovision to save about $6 million annually in travel-related costs.

Institute Tighter Spending Controls

A single individual should be appointed director of travel and entertainment to spearhead the effort to gain control of the T&E budget. More than a third of all U.S. companies now employ travel managers ("Businesses Use Savvy Managers" 4). The director should be familiar with the travel industry and should be well versed in both accounting and information technology. The director should also report to the vice president of operations. The director's first priorities should be to establish a written T&E policy and a cost-control system.

Electrovision currently has no written policy on travel and entertainment, a step that is widely recommended by air travel experts (Smith D4). Creating a policy would clarify management's position and serve as a vehicle for communicating the need for moderation.

Moreno creates a forceful tone by using action verbs in the third-level subheadings of this section. This approach is appropriate to the nature of the study and the attitude of the audience. However, in a status-conscious organization, the imperative verbs might sound a bit too presumptuous coming from a junior member of the staff.

Figure 11.15   *(continued)*

Breaks up text
with bulleted lists,
which not only call
attention to important
points but also add
visual interest

At a minimum, the policy should include the following:

- All travel and entertainment should be strictly related to business and should be approved in advance.

- Except under special circumstances to be approved on a case-by-case basis, employees should travel by coach and stay in mid-range business hotels.

- The T&E policy should apply equally to employees at all levels.

To implement the new policy, Electrovision will need to create a system for controlling T&E expenses. Each department should prepare an annual T&E budget as part of its operating plan. These budgets should be presented in detail so that management can evaluate how T&E dollars will be spent and can recommend appropriate cuts. To help management monitor performance relative to these budgets, the director of travel should prepare monthly financial statements showing actual T&E expenditures by department.

The director of travel should also be responsible for retaining a business-oriented travel service that will schedule all employee business trips and look for the best travel deals, particularly in airfares. In addition to centralizing Electrovision's reservation and ticketing activities, the agency will negotiate reduced group rates with hotels and rental car firms. The agency selected should have offices nationwide so that all Electrovision facilities can channel their reservations through the same company. This is particularly important in light of the dizzying array of often wildly different airfares available between some cities. It's not uncommon to find dozens of fares along commonly traveled routes (Rowe 30). In addition, the director can help coordinate travel across the company to secure group discounts whenever possible (Barker 31; Miller B6).

Specifies the
steps required
to implement
recommendations

Reduce Unnecessary Travel and Entertainment

One of the easiest ways to reduce expenses is to reduce the amount of traveling and entertaining that occurs. An analysis of last year's expenditures suggests that as much as 30 percent of Electrovision's travel and entertainment is discretionary. The professional staff spent $2.8 million attending seminars and conferences last year. Although these gatherings are undoubtedly beneficial, the company could save money by sending fewer representatives to each function and perhaps by eliminating some of the less valuable seminars.

Similarly, Electrovision could economize on trips between headquarters and divisions by reducing the frequency of such visits and by sending fewer people on each trip. Although there is often no substitute for face-to-face meetings, management could try to resolve more internal issues through telephone, electronic, and written communication.

Electrovision can also reduce spending by urging employees to economize. Instead of flying business class, employees can fly coach class or take advantage of discount fares. Rather than ordering a $50 bottle of wine, employees can select a less expensive bottle or dispense with

Reducing Electrovision's Travel and Entertainment Costs   P a g e   **6**

Moreno takes care not to overstep the boundaries of her analysis. For instance, she doesn't analyze the value of the seminars that employees attend every year, so she avoids any absolute statements about reducing travel to seminars.

Figure 11.15 *(continued)*

alcohol entirely. People can book rooms at moderately priced hotels and drive smaller rental cars.

Obtain Lowest Rates from Travel Providers

Apart from urging employees to economize, Electrovision can also save money by searching for the lowest available airfares, hotel rates, and rental car fees. Currently, few employees have the time or knowledge to seek out travel bargains. When they need to travel, they make the most convenient and comfortable arrangements. A professional travel service will be able to obtain lower rates from travel providers.

Judging by the experience of other companies, Electrovision may be able to trim as much as 30 to 40 percent from the travel budget simply by looking for bargains in airfares and negotiating group rates with hotels and rental car companies. Electrovision should be able to achieve these economies by analyzing its travel patterns, identifying frequently visited locations, and selecting a few hotels that are willing to reduce rates in exchange for guaranteed business. At the same time, the company should be able to save up to 40 percent on rental car charges by negotiating a corporate rate.

The possibilities for economizing are promising; however, making the best travel arrangements often requires trade-offs such as the following:

- The best fares might not always be the lowest. Indirect flights are usually cheaper, but they take longer and may end up costing more in lost work time.

- The cheapest tickets often require booking 14 or even 30 days in advance, which is often impossible for us.

- Discount tickets are usually nonrefundable, which is a serious drawback when a trip needs to be canceled at the last minute.

Replace Travel with Technological Alternatives

Less-expensive travel options promise significant savings, but the biggest cost reductions over the long term might come from replacing travel with virtual meeting technology. Both analysts and corporate users say that the early kinks that hampered online meetings have largely been worked out, and the latest systems are fast, easy to learn, and easy to use (Solheim 26). For example, Webex (a leading provider of webconferencing services) offers everything from simple, impromptu team meetings to major online events with up to 3,000 participants ("Online Meeting Solutions").

One of the first responsibilities of the new travel director should be an evaluation of these technologies and a recommendation for integrating them throughout Electrovision's operations.

Reducing Electrovision's Travel and Entertainment Costs   Page **7**

Points out possible difficulties to show that all angles have been considered and to build confidence in her judgment

Note how Moreno makes the transition from section to section. The first sentence under the second heading on this page refers to the subject of the previous paragraph and signals a shift in thought.

Figure 11.15 *(continued)*

The Impact of Reforms

By implementing tighter controls, reducing unnecessary expenses, negotiating more favorable rates, and exploring alternatives to travel, Electrovision should be able to reduce its T&E budget significantly. As Table 1 illustrates, the combined savings should be in the neighborhood of $6 million, although the precise figures are somewhat difficult to project.

Uses complete sentences to help readers focus immediately on the point of the table

Uses informative title in the table, which is consistent with the way headings are handled in this report and is appropriate for a report to a receptive audience

Table 1
Electrovision Can Trim Travel and Entertainment Costs by an Estimated $6 Million per Year

SOURCE OF SAVINGS	ESTIMATED SAVINGS
Switching from business-class to coach airfare	$2,300,000
Negotiating preferred hotel rates	940,000
Negotiating preferred rental car rates	460,000
Systematically searching for lower airfares	375,000
Reducing interdivisional travel	675,000
Reducing seminar and conference attendance	1,250,000
TOTAL POTENTIAL SAVINGS	**$6,000,000**

Includes financial estimates to help management envision the impact of the suggestions, even though estimated savings are difficult to project

To achieve the economies outlined in the table, Electrovision will incur expenses for hiring a director of travel and for implementing a T&E cost-control system. These costs are projected at $115,000: $105,000 per year in salary and benefits for the new employee and a one-time expense of $10,000 for the cost-control system. The cost of retaining a full-service travel agency is negligible, even with the service fees that many are now passing along from airlines and other service providers.

The measures required to achieve these savings are likely to be unpopular with employees. Electrovision personnel are accustomed to generous T&E allowances, and they are likely to resent having these privileges curtailed. To alleviate their disappointment

- Management should make a determined effort to explain why the changes are necessary.

- The director of corporate communication should be asked to develop a multifaceted campaign that will communicate the importance of curtailing T&E costs.

- Management should set a positive example by adhering strictly to the new policies.

- The limitations should apply equally to employees at all levels in the organization.

Note how Moreno calls attention in the first paragraph to items in the following table, without repeating the information in the table.

Figure 11.15   *(continued)*

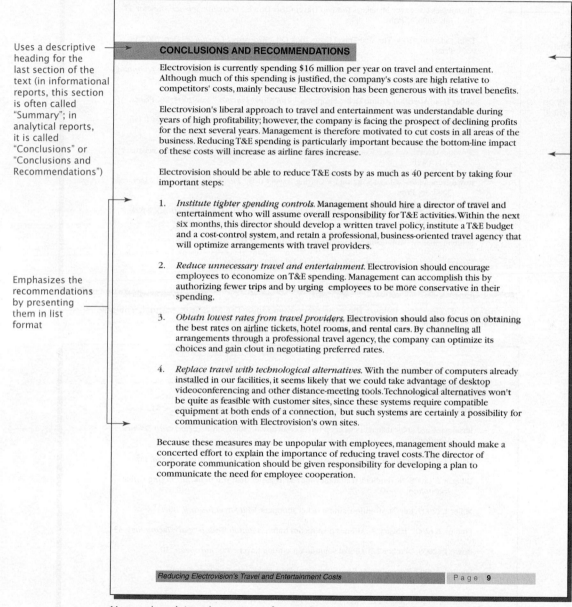

Uses a descriptive heading for the last section of the text (in informational reports, this section is often called "Summary"; in analytical reports, it is called "Conclusions" or "Conclusions and Recommendations")

Emphasizes the recommendations by presenting them in list format

Summarizes conclusions in the first two paragraphs—a good approach because Moreno organized her report around conclusions and recommendations, so readers have already been introduced to them

CONCLUSIONS AND RECOMMENDATIONS

Electrovision is currently spending $16 million per year on travel and entertainment. Although much of this spending is justified, the company's costs are high relative to competitors' costs, mainly because Electrovision has been generous with its travel benefits.

Electrovision's liberal approach to travel and entertainment was understandable during years of high profitability; however, the company is facing the prospect of declining profits for the next several years. Management is therefore motivated to cut costs in all areas of the business. Reducing T&E spending is particularly important because the bottom-line impact of these costs will increase as airline fares increase.

Electrovision should be able to reduce T&E costs by as much as 40 percent by taking four important steps:

1. *Institute tighter spending controls.* Management should hire a director of travel and entertainment who will assume overall responsibility for T&E activities. Within the next six months, this director should develop a written travel policy, institute a T&E budget and a cost-control system, and retain a professional, business-oriented travel agency that will optimize arrangements with travel providers.

2. *Reduce unnecessary travel and entertainment.* Electrovision should encourage employees to economize on T&E spending. Management can accomplish this by authorizing fewer trips and by urging employees to be more conservative in their spending.

3. *Obtain lowest rates from travel providers.* Electrovision should also focus on obtaining the best rates on airline tickets, hotel rooms, and rental cars. By channeling all arrangements through a professional travel agency, the company can optimize its choices and gain clout in negotiating preferred rates.

4. *Replace travel with technological alternatives.* With the number of computers already installed in our facilities, it seems likely that we could take advantage of desktop videoconferencing and other distance-meeting tools. Technological alternatives won't be quite as feasible with customer sites, since these systems require compatible equipment at both ends of a connection, but such systems are certainly a possibility for communication with Electrovision's own sites.

Because these measures may be unpopular with employees, management should make a concerted effort to explain the importance of reducing travel costs. The director of corporate communication should be given responsibility for developing a plan to communicate the need for employee cooperation.

Reducing Electrovision's Travel and Entertainment Costs   Page **9**

Moreno doesn't introduce any new facts in this section. In a longer report she might have divided this section into subsections, labeled "Conclusions" and "Recommendations," to distinguish between the two.

Figure 11.15 *(continued)*

Lists references alphabetically by the author's last name, and when the author is unknown, by the title of the reference (see Appendix B for additional details on preparing reference lists)

WORKS CITED

Barker, Julie. "How to Rein in Group Travel Costs." *Successful Meetings* Feb. 2011: 31. Print.

"Businesses Use Savvy Managers to Keep Travel Costs Down." *Christian Science Monitor* 17 July 2008: 4. Print.

Dahl, Jonathan. "2000: The Year Travel Costs Took Off." *Wall Street Journal* 29 Dec. 2007: B6. Print.

Gilligan, Edward P. "Trimming Your T&E Is Easier Than You Think." *Managing Office Technology* Nov. 2008: 39–40. Print.

Miller, Lisa. "Attention, Airline Ticket Shoppers." *Wall Street Journal* 7 July 2007: B6. Print.

Phillips, Edward H. "Airlines Post Record Traffic." *Aviation Week & Space Technology* 8 Jan. 2007: 331. Print.

"Product Overview: Cisco WebEx Meeting Center," *Webex.com.* 2011. WebEx, n.d. 2 February 2011. Web.

Rowe, Irene Vlitos. "Global Solution for Cutting Travel Costs." *European Business* 12 Oct. 2008: 30. Print.

Smith, Carol. "Rising, Erratic Airfares Make Company Policy Vital." *Los Angeles Times* 2 Nov. 2007: D4. Print.

Solheim, Shelley. "Web Conferencing Made Easy." *eWeek* 22 Aug. 2008: 26. Web.

"Travel Costs Under Pressure." *Purchasing* 15 Feb. 2007: 30. Print.

Moreno's list of references follows the style recommended in The MLA Style Manual. The box below shows how these sources would be cited following APA style.

REFERENCES

Barker, J. (2011, February). How to rein in group travel costs. *Successful Meetings,* 31.

Businesses use savvy managers to keep travel costs down. (2008, July 17). *Christian Science Monitor,* 4.

Dahl, J. (2007, December 29). 2000: The year travel costs took off. *Wall Street Journal,* B6.

Gilligan, E. (2008, November). Trimming your T&E is easier than you think. *Managing Office Technology,* 39–40.

Miller, L. (2007, July 7). Attention, airline ticket shoppers. *Wall Street Journal,* B6.

Phillips, E. (2007, January 8). Airlines post record traffic. *Aviation Week & Space Technology,* 331.

Rowe, I. (2008, October 12). Global solution for cutting travel costs. *European,* 30.

Smith, C. (2007, November 2). Rising, erratic airfares make company policy vital. *Los Angeles Times,* D4.

Solheim, S. (2008, August 22). Web conferencing made easy. *eWeek,* 26.

Travel costs under pressure. (2007, February 15). *Purchasing,* 30.

WebEx.com. (2011). *Product Overview: Cisco WebEx Meeting Center.* Retrieved 2 February 2011, from http://www.webex.com/product-overview/index.html.

Figure 11.15   *(continued)*

- **Letter of authorization.** If you received written authorization to prepare the report, you may want to include that letter or memo in your report.
- **Letter of transmittal.** The *letter* or *memo of transmittal* introduces the report on your behalf. The opening discusses scope, methods, and limitations. The body can highlight important sections of the report, suggest follow-up studies, offer details to help readers use the report, and acknowledge help from others. The close can include a note of thanks for the assignment, an expression of willingness to discuss the report, and an offer to assist with future projects (see page 322).
- **Table of contents.** The contents page lists report parts and text headings to indicate the location and hierarchy of the information in the report. List all prefatory parts that come after the contents page and all supplementary parts (see page 323).
- **List of illustrations.** Not all reports include a list of illustrations, but consider including one if the illustrations are particularly important and you want to call attention to them.
- **Synopsis.** A **synopsis**—sometimes called an **abstract**—is a brief overview (one page or less) of a report's most important points. The phrasing of a synopsis can be *informative* (presenting the main points in the order in which they appear in the text) if you're using the direct approach or *descriptive* (simply describing what the report is about, without "giving away the ending") if you're using the indirect approach.
- **Executive summary.** Instead of a synopsis or an abstract, a longer report may include an **executive summary**—a fully developed "mini" version of the report—for readers who lack the time or motivation to read the entire document.

Text of a Report

The heart of a report is the text, with its introduction, body, and close. If you have a synopsis or an executive summary, minimize redundancy by balancing your introduction with the material in your summary, as Moreno does in her report (Figure 11.15). Moreno's executive summary is fairly detailed, so she makes her introduction relatively brief.

Moreno's report also gives you a good idea of the types of supporting detail commonly included in the text body. Include only the essential supporting data in the body; put any additional detail in an appendix, if applicable.

In a long report, the close may be labeled "Summary" or "Conclusions and Recommendations." Because Moreno organized her report with the direct approach (so her audience has read the key message points in the body), her close is relatively brief. When using the indirect approach, you may use the close to present your recommendations and conclusions for the first time, in which case this section could be more extensive.

> If you include a synopsis or an executive summary, keep your introduction brief.

Supplementary Parts of a Report

Supplementary parts follow the text of a report and provide information for readers who seek more detailed discussion. Supplements are more common in long reports than in short ones. They typically include the following:

> The supplementary parts provide additional detail and reference materials.

- **Appendixes.** An appendix contains additional information for readers who want it—information related to the report but not included in the text because it is too lengthy, is too bulky, or lacks direct relevance. Be sure to list appendixes in your table of contents and refer to them as appropriate in the text.
- **Bibliography.** The bibliography lists the secondary sources you consulted. For more on citing sources, see Appendix B.
- **Index.** An index is an alphabetical list of names, places, and subjects mentioned in the report, along with the pages on which they occur. (See the index of this book for an example.)

Producing a Formal Proposal

Formal proposals contain many of the same components as other formal reports, but the special nature of proposals does require some unique elements (see Figure 11.16 on page 336).

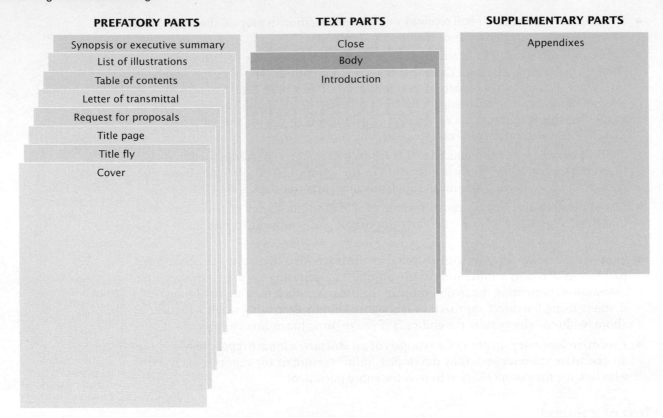

PREFATORY PARTS

- Synopsis or executive summary
- List of illustrations
- Table of contents
- Letter of transmittal
- Request for proposals
- Title page
- Title fly
- Cover

TEXT PARTS

- Close
- Body
- Introduction

SUPPLEMENTARY PARTS

- Appendixes

Figure 11.16   Parts of a Formal Proposal
Like formal reports, formal proposals can contain a wide variety of elements in addition to the main text.

Prefatory Parts of a Formal Proposal

The cover, title fly, title page, table of contents, and list of illustrations are handled the same way in formal proposals as in formal reports. However, other prefatory parts are handled quite differently:

- **Copy of or reference to the RFP.** Instead of having a letter of authorization, a solicited proposal should follow the instructions in the RFP. Some will instruct you to include the entire RFP in your proposal; others may want you to simply identify it by a name and tracking number.

- **Synopsis or executive summary.** Although you may include a synopsis or an executive summary, these components are often less useful in a formal proposal than in a report. In an unsolicited proposal, your transmittal letter will catch the reader's interest. In a solicited proposal, the introduction would provide an adequate preview of the contents.

- **Letter of transmittal.** If the proposal is solicited, treat the transmittal letter as a positive message, highlighting those aspects of your proposal that may give you a competitive advantage. If the proposal is unsolicited, the transmittal letter should follow the advice for persuasive messages (see Chapter 9). The letter must persuade the reader that you have something worthwhile to offer that justifies reading the entire proposal.

Follow the RFP's instructions for referring to or including the RFP in your introduction.

Text of a Proposal

The introduction of a proposal needs to summarize the problem or opportunity that your proposal intends to address.

Just as with reports, the text of a proposal is composed of an introduction, a body, and a close. The introduction presents and summarizes the problem you intend to solve and your solution. It highlights the benefits the reader will receive from the solution. The body explains the complete details of the solution: how the job will be done, how it will be broken into tasks, what method will be used to do it (including the required equipment, material, and personnel), when the work will begin and end, how much the entire job will cost (including a detailed breakdown), and why your company is qualified. The close emphasizes the benefits readers will realize from your solution and urges readers to act (see Figure 11.17).

Proofreading Reports and Proposals

After assembling your report or proposal in its final form, review it thoroughly one last time, looking for inconsistencies, errors, and missing components. Don't forget to proof your visuals thoroughly and make sure they are positioned correctly. For online reports, make sure all links work as expected and all necessary files are active and available. If you need specific tips on proofreading documents, look back at Chapter 5.

Be aware that at this point in the process, you are so familiar with the content of your report or proposal that your mind will fill in missing words, fix misspelled words, and subconsciously compensate for other flaws. Whenever possible, arrange for someone with "fresh eyes" to proofread the report or proposal. An ideal approach is to have a subject-matter expert check it for technical accuracy and a nontechnical reader review it for overall clarity and readability.[32]

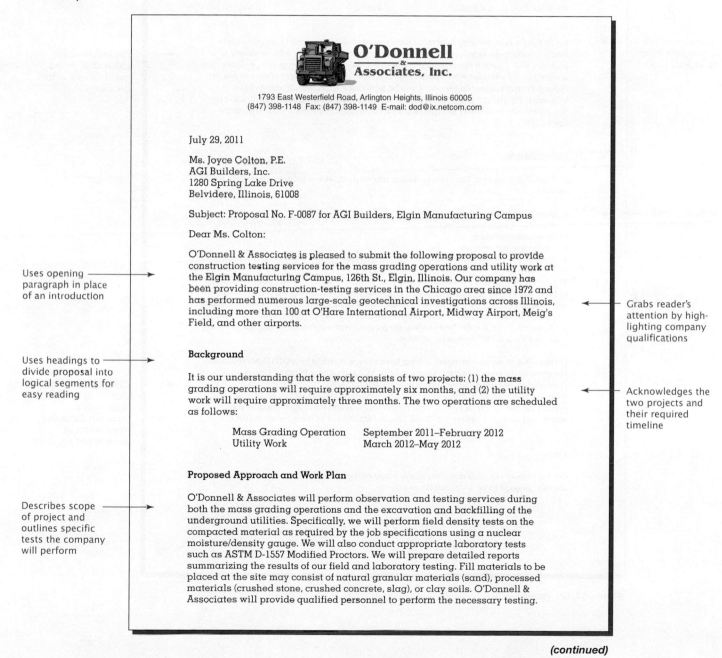

Uses opening paragraph in place of an introduction

Uses headings to divide proposal into logical segments for easy reading

Describes scope of project and outlines specific tests the company will perform

Grabs reader's attention by high-lighting company qualifications

Acknowledges the two projects and their required timeline

O'Donnell & Associates, Inc.

1793 East Westerfield Road, Arlington Heights, Illinois 60005
(847) 398-1148 Fax: (847) 398-1149 E-mail: dod@ix.netcom.com

July 29, 2011

Ms. Joyce Colton, P.E.
AGI Builders, Inc.
1280 Spring Lake Drive
Belvidere, Illinois, 61008

Subject: Proposal No. F-0087 for AGI Builders, Elgin Manufacturing Campus

Dear Ms. Colton:

O'Donnell & Associates is pleased to submit the following proposal to provide construction testing services for the mass grading operations and utility work at the Elgin Manufacturing Campus, 126th St., Elgin, Illinois. Our company has been providing construction-testing services in the Chicago area since 1972 and has performed numerous large-scale geotechnical investigations across Illinois, including more than 100 at O'Hare International Airport, Midway Airport, Meig's Field, and other airports.

Background

It is our understanding that the work consists of two projects: (1) the mass grading operations will require approximately six months, and (2) the utility work will require approximately three months. The two operations are scheduled as follows:

Mass Grading Operation	September 2011–February 2012
Utility Work	March 2012–May 2012

Proposed Approach and Work Plan

O'Donnell & Associates will perform observation and testing services during both the mass grading operations and the excavation and backfilling of the underground utilities. Specifically, we will perform field density tests on the compacted material as required by the job specifications using a nuclear moisture/density gauge. We will also conduct appropriate laboratory tests such as ASTM D-1557 Modified Proctors. We will prepare detailed reports summarizing the results of our field and laboratory testing. Fill materials to be placed at the site may consist of natural granular materials (sand), processed materials (crushed stone, crushed concrete, slag), or clay soils. O'Donnell & Associates will provide qualified personnel to perform the necessary testing.

(continued)

Figure 11.17   External Solicited Proposal
This proposal was submitted by Dixon O'Donnell, vice president of O'Donnell & Associates, a geotechnical engineering firm that conducts a variety of environmental testing services. The company is bidding on the mass grading and utility work specified by AGI Builders. As you review this document, pay close attention to the specific items addressed in the proposal's introduction, body, and closing.

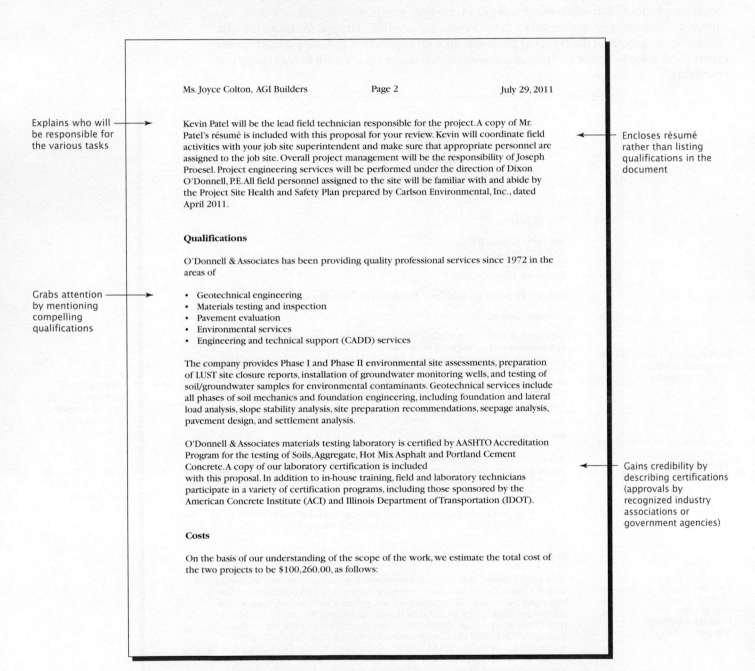

Explains who will be responsible for the various tasks →

Grabs attention by mentioning compelling qualifications →

← Encloses résumé rather than listing qualifications in the document

← Gains credibility by describing certifications (approvals by recognized industry associations or government agencies)

Ms. Joyce Colton, AGI Builders   Page 2   July 29, 2011

Kevin Patel will be the lead field technician responsible for the project. A copy of Mr. Patel's résumé is included with this proposal for your review. Kevin will coordinate field activities with your job site superintendent and make sure that appropriate personnel are assigned to the job site. Overall project management will be the responsibility of Joseph Proesel. Project engineering services will be performed under the direction of Dixon O'Donnell, P.E. All field personnel assigned to the site will be familiar with and abide by the Project Site Health and Safety Plan prepared by Carlson Environmental, Inc., dated April 2011.

Qualifications

O'Donnell & Associates has been providing quality professional services since 1972 in the areas of

- Geotechnical engineering
- Materials testing and inspection
- Pavement evaluation
- Environmental services
- Engineering and technical support (CADD) services

The company provides Phase I and Phase II environmental site assessments, preparation of LUST site closure reports, installation of groundwater monitoring wells, and testing of soil/groundwater samples for environmental contaminants. Geotechnical services include all phases of soil mechanics and foundation engineering, including foundation and lateral load analysis, slope stability analysis, site preparation recommendations, seepage analysis, pavement design, and settlement analysis.

O'Donnell & Associates materials testing laboratory is certified by AASHTO Accreditation Program for the testing of Soils, Aggregate, Hot Mix Asphalt and Portland Cement Concrete. A copy of our laboratory certification is included with this proposal. In addition to in-house training, field and laboratory technicians participate in a variety of certification programs, including those sponsored by the American Concrete Institute (ACI) and Illinois Department of Transportation (IDOT).

Costs

On the basis of our understanding of the scope of the work, we estimate the total cost of the two projects to be $100,260.00, as follows:

Figure 11.17   *(continued)*

Ms. Joyce Colton, AGI Builders   Page 3   July 29, 2011

Cost Estimates

Cost Estimate: Mass Grading	Units	Rate ($)	Total Cost ($)
Field Inspection			
Labor	1,320 hours	$38.50	$ 50,820.00
Nuclear Moisture Density Meter	132 days	35.00	4,620.00
Vehicle Expense	132 days	45.00	5,940.00
Laboratory Testing			
Proctor Density Tests (ASTM D-1557)	4 tests	130.00	520.00
Engineering/Project Management			
Principal Engineer	16 hours	110.00	1,760.00
Project Manager	20 hours	80.00	1,600.00
Administrative Assistant	12 hours	50.00	600.00
Subtotal			$ 65,860.00

Itemizes costs by project and gives supporting details

Cost Estimate: Utility Work	Units	Rate ($)	Total Cost ($)
Field Inspection			
Labor	660 hours	$ 38.50	$ 25,410.00
Nuclear Moisture Density Meter	66 days	5.00	2,310.00
Vehicle Expense	66 days	45.00	2,970.00
Laboratory Testing			
Proctor Density Tests (ASTM D-1557)	2 tests	130.00	260.00
Engineering/Project Management			
Principal Engineer	10 hours	110.00	1,100.00
Project Manager	20 hours	80.00	1,600.00
Administrative Assistant	15 hours	50.00	750.00
Subtotal			$ 34,400.00

Total Project Costs			**$100,260.00**

This estimate assumes full-time inspection services. However, our services may also be performed on an as-requested basis, and actual charges will reflect time associated with the project. We have attached our standard fee schedule for your review. Overtime rates are for hours in excess of 8.0 hours per day, before 7:00 a.m., after 5:00 p.m., and on holidays and weekends.

Provides alternative option in case full-time service costs exceed client's budget

Figure 11.17   *(continued)*

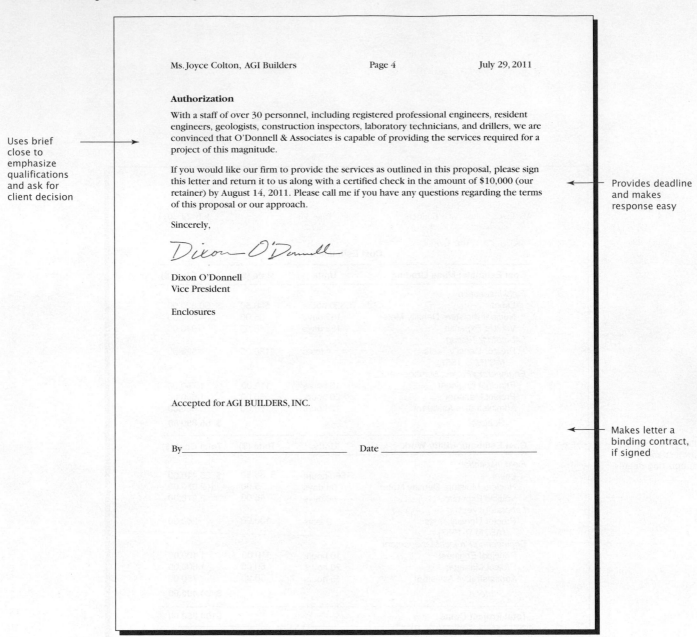

Uses brief close to emphasize qualifications and ask for client decision

Ms. Joyce Colton, AGI Builders   Page 4   July 29, 2011

Authorization

With a staff of over 30 personnel, including registered professional engineers, resident engineers, geologists, construction inspectors, laboratory technicians, and drillers, we are convinced that O'Donnell & Associates is capable of providing the services required for a project of this magnitude.

If you would like our firm to provide the services as outlined in this proposal, please sign this letter and return it to us along with a certified check in the amount of $10,000 (our retainer) by August 14, 2011. Please call me if you have any questions regarding the terms of this proposal or our approach.

Provides deadline and makes response easy

Sincerely,

Dixon O'Donnell

Dixon O'Donnell
Vice President

Enclosures

Accepted for AGI BUILDERS, INC.

Makes letter a binding contract, if signed

By_____   Date _____

Figure 11.17   *(continued)*

Distributing Your Reports and Proposals

If possible, have someone who hasn't seen the report before proofread it for you.

For physical distribution of important printed reports or proposals, consider spending the extra money for a professional courier or package delivery service. Doing so can help you stand out in a crowd, and it lets you verify receipt. Alternatively, if you've prepared the document for a single person or small group in your office or the local area, delivering it in person will give you the chance to personally "introduce" the report and remind readers why they're receiving it.

Many businesses use the Adobe portable document format (PDF) to distribute reports electronically.

For electronic distribution, unless your audience specifically requests a word processor file, provide documents in PDF format. Even with the recent discovery of potential vulnerabilities in PDF files, they are not as vulnerable to as many viruses as word processor files, and they let you control how your document is displayed on your audience's computer.

If your company or client expects you to distribute your reports via a web-based content management system, a shared workspace, or some other online location, double-check that you've uploaded the correct file(s) to the correct location. Verify the on-screen display of your reports after you've posted them, making sure graphics, charts, links, and other elements are in place and operational.

PEARSON mybcommlab

Are you an active learner? Go to mybcommlab.com to master Chapter 11's content. Chapter 11's interactive activities include:

- Customizable Study Plan and Chapter 11 practice quizzes
- Chapter 11 Simulation (Business Reports), which helps you think critically and prepare to make choices in the business world
- Chapter 11 Video Exercise (Writing Reports and Proposals: MELT), which shows you how textbook concepts are put into practice every day

- Flash Cards for mastering the definition of chapter terms
- Interactive Lessons that visually review key chapter concepts
- Document Makeovers for hands-on, scored practice in revising documents

---

CHAPTER REVIEW AND ACTIVITIES

Learning Objectives: Check Your Progress

1 OBJECTIVE List the topics commonly covered in the introduction, body, and close of informational reports, analytical reports, and proposals.

The introduction of a report highlights who authorized the report, its purpose and scope, the sources or methods used to gather information, important definitions, any limitations, and the order in which the various topics are covered. The body provides enough information to support its conclusion and recommendations, which can range from explanations of problems or opportunities to facts and trends to results of studies or investigations. The close summarizes key points, restates conclusions and recommendations if appropriate, and lists action items.

To a large extent, the content of proposals is dictated by the circumstances, particularly by whether the proposal is solicited or unsolicited. Proposals submitted in response to an RFP should always follow the instructions it contains. The introduction commonly includes a background or statement of the problem, an overview of the proposed solution (or, for indirect proposals, a statement that a solution is about to be presented), the scope of the proposals, and a description of how the proposal is organized. The body usually includes a description of the proposed solution, a work plan that outlines how and when the work will be accomplished, a statement of qualifications of the individual or organization presenting the proposal, and a discussion of costs. The close summarizes the key points, emphasizes the benefits that readers will realize from the proposed solution,

summarizes the merits of your approach, restates why you and your firm are a good choice, and asks for a decision from the reader.

2 OBJECTIVE Identify six guidelines for drafting effective website content.

Follow these six guidelines to draft effective online content: (1) Build trust by being accurate, current, complete, and authoritative; (2) adapt content to global audiences; (3) write web-friendly content that is compact and efficient; (4) present information in a concise, skimmable format; (5) make effective use of links; and (6) make the website a "living" document by adding fresh content and deleting content that is out of date or no longer relevant to the target audience.

3 OBJECTIVE Offer guidelines for becoming a valuable wiki contributor.

To become a valuable wiki contributor, let go of traditional expectations of authorship, including individual recognition and control; don't be afraid to edit and improve existing content; use page templates and other formatting options to make sure your content is formatted in the same style as the rest of the wiki; keep edits and comments separate by using the "talk page" to discuss content, rather than inserting comments directly into the text; take advantage of the sandbox to learn how use the wiki's writing and editing tools; and understand and follow the wiki's contributor guidelines.

4 OBJECTIVE Discuss six principles of graphic design that can improve the quality of your visuals, and identify the major types of business visuals.

When preparing visuals, (1) use elements of design consistently; (2) use color and other elements to show contrast effectively; (3) strive for visual balance, either formal or informal, that creates a feel that is appropriate for your overall message; (4) use design choices to draw attention to key elements; (5) understand and follow design conventions; and (6) strive for simplicity in your visuals.

The major types of business visuals include tables; line charts and surface charts; bar charts and pie charts; data visualization; flowcharts and organization charts; maps, drawings, diagrams, infographics, and photographs; and animation and video.

5 OBJECTIVE Summarize the four tasks involved in completing business reports and proposals.

The four completion tasks of revising, producing, proofreading, and distributing all need to be accomplished with care, given the size and complexity of many reports. The production stage for a formal report or proposal can involve creating a number of elements not found in most other business documents. Possible prefatory parts (those coming before the main text of the report or proposal) include a cover, a title fly, a title page, a letter of authorization, a letter of transmittal, a table of contents, a list of illustrations, and a synopsis (a brief overview of the report) or an executive summary (a miniature version of the report). Possible supplemental parts (those coming after the main text of the report or proposal) include one or more appendixes, a bibliography, and an index.

▮ Test Your Knowledge

To review chapter content related to each question, refer to the indicated Learning Objective.

1. What navigational elements can you use to help readers follow the structure and flow of information in a long report? [LO-1]
2. Why must the introduction of an unsolicited proposal include a statement of the problem or opportunity that the proposal addresses? [LO-1]
3. What is the purpose of a "sandbox" on a wiki? [LO-3]
4. How can you use the inverted pyramid style of writing to craft effective online content? [LO-2]
5. How does a synopsis differ from an executive summary? [LO-5]

▮ Apply Your Knowledge

To review chapter content related to each question, refer to the indicated Learning Objective.

1. Why is it important to write clear, descriptive headings and link titles with online content, as opposed to clever, wordplay headings? [LO-2]

2. Should the most experienced member of a department have final approval of the content for the department's wiki? Why or why not? [LO-3]
3. If you wanted to compare average monthly absenteeism for five divisions in your company over the course of a year, which type of visual would you use? Explain your choice. [LO-4]
4. For providing illustration in a report or proposal, when is a diagram a better choice than a photograph? [LO-4]
5. If a company receives a solicited formal proposal outlining the solution to a particular problem, is it ethical for the company to adopt the proposal's recommendations without hiring the firm that submitted the proposal? Why or why not? [LO-5]

▮ Practice Your Skills

Activities

Active links for all websites in this chapter can be found on mybcommlab; see your User Guide for instructions on accessing the content for this chapter. Each activity is labeled according to the primary skill or skills you will need to use. To review relevant chapter content, you can refer to the indicated Learning Objective. In some instances, supporting information will be found in another chapter, as indicated.

1. **Message Strategies: Informational Reports [LO-1]** You and a classmate are helping Linda Moreno prepare her report on Electrovision's travel and entertainment costs (see Figure 11.15). This time, however, the report is to be informational rather than analytical, so it will not include recommendations. Review the existing report and determine what changes would be needed to make it an informational report. Be as specific as possible. For example, if your team decides the report needs a new title, what title would you use? Draft a transmittal memo for Moreno to use in conveying this informational report to Dennis McWilliams, Electrovision's vice president of operations.

2. **Media Skills: Wiki Collaboration [LO-3], Chapter 5** To access this wiki exercise, go to http://real-timeupdates.com/bce5, click on "Student Assignments," and select "Chapter 11, page 310, Activity 2." Follow the instructions for evaluating this short article and revising it to make it more reader oriented. Refer to the guidelines in Chapter 5 (page 129) for reminders about editing and revising the work of other writers.

3. **Media Skills: Wiki Collaboration [LO-3], Chapter 5** To access this wiki exercise, go to http://real-time updates.com/bce5, click on "Student Assignments," and select "Chapter 11, Page 310, Activity 3." Follow the instructions for evaluating this wiki article and revising to make it more reader oriented. Refer to the guidelines in Chapter 5 (page 129) for reminders about editing and revising the work of other writers.

4. **Visual Communication: Choosing the Best Visual [LO-4]** You're preparing the annual report for FretCo Guitar Corporation. For each of the following types of information, select the appropriate chart or visual to illustrate the text. Explain your choices.

   a. Data on annual sales for the past 20 years
   b. Comparison of FretCo sales, product by product (electric guitars, bass guitars, amplifiers, acoustic guitars), for this year and last year
   c. Explanation of how a FretCo acoustic guitar is manufactured
   d. Explanation of how the FretCo Guitar Corporation markets its guitars
   e. Data on sales of FretCo products in each of 12 countries
   f. Comparison of FretCo sales figures with sales figures for three competing guitar makers over the past 10 years

5. **Visual Communication: Creating Visuals [LO-4]** As directed by your instructor, team up with other students, making sure that at least one of you has a digital camera or camera phone capable of downloading images to your word processing software. Find a busy location on campus or in the surrounding neighborhood, someplace with lots of signs, storefronts, pedestrians, and traffic. Scout out two different photo opportunities, one that maximizes the visual impression of crowding and clutter, and one that minimizes this impression. For the first, assume that you are someone who advocates reducing the crowding and clutter, so you want to show how bad it is.

   For the second, assume that you are a real estate agent or someone else who is motivated to show people that even though the location offers lots of shopping, entertainment, and other attractions, it's actually a rather calm and quiet neighborhood. Insert the two images in a word processing document and write a caption for each that emphasizes the two opposite messages just described. Finally, write a brief paragraph, discussing the ethical implications of what you've just done. Have you distorted reality or just presented it in ways that work to your advantage? Have you prevented audiences from gaining the information they would need to make informed decisions?

6. **Visual Communication: Creating Visuals [LO-4]** You work for C & S Holdings, a company that operates coin-activated, self-service car washes. Research shows that the farther customers live from a car wash, the less likely they are to visit. You know that 50 percent of customers at each of your car washes live within a 4-mile radius of the location, 65 percent live within 6 miles, 80 percent live within 8 miles, and 90 percent live within 10 miles. C & S's owner wants to open two new car washes in your city and has asked you to prepare a report recommending locations. Using a map of your city from an online or printed source, choose two possible locations for car washes and create a visual that depicts the customer base surrounding each location (make up whatever population data you need).

7. **Message Strategies: Informational Reports [LO-1]** Review a long business article in a journal or newspaper. Highlight examples of how the article uses headings, transitions, previews, and reviews to help the readers find their way.

8. **Message Strategies: Analytical Reports; Communication Ethics: Resolving Ethical Dilemmas [LO-1], Chapter 1** Your boss has asked you to prepare a feasibility report to determine whether the company should advertise its custom-crafted cabinetry in the weekly neighborhood newspaper. Based on your primary research, you think it should. As you draft the introduction to your report, however, you discover that the survey administered to the neighborhood newspaper subscribers was flawed. Several of the questions were poorly written and misleading. You used the survey results, among other findings, to justify your recommendation. The report is due in three days. What actions might you want to take, if any, before you complete your report?

9. **Completing: Producing Formal Reports [LO-5]** You are president of the Friends of the Library, a not-for-profit group that raises funds and provides volunteers to support your local library. Every February, you send a report of the previous year's activities and accomplishments to the County Arts Council, which provides an annual grant of $1,000 toward your group's summer reading festival. Now it's February 6, and you've completed your formal report. Here are the highlights:

   - Back-to-school book sale raised $2,000.
   - Holiday craft fair raised $1,100.
   - Promotion and prizes for summer reading festival cost $1,450.
   - Materials for children's program featuring local author cost $125.
   - New reference databases for library's career center cost $850.
   - Bookmarks promoting library's website cost $200.

   Write a letter of transmittal to Erica Maki, the council's director. Because she is expecting this report, you can use the direct approach. Be sure to express gratitude for the council's ongoing financial support.

Expand Your Skills

Critique the Professionals

Download the latest issue of the *International Trade Update* from http://trade.gov (look under "Publications"). What techniques does the report use to help readers find their way through the document or direct readers to other sources of information? What techniques are used to highlight key points in the document? Are these techniques effective? Using whatever medium your instructor requests, write a brief summary of your analysis.

Sharpen Your Career Skills Online

Bovée and Thill's Business Communication Web Search, at **http://businesscommunicationblog.com/websearch**, is a unique research tool designed specifically for business communication research. Use the Web Search function to find a website, video, PDF document, podcast, or presentation that offers advice on creating visuals for business reports. Write a brief e-mail message to your instructor or a post for your class blog, describing the item that you found and summarizing the career skills information you learned from it.

mybcommlab

If your course uses mybcommlab, log on to **www.mybcommlab .com** to access the following study and assessment aids associated with this chapter:

- Video applications
- Pre/post test

- Real-Time Updates
- Personalized study plan
- Peer review activity
- Model documents
- Quick Learning Guides
- Sample presentations

If you are not using mybcommlab, you can access Real-Time Updates and Quick Learning Guides through **http:// real-timeupdates.com/bce5**. The Quick Learning Guide (located under "Learn More" on the website) hits all the high points of this chapter in just two pages. This guide, especially prepared by the authors, will help you study for exams or review important concepts whenever you need a quick refresher.

CASES

▼ *Apply the three-step writing process to the following cases, as assigned by your instructor.*

Short Reports

1. Message Strategies: Informational Reports [LO-1] [LO-5]

You've been in your new job as human resources director for only a week, and already you have a major personnel crisis on your hands. Some employees in the marketing department got their hands on a confidential salary report and learned that, on average, marketing employees earn less than engineering employees. In addition, several top performers in the engineering group make significantly more than anybody in marketing. The report was instantly passed around the company by e-mail, and now everyone is discussing the situation. You'll deal with the data security issue later; for now, you need to address the dissatisfaction in the marketing group.

Case Table 11.1 lists the salary and employment data you were able to pull from the employee database. You also had the opportunity to interview the engineering and marketing directors to get their opinions on the pay situation; their answers are listed in Case Table 11.2.

CASE TABLE 11.1	Selected Employment Data for Engineers and Marketing Staff	
Employment Statistic	**Engineering Department**	**Marketing Department**
Average number of years of work experience	18.2	16.3
Average number of years of experience in current profession	17.8	8.6
Average number of years with company	12.4	7.9
Average number of years of college education	6.9	4.8
Average number of years between promotions	6.7	4.3
Salary range	$58–165k	$45–85k
Median salary	$77k	$62k

CASE TABLE 11.2 Summary Statements from Department Director Interviews

Question	Engineering Director	Marketing Director
1. Should engineering and marketing professionals receive roughly similar pay?	In general, yes, but we need to make allowances for the special nature of the engineering profession. In some cases, it's entirely appropriate for an engineer to earn more than a marketing person.	Yes.
2. Why or why not?	Several reasons: (1) Top engineers are extremely hard to find, and we need to offer competitive salaries; (2) the structure of the engineering department doesn't provide as many promotional opportunities, so we can't use promotions as a motivator the way marketing can; (3) many of our engineers have advanced degrees, and nearly all pursue continuous education to stay on top of the technology.	Without marketing, the products the engineers create wouldn't reach customers, and the company wouldn't have any revenue. The two teams make equal contributions to the company's success.
3. If we decide to balance pay between the two departments, how should we do it?	If we do anything to cap or reduce engineering salaries, we'll lose key people to the competition.	If we can't increase payroll immediately to raise marketing salaries, the only fair thing to do is freeze raises in engineering and gradually raise marketing salaries over the next few years.

Your task The CEO has asked for a short report, summarizing whatever data and information you have on engineering and marketing salaries. Feel free to offer your own interpretation of the situation as well (make up any information you need), but keep in mind that because you are a new manager with almost no experience in the company, your opinion might not have a lot of influence.

PORTFOLIO BUILDER

2. Message Strategies: Analytical Reports [LO-1] [LO-5] Like any other endeavor that combines hardnosed factual analysis and creative freethinking, the task of writing business plans generates a range of opinions.

Your task Find at least six sources of advice on writing successful business plans (focus on start-up businesses that are likely to seek outside investors). Use at least two books, two magazine or journal articles, and two websites, blogs, or other online resources. Analyze the advice you find and identify points where most or all the experts agree and points where they don't agree. Wherever you find points of significant disagreement, identify which opinion you find most convincing and explain why. Summarize your findings in a brief formal report.

PORTFOLIO BUILDER   TEAM SKILLS

3. Message Strategies: Analytical Reports [LO-1] [LO-5] Anyone looking at the fragmented 21st-century landscape of media and entertainment options might be surprised to learn that poetry was once a dominant medium for not only creative literary expression but also philosophical, political, and even scientific discourse. Alas, such is no longer the case.

Your task With a team of fellow students, your challenge is to identify opportunities to increase sales of poetry—any kind of poetry, in any medium. The following suggestions may help you get started:

- Research recent bestsellers in the poetry field and try to identify why they have been popular.
- Interview literature professors, professional poets, librarians, publishers, and bookstore personnel.
- Consider art forms and venues in which verse plays an essential role, including popular music and poetry slams.
- Conduct surveys and interviews to find out why consumers don't buy more poetry.
- Review professional journals that cover the field of poetry, including *Publishers Weekly* and *Poets & Writers*, from both business and creative standpoints.

Summarize your findings in a brief formal report; assume that your target readers are executives in the publishing industry.

PORTFOLIO BUILDER

4. Message Strategies: Informational Reports [LO-1] [LO-5] After 15 years in the corporate world, you're ready to strike out on your own. Rather than building a business from the ground up, however, you think that buying a franchise is a better idea. Unfortunately, some of the most lucrative franchise opportunities, such as the major fast-food chains, require significant start-up costs—some more than a half million dollars. Fortunately, you've met several potential investors who seem willing to help you get started in exchange for a share of ownership. Between your own savings and these investors, you estimate that you can raise from $350,000 to $600,000, depending on how much ownership share you want to concede to the investors.

You've worked in several functional areas already, including sales and manufacturing, so you have a fairly well-rounded business résumé. You're open to just about any type of business, too, as long as it provides the opportunity to grow; you don't want to be so tied down to the first operation that you can't turn it over to a hired manager and expand into another market.

Your task To convene a formal meeting with the investor group, you need to first draft a report that outlines the types of franchise opportunities you'd like to pursue. Write a brief report, identifying five franchises that you would like to explore further. (Choose five based on your own personal interests and the criteria identified above.) For each possibility, identify the nature of the business, the financial requirements, the level of support the company provides, and a brief statement of why you could run such a business successfully (make up any details you need). Be sure to carefully review the information you find about each franchise company to make sure you can qualify for it. For instance, McDonald's doesn't allow investment partnerships to buy franchises, so you won't be able to start up a McDonald's outlet until you have enough money to do it on your own.

For a quick introduction to franchising, see How Stuff Works (www.howstuffworks.com/franchising). You can learn more about the business of franchising at Franchising.com (www.franchising.com) and search for specific franchise opportunities at FranCorp Connect (www.francorpconnect .com). In addition, many companies that sell franchises, such as Subway, offer additional information on their websites.

Long Reports

5. Message Strategies: Informational Reports [LO-1] [LO-5]

Your company is the largest private employer in your metropolitan area, and the 43,500 employees in your workforce have a tremendous impact on local traffic. A group of city and county transportation officials recently approached your CEO with a request to explore ways to reduce this impact. The CEO has assigned you the task of analyzing the workforce's transportation habits and attitudes as a first step toward identifying potential solutions. He's willing to consider anything from subsidized bus passes to company-owned shuttle buses to telecommuting, but the decision requires a thorough understanding of employee transportation needs. Case Tables 11.3 through 11.7 summarize data you collected in an employee survey.

Your task Present the results of your survey in an informational report, using the data provided in the tables.

CASE TABLE 11.3   Employee Carpool Habits

Frequency of Use: Carpooling	Portion of Workforce
Every day, every week	10,138 (23%)
Certain days, every week	4,361 (10%)
Randomly	983 (2%)
Never	28,018 (64%)

CASE TABLE 11.4   Use of Public Transportation

Frequency of Use: Public Transportation	Portion of Workforce
Every day, every week	23,556 (54%)
Certain days, every week	2,029 (5%)
Randomly	5,862 (13%)
Never	12,053 (28%)

CASE TABLE 11.5   Effect of Potential Improvements to Public Transportation

Which of the Following Would Encourage You to Use Public Transportation More Frequently (check all that apply)	Portion of Respondents
Increased perception of safety	4,932 (28%)
Improved cleanliness	852 (5%)
Reduced commute times	7,285 (41%)
Greater convenience: fewer transfers	3,278 (18%)
Greater convenience: more stops	1,155 (6%)
Lower (or subsidized) fares	5,634 (31%)
Nothing could encourage me to take public transportation	8,294 (46%)

Note: This question was asked of respondents who use public transportation randomly or never, a subgroup that represents 17,915 employees, or 41 percent of the workforce.

CASE TABLE 11.6   Distance Traveled to/from Work

Distance You Travel to Work (one way)	Portion of Workforce
Less than 1 mile	531 (1%)
1–3 miles	6,874 (16%)
4–10 miles	22,951 (53%)
11–20 miles	10,605 (24%)
More than 20 miles	2,539 (6%)

CASE TABLE 11.7   Is Telecommuting an Option?

Does the Nature of Your Work Make Telecommuting a Realistic Option?	Portion of Workforce
Yes, every day	3,460 (8%)
Yes, several days a week	8,521 (20%)
Yes, random days	12,918 (30%)
No	18,601 (43%)

TEAM SKILLS   **PORTFOLIO** BUILDER

6. Message Strategies: Informational Reports [LO-1] [LO-5]
As a researcher in your state's consumer protection agency, you're frequently called on to investigate consumer topics and write reports for the agency's website. Thousands of consumers have arranged the purchase of cars online, and millions more do at least some of their research online before heading to a dealership. Some want to save time and money, some want to be armed with as much information as possible before talking to a dealer, and others want to completely avoid the often-uncomfortable experience of negotiating prices with car salespeople. In response, a variety of online services have emerged to meet these consumer needs. Some let you compare information on various car models, some connect you to local dealers to complete the transaction, and some complete nearly all the transaction details for you, including negotiating the price. Some search the inventory of thousands of dealers, whereas others search only a single dealership or a network of affiliated dealers. In other words, a slew of new tools are available for car buyers, but it's not always easy to figure out where to go and what to expect. That's where your report will help.

By visiting a variety of car-related websites and reading magazine and newspaper articles on the car-buying process, you've compiled a variety of notes related to the subject:

- **Process overview.** The process is relatively straightforward and fairly similar to other online shopping experiences, with two key differences. In general, a consumer identifies the make and model of car he or she wants, and then the online car-buying service searches the inventories of car dealers nationwide and presents the available choices. The consumer chooses a particular car from that list, and then the service handles the communication and purchase details with the dealer. When the paperwork is finished, the consumer visits the dealership and picks up the car. The two biggest differences with online auto buying are that (1) you can't actually complete the purchase over the Internet (in most cases, you must visit a local dealer to pick up the car and sign the papers, although in some cities, a dealer or a local car-buying service will deliver it to your home) and (2) in most states, it's illegal to purchase a new car from anyone other than a franchise dealer (that is, you can't buy directly from the manufacturer, the way you can buy a Dell computer directly from Dell, for instance).
- **Information you can find online** (not all information is available at all sites). You can find information on makes, models, colors, options, option packages (often, specific options are available only as part of a package; you need to know these constraints before you select your options), photos, specifications (everything from engine size to interior space), mileage estimates, performance data, safety information, predicted resale value, reviews, comparable models, insurance costs, consumer ratings, repair and reliability histories, available buyer incentives and rebates, true ownership costs (including costs for fuel, maintenance, repair, and so on), warranty, loan and lease payments, and maintenance requirements.
- **Advantages of shopping online.** Advantages of shopping online include shopping from the comfort and convenience of home, none of the dreaded negotiating at the dealership (in many cases), the ability to search far and wide for a specific car (even nationwide, on many sites), rapid access to considerable amounts of data and information, and reviews from both professional automotive journalists and other consumers. In general, online auto shopping reduces a key advantage that auto dealers used to have, which was control of most of the information in the purchase transaction. Now consumers can find out how reliable each model is, how quickly it will depreciate, how often it is likely to need repairs, what other drivers think of it, how much the dealer paid the manufacturer for it, and so on.
- **Changing nature of the business.** The relationship between dealers and third-party websites (such as CarsDirect.com and Vehix.com) continues to evolve. At first, the relationship was more antagonistic, as some third-party sites and dealers frequently competed for the same customers, and each side made bold proclamations about driving the other out of business. However, the relationship is more collaborative in many cases now, with dealers realizing that some third-party sites already have wide brand awareness and nationwide audiences. As the percentage of new car sales that originate via the Internet continues to increase, dealers are more receptive to working with third-party sites.
- **Comparing information from multiple sources.** Consumers shouldn't rely solely on information from a single website. Each site has its own way of organizing information, and many sites have their own ways of evaluating car models and connecting buyers with sellers.
- **Understanding what each site is doing.** Some sites search thousands of dealers, regardless of ownership connections. Others, such as AutoNation, search only affiliated dealers. A search for a specific model might yield only a half dozen cars on one site but dozens of cars on another site. Find out who owns the site and what their business objectives are, if you can; this will help you assess the information you receive.
- **Leading websites.** Consumers can check out a wide variety of websites, some of which are full-service operations, offering everything from research to negotiation; others provide more specific and limited services. For instance, CarsDirect (**www.carsdirect.com**) provides a full range of services, whereas Carfax (**www.carfax.com**) specializes in uncovering the repair histories of individual used cars. Case Table 11.8 on the next page lists some of the leading car-related websites.

Your task With a team assigned by your instructor, write an informational report based on your research notes. The purpose of the report is to introduce consumers to the basic concepts of integrating the Internet into their car-buying activities and to educate them about important issues.[33]

PORTFOLIO BUILDER

7. Message Strategies: Analytical Reports [LO-1] [LO-5]   As a college student and an active consumer, you may have considered

CASE TABLE 11.8 Leading Automotive Websites	
Site	**URL**
AutoAdvice	www.autoadvice.com
Autobytel	www.autobytel.com
Autos.com	www.autos.com
AutoVantage	www.autovantage.com
Autoweb	www.autoweb.com
CarBargains	www.carbargains.com
Carfax	www.carfax.com
CarPrices.com	www.carprices.com
Cars.com	www.cars.com
CarsDirect	www.carsdirect.com
CarSmart	www.carsmart.com
Consumer Reports	www.consumerreports.org
eBay Motors	www.motors.ebay.com
Edmunds	www.edmunds.com
iMotors	www.imotors.com
IntelliChoice	www.intellichoice.com
InvoiceDealers	www.invoicedealers.com
JDPower	www.jdpower.com
Kelly Blue Book	www.kbb.com
MSN Autos	http://autos.msn.com
PickupTrucks.com	www.pickuptrucks.com
The Car Connection	www.thecarconnection.com
Vehix.com	www.vehix.com
Yahoo! Autos	http//autos.yahoo.com

one or more of the following questions at some point in the past few years:

a. What criteria distinguish the top-rated MBA programs in the country? How well do these criteria correspond to the needs and expectations of business? Are the criteria fair for students, employers, and business schools?

b. Which of three companies you might like to work for has the strongest corporate ethics policies?

c. What will the music industry look like in the future? What's next after online stores such as Apple's iTunes and digital players such as the iPod?

Which industries and job categories are forecast to experience greatest growth—and therefore the greatest demand for workers—in the next 10 years?

e. What has been the impact of Starbucks's aggressive growth on small, independent coffee shops? On midsized chains or franchises? In the United States or in another country?

f. How large is the "industry" of major college sports? How much do the major football or basketball programs contribute—directly or indirectly—to other parts of a typical university?

g. How much have minor league sports—baseball, hockey, arena football—grown in small- and medium-market cities? What is the local economic impact when these municipalities build stadiums and arenas?

Your task Answer one of the preceding questions using secondary research sources for information. Be sure to document your sources, using the format your instructor indicates. Give conclusions and offer recommendations where appropriate.

Proposals

PORTFOLIO BUILDER

8. Message Strategies: Proposals [LO-1] [LO-5] Presentations can make—or break—both careers and businesses. A good presentation can bring in millions of dollars in new sales or fresh investment capital. A bad presentation might cause any number of troubles, from turning away potential customers to upsetting fellow employees to derailing key projects. To help business professionals plan, create, and deliver more effective presentations, you offer a three-day workshop that covers the essentials of good presentations:

- Understanding your audience's needs and expectations
- Formulating your presentation objectives
- Choosing an organizational approach
- Writing openings that catch your audience's attention
- Creating effective graphics and slides
- Practicing and delivering your presentation
- Leaving a positive impression on your audience
- Avoiding common mistakes with electronic slides
- Making presentations online using webcasting tools
- Handling questions and arguments from the audience
- Overcoming the top 10 worries of public speaking (including *How can I overcome stage fright?* and *I'm not the performing type; can I still give an effective presentation?*)

Workshop benefits: Students will learn how to prepare better presentations in less time and deliver them more effectively.

Who should attend: Top executives, project managers, employment recruiters, sales professionals, and anyone else who gives important presentations to internal or external audiences.

Your qualifications: 18 years of business experience, including 14 years in sales and 12 years of public speaking. Experience speaking to audiences as large as 5,000 people. More than a dozen speech-related articles published in professional journals. Have conducted successful workshops for nearly 100 companies.

Workshop details: Three-day workshop (9 A.M. to 3:30 P.M.) that combines lectures, practice presentations, and both individual and group feedback. Minimum number of students: 6. Maximum number of students per workshop: 12.

Pricing: The cost is $3,500, plus $100 per student; 10 percent discount for additional workshops.

Other information: Each attendee will have the opportunity to give three practice presentations that will last from 3 to 5 minutes. Everyone is encouraged to bring PowerPoint files containing slides from actual business presentations. Each attendee will also receive a workbook and a digital video recording of his or her final class presentation on DVD. You'll also be available for phone or e-mail coaching for six months after the workshop.

Your task Identify a company in your local area that might be a good candidate for your services. Learn more about the company by visiting its website so you can personalize your proposal. Using the information listed above, prepare a sales proposal that explains the benefits of your training and what students can expect during the workshop.

PORTFOLIO BUILDER

9. Message Strategies: Proposals [LO-1] [LO-5]   For years, a controversy has been brewing over the amount of junk food and soft drinks being sold through vending machines in local schools. Schools benefit from revenue-sharing arrangements, but many parents and health experts are concerned about the negative effects of these snacks and beverages. You and your brother have almost a decade of experience running espresso and juice stands in malls and on street corners, and you'd love to find some way to expand your business into schools. After a quick brainstorming session, the two of you craft a plan that makes good business sense while meeting the financial concerns of school administrators and the nutritional concerns of parents and dietitians. Here are the notes from your brainstorming session:

- Set up portable juice bars on school campuses, offering healthy fruit and vegetable drinks along with simple, healthy snacks
- Offer schools 30 percent of profits in exchange for free space and long-term contracts
- Provide job-training opportunities for students (during athletic events, etc.)
- Provide detailed dietary analysis of all products sold
- Establish a nutritional advisory board composed of parents, students, and at least one certified health professional
- Assure schools and parents that all products are safe (e.g., no stimulant drinks, no dietary supplements, and so on)
- Support local farmers and specialty food preparers by buying locally and giving these vendors the opportunity to test-market new products at your stands

Your task Based on the ideas listed, draft a formal proposal to the local school board, outlining your plan to offer healthier alternatives to soft drinks and prepackaged snack foods. Invent any details you need to complete your proposal.

PORTFOLIO BUILDER   TEAM SKILLS

10. Message Strategies: Proposals [LO-1] [LO-5]   It seems like everybody in your firm is frustrated. On the one hand, top executives complain about the number of lower-level employees who want promotions but just don't seem to "get it"

when it comes to dealing with customers and the public, recognizing when to speak out and when to be quiet, knowing how to push new ideas through the appropriate channels, and performing other essential but difficult-to-teach tasks. On the other hand, ambitious employees who'd like to learn more feel that they have nowhere to turn for career advice from people who've been there. In between, a variety of managers and midlevel executives are overwhelmed by the growing number of mentoring requests they're getting, sometimes from employees they don't even know.

You've been assigned the challenge of proposing a formal mentoring program—and a considerable challenge it is:

- The number of employees who want mentoring relationships far exceeds the number of managers and executives willing and able to be mentors; how will you select people for the program?
- The people most in demand for mentoring also tend to be some of the busiest people in the organization.
- After several years of belt tightening and staff reductions, the entire company feels overworked; few people can imagine adding another recurring task to their seemingly endless to-do lists.
- What's in it for the mentors? Why would they be motivated to help lower-level employees?
- How will you measure the success or failure of the mentoring effort?

Your task With a team assigned by your instructor, identify potential solutions to the issues (make up any information you need) and draft a proposal to the executive committee for a formal, companywide mentoring program that would match selected employees with successful managers and executives.

Improve Your Grammar, Mechanics, and Usage

You can download the text of this assignment from http://real-timeupdates.com/bce5; click on "Student Assignments" and then click on "Chapter 11. Improve Your Grammar, Mechanics, and Usage."

Level 1: Self-Assessment—Quotation Marks, Parentheses, Ellipses, Underscores, and Italics

Review Sections 2.10, 2.11, 2.12, and 3.2 in the Handbook of Grammar, Mechanics, and Usage and then complete the following 15 items.

In items 1–15, insert quotations marks, parentheses, and ellipses as needed, and add italics wherever necessary.

1. Be sure to read How to Sell by Listening in this month's issue of Fortune.
2. Her response see the attached memo is disturbing.
3. Contact is an overused word.
4. We will operate with a skeleton staff during the holiday break December 21 through January 2.
5. The SBP's next conference, the bulletin noted, will be held in Minneapolis.
6. Sara O'Rourke a reporter from The Wall Street Journal will be here on Thursday.

7. I don't care why you didn't fill my order; I want to know when you'll fill it.
8. The term up in the air means undecided.
9. Her assistant the one who just had the baby won't be back for four weeks.
10. Ask not what your country can do for you is the beginning of a famous quotation from John F. Kennedy.
11. Whom do you think Time magazine will select as its Person of the Year?
12. Do you remember who said And away we go?
13. Refinements in robotics may prove profitable. More detail about this technology appears in Appendix A.
14. The resignation letter begins Since I'll never regain your respect and goes on to explain why that's true.
15. You must help her distinguish between i.e. which means that is and e.g. which means for example.

Level 2: Workplace Applications

The following items may contain errors in grammar, capitalization, punctuation, abbreviation, number style, word division, and vocabulary. Rewrite each sentence, correcting all errors. If a sentence has no errors, write "Correct" for that number.

1. For the lst time, thank's to largely deals with the big chains like Stop & Shop, Sheila's Snak Treetz are showing a profit.
2. The premise for broadband, sometimes called simply 'high speed Internet', is that consumers need a more fast pipeline for getting digital information in our homes.
3. After moving into they're own factory, the Anderson's found theirselves in the market for an oven with airflow controls.
4. Cash-strapped entrepreneurs have learned penny-pinching, cost-cutting, credit-stretching techniques.
5. Designs in the Rough send out some 7 million catalogs a year yet until recently the company did'nt need a warehouse and they hadn't hardly any carrying costs.
6. Blockbuster estimates that 70 percent of the US population live within a 10 minute drive of a Blockbuster store.
7. Nestle Waters North America are the exclusive importer of globally-recognized brands such as: Perrier and Vittel from France and, S. Pelligrino from Italy,
8. The U.S. hispanic community; the largest Minority Group in the country; commands a impressive total purchasing power estimated at more than $500 billion dollars.
9. We conducted a six-month pilot in Chicago, to insure the affectiveness of the program.
10. A series of 7-Eleven television spots help make the term brain freeze part of every day American language.
11. The ad agencies accounts include the following consumer-brands; Walmart, Southwest airlines, FedEx, Land Rover, and Krispy Kreme.
12. PETsMART allows pets and their humans to together stroll the aisles of its stores; the number one Specialty Retailer of pet supplies.
13. Signature Fruit Co. has confirmed its closing it's ridley, CA peach plant this Fall.
    unite the company's 91 franchisees around a on corporate identity WingsToGo have setup a rate intranet.

15. It would be well for you to contract with an Internet service provider—a ISP - to both run and to maintain your website.

Level 3: Document Critique

The following document may contain errors in grammar, capitalization, punctuation, abbreviation, number style, word division, and vocabulary. As your instructor indicates, photocopy this page and correct all errors using standard proofreading marks (see Appendix C) or download the document and make the corrections in your word processing software.

Memco Construction
187 W. Euclid Avenue,
Glenview,
ILL 60025
www.memco.com

April 19, 2011

PROJECT: IDOT Letting Item #83 Contract No. 79371 DuPage County

Dear Mr. Estes—

Memco Construction is pleased to submit a road construction proposal for the above project. Our company has been providing quality materials and subcontracting services for highway reconstruction projects for over twenty-three years. Our most recent jobs in Illinois have included Illinois State Route 60 resurfacing, and reconstructing Illinois tollway 294.

Should you have any questions about this proposal please contact me at the company 847-672-0344, extension #30) or by e-mail at kbeirsdorf@memcocon.com.

Based on the scope of the work outlined: the total cost of this job is projected by us to run ninety-nine thousand, two hundred eighty-three dollars. Because material quantities can vary once a project gets underway a separate page will be attached by us to this letter detailing our per-unit fees. Final charges will be based on the exact quantity of materials used for the job, and anything that accedes this estimate will be added of course.

Our proposal assumes that the following items will be furnished by other contractors (at no cost to Memco). All forms, earthwork and clearing; All prep work; Water at project site; Traffic control setup, devices, and maintenance—Location for staging, stockpiling, and storing material and equipment at job sight.

If we win this bid, we are already to begin when the apropriate contracts have been signed by us and by you.

If you've have any questions, contact me at the phone number listed below.

Sincerely,
Kris Beiersdorf
Memco Construction
Office: (847) 352-9742, ext. 30
Fax: (847) 352-6595
E-mail: kbeiersdorf@memco.com

Developing Oral and Online Presentations

LEARNING OBJECTIVES

After studying this chapter, you will be able to

1 Highlight the importance of presentations in your business career and explain how to adapt the planning step of the three-step process to presentations

2 Describe the tasks involved in developing a presentation after completing the planning step

3 Describe the five major decisions required to enhance your presentation with effective visuals

4 Outline three special tasks involved in completing a presentation

5 Describe four important aspects of delivering a presentation in today's social media environment

---

PEARSON
mybcommlab

Access interactive videos, simulations, sample documents, Document Makeovers, and assessment quizzes in Chapter 12 of mybcommlab.com for mastery of this chapter's objectives.

" Successful speakers think about barriers. To connect with an audience, you must remove the many barriers that could interfere with the link between you and your audience. "

—Dr. Marc S. Friedman, *public speaking coach*

COMMUNICATION
Matters

With more than 30 years of experience in public speaking, teaching, and training, Marc Friedman has witnessed many technological changes that have transformed oral presentations. Although the right tools used in the right way can help a speaker build a strong connection with the audience, too often the technology gets in the way. Friedman says that holding an audience's attention is challenging enough in the best of circumstances, so any kind of communication barrier—from poorly designed slides to distracting laser pointers to excessive reliance on visual aids—makes the challenge that much greater. By all means, use the latest presentation tools whenever they can help, but don't let them interfere with the conversation you want to have with your audience.[1]

In any public speaking or presentation situation, try to remove the barriers that can prevent you from connecting with your audience.

1 LEARNING OBJECTIVE

Highlight the importance of presentations in your business career, and explain how to adapt the planning step of the three-step process to presentations

Oral presentation involve all of your communication skills, from research through nonverbal communication.

The three-step writing process can help you create more effective presentation and turn your public speaking anxiety into positive energy.

Creating a high-quality presentation for an important event can take many days, so be sure to allow enough time.

PLANNING A PRESENTATION

Oral presentations, delivered in person or online, offer important opportunities to put all your communication skills on display, including research, planning, writing, visual design, and interpersonal and nonverbal communication. Presentations also let you demonstrate your ability to think on your feet, grasp complex business issues, and handle challenging situations—all attributes that executives look for when searching for talented employees to promote.

If the thought of giving a speech or presentation makes you nervous, keep three points in mind. First, everybody gets nervous when speaking in front of groups. Second, being nervous is actually a good thing; it means you care about the topic, your audience, and your career success. Third, with practice, you can convert those nervous feelings into positive energy that helps you give more compelling presentations. You can take control of the situation by using the three-step writing process to prepare for successful presentations (see Figure 12.1).

Planning oral presentations is much like planning other business messages: You analyze the situation, gather information, select the right medium, and organize the information. Gathering information for oral presentations is essentially the same as it is for written communication projects. The other three planning tasks have some special applications when it comes to oral presentations; they are covered in the following sections.

On the subject of planning, be aware that preparing a professional-quality business presentation can take a considerable amount of time. Nancy Duarte, whose design firm has years of experience creating presentations for corporations, offers this rule of thumb: for a one-hour presentation that uses 30 slides, allow 36 to 90 hours to research, conceive, create, and practice.[2] Not every one-hour presentation justifies a week or two of preparation, of course, but the important presentations that can make your career or your company certainly can.

---

1 Plan →

Analyze the Situation

Define your purpose and develop a profile of your audience, including their likely emotional states and language preferences.

Gather Information

Determine audience needs and obtain the information necessary to satisfy those needs.

Select the Right Medium

Select the best medium or combination of media for delivering your presentation, including handouts and other support materials.

Organize the Information

Define your main idea, limit your scope and verify timing, select the direct or indirect approach, and outline your content.

2 Write →

Adapt to Your Audience

Adapt your content, presentation style, and room setup to the audience and the specific situation. Be sensitive to audience needs and expectations with a "you" attitude, politeness, positive emphasis, and bias-free language. Plan to establish your credibility as required.

Compose the Message

Outline an attention-getting introduction, body, and close. Prepare supporting visuals and speaking notes.

3 Complete

Revise the Message

Evaluate your content and speaking notes.

Master Your Delivery

Choose your delivery mode and practice your presentation

Prepare to Speak

Verify facilities and equipment, including online connection and software setups. Hire an interpreter if necessary.

Overcome Anxiety

Take steps to feel more confident and appear more confident on stage.

Figure 12.1   The Three-Step Process for Developing Oral and Online Presentations
Although you rarely "write" a presentation or speech in the sense of composing every word ahead of time, the tasks in the three-step writing process adapt quite well to the challenge of planning, creating, and delivering oral and online presentations.

Analyzing the Situation

As with written communications, analyzing the situation involves defining your purpose and developing an audience profile (see Table 12.1). The purpose of most of your presentations will be to inform or to persuade, although you may occasionally need to make a collaborative presentation, such as when you're leading a problem-solving or brainstorming session.

In addition to following the audience analysis advice in Chapter 3, try to anticipate the likely emotional state of your audience members. Figure 12.2 on the next page offers tips for dealing with a variety of audience mindsets.

As you analyze the situation, also consider the circumstances. Is the audience in the room or online? How many people will be present, and how will they be seated? Can you control the environment to minimize distractions? What equipment will you need? Such variables can influence not only the style of your presentation but the content itself.

Knowing your audience's state of mind will help you adjust both your message and your delivery.

Try to learn as much as you can about the setting and circumstances of your presentation, from the size of the audience to seating arrangements.

Selecting the Right Medium

The task of selecting the right medium might seem obvious. After all, you are speaking, so it's an oral medium. However, you have an array of choices these days, ranging from live, in-person presentations to *webcasts* (online presentations that people either view live or download later from your website), *screencasts* (recordings of activity on computer displays with audio voiceover), or *twebinars* (the use of Twitter as a *backchannel*—see page 370—for real-time conversation during a web-based seminar[3]).

Innovations in social media continue to reshape the nature of presentations.

● Access this chapter's slmulation entitled Business Presentations, located at mybcommlab.com.

Organizing Your Presentation

Organizing a presentation involves the same tasks as organizing a written message: Define your main idea, limit your scope, select the direct or indirect approach, and outline your content. Keep in mind that when people read written reports, they can skip back and forth if they're confused or don't need certain information. However, in an oral presentation, audiences are more or less trapped in your time frame and sequence. For some presentations, you should plan to be flexible and respond to audience feedback, such as skipping over sections the audience doesn't need to hear and going into more detail in other sections.

TABLE 12.1 Analyzing Audiences for Oral Presentations

Task	Actions
To determine audience size and composition	■ Estimate how many people will attend. ■ Identify what they have in common and how they differ. ■ Analyze the mix of men and women, age ranges, socioeconomic and ethnic groups, occupations, and geographic regions represented.
To predict the audience's probable reaction	■ Analyze why audience members are attending the presentation. ■ Determine the audience's general attitude toward the topic: interested, moderately interested, unconcerned, open-minded, or hostile. ■ Analyze the mood that people will be in when you speak to them. ■ Find out what kind of backup information will most impress the audience: technical data, historical information, financial data, demonstrations, samples, and so on. ■ Consider whether the audience has any biases that might work against you. ■ Anticipate possible objections or questions.
To gauge the audience's experience	■ Analyze whether everybody has the same background and level of understanding. ■ Determine what the audience already knows about the subject. ■ Decide what background information the audience will need to better understand the subject. ■ Consider whether the audience is familiar with the vocabulary you intend to use. ■ Analyze what the audience expects from you. ■ Think about the mix of general concepts and specific details you will need to present.

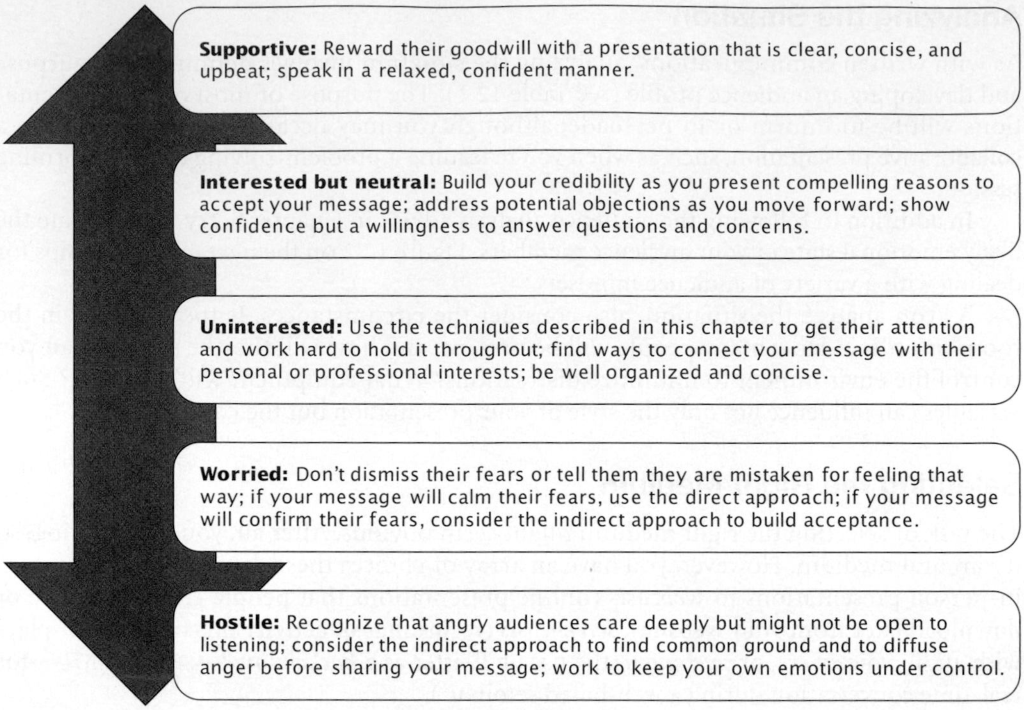

Supportive: Reward their goodwill with a presentation that is clear, concise, and upbeat; speak in a relaxed, confident manner.

Interested but neutral: Build your credibility as you present compelling reasons to accept your message; address potential objections as you move forward; show confidence but a willingness to answer questions and concerns.

Uninterested: Use the techniques described in this chapter to get their attention and work hard to hold it throughout; find ways to connect your message with their personal or professional interests; be well organized and concise.

Worried: Don't dismiss their fears or tell them they are mistaken for feeling that way; if your message will calm their fears, use the direct approach; if your message will confirm their fears, consider the indirect approach to build acceptance.

Hostile: Recognize that angry audiences care deeply but might not be open to listening; consider the indirect approach to find common ground and to diffuse anger before sharing your message; work to keep your own emotions under control.

Figure 12.2   Planning for Various Audience Mindsets
Try to assess the emotional state of your audience ahead of time so you can plan your presentation approach accordingly.

Defining Your Main Idea

If you can't express your main idea in a single sentence, you probably haven't defined it clearly enough.

If you've ever heard a speaker struggle to get his or her main point across ("What I really mean to say is . . ."), you know how frustrating such an experience can be for an audience. To avoid that struggle, figure out the one key message you want audience members to walk away with. Then compose a one-sentence summary that links your subject and purpose to your audience's frame of reference. Here are some examples:

> Convince management that reorganizing the technical support department will improve customer service and reduce employee turnover.

> Convince the board of directors that we should build a new plant in Texas to eliminate manufacturing bottlenecks and improve production quality.

> Address employee concerns regarding a new health-care plan by showing how the plan will reduce costs and improve the quality of their care.

Each of these statements puts a particular slant on the subject, one that directly relates to the audience's interests. By focusing on your audience's needs and using the "you" attitude, you help keep their attention and convince them that your points are relevant.

Limiting Your Scope

Limiting you scope ensures that your presentation fits the allotted time and your content meets audience needs and expectations.

Limiting your scope is important with any message, but it's particularly vital with presentations, for two reasons. First, for most presentations, you must work within strict time limits. For example, at DEMO and TechCrunch, two influential conferences in which entrepreneurs present their business plans to potential investors, presentations are limited to six and eight minutes, respectively.[4] Second, the longer you speak, the more difficult it is to hold the audience's attention levels, and the more difficult it is for your listeners to retain your key points.[5]

The only sure way to measure the length of your presentation is to complete a practice run.

The only sure way to know how much material you can cover in a given time is to practice your presentation after you complete it. As an alternative, if you're using conventional structured slides (see page 361) you can figure on 3 or 4 minutes per slide as a rough guide.[6] For instance, if you have 20 minutes, plan on being able to cover only 6 or 7 slides. Of course, be sure to factor in time for introductions, coffee breaks, demonstrations, question-and-answer sessions, and anything else that takes away from your speaking time.

If you're having trouble meeting a time limit or just want to keep your presentation as short as possible, consider a hybrid approach in which you present your key points in summary form and give people printed handouts with additional detail.[7] By the way, whenever you're up against a time or space constraint, try to view it as a creative challenge. Such limitations can force you to focus on the most essential message points that are important to your audience.[8] (See Case 1 on page 375 for the special twist on time-constrained presentations known as *pecha-kucha*.)

Choosing Your Approach

With a well-defined main idea to guide you and a clear idea about the scope of your presentation, you can begin to arrange your message. If you have 10 minutes or less, organize your presentation much as you would a letter or other brief message: Use the direct approach if the subject involves routine information or good news and use the indirect approach if the subject involves bad news or persuasion. Plan your introduction to arouse interest and to give a preview of what's to come. For the body of the presentation, be prepared to explain the who, what, when, where, why, and how of your subject. In the final section, review the points you've made and close with a statement that will help your audience remember the subject of your speech (see Figure 12.3).

Longer presentations are organized more like reports. If the purpose is to motivate or inform, you'll typically use the direct approach and a structure imposed naturally by the subject: comparison, importance, sequence, chronology, geography, or category (as discussed in Chapter 10). If your purpose is to analyze, persuade, or collaborate, organize your material around conclusions and recommendations or around a logical argument. Use the direct approach if the audience is receptive and the indirect approach if you expect resistance.

> Organize short presentations the same way you would a letter or brief memo; organize long presentations as you would a report or proposal.

Progress Update: August 2011

Purpose: To update the Executive Committee on our product development schedule.

I. Review goals and progress.
   A. Mechanical design:
     1. Goal: 100%
     2. Actual: 80%
     3. Reason for delay: Unanticipated problems with case durability
   B. Software development:
     1. Goal: 50%
     2. Actual: 60%
   C. Material sourcing:
     1. Goal: 100%
     2. Actual: 45% (and materials identified are at 140% of anticipated costs)
     3. Reason for delay: Purchasing is understaffed and hasn't been able to research sources adequately.
II. Discuss schedule options.
   A. Option 1: Reschedule product launch date.
   B. Option 2: Launch on schedule with more expensive materials.
III. Suggest goals for next month.
IV. Q&A

Figure 12.3   Effective Outline for a 10-Minute Presentation
Here is an outline of a short presentation that updates management on the status of a key project; the presenter has some bad news to deliver, so she opted for an indirect approach to lay out the reasons for the delay before sharing the news of the schedule slip.

Using a storytelling model can be a great way to catch and hold the audience's attention.

No matter what the length, look for opportunities to integrate storytelling (see page 95) into the structure of your presentation. The dramatic tension (not knowing what will happen to the "hero") at the heart of effective storytelling is a great way to capture and keep the audience's attention.

Preparing Your Outline

In addition to planning your speech, a presentation outline helps you plan your speaking notes.

A presentation outline helps you organize your message, and it serves as the foundation for delivering your speech. Prepare your outline in several stages:[9]

- State your purpose and main idea and then use these elements to guide the rest of your planning.
- Organize your major points and subpoints in logical order, expressing each major point as a single, complete sentence.
- Identify major points in the body first, then outline the introduction and close.

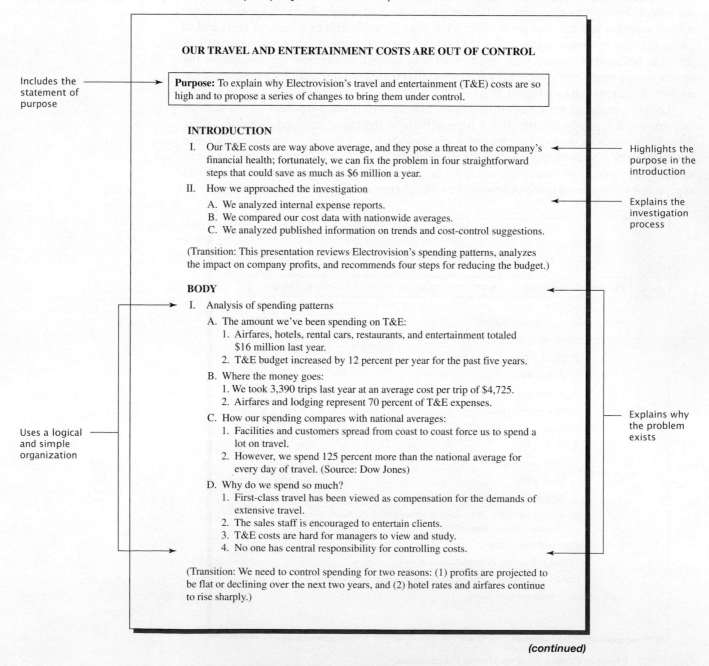

Includes the statement of purpose

OUR TRAVEL AND ENTERTAINMENT COSTS ARE OUT OF CONTROL

Purpose: To explain why Electrovision's travel and entertainment (T&E) costs are so high and to propose a series of changes to bring them under control.

INTRODUCTION

I. Our T&E costs are way above average, and they pose a threat to the company's financial health; fortunately, we can fix the problem in four straightforward steps that could save as much as $6 million a year. *(Highlights the purpose in the introduction)*

II. How we approached the investigation
   A. We analyzed internal expense reports.
   B. We compared our cost data with nationwide averages.
   C. We analyzed published information on trends and cost-control suggestions.
   (Explains the investigation process)

(Transition: This presentation reviews Electrovision's spending patterns, analyzes the impact on company profits, and recommends four steps for reducing the budget.)

BODY

I. Analysis of spending patterns
   A. The amount we've been spending on T&E:
      1. Airfares, hotels, rental cars, restaurants, and entertainment totaled $16 million last year.
      2. T&E budget increased by 12 percent per year for the past five years.
   B. Where the money goes:
      1. We took 3,390 trips last year at an average cost per trip of $4,725.
      2. Airfares and lodging represent 70 percent of T&E expenses.
   C. How our spending compares with national averages:
      1. Facilities and customers spread from coast to coast force us to spend a lot on travel.
      2. However, we spend 125 percent more than the national average for every day of travel. (Source: Dow Jones)
   D. Why do we spend so much?
      1. First-class travel has been viewed as compensation for the demands of extensive travel.
      2. The sales staff is encouraged to entertain clients.
      3. T&E costs are hard for managers to view and study.
      4. No one has central responsibility for controlling costs.

(Uses a logical and simple organization)
(Explains why the problem exists)

(Transition: We need to control spending for two reasons: (1) profits are projected to be flat or declining over the next two years, and (2) hotel rates and airfares continue to rise sharply.)

(continued)

Figure 12.4   Effective Outline for a 30-Minute Presentation
This outline clearly identifies the purpose and the distinct points to be made in the introduction, body, and close. Notice also how the speaker has written her major transitions in full-sentence form to be sure she can clearly phrase these critical passages when it's time to speak.

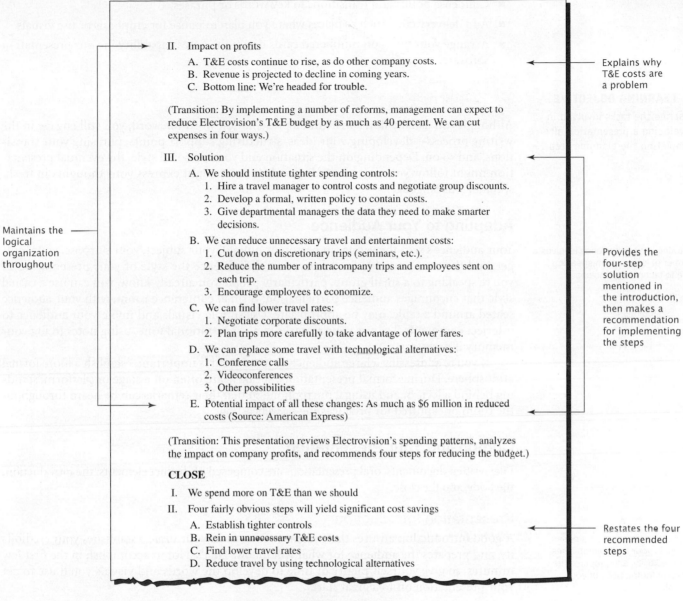

II. Impact on profits
    A. T&E costs continue to rise, as do other company costs.
    B. Revenue is projected to decline in coming years.
    C. Bottom line: We're headed for trouble.

Explains why T&E costs are a problem

(Transition: By implementing a number of reforms, management can expect to reduce Electrovision's T&E budget by as much as 40 percent. We can cut expenses in four ways.)

III. Solution
    A. We should institute tighter spending controls:
      1. Hire a travel manager to control costs and negotiate group discounts.
      2. Develop a formal, written policy to contain costs.
      3. Give departmental managers the data they need to make smarter decisions.
    B. We can reduce unnecessary travel and entertainment costs:
      1. Cut down on discretionary trips (seminars, etc.).
      2. Reduce the number of intracompany trips and employees sent on each trip.
      3. Encourage employees to economize.
    C. We can find lower travel rates:
      1. Negotiate corporate discounts.
      2. Plan trips more carefully to take advantage of lower fares.
    D. We can replace some travel with technological alternatives:
      1. Conference calls
      2. Videoconferences
      3. Other possibilities
    E. Potential impact of all these changes: As much as $6 million in reduced costs (Source: American Express)

Provides the four-step solution mentioned in the introduction, then makes a recommendation for implementing the steps

Maintains the logical organization throughout

(Transition: This presentation reviews Electrovision's spending patterns, analyzes the impact on company profits, and recommends four steps for reducing the budget.)

CLOSE

I. We spend more on T&E than we should

II. Four fairly obvious steps will yield significant cost savings

    A. Establish tighter controls
    B. Rein in unnecessary T&E costs
    C. Find lower travel rates
    D. Reduce travel by using technological alternatives

Restates the four recommended steps

mybcommlab

Apply Figure 12.4's key concepts by revising a new document. Go to Chapter 12 in mybcommlab.com and select Document Makeovers.

Figure 12.4

- Identify transitions between major points or sections, then write these transitions in full-sentence form.
- Prepare your bibliography or source notes; highlight those sources you want to identify by name during your talk.
- Choose a compelling title. Make it brief, action oriented, and focused on what you can do for the audience.[10]

Many speakers like to prepare both a detailed *planning outline* (see Figure 12.4) and a simpler *speaking outline* that provides all the cues and reminders they need in order to present their material. To prepare an effective speaking outline, follow these steps:[11]

You may find it helpful to create a simpler speaking outline from your planning outline.

- Start with the planning outline and then strip away anything you don't plan to say directly to your audience.

- Condense points and transitions to key words or phrases.
- Add delivery cues, such as places where you plan to pause for emphasis or use visuals.
- Arrange your notes on numbered cards or use the notes capability in your presentation software.

DEVELOPING A PRESENTATION

2 **LEARNING OBJECTIVE**
Describe the tasks involved in developing a presentation after completing the planning step

Although you usually don't write out a presentation word for word, you still engage in the writing process—developing your ideas, structuring support points, phrasing your transitions, and so on. Depending on the situation and your personal style, the eventual presentation might follow your initial words closely, or you might express your thoughts in fresh, spontaneous language.

Adapting to Your Audience

Adapting to your audience involves a number of issues, from speaking style to technology choices.

Your audience's size, the venue (in person or online), your subject, your purpose, your budget, and the time available for preparation all influence the style of your presentation. If you're speaking to a small group, particularly people you already know, you can use a casual style that encourages audience participation. A small conference room, with your audience seated around a table, may be appropriate. Use simple visuals and invite your audience to interject comments. Deliver your remarks in a conversational tone, using notes to jog your memory if necessary.

If you're addressing a large audience or if the event is important, establish a more formal atmosphere. During formal presentations, speakers are often on a stage or platform, standing behind a lectern and using a microphone so that their remarks can be heard throughout the room or captured for broadcasting or webcasting.

Composing Your Presentation

Like written documents, oral presentations are composed of distinct elements: the introduction, the body, and the close.

Presentation Introduction

An effective introduction arouses interest in your topic, establishes your credibility, and prepares the audience for the body of your presentation.

A good introduction arouses the audience's interest in your topic, establishes your credibility, and prepares the audience for what will follow. That's a lot to accomplish in the first few minutes, so give yourself plenty of time to develop the words and visuals you'll use to get your presentation off to a great start.

Spend some time thinking about the best technique to capture the audience's attention and interest with your opening remarks.

Getting Your Audience's Attention Some subjects are naturally more interesting to some audiences than others. If you will be discussing a matter of profound significance that will personally affect the members of your audience, chances are they'll listen, regardless of how you begin. All you really have to do is announce your topic, and you'll have their attention. Other subjects call for more imagination. Here are six ways to arouse audience interest:[12]

- Unite the audience around a common goal.
- Tell a compelling story that illustrates an important and relevant point. If your entire presentation is structured as a story, of course, you'll want to keep the interest high by not giving away the ending yet.
- Pass around an example or otherwise appeal to listeners' senses.
- Ask a question that will get your audience thinking about your message.
- Share an intriguing, unexpected, or shocking detail.
- Open with an amusing observation about yourself, the subject matter of the presentation, or the circumstances surrounding the presentation—but make sure any humorous remarks are relevant, appropriate, and not offensive to anyone in the audience.

Regardless of which technique you choose, make sure you can give audience members a reason to care and to believe that the time they're about to spend listening to you will be worth their while.[13]

Building Your Credibility   Audiences tend to decide within a few minutes whether you're worth listening to, so establishing your credibility quickly is vital.[14] If you're not a well-known expert or haven't already earned your audience's trust in other situations, you'll need to build credibility in your introduction. If someone else will introduce you, he or she can present your credentials. If you will be introducing yourself, keep your comments brief, but don't be afraid to mention your accomplishments. Your listeners will be curious about your qualifications, so tell them briefly who you are, why you're there, and how they'll benefit from listening to you. You might say something like this:

If someone else will be introducing you, ask this person to present your credentials.

> I'm Karen Whitney, a market research analyst with Information Resources Corporation. For the past five years, I've specialized in studying high-technology markets. Your director of engineering, John LaBarre, asked me to talk about recent trends in computer-aided design so that you'll have a better idea of how to direct your research efforts.

This speaker establishes credibility by tying her credentials to the purpose of her presentation. By mentioning her company's name, her specialization and position, and the name of the audience's boss, she lets her listeners know immediately that she is qualified to tell them something they need to know.

Previewing Your Message   In addition to getting the audience's attention and establishing your credibility, a good introduction gives your audience a preview of what's ahead. Your preview should summarize the main idea of your presentation, identify major supporting points, and indicate the order in which you'll develop those points. Of course, if you're using the indirect approach, you'll have to decide how much information to review in your introduction.

Offer a preview to help your audience understand the importance, the structure, and the content of your message.

Presentation Body

The bulk of your presentation is devoted to a discussion of the main points in your outline. No matter what organizational pattern you're using, your goals are to make sure that the organization of your presentation is clear and your that presentation holds the audience's attention.

Connecting Your Ideas   In written documents, you can show how ideas are related with a variety of design clues: headings, paragraph indentions, white space, and lists. However, with oral communication—particularly when you aren't using visuals for support—you have to rely primarily on spoken words to link various parts and ideas.

For the links between sentences and paragraphs, use one or two transitional words: *therefore, because, in addition, in contrast, moreover, for example, consequently, nevertheless,* or *finally.* To link major sections of a presentation, use complete sentences or paragraphs, such as "Now that we've reviewed the problem, let's take a look at some solutions." Every time you shift topics, be sure to stress the connection between ideas by summarizing what's been said and previewing what's to come. The longer your presentation, the more important your transitions. Your listeners need clear transitions to guide them to the most important points. Furthermore, they'll appreciate brief interim summaries to pick up any ideas they may have missed.

Use transitions to repeat key ideas, particularly in longer presentations.

Holding Your Audience's Attention   A successful introduction will have grabbed your audience's attention; now the body of your presentation needs to hold that attention. Here are a few helpful tips for keeping the audience tuned into your message:

- Keep relating your subject to your audience's needs.
- Anticipate—and answer—your audience's questions as you move along so people don't get confused or distracted.
- Use clear, vivid language and throw in some variety; repeating the same words and phrases over and over puts people to sleep.
- Show how your subject is related to ideas that audience members already understand, and give people a way to categorize and remember your points.[15]
- If appropriate, encourage participation by asking for comments or questions.
- Illustrate your ideas with visuals, which enliven your message, help you connect with audience members, and help them remember your message more effectively (see "Enhancing Your Presentation with Effective Visuals," pages 360–365).

The most important way to hold an audience's attention is to show how your message relates to their individual needs and concerns.

Presentation Close

Your close is critical because audiences tend to focus more carefully as they wait for you to wrap up, and they will leave with your final words ringing in their ears. Before closing your presentation, tell listeners that you're about to finish so that they'll make one final effort to listen intently. Don't be afraid to sound obvious. Consider saying something such as "In conclusion" or "To sum it all up." You want people to know that this is the final segment of your presentation.

Restating Your Main Points Repeat your main idea, emphasizing what you want your audience to do or to think, and stress the key motivating factor that will encourage them to respond that way. Reinforce your theme by restating your main supporting points, as this speaker did in a presentation on the company's executive compensation program:

> We can all be proud of the way our company has grown. However, if we want to continue that growth, we need to take four steps to ensure that our best people don't start looking for opportunities elsewhere:
>
> - First, increase the overall level of compensation
> - Second, establish a cash bonus program
> - Third, offer a variety of stock-based incentives
> - Fourth, improve our health insurance and pension benefits
>
> By taking these steps, we can ensure that our company retains the management talent it needs to face our industry's largest competitors.

Repetition of key ideas, as long as you don't overdo it, greatly improves the chance that your audience will hear your message in the way you intended.

Ending with Clarity and Confidence If you've been successful with the introduction and body of your presentation, your listeners now have the information they need, and they're in the right frame of mind to put that information to good use. Now you're ready to end on a strong note that confirms expectations about any actions or decisions that will follow the presentation—and to bolster the audience's confidence in you and your message one final time.

Some presentations require the audience to reach a decision or agree to take specific action, in which case the close provides a clear wrap-up. If the audience agrees on an issue covered in the presentation, briefly review the consensus. If they don't agree, make the lack of consensus clear by saying something like, "We seem to have some fundamental disagreement on this question." Then be ready to suggest a method of resolving the differences.

If you expect any action to occur as a result of your speech, be sure to explain who is responsible for doing what. List the action items and, if possible within the time available, establish due dates and assign responsibility for each task.

Make sure your final remarks are memorable and expressed in a tone that is appropriate to the situation. For example, if your presentation is a persuasive request for project funding, you might emphasize the importance of this project and your team's ability to complete it on schedule and within budget. Expressing confident optimism will send the message that you believe in your ability to perform. Conversely, if your purpose was to alert the audience to a problem or risk, false optimism will undermine your message.

Whatever final message is appropriate, think through your closing remarks carefully before stepping in front of the audience. You don't want to wind up on stage with nothing to say but "Well, I guess that's it."

Plan your final statement carefully so you can end on a strong, positive note.

Make sure your final remarks are memorable and have the right emotional tone.

3 LEARNING OBJECTIVE

Describe the five major decisions required to enhance your presentation with effective visuals

ENHANCING YOUR PRESENTATION WITH EFFECTIVE VISUALS

Visuals can improve the quality and impact of your oral presentation by creating interest, illustrating points that are difficult to explain in words alone, adding variety, and increasing the audience's ability to absorb and remember information.

You can select from a variety of visuals to enhance oral presentations. Don't overlook "old-school" technologies such as overhead transparencies, chalkboards, whiteboards, and flipcharts—they can all have value in the right circumstances. However, the medium of choice for most business presentations is an electronic presentation using Microsoft PowerPoint, Apple Keynote, Google Documents, or similar software. Electronic presentations are easy to edit and update; you can add sound, photos, video, and animation; they can be incorporated into online meetings, webcasts, and *webinars* (a common term for web-based seminars); and you can record self-running presentations for trade shows, websites, and other uses.

> Thoughtfully designed visuals create interest, illustrate complex points in your message, add variety, and help the audience absorb and remember information.

Electronic presentations are practically universal in business today, but their widespread use is not always welcome. You may have already heard the expression "death by PowerPoint," which refers to the agonizing experience of sitting through too many poorly conceived and poorly delivered presentations. In the words of presentation expert and author Garr Reynolds, "most presentations remain mind-numbingly dull, something to be endured by presenter and audience alike."[16]

That's the bad news. The good news is that presentations can be an effective communication medium and an experience that is satisfying, and sometimes even enjoyable, for presenter and audience alike. Start with the mindset of *simplicity* (clear ideas presented clearly) and *authenticity* (talking *with* your audience about things they care about, rather that talking at them or trying to be a "performer"), and you'll be well on your way to becoming an effective presenter.

> Focusing on making your presentations simple and authentic will help you avoid the "death by PowerPoint" stigma that presentations have in the mind of many professionals.

Choosing Structured or Free-Form Slides

Perhaps the most important design choice you face when creating slides is whether to use conventional, bullet point-intensive *structured slides* or the looser, visually oriented *free-form slides* that many presentation specialists now advocate. Compare the two rows of slides in Figure 12.5 on the next page. The structured slides in the top row follow the same basic format throughout the presentation. In fact, they're based directly on the templates built into PowerPoint, which tend to feature lots and lots of bullet points.

> Structured slides are usually based on templates that give all the slides in a presentation the same general look (which usually involves a lot of bullet points); free-form slides are much less rigid and emphasize visual appeal.

The free-form slides in the bottom row don't follow a rigid structure. However, free-form designs should not change randomly from one slide to the next. Effectively designed slides should still be unified by design elements such as color and font selections, as can be seen in Figures 12.5c and 12.5d. Also, note how Figure 12.5d combines visual and textual messages to convey the point about listening without criticizing. This complementary approach of pictures and words is a highlight of free-form design.

Because the amount of content varies so dramatically between the two design approaches, the number of slides in a presentation also varies dramatically. For instance, someone using structured slides might have 6 or 7 slides for a 20-minute presentation, but someone using free-form slides for the same presentation might have 60–80 slides or more and spend only 15 or 20 seconds on each one. In the extreme, a 20-minute free-form presentation could have *hundreds* of slides, with some slides sometimes displayed for less than a second.[17] Both design strategies have advantages and disadvantages, and one or the other can be a better choice for specific situations.

> Free-form slides often have far less content per slide than structured designs, which requires many more slides to cover a presentation of equal length.

Structured slides have the advantage of being easy to create; you simply choose an overall design scheme for the presentation, select a template for a new slide, and start typing. If you're in a schedule crunch, going the structured route might save the day because at least you'll have *something* ready to show. Given the speed and ease of creating them, structured slides can be a more practical choice for routine presentations such as project status updates. Also, because more information can usually be packed on each slide, carefully designed structured slides can be more effective at conveying complex ideas or sets of interrelated data to the right audiences. However, this opportunity to pack a lot of information into a single slide is often abused, with the result being slides that require too much study and explanation to be effective.

> Structured slides are often the best choice for project updates and other routine information presentations, particularly if the slides are intended to be used only once.

The goal of free-form slide design is to overcome the drawbacks of text-heavy structured design by fulfilling three criteria that researchers have identified as important for successful presentations: (1) providing complementary information through both textual and visual means; (2) limiting the amount of information delivered at any one time to prevent cognitive overload; and (3) helping viewers process information by identifying priorities and connections, such as by highlighting the most important data points in a graph.[18]

> Well-designed free-form slides help viewers understand, process, and remember the speaker's message.

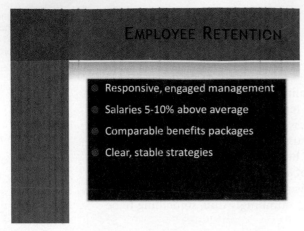

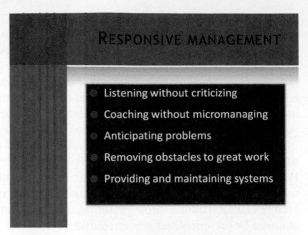

Figure 12.5a

Figure 12.5b

Figure 12.5c

Figure 12.5d

Figure 12.5 Structured Versus Free-Form Slide Design
Compare the rigid, predictable design of the two slides in the top row with the more dynamic free-form designs in the bottom row. Although the two free-form slides don't follow the same design structure, they are visually linked by color and font choices. (Note that Figure 12.5d is a humorous way of conveying the first bullet point in Figure 12.5b.)

With appropriate imagery, free-form designs can also create a more dynamic and engaging experience for the audience. Given their ability to excite and engage, free-form designs are particularly good for motivational, educational, and persuasive presentations—particularly when the slides will be used multiple times and therefore compensate for the extra time and effort required to create them.

In addition to the extra time and skill often required to create them, free-form slides place a greater burden on the presenter to convey the whole story because only the highlight points are displayed on the slides. Many presentation experts would argue that this is how it *should* be, however. Audiences come to hear you speak, not to read your slides.

> Use slide text to emphasize key points, not to convey your entire message.

Writing Readable Content

One of the most common mistakes beginners make—and one of the chief criticisms leveled at structured slide designs in general—is stuffing slides with too much text. Doing so creates several problems: It overloads the audience with too much information too fast; it takes attention away from the speaker by forcing people to read more; and it requires the presenter to use smaller type, which in turn makes the slides even harder to read.

Effective text slides supplement your words and help the audience follow the flow of ideas (see Figure 12.6). Use them to highlight key points, summarize and preview your message, signal major shifts in thought, illustrate concepts, or help create interest in your spoken message.

Designing Graphics for Slides

Visuals for presentations need to be simpler than visuals for printed documents. Detailed images that look fine on the printed page can be too dense and too complicated for presentations. Remember that your audience members will view your visuals from across the room—not from a foot or two away, as you do while you create them. Keep the level of detail at an absolute minimum, eliminating anything that is not absolutely essential. If necessary, break information into more than one illustration.

As much as possible, design visuals in a way that gives the viewer's eyes a clear path to follow, such as from left to right or from top to bottom. Avoid jumbled layouts that force the eye to traverse all over the screen to assemble the meaning of the visual. With the basic

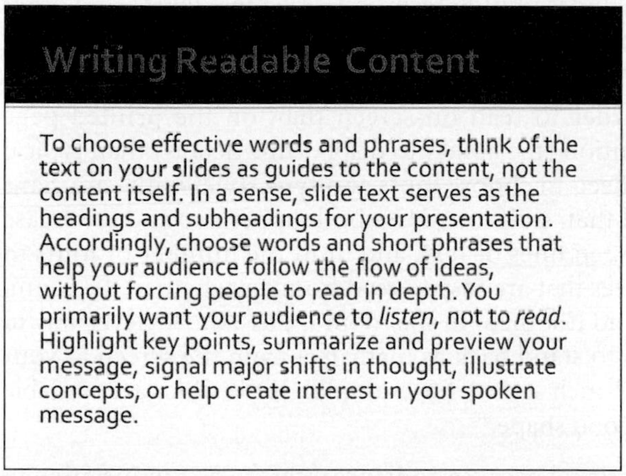

> Visuals for presentations need to be simpler than visuals for printed documents.

Writing Readable Content

To choose effective words and phrases, think of the text on your slides as guides to the content, not the content itself. In a sense, slide text serves as the headings and subheadings for your presentation. Accordingly, choose words and short phrases that help your audience follow the flow of ideas, without forcing people to read in depth. You primarily want your audience to *listen*, not to *read*. Highlight key points, summarize and preview your message, signal major shifts in thought, illustrate concepts, or help create interest in your spoken message.

Figure 12.6a

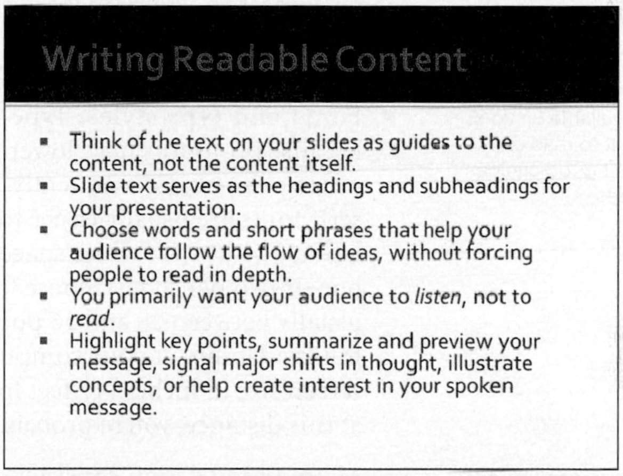

Writing Readable Content

- Think of the text on your slides as guides to the content, not the content itself.
- Slide text serves as the headings and subheadings for your presentation.
- Choose words and short phrases that help your audience follow the flow of ideas, without forcing people to read in depth.
- You primarily want your audience to *listen*, not to *read*.
- Highlight key points, summarize and preview your message, signal major shifts in thought, illustrate concepts, or help create interest in your spoken message.

Figure 12.6b

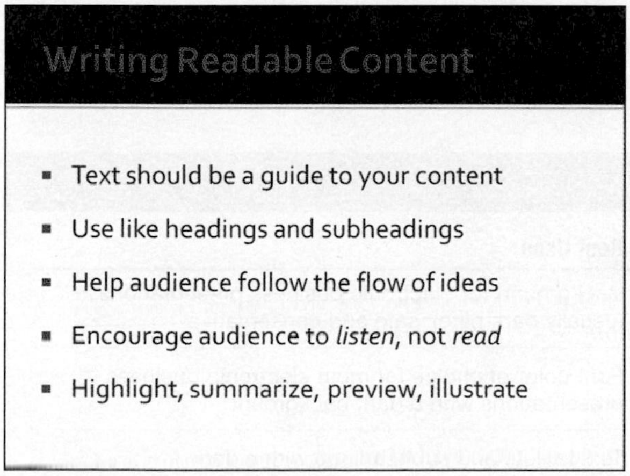

Writing Readable Content

- Text should be a guide to your content
- Use like headings and subheadings
- Help audience follow the flow of ideas
- Encourage audience to *listen*, not *read*
- Highlight, summarize, preview, illustrate

Figure 12.6c

Writing Readable Content

Use only enough text
to help your audience
follow the **flow** of **ideas**.

Figure 12.6d

Figure 12.6   Writing Readable Content
Effective text slides are clear, simple guides that help the audience understand and remember the speaker's message. Notice the progression toward simplicity in these slides: Figure 12.6a is a paragraph that would distract the audience for an extended period of time. Figure 12.6b simplifies the message somewhat, but these bullet points are too long, and the slide is too crowded. Figure 12.6c offers concise, readable bullets, although too many slides in a row in this structured design would become tedious. Figure 12.6d distills the message down to a single compelling thought, with three key words emphasized. It is easy to read, but the speaker will need to fill in the missing parts of the message.

mybcommlab

Apply Figure 12.6's key concepts by revising a new document. Go to Chapter 12 in mybcommlab.com and select Document Makeovers.

design in place, you can use design elements such as arrows, contrasting accent colors, and text labels to highlight key points.

Selecting Design Elements

As you create slides, pay close attention to the interaction of color, background and foreground designs, artwork, fonts, and type styles.

Color is more than just decoration; colors have meanings themselves, based on both cultural experience and the relationships that you established between the colors in your designs.

- **Color.** Color is a critical design element that can grab attention, emphasize important ideas, create contrast, and stimulate various emotions (see Table 12.2). Research shows that color visuals can account for 60 percent of an audience's acceptance or rejection of an idea. Color can increase willingness to read by up to 80 percent, and it can enhance learning and improve retention by more than 75 percent.[19] Color is powerful, so use it carefully.

Make sure the background of your slides stays in the background; it should never get in the way of the informational elements in the foreground.

- **Background designs and artwork.** All visuals have two layers of design: the *background* and the *foreground*. The background is the equivalent of paper in a printed report and "should be open, spacious, and simple," says design expert Nancy Duarte.[20] Be aware that many of the template designs in presentations software have backgrounds that are too distracting.

- **Foreground designs and artwork.** The foreground contains the unique text and graphic elements that make up each individual slide. Foreground elements can be either functional or decorative. *Functional artwork* includes photos, technical drawings, charts, and other visual elements containing information that's part of your message. In contrast, *decorative artwork* simply enhances the look of your slides and should be used sparingly, if at all.

Many of the fonts available on your computer are difficult to read on screen, so they aren't good choices for presentation slides.

- **Fonts and type styles.** Type is harder to read on-screen than on the printed page because projectors have lower resolution (the ability to display fine details) than typical office printers. Consequently, you need to choose fonts and type styles with care. Sans serif fonts are usually easier to read than serif fonts. Use both uppercase and lowercase letters, with extra white space between lines of text, and limit the number of fonts to one or two per slide. Choose font sizes that are easy to read from anywhere in the room, usually between 28 and 36 points, and test them in the room if possible. A clever way to test readability at your computer is to stand back as many feet from the screen as your screen size in inches (17 feet for a 17-inch screen, for example). If the slides are readable at this distance, you're probably in good shape.[21]

Design inconsistencies confuse and annoy audiences; don't change colors and other design elements randomly throughout your presentation.

Maintaining design consistency is critical because audiences start to assign meaning to visual elements beginning with the first slide. For instance, if yellow is used to call attention to the first major point in your presentation, viewers will expect the next occurrence of yellow to also signal an important point. The *slide master* feature makes consistency easy to achieve because it applies design choices to every slide in a presentation.

TABLE 12.2 Color and Emotion

Color	Emotional Associations	Best Uses
Blue	Peaceful, soothing, tranquil, cool, trusting	Background for electronic business presentations (usually dark blue); safe and conservative
White	Neutral, innocent, pure, wise	Font color of choice for most electronic business presentations with a dark background
Yellow	Warm, bright, cheerful, enthusiastic	Text bullets and subheadings with a dark background
Red	Passionate, dangerous, active, painful	For promoting action or stimulating the audience; seldom used as a background ("in the red" specifically refers to financial losses)
Green	Assertive, prosperous, envious, relaxed	Highlight and accent color (green symbolizes money in the United States but not in other countries).

Adding Animation and Multimedia

Today's presentation software offers many options for livening up your slides, including sound, animation, video clips, transition effects, and hyperlinks. Think about the impact that all these effects will have on your audience and use only those special effects that support your message.[22]

Functional animation involves motion that is directly related to your message, such as a highlight arrow that moves around the screen to emphasize specific points in a technical diagram. Such animation is also a great way to demonstrate sequences and procedures. In contrast, *decorative animation,* such as having a block of text cartwheel in from offscreen, needs to be used with great care. These effects don't add any functional value, and they easily distract audiences.

Transitions control how one slide replaces another, such as having the current slide gently fade out before the next slide fades in. Subtle transitions like this can ease your viewers' gaze from one slide to the next, but many of the transition effects now available are little more than distractions and are best avoided. **Builds** control the release of text, graphics, and other elements on individual slides. With builds, you can make key points appear one at a time rather than having all of them appear on a slide at once, thereby making it easier for you and the audience to focus on each new message point.

A **hyperlink** instructs your computer to jump to another slide in your presentation, to a website, or to another program entirely. Using hyperlinks is also a great way to build flexibility into your presentations so that you can instantly change the flow of your presentation in response to audience feedback.

Multimedia elements offer the ultimate in active presentations. Using audio and video clips can be a great way to complement your textual message. Just be sure to keep these elements brief and relevant, as supporting points for your presentation, not as replacements for it.

For the latest information on electronic presentation tools and techniques, visit http://real-timeupdates.com/bce5 and click on Chapter 12.

COMPLETING A PRESENTATION

The completion step for presentations involves a wider range of tasks than most printed documents require. Make sure you allow enough to time to test your presentation slides, verify equipment operation, practice your speech, and create handout materials. With a first draft of your presentation in hand, revise your slides to make sure they are readable, concise, consistent, and fully operational (including transitions, builds, animation, and multimedia). Complete your production efforts by finalizing your slides and support materials, choosing your presentation method, and practicing your delivery.

Finalizing Slides and Support Materials

Electronic presentation software can help you throughout the editing and revision process. As Figure 12.7 on the next page shows, the *slide sorter* view (different programs have different names for this feature) lets you see some or all of the slides in your presentation on a single screen. Use this view to add and delete slides, reposition slides, check slides for design consistency, and verify the operation of any effects. Moreover, the slide sorter is a great way to review the flow of your story.[23]

In addition to using content slides, you can help your audience follow the flow of your presentation by creating slides for your title, agenda and program details, and navigation:

- **Title slide(s).** You can make a good first impression with one or two title slides, the equivalent of a report's cover and title page (see Figures 12.8a and 12.8b on page 367).

- **Agenda and program details.** These slides communicate the agenda for your presentation and any additional information the audience might need (see Figures 12.8c and 12.8d).

- **Navigation slides.** To tell your audience where you're going and where you've been, you can use a series of **navigation slides** based on your outline or agenda. As you complete each section, repeat the agenda slide but indicate which material has been covered and which section you are about to begin (see Figure 12.9 on page 367). This sort of slide is sometimes referred to as a *moving blueprint.* As an alternative to the repeating agenda slide, you can insert a simple *bumper* slide at each major section break, announcing the title of the section you're about to begin.[24]

You can animate just about everything in an electronic presentation, but resist the temptation to do so; make sure an animation has a purpose.

If you use transitions between slides, make sure they are subtle; they should do nothing more than ease the eye from one slide to the next.

Hyperlinks let you build flexibility into your presentations.

4 LEARNING OBJECTIVE
Outline three special tasks involved in completing a presentation

Navigation slides help your audience keep track of what you've covered already and what you plan to cover next.

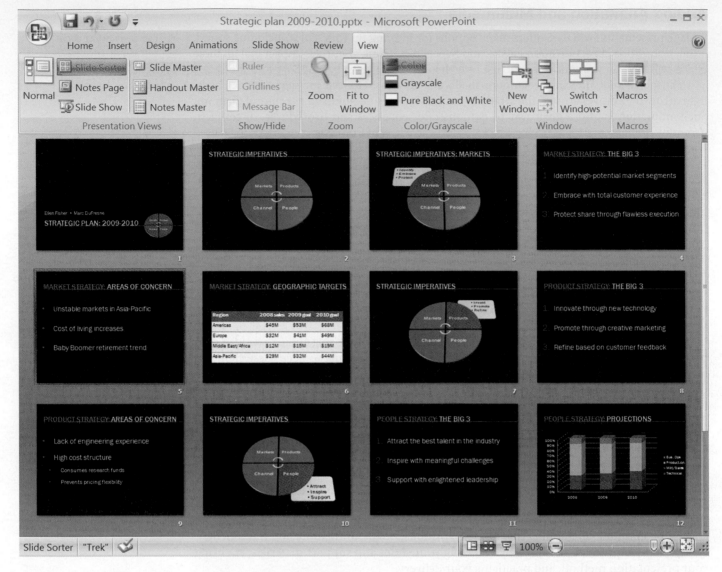

Figure 12.7   Slide Sorter View
Examining *thumbnails* of slides on one screen is the best way to check the overall design of your final product. The slide sorter also makes it easy to ponder the order and organization of your presentation; you can change the position of any slide simply by clicking and dragging it to a new position.

Use handout materials to support the points made in your presentation and to offer the audience additional information on your topic.

With your slides working properly and in clear, logical order, consider whether printed handouts or other support materials could help your audience grasp and act on your message. As mentioned on page 355, for example, a detailed handout that is well-integrated with your spoken message points is a good way to make the best use of your limited time in front of the audience.

Choosing Your Presentation Method

With all your materials ready, your next step is to decide which method of speaking you want to use. In nearly all situations, the best choice is speaking from notes, rather than reciting from memory or reading a prepared statement word for word. Even if you can memorize your entire speech, your presentation will sound stiff and overly formal because you are "delivering lines," rather than talking to your audience. Worse yet, you might forget your lines. However, memorizing a quotation, an opening statement, or a few concluding remarks can bolster your confidence and strengthen your delivery.

Reading your speech is sometimes necessary, such as when delivering legal information, policy statements, or other messages that must be conveyed in an exact manner. However, for all other business presentations, reading is a poor choice because it limits your interaction with the audience and lacks the fresh, dynamic feel of natural talking. If you

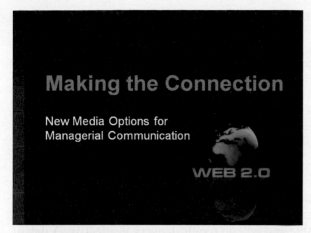

Figure 12.8a Title slide

Figure 12.8b Title slide 2

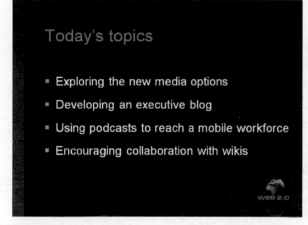

Figure 12.8c Agenda

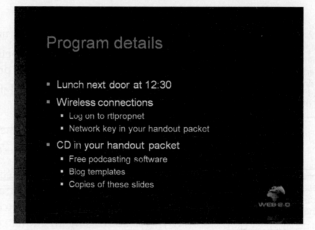

Figure 12.8d Program details

Figure 12.8   Navigation and Support Slides
You can use a variety of navigation and support slides to introduce yourself and your presentation, to let the audience know what your presentation will cover, and to provide essential details.

must read a prepared speech, practice enough so that you can still maintain eye contact with your audience. Print your speech with triple-spaced lines, wide margins, and large type.

Speaking from notes, with the help of an outline, note cards, or visuals, is usually the most effective and easiest delivery mode. This approach gives you something to refer to and

Figure 12.9a "Muting" topics already covered

Figure 12.9b Highlighting the next topic

Figure 12.9   Moving Blue print Slides
Here are two of the ways you can use a *blueprint slide* as a navigational aid to help your audience stay on track with the presentation. Figure 12.9a visually "mutes" and checks off the sections of the presentation that have already been covered. In contrast, Figure 12.9b uses a sliding highlight box to indicate the next section to be covered.

Speaking from carefully prepared notes is the easiest and most effective delivery mode for most speakers.

still allows for plenty of eye contact, interaction with the audience, and improvisation in response to audience feedback.

Another important decision at this point is preparing the venue where you will speak. In many instances, you won't have much of a choice, such as when presenting at a conference or when visiting a client's offices. However, if you do have some control over the environment, think carefully about the seating for the audience, your position in the room, and the lighting. For instance, dimming the lights is common practice for many presenters, but dimming the lights too far can hamper the nonverbal communication between you and your audience and therefore limit opportunities for interaction.[25]

Practicing Your Delivery

The more you practice, the more confidence you'll have in yourself and your material.

Practicing your presentation is essential. Practice helps ensure that you appear polished and confident, and it lets you verify the operation of visuals and equipment. A test audience can tell you if your slides are understandable and whether your delivery is effective. A day or two before you're ready to step on stage for an important talk, make sure you and your presentation are ready:

Make sure you're comfortable with the equipment you'll be expected to use; you don't want to be fumbling with controls while the audience is watching and waiting.

- Can you present your material naturally, without reading your slides?
- Could you still make a compelling and complete presentation if you experience an equipment failure and have to proceed without using your slides at all?
- Is the equipment working, and do you know how to work it?
- Is your timing on track?
- Can you easily pronounce all the words you plan to use?
- Have you anticipated likely questions and objections?

You'll know you've practiced enough when you can present the material at a comfortable pace and in a natural, conversational tone.

With experience, you'll get a feel for how much practice is enough in any given situation. Practicing helps keep you on track, helps you maintain a conversational tone with your audience, and boosts your confidence and composure.

If you're addressing an audience that doesn't speak your language, consider using an interpreter. Send your interpreter a copy of your speech and visuals as far in advance of your presentation as possible. If your audience is likely to include persons with hearing impairments, be sure to team up with a sign-language interpreter as well.

When you deliver an oral presentation to people from other cultures, you may need to adapt the content of your presentation. It is also important to take into account any cultural differences in appearance, mannerisms, and other customs. Your interpreter or host will be able to suggest appropriate changes for a specific audience or occasion.

5 LEARNING OBJECTIVE
Describe four important aspects of delivering a presentation in today's social media environment

DELIVERING A PRESENTATION

It's show time. This section offers practical advice for four important aspects of delivery: overcoming anxiety, handling questions responsively, embracing the backchannel, and giving presentations online.

> "Put your love, passion, imagination, and spirit behind it. Without enthusiasm, there is no creativity. It may be a quiet enthusiasm, or it may be loud. It doesn't matter, so long as it is real."
> —Garr Reynolds[26]
> **PASSION** *Matters*

Preparation is the best antidote for anxiety; it gives you confidence that you know your material and that you recover from any glitches you might encounter.

Overcoming Anxiety

Keep in mind that nervousness is an indication that you care about your audience, your topic, and the occasion. These techniques will help you convert anxiety into positive energy:[27]

- **Stop worrying about being perfect.** Everyone makes mistakes, whether it's tripping over a hard-to-pronounce word or literally tripping while on stage. Successful speakers focus on making an authentic connection with their listeners, rather than on trying to deliver a note-perfect presentation.

- **Prepare more material than necessary.** Combined with having a genuine interest in your topic, having extra knowledge will reduce your anxiety.

- **Practice.** The more familiar you are with your material, the less panic you'll feel.

- **Visualize your success.** Visualize mental images of yourself in front of the audience, feeling confident, prepared, and able to handle any situation that might arise.[28] Remember that your audience wants you to succeed, too.

- **Remember to breathe.** Tension can lead people to breathe in a rapid and shallow fashion, which can create a lightheaded feeling. Breathe slowly and deeply to maintain a sense of calm and confidence.

- **Be ready with your opening line.** Have your first sentence memorized and on the tip of your tongue.

- **Be comfortable.** Dress appropriately but as comfortably as possible. Drink plenty of water ahead of time to hydrate your voice (bring a bottle of water with you, too).

- **Take a three-second break.** If you sense that you're starting to race, pause and arrange your notes or perform some other small task while taking several deep breaths. Then start again at your normal pace. If you feel that you're losing your audience, try to pull them back by asking for comments or questions.

- **Concentrate on your message and your audience, not on yourself.** When you're busy thinking about your subject and observing your audience's response, you tend to forget your fears.

- **Maintain eye contact with friendly audience members.** Eye contact not only makes you appear sincere, confident, and trustworthy but can give you positive feedback as well.

- **Keep going.** Things usually get better as you move along, with each successful minute giving you more and more confidence.

Handling Questions Responsively

The question-and-answer (Q&A) period is one of the most important parts of an oral presentation. It gives you a chance to obtain important information, to emphasize your main idea and supporting points, and to build enthusiasm for your point of view. When you're speaking to high-ranking executives in your company, the Q&A period will often consume most of the time allotted for your presentation.[29]

Whether or not you can establish ground rules for Q&A depends on the audience and the situation. If you're presenting to a small group of upper managers or potential investors, for example, you will probably have no say in the matter: Audience members will likely ask as many questions as they want, whenever they want, to get the information they need. On the other hand, if you are presenting to your peers or a large public audience, establish some guidelines, such as the number of questions allowed per person and the overall time limit for questions.

Don't assume that you can handle whatever comes up without some preparation.[30] Learn enough about your audience members to get an idea of their concerns and think through answers to potential questions.

When people ask questions, pay attention to nonverbal signals to help determine what each person really means. Repeat the question to confirm your understanding and to ensure that the entire audience has heard it. If the question is vague or confusing, ask for clarification; then give a simple, direct answer.

If you are asked a difficult or complex question, avoid the temptation to sidestep it. Offer to meet with the questioner afterward if the issue isn't relevant to the rest of the audience or if giving an adequate answer would take too long. If you don't know the answer, don't pretend that you do. Instead, offer to get a complete answer as soon as possible.

Be on guard for audience members who use questions to make impromptu speeches or to take control of your presentation. Without offending anyone, find a way to stay in control.

Don't leave the question-and-answer period to chance: Anticipate potential questions and think through your answers.

If you don't have the complete answer to an important question, offer to provide it after the presentation.

You might admit that you and the questioner have differing opinions and, before calling on someone else, offer to get back to the questioner after you've done more research.[31]

If you ever face hostile questions, respond honestly and directly while keeping your cool.

If a question ever puts you on the hot seat, respond honestly but keep your cool. Look the person in the eye, answer the question as well as you can, and keep your emotions under control. Defuse hostility by paraphrasing the question and asking the questioner to confirm that you've understood it correctly. Maintain a businesslike tone of voice and a pleasant expression.[32]

When the time allotted for your presentation is almost up, prepare the audience for the end by saying something like, "Our time is almost up. Let's have one more question." After you reply to that last question, summarize the main idea of the presentation and thank people for their attention. Conclude with the same confident demeanor you've had from the beginning.

Embracing the Backchannel

Twitter and other social media are dramatically changing business presentations by making it easy for all audience members to participate in the backchannel.

Many business presentations these days involve more than just the spoken conversation between the speaker and his or her audience. Using Twitter and other electronic media, audience members often carry on their own parallel communication during a presentation via the **backchannel**, which presentation expert Cliff Atkinson defines as "a line of communication created by people in an audience to connect with others inside or outside the room, with or without the knowledge of the speaker."[33] Chances are you've participated in a backchannel already, such as when texting with your classmates or live-blogging during a lecture.

The backchannel presents both risks and rewards for business presenters. On the negative side, for example, listeners can research your claims the instant you make them and spread the word quickly if they think your information is shaky. The backchannel also gives contrary audience members more leverage, which can lead to presentations spinning out of control. On the plus side, listeners who are excited about your message can build support for it, expand on it, and spread it to a much larger audience in a matter of seconds. You can also get valuable feedback during and after presentations.[34]

Resist the urge to ignore or fight the backchannel; instead, learn how to use it to your advantage.

By embracing the backchannel, rather than trying to fight it or ignore it, presenters can use this powerful force to their advantage. Follow these tips to make the backchannel work for you:[35]

- **Integrate social media into the presentation process.** For example, you can set up a formal backchannel yourself using tools such as BackNoise (**http://backnoise.com**), create a website for the presentation so that people can access relevant resources during or after the presentation, create a Twitter hashtag that everyone can use when sending tweets, or display the Twitterstream during Q&A so that everyone can see the questions and comments on the backchannel.

- **Monitor and ask for feedback.** Using a free service such as Tweetdeck, which organizes tweets by hashtag and other variables, you can monitor in real time what the people in the audience are writing about. To avoid trying to monitor the backchannel while speaking, you can schedule "Twitter breaks," during which you review comments and respond as needed.

- **Review comments point by point to improve your presentation.** After a presentation is over, review comments on audience members' Twitter accounts and blogs to see which parts confused them, which parts excited them, and which parts seemed to have little effect (based on few or no comments).

- **Automatically tweet key points from your presentation while you speak.** Add-ons for presentation software can send out prewritten tweets as you show specific slides during a presentation. By making your key points readily available, you make it easy for listeners to retweet and comment on your presentation.

- **Establish expectations with the audience.** Explain that you welcome audience participation, but to ensure a positive experience for everyone, comments should be civil, relevant, and productive.

REAL-TIME UPDATES
Learn More by Watching This Video

Maximize the rewards of the backchannel and minimize the risks

This webinar hosted by author Cliff Atkinson outlines the principles of the social media backchannel and analyzes a real-life presentation where the backchannel spurred an audience revolt and what presenters can learn from this. Go to **http://real-timeupdates.com/bce5** and click on "Learn More." If you are using mybcommlab, you can access Real-Time Updates within each chapter or under Student Study Tools.

Giving Presentations Online

In some companies, online presentations have already become a routine matter, conducted via internal groupware, virtual meeting systems, or webcast systems designed specifically for online presentations. Your audience members will view your presentation either on their individual computer screens or via a projector in a conference room.

The benefits of online presentations are considerable, including the opportunity to communicate with a geographically dispersed audience at a fraction of the cost of travel and the ability for a project team or an entire organization to meet at a moment's notice. However, the challenges for a presenter can be significant, thanks to that layer of technology between you and your audience. Many of those "human moments" that guide and encourage you through an in-person presentation won't travel across the digital divide. For instance, it's often difficult to tell whether audience members are bored or confused because your view of them is usually confined to small video images (and sometimes not even that).

Online presentations give you a way to reach more people in less time, but they require special preparation and skills.

To ensure successful online presentations, keep the following advice in mind:

- **Consider sending preview study materials ahead of time.** Doing so allows audience members to familiarize themselves with any important background information. Also, by using a free service such as SlideShare (www.slideshare.net), you can distribute your presentation slides to either public or private audiences, and you can record audio narrative to make your presentations function on their own.[36] Some presenters advise against giving out your slides ahead of time, however, because doing so gives away the ending of your presentation, so to speak.

- **Keep your presentation as simple as possible.** Break complicated slides down into multiple slides if necessary, and keep the direction of your discussion clear so that no one gets lost.

- **Ask for feedback frequently.** You won't have as much of the visual feedback that alerts you when audience members are confused, and many online viewers will be reluctant to call attention to themselves by interrupting you to ask for clarification. Setting up a backchannel via Twitter or as part of your online meeting system will help in this regard.

- **Consider the viewing experience from the audience members' point of view.** Will they be able to see what you think they can see? For instance, webcast video is typically displayed in a small window on-screen, so viewers may miss important details.

- **Allow plenty of time for everyone to get connected and familiar with the screen they're viewing.** Build extra time into your schedule to ensure that everyone is connected and ready to start.

Last but not least, don't get lost in the technology. Use these tools whenever they'll help but remember that the most important aspect of any presentation is getting the audience to receive, understand, and embrace your message. For the latest information on online presentations, visit **http://real-timeupdates.com/bce5** and click on Chapter 12.

PEARSON mybcommlab   Are you an active learner? Go to mybcommlab.com to master Chapter 12's content. Chapter 12's interactive activities include:

- Customizable Study Plan and Chapter 12 practice quizzes
- Chapter 12 Simulation (Business Presentations), which helps you think critically and prepare to make choices in the business world
- Chapter 12 Video Exercise (Effective Oral Presentations), which shows you how textbook concepts are put into practice every day

- Flash Cards for mastering the definition of chapter terms
- Interactive Lessons that visually review key chapter concepts
- Document Makeovers for hands-on, scored practice in revising documents

CHAPTER REVIEW AND ACTIVITIES

Learning Objectives: Check Your Progress

1 OBJECTIVE Highlight the importance of presentations in your business career, and explain how to adapt the planning step of the three-step process to presentations.

Oral and online presentations give the opportunity to use all your communication skills, from research to writing to speaking. Presentations also demonstrate your ability to think quickly, to adapt to challenging situations, and to handle touchy questions and complex issues.

The tasks in planning oral presentations are generally the same as with any other business message, but three tasks require special consideration. First, when analyzing the situation, in addition to understanding the audience's information needs, you also need to anticipate the likely emotional states of your listeners during the presentation. Second, although some presentations consist only of the purely oral medium of spoken communication, presentations increasingly involve integration with a variety of electronic media. Third, organizing your presentation takes on special importance with oral presentations because audience members are more or less at your mercy during the presentation and can't flip or click back and forth as they can with printed or electronic media. Limiting the scope is particularly vital, because many presentations must fit strict time limits, and keeping presentations as short as possible is always a good idea in order to keep from losing the audience's attention.

2 OBJECTIVE Describe the tasks involved in developing a presentation after completing the planning step.

Although you usually don't write out a presentation word for word, you still engage in the writing process—developing your ideas, structuring support points, phrasing your transitions, and so on. Adapting to the audience is crucial because presentation audiences and venues can vary widely, from small, informal gatherings to formal keynote speeches in large auditoriums to virtual presentations given entirely online. To compose a presentation, break it down into three essential parts: an introduction that arouses the audience's interest in your topic, establishes your credibility, and prepares the audience for what will follow; a body that conveys your information in a way that maintains audience interest and makes it easy to connect one idea to the next; and a close that restates your main points, wraps up any unfinished business, and lets you end with clarity and confidence.

3 OBJECTIVE Describe the five major decisions required to enhance your presentation with effective visuals.

First, choose between structured and free-form slides. Structured slides follow the same design plan for most or all the slides in a presentation, are often created by using the templates provided with presentation software, and tend to convey most of their information through bullet points. In contrast, visually oriented free-form slides do not follow any set design scheme from slide to slide, although they should have a unified sense of color, font selection, and other design elements. Second, for any slides that have textual content, be sure to strictly limit the word count and keep the font size large enough to read easily. Third, make sure any graphic elements are simple and clear enough to be easily grasped from anywhere in the room. Fourth, choose and use design elements—color, background and foreground designs, artwork, fonts, and type styles—in a way that enhances, not obscures, your message. Fifth, add animation and multimedia elements if they will help build audience interest and understanding.

4 OBJECTIVE Outline three special tasks involved in completing a presentation.

The completion state for presentations involves a wider range of tasks than printed documents require. Three tasks require particular attention. First, finalize your slides and support materials using the slide sorter to get a big picture view of your presentation and creating title slide(s), agenda and program detail slides, and navigation slides. Second, choose your presentation method: memorizing your material word for word, reading a printout of your material, or speaking from notes. Speaking from notes is the best choice for most presentations. Third, practice your delivery. Practice helps ensure a smooth presentation, and it boosts your confidence, too.

5 OBJECTIVE Describe four important aspects of delivering a presentation in today's social media environment.

First, take steps to reduce your anxiety, which include not trying to be perfect, preparing more material than is necessary, practicing extensively, visualizing success, breathing deeply and slowly, being ready with an opening line, dressing as comfortably as appropriate, taking a very short break if you're rushing, concentrating on your message, maintaining eye contact, and plowing ahead no matter what happens.

Second, handle questions responsively. First, determine whether you can set boundaries for the Q&A period. Prepare answers to potential questions. Pay attention to nonverbal signals and be sure to respond to all questions. Don't let questioners take control of the presentation. Face hostile questions head-on without getting defensive. Finally, alert the audience when the Q&A period is almost over.

Third, embrace the backchannel, the parallel conversation that might be going on among audience members on Twitter and other media. To take advantage of the backchannel, you can integrate social media into your presentation, monitor and ask for feedback, review point by point comments to improve your presentation, automatically tweet key points from your presentation while you speak, and establish expectations with the audience.

Fourth, to ensure a successful online presentation, consider sending preview materials ahead of time, keep your content and presentation as simple as possible, ask for feedback frequently, consider the viewing experience from the audience's side, and give participants time to get connected.

Test Your Knowledge

To review chapter content related to each question, refer to the indicated Learning Objective.

1. What skills do presentations give you the opportunity to practice and demonstrate? [LO-1]
2. What three goals should you accomplish during the introduction of a presentation? [LO-2]
3. What techniques can you use to get an audience's attention during your introduction? [LO-2]
4. What three tasks should you accomplish in the close of your presentation? [LO-2]
5. What steps can you take to ensure success with online presentations? [LO-5]

Apply Your Knowledge

To review chapter content related to each question, refer to the indicated Learning Objective.

1. Why is it important to limit the scope of presentations? [LO-1]
2. Is it ethical to use design elements and special effects to persuade an audience? Why or why not? [LO-3]
3. How can visually oriented free-form slides help keep an audience engaged in a presentation? [LO-3]
4. How does embracing the backchannel reflect the "you" attitude? [LO-5]
5. Why is speaking from notes usually the best method of delivery? [LO-4]

Practice Your Skills

Activities

Active links for all websites in this chapter can be found on mybcommlab; see your User Guide for instructions on accessing the content for this chapter. Each activity is labeled according to the primary skill or skills you will need to use. To review relevant chapter content, you can refer to the indicated Learning Objective. In some instances, supporting information will be found in another chapter, as indicated.

1. **Presentations: Planning a Presentation [LO-1]**   Select one of the following topics:

   a. What I expect to learn in this course
   b. Past public speaking experiences: the good, the bad, and the ugly

   c. I would be good at teaching _____.
   d. I am afraid of _____.
   e. It's easy for me to _____.
   f. I get angry when _____.
   g. I am happiest when I _____.
   h. People would be surprised if they knew that I _____ .
   i. My favorite older person
   j. My favorite charity
   k. My favorite place
   l. My favorite sport
   m. My favorite store
   n. My favorite television show
   o. The town you live in suffers from a great deal of juvenile vandalism. Explain to a group of community members why juvenile recreational facilities should be built instead of a juvenile detention complex.
   p. You are speaking to the Humane Society. Support or oppose the use of animals for medical research purposes.
   q. You are talking to civic leaders of your community. Try to convince them to build an art gallery.
   r. You are speaking to a first-grade class at an elementary school. Explain why they should brush their teeth after meals.
   s. You are speaking to a group of traveling salespeople. Convince them that they should wear their seatbelts while driving.
   t. You are speaking to a group of elderly people. Convince them to adopt an exercise program.
   u. Energy issues (supply, conservation, alternative sources, national security, global warming, pollution, etc.)
   v. Financial issues (banking, investing, family finances, etc.)
   w. Government (domestic policy, foreign policy, Social Security taxes, welfare, etc.)
   x. Interesting new technologies (virtual reality, geographic information systems, nanotechnology, bioengineering, etc.)
   y. Politics (political parties, elections, legislative bodies and legislation, the presidency, etc.)
   z. Sports (amateur and professional, baseball, football, golf, hang gliding, hockey, rock climbing, tennis, etc.)

   Research your topic as needed and prepare a brief presentation (5–10 minutes) to be given to your class.

2. **Presentations: Developing a Presentation; Collaboration: Team Projects [LO-2], Chapter 2**   You've been asked to give an informative 10-minute talk on vacation opportunities in your home state. Draft your introduction, which should last no more than 2 minutes. Then pair off with a classmate and analyze each other's introductions. How well do these two introductions arouse the audience's interest, build credibility, and preview the presentation? Suggest how these introductions might be improved.

3. **Presentations: Developing a Presentation [LO-2]**   Locate the transcript of a speech, either online or through your

school library. Good sources include Yahoo's directory of commencement speeches (http://dir.yahoo.com/Education/Graduation/Speeches) and the publication *Vital Speeches of the Day*. (Recent years of *Vital Speeches of the Day* are available in the ProQuest database; ask at your library.) Many corporate websites also have archives of executives' speeches; look in the "investor relations" section. Examine both the introduction and the close of the speech you've chosen and then analyze how these two sections work together to emphasize the main idea. What action does the speaker want the audience to take? Next, identify the transitional sentences or phrases that clarify the speech's structure for the listener, especially those that help the speaker shift between supporting points. Using these transitions as clues, list the main message and supporting points; then indicate how each transitional phrase links the current supporting point to the succeeding one. Prepare a two- to three-minute presentation summarizing your analysis for your class.

4. **Presentations: Designing Presentation Visuals [LO-4]** Look through recent issues (print or online) of *BusinessWeek*, *Fortune*, or other business publications for articles discussing challenges that a specific company or industry is facing. Using the articles and the guidelines discussed in this chapter, create three to five slides summarizing these issues. If you don't have access to computer presentation software or a word processor, you can draw the slides on plain paper.

5. **Presentations: Designing Presentation Visuals [LO-4]** To access this PowerPoint presentation, go to http://real-timeupdates.com/bce5, click on "Student Assignments," and select "Chapter 12, Page 342, Activity 4." Download and watch the presentation in slide show mode or the equivalent in your software. After you've watched the presentation, identify at least three ways in which various animations, builds, and transitions either enhanced or impeded your understanding of the subject matter.

6. **Presentations: Designing Presentation Visuals [LO-4]** Find a business-related slide presentation on SlideShare (www.slideshare.net) and analyze the design. Do you consider it structured or free form? Does the design help the audience understand and remember the message? Why or why not? What improvements would you suggest to the design?

7. **Presentations: Mastering Delivery; Nonverbal Communication: Analyzing Nonverbal Signals [LO-5], Chapter 2** Observe and analyze the delivery of a speaker in a school, work, or other setting. What type of delivery did the speaker use? Was this delivery appropriate for the occasion? What nonverbal signals did the speaker use to emphasize key points? Were these signals effective? Which nonverbal signals would you suggest to further enhance the delivery of this oral presentation? Why?

8. **Presentations: Delivering a Presentation; communication Ethics: Making Ethical Choices [LO-5], Chapter 1** Think again about the oral presentation you observed and analyzed in the previous activity. How could the speaker have used nonverbal signals to unethically manipulate the audience's attitudes or actions?

9. **Presentations: Delivering a Presentation; Collaboration: Team Projects; Media Skills: Microblogging [LO-5], Chapter 2, Chapter 6** In a team of six students, develop a 10-minute slide presentation on any topic that interests you. Nominate one person to give the presentation; the other five will participate via a Twitter backchannel. Create a webpage that holds at least one downloadable file that will be discussed during the presentation, and set up a backchannel on BackNoise (http://backnoise.com) or a similar service. Practice using the backchannel, including using a hashtag for the meeting and having the presenter ask for audience feedback during a "Twitter break." Be ready to discuss your experience with the entire class. For information on getting started on Twitter, visit http://real-timeupdates.com/bce5, click on "Student Assignments," and then click on "Twitter Screencast."

Expand Your Skills

Critique the Professionals

Visit the TED website at www.ted.com/talks and listen to any presentation that interests you. Compare the speaker's delivery and visual support materials with the concepts presented in this chapter. What works? What doesn't work? Using whatever medium your instructor requests, write a brief summary of your analysis.

Sharpen Your Career Skills Online

Bovée and Thill's Business Communication Web Search, at http://businesscommunicationblog.com/websearch, is a unique research tool designed specifically for business communication research. Use the Web Search function to find a website, video, PDF document, podcast, or presentation that offers advice on creating and delivering business presentations. Write a brief e-mail message to your instructor or a post for your class blog, describing the item that you found and summarizing the career skills information you learned from it.

mybcommlab

If your course uses mybcommlab, log on to www.mybcommlab.com to access the following study and assessment aids associated with this chapter:

- Video applications
- Pre/post test
- Real-Time Updates
- Personalized study plan
- Peer review activity
- Model documents
- Quick Learning Guides
- Sample presentations

If you are not using mybcommlab, you can access Real-Time Updates and Quick Learning Guides through http://real-timeupdates.com/bce5. The Quick Learning Guide (located under "Learn More" on the website) hits all the high points of this chapter in just two pages. This guide, especially prepared by the authors, will help you study for exams or review important concepts whenever you need a quick refresher.

CASES

▼ *Apply the three-step writing process to the following cases, as assigned by your instructor.*

PRESENTATION SKILLS   PORTFOLIO BUILDER

1. Presentations: Planning a Presentation [LO-1]   Pecha-kucha (Japanese for "chatter") is a style of presentation that might be the ultimate in creative constraint: The speaker is limited to 20 slides, each of which is displayed for exactly 20 seconds before automatically advancing. Pecha-kucha Nights, which are open to the public, are now put on in cities all over the world. Visit www .pecha-kucha.org for more information on these events or to view some archived presentations.

Your task Select one of the subjects from Activity 1 on page 341 and develop a *pecha-kucha* style presentation with 20 slides, each designed to be displayed for 20 seconds. Use the slide timing capabilities in your presentation software to control the timing. Make sure you practice before presenting to your class so that you can hit the precise timing requirements.[37]

PRESENTATION SKILLS   SOCIAL NETWORKING SKILLS

2. Presentations: Planning a Presentation [LO-1]   You know those times when you're craving Thai food or the perfect fruit smoothie, but you don't know where to go? Or when you're out shopping or clubbing and want to let your friends know where you are? Foursquare's location-based services connect you with friends and companies that offer products and services of interest.

Your task Create a brief presentation explaining the Foursquare concept and its features and benefits. List two Foursquare competitors and give a brief assessment of which of the three you would recommend to your classmates.[38]

PRESENTATION SKILLS   TEAM SKILLS

3. Presentations: Planning a Presentation [LO-1]   In your job as a business development researcher for a major corporation, you're asked to gather and process information on a wide variety of subjects. Management has gained confidence in your research and analysis skills and would now like you to begin making regular presentations at management retreats and other functions. Topics are likely to include the following:

- Offshoring of U.S. jobs
- Foreign ownership of U.S. firms
- Employment issues involving workers from other countries

- Tax breaks offered by local and state governments to attract new businesses
- Economic impact of environmental regulations

Your task With a team assigned by your instructor, choose one of the topics from the list and conduct enough research to familiarize yourself with the topic. Identify at least three important issues that anyone involved with this topic should know about. Prepare a 10-minute presentation that introduces the topic, comments on its importance to the U.S. economy, and discusses the issues you've identified. Assume that your audience is a cross-section of business managers who don't have any particular experience in the topic you've chosen.

PRESENTATION SKILLS   PORTFOLIO BUILDER

4. Presentations: Designing Presentation Visuals [LO-4] Depending on the sequence your instructor chose for this course, you've probably covered 8 to 10 chapters at this point and learned or improved many valuable skills. Think through your progress and identify five business communication skills that you've either learned for the first time or developed during this course.

Your task Create a six-slide presentation, with a title slide and five slides that describe each of the five skills you've identified. Be sure to explain how each skill could help you in your career. Use any visual style that you feel is appropriate for the assignment.

Improve Your Grammar, Mechanics, and Usage

You can download the text of this assignment from **http:// real-timeupdates.com/bce5**; click on "Student Assignments" and then click on "Chapter 12. Improve Your Grammar, Mechanics, and Usage."

Level 1: Self-Assessment—Capitals and Abbreviations

Review Sections 3.1 and 3.3 in the Handbook of Grammar, Mechanics, and Usage and then complete the following 15 items.

In items 1–15, capitalize any words that should be capitalized, spell out any abbreviations that should be spelled out, and insert abbreviations where appropriate.

1. Dr. paul hansen is joining our staff.
2. New caressa skin cream should be in a position to dominate that market.

3. Send this report to Mister h. k. danforth, rural route 1, warrensburg, new york 12885.
4. You are responsible for training my new assistant to operate the xerox machine.
5. She received her master of business administration degree from the university of michigan.
6. The building is located on the corner of madison and center streets.
7. Call me at 8 tomorrow morning, pacific standard time, and I'll have the information you need.
8. When jones becomes ceo next month, we'll need your input asap.
9. Address it to art bowers, chief of production.
10. Please rsvp to sony corp. just as soon as you know your schedule.
11. The data-processing department will begin work on feb. 2, just one wk. from today.
12. You are to meet him on friday at the un building in nyc.
13. Whenever you can come, professor, our employees will greatly enjoy your presentation.
14. At 50 per box, our std. contract forms are $9 a box, and our warranty forms are $7.95 a box.
15. We plan to establish a sales office on the west coast.

Level 2: Workplace Applications

The following items may contain errors in grammar, capitalization, punctuation, abbreviation, number style, word division, and vocabulary. Rewrite each sentence, correcting all errors. If a sentence has no errors, write "Correct" for that number.

1. Mc'Donalds and Sears' have partnered with the television program, "Its Showtime At The Apollo." To offer talented kids the opportunity too appear on national television.
2. Tiffany & Co., the internationally-renowned jeweler and specialty retailer plan to open a 5000 square feet store in Walnut Creek, CA next year.
3. If none of the solutions seem satisfying, pick the more easier one.
4. Ken Baker, the west coast bureau chief for Us magazine, will be responsible for overseeing all of magazine reporting in Hollywood, conducting high profile, celebrity interviews, for identifying news stories, and assist in the generation of cover concepts.
5. With experience managing numerous enthusiast brands, including "Kawasaki" and "Skechers," Juxt Interactive are cementing their role as a leader in strategic, integrated campaigns.
6. You're message, tone, and product positioning has to be right on to be excepted and successful.
7. As I begun to put the team together, it became apparent to myself that my idea was ahead of it's time.

8. Many think that the primary market for newspapers are the readers, however advertisers generate the majority of revenues.
9. REIs second website, **www.rei-outlet.com**, features items that are not available at REI's physical stores, catalog, or main website.
10. The company's C.E.O., who we had saw at the awards dinner wednesday night, was fired the next day.
11. A designer of high priced purses such as Kate Spade or Louis Vitton generally limit distribution to exclusive boutiques or high end retail stores: such as Neiman-Marcus.
12. There is many indications that an economic recovery is underway, and will continue to stabilize and build however modestly.
13. We bought the equipment at a second hand store which turned out to be shoddy and defective.
14. Experts site 2 principle reasons for Webvan's failure; consumer resistance and over expansion.
15. Implementation of the over time hours guidelines will be carried out by the Human Resources Staff members.

Level 3: Document Critique

The following document may contain errors in grammar, capitalization, punctuation, abbreviation, number style, word division, and vocabulary. As your instructor indicates, photocopy this page and correct all errors using standard proofreading marks (see Appendix C) or download the document and make the corrections in your word processing software.

Date: Thu, 25 April, 2011
FROM: Steve Pendergrass <spender@manchcc.edu>
TO: Gregory Hansford gregory.<hansford@manchcc.edu>
Subject: Library Hours

Dear Mr. Hansford,

There is a favorite place in which Manchester students study on our campus: the library because of the quiet atmosphere excellent resources, and helpful staff. With a ajustment in library hours there assets could be taken advantage of by more students.

In an informal survey of the students in my English class, a desire for the library to be open more hours on the weekends became evident. Many students find weekends best for researching term papers: because that's when large blocks of time can be found in their schedules.

I'd like to sight several reasons for the change I am about to propose to encourage your interest and desire for my suggestion. Understandable, librarians need a day off. Perhaps students and librarians could both be accomodated if the library closed at five p.m. on Friday night. Friday night is the time most students like to relax and attend sports events or parties. The libary could then be open on Saturdays from ten a.m. until 4:30 p.m. To make this arrangement fair to librarians; perhaps their schedules could be staggered so that nobody would have to work every Saturday or those scheduled to work on Saturdays could be given Mondays or Fridays off.

Consider implementing this new schedule this Fall. Another much-appreciated service for students will be performed if you do this.

Sincerely:

Steve Pendergrass, student

UNIT
5

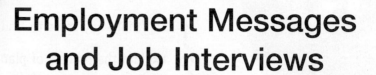

Employment Messages and Job Interviews

Building Careers and Writing Résumés

LEARNING OBJECTIVES

After studying this chapter, you will be able to

1 List eight key steps to finding the ideal opportunity in today's job market

2 Explain the process of planning your résumé, including how to choose the best résumé organization

3 Describe the tasks involved in writing your résumé and list the major sections of a traditional résumé

4 Characterize the completing step for résumés, including the six most common formats in which you can produce a résumé

PEARSON
mybcommlab

Access interactive videos, simulations, sample documents, Document Makeovers, and assessment quizzes in Chapter 13 of mybcommlab.com for mastery of this chapter's objectives.

COMMUNICATION *Matters*

" Starting a job search is like becoming a sales rep for a short period of time, but you're not selling a product, you're selling yourself. "
—Mitchell Schneir, *Recruiting Consultant, RSA*

Be ready to promote yourself and to explain how your "features and benefits" meet a company's needs.

With 20 years of experience in employee recruiting, RSA's Mitchell Schneir understands that securing the right career opportunity is largely a process of persuasive communication. He also emphasizes the importance of knowing yourself and your target audience. "Know your product, industry, selling points, customers, and marketplace. Give potential employers a reason to hire you."[1] By using the skills you've developed in this course, particularly the techniques of persuasive messages, you can "sell yourself" into the ideal career opportunity.

Many job seekers are uncomfortable with the idea of selling themselves during the job hunt, which is a natural reaction. If you feel this way, remember that you are engaging in a business transaction, offering valuable skills and knowledge in exchange for career opportunities and compensation.

FINDING THE IDEAL OPPORTUNITY IN TODAY'S JOB MARKET

Finding and landing the ideal job can be a complex process, with lots of stress and frustration along the way. The good news is that it is all about communication, so the skills you're developing in this course will give you a competitive advantage. This section offers a general job-search strategy with advice that applies to just about any career path you might want to pursue. As you craft your personal strategy, keep these two guidelines in mind:

- **Get organized.** Your job search could last many months and involve multiple contacts with dozens of companies. You need to keep all the details straight to make sure you don't miss opportunities or make mistakes such as losing someone's e-mail address or forgetting an appointment.

- **Start now and stick to it.** Even if you are a year or more away from graduation, now is not too early to get started with some of the essential research and planning tasks. If you wait until the last minute, you will miss opportunities and you won't be as prepared as the candidates you'll be competing against.

Writing the Story of You

If all you want to do is "get a job," you will struggle to focus your job search efforts and to present yourself as a compelling candidate. And if you do get a job, chances are you'll wind up with something you don't like and will have to start the process all over again before long.

To avoid that situation, take the time you have now to explore the possibilities, to find your passion, and to identify appealing career paths. If you haven't yet, read the career-planning Prologue that starts on page 25 and particularly the "What Do You Want to Do?" section on page 27 to help identify the nature of the work you'd like to do, if not a specific profession.

Next, using the advice on creating a personal brand on page 30, begin writing the "story of you," the things you are passionate about, the skills you possess, your ability to help an organization reach its goals, the path you've been on so far, and the path you want to follow in the future. Think in terms of an image or a theme you'd like to project. Are you academically gifted? An effective leader? A well-rounded professional with wide-ranging talents? A creative problem solver? A technical wizard? Writing your story is a valuable planning exercise that helps you think about where you want to go and how to present yourself to target employers.

Learning to Think Like an Employer

Now that you know your side of the hiring equation a little better, switch sides and look at it from an employer's perspective. To begin with, recognize that companies take risks with every hiring decision—the risk that the person hired doesn't meet expectations and the risk that they let a better candidate slip through their fingers. Many companies judge the success of their recruiting efforts by *quality of hire*, a measure of how closely new employees meet the company's needs.[2] What steps can you take to present yourself as the low-risk, high-reward choice, as someone who can make a meaningful contribution to the organization?

Of course, your perceived ability to perform the job is an essential part of your potential quality as a new hire. However, hiring managers consider more than just your ability to handle the job. They want to know if you'll be reliable and motivated, if you're somebody who "gets it" when it comes to being a professional in today's workplace. A great way to get inside the heads of corporate recruiters is to "listen in" on their professional conversations by reading periodicals such as *Workforce Management* (www.workforce.com) and blogs such as Fistful of Talent (www.fistfuloftalent.com) and The HR Capitalist (www.hrcapitalist.com).

Researching Industries and Companies of Interest

Learning more about professions, industries, and individual companies is easy to do with the library and online resources available to you. Don't limit your research to easily available sources, however. Companies are likely to be impressed by creative research, such as interviewing their customers to learn more about how the firm does business. "Detailed research,

1 LEARNING OBJECTIVE

List eight key steps to finding the ideal opportunity in today's job market

If you haven't already, read the Prologue, "Building a Career with Your Communication Skills," before studying this chapter.

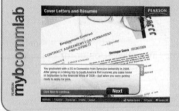

- Access this chapter's simulation entitled Cover Letters and Résumés, located at mybcommlab.com.

What's your story? Employers will want to know where you've been and where you want to go.

Employers judge their recruiting success by *quality of hire*, and you can take steps to be—and look like—a high-quality hire.

Follow the online conversations of professional recruiters to learn what their hot-button issues are.

including talking to our customers, is so rare it will almost guarantee you get hired," explains the recruiting manager at Alcon Laboratories.[3]

Table 13.1 lists some of the many websites where you can learn more about companies and find job openings. Start with The Riley Guide, **www.rileyguide.com**, which offers advice for online job searches as well as links to hundreds of specialized websites that post openings in specific industries and professions. Your college's career center placement office probably maintains an up-to-date list as well.

Employers expect you to be familiar with important developments in their industries, so stay on top of business news.

To learn more about contemporary business topics, peruse some of these leading business periodicals and newspapers with significant business sections (in some cases, you may need to go through your library's online databases in order to access back issues):

- *Wall Street Journal*: **http://online.wsj.com/public/us**
- *New York Times*: **www.nyt.com**

TABLE 13.1 Selected Job Search Websites

Website*	URL	Highlights
Riley Guide	www.rileyguide.com	Vast collection of links to both general and specialized job sites for every career imaginable; don't miss this one—it could save you hours of searching
TweetMyJobs.com	http://tweetmyjobs.com	The largest Twitter job board, with thousands of channels segmented by geography, job type, and industry
CollegeRecruiter.com	www.collegerecruiter.com	Focused on opportunities for graduates with less than three years of work experience
Monster	http://home.monster.com	One of the most popular job sites, with hundreds of thousands of openings, many from hard-to-find small companies; extensive collection of advice on the job search process
MonsterCollege	http://college.monster.com	Focused on job searches for new college grads; your school's career center site probably links here
CareerBuilder	www.careerbuilder.com	One of the largest job boards; affiliated with more than 150 newspapers around the country
Jobster	www.jobster.com	Uses social networking to link employers with job seekers
USAJOBS	www.usajobs.opm.gov	The official job search site for the U.S. government, featuring everything from jobs for economists to astronauts to border patrol agents
IMDiversity	www.imdiversity.com	Good resource on diversity in the workplace, with job postings from companies that have made a special commitment to promoting diversity in their workforces
Dice.com	www.dice.com	One of the best sites for high-technology jobs
Net-Temps	www.net-temps.com	Popular site for contractors and freelancers looking for short-term assignments
Internship Programs.com	http://internshipprograms.com	Posts listings from companies looking for interns in a wide variety of professions
Simply Hired Indeed	www.simplyhired.com www.indeed.com	Specialized search engines that look for job postings on hundreds of websites worldwide; they find many postings that aren't listed on job board sites such as Monster

*Note: This list represents only a small fraction of the hundreds of job-posting sites and other resources available online; be sure to check with your college's career center for the latest information.

- *USA Today*: www.usatoday.com
- *BusinessWeek*: www.businessweek.com
- *Business 2.0*: http://money.cnn.com/magazines/business2
- *Fast Company*: www.fastcompany.com
- *Fortune*: http://money.cnn.com/magazines/fortune
- *Forbes*: www.forbes.com

In addition, thousands of bloggers, microbloggers, and podcasters offer news and commentary on the business world. To identify some that you might find helpful, start with directories such as Technorati (http://technorati.com/business) for blogs or Podcast Alley (www.podcastalley.com; select the "Business" genre) for podcasts. AllTop (http://alltop .com) is another good resource for finding people who write about topics that interest you. In addition to learning more about professions and opportunities, this research will help you get comfortable with the jargon and buzzwords currently in use in a particular field—including essential *keywords* to use in your résumé (see page 392).

Translating Your General Potential into a Specific Solution for Each Employer

An important aspect of the quality-of-hire challenge is trying to determine how well a candidate's attributes and experience will translate to the challenges of a specific position. As Jim Schaper, CEO of the Alpharetta, Georgia, software company Infor Global Solutions, puts it, "We try to determine if newly minted graduates can apply knowledge they've already gained."[4] Customizing your résumé to each job opening is an important step in showing employers that you will be a good fit. From your initial contact all the way through the interviewing process, in fact, you will have opportunities to impress recruiters by explaining how your general potential translates to the specific needs of the position.

> An essential task in your job search is presenting your skills and accomplishments in a way that is relevant to the employer's business challenges.

For example, instead of following up with just a simple thank-you note after interviewing with Detroit-based InStar Services, Mary Berman offered a plan showing how she could help the company during her first 60 days on the job.[5] Berman could offer such a plan because she researched the company to know what its needs were and she understands her own capabilities well enough to match them to the company's needs.

Taking the Initiative to Find Opportunities

When it comes to finding the right opportunities for you, the easiest ways are not always the most productive ways. The major job boards such as Monster and classified services such as Craigslist might have thousands of openings—but thousands of job seekers are looking at and applying for these same openings. Moreover, posting job openings on these sites is often a company's last resort, after it has exhausted other possibilities.

> Don't hesitate to contact interesting companies even if they haven't advertised job openings to the public yet—they might be looking for somebody just like you.

Instead of searching through the same job openings as everyone else, take the initiative and go find opportunities. Identify the companies you want to work for and focus your efforts on them. Get in touch with their human resources departments (or individual managers if possible), describe what you can offer the company, and ask to be considered if any opportunities come up.[6] Your message might appear right when a company is busy looking for someone but hasn't yet advertised the opening to the outside world.

> Start thinking like a networker now; your classmates could turn out to be some of your most important business contacts.

Building Your Network

Networking is the process of making informal connections with mutually beneficial business contacts. Networking takes place wherever and whenever people talk: at industry functions, at social gatherings, at alumni reunions—and all over the Internet, from LinkedIn to Facebook to Twitter. Networking is more essential than ever, because the vast majority of job openings are never advertised to the general

REAL-TIME UPDATES
Learn More by Reading This Article

100 Twitter tools for job searchers

From specialized search tools to job listing feeds in specific professions, these Twitter tools can help you navigate today's job market. Go to **http://real-timeupdates.com/ bce5** and click on "Learn More." If you are using mybcommlab, you can access Real-Time Updates within each chapter or under Student Study Tools.

REAL-TIME UPDATES
Learn More by Watching This Video

Tweet your way to a sweet job

This simple introduction to Twitter focuses on using the microblogging service for career networking. Go to **http://real-timeupdates.com/bce5** and click on "Learn More." If you are using mybcommlab, you can access Real-Time Updates within each chapter or under Student Study Tools.

public. To avoid the time and expense of sifting through thousands of applications and the risk of hiring complete strangers, most companies prefer to ask their employees for recommendations first.[7] The more people who know you, the better chance you have of being recommended for one of these hidden job openings.

Start building your network now, before you need it. Your classmates could end up being some of your most valuable contacts, if not right way then possibly later in your career. Then branch out by identifying people with similar interests in your target professions, industries, and companies. Read news sites, blogs, and other online sources. Follow industry leaders on Twitter. You can also follow individual executives at your target companies to learn about their interests and concerns.[8] Connect with people on LinkedIn and Facebook, particularly in groups dedicated to particular career interests. You can introduce yourself via private messages, as long as you are respectful of people and don't take up much of their time.[9] Participate in student business organizations, especially those with ties to professional organizations. Visit *trade shows* to learn about various industries and rub shoulders with people who work in those industries.[10] Don't overlook volunteering; you not only meet people but also demonstrate your ability to solve problems, manage projects, and lead others. You can do some good while creating a network for yourself.

Remember that networking is about people helping each other, not just about other people helping you. Pay close attention to networking etiquette: Try to learn something about the people you want to connect with, don't overwhelm others with too many messages or requests, be succinct in all your communication efforts, don't give out other people's names and contact information without their permission to do so, never e-mail your résumé to complete strangers, and remember to say thank you every time someone helps you.[11]

To become a valued network member, you need to be able to help others in some way. You may not have any influential contacts yet, but because you're actively researching a number of industries and trends in your own job search, you probably have valuable information you can share via your social networks, blog, or Twitter account. Or you might simply be able to connect one person with another who can help. The more you network, the more valuable you become in your network—and the more valuable your network becomes to you.

Finally, be aware that your online network reflects on who you are in the eyes of potential employers, so exercise some judgment in making connections. Also, some employers are beginning to contact people in a candidate's network for background information, even if the candidate doesn't list those people as references.[12]

Put your network in place before you need it.

Networking is a mutually beneficial activity, so look for opportunities to help others in some way.

Seeking Career Counseling

Don't overlook the many resources available through your college's career center.

Don't let a silly mistake knock you out of contention for a great job.

Your college's career center probably offers a wide variety of services, including individual counseling, job fairs, on-campus interviews, and job listings. Counselors can give you advice on career planning and provide workshops on job search techniques, résumé preparation, job readiness training, interview techniques, self-marketing, and more.[13] You can also find career planning advice online. Many of the websites listed in Table 13.1 offer articles and online tests to help you choose a career path, identify essential skills, and prepare to enter the job market.

Avoiding Mistakes

While you're making all these positive moves to show employers you will be a quality hire, take care to avoid the simple blunders that can torpedo a job search—not catching mistakes in your résumé, misspelling the name of a manager you're writing to, showing up late for an interview, tweeting something unprofessional, failing to complete application forms correctly, asking for information that you can easily find

REAL-TIME UPDATES
Learn More by Reading This Article

Follow these people to a new career

Alison Doyle maintains a great list of career experts to follow on Twitter. Go to **http://real-timeupdates.com/bce5** and click on "Learn More." If you are using mybcommlab, you can access Real-Time Updates within each chapter or under Student Study Tools.

yourself on a company's website, or making any other error that could flag you as someone who is careless or disrespectful.

To understand why even a minor mistake can hurt your chances, look at the situation from a recruiter's point of view. At KeyBank, for instance, a recruiter typically has 25 to 30 open positions at any given time.[14] If a hundred people are applying for each position—and the number can be much higher in a slow job market—a single recruiter could be considering 2,500 to 3,000 candidates at once. As recruiters narrow down the possibilities, even an innocent or inconsequential mistake on your part can give them a reason to bump you out of the candidate pool.

REAL-TIME UPDATES
Learn More by Reading This Article

Try these Facebook applications in your job search

These Facebook applications can supply automated job alerts, let you upload your résumé, and perform other helpful functions for your job search. Go to **http://real-timeupdates.com/bce5** and click on "Learn More." If you are using mybcommlab, you can access Real-Time Updates within each chapter or under Student Study Tools.

PLANNING YOUR RÉSUMÉ

Although you will create many messages during your career search, your résumé will be the most important document in this process. You will be able to use it directly in many instances, adapt it to a variety of uses such an e-portfolio or a social media résumé, and reuse pieces of it in social networking profiles and online application forms.

Writing a résumé is one of those projects that really benefits from multiple planning, writing, and completing sessions spread out over several days or weeks. You are trying to summarize a complex subject (yourself!) and present a compelling story to complete strangers in a brief document. Follow the three-step writing process (see Figure 13.1) and give yourself plenty of time.

2 LEARNING OBJECTIVE

Explain the process of planning your résumé, including how to choose the best résumé organization

---

1 Plan → 2 Write → 3 Complete

1 Plan

Analyze the Situation

Recognize that the purpose of your résumé is to get an interview, not to get a job.

Gather Information

Research target industries and companies so that you know what they're looking for in new hires; learn about various jobs and what to expect; learn about the hiring manager, if possible.

Select the Right Medium

Start with a traditional paper résumé and develop scannable, electronic plain-text, HTML, or PDF versions, as needed. Consider using PowerPoint and video for your e-portfolio.

Organize the Information

Chose an organizational model that highlights your strengths and downplays your shortcomings; use the chronological approach unless you have a strong reason not to.

2 Write

Adapt to Your Audience

Plan your wording carefully so that you can catch a recruiter's eye within seconds; translate your education and experience into attributes that target employers find valuable.

Compose the Message

Write clearly and succinctly, using active, powerful language that is appropriate to the industries and companies you're targeting; use a professional tone in all communications, even when using e-mail.

3 Complete

Revise the Message

Evaluate content and review readability and then edit and rewrite for conciseness and clarity.

Produce the Message

Use effective design elements and suitable layout for a clean, professional appearance; seamlessly combine text and graphical elements.

Proofread the Message

Review for errors in layout, spelling, and mechanics; mistakes can cost you interview opportunities.

Distribute the Message

Deliver your résumé, following the specific instructions of each employer or job board website.

Figure 13.1   Three-Step Writing Process for Résumés
Following the three-step writing process will help you create a successful résumé in a short time. Remember to pay particular attention to the "you" attitude and presentation quality; your résumé will probably get tossed aside if it doesn't speak to audience needs or if it contains mistakes.

Analyzing Your Purpose and Audience

Once you view your résumé as a persuasive business message, it's easier to decide what should and shouldn't be in it.

A **résumé** is a structured, written summary of a person's education, employment background, and job qualifications. Before you begin writing a résumé, make sure you understand its true function—as a brief, persuasive business message intended to stimulate an employer's interest in meeting you and learning more about you (see Table 13.2). In other words, the purpose of a résumé is not to get you a job but rather to get you an interview.[15]

As you conduct your research on various professions, industries, companies, and individual managers, you will have a better perspective on your target readers and their information needs. Learn as much as you can about the individuals who may be reading your résumé. Many professionals and managers are bloggers, Twitter users, and LinkedIn members, for example, so you can learn more about them online even if you've never met them. Any bit of information can help you craft a more effective message.

Thanks to Twitter, LinkedIn, and other social media, you can often learn valuable details about individual managers in your target employers.

By the way, if employers ask to see your "CV," they're referring to your *curriculum vitae*, the term used instead of *résumé* in academic professions and in many countries outside the United States. Résumés and CVs are essentially the same, although CVs can be much more detailed. If you need to adapt a U.S.-style résumé to CV format, or vice versa, career expert Alison Doyle offers advice on her website, www.alisondoyle.com.

Gathering Pertinent Information

If you haven't been building an employment portfolio thus far, you may need to do some research on yourself at this point. Gather all the pertinent personal history you can think of, including all the specific dates, duties, and accomplishments from any previous jobs you've held. Collect every piece of relevant educational experience that adds to your qualifications—formal degrees, skills certificates, academic awards, or scholarships. Also, gather any relevant information about school or volunteer activities that might be relevant to your job search, including offices you have held in any club or professional organization, presentations given, and online or print publications. You probably won't use every piece of information you come up with, but you'll want to have it at your fingertips before you begin composing your résumé.

Selecting the Best Medium

You should expect to produce your résumé in several media and formats. "Producing Your Résumé" on page 363 explores the various options.

Organizing Your Résumé Around Your Strengths

Although you will see a number of ways to organize a résumé, most are some variation of chronological, functional, or a combination of the two. The right choice depends on your background and your goals.

TABLE 13.2 Fallacies and Facts About Résumés	
Fallacy	**Fact**
The purpose of a résumé is to list all your skills and abilities.	The purpose of a résumé is to kindle employer interest and generate an interview.
A good résumé will get you the job you want.	All a résumé can do is get you in the door.
Your résumé will always be read carefully and thoroughly.	In most cases, your résumé needs to make a positive impression within 30 or 45 seconds; only then will someone read it in detail. Moreover, it will likely be screened by a computer looking for keywords first—and if it doesn't contain the right keywords, a human being may never see it.
The more good information you present about yourself in your résumé, the better, so stuff your résumé with every positive detail you can think of.	Recruiters don't need that much information about you at the initial screening stage, and they probably won't read it.
If you want a really good résumé, have it prepared by a résumé service.	You have the skills needed to prepare an effective résumé, so prepare it yourself—unless the position is especially high level or specialized. Even then, you should check carefully before using a service.

The Chronological Résumé

In a **chronological résumé**, the work experience section dominates and is placed immediately after your contact information and introductory statement. The chronological approach is the most common way to organize a résumé, and many employers prefer this format because it presents your professional history in a clear, easy-to-follow arrangement.[16] If you're just graduating from college and have limited professional experience, you can vary this chronological approach by putting your educational qualifications before your experience.

Develop your work experience section by listing your jobs in reverse chronological order, beginning with the most recent position. For each job, start by listing the employer's name and location, your official job title, and the dates you held the position (write "to present" if you are still in your most recent position). Next, in a short block of text, highlight your accomplishments in a way that is relevant to your readers. This may require "translating" the terminology used in a particular industry or profession into terms that are more meaningful to your target readers. If the general responsibilities of the position are not obvious from the job title, provide a little background to help readers understand what you did. See Figures 13.2 (below) and 13.3 (on the next page) for examples of ineffective and effective approaches.

> The chronological résumé is the most common approach, but it might not be right for you at this stage in your career.

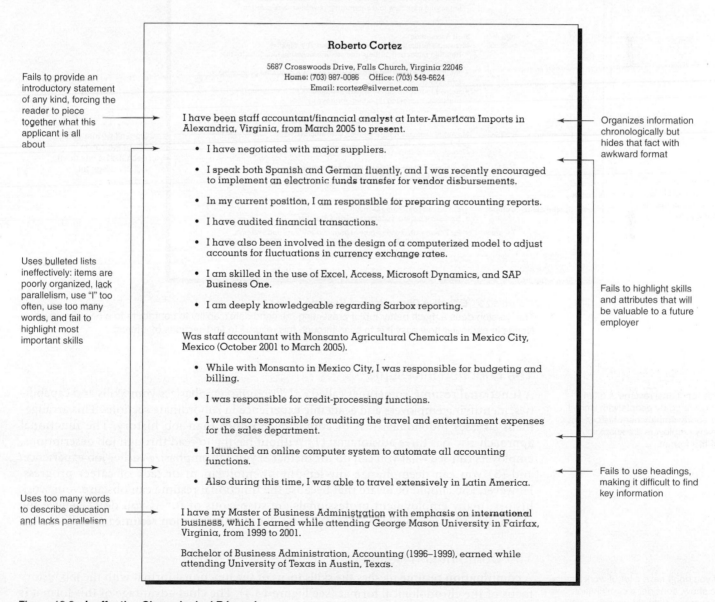

Roberto Cortez

5687 Crosswoods Drive, Falls Church, Virginia 22046
Home: (703) 987-0086   Office: (703) 549-6624
Email: rcortez@silvernet.com

Fails to provide an introductory statement of any kind, forcing the reader to piece together what this applicant is all about

I have been staff accountant/financial analyst at Inter-American Imports in Alexandria, Virginia, from March 2005 to present.

- I have negotiated with major suppliers.

- I speak both Spanish and German fluently, and I was recently encouraged to implement an electronic funds transfer for vendor disbursements.

- In my current position, I am responsible for preparing accounting reports.

- I have audited financial transactions.

- I have also been involved in the design of a computerized model to adjust accounts for fluctuations in currency exchange rates.

- I am skilled in the use of Excel, Access, Microsoft Dynamics, and SAP Business One.

- I am deeply knowledgeable regarding Sarbox reporting.

Uses bulleted lists ineffectively: items are poorly organized, lack parallelism, use "I" too often, use too many words, and fail to highlight most important skills

Organizes information chronologically but hides that fact with awkward format

Fails to highlight skills and attributes that will be valuable to a future employer

Was staff accountant with Monsanto Agricultural Chemicals in Mexico City, Mexico (October 2001 to March 2005).

- While with Monsanto in Mexico City, I was responsible for budgeting and billing.

- I was responsible for credit-processing functions.

- I was also responsible for auditing the travel and entertainment expenses for the sales department.

- I launched an online computer system to automate all accounting functions.

- Also during this time, I was able to travel extensively in Latin America.

Uses too many words to describe education and lacks parallelism

Fails to use headings, making it difficult to find key information

I have my Master of Business Administration with emphasis on international business, which I earned while attending George Mason University in Fairfax, Virginia, from 1999 to 2001.

Bachelor of Business Administration, Accounting (1996–1999), earned while attending University of Texas in Austin, Texas.

Figure 13.2   Ineffective Chronological Résumé
This chronological résumé exhibits a wide range of problems. The language is self-centered and unprofessional, and the organization forces the reader to dig out essential details—and today's recruiters don't have the time or the patience for that. Compare this with the improved version in Figure 13.3.

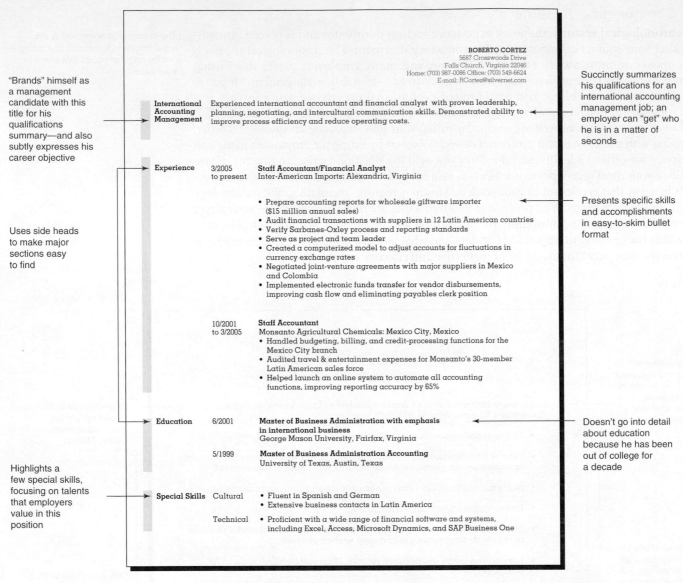

"Brands" himself as a management candidate with this title for his qualifications summary—and also subtly expresses his career objective

Uses side heads to make major sections easy to find

Highlights a few special skills, focusing on talents that employers value in this position

Succinctly summarizes his qualifications for an international accounting management job; an employer can "get" who he is in a matter of seconds

Presents specific skills and accomplishments in easy-to-skim bullet format

Doesn't go into detail about education because he has been out of college for a decade

ROBERTO CORTEZ
5687 Crosswoods Drive
Falls Church, Virginia 22046
Home: (703) 987-0086 Office: (703) 549-6624
E-mail: RCortez@silvernet.com

International Accounting Management

Experienced international accountant and financial analyst with proven leadership, planning, negotiating, and intercultural communication skills. Demonstrated ability to improve process efficiency and reduce operating costs.

Experience   3/2005 to present   **Staff Accountant/Financial Analyst**
Inter-American Imports: Alexandria, Virginia

- Prepare accounting reports for wholesale giftware importer ($15 million annual sales)
- Audit financial transactions with suppliers in 12 Latin American countries
- Verify Sarbanes-Oxley process and reporting standards
- Serve as project and team leader
- Created a computerized model to adjust accounts for fluctuations in currency exchange rates
- Negotiated joint-venture agreements with major suppliers in Mexico and Colombia
- Implemented electronic funds transfer for vendor disbursements, improving cash flow and eliminating payables clerk position

10/2001 to 3/2005   **Staff Accountant**
Monsanto Agricultural Chemicals: Mexico City, Mexico
- Handled budgeting, billing, and credit-processing functions for the Mexico City branch
- Audited travel & entertainment expenses for Monsanto's 30-member Latin American sales force
- Helped launch an online system to automate all accounting functions, improving reporting accuracy by 65%

Education   6/2001   **Master of Business Administration with emphasis in international business**
George Mason University, Fairfax, Virginia

5/1999   **Master of Business Administration Accounting**
University of Texas, Austin, Texas

Special Skills   Cultural   - Fluent in Spanish and German
- Extensive business contacts in Latin America

Technical   - Proficient with a wide range of financial software and systems, including Excel, Access, Microsoft Dynamics, and SAP Business One

Figure 13.3   Effective Chronological Résumé
This version does a much better job of presenting the candidate's ability to contribute to a new employer. Notice in particular how easy it is to scan through this résumé to find sections of interest.

The Functional Résumé

The functional résumé is often considered by people with limited or spotty employment history, but many employers are suspicious of this format.

A **functional résumé**, sometimes called a *skills résumé*, emphasizes your skills and capabilities, identifying employers and academic experience in subordinate sections. This arrangement stresses individual areas of competence rather than job history. The functional approach also has three advantages: (1) Without having to read through job descriptions, employers can see what you can do for them, (2) you can emphasize earlier job experience, and (3) you can deemphasize any lengthy unemployment or lack of career progress. However, you should be aware that because the functional résumé can obscure your work history, many employment professionals are suspicious of it.[17] If you don't believe the chronological format will work for you, consider the combination résumé instead.

The Combination Résumé

If you don't have a lot of work history to show, consider a combination résumé to highlight your skills while still providing a chronological history of your employment.

A **combination résumé** meshes the skills focus of the functional format with the job history focus of the chronological format (see Figure 13.4). The chief advantage of this format is that it allows you to focus attention on your capabilities when you don't have a long or steady employment history, without raising concerns that you might be hiding something about your past.

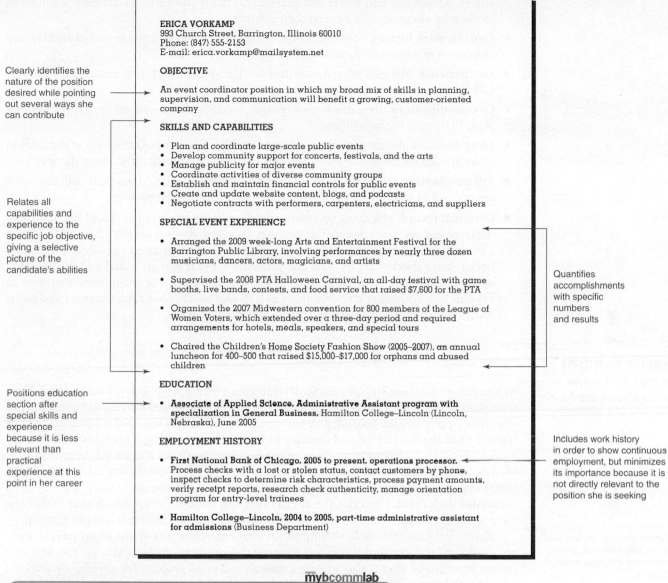

Clearly identifies the nature of the position desired while pointing out several ways she can contribute

Relates all capabilities and experience to the specific job objective, giving a selective picture of the candidate's abilities

Positions education section after special skills and experience because it is less relevant than practical experience at this point in her career

ERICA VORKAMP
993 Church Street, Barrington, Illinois 60010
Phone: (847) 555-2153
E-mail: erica.vorkamp@mailsystem.net

OBJECTIVE

An event coordinator position in which my broad mix of skills in planning, supervision, and communication will benefit a growing, customer-oriented company

SKILLS AND CAPABILITIES

- Plan and coordinate large-scale public events
- Develop community support for concerts, festivals, and the arts
- Manage publicity for major events
- Coordinate activities of diverse community groups
- Establish and maintain financial controls for public events
- Create and update website content, blogs, and podcasts
- Negotiate contracts with performers, carpenters, electricians, and suppliers

SPECIAL EVENT EXPERIENCE

- Arranged the 2009 week-long Arts and Entertainment Festival for the Barrington Public Library, involving performances by nearly three dozen musicians, dancers, actors, magicians, and artists

- Supervised the 2008 PTA Halloween Carnival, an all-day festival with game booths, live bands, contests, and food service that raised $7,600 for the PTA

- Organized the 2007 Midwestern convention for 800 members of the League of Women Voters, which extended over a three-day period and required arrangements for hotels, meals, speakers, and special tours

- Chaired the Children's Home Society Fashion Show (2005–2007), an annual luncheon for 400–500 that raised $15,000–$17,000 for orphans and abused children

EDUCATION

- **Associate of Applied Science, Administrative Assistant program with specialization in General Business,** Hamilton College–Lincoln (Lincoln, Nebraska), June 2005

EMPLOYMENT HISTORY

- **First National Bank of Chicago, 2005 to present, operations processor.** Process checks with a lost or stolen status, contact customers by phone, inspect checks to determine risk characteristics, process payment amounts, verify receipt reports, research check authenticity, manage orientation program for entry-level trainees

- **Hamilton College–Lincoln, 2004 to 2005, part-time administrative assistant for admissions** (Business Department)

Quantifies accomplishments with specific numbers and results

Includes work history in order to show continuous employment, but minimizes its importance because it is not directly relevant to the position she is seeking

mybcommlab

Apply Figure 13.4's key concepts by revising a new document. Go to Chapter 13 in mybcommlab.com and select Document Makeovers.

Figure 13.4   Combination Résumé
With her limited work experience in her field of interest, Erica Vorkamp opted for a combination résumé to highlight her skills. Her employment history is complete and easy to find, but it isn't featured to the same degree as the other elements.

As you look at a number of sample résumés, you'll probably notice many variations on the three basic formats presented here. Study these other options in light of the effective communication principles you've learned in this course and the unique circumstances of your job search. If you find one that seems like the best fit for your unique situation, by all means use it.

Addressing Areas of Concern

Many people have gaps in their careers or other issues that could be a concern for employers. Here are some common issues and suggestions for handling them in a résumé:[18]

- **Frequent job changes.** If you've had a number of short-term jobs of a similar type, such as independent contracting and temporary assignments, try to group them under a single heading. Also, if past job positions were eliminated as a result of layoffs or mergers, find a subtle way to convey that information (if not in your résumé, then in your cover

Frequent job changes and gaps in your work history are two of the more common issues that employers may perceive as weaknesses.

letter). Reasonable employers understand that many professionals have been forced to job hop by circumstances beyond their control.

- **Gaps in work history.** Mention relevant experience and education you gained during employment gaps, such as volunteer or community work.
- **Inexperience.** Mention related volunteer work and membership in professional groups. List relevant course work and internships.
- **Overqualification.** Tone down your résumé, focusing exclusively on the experience and skills that relate to the position.
- **Long-term employment with one company.** Itemize each position held at the firm to show growth within the organization and increasing responsibilities along the way.
- **Job termination for cause.** Be honest with interviewers and address their concerns with proof, such as recommendations and examples of completed projects.
- **Criminal record.** You don't necessarily need to disclose a criminal record or time spent incarcerated on your résumé, but you may be asked about it on job application forms. Laws regarding what employers may ask (and whether they can conduct a criminal background check) vary by state and profession, but if you are asked and the question applies to you, you are legally bound to answer truthfully. Use the interview process to explain any mitigating circumstances and to emphasize your rehabilitation and commitment to being a law-abiding, trustworthy employee.[19]

<table>
<tr><td>

3 LEARNING OBJECTIVE

Describe the tasks involved in writing your résumé, and list the major sections of a traditional résumé

</td></tr>
</table>

WRITING YOUR RÉSUMÉ

As you follow the three-step process to develop your résumé, keep four points in mind. First, treat your résumé with the respect it deserves. A single mistake or oversight can cost you interview opportunities. Second, give yourself plenty of time. Don't put off preparing your résumé until the last second and then try to write it in one sitting. Third, learn from good models. You can find sample résumés online at college websites and on job boards such as Monster and CareerBuilder. Fourth, don't get frustrated by the conflicting advice you'll read about résumés. Résumés are as much art as science, and there is more than one way to be successful with them. Consider the alternatives and choose the approach that makes the most sense to you, given everything you know about successful business communication.

> If you're uncomfortable writing your own résumé, see if you can trade with a classmate and write each other's résumé.

If you feel uncomfortable writing about yourself, you're not alone. Many people, even accomplished writers, find it difficult to write their own résumés. If you get stuck, find a classmate or friend who is also writing a résumé and swap projects for a while. By working on each other's résumés, you might be able to speed up the process for both of you.

Keeping Your Résumé Honest

Estimates vary, but one comprehensive study uncovered lies about work history in more than 40 percent of the résumés tested.[20] And dishonest applicants are getting bolder all the time—going so far as to buy fake diplomas online, pay a computer hacker to insert their names into prestigious universities' graduation records, and sign up for services that offer phony employment verification.[21]

> Résumé fraud has reached epidemic proportions, but employers are fighting back with more rigorous screening techniques.

Applicants with integrity know they don't need to stoop to lying. If you are tempted to stretch the truth, bear in mind that professional recruiters have seen every trick in the book, and frustrated employers are working aggressively to uncover the truth. Nearly all employers do some form of background checking, from contacting references and verifying employment to checking criminal records and sending résumés through verification services.[22] Employers are also beginning to craft certain interview questions specifically to uncover dishonest résumé entries.[23]

More than 90 percent of companies that find lies on résumés refuse to hire the offending applicants, even if that means withdrawing formal job offers.[24] And if you do sneak past these filters and get hired, you'll probably be exposed on the job when you can't live up to your own résumé. Given the networked nature of today's job market, lying on a résumé could haunt you for years—and you could be forced to keep lying throughout your career to hide the original misrepresentations on your résumé.[25]

Adapting Your Résumé to Your Audience

The importance of adapting your résumé to your target readers' needs and interests cannot be overstated. In a competitive job market, the more you look like a good fit, the better your chances will be of securing interviews. Address your readers' business concerns by showing how your capabilities meet the demands and expectations of the position and the organization as a whole. For example, an in-house public relations (PR) department and an independent PR agency perform many of the same tasks, but the outside agency must also sell its services to multiple clients. Consequently, it needs employees who are skilled at attracting and keeping paying customers, in addition to being skilled at PR.

Translate your past accomplishments into a compelling picture of what you can do for employers in the future.

Adapting to your readers can mean customizing your résumé, sometimes for each job opening. However, the effort can pay off with more interviewing opportunities.

Use what you've learned about your target readers to express your experience in the terminology of the hiring organization. For instance, military experience can help you develop many skills that are valuable in business, but military terminology can sound like a foreign language to people who aren't familiar with it. Isolate the important general concepts and present them in common business language. Similarly, educational achievements in other countries might not align with the standard U.S. definitions of high schools, community colleges, technical and trade schools, and universities. If necessary, include a brief statement explaining how your degree or certificate relates to U.S. expectations—or how your U.S. degree relates to expectations in other countries, if you're applying for work abroad.

Military service and other specialized experiences may need to be "translated" into terms more readily understandable by your target readers.

Composing Your Résumé

Write your résumé using a simple and direct style. Use short, crisp phrases instead of whole sentences and focus on what your reader needs to know. Avoid using the word *I*, which can sound both self-involved and repetitive by the time you outline all your skills and accomplishments. Instead, start your phrases with strong action verbs such as these:[26]

Draft your résumé using short, crisp phrases built around strong verbs and nouns.

accomplished	coordinated	initiated	participated	set up
achieved	created	installed	performed	simplified
administered	demonstrated	introduced	planned	sparked
approved	developed	investigated	presented	streamlined
arranged	directed	launched	proposed	strengthened
assisted	established	maintained	raised	succeeded
assumed	explored	managed	recommended	supervised
budgeted	forecasted	motivated	reduced	systematized
chaired	generated	negotiated	reorganized	targeted
changed	identified	operated	resolved	trained
compiled	implemented	organized	saved	transformed
completed	improved	oversaw	served	upgraded

For instance, you might say, "Created a campus organization for students interested in entrepreneurship" or "Managed a fast-food restaurant and four employees." Whenever you can, quantify the results so that your claims don't come across as empty puffery. Don't just say you're a team player or detail oriented—show you are by offering concrete proof.[27] Here are some examples of phrasing accomplishments using active statements that show results:

Instead of This	Write Active Statements That Show Results
Responsible for developing a new filing system	Developed a new filing system that reduced paperwork by 50 percent
I was in charge of customer complaints and all ordering problems	Handled all customer complaints and resolved all product order discrepancies

I won a trip to Europe for opening the most new customer accounts in my department	Generated the highest number of new customer accounts in my department
Member of special campus task force to resolve student problems with existing cafeteria assignments	Assisted in implementing new campus dining program that balances student wishes with cafeteria capacity

Providing specific supporting evidence is vital but make sure you don't go overboard with small details.[28]

Include relevant *keywords* in your introductory statement, work history, and education sections.

In addition to clear writing with specific examples, the particular words and phrases you use throughout your résumé are critically important. The majority of résumés are now subjected to *keyword searches* in an applicant tracking system or other database, in which a recruiter searches for résumés most likely to match the requirements of a particular job. Résumés that don't match the requirements closely may never be seen by a human reader, so it is essential to use the words and phrases that a recruiter is most likely to search on. (Although most experts used to advise including a separate *keyword summary* as a stand-alone list, the trend nowadays is to incorporate your keywords into your introductory statement and other sections of your résumé.[29])

Identifying these keywords requires some research, but you can uncover many of them while you are researching various industries and companies (see page 381). The trick is to study job descriptions carefully and to understand your target audience's needs. In contrast to the action verbs that catch a human reader's attention, keywords that catch a computer's attention are usually nouns that describe the specific skills, attributes, and experiences an employer is looking for in a candidate. Keywords can include the business and technical terms associated with a specific profession, industry-specific jargon, names or types of products or systems used in a profession, job titles, and college degrees.[30] Follow the Real-Time Updates link on this page to see a helpful list of ideas for compiling keywords for your career search.

Name and Contact Information

Be sure to provide complete and accurate contact information; mistakes in this section of the résumé are surprisingly common.

Employers obviously need to know who you are and where you can be reached. Your name and contact information constitute the heading of your résumé, so include the following:

- Name
- Physical address (both permanent and temporary, if you're likely to move during the job search process; however, if you're posting a résumé in an unsecured location online, leave off your physical address for security purposes)
- E-mail address
- Phone number(s)
- The URL of your personal webpage, e-portfolio, or social media résumé (if you have one)

Get a professional-sounding e-mail address for business correspondence (such as *firstname.lastname@something.com*), if you don't already have one.

If the only e-mail address you have is through your current employer, get a free personal e-mail address from one of the many services that offer them. Using company resources for a job search is not fair to your current employer, and it sends a bad signal to potential employers. Also, if your personal e-mail address is anything like precious.princess@something.com or PsychoDawg@something.com, get a new e-mail address for your business correspondence.

REAL-TIME UPDATES
Learn More by Reading This Article

Find the keywords that will light up your résumé

This list of tips and tools will help you find the right keywords to customize your résumé for every opportunity. Go to **http://real-timeupdates.com/bce5** and click on "Learn More." If you are using mybcommlab, you can access Real-Time Updates within each chapter or under Student Study Tools.

Introductory Statement

Of all the parts of a résumé, the brief introductory statement that follows your name and contact information probably generates the most disagreement. You can put one of three things here:[31]

- **Career objective.** A career objective identifies either a specific job you want to land or a general career track you would like to pursue. Some experts advise against including a career objective because it can categorize you so narrowly that you miss out on interesting opportunities, and it is essentially about fulfilling your desires, not about meeting the employer's needs. In the past, most résumés included a career objective, but in recent years more job seekers are using a qualifications summary or a career summary. However, if you have little or no work experience in your target profession, a career objective might be your best option. If you do opt for an objective, word it in a way that relates your qualifications to employer needs (see Figure 13.4 on page 389).

> You can choose to open with a career objective, a qualifications summary, or a career summary.

- **Qualifications summary.** A qualifications summary offers a brief view of your key qualifications. The goal is to let a reader know within a few seconds what you can deliver. You can title this section generically as "Qualifications Summary" or "Summary of Qualifications," or, if you have one dominant qualification, you can use that as the title (see the career summary in Figure 13.3 on page 388 for an example). Consider using a qualifications summary if you have one or more important qualifications but don't yet have a long career history. Also, if you haven't been working long but your college education has given you a dominant professional "theme," such as multimedia design or statistical analysis, you can craft a qualifications summary that highlights your educational preparedness.

> If you have a reasonably focused skill set but don't yet have a long career history, a qualifications summary is probably the best type of introductory statement for you.

- **Career summary.** A career summary offers a brief recap of your career with the goal of presenting increasing levels of responsibility and performance. A career summary can be particularly useful for executives who have demonstrated the ability to manage increasingly larger and more complicated business operations—a key consideration when companies look to hire upper-level managers.

Whichever option you chose, make sure it includes many of the essential keywords you identified in your research—and adapt these words and phrases to each job opportunity as needed.

Education

If you're still in college or have recently graduated, education is probably your strongest selling point. Present your educational background in depth, choosing facts that support your "theme." Give this section a heading such as "Education," "Technical Training," or "Academic Preparation," as appropriate. Then, starting with the most recent, list the name and location of each school you have attended, the month and year of your graduation (say "anticipated graduation in _____" if you haven't graduated yet), your major and minor fields of study, significant skills and abilities you've developed in your course work, and the degrees or certificates you've earned. If you're still working toward a degree, include in parentheses the expected date of completion. Showcase your qualifications by listing courses that have directly equipped you for the job you are seeking and indicate any scholarships, awards, or academic honors you've received.

> If you are early in your career, your education is probably your strongest selling point.

The education section should also include relevant training sponsored by business or government organizations. Mention high school or military training only if the associated achievements are pertinent to your career goals.

Whether you list your grade point average depends on the job you want and the quality of your grades. If you don't show your GPA on your résumé—and there's no rule saying you have to—be prepared to answer questions about it during the interview process because many employers will assume that your GPA is not spectacular if you didn't list it on your résumé. If you choose to show a grade point average, be sure to mention the scale, especially if it isn't a four-point scale. If your grades are better within your major than in other courses, you can also list your GPA as "Major GPA" and include only those courses within your major.

Work Experience, Skills, and Accomplishments

Like the education section, the work experience section should focus on your overall theme in a way that shows how your past can contribute to an employer's future. Use keywords to call attention to the skills you've developed on the job and to your ability to handle increasing responsibility.

> When you describe past job responsibilities, identify the skills and knowledge that you can apply to a future job.

List your jobs in reverse chronological order, starting with the most recent. Include military service and any internships and part-time or temporary jobs related to your career objective. Include the name and location of the employer, and if readers are unlikely to recognize the organization, briefly describe what it does. When you want to keep the name of your current employer confidential, you can identify the firm by industry only ("a large video game developer"). If an organization's name or location has changed since you worked there, state the current name and location and include the old information preceded by "formerly . . ." Before or after each job listing, state your job title and give the years you worked in the job; use the phrase "to present" to denote current employment. Indicate whether a job was part time.

Devote the most space to the jobs that are related to your target position. If you were personally responsible for something significant, be sure to mention it. Facts about your skills and accomplishments are the most important information you can give a prospective employer, so quantify them whenever possible.

One helpful exercise is to write a 30-second "commercial" for each major skill you want to highlight. The commercial should offer proof that you really do possess the skill. For your résumé, distill the commercials down to brief phrases; you can use the more detailed proof statements in cover letters and as answers to interview questions.[32]

If you have a number of part-time, temporary, or entry-level jobs that don't relate to your career objective, you have to use your best judgment when it comes to including or excluding them. Too many minor and irrelevant work details can clutter your résumé, particularly if you've been in the professional workforce for a few years. However, if you don't have a long employment history, including these jobs shows your ability and willingness to keep working.

Activities and Achievements

Include activities and achievements outside of a work context only if they make you a more attractive job candidate. For example, traveling, studying, or working abroad and fluency in multiple languages could weigh heavily in your favor with employers who do business internationally.

Because many employers are involved in their local communities, they tend to look positively on applicants who are active and concerned members of their communities as well. Consider including community service activities that suggest leadership, teamwork, communication skills, technical aptitude, or other valuable attributes.

You should generally avoid indicating membership or significant activity in religious or political organizations (unless, of course, you're applying to such an organization) because doing so might raise concerns for people with differing beliefs or affiliations. However, if you want to highlight skills you developed while involved with such a group, you can refer to it generically as a "not-for-profit organization."

Finally, if you have little or no job experience and not much to discuss outside of your education, indicating involvement in athletics or other organized student activities lets employers know that you don't spend all your free time hanging around your apartment playing video games. Also consider mentioning publications, projects, and other accomplishments that required relevant business skills.

Personal Data and References

In nearly all instances, your résumé should not include any personal data beyond the information described in the previous sections. When applying to U.S. companies, never include any of the following: physical characteristics, age, gender, marital status, sexual orientation, religious or political affiliations, race, national origin, salary history, reasons for leaving jobs, names of previous supervisors, names of references, Social Security number, or student ID number.

Note that standards can vary in other countries. For example, you might be expected to include your citizenship, nationality, or marital status.[33] However, verify such requirements before including any personal data.

The availability of references is usually assumed, so you don't need to put "References available upon request" at the end of your résumé. However, be sure to have a list of several references ready when you begin applying for jobs. Prepare your reference sheet with your name and contact information at the top. For a finished look, use the same design and layout you use for your résumé. Then list three or four people who have agreed to serve as references. Include each person's name, job title, organization, address, telephone number, e-mail address (if the reference prefers to be contacted by e-mail), and the nature of your relationship.

COMPLETING YOUR RÉSUMÉ

Completing your résumé involves revising it for optimum quality, producing it in the various forms and media you'll need, and proofreading it for any errors before distributing it or publishing it online. Producing and distributing a résumé used to be fairly straightforward; you printed it on quality paper and mailed or faxed it to employers. However, the advent of *applicant tracking systems* (databases that let managers sort through incoming applications to find the most promising candidates), social media, and other innovations has dramatically changed the nature of résumé production and distribution. Be prepared to produce several versions of your résumé, in multiple formats and multiple media.

Even if most or all of your application efforts take place online, starting with a traditional paper résumé is still useful, for several reasons. First, a traditional printed résumé is a great opportunity to organize your background information and identify your unique strengths. Second, the planning and writing tasks involved in creating a conventional résumé will help you generate blocks of text that you can reuse in multiple ways throughout the job search process. Third, you'll never know when someone might ask for your résumé during a networking event or other in-person encounter, and you don't want to let that interest fade in the time it might take for the person to get to your information online.

Revising Your Résumé

Ask professional recruiters to list the most common mistakes they see on résumés, and you'll hear the same things over and over again. Take care to avoid these flaws:

- Too long or too wordy
- Too short or sketchy
- Difficult to read
- Poorly written
- Displaying weak understanding of the business world in general or of a particular industry or company
- Poor-quality printing or cheap paper
- Full of spelling and grammar errors
- Boastful
- Gimmicky design

The ideal length of your résumé depends on the depth of your experience and the level of the positions for which you are applying. As a general guideline, if you have fewer than 10 years of professional experience, try to keep your conventional résumé to one page. For online résumé formats, you can always provide links to additional information. If you have more experience and are applying for a higher-level position, you may need to prepare a somewhat longer résumé.[34] For highly technical positions, longer résumés are often the norm as well because the qualifications for such jobs can require more description.

Producing Your Résumé

No matter how many media and formats you eventually choose for producing your résumé, a clean, professional-looking design is a must. Unless you have some experience in graphic design and you're applying in a field such as advertising or retail merchandising, where visual creativity is viewed as an asset, resist the urge to "get creative" with your résumé layout.[35] Recruiters and hiring managers want to skim your essential information in a matter of seconds, and anything that distracts or delays them will work against you. Moreover, complex layouts can confuse an applicant tracking system, which can result in your information getting garbled.

Fortunately, good résumé design is not difficult to achieve. As you can see in Figures 13.3 and 13.4, good designs feature simplicity, order, effective use of white space, and clear typefaces. Make subheadings easy to find and easy to read, placing them either above each section or in the left margin. Use lists to itemize your most important qualifications. Color is not necessary by any means, but if you add color, make it subtle and sophisticated, such as

4 LEARNING OBJECTIVE
Characterize the completing step for résumés, including the six most common formats in which you can produce a résumé

Most of your application efforts will take place online, but starting with a traditional paper résumé is still useful.

Avoid the common errors that will get your résumé excluded from consideration.

If your employment history is brief, keep your résumé to one page.

Effective résumé designs are simple, clean, and professional—not gaudy, "clever," or cute.

Be prepared to produce several versions of your résumé in multiple media.

for a thin horizontal line under your name and address. The most common way to get into trouble with résumé design is going overboard (see Figure 13.5).

Depending on the companies you apply to, you might want to produce your résumé in as many as six formats (all are explained in the following sections):

- Printed traditional résumé
- Printed scannable résumé
- Electronic plain-text file
- Microsoft Word file
- Online résumé
- PDF file

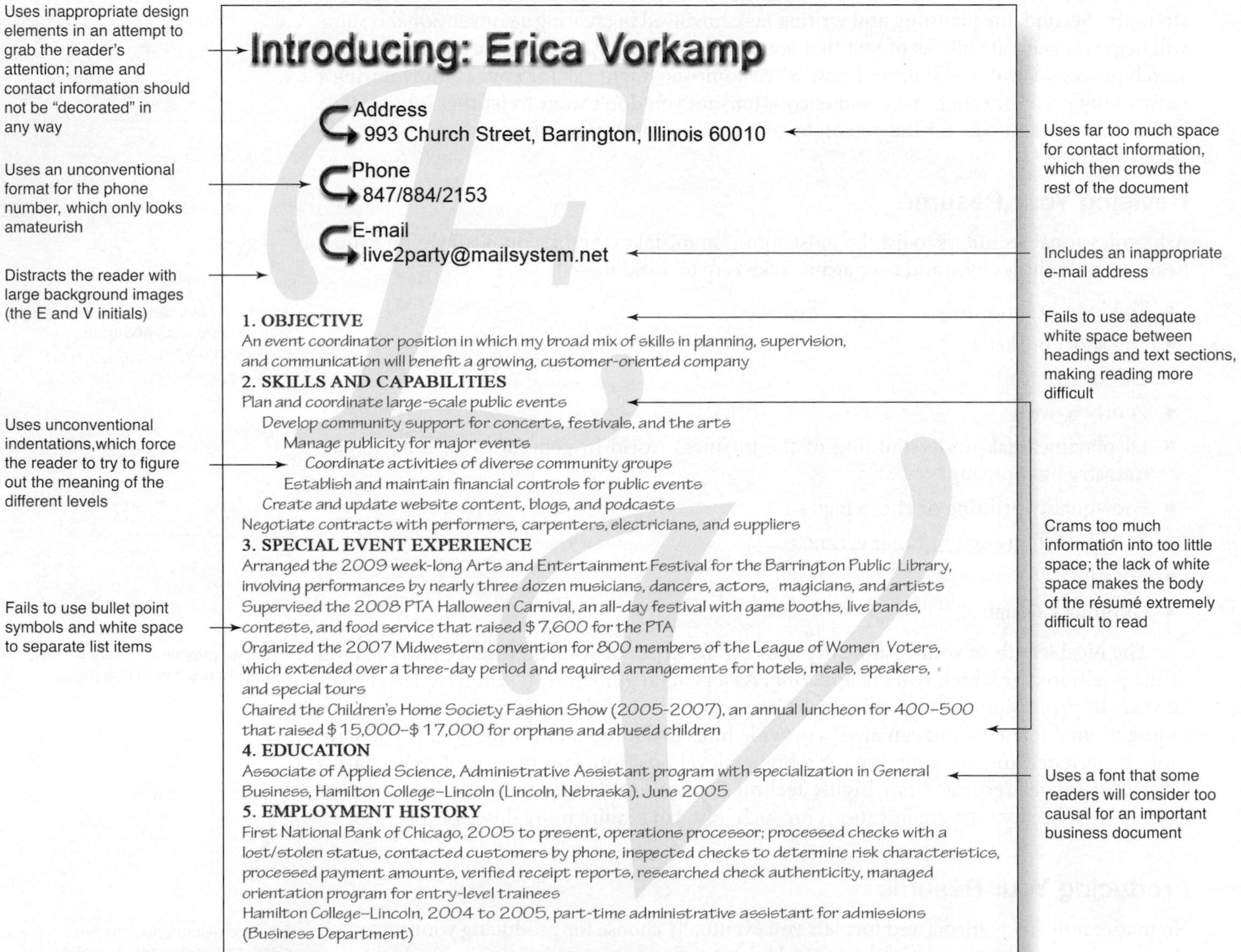

Uses inappropriate design elements in an attempt to grab the reader's attention; name and contact information should not be "decorated" in any way

Uses an unconventional format for the phone number, which only looks amateurish

Distracts the reader with large background images (the E and V initials)

Uses unconventional indentations, which force the reader to try to figure out the meaning of the different levels

Fails to use bullet point symbols and white space to separate list items

Introducing: Erica Vorkamp

Address
993 Church Street, Barrington, Illinois 60010

Phone
847/884/2153

E-mail
live2party@mailsystem.net

1. OBJECTIVE
An event coordinator position in which my broad mix of skills in planning, supervision, and communication will benefit a growing, customer-oriented company

2. SKILLS AND CAPABILITIES
Plan and coordinate large-scale public events
Develop community support for concerts, festivals, and the arts
Manage publicity for major events
Coordinate activities of diverse community groups
Establish and maintain financial controls for public events
Create and update website content, blogs, and podcasts
Negotiate contracts with performers, carpenters, electricians, and suppliers

3. SPECIAL EVENT EXPERIENCE
Arranged the 2009 week-long Arts and Entertainment Festival for the Barrington Public Library, involving performances by nearly three dozen musicians, dancers, actors, magicians, and artists
Supervised the 2008 PTA Halloween Carnival, an all-day festival with game booths, live bands, contests, and food service that raised $7,600 for the PTA
Organized the 2007 Midwestern convention for 800 members of the League of Women Voters, which extended over a three-day period and required arrangements for hotels, meals, speakers, and special tours
Chaired the Children's Home Society Fashion Show (2005-2007), an annual luncheon for 400–500 that raised $15,000–$17,000 for orphans and abused children

4. EDUCATION
Associate of Applied Science, Administrative Assistant program with specialization in General Business, Hamilton College–Lincoln (Lincoln, Nebraska), June 2005

5. EMPLOYMENT HISTORY
First National Bank of Chicago, 2005 to present, operations processor; processed checks with a lost/stolen status, contacted customers by phone, inspected checks to determine risk characteristics, processed payment amounts, verified receipt reports, researched check authenticity, managed orientation program for entry-level trainees
Hamilton College–Lincoln, 2004 to 2005, part-time administrative assistant for admissions (Business Department)

Uses far too much space for contact information, which then crowds the rest of the document

Includes an inappropriate e-mail address

Fails to use adequate white space between headings and text sections, making reading more difficult

Crams too much information into too little space; the lack of white space makes the body of the résumé extremely difficult to read

Uses a font that some readers will consider too casual for an important business document

mybcommlab

Apply Figure 13.5's key concepts by revising a new document. Go to Chapter 13 in mybcommlab.com and select Document Makeovers.

Figure 13.5   Ineffective Résumé Design
This résumé tries too hard to be creative and eye-catching, resulting in a document that is difficult to read—and that probably won't get read. Recruiters have seen every conceivable design gimmick, so don't try to stand out from the crowd with unusual design. Instead, provide compelling, employer-focused information that is easy to find.

Unfortunately, there is no single format or medium that works for all the situations you will encounter, and employer expectations continue to change as technology evolves. Find out what each employer or job posting website expects, and provide your résumé in that specific format.

As you produce your résumé in various formats, you will encounter the question of whether to include a photograph of yourself on or with your résumé. For print or electronic documents that you will be submitting to employers or job websites, the safest advice is to avoid photos. The reason is that seeing visual cues of the age, ethnicity, and gender of candidates early in the selection process exposes employers to complaints of discriminatory hiring practices. In fact, some employers won't even look at résumés that include photos, and some applicant tracking systems automatically discard résumés with any kind of extra files.[36] However, photographs are acceptable for social media résumés and other online formats where you are not actually submitting a résumé to an employer.

In addition to these six main formats, some applicants create PowerPoint presentations or videos to supplement a conventional résumé. Two key advantages of a PowerPoint supplement are flexibility and multimedia capabilities. For instance, you can present a menu of choices on the opening screen and allow viewers to click through to sections of interest. (Note that most of the things you can accomplish with PowerPoint can be done with an online résumé, which is probably more convenient for most readers.)

A video résumé can be a compelling supplement as well, but be aware that some employment law experts advise employers not to view videos, at least not until after candidates have been evaluated solely on their credentials. The reason for this caution is the same as with photographs. In addition, videos are more cumbersome to evaluate than paper or electronic résumés, and some recruiters refuse to watch them.[37]

> Do not include or enclose a photo in résumés that you send to employers or post on job websites.

Producing a Traditional Printed Résumé

When printing a traditional paper résumé, avoid the low-cost bond paper intended for general office use and gimmicky papers with borders and backgrounds. Choose a heavier, higher-quality paper designed specifically for résumés and other important documents. White or slightly off-white is the best color choice. This paper is more expensive than general office paper, but you don't need much, and it's a worthwhile investment. Make sure the printer you use is well maintained and has adequate toner or ink.

> Use high-quality paper when printing your résumé.

Printing a Scannable Résumé

You might encounter a company that prefers *scannable résumés*, a type of printed résumé that is specially formatted to be compatible with optical scanning systems that convert printed documents to electronic text. These systems were quite common just a few years ago, but their use appears to be declining rapidly as more employers prefer e-mail delivery or website application forms.[38] A scannable résumé differs from the traditional format in two major ways: it should always include a keyword summary (employers search on these terms to find promising candidates), and it should be formatted in a simpler fashion that avoids underlining, special characters, and other elements that can confuse the scanning system. If you need to produce a scannable résumé, search online for "formatting a scannable résumé" to get detailed instructions.

> Some employers still prefer résumés in scannable format, but most now want electronic submissions.

Creating a Plain-Text File of Your Résumé

A *plain-text file* (sometimes known as an ASCII text file) is an electronic version of your résumé that has no font formatting, no bullet symbols, no colors, no lines or boxes, or other special formatting. The plain-text version can be used in two ways. First, you can include it in the body of an e-mail message, for employers who want e-mail delivery but don't want file attachments. Second, you can copy and paste the sections into the application forms on an employer's website.

A plain-text version is easy to create with your word processor. Start with the file you used to create your scannable résumé, use the "Save As" choice to save it as "plain text" or whichever similarly labeled option your software has, and verify the result by using a basic text editor (such as Microsoft Notepad). If necessary, reformat the page manually, moving text and inserting space as needed. For simplicity's sake, left-justify all your headings rather than trying to center them manually.

> A plain-text version of your résumé is simply a computer file without any of the formatting that you typically apply using a word processor.

> Make sure you verify the plain-text file that you create with your word processor; it might need a few manual adjustments using a text editor such as Notepad.

Creating a Word File of Your Résumé

Some employers and websites want your résumé in Microsoft Word format; make sure your computer is thoroughly scanned for viruses first, however.

In some cases, an employer or job-posting website will want you to upload a Microsoft Word file or attach it to an e-mail message. (Although there are certainly other word processors on the market, Microsoft Word is the de facto standard in business these days.) This method of transferring information preserves the design and layout of your résumé and saves you the trouble of creating a plain-text version. However, before you submit a Word file to anyone, make sure your computer is free of viruses. Infecting a potential employer's computer will not make a good first impression.

Creating a PDF Version of Your Résumé

Creating a PDF file is a simple procedure, but you need the right software. Adobe Acrobat (not the free Adobe Reader) is the best-known program, but many others are available, including some free versions. You can also use Adobe's online service, at **http://createpdf .adobe.com**, to create PDFs without buying software.

Creating an Online Résumé

You have many options for creating an online résumé, from college-hosted e-portfolios to multimedia résumés on commercial websites.

A variety of terms are used to describe online résumés, including *personal webpage, e-portfolio, social media résumé,* and *multimedia résumé.* Whatever the terminology used on a particular site, all these formats provide the opportunity to expand on the information contained in your basic résumé with links to projects, publications, screencasts, online videos, course lists, social networking profiles, and other elements that give employers a more complete picture of who you are and what you can offer (see Figure 13.6).

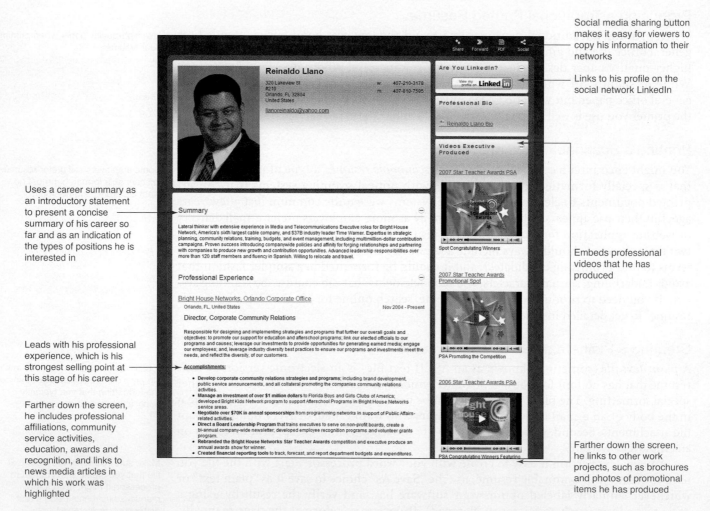

Social media sharing button makes it easy for viewers to copy his information to their networks

Links to his profile on the social network LinkedIn

Embeds professional videos that he has produced

Uses a career summary as an introductory statement to present a concise summary of his career so far and as an indication of the types of positions he is interested in

Leads with his professional experience, which is his strongest selling point at this stage of his career

Farther down the screen, he includes professional affiliations, community service activities, education, awards and recognition, and links to news media articles in which his work was highlighted

Farther down the screen, he links to other work projects, such as brochures and photos of promotional items he has produced

Figure 13.6 Online Résumé
Reinaldo Llano, a corporate communications executive in the media industry, used the résumé hosting website VisualCV to create and present this multimedia/social media résumé.

A good place to start is your college's career center. Ask whether the career center (or perhaps the information technology department) hosts online résumés or e-portfolios for students. For example, Penn State's e-portfolio service (see http://portfolio.psu.edu/gallery for examples) hosts student portfolios and offers helpful information on designing and creating an online portfolio.

A commercial hosting service is another good possibility for an online résumé. For instance, the free service VisualCV (www.visualcv.com) lets you build an online résumé with video clips and other multimedia elements. This site is a good place to see numerous examples, from students just about to enter the workforce full-time all the way up to corporate CEOs.[39]

Regardless of the approach you take to creating an online résumé, keep these helpful tips in mind:

- **Remember that your online presence is a career-management tool.** The way you are portrayed online can work for you or against you, and it's up to you to create a positive impression. Most employers now conduct online searches to learn more about promising candidates, and 70 percent of those who do have rejected applicants because of information they dug up online.[40]

- **Take advantage of social networking.** Use whatever tools are available to direct people to your online résumé, such as including your URL on the "Info" tab on your Facebook page.

- **During the application process, don't expect or ask employers to retrieve a résumé from your website.** Submit your résumé using whatever method and medium each employer prefers. If employers then want to know more about you, they will likely do a web search on you and find your site, or you can refer them to your site in your résumé or application materials.

Proofreading Your Résumé

Employers view your résumé as a concrete example of your attention to quality and detail. Your résumé doesn't need to be good or pretty good—it needs to be *perfect*. Although it may not seem fair, just one or two errors in a job application package are enough to doom a candidate's chances.[41]

Your résumé is one of the most important documents you'll ever write, so don't rush or cut corners when it comes to proofreading. Check all headings and lists for clarity and parallelism and be sure that your grammar, spelling, and punctuation are correct. Ask at least three other people to read it, too. As the creator of the material, you could stare at a mistake for weeks and not see it.

Your résumé can't be "pretty good" or "almost perfect"—it needs to be perfect, *so proofread it thoroughly and ask several other people to verify it, too.*

Distributing Your Résumé

How you distribute your résumé depends on the number of employers you target and their preferences for receiving résumés. Employers usually list their requirements on their websites, so verify this information and follow it carefully. Beyond that, here are some general distribution tips:

- **Mailing printed résumés.** Take some care with the packaging. Spend a few extra cents to mail these documents in a flat 9 × 12 envelope, or better yet, use a Priority Mail flat-rate envelope, which gives you a sturdy cardboard mailer and faster delivery for just a few more dollars.

- **E-mailing your résumé.** Some employers want applicants to include the text of their résumés in the body of an e-mail message; others prefer an attached Microsoft Word file. If you have a reference number or a job ad number, include it in the subject line of your e-mail message.

- **Submitting your résumé to an employer's website.** Many employers, including most large companies, now prefer or require applicants to submit their résumés online. In some instances, you will be asked to upload a complete file. In others, you will need to copy and paste sections of your résumé into individual boxes in an online application form.

- **Posting your résumé on job websites.** You can post your résumé on general-purpose job websites such as Monster (www.monster.com) and CareerBuilder

When distributing your résumé, pay close attention to the specific instructions provided by every employer, job website, or other recipient.

Don't post a résumé on any public website unless you understand its privacy and security policies.

(www. careerbuilder.com), on more specialized websites such as Jobster (**www.jobster** **.com**) or Jobfox (**www.jobfox.com**), or with staffing services such as Volt (**http://jobs** **.volt.com**). Before you upload your résumé to any site, however, learn about its confidentiality protection. Some sites allow you to specify levels of confidentiality, such as letting employers search your qualifications without seeing your personal contact information or preventing your current employer from seeing your résumé. Don't post your résumé to any website that doesn't give you the option of restricting the display of your contact information. (Only employers that are registered clients of the service should be able to see your contact information.)[42]

For the latest information on résumé writing and distribution, visit **http://real-timeupdates** **.com/bce5** and click on Chapter 13.

PEARSON **mybcommlab**

Are you an active learner? Go to mybcommlab.com to master Chapter 13's content. Chapter 13's interactive activities include:

- Customizable Study Plan and Chapter 13 practice quizzes
- Chapter 13 Simulation (Cover Letters and Résumés), which helps you think critically and prepare to make choices in the business world
- Chapter 13 Video Exercise (Building Careers & Writing Résumés: Giant Robot Magazine), which shows you how textbook concepts are put into practice every day

- Flash Cards for mastering the definition of chapter terms
- Interactive Lessons that visually review key chapter concepts
- Document Makeovers for hands-on, scored practice in revising documents

---

CHAPTER REVIEW AND ACTIVITIES

Learning Objectives: Check Your Progress

1 OBJECTIVE **List eight key steps to finding the ideal opportunity in today's job market.**

The eight steps discussed in the chapter are (1) writing the story of you, which involves describing where you have been in your career so far and where you would like to go in the future; (2) learning to think like an employer so you can present yourself as a quality hire; (3) researching industries and companies of interest to identify promising opportunities and to learn the language of the hiring managers; (4) translating your general potential into a specific solution for each employer so that you look like a good fit for each opening; (5) taking the initiative to approach interesting companies even if they haven't yet posted any job openings; (6) building your network so you and your connections can help each other in the job search process; (7) seeking career counseling if appropriate; and (8) avoiding the easily avoidable mistakes that can ruin your chances of getting a job.

2 OBJECTIVE **Explain the process of planning your résumé, including how to choose the best résumé organization.**

Planning a résumé starts with recognizing what it is: a persuasive message designed to get you job interviews. Gathering the necessary information involves learning about target industries, professions, companies, and specific positions, as well as gathering information about yourself. Choosing the best résumé organization depends on your background and your goals. A chronological résumé helps employers easily locate necessary information, highlights your professional growth and career progress, and emphasizes continuity and stability. If you can use the chronological format, you should because it is the approach employers tend to prefer. A functional résumé helps employers easily see what you can do for them, allows you to emphasize earlier job experience, and lets you downplay any lengthy periods of unemployment or a lack of career progress. However, many employers are suspicious of functional résumés for this very reason. The combination approach uses the best features of the other two and is often the best choice for recent graduates.

3 OBJECTIVE Describe the tasks involved in writing your résumé, and list the major sections of a traditional résumé.

Adapting to the audience is crucial, because readers are looking to see how well you understand their businesses and can present a solution to their talent needs. The major sections of a traditional résumé are (1) your name and contact information; (2) an introductory statement, which can be a career objective, a qualifications summary, or a career summary; (3) your education; (4) your work experience; and (5) activities and achievements that are professionally relevant. Most résumés do not need to include any personal data.

4 OBJECTIVE Characterize the completing step for résumés, including the six most common formats in which you can produce a résumé.

Quality is paramount with résumés, so the tasks of revising and proofing are particularly important. The six common résumé formats are traditional printed résumé, scannable résumé, electronic plain-text file, Microsoft Word file, PDF, and online résumé (which might be called a personal webpage, an e-portfolio, or a social media résumé).

◼ Test Your Knowledge

To review chapter content related to each question, refer to the indicated Learning Objective.

1. Why is networking an essential part of your lifelong career planning? [LO-1]
2. Why do most employers prefer chronological résumés over functional résumés? [LO-2]
3. What is a résumé, and why is it important to adopt a "you" attitude when preparing one? [LO-2]
4. Why is it important to find and use relevant keywords in your résumé? [LO-3]
5. What are the advantages of an online résumé? [LO-4]

◼ Apply Your Knowledge

To review chapter content related to each question, refer to the indicated Learning Objective.

1. Some people don't have a clear career path when they enter the job market. If you're in this situation, how would your uncertainty affect the way your write your résumé? [LO-1]
2. Can you use a qualifications summary if you don't yet have extensive professional experience in your desired career? Why or why not? [LO-3]
3. How should you present a past job that is unrelated to your current career plans? [LO-3]

4. Between your sophomore and junior years, you quit school for a year to earn the money to finish college. You worked as a loan-processing assistant in a finance company, checking references on loan applications, typing, and filing. Your manager made a lot of the fact that he had never attended college. He seemed to resent you for pursuing your education, but he never criticized your work, so you thought you were doing okay. After you'd been working there for six months, he fired you, saying that you had failed to be thorough enough in your credit checks. You were actually glad to leave, and you found another job right away, at a bank doing similar duties. Now that you've graduated from college, you're writing your résumé. Will you include the finance company job in your work history? Explain. [LO-3]
5. You've completed an attractive, professional-quality online résumé but haven't created a conventional résumé yet. You run across an intriguing job opportunity for which the hiring manager asks interested applicants to e-mail résumés as Microsoft Word attachments. You don't want to let this opportunity slip by. Should you e-mail the manager a link to your online résumé and explain that you haven't had time to create a conventional résumé yet? Why or why not? [LO-4]

◼ Practice Your Skills

Activities

Active links for all websites in this chapter can be found on mybcommlab; see your User Guide for instructions on accessing the content for this chapter. Each activity is labeled according to the primary skill or skills you will need to use. To review relevant chapter content, you can refer to the indicated Learning Objective. In some instances, supporting information will be found in another chapter, as indicated.

1. **Career Management: Researching Career Opportunities [LO-1]**   Based on the preferences you identified in the self-assessment in the Prologue (see page 28) and the academic, professional, and personal qualities you have to offer, perform an online search for a career opportunity that matches your interests and qualifications (starting with any of the websites listed in Table 13.1). Draft a one-page report indicating how the career you select and the job openings you find match your strengths and preferences.
2. **Message Strategies: Planning a Résumé [LO-2]**   Identify a position in an interesting career field that you could potentially be qualified for upon graduation. Using at least three different sources, including the description in an online job posting, create a list of ten keywords that should be included in a résumé customized for this positioning.
3. **Message Strategies: Writing a Résumé [LO-3]**   Rewrite this résumé so that it follows the guidelines presented in this chapter.

Sylvia Manchester

765 Belle Fleur Blvd.

New Orleans, LA 70113

(504) 555-9504

smanchester@rcnmail.com

PERSONAL: Single, excellent health, 5'7", 136 lbs.; hobbies include cooking, dancing, and reading.

JOB OBJECTIVE: To obtain a responsible position in marketing or sales with a good company.

Education: BA degree in biology, University of Louisiana, 1998. Graduated with a 3.0 average. Member of the varsity cheerleading squad. President of Panhellenic League. Homecoming queen.

WORK EXPERIENCE

Fisher Scientific Instruments, 2004 to now, field sales representative. Responsible for calling on customers and explaining the features of Fisher's line of laboratory instruments. Also responsible for writing sales letters, attending trade shows, and preparing weekly sales reports.

Fisher Scientific Instruments, 2001–2003, customer service representative. Was responsible for handling incoming phone calls from customers who had questions about delivery, quality, or operation of Fisher's line of laboratory instruments. Also handled miscellaneous correspondence with customers.

Medical Electronics, Inc., 1998–2001, administrative assistant to the vice president of marketing. In addition to handling typical secretarial chores for the vice president of marketing, I was in charge of compiling the monthly sales reports, using figures provided by members of the field sales force. I also was given responsibility for doing various market research activities.

New Orleans Convention and Visitors Bureau, 1995–1998, summers, tour guide. During the summers of my college years, I led tours of New Orleans for tourists visiting the city. My duties included greeting conventioneers and their spouses at hotels, explaining the history and features of the city during an all-day sightseeing tour, and answering questions about New Orleans and its attractions. During my fourth summer with the bureau, I was asked to help train the new tour guides. I prepared a handbook that provided interesting facts about the various tourist attractions, as well as answers to the most commonly asked tourist questions. The Bureau was so impressed with the handbook they had it printed up so that it could be given as a gift to visitors.

University of Louisiana, 1995–1998, part-time clerk in admissions office. While I was a student in college, I worked 15 hours a week in the admissions office. My duties included filing, processing

applications, and handling correspondence with high school students and administrators.

4. **Message Strategies: Writing a Résumé; Collaboration: Team Projects [LO-3], Chapter 2** Working with another student, change the following statements to make them more effective for a résumé by using action verbs and concrete keywords.

  a. Have some experience with database design.
  b. Assigned to a project to analyze the cost accounting methods for a large manufacturer.
  c. I was part of a team that developed a new inventory control system.
  d. Am responsible for preparing the quarterly department budget.
  e. Was a manager of a department with seven employees working for me.
  f. Was responsible for developing a spreadsheet to analyze monthly sales by department.
  g. Put in place a new program for ordering supplies.

5. **Message Strategies: Writing a Résumé [LO-3]** Using your team's answers to Activity 3, make the statements stronger by quantifying them (make up any numbers you need).

6. **Message Strategies: Writing a Résumé; Communication Ethics: Resolving Ethical Dilemmas [LO-3], Chapter 1** Assume that you achieved all the tasks shown in Activity 3, not as an individual employee but as part of a work team. In your résumé, must you mention other team members? Explain your answer.

▌Expand Your Skills

Critique the Professionals

Locate an example of an online résumé (a sample or an actual résumé). Try Monster (www.monster.com) and VisualCV (www.visualcv.com), among other sites. Analyze the résumé following the guidelines presented in this chapter. Using whatever medium your instructor requests, write a brief analysis (no more than one page) of the résumé's strengths and weaknesses, citing specific elements from the résumé and support from the chapter. If you are analyzing a real résumé, do not include any personally identifiable data, such as the person's name, e-mail address, or phone number, in your report.

Sharpen Your Career Skills Online

Bovée and Thill's Business Communication Web Search, at http://businesscommunicationblog.com/websearch, is a unique research tool designed specifically for business communication research. Use the Web Search function to find a website, video, PDF document, podcast, or presentation that offers advice on creating effective online résumés. Write a brief e-mail message to your instructor or a post for your class blog, describing the item that you found and summarizing the career skills information you learned from it.

mybcommlab

If your course uses mybcommlab, log on to www.mybcommlab.com to access the following study and assessment aids associated with this chapter:

- Video applications
- Pre/post test
- Real-Time Updates
- Personalized study plan

- Peer review activity
- Model documents
- Quick Learning Guides
- Sample presentations

If you are not using mybcommlab, you can access Real-Time Updates and Quick Learning Guides through http://real-timeupdates.com/bce5. The Quick Learning Guide (located under "Learn More" on the website) hits all the high points of this chapter in just two pages. This guide, especially prepared by the authors, will help you study for exams or review important concepts whenever you need a quick refresher.

CASES

▼ *Apply the three-step writing process to the following cases, as assigned by your instructor.*

1. Career Management: Researching Career Opportunities [LO-1]
Chances are you won't be able to land your dream job right out of college, but that doesn't mean you shouldn't start planning right now to make that dream come true.

Your task Using online job search tools, find a job that sounds just about perfect for you, even if you're not yet qualified for it. It might even be something that would take 10 or 20 years to reach. Don't settle for something that's not quite right; find a job that is so "you" and so exciting that you would jump out of bed every morning, eager to go to work (such jobs really do exist!). Start with the job description you found online and then supplement it with additional research so that you get a good picture of what this job and career path are all about. Compile a list of all the qualifications you would need to have a reasonable chance of landing such a job. Now compare this list with your current résumé. Write a brief e-mail to your instructor that identifies all the areas in which you would need to improve your skills, work experience, education, and other qualifications in order to land your dream job.

2. Message Strategies: Planning a Résumé [LO-2] Think about yourself. What are some things that come easily to you? What do you enjoy doing? In what part of the country would you like to live? Do you like to work indoors? Outdoors? A combination of the two? How much do you like to travel? Would you like to spend considerable time on the road? Do you like to work closely with others or more independently? What conditions make a job unpleasant? Do you delegate responsibility easily, or do you like to do things yourself? Are you better with words or numbers? Better at speaking or writing? Do you like to work under fixed deadlines? How important is job security to you? Do you want your supervisor to state clearly what is expected of you, or do you like having the freedom to make many of your own decisions?

Your task After answering these questions, gather information about possible jobs that suit your current qualifications by consulting reference materials (from your college library or placement center) and by searching online. Next, choose a location, a company, and a job that interest you. Write a résumé that matches your qualifications and the job description; use whatever format and media your instructor specifies.

3. Message Strategies: Completing a Résumé [LO-4] Creating presentations and other multimedia supplements can be a great way to expand on the brief overview that a résumé provides.

Your task Starting with any version of a résumé that you've created for yourself, create an electronic presentation that expands on your résumé information to give potential employers a more complete picture of what you can contribute. Include samples of your work, testimonials from current or past employers and colleagues, videos of speeches you've made, and anything else that tells the story of the professional "you." If you have a specific job or type of job in mind, focus on that. Otherwise, present a more general picture that shows why you would be a great employee for any company to consider. Be sure to review the information from Chapter 12 about creating professional-quality presentations.

Improve Your Grammar, Mechanics, and Usage

You can download the text of this assignment from http://real-timeupdates.com/bce5; click on "Student Assignments" and then click on "Chapter 13. Improve Your Grammar, Mechanics, and Usage."

Level 1: Self-Assessment—Numbers

Review Section 3.4 in the Handbook of Grammar, Mechanics, and Usage and then complete the following 15 items.

For items 1–15, correct number styles wherever necessary.

1. We need to hire one office manager, four book-keepers, and twelve clerk-typists.
2. The market for this product is nearly six million people in our region alone.
3. Make sure that all 1835 pages are on my desk no later than nine o'clock a.m.
4. 2004 was the year that José Guiterez sold more than $50 thousand dollars worth of stock.
5. Our deadline is 4/7, but we won't be ready before 4/11.
6. 95 percent of our customers are men.
7. More than 1/2 the U.S. population is female.
8. Cecile Simmons, thirty-eight, is the first woman in this company to be promoted to management.
9. Last year, I wrote 20 15-page reports, and Michelle wrote 24 three-page reports.
10. Of the 15 applicants, seven are qualified.
11. Our blinds should measure 38 inches wide by 64 and one-half inches long by 7/16 inches deep.
12. Deliver the couch to seven eighty-three Fountain Rd., Suite three, Procter Valley, CA 92074.
13. Here are the corrected figures: 42.7% agree, 23.25% disagree, 34% are undecided, and the error is .05%
14. You have to agree that 50,000,000 U.S. citizens cannot be wrong.
15. We need a set of shelves 10 feet, eight inches long.

Level 2: Workplace Applications

The following items may contain errors in grammar, capitalization, punctuation, abbreviation, number style, word division, and vocabulary. Rewrite each sentence, correcting all errors. If a sentence has no errors, write "Correct" for that number.

1. Speaking at a recent software conference Alan Nichols; ceo of Tekco Systems; said the companys' goal is to reduce response time to 2 to 4 hrs., using software as an enabler.
2. Selling stocks short are the latest rage on wall street, where lately things have just gone from bad to worst.
3. As Electronic Commerce grows people are trying to find new ways to make money off of it.
4. We give a notification not only to the customer but also our salespeople that the product has been shipped because they will want to follow up.
5. When deciding between these various suppliers, we found that each of them offer both advantages and also disadvantages.
6. I found the book, "Marketing is Easy, Selling is Hard," for three different prices on the Internet: $14, $13.25, and $12.00.
7. United Agra Products, a distributor of fertilizers and seeds, in transmission of customer orders over it's private network faced the possibility of serious bottlenecks.

8. The answers you receive on your questionnaire, are influenced by the types of question you ask, the way they are asked, and your subjects cultural and language background.
9. The creation of hazardous by products, like silver in film processing, require us to collect our used chemicals for disposal at a hazardous-waste-facility.
10. As a source of ingredients for our products, we try to establish relationships with small cooperative or farming communities - often in developing countries– because, we believe that the best way to improve peoples' lives is to give them a chance at self reliance.
11. A entrepreneur really should never be in any organization that get's so big that it looses intimacy.
12. Racecar Driver Eddie Cheever, is founder of Aleanza Marketing Group, a seven-person company that handles $10 million dollars in sponsorship campaigns for Cheevers' team Red Bull Cheever Racing.
13. Over the last six years, Business Cluster Development have started 13 technology related incubators, that they call 'business clusters.'
14. In an interview, Gary Hoover said "When I dreamed up Bookstop, we asked people, "If there was a bookstore that carried a huge selection of books and had them all at discount prices, would you go there"? and we got a lot of yawns".
15. The chief attraction of vending machines are their convenience, they are open 24 hours a day, on the other hand, vending machine prices are no bargain.

Level 3: Document Critique

The following document may contain errors in grammar, capitalization, punctuation, abbreviation, number style, word division, and vocabulary. As your instructor indicates, photocopy this page and correct all errors using standard proofreading marks (see Appendix C) or download the document and make the corrections in your word processing software.

The Executive Summary (excerpt)

Purpose of the Proposal

This document will acquaint the reader with 3 principle topics by

- Showing what the San Diego State University (SDSU) Suntrakker project is

- Showing that the team-oriented, inerdepartmental diciplines at SDSU possesses the tenacity and knowhow to build and race a solar-powered vehical in the World solar Challenge Race in Austrailia next year;

- Define and articulate how this business team expect to promote and generate the neccesary support; funds, and materials from the student body, alumni, community and local businesses to sieze and executive this opportunity;

Project Profile

The Suntrakker Solar Car project was conceived by a small group of San Diego State university engineering students motivated by the successof of the General motors "Sunrayce," committed itself to designing and building a superior solar-powered vehicle to compete in the world Solar Challenge.

From modest Beginnings, the Suntrakker project quickly revolved into a cross-disciplinary educational effort encompassing students from many colleges of San Diego State University. The project has provides students participants and volunteers with valuable real life experiences and has brought them together in an effort that benefits not only the students and the university but also the environment.

Sponsors of this project are not only contributing to the successful achievment of the overall Suntrakker project but will also enhance their goodwill, advertising, and name promotion by association with the project. In addition, the Suntrakker offers a unique opportunity for the companies who can donate parts and accessories to showcase their name and test field their products in public in this highly publicized international contest.

CHAPTER 14

Applying and Interviewing for Employment

LEARNING OBJECTIVES

After studying this chapter, you will be able to

1 Explain the purposes of application letters and describe how to apply the AIDA organizational approach to them

2 Describe the typical sequence of job interviews, the major types of interviews, and what employers look for during an interview

3 List six tasks you need to complete to prepare for a successful job interview

4 Explain how to succeed in all three stages of an interview

5 Identify the most common employment messages that follow an interview and explain when you would use each one

---

PEARSON mybcommlab

Access interactive videos, simulations, sample documents, Document Makeovers, and assessment quizzes in Chapter 14 of mybcommlab.com for mastery of this chapter's objectives.

COMMUNICATION *Matters*

"Avoid becoming so focused on saying the 'right thing' that you don't give an accurate portrayal of your skills and interests . . . The hiring manager is trying to get to know you, so do your best to provide a glimpse into what type of employee you'll be.

—Max Messmer, *Chairman and CEO, Robert Half International*[1]

www.rhi.com

Staffing expert Max Messmer appreciates the stress that interviewees feel but encourages them to focus on portraying their value to the company.

Max Messmer's observation about employment interviewing highlights an important point that is too easy to forget during the often-stressful process of looking for a job: An interview should be approached as a business conversation in which both parties get to know each other better. Don't view it as a test in which you try to guess the "right" answers or as an interrogation in which you have to defend your background and skills. Treat interviews as opportunities to share information. After all, you need to determine which company is the right employer for you, just as companies need to determine whether you are the right employee for them. You'll learn more this way, and you'll lower the stress level, too.

This chapter will give you a foundation for successful interviewing, along with tips on writing effective application letters and other important employment-related messages.

SUBMITTING YOUR RÉSUMÉ

Your résumé (see Chapter 13) is the centerpiece of your job search package, but it needs support from several other employment messages, including application letters job-inquiry letters, application forms, and follow-up notes.

Writing Application Letters

Whenever you mail, e-mail, hand-deliver, or upload your résumé, you should include an **application letter**, also known as a *cover letter*, to let readers know what you're sending, why you're sending it, and how they can benefit from reading it. (Even though this message is often not a printed letter anymore, many professionals still refer to it as a letter.) Take the same care with your application letter that you took with your résumé. A poorly written application letter can prompt employers to skip over your résumé, even if you are a good fit for a job.[2] Staffing specialist Abby Kohut calls the application letter "a writing-skills evaluation in disguise" and emphasizes that even a single error can get you bounced from contention.[3]

The best approach for an application letter depends on whether you are applying for an identified job opening or are *prospecting*—taking the initiative to write to companies even though they haven't announced a job opening that is right for you.[4] In many ways, the difference between the two is like the difference between solicited and unsolicited proposals (see page 257). Figure 14.1 on the next page shows an application message written in response to a posted job opening. The writer knows exactly what qualifications the organization is seeking and can "echo" those attributes back in his letter.

Writing a prospecting letter is more challenging because you don't have the clear target you have with a solicited letter. You will need to do more research to identify the qualities that a company would probably seek for the position you hope to occupy (see Figure 14.2 on page 377). Also, search for news items that involve the company, its customers, the profession, or the individual manager to whom you are writing. Using this information in your application letter helps you establish common ground with your reader—and it shows that you are tuned in to what is going on in the industry.

For either type of letter, follow these tips to be more effective:[5]

- If the name of an individual manager is at all findable, address your letter to that person, rather than something generic such as "Dear Hiring Manager." Search LinkedIn, the company's website, industry directories, Twitter, and anything else you can think of to find an appropriate name. Ask the people in your network if they know a name. If another applicant finds a name and you don't, you're at a disadvantage.

- Clearly identify the opportunity you are applying for or expressing interest in.

- Show that you understand the company and its marketplace.

- Never volunteer salary history or requirements unless an employer has asked for this information.

- Keep it short—no more than three paragraphs. Keep in mind that all you are trying to do at this point is move the conversation forward one step.

- Show some personality, while maintaining a business-appropriate tone. The letter gives you the opportunity to balance the facts-only tone of your résumé.

- Project confidence without being arrogant.

Because application letters are persuasive messages, the AIDA approach you learned in Chapter 9 is ideal, as the following sections explain.

Getting Attention

The opening paragraph of your application letter must accomplish two essential tasks: (1) explaining why you are writing and (2) giving the recipient a reason to keep reading by demonstrating that you have some immediate potential for meeting the company's needs. Consider this opening:

> With the recent slowdown in corporate purchasing, I can certainly appreciate the challenge of new fleet sales in this business environment. With my high energy level and

1 LEARNING OBJECTIVE

Explain the purposes of application letters and describe how to apply the AIDA organizational approach to them

Always accompany your résumé with an application message (letter or e-mail) that motivates the recipient to read the résumé.

Resist the temptation to stand out with gimmicky application letters; impress with knowledge and professionalism instead.

The opening paragraph of your application letter needs to clearly convey the reason you're writing and give the recipient a compelling reason to keep reading.

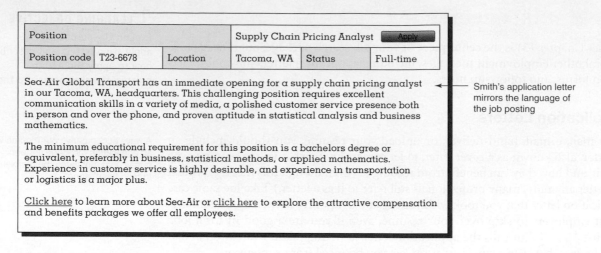

Position			Supply Chain Pricing Analyst		[Apply]
Position code	T23-6678	Location	Tacoma, WA	Status	Full-time

Sea-Air Global Transport has an immediate opening for a supply chain pricing analyst in our Tacoma, WA, headquarters. This challenging position requires excellent communication skills in a variety of media, a polished customer service presence both in person and over the phone, and proven aptitude in statistical analysis and business mathematics.

The minimum educational requirement for this position is a bachelors degree or equivalent, preferably in business, statistical methods, or applied mathematics. Experience in customer service is highly desirable, and experience in transportation or logistics is a major plus.

<u>Click here</u> to learn more about Sea-Air or <u>click here</u> to explore the attractive compensation and benefits packages we offer all employees.

Smith's application letter mirrors the language of the job posting

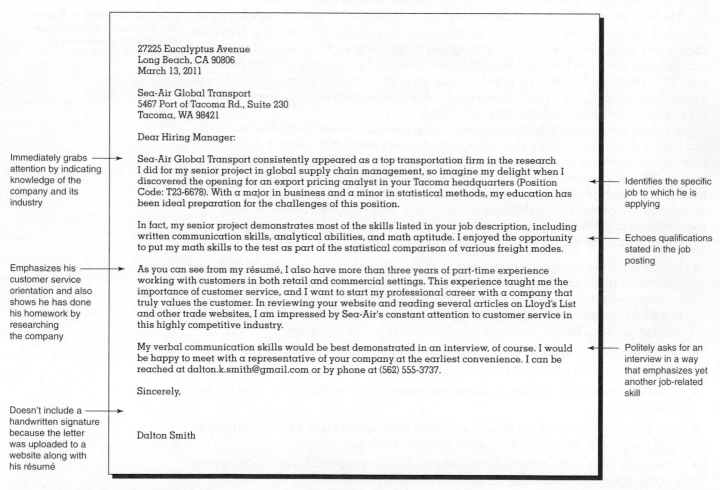

27225 Eucalyptus Avenue
Long Beach, CA 90806
March 13, 2011

Sea-Air Global Transport
5467 Port of Tacoma Rd., Suite 230
Tacoma, WA 98421

Dear Hiring Manager:

Sea-Air Global Transport consistently appeared as a top transportation firm in the research I did for my senior project in global supply chain management, so imagine my delight when I discovered the opening for an export pricing analyst in your Tacoma headquarters (Position Code: T23-6678). With a major in business and a minor in statistical methods, my education has been ideal preparation for the challenges of this position.

In fact, my senior project demonstrates most of the skills listed in your job description, including written communication skills, analytical abilities, and math aptitude. I enjoyed the opportunity to put my math skills to the test as part of the statistical comparison of various freight modes.

As you can see from my résumé, I also have more than three years of part-time experience working with customers in both retail and commercial settings. This experience taught me the importance of customer service, and I want to start my professional career with a company that truly values the customer. In reviewing your website and reading several articles on Lloyd's List and other trade websites, I am impressed by Sea-Air's constant attention to customer service in this highly competitive industry.

My verbal communication skills would be best demonstrated in an interview, of course. I would be happy to meet with a representative of your company at the earliest convenience. I can be reached at dalton.k.smith@gmail.com or by phone at (562) 555-3737.

Sincerely,

Dalton Smith

Immediately grabs attention by indicating knowledge of the company and its industry

Emphasizes his customer service orientation and also shows he has done his homework by researching the company

Doesn't include a handwritten signature because the letter was uploaded to a website along with his résumé

Identifies the specific job to which he is applying

Echoes qualifications stated in the job posting

Politely asks for an interview in a way that emphasizes yet another job-related skill

Figure 14.1 Solicited Application Message
In this response to an online job posting, Dalton Smith highlights his qualifications while mirroring the requirements specified in the posting. Following the AIDA model, he grabs attention immediately by letting the reader know that he is familiar with the company and the global transportation business.

16 months of new-car sales experience, I believe I can produce the results you listed as vital in the job posting on your website.

This applicant does a smooth job of mirroring the company's stated needs while highlighting his personal qualifications and providing evidence that he understands the broader market. He balances his relative lack of experience with enthusiasm and knowledge of the

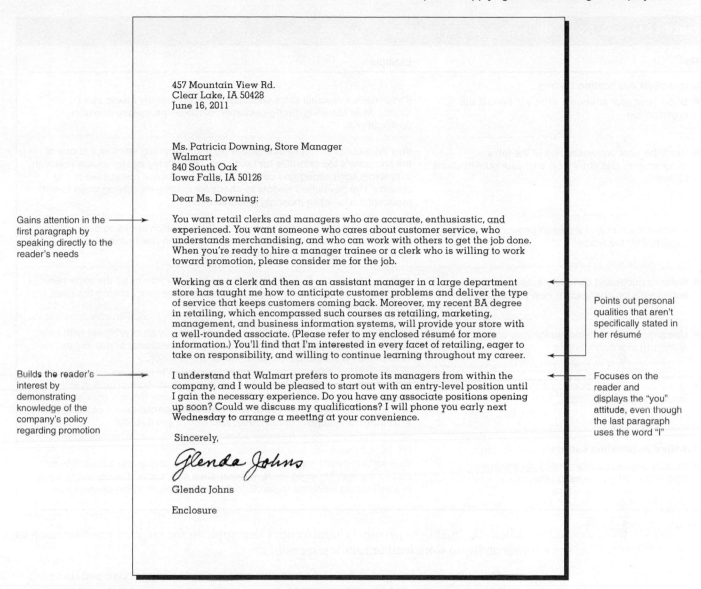

Gains attention in the first paragraph by speaking directly to the reader's needs

Builds the reader's interest by demonstrating knowledge of the company's policy regarding promotion

457 Mountain View Rd.
Clear Lake, IA 50428
June 16, 2011

Ms. Patricia Downing, Store Manager
Walmart
840 South Oak
Iowa Falls, IA 50126

Dear Ms. Downing:

You want retail clerks and managers who are accurate, enthusiastic, and experienced. You want someone who cares about customer service, who understands merchandising, and who can work with others to get the job done. When you're ready to hire a manager trainee or a clerk who is willing to work toward promotion, please consider me for the job.

Working as a clerk and then as an assistant manager in a large department store has taught me how to anticipate customer problems and deliver the type of service that keeps customers coming back. Moreover, my recent BA degree in retailing, which encompassed such courses as retailing, marketing, management, and business information systems, will provide your store with a well-rounded associate. (Please refer to my enclosed résumé for more information.) You'll find that I'm interested in every facet of retailing, eager to take on responsibility, and willing to continue learning throughout my career.

I understand that Walmart prefers to promote its managers from within the company, and I would be pleased to start out with an entry-level position until I gain the necessary experience. Do you have any associate positions opening up soon? Could we discuss my qualifications? I will phone you early next Wednesday to arrange a meeting at your convenience.

Sincerely,

Glenda Johns

Glenda Johns

Enclosure

Points out personal qualities that aren't specifically stated in her résumé

Focuses on the reader and displays the "you" attitude, even though the last paragraph uses the word "I"

Figure 14.2   Unsolicited Application Letter
Glenda Johns's experience as a clerk and an assistant manager gives her a good idea of the qualities that Walmart is likely to be looking for in future managers. She uses these insights to craft the opening of her letter.

industry. Table 14.1 on the next page suggests some other ways that you can spark interest and grab attention in your opening paragraph.

Building Interest and Increasing Desire

The middle section of your letter presents your strongest selling points in terms of their potential benefit to the organization, thereby building interest in you and creating a desire to interview you. Be specific and back up your assertions with convincing evidence:

Poor: I completed three college courses in business communication, earning an A in each course, and have worked for the past year at Imperial Construction.

Improved: Using the skills gained from three semesters of college training in business communication, I developed a collection system for Imperial Construction that reduced annual bad-debt losses by 25 percent.

When writing a solicited letter, be sure to discuss each requirement listed in the job posting. If you are deficient in any of these requirements, stress other solid selling points to help strengthen your overall presentation. Don't restrict your message to just core job duties,

Use the middle section of your application letter to expand on your opening and present a more complete picture of your strengths.

TABLE 14.1   Tips for Getting Attention in Application Letters

Tip	Example
Unsolicited Application Letters	
■ Show how your strongest skills will benefit the organization.	If your need a regional sales specialist who consistently meets sales targets while fostering strong customer relationships, please consider my qualifications.
■ Describe your understanding of the job's requirements and show how well your qualifications fit them.	Your annual report stated that improving manufacturing efficiency is one of the company's top priorities for next year. Through my postgraduate research in systems engineering and consulting work for several companies in the industry, I've developed reliable methods for quickly identifying ways to cut production time while reducing resource use.
■ Mention the name of a person known to and highly regarded by the reader.	When Janice McHugh of your franchise sales division spoke to our business communication class last week, she said you often need promising new marketing graduates at this time of year.
■ Refer to publicized company activities, achievements, changes, or new procedures.	Today's issue of the *Detroit News* reports that you may need the expertise of computer programmers versed in robotics when your Lansing tire plant automates this spring.
■ Use a question to demonstrate your understanding of the organization's needs.	Can your fast-growing market research division use an interviewer with two years of field survey experience, a B.A. in public relations, and a real desire to succeed? If so, please consider me for the position.
■ Use a catchphrase opening if the job requires ingenuity and imagination.	*Haut monde*—whether referring to French, Italian, or Arab clients, it still means "high society." As an interior designer for your Beverly Hills showroom, not only could I serve and sell to your distinguished clientele, but I could do it in all these languages. I speak, read, and write them fluently.
Solicited Application Letters	
■ Identify where you discovered the job opening; describe what you have to offer.	Your ad in the April issue of *Travel & Leisure* for a cruise-line social director caught my eye. My eight years of experience as a social director in the travel industry would allow me to serve your new Caribbean cruise division well.

either. Also highlight personal characteristics that apply to the targeted position, such as your ability to work hard or handle responsibility:

> While attending college full time, I worked part-time during the school year and up to 60 hours a week each summer in order to be totally self-supporting while in college. I can offer your organization the same level of effort and perseverance.

Don't bring up salary in your application letter unless the recipient has asked you to include your salary requirements.

Mention your salary requirements only if the organization has asked you to state them. If you don't know the salary that's appropriate for the position and someone with your qualifications, you can find typical salary ranges at the Bureau of Labor Statistics website, **www.bls.gov**, or a number of commercial websites. If you do state a target salary, tie it to the value you would offer:

> For the past two years, I have been helping a company similar to yours organize its database marketing efforts. I would therefore like to receive a salary in the same range (the mid-60s) for helping your company set up a more efficient customer database.

Toward the end of this section, refer the reader to your résumé by citing a specific fact or general point covered there:

> As you can see in the attached résumé, I've been working part time with a local publisher since my sophomore year. During that time, I've used client interactions as an opportunity to build strong customer service skills.

Motivating Action

In the final paragraph of your application letter, respectfully ask for specific action and make it easy for the reader to respond.

The final paragraph of your application letter has two important functions: to ask the reader for a specific action (usually an interview) and to facilitate a reply. Offer to come to the employer's office at a convenient time or, if the firm is some distance away, to meet with its nearest representative or arrange a telephone interview. Include your e-mail address and phone number, as well as the best time to reach you. Alternatively, you can take the initiative and say that you will follow up with a phone call. Refer again to your strongest selling point and, if desired, your date of availability:

> After you have reviewed my qualifications, could we discuss the possibility of putting my marketing skills to work for your company? Because I will be on spring break the week of March 8, I would like to arrange a time to talk then. I will call in late February to schedule a convenient time when we could discuss employment opportunities at your company.

REAL-TIME UPDATES
Learn More by Reading This Article

How much are you worth?

Find real-life salary ranges for a wide range of jobs. Go to **http://real-timeupdates.com/bce5** and click on "Learn More." If you are using mybcommlab, you can access Real-Time Updates within each chapter or under Student Study Tools.

Following Up After Submitting a Résumé

Deciding if, when, and how to follow up after submitting your résumé and application letter is one of the trickiest parts of a job search. First and foremost, keep in mind that employers continue to evaluate your communication efforts and professionalism during this phase, so don't say or do anything to leave a negative impression. Second, adhere to whatever instructions the employer has provided. If a job posting says "no calls," for example, don't call. Third, if the job posting lists a *close date*, don't call or write before then, because the company is still collecting applications and will not have made a decision about inviting people for interviews. Wait a week or so after the close date. If no close date is given and you have no other information to suggest a timeline, you can generally contact the company starting a week or two after submitting your résumé.[6]

Think creatively about a follow-up letter; show that you've continued to add to your skills or that you've learned more about the company or the industry.

A single instance of poor etiquette can undo all your hard work in a job search, so maintain your professional behavior every step of the way.	**ETIQUETTE** *Matters*

When you follow up by e-mail or telephone, you can share an additional piece of information that links your qualifications to the position (keep an eye out for late-breaking news about the company, too) and ask a question about the hiring process as a way to gather some information about your status. Good questions to ask include:[7]

- Has a hiring decision been made yet?
- Can you tell me what to expect next in terms of the hiring process?
- What is the company's timeframe for filling this position?
- Could I follow up in another week if you haven't had the chance to contact me yet?
- Can I provide any additional information regarding my qualifications for the position?

Whatever the circumstances, a follow-up message can demonstrate that you're sincerely interested in working for the organization, persistent in pursuing your goals, and committed to upgrading your skills.

If you don't land a job at your dream company on the first attempt, don't give up. You can apply again if a new opening appears, or you can send an updated résumé with a new unsolicited application letter that describes how you have gained additional experience, taken a relevant course, or otherwise improved your skill set. Many leading employers take note of applicants who came close but didn't quite make it and may extend offers when positions open up in the future.[8]

- Access this chapter's simulation entitled Interviewing, located at mybcommlab.com.

2 LEARNING OBJECTIVE

Describe the typical sequence of job interviews, the major types of interviews, and what employers look for during an interview

UNDERSTANDING THE INTERVIEWING PROCESS

An **employment interview** is a formal meeting during which both you and the prospective employer ask questions and exchange information. The employer's objective is to find the best talent to fill available job openings, and your objective is to find the right match for your goals and capabilities.

Start preparing early for your interviews—and be sure to consider a wide range of options.

As you get ready to begin interviewing, keep two vital points in mind. First, recognize that the process takes time. Start your preparation and research early; the best job offers usually go to the best-prepared candidates. Second, don't limit your options by looking at only a few companies. By exploring a wide range of firms and positions, you might uncover great opportunities that you would not have found otherwise. You'll increase the odds of getting more job offers, too.

The Typical Sequence of Interviews

Most employers interview an applicant multiple times before deciding to make a job offer. At the most selective companies, you might have a dozen or more individual interviews across several stages.[9] Depending on the company and the position, the process may stretch out over many weeks, or it may be completed in a matter of days.[10]

During the screening stage of interviews, use the limited time available to differentiate yourself from other candidates.

Employers start with the *screening stage*, in which they filter out applicants who are unqualified or otherwise not a good fit for the position. Screening can take place on your school's campus, at company offices, via telephone (including Skype or another Internet-based phone service), or through a computer-based screening system. Time is limited in screening interviews, so keep your answers short while providing a few key points that differentiate you from other candidates. If your screening interview will take place by phone, try to schedule it for a time when you can be focused and free from interruptions.[11]

During the selection stage, continue to show how your skills and attributes can help the company.

The next stage of interviews, the *selection stage*, helps the organization identify the top candidates from all those who qualify. During these interviews, show keen interest in the job, relate your skills and experience to the organization's needs, listen attentively, and ask insightful questions that show you've done your research.

During the final stage, the interviewer may try to sell you on working for the firm.

If the interviewers agree that you're a good candidate, you may receive a job offer, either on the spot or a few days later by phone, mail, or e-mail. In other instances, you may be invited back for a final evaluation, often by a higher-ranking executive. The objective of the *final stage* is often to sell you on the advantages of joining the organization.

Common Types of Interviews

Employers can use a variety of interviewing methods, and you need to recognize the different types and be prepared for each one. These methods can be distinguished by the way they are structured, the number of people involved, and the purpose of the interview.

Structured Versus Unstructured Interviews

A structured interview follows a set sequence of questions, allowing the interview team to compare answers from all candidates.

In a **structured interview**, the interviewer (or a computer program) asks a series of questions in a predetermined order. Structured interviews help employers identify candidates who don't meet basic job criteria, and they allow the interview team to compare answers from multiple candidates.[12]

In an open-ended interview, the interviewer adapts the line of questioning based on your responses and questions.

In contrast, in an **open-ended interview**, the interviewer adapts his or her line of questioning based on the answers you give and any questions you ask. Even though it may feel like a conversation, remember that it's still an interview, so keep your answers focused and professional.

Panel and Group Interviews

In a panel interview, you meet with several interviewers at once; in a group interview, you and several other candidates meet with one or more interviewers at once.

Although one-on-one interviews are the most common format, some employers use panel or group interviews as well. In a **panel interview**, you meet with several interviewers at once.[13] Try to make a connection with each person on the panel and keep in mind that each person has a different perspective, so tailor your responses accordingly.[14] For example, an upper-level manager is likely to be interested in your overall business sense and strategic perspective, whereas a potential colleague might be more interested in your technical skills and ability to work in a team. In a **group interview**, one or more interviewers meet with several candidates simultaneously. A key purpose of a group interview is to observe how the candidates interact.[15]

Behavioral, Situational, Working, and Stress Interviews

Perhaps the most common type of interview these days is the **behavioral interview**, in which you are asked to relate specific incidents and experiences from your past.[16] Generic interview questions can often be answered with "canned" responses, but behavioral questions require candidates to use their own experiences and attributes to craft answers. Studies show that behavioral interviewing is a much better predictor of success on the job than traditional interview questions.[17] To prepare for a behavioral interview, review your work or college experiences to recall several instances in which you demonstrated an important job-related attribute or dealt with a challenge such as uncooperative team members or heavy workloads. Get ready with responses that quickly summarize the situation, the actions you took, and the outcome of those actions.[18]

> In a behavioral interview, you are asked to describe how you handled situations from your past.

A **situational interview** is similar to a behavioral interview except that the questions focus on how you would handle various hypothetical situations on the job. The situations will likely relate to the job you're applying for, so the more you know about the position, the better prepared you'll be.

> In situational interviews, you're asked to explain how you would handle various hypothetical situations.

A **working interview** is the most realistic type of interview: You actually perform a job-related activity during the interview. You may be asked to lead a brainstorming session, solve a business problem, engage in role playing, or even make a presentation.[19]

> In a working interview, you actually perform work-related tasks.

The most unnerving type of interview is the **stress interview**, during which you might be asked questions designed to unsettle you or might be subjected to long periods of silence, criticism, interruptions, and or even hostile reactions by the interviewer. The theory behind this approach is that you'll reveal how well you handle stressful situations, although some experts find the technique of dubious value.[20] If you find yourself in a stress interview, recognize what is happening and collect your thoughts for a few seconds before you respond.

> Stress interviews help recruiters see how you handle yourself under pressure.

Interview Media

Expect to be interviewed through a variety of media. Employers trying to cut travel costs and the demands on staff time now interview candidates via telephone, e-mail, instant messaging, virtual online systems, and videoconferencing, in addition to traditional face-to-face meetings (see Figure 14.3).

> Expect to use a variety of media when you interview, from in-person conversations to virtual meetings.

Figure 14.3 Finding Real Jobs in a Virtual World
Virtual job fairs, such as the Working Worlds event hosted by Luxembourg's GAX Technologies, allow candidates and recruiters to interact without the time and expense of travel.

REAL-TIME UPDATES
Learn More by Watching This Video

Video interviewing on Skype

Chances are you'll have at least one video interview using Skype or another Internet-based phone service. Watch this video for essential tips on preparing and participating in an online video interview. Go to **http://real-timeupdates .com/bce5** and click on "Learn More." If you are using mybcommlab, you can access Real-Time Updates within each chapter or under Student Study Tools.

To succeed at a telephone interview, make sure you treat it as seriously as an in-person interview. Be prepared with a copy of all the materials you have sent to the employer, including your résumé and any correspondence. In addition, prepare some note cards with key message points you'd like to make and questions you'd like to ask. If possible, arrange to speak on a landline so you don't have to worry about mobile phone reception problems. And remember that you won't be able to use a pleasant smile, a firm handshake, and other nonverbal signals to create a good impression. A positive, alert tone of voice is therefore vital.[21]

E-mail and IM are also sometimes used in the screening stage. Although you have almost no opportunity to send and receive nonverbal signals with these formats, you do have the major advantage of being able to review and edit each response before you send it. Maintain a professional style in your responses, and be sure to ask questions that demonstrate your knowledge of the company and the position.[22]

> Treat a telephone interview as seriously as you would an in-person interview.

> When interviewing via e-mail or IM, be sure to take a moment to review your responses before sending them.

> In a video interview, speak to the camera as though you are addressing the interviewer in person.

> Computer-based virtual interviews range from simple structured interviews to realistic job simulations to meetings in virtual worlds.

Many employers use video technology for both live and recorded interviews. For instance, the online retailer Zappos uses video interviews on Skype to select the top two or three finalists for each position and then invites those candidates for in-person interviews.[23] With recorded video interviews, an online system asks a set of questions and records the respondent's answers. Recruiters then watch the videos as part of the screening process.[24] Prepare for a video interview as you would for an in-person interview—including dressing and grooming—and take the extra steps needed to become familiar with the equipment and the process. If you're interviewing from home, arrange your space so that the webcam doesn't pick up anything distracting or embarrassing in the background. During any video interview, remember to sit up straight and focus on the camera.

Online interviews can range from simple structured questionnaires and tests to sophisticated job simulations that are similar to working interviews (see Figure 14.4). In the banking industry, for example, Atlanta-based SunTrust and Cleveland-based National City use computerized simulations to see how well candidates can perform job-related tasks and

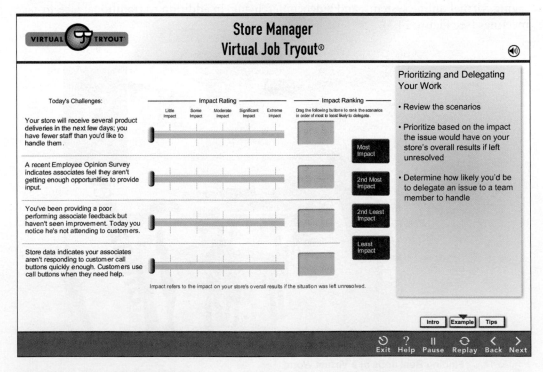

Figure 14.4   Job Task Simulations
Computer-based job simulations are an increasingly popular approach to testing job-related skills.

decision-making scenarios. These simulations help identify good candidates, give applicants an idea of what the job is like, and reduce the risk of employment discrimination lawsuits because they closely mimic actual job skills.[25]

What Employers Look For in an Interview

Interviews give employers the chance to go beyond the basic data of your résumé to get to know you and to answer two essential questions. The first is whether you can handle the responsibilities of the position. Naturally, the more you know about the demands of the position, and the more you've thought about how your skills match those demands, the better you'll be able to respond.

The second essential question is whether you will be a good fit with the organization and the target position. This line of inquiry includes both a general and a specific aspect. The general aspect concerns your overall personality and approach to work. All good employers want people who are confident, dedicated, positive, curious, courteous, ethical, and willing to commit to something larger than their own individual goals.

The specific aspect involves the fit with a particular company and position. Just like people, companies have different "personalities." Some are intense; others are more laid back. Some emphasize teamwork; others expect employees to forge their own way and even to compete with one another. Expectations also vary from job to job within a company and from industry to industry. An outgoing personality is essential for sales but less so for research, for instance.

Suitability for a specific job is judged on the basis of such factors as
- Academic preparation
- Work experience
- Job-related personality traits

Compatibility with an organization and a position is judged on the basis of personal background, attitudes, and style.

Preemployment Testing and Background Checks

In an effort to improve the predictability of the selection process, many employers now conduct a variety of preemployment evaluations and investigations. Here are types of assessments you are likely to encounter during your job search:[26]

Preemployment tests attempt to provide objective, quantitative information about a candidate's skills, attitudes, and habits.

- **Integrity tests.** Integrity tests attempt to measure how truthful and trustworthy a candidate is likely to be.
- **Personality tests.** Personality tests are designed to gauge such aspects as attitudes toward work, interests, managerial potential, dependability, commitment, and motivation.
- **Cognitive tests.** Cognitive tests measure a variety of attributes involved in acquiring, processing, analyzing, using, and remembering information. Typical tests involve reading comprehension, mathematics, problem solving, and decision making.
- **Job knowledge and job skills tests.** These assessments measure the knowledge and skills required to succeed in a particular position. An accounting candidate, for example, might be tested on accounting principles and legal matters (knowledge) and asked to create a simple balance sheet or income statement (skills).
- **Substance tests.** A majority of companies perform some level of drug and alcohol testing. Many employers believe such testing is necessary to maintain workplace safety, ensure productivity, and protect companies from lawsuits, but others view it as an invasion of employee privacy.
- **Background checks.** In addition to testing, most companies conduct some sort of background check, including reviewing your credit record, checking to see whether you have a criminal history, and verifying your education. Moreover, you should assume that every employer will conduct a general online search on you. To help prevent a background check from tripping you up, verify that your college transcripts are current, look for any mistakes or outdated information in your credit record, plug your name into multiple search engines to see whether anything embarrassing shows up, and scour your social network profiles and connections for potential problems.

Preemployment assessments are a complex and controversial aspect of workforce recruiting. For instance, even though personality testing is widely used, some research suggests that current tests are not a reliable predictor of job success.[27] However, expect to see more innovation in this area and greater use of testing in general in the future as companies try to reduce the risks and costs of poor hiring decisions.

List six tasks you need to complete to prepare for a successful job interview

PREPARING FOR A JOB INTERVIEW

Now that you're armed with insights into the interviewing and assessment process, you're ready to begin preparing for your interviews. Preparation will help you feel more confident and perform better under pressure, and preparation starts with learning about the organization.

Learning About the Organization

Interviewers expect you to know some basic information about the company and its industry.

Today's employers expect serious candidates to demonstrate an understanding of the company's operations, its markets, and its strategic and tactical challenges.[28] You've already done some initial research to identify companies of interest, but when you're invited to interview, it's time to dig a little deeper (see Table 14.2). Making this effort demonstrates your interest in the company, and it identifies you as a business professional who knows the importance of investigation and analysis.

Thinking Ahead About Questions

Planning ahead for the interviewer's questions will help you handle them more confidently and successfully. In addition, you will want to prepare insightful questions of your own.

TABLE 14.2   Investigating an Organization and a Job Opportunity

Where to Look and What You Can Learn

- *Company website, blogs, and social media accounts:* Overall information about the company, including key executives, products and services, locations and divisions, employee benefits, job descriptions
- *Competitors' websites, blogs, and social media accounts:* Similar information from competitors, including the strengths these companies claim to have
- *Industry-related websites and blogs:* Objective analysis and criticism of the company, its products, its reputation, and its management
- *Marketing materials (print and online):* The company's marketing strategy and customer communication style
- *Company publications (print and online):* Key events, stories about employees, new products
- *Your social network contacts:* Names and job titles of potential contacts within a company
- *Periodicals (newspapers and trade journals, both print and online):* In-depth stories about the company and its strategies, products, successes, and failures; you may find profiles of top executives
- *Career center at your college:* Often provides a wide array of information about companies that hire graduates
- *Current and former employees:* Insights into the work environment

Points to Learn About the Organization

- Full name
- Location (headquarters and divisions, branches, subsidiaries, or other units)
- Ownership (public or private; whether it is owned by another company)
- Brief history
- Products and services
- Industry position (whether the company is a leader or a minor player; whether it is an innovator or more of a follower)
- Key financial points (such as stock price and trends, if a public company)
- Growth prospects (whether the company is investing in its future through research and development; whether it is in a thriving industry)

Points to Learn About the Position

- Title
- Functions and responsibilities
- Qualifications and expectations
- Possible career paths
- Salary range
- Travel expectations and opportunities
- Relocation expectations and opportunities

Planning for the Employer's Questions

Many general interview questions are "stock" queries that you can expect to hear again and again during your interviews. Get ready to face these five at the very least:

- **What is the hardest decision you've ever had to make?** Be prepared with a good example (that isn't too personal), explaining why the decision was difficult, how you made the choice you made, and what you learned from the experience.

- **What is your greatest weakness?** This question seems to be a favorite of some interviewers, although it probably rarely yields useful information. One good strategy is to mention a skill or attribute you haven't had the opportunity to develop yet but would like to in your next position.[29]

- **Where do you want to be five years from now?** This question tests (1) whether you're merely using this job as a stopover until something better comes along and (2) whether you've given thought to your long-term goals. Your answer should reflect your desire to contribute to the employer's long-term goals, not just your own goals. Whether this question often yields useful information is also a matter of debate, but be prepared to answer it.[30]

- **What didn't you like about previous jobs you've held?** Answer this one carefully: The interviewer is trying to predict whether you'll be an unhappy or difficult employee.[31] Describe something that you didn't like in a way that puts you in a positive light, such as having limited opportunities to apply your skills or education. Avoid making negative comments about former employers or colleagues.

- **Tell me something about yourself.** One good strategy is to *briefly* share the "story of you" (see page 381), quickly summarizing where you have been and where would like to go—in a way that aligns your interests with the company's. Alternatively, you can focus on a specific skill that you know is valuable to the company, share something business-relevant that you are passionate about, or offer a short summary of what colleagues or customers think about you.[32] Whatever tactic you choose, this is not the time to be shy or indecisive, so be ready with a confident, memorable answer.

Continue your preparation by planning a brief answer to each question in Table 14.3 on the next page. You can also find typical interview questions at websites such as InterviewUp, **www.interviewup.com**, where candidates share actual questions they have faced in recent interviews.[33]

As you prepare answers, look for ways to frame your responses as brief stories (30 to 90 seconds) rather than simple declarative answers.[34] Cohesive stories tend to stick in the listener's mind more effectively than disconnected facts and statements.

You can expect to face a number of common questions in your interviews, so be sure to prepare for them.

Look for ways to frame your responses as brief stories rather than as dry facts or statements.

Planning Questions of Your Own

Remember that an interview is a two-way conversation: The questions you ask are just as important as the answers you provide. By asking insightful questions, you can demonstrate your understanding of the organization, you can steer the discussion into areas that allow you to present your qualifications to best advantage, and you can verify for yourself whether this is a good opportunity. Plus, interviewers expect you to ask questions and tend to look negatively on candidates who don't have any questions to ask. For a list of good questions that you might use as a starting point, see Table 14.4 on page 419.

Preparing questions of your own helps you understand the company and the position, and it sends an important signal that you are truly interested.

Bolstering Your Confidence

Interviewing is stressful for everyone, so some nervousness is natural. However, you can take steps to feel more confident. Start by reminding yourself that you have value to offer the employer, and the employer already thinks highly enough of you to invite you to an interview.

If some aspect of your appearance or background makes you uneasy, correct it if possible or offset it by emphasizing

REAL-TIME UPDATES
Learn More by Watching This Video

Study the classics to ace your next interview

No, not Homer and Ovid—classic interview questions. Prepare answers to these old standbys so you can respond with clarity and confidence. Go to **http://real-timeupdates.com/bce5** and click on "Learn More." If you are using mybcommlab, you can access Real-Time Updates within each chapter or under Student Study Tools.

TABLE 14.3   Twenty-Five Common Interview Questions

Questions About College

1. What courses in college did you like most? Least? Why?
2. Do you think your extracurricular activities in college were worth the time you spent on them? Why or why not?
3. When did you choose your college major? Did you ever change your major? If so, why?
4. Do you feel you did the best scholastic work you are capable of?
5. How has your college education prepared you for this position?

Questions About Employers and Jobs

6. What jobs have you held? Why did you leave?
7. What percentage of your college expenses did you earn? How?
8. Why did you choose your particular field of work?
9. What are the disadvantages of your chosen field?
10. Have you served in the military? What rank did you achieve? What jobs did you perform?
11. What do you think about how this industry operates today?
12. Why do you think you would like this particular type of job?

Questions About Work Experiences and Expectations

13. Do you prefer to work in any specific geographic location? If so, why?
14. What motivates you? Why?
15. What do you think determines a person's progress in a good organization?
16. Describe an experience in which you learned from one of your mistakes.
17. Why do you want this job?
18. What have you done that shows initiative and willingness to work?
19. Why should I hire you?

Questions About Work Habits

20. Do you prefer working with others or by yourself?
21. What type of boss do you prefer?
22. Have you ever had any difficulty getting along with colleagues or supervisors? With instructors? With other students?
23. What would you do if you were given an unrealistic deadline for a task or project?
24. How do you feel about overtime work?
25. How do you handle stress or pressure on the job?

The best way to build your confidence is to prepare thoroughly and address shortcomings as best you can—in other words, take action.

positive traits such as warmth, wit, intelligence, or charm. Instead of dwelling on your weaknesses, focus on your strengths. Instead of worrying about how you will perform in the interview, focus on how you can help the organization succeed. As with public speaking, the more prepared you are, the more confident you'll be.

Polishing Your Interview Style

Staging mock interviews with a friend is a good way to hone your style.

Competence and confidence are the foundation of your interviewing style, and you can enhance them by giving the interviewer an impression of poise, good manners, and good judgment. You can develop an adept style by staging mock interviews with a friend or using an interview simulator. Record these mock interviews so you can evaluate yourself. Your college's career center may have computer-based systems for practicing interviews as well (see Figure 14.5).

TABLE 14.4   Ten Questions to Ask the Interviewer

Question	Reason For Asking
1. What are the job's major responsibilities?	A vague answer could mean that the responsibilities have not been clearly defined, which is almost guaranteed to cause frustration if you take the job.
2. What qualities do you want in the person who fills this position?	This will help you go beyond the job description to understand what the company really wants.
3. How do you measure success for someone in this position?	A vague or incomplete answer could mean that the expectations you will face are unrealistic or ill defined.
4. What is the first problem that needs the attention of the person you hire?	Not only will this help you prepare, but it can signal whether you're about to jump into a problematic situation.
5. Would relocation be required now or in the future?	If you're not willing to move often or at all, you need to know those expectations now.
6. Why is this job now vacant?	If the previous employee got promoted, that's good sign. If the person quit, that might not be such a good sign.
7. What makes your organization different from others in the industry?	The answer will help you assess whether the company has a clear strategy to succeed in its industry and whether top managers communicate it to lower-level employees.
8. How would you define your organization's managerial philosophy?	You want to know whether the managerial philosophy is consistent with your own working values.
9. What is a typical workday like for you?	The interviewer's response can give you clues about daily life at the company.
10. What systems and policies are in place to help employees stay up to date in their professions and continue to expand their skills?	If the company doesn't have a strong commitment to employee development, chances are it isn't going to stay competitive very long.

Figure 14.5   Interview Simulators
Experts advise you to practice your interview skills as much as possible. You can use a friend or classmate as a practice partner, or you might be able to use one of the interview simulators now available, such as this system from Perfect Interview. Ask at your career center, or search online for "practice interviews" or "interview simulators."

TABLE 14.5 Warning Signs: 25 Traits That Interviewers Don't Like to See	
1. Poor personal appearance	13. Poor scholastic record; just got by
2. Overbearing, overaggressive, or conceited demeanor; a "superiority complex"; a know-it-all attitude	14. Unwillingness to start at the bottom; expecting too much too soon
3. Inability to express ideas clearly; poor voice, diction, or grammar	15. Tendency to make excuses
4. Lack of knowledge or experience	16. Evasive answers; hedging on unfavorable factors in record
5. Poor preparation for the interview	17. Lack of tact
6. Lack of interest in the job	18. Lack of maturity
7. Lack of planning for career; lack of purpose or goals	19. Lack of courtesy; being ill mannered
8. Lack of enthusiasm; passive and indifferent demeanor	20. Condemnation of past employers
9. Lack of confidence and poise; appearance of being nervous and ill at ease	21. Lack of social skills
10. Insufficient evidence of achievement	22. Marked dislike for schoolwork
11. Failure to participate in extracurricular activities	23. Lack of vitality
12. Overemphasis on money; interested only in the best dollar offer	24. Failure to took interviewer in the eye
	25. Limp, weak handshake

Evaluate the length and clarity of your answers, your nonverbal behavior, and the quality of your voice.

After each practice session, look for opportunities to improve. Have your mock interview partner critique your performance, or critique yourself if you're able to record your practice interviews, using the list of warning signs shown in Table 14.5. Pay close attention to the length of your planned answers as well. Interviewers want you to give complete answers but they don't want you to take up valuable time or test their patience by chatting about minor or irrelevant details.[35]

In addition to reviewing your answers, evaluate your nonverbal behavior, including your posture, eye contact, facial expressions, and hand gestures and movements. Do you come across as alert and upbeat or passive and withdrawn? Pay close attention to your speaking voice as well. If you tend to speak in a monotone, for instance, practice speaking in a livelier style, with more inflection and emphasis. And watch out for "filler words" such as *uh* and *um*. Many people start sentences with a filler without being conscious of doing so. Train yourself to pause silently for a moment instead as you gather your thoughts and plan what to say.

Presenting a Professional Image

Dress conservatively and be well groomed for every interview.

Clothing and grooming are important elements of preparation because they reveal something about a candidate's personality, professionalism, and ability to sense the unspoken "rules" of a situation. Your research into various industries and professions should give you insight into expectations for business attire. If you're not sure what to wear, ask someone who works in the same industry or even visit the company at the end of the day and see what employees are wearing as they leave the office. You don't need to spend a fortune on interview clothes, but your clothes must be clean, pressed, and appropriate (see Figure 14.6). The following look will serve you well in just about any interview situation:[36]

- Neat, "adult" hairstyle
- Conservative business suit (for women, that means no exposed midriffs, short skirts, or plunging necklines) in dark solid color or a subtle pattern such as pinstripes
- White shirt for men; coordinated blouse for women
- Conservative tie (classic stripes or subtle patterns) for men
- Limited jewelry (men, especially, should wear very little jewelry)
- No visible piercings other than one or two earrings (for women only)

Figure 14.6   Professional Appearance for Job Interviews
Make a positive first impression with careful grooming and attire. You don't need to spend a fortune on new clothes, but you do need to look clean, prepared, and professional.

- No visible tattoos
- Stylish but professional-looking shoes (no extreme high heels or casual shoes)
- Clean hands and nicely trimmed fingernails
- Little or no perfume or cologne (some people are allergic and many people are put off by strong smells)
- Subtle makeup (for women)
- Exemplary personal hygiene

Remember that an interview is not the place to express your individuality or to let your inner rebel run wild. Send a clear signal that you understand the business world and know how to adapt to it. You won't be taken seriously otherwise.

> If you want to be taken seriously, dress and act seriously.

Being Ready When You Arrive

When you go to your interview, bring a small notebook, a pen, a list of the questions you want to ask, several copies of your résumé (protected in a folder), an outline of what you have learned about the organization, and any past correspondence about the position. You may also want to take a small calendar, a transcript of your college grades, a list of references, and a portfolio containing samples of your work, performance reviews, and certificates of achievement.[37] Carry all these items in a good-quality briefcase.

> Be ready to go the minute you arrive at the interviewing site; don't fumble around for your résumé or your list of questions.

Be sure you know when and where the interview will be held. The worst way to start any interview is to be late. Verify the route and time required to get there, even if that means traveling there ahead of time. Plan to arrive early.

When you arrive, you may have to wait for a while. Use this time to review the key messages about yourself you want to get across in the interview. Conduct yourself professionally while waiting. Show respect for everyone you encounter and avoid chewing gum, eating, or drinking. Anything you do or say at this stage may get back to the interviewer, so make sure your best qualities show from the moment you enter the premises.

Explain how to succeed in all
three stages of an interview

INTERVIEWING FOR SUCCESS

At this point, you have a good sense of the overall process and know how to prepare for your interviews. The next step is to get familiar with the three stages of every interview: the warm-up, the question-and-answer session, and the close.

The Warm-Up

The first minute of the interview is crucial, so stay alert and be on your best business behavior.

Of the three stages, the warm-up is the most important, even though it may account for only a small fraction of the time you spend in the interview. Studies suggest that many interviewers, particularly those who are poorly trained in interviewing techniques, make up their minds within the first 20 seconds of contact with a candidate.[38] Don't let your guard down if it appears that the interviewer wants to engage in what feels like small talk; these exchanges are every bit as important as structured questions.

Body language is crucial at this point. Stand or sit up straight, maintain regular but natural eye contact, and don't fidget. When the interviewer extends a hand, respond with a firm but not overpowering handshake. Repeat the interviewer's name when you're introduced ("It's a pleasure to meet you, Ms. Litton"). Wait until you're asked to be seated or the interviewer has taken a seat. Let the interviewer start the discussion, and be ready to answer one or two substantial questions right away. The following are some common openers:[39]

Recognize that you could face substantial questions as soon as your interview starts, so make sure you are prepared and ready to go.

- Why do you want to work here?
- What do you know about us?
- Tell me a little about yourself.

The Question-and-Answer Stage

Questions and answers usually consume the greatest part of the interview. Depending on the type of interview, the interviewer will likely ask about your qualifications, discuss some of the points mentioned in your résumé, and ask about how you have handled particular situations in the past or would handle them in the future. You'll also be asking questions of your own.

Answering and Asking Questions

Listen carefully to questions before you answer.

Let the interviewer lead the conversation, and never answer a question before he or she has finished asking it. Not only is this type of interruption rude, but the last few words of the question might alter how you respond. As much as possible, avoid one-word, yes-or-no answers. Use the opportunity to expand on a positive response or explain a negative response. If you're asked a difficult question, pause before responding. Think through the implications of the question. For instance, the recruiter may know that you can't answer a question and only wants to know how you'll respond under pressure.

Whenever you're asked if you have any questions, or whenever doing so naturally fits the flow of the conversation, ask a question from the list you've prepared. Probe for what the company is looking for in its new employees so that you can show how you meet the firm's needs. Also try to zero in on any reservations the interviewer might have about you so that you can dispel them.

Listening to the Interviewer

Paying attention to both verbal and nonverbal messages can help you turn the question-and-answer stage to your advantage.

Paying attention when the interviewer speaks can be as important as giving good answers or asking good questions. Review the tips on listening offered in Chapter 2. The interviewer's facial expressions, eye movements, gestures, and posture may tell you the real meaning of what is being said. Be especially aware of how your answers are received. Does the interviewer nod in agreement or smile to show approval? If so, you're making progress. If not, you might want to introduce another topic or modify your approach.

Handling Discriminatory Questions

Federal, state, and local laws prohibit a wide variety of interview questions.

A variety of federal, state, and local laws prohibit employment discrimination on the basis of race, ethnicity, gender, age (at least if you're between 40 and 70), marital status, religion,

TABLE 14.6 Interview Questions That May and May Not Be Asked

Interviewers May Ask This ...	But Not This
What is your name?	What was your maiden name?
Are you over 18?	When were you born?
Did you graduate from high school?	When did you graduate from high school?
[No questions about race are allowed.]	What is your race?
Can you perform [specific tasks]?	Do you have physical or mental disabilities?
	Do you have a drug or alcohol problem?
	Are you taking any prescription drugs?
Would you be able to meet the job's requirement to frequently work weekends?	Would working on weekends conflict with your religion?
Do you have the legal right to work in the United States?	What country are you a citizen of?
Have you ever been convicted of a felony?	Have you ever been arrested?
This job requires that you speak Spanish. Do you?	What language did you speak in your home when you were growing up?

national origin, or disability. Interview questions designed to elicit information on these topics are potentially illegal.[40] Table 14.6 compares some specific questions that employers are and are not allowed to ask during an employment interview.

If an interviewer asks a potentially unlawful question, consider your options carefully before you respond. You can answer the question as it was asked, you can ask tactfully whether the question might be prohibited, you can simply refuse to answer it, or you can try to answer "the question behind the question."[41] For example, if an interviewer inappropriately asks whether you are married or have strong family ties in the area, he or she might be trying to figure out if you're willing to travel or relocate—both of which are acceptable questions. Only you can decide which is the right choice based on the situation.

Think about how you might respond if you were asked a potentially unlawful question.

Even if you do answer the question as it was asked, think hard before accepting a job offer from this company if you have alternatives. Was the off-limits question possibly accidental (it happens) and therefore not really a major concern? If you think it was intentional, would you want to work for an organization that condones illegal or discriminatory questions or that doesn't train its employees to avoid them?

If you believe an interviewer's questions to be unreasonable, unrelated to the job, or an attempt to discriminate, you have the option of filing a complaint with the EEOC (www.eeoc.gov) or with the agency in your state that regulates fair employment practices.

The Close

Like the warm-up, the end of the interview is more important than its brief duration would indicate. These last few minutes are your last opportunity to emphasize your value to the organization and to correct any misconceptions the interviewer might have. Be aware that many interviewers will ask whether you have any more questions at this point, so save one or two from your list.

Concluding Gracefully

You can usually tell when the interviewer is trying to conclude the session. He or she may ask whether you have any more questions, check the time, summarize the discussion, or simply tell you that the allotted time for the interview is up. When you get the signal, be sure to thank the interviewer for the opportunity and express your interest in the organization. If you can do so comfortably, try to pin down what will happen next, but don't press for an immediate decision.

Conclude an interview with courtesy and enthusiasm.

If this is your second or third visit to the organization, the interview may end with an offer of employment. If you have other offers or need time to think about this offer, it's perfectly acceptable to thank the interviewer for the offer and ask for some time to consider it. If no job offer is made, the interview team may not have reached a decision yet, but you may tactfully ask when you can expect to know the decision.

Discussing Salary

If you receive an offer during the interview, you'll naturally want to discuss salary. However, let the interviewer raise the subject. If asked your salary requirements during the interview or on a job application, you can say that your requirements are open or negotiable or that you would expect a competitive compensation package.[42]

How far you can negotiate depends on several factors, including market demand for your skills, the strength of the job market, the company's compensation policies, the company's financial health, and whether you have other job offers. Remember that you're negotiating a business deal, not asking for personal favors, so focus on the unique value you can bring to the job. The more information you have, the stronger your position will be.

If salary isn't negotiable, look at the overall compensation and benefits package. You may find flexibility in a signing bonus, profit sharing, retirement benefits, health coverage, vacation time, and other valuable elements.[43]

Interview Notes

Maintain a notebook or simple database with information about each company, interviewers' answers to your questions, contact information for each interviewer, the status of thank-you notes and other follow-up communication, and upcoming interview appointments. Carefully organized notes will help you decide which company is the right fit for you when it comes time to choose from among the job offers you receive.

For the latest information on interviewing strategies, visit **http://real-timeupdates.com/bce5** and click on Chapter 14.

FOLLOWING UP AFTER AN INTERVIEW

Staying in contact with a prospective employer after an interview shows that you really want the job and are determined to get it. Doing so also gives you another chance to demonstrate your communication skills and sense of business etiquette. Following up brings your name to the interviewer's attention once again and reminds him or her that you're actively looking and waiting for the decision.

Any time you hear from a company during the application or interview process, be sure to respond quickly. Companies flooded with résumés may move on to another candidate if you they don't hear back from you within 24 hours.[44]

Thank-You Message

Write a thank-you message within two days of the interview, even if you feel you have little chance of getting the job. In addition to demonstrating good etiquette, a thank-you message gives you the opportunity to reinforce the reasons you are a good choice for the position and lets you respond to any negatives that might've arisen in the interview.[45] Acknowledge the interviewer's time and courtesy, convey your continued interest, reinforce the reasons that you are a good fit for the position, and ask politely for a decision (see Figure 14.7).

Depending on the company and the relationship you've established with the interviewer, the thank-you message can be handled via letter or e-mail. Be brief and sound positive without sounding overconfident.

Message of Inquiry

If you're not advised of the interviewer's decision by the promised date or within two weeks, you might make an inquiry. A message of inquiry (which can be handled by e-mail

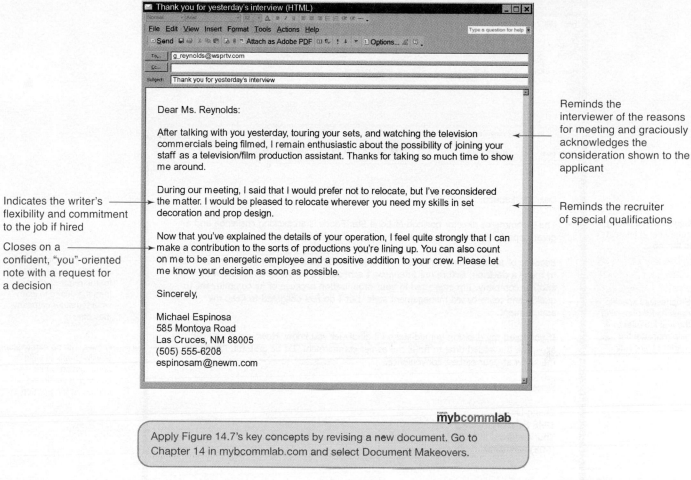

Reminds the interviewer of the reasons for meeting and graciously acknowledges the consideration shown to the applicant

Indicates the writer's flexibility and commitment to the job if hired

Reminds the recruiter of special qualifications

Closes on a confident, "you"-oriented note with a request for a decision

Email content:

Dear Ms. Reynolds:

After talking with you yesterday, touring your sets, and watching the television commercials being filmed, I remain enthusiastic about the possibility of joining your staff as a television/film production assistant. Thanks for taking so much time to show me around.

During our meeting, I said that I would prefer not to relocate, but I've reconsidered the matter. I would be pleased to relocate wherever you need my skills in set decoration and prop design.

Now that you've explained the details of your operation, I feel quite strongly that I can make a contribution to the sorts of productions you're lining up. You can also count on me to be an energetic employee and a positive addition to your crew. Please let me know your decision as soon as possible.

Sincerely,

Michael Espinosa
585 Montoya Road
Las Cruces, NM 88005
(505) 555-6208
espinosam@newm.com

mybcommlab

Apply Figure 14.7's key concepts by revising a new document. Go to Chapter 14 in mybcommlab.com and select Document Makeovers.

Figure 14.7   Thank-You Message
In three brief paragraphs, Michael Espinosa acknowledges the interviewer's time and consideration, expresses his continued interest in the position, explains a crucial discussion point that he has reconsidered, and asks for a decision.

if the interviewer has given you his or her e-mail address) is particularly appropriate if you've received a job offer from a second firm and don't want to accept it before you have an answer from the first. The following message illustrates the general model for a direct request:

> When we talked on April 7 about the fashion coordinator position in your Park Avenue showroom, you indicated that a decision would be made by May 1. I am still enthusiastic about the position and eager to know what conclusion you've reached.

Identifies the position and introduces the main idea

> To complicate matters, another firm has now offered me a position and has asked that I reply within the next two weeks.

Places the reason for the request second

> Because your company seems to offer a greater challenge, I would appreciate knowing about your decision by Thursday, May 12. If you need more information before then, please let me know.

Makes a courteous request for specific action last, while clearly stating a preference for this organization

Request for a Time Extension

If you receive a job offer while other interviews are still pending, you can ask the employer for a time extension. Open with a strong statement of your continued interest in the job, ask for more time to consider the offer, provide specific reasons for the request, and assure the reader that you will respond by a specific date (see Figure 14.8 on the next page).

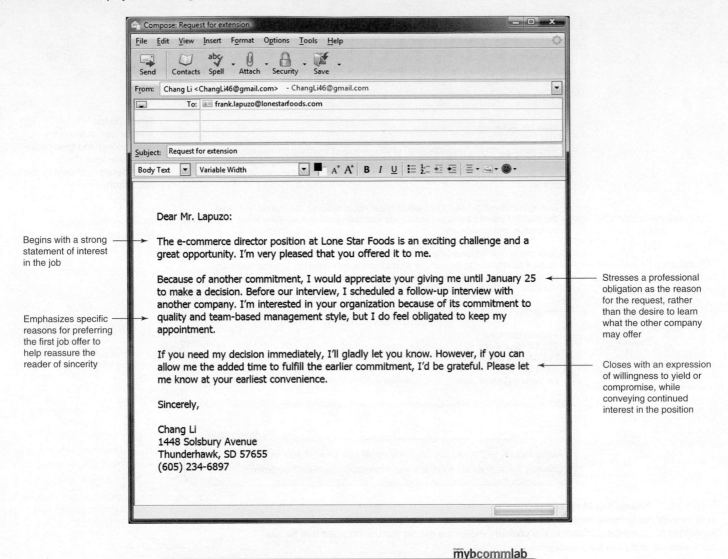

Begins with a strong statement of interest in the job

Emphasizes specific reasons for preferring the first job offer to help reassure the reader of sincerity

Stresses a professional obligation as the reason for the request, rather than the desire to learn what the other company may offer

Closes with an expression of willingness to yield or compromise, while conveying continued interest in the position

Figure 14.8   Request for a Time Extension
If you need to request more time to make a decision about a job offer, make sure to reaffirm that you are still interested in the job.

Letter of Acceptance

Use the model for positive messages when you write a letter of acceptance.

When you receive a job offer that you want to accept, reply within five days. Begin by accepting the position and expressing thanks. Identify the job that you're accepting. In the next paragraph, cover any necessary details. Conclude by saying that you look forward to reporting for work. As always, a positive letter should convey your enthusiasm and eagerness to cooperate:

Confirms the specific terms of the offer with a good-news statement at the beginning

> I'm delighted to accept the graphic design position in your advertising department at the salary of $2,875 per month.

Covers miscellaneous details in the middle

> Enclosed are the health insurance forms you asked me to complete and sign. I've already given notice to my current employer and will be able to start work on Monday, January 18.

Closes with another reference to the good news and a look toward the future

> The prospect of joining your firm is exciting. Thank you for giving me this opportunity, and I look forward to making a positive contribution.

Written acceptance of a job offer can be considered a legally binding contract.

Be aware that a job offer and a written acceptance of that offer can constitute a legally binding contract, for both you and the employer. Before you send an acceptance letter, be sure you want the job.

Letter Declining a Job Offer

After all your interviews, you may find that you need to write a letter declining a job offer. Use the techniques for negative messages (see Chapter 8): Open warmly, state the reasons for refusing the offer, decline the offer explicitly, and close on a pleasant note that expresses gratitude. By taking the time to write a sincere, tactful letter, you leave the door open for future contact:

If you decide to decline a job offer, do so tactfully, using the model for negative messages.

> One of the most interesting interviews I have ever had was the one last month at your Durham facility. I'm flattered that you would offer me the computer analyst position that we talked about.

Uses a buffer in the opening paragraph

> I was fortunate to receive two job offers during my search. Because my desire to work abroad can more readily be satisfied by another company, I have accepted that job offer.

Precedes the bad news with tactfully phrased reasons for the applicant's unfavorable decision and leaves the door open

> I deeply appreciate the time you spent talking with me. Thank you again for your consideration and kindness.

Lets the reader down gently with a sincere and cordial ending

Letter of Resignation

If you get a job offer while currently employed, you can maintain good relations with your current employer by writing a thoughtful letter of resignation to your immediate supervisor. Follow the advice for negative messages and make the letter sound positive, regardless of how you feel. Say something favorable about the organization, the people you work with, or what you've learned on the job. Then state your intention to leave and give the date of your last day on the job. Be sure you give your current employer at least two weeks' notice.

Letters of resignation should always be written in a gracious and professional style that avoids criticism of your employer or your colleagues.

> My sincere thanks to you and to all the other Emblem Corporation employees for helping me learn so much about serving the public these past two years. You have given me untold help and encouragement.

Uses an appreciative opening to serve as a buffer

> You may recall that when you first interviewed me, my goal was to become a customer relations supervisor. Because that opportunity has been offered to me by another organization, I am submitting my resignation. I will miss all of you, but I want to take advantage of this opportunity.

States reasons before the bad news itself, using tactful phrasing to help keep the relationship friendly, should the writer later want letters of recommendation

> I would like to terminate my work here two weeks from today but can arrange to work an additional week if you want me to train a replacement.

Discusses necessary details in an extra paragraph

> My sincere thanks and best wishes to all of you.

Tempers any disappointment with a cordial close

PEARSON **mybcommlab**   Are you an active learner? Go to mybcommlab.com to master Chapter 14's content. Chapter 14's interactive activities include:

- Customizable Study Plan and Chapter 14 practice quizzes
- Chapter 14 Simulation (Interviewing), which helps you think critically and prepare to make choices in the business world
- Chapter 14 Video Exercise (Interviewing Skills), which shows you how textbook concepts are put into practice every day

- Flash Cards for mastering the definition of chapter terms
- Interactive Lessons that visually review key chapter concepts
- Document Makeovers for hands-on, scored practice in revising documents

CHAPTER REVIEW AND ACTIVITIES

Learning Objectives: Check Your Progress

1 OBJECTIVE Explain the purposes of application letters, and describe how to apply the AIDA organizational approach to them.

The purposes of an application letter are to introduce your résumé, persuade an employer to read it, and request an interview. With the AIDA model, get attention in the opening paragraph by showing how your work skills could benefit the organization, by explaining how your qualifications fit the job, or by demonstrating an understanding of the organization's needs. Build interest and desire by showing how you can meet the job requirements and, near the end of this section, be sure to refer your reader to your résumé. Finally, motivate action by making your request easy to fulfill and by including all necessary contact information.

2 OBJECTIVE Describe the typical sequence of job interviews, the major types of interviews, and what employers look for during an interview.

The typical sequence of interviews involves three stages. During the screening stage, employers filter out unqualified applicants and identify promising candidates. During the selection stage, the pool of applicants is narrowed through a variety of structured and unstructured interviewing methods. In the final stage, employers select the candidates who will receive offers and, if necessary, promote the benefits of joining the company.

Interviews can be distinguished by the way they are structured (structured or unstructured interviews), the number of people involved (one-on-one, panel, or group interviews), and the purpose of the interview (behavioral, situational, working, or stress interviews). The behavioral interview, probably the most common in terms of purpose, requires candidates to use their own experiences and attributes to craft answers. The situational interview is similar, but instead of using incidents from the candidate's past, it explores how the candidate would respond to hypothetical situations in the future.

Employers look for two things during an employment interview. First, they seek evidence that an applicant is qualified for the position. Second, they seek reassurance that an applicant will be a good fit with the "personality" of the organization and the position.

3 OBJECTIVE List six tasks you need to complete to prepare for a successful job interview.

To prepare for a successful job interview, (1) complete the research you started when planning your résumé, (2) think ahead about questions you'll need to answer and questions you'll want to ask, (3) bolster your confidence by focusing on your strengths and preparing thoroughly, (4) polish your interviewing style, (5) present a professional image with businesslike clothing and good grooming, and (6) arrive on time and ready to begin.

4 OBJECTIVE Explain how to succeed in all three stages of an interview.

All employment interviews have three stages. The warm-up stage is the most important because first impressions greatly influence an interviewer's decision. The question-and-answer stage, during which you will answer and ask questions, is the longest. The close is your final opportunity to promote your value to the organization and counter any misconceptions the interviewer may have.

5 OBJECTIVE Identify the most common employment messages that follow an interview, and explain when you would use each one.

Following an interview, send a *thank-you message* to show appreciation, emphasize your strengths, and politely ask for a decision. Send an *inquiry* if you haven't received the interviewer's decision by the date promised or within one or two weeks of the interview—especially if you've received a job offer from another firm. You can *request a time extension* if you need more time to consider an offer. Send a *letter of acceptance* after receiving a job offer that you want to take. Send a *letter declining a job offer* when you want to refuse an offer tactfully. Finally, if you are currently employed, send a *letter of resignation* after you have accepted the offer of another job.

Test Your Knowledge

To review chapter content related to each question, refer to the indicated Learning Objective.

1. What information or questions can you use when writing a follow-up message after submitting a résumé? [LO-1]
2. How does a structured interview differ from an open-ended interview? [LO-2]
3. What should your objective be for an interview during the selection stage? [LO-2]
4. Why are the questions you ask during an interview as important as the answers you give to the interviewer's questions? [LO-3]
5. What are the three stages of every interview, and which is the most important? [LO-4]

Apply Your Knowledge

To review chapter content related to each question, refer to the indicated Learning Objective.

1. How can you prepare for a situational or behavioral interview if you have no experience with the job for which you are interviewing? [LO-2]

2. How can you distinguish yourself from other candidates in a screening interview and still keep your responses short and to the point? Explain. [LO-2]

3. If you lack one important qualification for a job but have made it past the initial screening stage, how should you prepare to handle this issue during the next round of interviews? Explain your answer. [LO-3]

4. If you want to switch jobs because you can't work with your supervisor, how can you explain this situation to a prospective employer? [LO-4]

5. Why is it important to distinguish unethical or illegal interview questions from acceptable questions? Explain. [LO-4]

Practice Your Skills

Activities

Active links for all websites in this chapter can be found on mybcommlab; see your User Guide for instructions on accessing the content for this chapter. Each activity is labeled according to the primary skill or skills you will need to use. To review relevant chapter content, you can refer to the indicated Learning Objective. In some instances, supporting information will be found in another chapter, as indicated.

1. **Message Strategies: Employment Messages [LO-1]** Revise this message so that it follows this chapter's guidelines.

   I'm writing to let you know about my availability for the brand manager job you advertised. As you can see from my enclosed résumé, my background is perfect for the position. Even though I don't have any real job experience, my grades have been outstanding considering that I went to a top-ranked business school.

   I did many things during my undergraduate years to prepare me for this job:

   - Earned a 3.4 out of a 4.0 with a 3.8 in my business courses
   - Elected representative to the student governing association
   - Selected to receive the Lamar Franklin Award
   - Worked to earn a portion of my tuition

   I am sending my résumé to all the top firms, but I like yours better than any of the rest. Your reputation is tops in the industry, and I want to be associated with a business that can pridefully say It's the best.

   If you wish for me to come in for an interview, I can come on a Friday afternoon or anytime on weekends when I don't have classes. Again, thanks for considering me for your brand manager position.

2. **Message Strategies: Employment Messages [LO-1]** Revise this message so that it follows this chapter's guidelines.

   Did you receive my résumé? I sent it to you at least two months ago and haven't heard anything. I know you keep résumés on file, but I just want to be sure that you keep me in mind. I heard you are hiring health-care managers and certainly would like to be considered for one of those positions.

   Since I last wrote you, I've worked in a variety of positions that have helped prepare me for management. To wit, I've become lunch manager at the restaurant where I work, which involved a raise in pay. I now manage a waitstaff of 12 girls and take the lunch receipts to the bank every day.

   Of course, I'd much rather be working at a real job, and that's why I'm writing again. Is there anything else you would like to know about me or my background? I would really like to know more about your company. Is there any literature you could send me? If so, I would really appreciate it.

   I think one reason I haven't been hired yet is that I don't want to leave Atlanta. So I hope when you think of me, it's for a position that wouldn't require moving. Thanks again for considering my application.

3. **Career Management: Preparing for Interviews [LO-2]** Google yourself, Bing yourself, scour your social networking profiles, review your Twitter messages, and explore every other possible online source you can think of that might have something about you. If you find anything potentially embarrassing, remove it if possible. Write a summary of your search-and-destroy mission (you can skip any embarrassing details in your report to your instructor!).

4. **Career Management: Researching Target Employers [LO-3]** Select a large company (one on which you can easily find information) where you might like to work. Use online sources to gather some preliminary research on the company; don't limit your search to the company's own website.

   a. What did you learn about this organization that would help you during an interview there?
   b. What Internet sources did you use to obtain this information?
   c. Armed with this information, what aspects of your background do you think might appeal to this company's recruiters?
   d. If you choose to apply for a job with this company, what keywords would you include on your résumé? Why?

5. **Career Management: Interviewing [LO-3]** Write a short e-mail to your instructor, discussing what you believe are your greatest strengths and weaknesses from an employment perspective. Next, explain how these strengths and weaknesses would be viewed by interviewers evaluating your qualifications.

6. **Career Management: Interviewing [LO-3]** Prepare written answers to 10 of the questions listed in Table 14.3 on page 418.

7. **Career Management: Interviewing; Collaboration: Team Projects [LO-4], Chapter 2** Divide the class into two groups. Half the class will be recruiters for a large

chain of national department stores, looking to fill 15 manager-trainee positions. The other half of the class will be candidates for the job. The company is specifically looking for candidates who demonstrate these three qualities: initiative, dependability, and willingness to assume responsibility.

   a. Have each recruiter select and interview an applicant for 10 minutes.
   b. Have all the recruiters discuss how they assessed the applicant in each of the three desired qualities. What questions did they ask or what did they use as an indicator to determine whether the candidate possessed the quality?
   c. Have all the applicants discuss what they said to convince the recruiters that they possessed each of the three desired qualities.

8. **Message Strategies: Employment Messages [LO-5]** Revise this message so that it follows this chapter's guidelines.

   I have recently received a very attractive job offer from the Warrington Company. But before I let them know one way or another, I would like to consider any offer that your firm may extend. I was quite impressed with your company during my recent interview, and I am still very interested in a career there.

   I don't mean to pressure you, but Warrington has asked for my decision within 10 days. Could you let me know by Tuesday whether you plan to offer me a position? That would give me enough time to compare the two offers.

9. **Message Strategies: Employment Messages [LO-5]** Revise this message so that it follows this chapter's guidelines.

   Thank you for the really marvelous opportunity to meet you and your colleagues at Starret Engine Company. I really enjoyed touring your facilities and talking with all the people there. You have quite a crew! Some of the other companies I have visited have been so rigid and uptight that I can't imagine how I would fit in. It's a relief to run into a group of people who seem to enjoy their work as much as all of you do.

   I know that you must be looking at many other candidates for this job, and I know that some of them will probably be more experienced than I am. But I do want to emphasize that my two-year hitch in the Navy involved a good deal of engineering work. I don't think I mentioned all my shipboard responsibilities during the interview.

   Please give me a call within the next week to let me know your decision. You can usually find me at my dormitory in the evening after dinner (phone: 877-9080).

10. **Message Strategies: Employment Messages [LO-5]** Revise this message so that it follows this chapter's guidelines.

    I'm writing to say that I must decline your job offer. Another company has made me a more generous offer, and I have decided to accept. However, if things don't work out for me there, I will let you know. I sincerely appreciate your interest in me.

11. **Message Strategies: Employment Messages, Communication Ethics: Resolving Ethical Dilemmas [LO-5],**

Chapter 1   You have decided to accept a new position with a competitor of your company. Write a letter of resignation to your supervisor, announcing your decision. In an e-mail message to your instructor, address the following questions:

   a. Will you notify your employer that you are joining a competing firm? Explain.
   b. Will you use the direct or indirect approach? Explain.
   c. Will you send your letter by e-mail, send it by regular mail, or place it on your supervisor's desk?

Expand Your Skills

Critique the Professionals

Visit LinkedIn Answers at www.linkedin.com/answers (open a free LinkedIn account if required). In the "Browse" panel, click on "Career and Education" and then "Job Search." Browse both "Open Questions" and "Closed Questions" to find three job search insights that you didn't know before. Using whatever medium your instructor requests, write a brief summary (no more than one page) of what you learned.

Sharpen Your Career Skills Online

Bovée and Thill's Business Communication Web Search, at http://businesscommunicationblog.com/websearch, is a unique research tool designed specifically for business communication research. Use the Web Search function to find a website, video, PDF document, podcast, or presentation that offers advice on successful interviewing techniques. Write a brief e-mail message to your instructor or a post for your class blog, describing the item that you found and summarizing the career skills information you learned from it.

mybcommlab

If your course uses mybcommlab, log on to www.mybcommlab.com to access the following study and assessment aids associated with this chapter:

- Video applications
- Pre/post test
- Real-Time Updates
- Personalized study plan
- Peer review activity
- Model documents
- Quick Learning Guides
- Sample presentations

If you are not using mybcommlab, you can access Real-Time Updates and Quick Learning Guides through http://real-timeupdates.com/bce5. The Quick Learning Guide (located under "Learn More" on the website) hits all the high points of this chapter in just two pages. This guide, especially prepared by the authors, will help you study for exams or review important concepts whenever you need a quick refresher.

CASES

Apply the three-step writing process to the following cases, as assigned by your instructor.

Writing Application Letters

E-MAIL SKILLS

1. Message Strategies: Employment Messages [LO-1]   Use one of the websites listed in Table 13.1 on page 350 to find a job opening in your target profession. If you haven't narrowed down to one career field yet, chose a business job for which you will have at least some qualifications at the time of your graduation.

Your task Write an e-mail message that would serve as your application letter if you were to apply for this job. Base your message on your actual qualifications for the position, and be sure to "echo" the requirements listed in the job description. Include the job description in your e-mail message when you submit it to your instructor.

E-MAIL SKILLS

2. Message Strategies: Employment Messages [LO-1]   You've studied with vigor and resolve for four years, and you're just about to graduate with your business degree. While cruising the web to relax one night, you stumble on something called Google Earth. You're hooked instantly by the ability to zoom all around the globe and look at detailed satellite photos of places you've been to or dreamed of visiting. You can even type in the address of your apartment and get an aerial view of your neighborhood. You're amazed at the three-dimensional renderings of major cities. Plus, the photographs and maps are linked to Google's other search technologies, allowing you to locate everything from ATMs to coffee shops in your neighborhood.

You've loved maps since you were a kid, and discovering Google Earth is making you wish you had majored in geography. Knowing how important it is to follow your heart, you decide to apply to Google anyway, even though you don't have a strong background in geographic information systems. What you do have is a ton of passion for maps and a good head for business.[46]

Your task Visit http://earth.google.com and explore the system's capabilities. (You can download a free copy of the software.) In particular, look at the business and government applications of the technology, such as customized aerial photos and maps for real estate sales, land use and environmental impact analysis, and emergency planning for homeland security agencies. Be sure to visit the Community pages, where you can learn more about the many interesting applications of this technology. Draft an application e-mail to Google, asking to be considered for the Google Earth team. Think about how you could help the company develop the commercial potential of this product line and make sure your enthusiasm shines through in the message. Make up any information you need to write the message.

Interviewing

BLOGGING SKILLS   TEAM SKILLS

3. Career Management: Researching Target Employers [LO-3] Research is a critical element of the job search process. With information in hand, you increase the chance of finding the right opportunity (and avoiding bad choices), and you impress interviewers in multiple ways by demonstrating initiative, curiosity, research and analysis skills, an appreciation for the complex challenges of running a business, and willingness to work to achieve results.

Your task With a small team of classmates, use online job listings (see Table 13.1) to identify an intriguing job opening that at least one member of the team would seriously consider pursuing as graduation approaches. (You'll find it helpful if the career is related to at least one team member's college major or on-the-job experience so that the team can benefit from some knowledge of the profession in question.) Next, research the company, its competitors, its markets, and this specific position to identify five questions that would (1) help the team member decide if this is a good opportunity and (2) show an interviewer that you've really done your homework. Go beyond the basic and obvious questions to identify current, specific, and complex issues that only deep research can uncover. For example, is the company facing significant technical, financial, legal, or regulatory challenges that threaten its ability to grow or perhaps even survive in the long term? Or is the market evolving in a way that positions this particular company for dramatic growth? In a post for your class blog, list your five questions, identify how you uncovered the issue, and explain why each is significant.

TEAM SKILLS

4. Career Management: Interviewing [LO-4]   Interviewing is a skill that can be improved through practice and observation.

Your task You and all other members of your class are to write letters of application for an entry-level or management-trainee position that requires an engaging personality and intelligence but a minimum of specialized education or experience. Sign your letter with a fictitious name that conceals your identity. Next, polish (or create) a résumé that accurately identifies you and your educational and professional accomplishments.

Now, three members of the class who volunteer as interviewers divide up all the anonymously written application letters. Then each interviewer selects a candidate who seems the most convincing in his or her letter. At this time, the selected candidates identify themselves and give the interviewers their résumés.

Each interviewer then interviews his or her chosen candidate in front of the class, seeking to understand how the items on the résumé qualify the candidate for the job. At the end of the interviews, the class decides who gets the job and discusses why this candidate was successful. Afterward, retrieve your letter, sign it with the right name, and submit it to the instructor for credit.

TEAM SKILLS

5. Career Management: Interviewing [LO-4]   Select a company in an industry in which you might like to work and then identify an interesting position within the company. Study the company and prepare for an interview with that company.

Your task Working with a classmate, take turns interviewing each other for your chosen positions. Interviewers should take notes during the interview. When the interview is complete, critique each other's performance. (Interviewers should critique how well candidates prepared for the interview and answered the questions; interviewees should critique the quality of the questions asked.) Write a follow-up letter thanking your interviewer and submit the letter to your instructor.

Following Up After an Interview

LETTER WRITING SKILLS

6. Message Strategies: Employment Messages [LO-5]   Due to a mix-up in your job application scheduling, you accidentally applied for your third-choice job before going after the one you really wanted. What you want to do is work in retail marketing with the upscale department store Neiman Marcus in Dallas; what you have been offered is a job with Longhorn Leather and Lumber, 65 miles away in the small town of Commerce, Texas.

You review your notes. Your Longhorn interview was three weeks ago with the human resources manager, R. P. Bronson, who has just written to offer you the position. The store's address is 27 Sam Rayburn Drive, Commerce, TX 75428. Mr. Bronson notes that he can hold the position open for 10 days. You have an interview scheduled with Neiman Marcus next week, but it is unlikely that you will know the store's decision within this 10-day period.

Your task Write to Mr. Bronson, requesting a reasonable delay in your consideration of his job offer.

LETTER WRITING SKILLS   E-MAIL SKILLS

7. Message Strategies: Employment Messages [LO-5]   Fortunately for you, your interview with Neiman Marcus (see Case 6) went well, and you've just received a job offer from the company.

Your task Write a letter to R.P. Pronson at Longhorn Leather and Lumber, declining his job offer, and write an e-mail message to Clarissa Bartle at Neiman Marcus, accepting her job offer. Make up any information you need when accepting the Neiman Marcus offer.

 ## Improve Your Grammar, Mechanics, and Usage

You can download the text of this assignment from **http://real-timeupdates.com/bce5**; click on "Student Assignments" and then click on "Chapter 14. Improve Your Grammar, Mechanics, and Usage."

Level 1: Self-Assessment—Vocabulary

Review Sections 4.1, 4.2, and 4.3 in the Handbook of Grammar, Mechanics, and Usage and then complete the following 15 items.

In items 1–7, indicate the correct word provided in parentheses.

1. Everyone (accept/except) Barbara King has registered for the company competition.
2. We need to find a new security (device/devise).
3. The Jennings are (loath/loathe) to admit that they are wrong.
4. The judge has ruled that this town cannot enforce such a local (ordinance/ordnance).
5. To stay on schedule, we must give (precedence/precedents) to the Marley project.
6. This month's balance is greater (than/then) last month's.
7. That decision lies with the director, (who's/whose) in charge of this department.

In items 8–15, correct any errors you find:

8. In this department, we see alot of mistakes like that.
9. In my judgement, you'll need to redo the cover.
10. He decided to reveal the information, irregardless of the consequences.
11. Why not go along when it is so easy to accomodate his demands?
12. When you say that, do you mean to infer that I'm being unfair?
13. She says that she finds this sort of ceremony embarassing.
14. All we have to do is try and get along with him for a few more days.
15. A friendly handshake should always preceed negotiations.

Level 2: Workplace Applications

The following items may contain errors in grammar, capitalization, punctuation, abbreviation, number style, word division, and vocabulary. Rewrite each sentence, correcting all errors. If a sentence has no errors, write "Correct" for that number.

1. An entrepreneur and their business, are so closely tied together that a bank will want to see how they handle their personal affairs, before granting a small business line of credit.
2. The companys' annual meeting will be held from 2–4 PM on May 3d in the Santa Fe room at the Marriott hotel.
3. Well over four hundred outstanding students from coast-to-coast, have realized their dreams of a college education thanks to the NASE Scholarship program.
4. If you're home is you're principle place of business you can deduct generally the cost of traveling from you're home, to any business destination.
5. Companies like McLeod USA sprung into being in the 1990's to provide cut rate phone services to small- and medium-size businesses in competition with the established baby bells.
6. Some question whether a 'new economy' exists and if so how it differs from the old economy?

7. When the music industry claimed by stealing intellectual property Napster were committing piracy - Napster argued that it was'nt doing anything illegal or un-ethical.

8. The World Bank plays an important roll in todays fast changing closely-meshed global economy.

9. When it comes to consumer rights the F.D.A., F.T.C., and Agriculture department are concerned not only with safety but also accurate information.

10. Fujitsu, a $50 billion company with 190,000 employees, dominates the Japanese computer industry.

11. The fortune 500 ranks not only corporations by size but also offers brief company descriptions; along with industry statistics, and additional measures of corporate performance.

12. Having bought 55 companies over the past decade, plans to make ten to 15 new acquisitions each year are being made by Cisco Systems.

13. In 1984 Michael Dell decided to sell P.C.'s direct and built to order, now everybody in the industry are trying to imitate Dells' strategy.

14. Resulting in large cost savings for the company, American Express have reduced the number of field office's from 85 to 7 by using virtual teams.

15. In Europe and Asia, people are using mobile phones to send text messages to other users; exchange e-mail; read the morning news; surfing certain websites; and to make purchases such as movie tickets and charge it to they're monthly phone bill.

Level 3: Document Critique

The following document may contain errors in grammar, capitalization, punctuation, abbreviation, number style, word division, and vocabulary. As your instructor indicates, photocopy this page and correct all errors using standard proofreading marks (see Appendix C) or download the document and make the corrections in your word processing software.

Morgan Mitras

2397 Glencrest ridge, Fort Worth, TEX 76119

(817/ 226-1804)

February 2 2011:

Norton Acctg. Group

Ms Nancy Remington, Human Resources

3778 Parkway North

Indianapolis, Indiana 46205

Dear Ms. Remington—

With your companys' reputation for quality, customer service, employee empowerment, you'll will want to hire someone who is not only accurrate and efficient but also self motivated and results-oriented—someone who is able to make decisions as well as coperate with team members and clients. The ad you placed in the February 1st issue of The Wall Street Journal for someone to fill a financial management position really has me very excited and eager.

During my 3 years at Tandy corporation -see attached résumé- I've conducted internal auditing for accounts valued at $450 million dollars. Some of my many, countless accomplishments include

- Increasing both internal and client support for the auditing process

- I save the company over 2.5 million dollars when I discovered billing errors

- Suggest ways accounts receivable processes could be streamlined

In addition it might be that Norton Accounting may appreciate my ability to complete projects on time as well as keeping them under budget. One of my priorities is a position in which my expereince will be broaden: so any opportunity to travel would be welcomed by me!

I'll be in your area during the weak of February 20; I'll call your office on Feb. 8 to see whether we can arrange to meet. I hope you'll give me a chance, please.

Sincerely,

Morgan Mitras,

Applicant

Appendix A

Format and Layout of Business Documents

The format and layout of business documents vary from country to country. In addition, many organizations develop their own variations of standard styles, adapting documents to the types of messages they send and the kinds of audiences they communicate with. The formats described here are the most common approaches used in U.S. business correspondence, but be sure to follow whatever practices are expected at your company.

FIRST IMPRESSIONS

Your documents tell readers a lot about you and about your company's professionalism. So all your documents must look neat, present a professional image, and be easy to read. Your audience's first impression of a document comes from the quality of its paper, the way it is customized, and its general appearance.

Paper

To give a quality impression, businesspeople consider carefully the paper they use. Several aspects of paper contribute to the overall impression:

- **Weight.** Paper quality is judged by the weight of four reams (each a 500-sheet package) of letter-size paper. The weight most commonly used by U.S. business organizations is 20-pound paper, but 16- and 24-pound versions are also used.

- **Cotton content.** Paper quality is also judged by the percentage of cotton in the paper. Cotton doesn't yellow over time the way wood pulp does, plus it's both strong and soft. For letters and outside reports, use paper with a 25 percent cotton content. For memos and other internal documents, you can use a lighter-weight paper with lower cotton content. Airmail-weight paper may save money for international correspondence, but make sure it isn't too flimsy.[1]

- **Size.** In the United States, the standard paper size for business documents is 8½ by 11 inches. Standard legal documents are 8½ by 14 inches. Executives sometimes have heavier 7-by-10-inch paper on hand (with matching envelopes) for personal messages such as congratulations.[2] They may also have a box of note cards imprinted with their initials and a box of plain folded notes for condolences or for acknowledging formal invitations.

- **Color.** White is the standard color for business purposes, although neutral colors such as gray and ivory are sometimes used. Memos can be produced on pastel-colored paper to distinguish them from external correspondence. In addition, memos are sometimes produced on various colors of paper for routing to separate departments. Light-colored papers are appropriate, but bright or dark colors make reading difficult and may appear too frivolous.

Customization

For letters to outsiders, U.S. businesses commonly use letterhead stationery, which may be either professionally printed or designed in-house using word processing templates and graphics. Letterhead typically contains the company name, logo, address, telephone and fax numbers, general e-mail address, and website URL.

In the United States, businesses always use letterhead for the first page of a letter. Successive pages are usually plain sheets of paper that match the letterhead in color and quality. Some companies use a specially printed second-page letterhead that bears only the company's name.

Appearance

Nearly all business documents are produced using an inkjet or laser printer; make sure to use a clean, high-quality printer. Certain documents, however, should be handwritten (such as a short informal memo or a note of condolence). Be sure to handwrite, print, or type the envelope to match the document. However, even a letter on the best-quality paper with the best-designed letterhead may look unprofessional if it's poorly produced. So pay close attention to all the factors affecting appearance, including the following:

- **Margins.** Business letters typically use 1-inch margins at the top, bottom, and sides of the page, although these parameters are sometimes adjusted to accommodate letterhead elements.

- **Line length.** Lines are rarely justified, because the resulting text looks too formal and can be difficult to read.

- **Character spacing.** Use proper spacing between characters and after punctuation. For example, U.S. conventions include leaving one space after commas, semicolons, colons, and sentence-ending periods. Each letter in a person's initials is followed by a period and a single space. However, abbreviations such as U.S.A. or MBA may or may not have periods, but they never have internal spaces.

- **Special symbols.** Take advantage of the many special symbols available with your computer's selection of fonts. In addition, see if your company has a style guide for documents, which may include particular symbols you are expected to use.

- **Corrections.** Messy corrections are unacceptable in business documents. If you notice an error after printing a document with your word processor, correct the mistake and reprint. (With informal memos to members of your own team or department, the occasional small correction in pen or pencil is acceptable, but never in formal documents.)

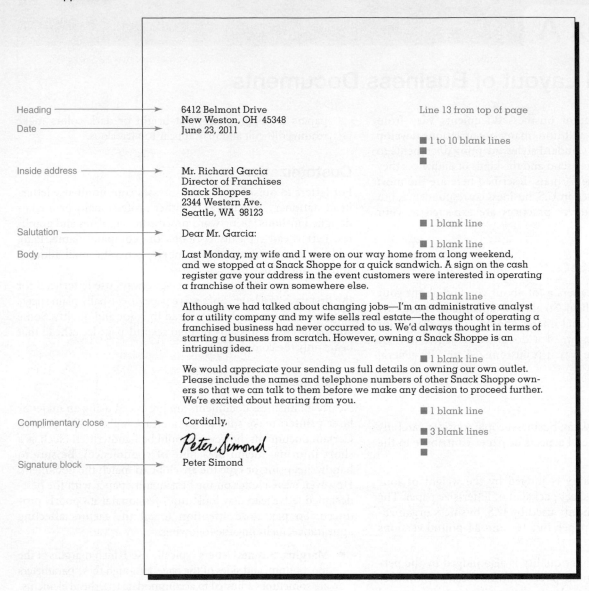

Heading → 6412 Belmont Drive
New Weston, OH 45348
Date → June 23, 2011

Line 13 from top of page

■ 1 to 10 blank lines
■
■

Inside address → Mr. Richard Garcia
Director of Franchises
Snack Shoppes
2344 Western Ave.
Seattle, WA 98123

■ 1 blank line

Salutation → Dear Mr. Garcia:

■ 1 blank line

Body → Last Monday, my wife and I were on our way home from a long weekend, and we stopped at a Snack Shoppe for a quick sandwich. A sign on the cash register gave your address in the event customers were interested in operating a franchise of their own somewhere else.

■ 1 blank line

Although we had talked about changing jobs—I'm an administrative analyst for a utility company and my wife sells real estate—the thought of operating a franchised business had never occurred to us. We'd always thought in terms of starting a business from scratch. However, owning a Snack Shoppe is an intriguing idea.

■ 1 blank line

We would appreciate your sending us full details on owning our own outlet. Please include the names and telephone numbers of other Snack Shoppe owners so that we can talk to them before we make any decision to proceed further. We're excited about hearing from you.

■ 1 blank line

Complimentary close → Cordially,

■ 3 blank lines
■
■

Peter Simond

Signature block → Peter Simond

Figure A.1   Standard Letter Parts

LETTERS

All business letters have certain elements in common. Several of these elements appear in every letter; others appear only when desirable or appropriate. In addition, these letter parts are usually arranged in one of three basic formats.

Standard Letter Parts

The letter in Figure A.1 shows the placement of standard letter parts. The writer of this business letter had no letterhead available but correctly included a heading. All business letters typically include these seven elements.

Heading

The elements of the letterhead make up the heading of a letter in most cases. If letterhead stationery is not available, the heading includes a return address (but no name) and starts 13 lines from the top of the page, which leaves a 2-inch top margin.

Date

If you're using letterhead, place the date at least one blank line beneath the lowest part of the letterhead. Without letterhead, place the date immediately below the return address. The standard method of writing the date in the United States uses the full name of the month (no abbreviations), followed by the day (in numerals, without *st*, *nd*, *rd*, or *th*), a comma, and then the year: July 14, 2011 (7/14/2011). Some organizations follow other conventions (see Table A.1). To maintain the utmost clarity in international correspondence, always spell out the name of the month in dates.[3]

Inside Address

The inside address identifies the recipient of the letter. For U.S. correspondence, begin the inside address at least one line below the date. Precede the addressee's name with a courtesy title, such as *Dr.*, *Mr.*, or *Ms.* The accepted courtesy title for women in business is *Ms.*, although a woman known to prefer the title *Miss* or *Mrs.* is always accommodated. If you don't know

TABLE A.1 Common Date Forms

Convention	Description	Date—Mixed	Date—All Numerals
U.S. standard	Month (spelled out) day, year	July 14, 2011	7/14/11
U.S. government and some U.S. industries	Day (in numerals) month (spelled out) year	14 July 2011	14/7/11
European	Replace U.S. solidus (diagonal line) with periods	14 July 2011	14.7.2011
International standard	Year month day	2011 July 14	2011,7,14

whether a person is a man or a woman (and you have no way of finding out), omit the courtesy title. For example, *Terry Smith* could be either a man or a woman. The first line of the inside address would be just *Terry Smith*, and the salutation would be *Dear Terry Smith*. The same is true if you know only a person's initials, as in *S. J. Adams*.

Spell out and capitalize titles that precede a person's name, such as *Professor* or *General* (see Table A.2 on the next page for the proper forms of address). The person's organizational title, such as *Director*, may be included on this first line (if it is short) or on the line below; the name of a department may follow. In addresses and signature lines, don't forget to capitalize any professional title that follows a person's name:

> Mr. Ray Johnson, Dean
>
> Ms. Patricia T. Higgins
>
> Assistant Vice President

However, professional titles not appearing in an address or signature line are capitalized only when they directly precede the name:

> President Kenneth Johanson will deliver the speech.
>
> Maria Morales, president of ABC Enterprises, will deliver the speech.
>
> The Honorable Helen Masters, senator from Arizona, will deliver the speech.

If the name of a specific person is unavailable, you may address the letter to the department or to a specific position within the department. Also, be sure to spell out company names in full, unless the company itself uses abbreviations in its official name.

Other address information includes the treatment of buildings, house numbers, and compass directions (see Table A.3 on the next page). The following example shows all the information that may be included in the inside address and its proper order for U.S. correspondence:

> Ms. Linda Coolidge, Vice President
> Corporate Planning Department
> Midwest Airlines
> Kowalski Building, Suite 21-A
> 7279 Bristol Ave.
> Toledo, OH 43617

Canadian addresses are similar, except that the name of the province is usually spelled out:

> Dr. H. C. Armstrong
> Research and Development

Commonwealth Mining Consortium
The Chelton Building, Suite 301
585 Second St. SW
Calgary, Alberta T2P 2P5

The order and layout of address information vary from country to country. So when addressing correspondence for other countries, carefully follow the format and information that appear in the company's letterhead. However, when you're sending mail from the United States, be sure that the name of the destination country appears on the last line of the address in capital letters. Use the English version of the country name so that your mail is routed from the United States to the right country. Then, to be sure your mail is routed correctly within the destination country, use the foreign spelling of the city name (using the characters and diacritical marks that would be commonly used in the region). For example, the following address uses *Köln* instead of *Cologne*:

H. R. Veith, Director	Addressee
Eisfieren Glaswerk	Company name
Blaubachstrasse 13	Street address
Postfach 10 80 07	Post office road
D-5000 Köln I	District, city
GERMANY	Country

For additional examples of international addresses, see Table A.4 on page A-5.

Be sure to use organizational titles correctly when addressing international correspondence. Job designations vary around the world. In England, for example, a managing director is often what a U.S. company would call its chief executive officer or president, and a British deputy is the equivalent of a vice president. In France, responsibilities are assigned to individuals without regard to title or organizational structure, and in China the title *project manager* has meaning, but the title *sales manager* may not.

To make matters worse, businesspeople in some countries sign correspondence without their names typed below. In Germany, for example, the belief is that employees represent the company, so it's inappropriate to emphasize personal names.[4] Use the examples in Table A.4 as guidelines when addressing correspondence to countries outside the United States.

Salutation

In the salutation of your letter, follow the style of the first line of the inside address. If the first line is a person's name, the salutation is *Dear Mr.* or *Ms. Name*. The formality of the salutation depends on your relationship with the addressee. If in conversation you would say "Mary," your letter's salutation

TABLE A.2 Forms of Address

Person	In Address	In Salutation
Personal Titles		
Man	Mr. [first & last name]	Dear Mr. [last name]:
Woman*	Ms. [first & last name]	Dear Ms. [last name]:
Two men (or more)	Mr. [first & last name] and Mr. [first & last name]	Dear Mr. [last name] and Mr. [last name] *or* Messrs. [last name] and [last name]:
Two women (or more)	Ms. [first & last name] and Ms. [first & last name]	Dear Ms. [last name] and Ms. [last name] *or* Mses. [last name] and [last name]:
One woman and one man	Ms. [first & last name] and Mr. [first & last name]	Dear Ms. [last name] and Mr. [last name]:
Couple (married with same last name)	Mr. [husband's first name] and Mrs. [wife's first name] [couple's last name]	Dear Mr. and Mrs. [last name]:
Couple (married with different last names)	Mr. [first & last name of husband] Ms. [first & last name of wife]	Dear Mr. [husband's last name] and Ms. [wife's last name]:
Couple (married professionals with same title and same last name)	[title in plural form] [husband's first name] and [wife's first name] [couple's last name]	Dear [title in plural form] [last name]:
Couple (married professionals with different titles and same last name)	[title] [first & last name of husband] and [title] [first & last name of wife]	Dear [title] and [title] [last name]:
Professional Titles		
President of a college or university	[title] [first & last name], President	Dear [title] [last name]:
Dean of a school of college	Dean [first & last name] *or* Dr., Mr., *or* Ms. [first & last name], Dean of [title]	Dear Dean [last name]: *or* Dear Dr., Mr., *or* Ms. [last name]:
Professor	Professor *or* Dr. [first & last name]	Dear Professor *or* Dr. [last name]:
Physician	[first & last name], M.D.	Dear Dr. [last name]:
Lawyer	Mr. *or* Ms. [first & last name] Attorney at Law	Dear Mr. *or* Ms. [last name]:
Military personnel	[full rank, first & last name, abbreviation of service designation] (add *Retired* if applicable)	Dear [rank][last name]:
Company or corporation	[name of organization]	Ladies and Gentlemen: *or* Gentlemen and Ladies:
Governmental Titles		
President of the United States	The president	Dear Mr. *or* Madam President:
Senator of the United States	Honorable [first & last name]	Dear Senator [last name]:
Cabinet member	Honorable [first & last name]	Dear Mr. *or* Madam Secretary:
Postmaster General		Dear Mr. *or* Madam Postmaster General:
Attorney General		Dear Mr. *or* Madam Attorney General:
Mayor	Honorable [first & last name], Mayor of [name of city]	Dear Mayor [last name]:
Judge	The Honorable [first & last name]	Dear Judge [last name]:

*Use *Mrs.* or *Miss* only if the recipient has specifically requested that you use one of these titles; otherwise *always* use *Ms.* in business correspondence. Also, never refer to a married woman by her husband's name (e.g., Mrs. Robert Washington) unless she specifically requests that you do so.

TABLE A.3 Inside Address Information

Description	Example
Capitalize building names.	Empire State Building
Capitalize locations within buildings (apartments, suites, rooms).	Suite 1073
Use numerals for all house or building numbers, except the number one.	One Trinity Lane; 637 Adams Ave., Apt. 7
Spell out compass directions that fall within a street address	1074 West Connover St.
Abbreviate compass directions that follow the street address	783 Main St., N.E., Apt. 27

TABLE A.4 International Addresses and Salutations

Country	Postal Address	Address Elements	Salutations
Argentina	Sr. Juan Pérez Editorial Internacional S.A. Av. Sarmiento 1337, 8° P.C. C1035AAB BUENOS AIRES–CF ARGENTINA	S.A. = Sociedad Anónima (corporation) Av. Sarmiento (name of street) 1337 (building number) 8° – 8th. P = Piso (floor) C (room or suite) C1035AAB (postcode + city) CF = Capital Federal (federal capital)	Sr. = Señor (Mr.) Sra. = Señora (Mrs.) Srta. = Señorita (Miss) Don't use given names except with people you know well.
Australia	Mr. Roger Lewis International Publishing Pty. Ltd. 166 Kent Street, Level 9 GPO Box 3542 SYDNEY NSW 200 AUSTRALIA	Pty. Ltd. – Proprietory Limited (corp.) 166 (building number) Kent Street (name of street) Level (floor) GPO Box (P.O. box) City + state (abbrev.) + postcode	Mr. and Mrs. used on first contact. Ms. not common (avoid use). Business is informal—use given name freely.
Austria	Herrn Dipl.-Ing.J.Gerdenitsch International Verlag Ges.m.b.H. Glockengasse 159 1010 WIEN AUSTRIA	Herrn – To Mr. (separate line) Dipl.-Ing. (engineering degree) Ges.m.b.H. (a corporation) Glockengasse (street name) 159 (building number) 1010 (postcode + city) WIEN (Vienna)	Herr (Mr.) Frau (Mrs.) Fräulein (Miss) obsolete in business, so do not use. Given names are almost never used in business.
Brazil	Ilmo. Sr. Gllberto Rabello Ribeiro Editores Internacionais S.A. Rua da Ajuda, 228–6° Andar Caixa Postal 2574 20040–000 RIO DE JANEIRO–RJ BRAZIL	Ilmo. = Ilustrissimo (honorific) Ilma. = Ilustrissima (hon. female) S.A. – Sociedade Anônima (corporation) Rua = street, da Ajuda (street name) 228 (building number) 6° = 6th. Andar (floor) Caixa Postal (P.O. box) 20040–000 (postcode + city)–RJ (state abbrev.)	Sr. = Senhor (Mr.) Sra. = Senhora (Mrs.) Srta. = Senhorita (Miss) Family name at end, e.g., Senhor Ribeiro (Rabello is mother's family name) Given names readily used in business.
China	Xia Zhlyl International Publishing Ltd. 14 Jianguolu Chaoyangqu BEIJING 100025 CHINA	Ltd. (limited liability corporation) 14 (building number) Jianguolu (street name), lu (street) Chaoyangqu (district name) (city + postcode)	Family name (single syllable) first. Given name (2 syllables) second, sometimes reversed. Use Mr. or Ms. at all times (Mr. Xia).
France	Monsieur LEFÈVRE Alain Éditions Internationales S.A. Siège Social Immeuble Le Bonaparte 64–68, av. Galliéni B.P. 154 75942 PARIS CEDEX 19 FRANCE	S.A. = Société Anonyme (corporation) Siège Social (head office) Immeuble (building + name) 64–68 (building occupies 64, 66, 68) av. = avenue (no initial capital) B.P. = Boîte Postale (P.O. box) 75942 (postcode + city) CEDEX (postcode for P.O. box)	Monsieur (Mr.) Madame (Mrs.) Mademoiselle (Miss) Best not to abbreviate. Family name is sometimes in all caps with given name following.
Germany	Herrn Gerhardt Schneider International Verlag GmbH Schillerstraße 159 44147 DORTMUND GERMANY	Herrn = To Mr. (on a separate line) GmbH (inc.—incorporated) –straße (street—'ß' often written 'ss') 159 (building number) 44147 (postcode – city)	Herr (Mr.) Frau (Mrs.) Fräulein (Miss) obsolete in business. Business is formal: (1) do not use given names unless invited, and (2) use academic titles precisely.
India	Sr. Shyam Lal Gupta International Publishing (Pvt.) Ltd. 1820 Rehaja Centre 214, Darussalam Road Andheri East BOMBAY–400049 INDIA	(Pvt.) (privately owned) Ltd. (limited liability corporation) 1820 (possibly office #20 on 18th floor) Rehaja Centre (building name) 214 (building number) Andheri East (suburb name) (city + hyphen + postcode)	Shri (Mr.), Shrimati (Mrs.) but English is common business language, so use Mr., Mrs., Miss. Given names are used only by family and close friends.
Italy	Egr. Sig. Giacomo Mariotti Edizioni Internazionali S.p.A. Via Terenzio, 21 20138 MILANO ITALY	Egr. = Egregio (honorific) Sig. = Signor (not nec. a separate line) S.p.A. = Società per Azioni (corp.) Via (street) 21 (building number) 20138 (postcode + city)	Sig. = Signore (Mr.) Sig.ra = Signora (Mrs.) Sig.a (Ms.) Women in business are addressed as Signora. Use given name only when invited.

(Continued)

TABLE A.4 (*Continued*)

Country	Postal Address	Address Elements	Salutations
Japan	Mr. Taro Tanaka Kokusai Shuppan K.K. 10–23, 5-chome, Minamiazabu Minato-ku TOKYO 106 JAPAN	K.K. = Kabushiki Kaisha (corporation) 10 (lot number) 23 (building number) 5-chome (area #5) Minamiazabu (neighborhood name) Minato-ku (city district) (city + postcode)	Given names not used in business. Use family name + job title. Or use family name + "-san" (Tanaka-san) or more respectfully, add "-sama" or "-dono."
Korea	Mr. Kim Chang-ik International Publishers Ltd. Room 206, Korea Building 33–4 Nonhyon-dong Kangnam-ku SEOUL 135–010 KOREA	English company names common Ltd. (a corporation) 206 (office number inside the building) 33–4 (area 4 of subdivision 33) -dong (city neighborhood name) -ku (subdivision of city) (city + postcode)	Family name is normally first but sometimes placed after given name. A two-part name is the given name. Use Mr. or Mrs. in letters, but use job title in speech.
Mexico	Sr. Francisco Pérez Martínez Editores Internacionales S.A. Independencia No. 322 Col. Juárez 06050 MEXICO D.F.	S.A. – Sociedad Anónima (corporation) Independencia (street name) No. = Número (number) 322 (building number) Col. = Colonia (city district) Juárez (locality name) 06050 (postcode + city) D.F. = Distrito Federal (federal capital)	Sr. = Señor (Mr.) Sra. = Señora (Mrs.) Srta. = Señorita (Miss) Family name in middle: e.g., Sr. Pérez (Martínez is mother's family). Given names are used in business.
South Africa	Mr. Mandla Ntuli International Publishing (Pty.) Ltd. Private Bag X2581 JOHANNESBURG 2000 SOUTH AFRICA	Pty. = Proprietory (privately owned) Ltd. (a corporation) Private Bag (P.O. Box) (city + postcode) or (postcode + city)	Mnr. = Meneer (Mr.) Mev. = Mevrou (Mrs.) Mejuffrou (Miss) is not used in business. Business is becoming less formal, so the use of given names is possible.
United Kingdom	Mr. N. J. Lancaster International Publishing Ltd. Kingsbury House 12 Kingsbury Road EDGEWARE Middlesex HA8 9XG ENGLAND	N. J. (initials of given names) Ltd. (limited liability corporation) Kingsbury House (building name) 12 (building number) Kingsbury Road (name of street/road) EDGEWARE (city—all caps) Middlesex (county—not all caps) HA8 9XG	Mr. and Ms. used mostly. Mrs. and Miss sometimes used in North and by older women. Given names—called Christian names—are used in business after some time. Wait to be invited.

should be *Dear Mary*, followed by a colon. Otherwise, include the courtesy title and last name, followed by a colon. Presuming to write *Dear Lewis* instead of *Dear Professor Chang* demonstrates a disrespectful familiarity that the recipient will probably resent.

If the first line of the inside address is a position title such as *Director of Personnel*, then use *Dear Director*. If the addressee is unknown, use a polite description, such as *Dear Alumnus*, *Dear SPCA Supporter*, or *Dear Voter*. If the first line is plural (a department or company), then use *Ladies and Gentlemen* (look again at Table A.2). When you do not know whether you're writing to an individual or a group (for example, when writing a reference or a letter of recommendation), use *To whom it may concern*.

In the United States some letter writers use a "salutopening" on the salutation line. A salutopening omits *Dear* but includes the first few words of the opening paragraph along with the recipient's name. After this line, the sentence continues a double space below as part of the body of the letter, as in these examples:

Thank you, Mr. Brown,
for your prompt payment of your bill.   Salutopening Body
Congratulations, Ms. Lake!
Your promotion is well deserved.   Salutopening Body

Whether your salutation is informal or formal, be especially careful that names are spelled correctly. A misspelled name is glaring evidence of carelessness, and it belies the personal interest you're trying to express.

Body

The body of the letter is your message. Almost all letters are single-spaced, with one blank line before and after the salutation or salutopening, between paragraphs, and before the complimentary close. The body may include indented lists, entire paragraphs indented for emphasis, and even subheadings. If it does, all similar elements should be treated in the same way. Your department or company may select a format to use for all letters.

Complimentary Close

The complimentary close begins on the second line below the body of the letter. Alternatives for wording are available, but currently the trend seems to be toward using one-word closes, such as *Sincerely* and *Cordially*. In any case, the complimentary close reflects the relationship between you and the person you're writing to. Avoid cute closes, such as *Yours for bigger profits*. If your audience doesn't know you well, your sense of humor may be misunderstood.

Signature Block

Leave three blank lines for a written signature below the complimentary close, and then include the sender's name (unless it appears in the letterhead). The person's title may appear on the same line as the name or on the line below:

Cordially,

Raymond Dunnigan
Director of Personnel

Your letterhead indicates that you're representing your company. However, if your letter is on plain paper or runs to a second page, you may want to emphasize that you're speaking legally for the company. The accepted way of doing that is to place the company's name in capital letters a double space below the complimentary close and then include the sender's name and title four lines below that:

Sincerely,
WENTWORTH INDUSTRIES

(Ms.) Helen B. Taylor
President

If your name could be taken for either a man's or a woman's, a courtesy title indicating gender should be included, with or without parentheses. Also, women who prefer a particular courtesy title should include it:

Mrs. Nancy Winters
(Ms.) Juana Flores
Ms. Pat Li
(Mr.) Jamie Saunders

Additional Letter Parts

Letters vary greatly in subject matter and thus in the identifying information they need and the format they adopt. The letter in Figure A.2 on the next page shows how these additional parts should be arranged. The following elements may be used in any combination, depending on the requirements of the particular letter:

- **Addressee notation.** Letters that have a restricted readership or that must be handled in a special way should include such addressee notations as *PERSONAL, CONFIDENTIAL, or PLEASE FORWARD*. This sort of notation appears a double space above the inside address, in all-capital letters.

- **Attention line.** Although not commonly used today, an attention line can be used if you know only the last name of the person you're writing to. It can also direct a letter to a position title or department. Place the attention line on the first line of the inside address and put the company name on the second.[5] Match the address on the envelope with the style of the inside address. An attention line may take any of the following forms or variants of them:

Attention Dr. McHenry

Attention Director of Marketing

Attention Marketing Department

- **Subject line.** The subject line tells recipients at a glance what the letter is about (and indicates where to file the letter for future reference). It usually appears below the salutation, either against the left margin, indented (as a paragraph in the body), or centered. It can be placed above the salutation or at the very top of the page, and it can be underscored. Some businesses omit the word *Subject*, and some organizations replace it with *Re:* or *In re:* (meaning "concerning" or "in the matter of"). The subject line may take a variety of forms, including the following:

Subject: RainMaster Sprinklers

About your February 2, 2011, order

FALL 2011 SALES MEETING

Reference Order No. 27920

- **Second-page heading.** Use a second-page heading whenever an additional page is required. Some companies have second-page letterhead (with the company name and address on one line and in a smaller typeface). The heading bears the name (person or organization) from the first line of the inside address, the page number, the date, and perhaps a reference number. Leave two blank lines before the body. Make sure that at least two lines of a continued paragraph appear on the first and second pages. Never allow the closing lines to appear alone on a continued page. Precede the complimentary close or signature lines with at least two lines of the body. Also, don't hyphenate the last word on a page. All the following are acceptable forms for second-page headings:

Ms. Melissa Baker
May 10, 2011
Page 2

Ms. Melissa Baker, May 10, 2011, Page 2

Ms. Melissa Baker   -2-   May 10, 2011

- **Company name.** If you include the company's name in the signature block, put it a double space below the complimentary close. You usually include the company's name in the signature block only when the writer is serving as the company's official spokesperson or when letterhead has not been used.

- **Reference initials.** When businesspeople keyboard their own letters, reference initials are unnecessary, so they are becoming rare. When one person dictates a letter and another person produces it, reference initials show who helped prepare it. Place initials at the left margin, a double space below the signature block. When the signature block includes the writer's name, use only the preparer's initials. If the signature block includes only the department, use both sets of initials, usually in one of the following forms: *RSR/sm, RSR:sm, or RSR:SM* (writer/preparer). When the writer and the signer are different people, at least the file copy should bear both their initials as well as the typist's: *JFS/RSR/sm* (signer/writer/preparer).

- **Enclosure notation.** Enclosure notations appear at the bottom of a letter, one or two lines below the reference initials. Some common forms include the following:

Enclosure

Enclosures (2)

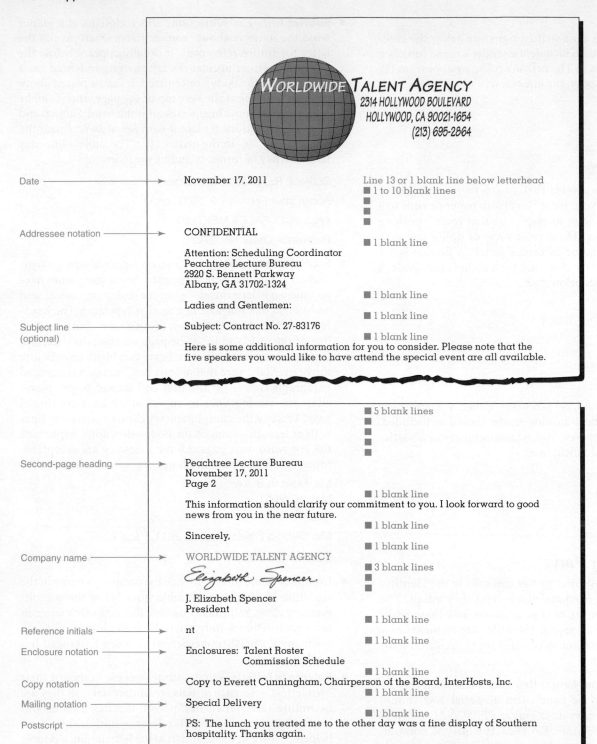

WORLDWIDE TALENT AGENCY
2314 HOLLYWOOD BOULEVARD
HOLLYWOOD, CA 90021-1654
(213) 695-2864

Date → November 17, 2011   Line 13 or 1 blank line below letterhead
                                            ■ 1 to 10 blank lines
                                            ■
                                            ■
                                            ■

Addressee notation → CONFIDENTIAL   ■ 1 blank line

Attention: Scheduling Coordinator
Peachtree Lecture Bureau
2920 S. Bennett Parkway
Albany, GA 31702-1324   ■ 1 blank line

Ladies and Gentlemen: ■ 1 blank line

Subject line → Subject: Contract No. 27-83176   ■ 1 blank line
(optional)
Here is some additional information for you to consider. Please note that the
five speakers you would like to have attend the special event are all available.

                                            ■ 5 blank lines
                                            ■
                                            ■
                                            ■
                                            ■

Second-page heading → Peachtree Lecture Bureau
November 17, 2011
Page 2   ■ 1 blank line

This information should clarify our commitment to you. I look forward to good
news from you in the near future.   ■ 1 blank line

Sincerely,   ■ 1 blank line

Company name → WORLDWIDE TALENT AGENCY   ■ 3 blank lines
                                            ■
Elizabeth Spencer   ■

J. Elizabeth Spencer
President

Reference initials → nt   ■ 1 blank line

Enclosure notation → Enclosures: Talent Roster   ■ 1 blank line
                       Commission Schedule
                                            ■ 1 blank line
Copy notation → Copy to Everett Cunningham, Chairperson of the Board, InterHosts, Inc.
                                            ■ 1 blank line
Mailing notation → Special Delivery
                                            ■ 1 blank line
Postscript → PS: The lunch you treated me to the other day was a fine display of Southern
hospitality. Thanks again.

Figure A.2   Additional Letter Parts

Enclosures: Résumé

   Photograph

   Brochure

■ **Copy notation.** Copy notations may follow reference initials or enclosure notations. They indicate who's receiving a *courtesy copy* (*cc*). Recipients are listed in order of rank or (rank being equal) in alphabetical order. Among the forms used are the following:

cc: David Wentworth, Vice President

Copy to Hans Vogel

748 Chesterton Road

Snohomish, WA 98290

■ **Mailing notation.** You may place a mailing notation (such as *Special Delivery* or *Registered Mail*) at the bottom of the letter, after reference initials or enclosure notations (whichever is last) and before copy notations. Or you may place it at the top of the letter, either above the inside address on the left side or just below the date on the right side. For greater visibility, mailing notations may appear in capital letters.

- **Postscript.** A postscript is presented as an afterthought to the letter, a message that requires emphasis, or a personal note. It is usually the last thing on any letter and may be preceded by *P.S., PS., PS:,* or nothing at all. A second afterthought would be designated *P.P.S.* (post postscript).

Letter Formats

A letter format is the way of arranging all the basic letter parts. Sometimes a company adopts a certain format as its policy; sometimes the individual letter writer or preparer is allowed to choose the most appropriate format. In the United States, three major letter formats are commonly used:

- **Block format.** Each letter part begins at the left margin. The main advantage is quick and efficient preparation (see Figure A.3).

- **Modified block format.** Same as block format, except that the date, complimentary close, and signature block start near the center of the page (see Figure A.4 on the next page). The modified block format does permit indentions as an option. This format mixes preparation speed with traditional placement of some letter parts. It also looks more balanced on the page than the block format does.

- **Simplified format.** Instead of using a salutation, this format often weaves the reader's name into the first line or two of the body and often includes a subject line in capital letters (see Figure A.5 on page 445). This format does not include a complimentary close, so your signature appears immediately below the body text. Because certain letter parts are eliminated, some line spacing is changed.

These three formats differ in the way paragraphs are indented, in the way letter parts are placed, and in some punctuation. However, the elements are always separated by at least one blank line, and the printed name is always

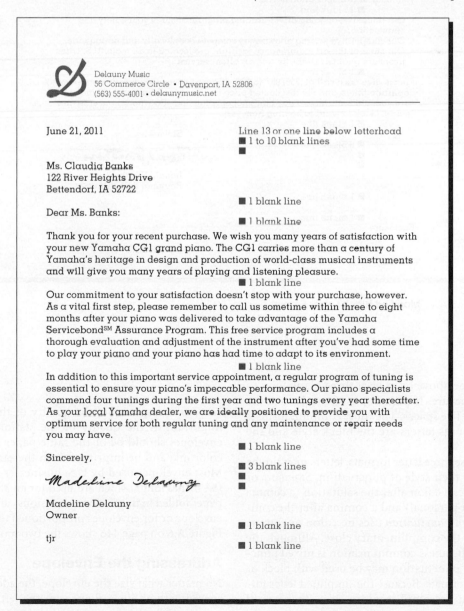

Figure A.3 Block Letter Format

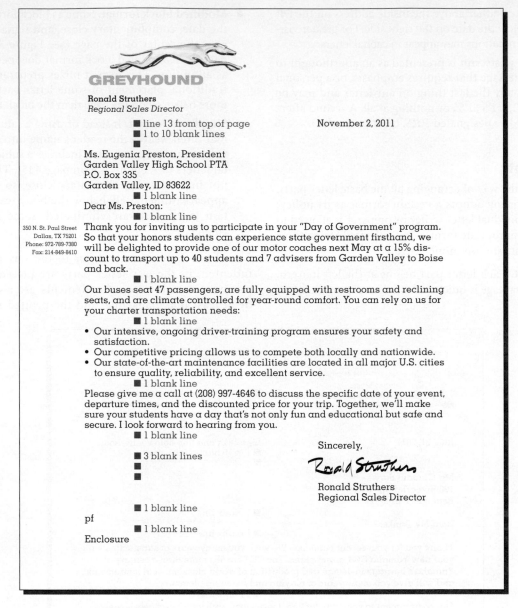

Figure A.4　Modified Block Letter Format

separated from the line above by at least three blank lines to allow space for a signature. If paragraphs are indented, the indention is normally five spaces. The most common formats for intercultural business letters are the block style and the modified block style.

In addition to these three letter formats, letters may also be classified according to their style of punctuation. *Standard*, or *mixed, punctuation* uses a colon after the salutation (a comma if the letter is social or personal) and a comma after the complimentary close. *Open punctuation* uses no colon or comma after the salutation or the complimentary close. Although the most popular style in business communication is mixed punctuation, either style of punctuation may be used with block or modified block letter formats. Because the simplified letter format has no salutation or complimentary close, the style of punctuation is irrelevant.

ENVELOPES

For a first impression, the quality of the envelope is just as important as the quality of the stationery. Letterhead and envelopes should be of the same paper stock, have the same color ink, and be imprinted with the same address and logo. Most envelopes used by U.S. businesses are No. 10 envelopes (9½ inches long), which are sized for an 8½-by-11-inch piece of paper folded in thirds. Some occasions call for a smaller, No. 6¾, envelope or for envelopes proportioned to fit special stationery. Figure A.6 on page 446 shows the two most common sizes.

Addressing the Envelope

No matter what size the envelope, the address is always single-spaced with all lines aligned on the left. The address on the envelope is in the same style as the inside address and presents

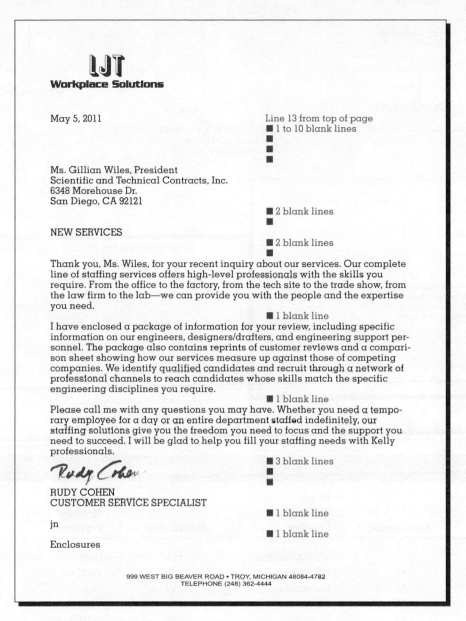

Figure A.5   Simplified Letter Format

the same information. The order to follow is from the smallest division to the largest:

1. Name and title of recipient
2. Name of department or subgroup
3. Name of organization
4. Name of building
5. Street address and suite number, or post office box number
6. City, state, or province, and zip code or postal code
7. Name of country (if the letter is being sent abroad)

Because the U.S. Postal Service uses optical scanners to sort mail, envelopes for quantity mailings, in particular, should be addressed in the prescribed format. Everything is in capital letters, no punctuation is included, and all mailing instructions of interest to the post office are placed above the address area (see Figure A.6). Canada Post requires a similar format, except that only the city is all in capitals, and the postal code is placed on the line below the name of the city. The post office scanners read addresses from the bottom up, so if a letter is to be sent to a post office box rather than to a street address, the street address should appear on the line above the box number. Figure A.6 also shows the proper spacing for addresses and return addresses.

The U.S. Postal Service and the Canada Post Corporation have published lists of two-letter mailing abbreviations for states, provinces, and territories (see Table A.5 on the next page). Postal authorities prefer no punctuation with these abbreviations. Quantity mailings should always follow post office requirements. For other letters, a reasonable compromise is to use traditional punctuation, uppercase and lowercase letters for names and street addresses, but two-letter state or province abbreviations, as shown here:

Mr. Kevin Kennedy

2107 E. Packer Dr.

Amarillo, TX 79108

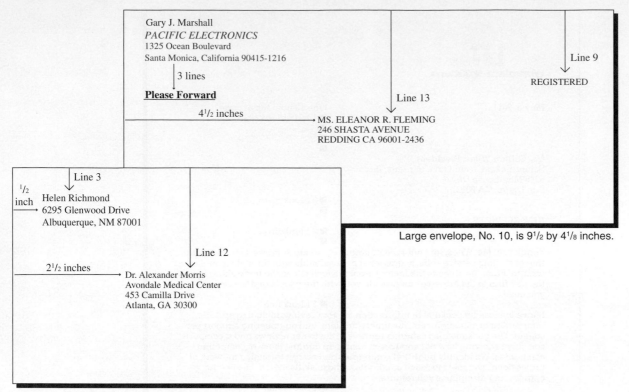

Figure A.6   **Prescribed Envelope Format**

State/Territory/Province	Abbreviation	State/Territory/Province	Abbreviation	State/Territory/Province	Abbreviation
TABLE A.5 Two-Letter Mailing Abbreviations for the United States and Canada					
United States		Massachusetts	MA	Utah	UT
Alabama	AL	Michigan	MI	Vermont	VT
Alaska	AK	Minnesota	MN	Virginia	VA
American Samoa	AS	Mississippi	MS	Virgin Islands	VI
Arizona	AZ	Missouri	MO	Washington	WA
Arkansas	AR	Montana	MT	West Virginia	WV
California	CA	Nebraska	NE	Wisconsin	WI
Canal Zone	CZ	Nevada	NV	Wyoming	WY
Colorado	CO	New Hampshire	NH	**Canada**	
Connecticut	CT	New Jersey	NJ	Alberta	AB
Delaware	DE	New Mexico	NM	British Columbia	BC
District of Columbia	DC	New York	NY	Labrador	NL
Florida	FL	North Carolina	NC	Manitoba	MB
Georgia	GA	North Dakota	ND	New Brunswick	NB
Guam	GU	Northern Mariana	MP	Newfoundland	NL
Hawaii	HI	Ohio	OH	Northwest Territories	NT
Idaho	ID	Oklahoma	OK	Nova Scotia	NS
Illinois	IL	Oregon	OR	Nunavur	NU
Indiana	IN	Pennsylvania	PA	Ontario	ON
Iowa	IA	Puerto Rico	PR	Prince Edward Island	PE
Kansas	KS	Rhode Island	RI	Quebec	PQ
Kentucky	KY	South Carolina	SC	Saskatchewan	SK
Louisiana	LA	South Dakota	SD	Yukon Territory	YT
Maine	ME	Tennessee	TN		
Maryland	MD	Texas	TX		

Canadian postal codes are alphanumeric, with a three-character "area code" and a three-character "local code" separated by a single space (K2P 5A5). Zip and postal codes should be separated from state and province names by one space. Canadian postal codes may be treated the same or may be put in the bottom line of the address all by itself.

Folding to Fit

The way a letter is folded also contributes to the recipient's overall impression of your organization's professionalism. When sending a standard-size piece of paper in a No. 10 envelope, fold it in thirds, with the bottom folded up first and the top folded down over it (see Figure A.7); the open end should be at the top of the envelope and facing out. Fit smaller stationery neatly into the appropriate envelope simply by folding it in half or in thirds. When sending a standard-size letterhead in a No. 6¾ envelope, fold it in half from top to bottom and then in thirds from side to side.

International Mail

Postal service differs from country to country, so it's always a good idea to investigate the quality and availability of various services before sending messages and packages internationally. Also, compare the services offered by delivery companies such as UPS and FedEx to find the best rates and options for each destination and type of shipment. No matter which service you choose, be aware that international mail requires more planning than domestic mail. For example, for anything beyond simple letters, you generally need to prepare *customs forms* and possibly other documents, depending on the country of destination and the type of shipment. You are responsible for following the laws of the United States and any countries to which you send mail and packages.

The U.S. Postal Service currently offers four classes of international delivery, listed here from the fastest (and most expensive) to the slowest (and least expensive):

- **Global Express Guaranteed** is the fastest option. This service, offered in conjunction with FedEx, provides delivery in one to three business days to more than 190 countries and territories.
- **Express Mail International** guarantees delivery in three to five business days to a limited number of countries, including Australia, China, Hong Kong, Japan, and South Korea.
- **Priority Mail International** offers delivery guarantees of 6 to 10 business days to more than 190 countries and territories.
- **First Class Mail International** is an economical way to send correspondence and packages weighing up to four pounds to virtually any destination worldwide.

To prepare your mail for international delivery, follow the instructions provided at www.usps.com/international. There you'll find complete information on the international services available through the U.S. Postal Service, along with advice on addressing and packaging mail, completing customs forms, and calculating postage rates and fees. The *International Mail Manual*, also available on this website, offers the latest information and regulations for both outbound and inbound international mail. For instance, you can click on individual country names to see current information about restricted or prohibited items and materials, required customs forms, and rates for various classes of service.[5] Various countries have specific and often extensive lists of items that may not be sent by mail at all or that must be sent using particular postal service options.

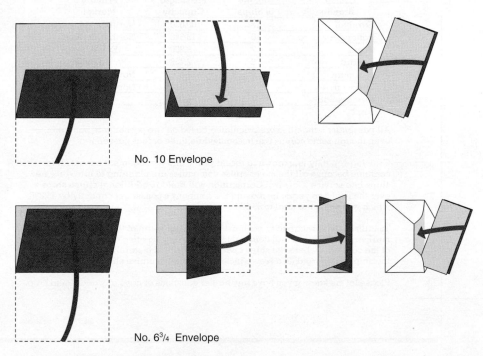

No. 10 Envelope

No. 6³/₄ Envelope

Figure A.7   Folding Standard-Size Letterhead

MEMOS

Electronic media have replaced most internal printed memos in many companies, but you may have occasion to send printed memos from time to time. These can be simple announcements or messages, or they can be short reports using the memo format (see Figure A.8).

On your document, include a title such as MEMO or INTEROFFICE CORRESPONDENCE (all in capitals) centered at the top of the page or aligned with the left margin. Also at the top, include the words *To, From, Date,* and *Subject*—followed by the appropriate information—with a blank line between as shown here:

MEMO

TO:
FROM:
DATE:
SUBJECT:

Sometimes the heading is organized like this:

MEMO

TO:	DATE:
FROM:	SUBJECT:

The following guidelines will help you effectively format specific memo elements:

- **Addressees.** When sending a memo to a long list of people, include the notation *See distribution list* or *See below* in the *To* position at the top; then list the names at the end of the memo. Arrange this list alphabetically, except when high-ranking officials deserve more prominent placement. You can also address memos to groups of people—*All Sales Representatives, Production Group, New Product Team.*

- **Courtesy titles.** You need not use courtesy titles anywhere in a memo; first initials and last names, first names, or even initials alone are often sufficient. However, use a courtesy

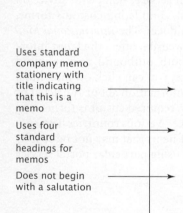

Uses standard company memo stationery with title indicating that this is a memo

Uses four standard headings for memos

Does not begin with a salutation

Carnival
INTERNAL MEMORANDUM

TO: Lauren Eastman
FROM: Brad Lymans
DATE: June 11, 2011
SUBJECT: Capacity for Carnival Corporation Cruise Ships

Here is the capacity data you requested along with a brief explanation of the figures:

Cruise Brand	Number of Ships	Passenger Capacity	Primary Market
Carnival	15	30,020	North America
Holland America	10	13,348	North America
Costa	7	9,200	Europe
Cunard	2	2,458	Worldwide
Seabourn	6	1,614	North America
Windstar	4	756	North America
Airtours-Sun	4	4,352	Europe
Total	48	61,748	

All passenger capacities are calculated based on two passengers per cabin, even though some cabins can accommodate three or four passengers.

Cruising capacity has grown in recent years, and management expects it to continue because all the major cruise companies are planning to introduce new ships into service. Carnival Corporation will build 16 additional cruise ships over the next five years, increasing the company's passenger capacity by 36,830, which will bring the total to 98,578.

To utilize this new capacity, we must increase our share of the overall vacation market. Keep in mind that demand for cruises may be affected by (1) the strength of the countries where the ships operate; (2) political instability in areas where the ships travel; and (3) adverse incidents involving cruise ships in general.

Please let me know if you have any further questions or need any additional data.

Does not include a complimentary close or a signature block

Figure A.8   Short Report Using the Memo Format

title if you would use one in a face-to-face encounter with the person.

- **Subject line.** The subject line of a memo helps busy colleagues quickly find out what your memo is about, so take care to make it concise and compelling.

- **Body.** Start the body of the memo on the second or third line below the heading. Like the body of a letter, it's usually single-spaced with blank lines between paragraphs. Indenting paragraphs is optional. Handle lists, important passages, and subheadings as you do in letters.

- **Second page.** If the memo carries over to a second page, head the second page just as you head the second page of a letter.

- **Writer's initials.** Unlike a letter, a memo doesn't require a complimentary close or a signature, because your name is already prominent at the top. However, you may initial the memo—either beside the name appearing at the top of the memo or at the bottom of the memo.

- **Other elements.** Treat elements such as reference initials and copy notations just as you would in a letter. One difference between letters and memos is that while letters use the term *enclosure* to refer to other pieces included with the letter, memos usually use the word *attachment*.

Memos may be delivered by hand, by the post office (when the recipient works at a different location), or through interoffice mail. Interoffice mail may require the use of special reusable envelopes that have spaces for the recipient's name and department or room number; the name of the previous recipient is simply crossed out. If a regular envelope is used, the words *Interoffice Mail* appear where the stamp normally goes, so that it won't accidentally be stamped and mailed with the rest of the office correspondence.

Informal, routine, or brief reports for distribution within a company are often presented in memo form. Don't include report parts such as a table of contents and appendixes, but write the body of the memo report just as carefully as you'd write a formal report.

REPORTS

Enhance the effectiveness of your reports by paying careful attention to their appearance and layout. Follow whatever guidelines your organization prefers, always being neat and consistent throughout. If it's up to you to decide formatting questions, the following conventions may help you decide how to handle margins, headings, and page numbers.

Margins

All margins on a report page should be at least 1 inch wide. The top, left, and right margins are usually the same, but the bottom margins can be 1½ times deeper. Some special pages also have deeper top margins. Set top margins as deep as 2 inches for pages that contain major titles: prefatory parts (such as the table of contents or the executive summary), supplementary parts (such as the reference notes or bibliography), and textual parts (such as the first page of the text or the first page of each chapter).

If you're going to bind your report at the left or at the top, add half an inch to the margin on the bound edge (see Figure A.9): The

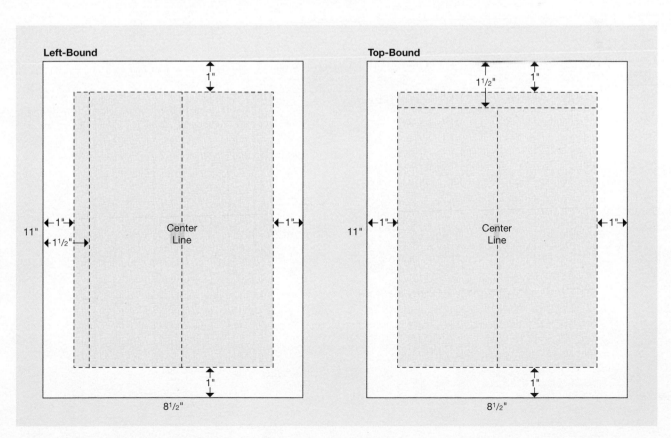

Figure A.9   Margins for Formal Reports

space taken by the binding on left-bound reports makes the center point of the text a quarter inch to the right of the center of the paper. Be sure to center headings between the margins, not between the edges of the paper.

Headings

If you don't have a template supplied by your employer, choose a design for headings and subheadings that clearly distinguishes the various levels in the hierarchy. The first-level headings should be the most prominent, on down to the lowest-level subheading.

Page Numbers

Every page in a report is counted; however, not all pages show numbers. The first page of the report, normally the title page, is unnumbered. All other pages in the prefatory section are numbered with a lowercase roman numeral, beginning with *ii* and continuing with *iii, iv, v,* and so on. Start numbering again with arabic numerals (1, 2, and so on) starting at the first page of the body.

You have many options for placing and formatting the page numbers, although these choices are usually made for you in a template. If you're not using a standard company template, position the page number where it is easy to see as the reader flips through the report. If the report will be stapled or otherwise bound along the left side, for instance, the best place for the page number is the upper right or lower right corner.

Appendix B

Documentation of Report Sources

By providing information about your sources, you improve your own credibility as well as the credibility of the facts and opinions you present. Documentation gives readers the means for checking your findings and pursuing the subject further. Also, documenting your report is the accepted way to give credit to the people whose work you have drawn from.

What style should you use to document your report? Experts recommend various forms, depending on your field or discipline. Moreover, your employer or client may use a form different from those the experts suggest. Don't let this discrepancy confuse you. If your employer specifies a form, use it; the standardized form is easier for colleagues to understand. However, if the choice of form is left to you, adopt one of the styles described here. Whatever style you choose, be consistent within any given report, using the same order, punctuation, and format from one reference citation or bibliography entry to the next.

A wide variety of style manuals provide detailed information on documentation. These publications explain the three most commonly used styles:

- American Psychological Association, *Publication Manual of the American Psychological Association*, 6th ed. (Washington, D.C.: American Psychological Association, 2009). Details the author-date system, which is preferred in the social sciences and often in the natural sciences as well.

- *The Chicago Manual of Style*, 16th ed. (Chicago: University of Chicago Press, 2010). Often referred to only as "*Chicago*" and widely used in the publishing industry; provides detailed treatment of source documentation and many other aspects of document preparation.

- Joseph Gibaldi, *MLA Style Manual and Guide to Scholarly Publishing*, 3rd ed. (New York: Modern Language Association, 2008). Serves as the basis for the note and bibliography style used in much academic writing and is recommended in many college textbooks on writing term papers; provides a lot of examples in the humanities.

For more information on these three guides, visit http://real-timeupdates.com/bce5 and click on Appendix B. Although many schemes have been proposed for organizing the information in source notes, all of them break the information into parts: (1) information about the author (name), (2) information about the work (title, edition, volume number), (3) information about the publication (place, publisher), (4) information about the date, and (5) information on relevant page ranges.

The following sections summarize the major conventions for documenting sources in three styles: *The Chicago Manual of Style* (Chicago), the *Publication Manual of the American Psychological Association* (APA), and the *MLA Style Manual* (MLA).

CHICAGO HUMANITIES STYLE

The Chicago Manual of Style recommends two types of documentation systems. The *documentary-note*, or *humanities*, style gives bibliographic citations in notes—either footnotes (when printed at the bottom of a page) or endnotes (when printed at the end of the report). The humanities system is often used in literature, history, and the arts. The other system recommended by *Chicago* is the *author-date* system, which cites the author's last name and the date of publication in the text, usually in parentheses, reserving full documentation for the reference list (or bibliography). For the purpose of comparing styles, this section concentrates on the humanities system, which is described in detail in *Chicago*.

In-Text Citation—Chicago Humanities Style

To document report sources in text, the humanities system relies on superscripts—arabic numerals placed just above the line of type at the end of the reference:

> Toward the end of his speech, Myers sounded a note of caution, saying that even though the economy is expected to grow, it could easily slow a bit.[10]

The superscript lets the reader know how to look for source information in either a footnote or an endnote (see Figure B.1 on the next page). Some readers prefer footnotes so that they can simply glance at the bottom of the page for information. Others prefer endnotes so that they can read the text without a clutter of notes on the page. Also, endnotes relieve the writer from worrying about how long each note will be and how much space it will take away from the page. Both footnotes and endnotes are handled automatically by today's word processing software.

For the reader's convenience, you can use footnotes for **content notes** (which may supplement your main text with asides about a particular issue or event, provide a cross-reference to another section of your report, or direct the reader to a related source). Then you can use endnotes for **source notes** (which document direct quotations, paraphrased passages, and visual aids). Consider which type of note is most common in your report, and then choose whether to present these notes all as endnotes or all as footnotes. Regardless of the method you choose for referencing textual information in your report, notes for visual aids (both content notes and source notes) are placed on the same page as the visual.

Bibliography—Chicago Humanities Style

The humanities system may or may not be accompanied by a bibliography (because the notes give all the necessary bibliographic information). However, endnotes are arranged

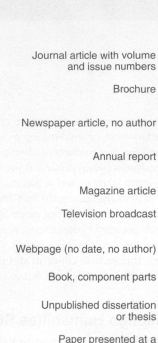

	NOTES
Journal article with volume and issue numbers	1. Jonathan Clifton, "Beyond Taxonomies of Influence," *Journal of Business Communication* 46, no. 1 (2009): 57–79.
Brochure	2. BestTemp Staffing Services, *An Employer's Guide to Staffing Services,* 2d ed. (Denver: BestTemp Information Center, 2008), 31.
Newspaper article, no author	3. "Might Be Harder Than It Looks," *Los Angeles Times,* 30 January 2009, sec. A, p. 22.
Annual report	4. The Walt Disney Company, *2007 Annual Report* (Burbank, Calif.: The Walt Disney Company, 2008), 48.
Magazine article	5. Kerry A. Dolan, "A Whole New Crop" *Forbes,* 2 June 2008, 72–75.
Television broadcast	6. Daniel Han, "Trade Wars Heating Up Around the Globe," *CNN Headline News* (Atlanta: CNN, 5 March 2002).
Webpage (no date, no author)	7. Nordstrom, "Company History," Nordstrom.com (accessed 16 August 2010).
Book, component parts	8. Sonja Kuntz, "Moving Beyond Benefits," in *Our Changing Workforce,* ed. Randolf Jacobson (New York: Citadel Press, 2001), 213–27.
Unpublished dissertation or thesis	9. George H. Morales, "The Economic Pressures on Industrialized Nations in a Global Economy" (Ph.D. diss., University of San Diego, 2001), 32–47.
Paper presented at a meeting	10. Charles Myers, "HMOs in Today's Environment" (paper presented at the Conference on Medical Insurance Solutions, Chicago, Ill., August 2001), 16–17.
Online magazine article	11. Leo Babauta, "17 Tips to Be Productive with Instant Messaging," in *Web Worker Daily* [online] (San Francisco, 2007 [updated 14 November 2007; cited 14 February 2008]); available from http://webworkerdaily.com.
Online encyclopedia	12. "Capitalism," *Encyclopædia Britannica Online* http://www.britannica.com/EBchecked/topic/93927/capitalism (accessed 16 August 2010).
Online encyclopedia Interview	13. Georgia Stainer, general manager, Day Cable and Communications, interview by author, Topeka, Kan., 2 March 2000.
Newspaper article, one author	14. Evelyn Standish, "Global Market Crushes OPEC's Delicate Balance of Interests," *Wall Street Journal,* 19 January 2002, sec. A, p. 1.
Book, two authors	15. Miriam Toller and Jay Fielding, *Global Business for Smaller Companies* (Rocklin, Calif.: Prima Publishing, 2001), 102–3.
Government publication	16. U.S. Department of Defense, *Stretching Research Dollars: Survival Advice for Universities and Government Labs* (Washington, D.C.: GPO, 2002), 126.
Blog post	17. David Meerman Scott, "Offering Unique Experiences Generates Attention for Nonprofits," WebInkNow (blog), 9 August 2010, http://www.webinknow.com.

Figure B.1   Sample Endnotes—*Chicago* Humanities Style

in order of appearance in the text, so an alphabetical bibliography can be valuable to your readers. The bibliography may be titled *Bibliography, Reference List, Sources, Works Cited* (if you include only those sources you actually cited in your report), or *Works Consulted* (if you include uncited sources as well). This list of sources may also serve as a reading list for those who want to pursue the subject of your report further, so you may want to annotate each entry—that is, comment on the subject matter and viewpoint of the source, as well as on its usefulness to readers. Annotations may be written in either complete or incomplete sentences. (See the annotated list of style manuals earlier in this appendix.) A bibliography may also be more manageable if you subdivide it into categories (a classified bibliography), either by type of reference (such as books, articles, and unpublished material) or by

subject matter (such as government regulation, market forces, and so on). Following are the major conventions for developing a bibliography according to *Chicago* style (see Figure B.2):

- Exclude any page numbers that may be cited in source notes, except for journals, periodicals, and newspapers.
- Alphabetize entries by the last name of the lead author (listing last name first). The names of second and succeeding authors are listed in normal order. Entries without an author name are alphabetized by the first important word in the title.
- Format entries as hanging indents (indent second and succeeding lines three to five spaces).

BIBLIOGRAPHY

Online encyclopedia	"Capitalism," *Encyclopædia Britannica Online* http://www.britannica.com/EBchecked/topic/93927/capitalism (accessed 16 August 2010).
Journal article with volume and issue numbers	Clifton, Jonathan. "Beyond Taxonomies of Influence." *Journal of Business Communication* 46, no. 1 (2009): 57–79.
Website	"Company History," Nordstrom (accessed 16 August 2010) http://www.nordstrom.com.
Online magazine article	Babauta, Leo. "17 Tips to Be Productive with Instant Messaging," In *Web Worker Daily* [online], San Francisco, 2007 [updated 14 November 2007, cited 14 February 2008]. Available from http://webworkerdaily.com.
Brochure	BestTemp Staffing Services. *An Employer's Guide to Staffing Services.* 2d ed. Denver: BestTemp Information Center, 2008.
Newspaper article, no author	"Might Be Harder Than It Looks." *Los Angeles Times,* 30 January 2009, sec. A, p. 22.
Magazine article	Dolan, Kerry A. "A Whole New Crop," *Forbes,* 2 June 2008, 72–75.
Television broadcast	Han, Daniel. "Trade Wars Heating Up Around the Globe." *CNN Headline News.* Atlanta: CNN, 5 March 2002.
Book, component parts	Kuntz, Sonja. "Moving Beyond Benefits." In *Our Changing Workforce*, edited by Randolf Jacobson. New York: Citadel Press, 2001.
Unpublished dissertation or thesis	Morales, George H. "The Economic Pressures on Industrialized Nations in a Global Economy." Ph.D. diss., University of San Diego, 2001.
Paper presented at a meeting	Myers, Charles. "HMOs in Today's Environment." Paper presented at the Conference on Medical Insurance Solutions, Chicago, Ill., August 2001.
Blog post	Scott, David Meerman. "Offering Unique Experiences Generates Attention for Nonprofits," WebInkNow (blog), 9 August 2010, http://www.webinknow.com.
Interview	Stainer, Georgia, general manager, Day Cable and Communications. Interview by author. Topeka, Kan., 2 March 2000.
Newspaper article, one author	Standish, Evelyn. "Global Market Crushes OPEC's Delicate Balance of Interests." *Wall Street Journal,* 19 January 2002, sec. A, p. 1.
Book, two authors	Toller, Miriam, and Jay Fielding. *Global Business for Smaller Companies.* Rocklin, Calif.: Prima Publishing, 2001.
Government publication	U.S. Department of Defense. *Stretching Research Dollars: Survival Advice for Universities and Government Labs.* Washington, D.C.: GPO, 2002.
Annual report	The Walt Disney Company, *2007 Annual Report,* Burbank, Calif.: The Walt Disney Company, 2008.

Figure B.2   Sample Bibliography—Chicago Humanities Style

- Arrange entries in the following general order: (1) author name, (2) title information, (3) publication information, (4) date, (5) periodical page range.

- Use quotation marks around the titles of articles from magazines, newspapers, and journals. Capitalize the first and last words, as well as all other important words (except prepositions, articles, and coordinating conjunctions).

- Use italics to set off the names of books, newspapers, journals, and other complete publications. Capitalize the first and last words, as well as all other important words.

- For journal articles, include the volume number and the issue number (if necessary). Include the year of publication inside parentheses and follow with a colon and the page range of the article: *Journal of Business Communication* 46, no. 1 (2009): 57–79. (In this source, the volume is 46, the number is 1, and the page range is 57–79.)

- Use brackets to identify all electronic references: [Online database] or [CD-ROM].

- Explain how electronic references can be reached: Available from www.spaceless.com/WWWVL.

- Give the citation date for online references: Cited 23 August 2010.

APA STYLE

The American Psychological Association (APA) recommends the author-date system of documentation, which is popular in the physical, natural, and social sciences. When using this system, you simply insert the author's last name and the year of publication within parentheses following the text discussion of the material cited. Include a page number if you use a direct quotation. This approach briefly identifies the source so that readers can locate complete information in the alphabetical reference list at the end of the report. The author-date system is both brief and clear, saving readers time and effort.

In-Text Citation—APA Style

To document report sources in text using APA style, insert the author's surname and the date of publication at the end of a statement. Enclose this information in parentheses. If the author's name is referred to in the text itself, then the name can be omitted from parenthetical material.

> Some experts recommend both translation and back-translation when dealing with any non-English-speaking culture (Clifton, 2009).

> Toller and Fielding (2001) make a strong case for small companies succeeding in global business.

Personal communications and interviews conducted by the author would not be listed in the reference list at all. Such citations would appear in the text only.

> Increasing the role of cable companies is high on the list of Georgia Stainer, general manager at Day Cable and Communications (personal communication, March 2, 2009).

List of References—APA Style

For APA style, list only those works actually cited in the text (so you would not include works for background or for further reading). Following are the major conventions for developing a reference list according to APA style (see Figure B.3):

- Format entries as hanging indents.
- List all author names in reversed order (last name first), and use only initials for the first and middle names.
- Arrange entries in the following general order: (1) author name, (2) date, (3) title information, (4) publication information, (5) periodical page range.
- Follow the author name with the date of publication in parentheses.
- List titles of articles from magazines, newspapers, and journals without underlines or quotation marks. Capitalize only the first word of the title, any proper nouns, and the first word to follow an internal colon.
- Italicize titles of books, capitalizing only the first word, any proper nouns, and the first word to follow a colon.
- Italicize titles of magazines, newspapers, journals, and other complete publications. Capitalize all the important words in the title.
- For journal articles, include the volume number (in italics) and, if necessary, the issue number (in parentheses). Finally,

include the page range of the article: *Journal of Business Communication, 46*(1), 57–79. (In this example, the volume is 46, the number is 1, and the page range is 57–79.)

- Include personal communications (such as letters, memos, e-mail, and conversations) only in text, not in reference lists.
- Electronic references include author, date of publication, title of article, name of publication (if one), volume, date of retrieval (month, day, year), and the source.
- For electronic references, indicate the actual year of publication and the exact date of retrieval.
- For webpages with extremely long URLs, use your best judgment to determine which URL from the site to use. For example, rather than giving the URL of a specific news release with a long URL, you can provide the URL of the "Media relations" webpage.
- APA citation guidelines for social media are still evolving. For the latest information, visit the APA Style Blog at http://blog.apastyle.org/apastyle.
- For online journals or periodicals that assign a digital object identifier (DOI), include that instead of a conventional URL. If no DOI is available, include the URL of the publication's home page (such as http://online.wsj.com for the *Wall Street Journal*).

MLA STYLE

The style recommended by the Modern Language Association of America is used widely in the humanities, especially in the study of language and literature. Like APA style, MLA style uses brief parenthetical citations in the text. However, instead of including author name and year, MLA citations include author name and page reference.

In-Text Citation—MLA Style

To document report sources in text using MLA style, insert the author's last name and a page reference inside parentheses following the cited material: (Matthews 63). If the author's name is mentioned in the text reference, the name can be omitted from the parenthetical citation: (63). The citation indicates that the reference came from page 63 of a work by Matthews. With the author's name, readers can find complete publication information in the alphabetically arranged list of works cited that comes at the end of the report.

> Some experts recommend both translation and back-translation when dealing with any non-English-speaking culture (Clifton 57).

> Toller and Fielding make a strong case for small companies succeeding in global business (102–03).

List of Works Cited—MLA Style

The *MLA Style Manual* recommends preparing the list of works cited first so that you will know what information to give in the parenthetical citation (for example, whether to add a short title

	REFERENCES
Journal article with volume and issue numbers	Clifton, J. (2009). Beyond taxonomies of influence. *Journal of Business Communication 46* (1), 57.
Webpage (no date, no author)	(n.d.) Company history. Retrieved from http://about.nordstrom.com/aboutus/company hist/companyhist.asp
Online magazine article	Babauta, L. (2007, November 14). 17 tips to be productive with instant messaging. *Web Worker Daily*. Retrieved from http://webworkerdaily.com
Brochure	BestTemp Staffing Services. (2008). *An employer's guide to staffing services* (2d ed.) [Brochure]. Denver: BestTemp Information Center.
Newspaper article, no author	Might be harder than it looks. (2009, January 30). *Los Angeles Times,* p. A22.
Magazine article	Dolan, K. A. (2008, June 2). A whole new crop. *Forbes*, 72–75.
Television broadcast	Han, D. (2002, March 5). Trade wars heating up around the globe. *CNN Headline News*. [Television broadcast]. Atlanta, GA: CNN.
Book, component parts	Kuntz, S. (2001). Moving beyond benefits. In Randolph Jacobson (Ed.), *Our changing workforce* (pp. 213–227). New York: Citadel Press.
Unpublished dissertation or thesis	Morales, G. H. (2001). *The economic pressures on industrialized nations in a global economy* (Unpublished doctoral dissertation). University of San Diego.
Paper presented at a meeting	Myers, C. (2001, August). *HMOs in today's environment*. Paper presented at the Conference on Medical Insurance Solutions, Chicago, IL.
Blog post	Scott, D. (2010, August 9). Offering unique experiences generates attention for nonprofits. Retrieved from http://www.webinknow.com. (2010, August 16).
Online encyclopedia article, no author	Capitalism. (2010). In *Encyclopædia Britannica Online*. Retrieved August 16, 2010, from http://www.britannica.com/EBchecked/topic/93927/capitalism
Newspaper article, one author	Standish, E. (2002, January 19). Global market crushes OPEC's delicate balance of interests. *Wall Street Journal*, p. A1.
Book, two authors	Toller, M., & Fielding, J. (2001). *Global business for smaller companies*. Rocklin, CA: Prima Publishing.
Government publication	U.S. Department of Defense. (2002). *Stretching research dollars: Survival advice for universities and government labs*. Washington, DC: U.S. Government Printing Office.
Annual report	The Walt Disney Company. (2008). *2007 Annual Report*. Burbank, Calif.: The Walt Disney Company.
Interview	*Cited in text only, not in the list of references.*

Figure B.3   Sample References—APA Style

if you're citing more than one work by the same author, or whether to give an initial or first name if you're citing two authors who have the same last name). The list of works cited appears at the end of your report, contains all the works that you cite in your text, and lists them in alphabetical order. Following are the major conventions for developing a reference list according to MLA style (see Figure B.4 on the next page):

- Format entries as hanging indents.
- Arrange entries in the following general order: (1) author name, (2) title information, (3) publication information, (4) date, (5) periodical page range.

- List the lead author's name in reverse order (last name first), using either full first names or initials. List second and succeeding author names in normal order.
- Use quotation marks around the titles of articles from magazines, newspapers, and journals. Capitalize all important words.
- Italicize the names of books, newspapers, journals, and other complete publications, capitalizing all main words in the title.
- For journal articles, include the volume number and the issue number (if necessary). Include the year of publication

WORKS CITED

Online magazine article	Babauta, Leo. "17 Tips to Be Productive with Instant Messaging," *Web Worker Daily* 14 Nov. 2007. 14 Feb. 2008. <http://webworkerdaily.com>.
Brochure	BestTemp Staffing Services. *An Employer's Guide to Staffing Services.* 2d ed. Denver: BestTemp Information Center, 2008.
Journal article with volume and issue numbers	Clifton, Jonathan. "Beyond Taxonomies of Influence." *Journal of Business Communication* 46, 1 (2009): 57–79. Print.
Webpage (no date, no author)	"Company History." *Nordstom.com.* Nordstrom, n.d. Web 16 Aug. 2010.
Newspaper article, no author	"Might Be Harder Than It Looks." *Los Angeles Times,* 30 Jan. 2009: A22. Print.
Magazine article	Dolan, Kerry A. "A Whole New Crop." *Forbes,* 2 June 2008: 72–75. Print.
Television broadcast	Han, Daniel. "Trade Wars Heating Up Around the Globe." *CNN Headline News.* CNN, Atlanta. 5 Mar. 2002. Television.
Book, component parts	Kuntz, Sonja. "Moving Beyond Benefits." *Our Changing Workforce.* Ed. Randolf Jacobson. New York: Citadel Press, 2001. 213–27. Print.
Unpublished dissertation or thesis	Morales, George H. "The Economic Pressures on Industrialized Nations in a Global Economy." Diss. U of San Diego, 2001. Print.
Paper presented at a meeting	Myers, Charles. "HMOs in Today's Environment." Conference on Medical Insurance Solutions. Chicago. 13 Aug. 2001. Address.
Blog post	Scott, David. "Offering Unique Experiences Generates Attention for Nonprofits." WebInkNow.com. WebInkNow, 9 Aug. 2010. Web. Aug. 16, 2010.
Interview	Stainer, Georgia, general manager, Day Cable and Communications. Telephone interview. 2 Mar. 2010.
Newspaper article, one author	Standish, Evelyn. "Global Market Crushes OPEC's Delicate Balance of Interests." *Wall Street Journal,* 19 Jan. 2002: A1. Print.
Book, two authors	Toller, Miriam, and Jay Fielding. *Global Business for Smaller Companies.* Rocklin, CA: Prima Publishing, 2001. Print.
Government publication	United States. Department of Defense. *Stretching Research Dollars: Survival Advice for Universities and Government Labs.* Washington: GPO, 2002. Print.
Annual report	The Walt Disney Company, *2007 Annual Report.* Calif.: The Walt Disney Company, 2008. Print.

Figure B.4   Sample Works Cited—MLA Style

inside parentheses and follow with a colon and the page range of the article: *Journal of Business Communication* 46, 1 (2009): 57. (In this source, the volume is 46, the number is 1, and the page is 57.)

- Electronic sources are less fixed than print sources, and they may not be readily accessible to readers. So citations for electronic sources must provide more information. Always try to be as comprehensive as possible, citing whatever information is available (however, see the note in the right column about extremely long URLs).

- The date for electronic sources should contain both the date assigned in the source (if no date is shown, write "n.d." instead) and the date accessed by the researcher.

- The URL for electronic sources must be as accurate and complete as possible, from access-mode identifier (such as http or ftp) to all relevant directory and file names. If the URL is extremely long, however, use the URL of the website's home page or the URL of the site's search page if you used the site's search function to find the article. Beginning with its 2009 edition, the MLA Style Manual no longer requires writers to include URLs for materials retrieved online. However, follow whatever guidelines your instructor gives you in this regard.

- Also beginning in 2009, MLA style requires you to indicate the medium of publication. For most sources, this will be "Web" or "Print," but you may also cite "CD-ROM" and other media, as appropriate.

Appendix C

Correction Symbols

Instructors often use these short, easy-to-remember correction symbols and abbreviations when evaluating students' writing. You can use them too, to understand your instructor's suggestions and to revise and proofread your own letters, memos, and reports. Refer to the Handbook of Grammar, Mechanics, and Usage (pp. 467–496) for further information.

CONTENT AND STYLE

Acc	Accuracy. Check to be sure information is correct.
ACE	Avoid copying examples.
ACP	Avoid copying problems.
Adp	Adapt. Tailor message to reader.
App	Follow proper organization approach. (Refer to Chapter 4.)
Assign	Assignment. Review instructions for assignment.
AV	Active verb. Substitute active for passive.
Awk	Awkward phrasing. Rewrite.
BC	Be consistent.
BMS	Be more sincere.
Chop	Choppy sentences. Use longer sentences and more transitional phrases.
Con	Condense. Use fewer words.
CT	Conversational tone. Avoid using overly formal language.
Depers	Depersonalize. Avoid attributing credit or blame to any individual or group.
Dev	Develop. Provide greater detail.
Dir	Direct. Use direct approach; get to the point.
Emph	Emphasize. Develop this point more fully.
EW	Explanation weak. Check logic; provide more proof.
Fl	Flattery. Avoid compliments that are insincere.
FS	Figure of speech. Find a more accurate expression.
GNF	Good news first. Use direct order.
GRF	Give reasons first. Use indirect order.
GW	Goodwill. Put more emphasis on expressions of goodwill.
H/E	Honesty/ethics. Revise statement to reflect good business practices.
Imp	Imply. Avoid being direct.
Inc	Incomplete. Develop further.
Jar	Jargon. Use less specialized language.
Log	Logic. Check development of argument.

Neg	Negative. Use more positive approach or expression.
Obv	Obvious. Do not state point in such detail.
OC	Overconfident. Adopt humbler language.
OM	Omission.
Org	Organization. Strengthen outline.
OS	Off the subject. Close with point on main subject.
Par	Parallel. Use same structure.
Pom	Pompous. Rephrase in down-to-earth terms.
PV	Point of view. Make statement from reader's perspective rather than your own.
RB	Reader benefit. Explain what reader stands to gain.
Red	Redundant. Reduce number of times this point is made.
Ref	Reference. Cite source of information.
Rep	Repetitive. Provide different expression.
RS	Resale. Reassure reader that he or she has made a good choice.
SA	Service attitude. Put more emphasis on helping reader.
Sin	Sincerity. Avoid sounding glib or uncaring.
SL	Stereotyped language. Focus on individual's characteristics instead of on false generalizations.
Spec	Specific. Provide more specific statement.
SPM	Sales promotion material. Tell reader about related goods or services.
Stet	Let stand in original form.
Sub	Subordinate. Make this point less important.
SX	Sexist. Avoid language that contributes to gender stereotypes.
Tone	Tone needs improvement.
Trans	Transition. Show connection between points.
UAE	Use action ending. Close by stating what reader should do next.
UAS	Use appropriate salutation.
UAV	Use active voice.
Unc	Unclear. Rewrite to clarify meaning.
UPV	Use passive voice.
USS	Use shorter sentences.
V	Variety. Use different expression or sentence pattern.
W	Wordy. Eliminate unnecessary words.
WC	Word choice. Find a more appropriate word.
YA	"You" attitude. Rewrite to emphasize reader's needs.

GRAMMAR, MECHANICS, AND USAGE

Ab	Abbreviation. Avoid abbreviations in most cases; use correct abbreviation.
Adj	Adjective. Use adjective instead.
Adv	Adverb. Use adverb instead.
Agr	Agreement. Make subject and verb or noun and pronoun agree.
Ap	Appearance. Improve appearance.
Apos	Apostrophe. Check use of apostrophe.
Art	Article. Use correct article.
BC	Be consistent.
Cap	Capitalize.
Case	Use cases correctly.
CoAdj	Coordinate adjective. Insert comma between coordinate adjectives; delete comma between adjective and compound noun.
CS	Comma splice. Use period or semicolon to separate clauses.
DM	Dangling modifier. Rewrite so that modifier clearly relates to subject of sentence.
Exp	Expletive. Avoid expletive beginnings, such as it is, there are, there is, this is, and these are.
F	Format. Improve layout of document.
Frag	Fragment. Rewrite as complete sentence.
Gram	Grammar. Correct grammatical error.
HCA	Hyphenate compound adjective.
lc	Lowercase. Do not use capital letter.
M	Margins. Improve frame around document.
MM	Misplaced modifier. Place modifier close to word it modifies.
NRC	Nonrestrictive clause (or phrase). Separate from rest of sentence with commas.
P	Punctuation. Use correct punctuation.
Par	Parallel. Use same structure.
PH	Place higher. Move document up on page.
PL	Place lower. Move document down on page.
Prep	Preposition. Use correct preposition.
RC	Restrictive clause (or phrase). Remove commas that separate clause from rest of sentence.
RO	Run-on sentence. Separate two sentences with comma and coordinating conjunction or with semicolon.
SC	Series comma. Add comma before *and*.
SI	Split infinitive. Do not separate *to* from rest of verb.
Sp	Spelling error. Consult dictionary.
S-V	Subject-verb pair. Do not separate with comma.
Syl	Syllabification. Divide word between syllables.
WD	Word division. Check dictionary for proper end-of-line hyphenation.
WW	Wrong word. Replace with another word.

PROOFREADING MARKS

Symbol	Meaning	Symbol Used in Context	Corrected Copy
⹀	Align horizontally	meaningful result	meaningful result
‖	Align vertically	1. Power cable 2. Keyboard	1. Power cable 2. Keyboard
(bf)	Boldface	Recommendations (bf)	**Recommendations**
≡	Capitalize	Pepsico, Inc.	PepsiCo, Inc.
⊐⊏	Center	Awards Banquet	Awards Banquet
◡	Close up space	self- confidence	self-confidence
ℓ	Delete	harrassment and abuse	harassment
(ds)	Double-space	text in first line text in second line (ds)	text in first line text in second line
∧	Insert	turquoise shirts (and white)	turquoise and white shirts
∀	Insert apostrophe	our teams goals	our team's goals
⋏	Insert comma	a, b and c	a, b, and c
⹀∧	Insert hyphen	third quarter sales	third-quarter sales
⊙	Insert period	Harrigan et al	Harrigan et al.
∀ ∀	Insert quotation marks	This team isn't cooperating.	This "team" isn't cooperating.
#	Insert space	real estate test case	real estate test case
(ital)	Italics	Quarterly Report (ital)	*Quarterly Report*
/	Lowercase	TULSA, South of here	Tulsa, south of here
⌣	Move down	Sincerely,	Sincerely,
⊏	Move left	Attention: Security	Attention: Security
⊐	Move right	February 2, 2010	February 2, 2010
⌐	Move up	THIRD-QUARTER SALES	THIRD-QUARTER SALES
(STET)	Restore	staff talked openly and frankly (STET)	staff talked openly
⌇	Run lines together	Manager, Distribution	Manager, Distribution
(ss)	Single space	text in first line text in second line (ss)	text in first line text in second line
⬭	Spell out	(COD)	cash on delivery
(sp)	Spell out	(sp) Assn. of Biochem. Engrs.	Association of Biochemical Engineers
⌐	Start new line	Marla Fenton, Manager, Distribution	Marla Fenton, Manager, Distribution
¶	Start new paragraph	¶ The solution is easy to determine but difficult to implement in a competitive environment like the one we now face.	The solution is easy to determine but difficult to implement in a competitive environment like the one we now face.
∼	Transpose	airy, light, casual tone	light, airy, casual tone

Video Guide

Your instructor may elect to show you one or more of the videos described on the following pages. These programs supplement course concepts with real-life examples of businesspeople meeting important communication challenges. This video guide includes several review and analysis questions as well as exercises for each video. Be sure to review the appropriate page ahead of time so that you'll know what to look for when you watch the video. (To access backup copies of the online articles mentioned in the follow-up assignments and research projects, visit and click on "Student Assignments.")

EFFECTIVE COMMUNICATION

Learning Objectives

After viewing this video, you will be able to

1. Recognize the importance of communication in the business environment
2. Recognize the elements that distinguish effective from ineffective communication
3. Understand why brevity is an important part of effective communication

Background Information

Effective communication delivers a number of business benefits, including stronger decision making and faster problem solving, earlier warning of potential problems, increased productivity and steadier workflow, stronger business relationships, clearer and more persuasive marketing messages, enhanced professional images for both employers and companies, lower employee turnover and higher employee satisfaction, better financial results, and higher return for investors. To be considered effective, communication efforts need to provide practical information, give facts rather than vague impressions, present information concisely, clarify expectations and responsibilities, and offer persuasive arguments and recommendations.

The Video

This video portrays a new employee at an advertising agency as he learns the importance of effective communication—and learns how to improve his communication efforts. As he goes through a typical day accompanied by a "message mentor," he observes the results of both effective and ineffective communication.

Discussion Questions

1. Why might new hires fresh out of college face challenges in learning how to communicate in the workplace?
2. How should you handle situations in which you are asked to provide solid information but the only information available to you is imprecise and potentially unreliable?
3. How can effective communication improve employee morale?
4. How can you judge how much information to provide your audience in any given situation?
5. Can communication efforts be both effective and unethical? For example, what about a marketing campaign that uses compelling information to persuade people to buy an inferior product when a better product is available from the competition?

Follow-Up Assignment

Most companies make an effort to define external communication strategies, but many don't have a formal strategy for internal communication—which is every bit as essential to their success. Read the article, "Internal Communication Strategies—The Neglected Strategic Element," at http://workhelp.org/joomla/content/view/171/46/ and then answer the following questions:

1. What are the advantages of effective internal communication?
2. How does communication help align the efforts of everyone in the organization toward common goals?
3. Why is it important to have a companywide strategy for internal communication?

For Further Research

The *HR Magazine* article "Great Communicators, Great Communication" emphasizes the role communication plays in creating great workplaces. Visit www.shrm.org, use the search function to find the article, and then summarize the steps companies have taken to be included among the magazine's list of the 50 best small and medium companies to work for in the United States.

ETHICAL COMMUNICATION

Learning Objectives

After viewing this video, you will be able to

1. Describe a process for deciding what is ethical or unethical
2. Explain the importance of meeting your personal and professional responsibilities in an ethical manner
3. Discuss the possible consequences of ethical and unethical choices and talk about the impact of these choices on direct and related audiences

Background Information

Communication is ethical when it includes all relevant information, when it's true in every sense, and when it isn't deceptive in any way. In contrast, communication is unethical when it includes false information, fails to include important information, or otherwise misleads an audience. To avoid unethical choices in your communication efforts, you must consider not only legal issues but also the needs of your audience and the expectations of society and your employer. In turn, companies that demonstrate high standards of ethics maintain credibility with employees, customers, and other stakeholders.

The Video

This video identifies two important tools in a communicator's toolbox: honesty and objectivity. These tools help businesspeople resolve ethical dilemmas and avoid ethical lapses, both within the company and during interactions with outside audiences. Poor ethical choices can damage a company's credibility and put employees, customers, and the surrounding community at risk. Unfortunately, some ethical choices are neither clear nor simple, and you may face situations in which the needs of one group or individual must be weighed against the needs of another.

Discussion Questions

1. Would you ever consider compromising your ethics for self-gain? If so, under what circumstance? If not, why?
2. The video mentions the role of misrepresentations in the collapse of Enron. If you were the head of communications at Enron and had some knowledge of the true nature of the company's financial condition, what would you have done?
3. Identify risks involved when you choose to act in an unethical manner.
4. How can you be an effective business communicator without credibility?
5. Is it ethical to call in sick to work, even though you are not ill? What happens to your credibility if someone finds out you were not sick?

Follow-Up Assignment

Many businesses, from small companies to large corporations, formulate codes of ethics that outline ethical standards for employees. Download IBM's Business Conduct Guidelines from www.ibm.com/investor/pdf/BCG2009.pdf and answer the following questions:

1. What does IBM want employees to do if they are aware of unethical situations within the organization?
2. How does IBM view misleading statements or innuendoes about competitors?
3. What advice does IBM give employees on the subject of receiving gifts from people outside the company?

For Further Research

As magazines venture deeper into the digital realm, they are encountering some important ethical questions about the separation of journalism and advertising. Read the article at www.pbs.org/mediashift/2010/04/the-ethics-of-digital-magazine-advertising-118.html. How much responsibility does a magazine publisher have in terms of alerting readers about the presence of embedded or linked advertising? How much responsibility do readers have regarding recognizing when they are consuming editorial content and when they are consuming advertising content?

BUSINESS ETIQUETTE

Learning Objectives

After viewing this video, you will be able to

1. Recognize the negative impact that poor etiquette can have in the workplace
2. Identify the five goals that every bad-news message should seek to achieve
3. Identify situations in which the indirect approach is likely to be more effective than the direct approach

Background Information

Etiquette strikes some people as a fine idea for tea parties but something that has little relevance in the contemporary workplace. However, the stresses and strains of today's business environment make etiquette more important than ever. Poor etiquette harms relationships, hinders communication, lowers morale and productivity, and limits career potential. Successful professionals know that taking the time and effort to treat others with respect—through their words and their actions—pays off for everyone in the long run.

The Video

This video shows a young employee learning firsthand the value of business etiquette. A business associate whom he has offended through clumsy communication turns the tables and helps him understand the negative effect that poor etiquette has on people in the workplace. She then helps him grasp the steps needed to present himself respectably and to communicate in ways that get his point across without unnecessarily stirring up negative emotions.

Discussion Questions

1. Is paying attention to standards of etiquette likely to save time or cost time in the workplace? Why?
2. If you need to deliver bad news to a person with whom you will probably never interact again, how can you justify taking extra time and effort to communicate carefully and respectfully? Are you wasting your company's money by spending time on such efforts?
3. How does a well-written buffer in an indirect negative message help the receiver accept the bad news?
4. Can a buffer also make the task of delivering negative messages less stressful? Why or why not?
5. Is the indirect approach to negative messages deceptive? Shouldn't communication always be straightforward and direct? Be prepared to explain your answer.

Follow-Up Assignment

Visit www.executiveplanet.com and click on any country that interests you. Explore the Public Behaviour section(s) for that country and identify three tips that would help anyone from the United States who is preparing to do business there.

For Further Research

Take the brief business etiquette quiz at http://www.gradview.com/articles/careers/etiquette.html. Were you able to figure out answers to these situations? Do you agree with the responses that the website identifies as being correct?

LEARNING TO LISTEN: SECOND CITY COMMUNICATIONS

Creativity: Second City Communications

Learning Objectives

After viewing this video, you will be able to

1. Understand the functions of interpersonal communication in the workplace
2. Identify the ways to overcome barriers to effective communication
3. Discuss the importance of active listening both socially and professionally

Background Information

Chicago's Second City Improv is more than the world's best-known comedy theater. Second City now brings its famous brand of humor to corporate giants such as Coca-Cola, Motorola, and Microsoft. With over 40 years of experience in corporate services, Second City's teachers help business professionals develop communication skills through lessons in improvisational theater. Business communications training is Second City's fastest-growing practice, fueled by the demands of more than 200 Fortune 500 companies. Workshops are tailored to clients' needs in such areas as listening and giving presentations, collaborative leadership and team skills, interviewing, breaking down barriers to successful communication, and using humor to convey important messages. The next time you watch improvisational sketch comedy, ask yourself how a lesson in the art of "improv" might give your career a boost.

The Video

In these two video segments, you'll see Second City's training techniques in action. The first segment addresses the need to listen actively, and the second explores techniques for encouraging innovation. The second clip is less focused on communication, but you can see how the techniques for stimulating innovation work equally well for fostering meaningful, two-way conversation that encourages people to open up rather than shut down.

Discussion Questions

1. How do the exercises featured in this video address the contrasting needs of the trial lawyer, the divorce lawyer, and the media buyer?
2. Would ABC's talkative guest Kay Jarman, the 47-year-old award-winning salesperson, be a good candidate for Second City's training workshop?
3. What other workshops might Tom Yorton want to offer companies in response to the current economic and political climate?
4. How might the "Yes and" rule of improvisation be used to train customer service representatives at an L.L. Bean or a Dell call center? Without physical cues, such as facial expression and body language, is the "Yes and" rule still effective?
5. As president and managing director of Second City Communications, Tom Yorton says the following: "You have to be willing to fail to be able to get the results you want . . . to connect with an audience." Do you agree that this statement is as true in business as it is in comedy? Support your chosen position.

Follow-Up Assignment

Review the current course catalog available from Second City's website (www.secondcity.com). How could such training help you in a business career?

For Further Research

The importance of active listening is at the core of *consultative selling*, an approach that emphasizes posing questions to the potential buyer in order to identify needs and expectations—rather than rattling off a prepared sales speech. PublicSpeaking Skills.com (www.publicspeakingskills.com) is one of many companies that offer training in consultative selling. Review the description of the company's Consultative Selling Skills course. Do the principles espoused match the concept of the "you" attitude and the elements of ethical communication that you've learned so far?

COMMUNICATING IN THE GLOBAL WORKPLACE

Learning Objectives

After viewing this video, you will be able to

1. Discuss the challenges of communicating in the global workplace
2. Identify barriers to effective communication across borders
3. Explain the critical role of time in global communication efforts

Background Information

Many businesses are crossing national boundaries to engage in international business. However, operating in a global environment presents a variety of challenges related to culture and communication. Understanding and respecting these challenges can mean the difference between success and failure, so executives must make sure that employees are educated on cultural issues before attempting to do business in other countries.

The Video

This video identifies the challenges to effective communication in the global marketplace, including the barriers posed by language, culture, time, and technology. You will see that a significant amount of research needs to be conducted before a company can engage in successful global business ventures. For instance, if communicators are unaware of differences in gestures, expressions, and dialect, they can inadvertently offend or confuse their audiences. In addition, time zone differences require organizations to plan carefully in advance so that they can develop, translate, and deliver information in a timely manner.

Discussion Questions

1. Language can be a barrier to effective communication. What steps can a company take to minimize language barriers across borders?

2. What characteristics of a country's culture need to be researched to ensure business success across borders?

3. How does a company ensure that a message is properly translated into the local language and dialect of the people it conducts business with?

4. What challenges does a company face when trying to hold a conference call or video meeting with affiliates and employees around the world?

5. The video mentions that some companies have trusted contacts in a country they wish to do business with, while other companies rely on a significant amount of research to learn more about culture and other local characteristics. What method do you feel is most effective for gathering useful, accurate, and up-to-date information regarding cultural issues?

Follow-Up Assignment
The Coca-Cola Company has local operations in more than 200 countries throughout the world. Visit www.coca-cola.com and click on "Change Country" at the top of the page to learn more about the company's business activities in a variety of countries. What steps does Coke take to communicate through its website with customers around the world? Does the company strive to develop products that meet local tastes and needs? If so, how and why?

For Further Research
Choose a country other than the United States and research your selection, using both online and library resources to identify important cultural characteristics specific to that country. For example, you might want to gather information about gestures and other nonverbal communication that would be considered offensive, about work habits, or about laws related to conducting business in that country. The characteristics you identify should be useful and accurate.

Based on what you've learned about this country and your personal beliefs, values, and life experiences, is there any risk that you might have a prejudiced or ethnocentric viewpoint regarding people from this country? Why or why not?

IMPACT OF CULTURE ON BUSINESS: SPOTLIGHT ON LATIN AMERICA
Learning Objectives
After viewing this video, you will be able to

1. List key aspects of Latin American cultures and indicate the influences on their development
2. Identify factors that might lead to cultural change in Latin America
3. Explain some of the major cultural contrasts within Latin America and their impact on international business operations

Background Information
To a large degree, culture defines the way all human beings interpret and respond to life's changing circumstances. When you interact with people from your own culture, your shared experiences and expectations usually enhance the communication process by providing a common language and frame of reference. However, when you communicate across cultural boundaries, a lack of awareness of your audience's culture—and the subconscious ways that your own culture shapes your perceptions—can result in partial or even total failure of the communication process. Moreover, culture is rarely static, so impressions you may have gathered at one point in your life may need to be revisited and revised over time.

The Video
This video takes a broad look at Latin America's various countries and cultures and explores the business implications of cultural similarities and differences. You'll learn how cultural groups that may appear identical on the surface can in fact have subtle but profound differences. Although communication is just one of many topics discussed in the video, you will get a sense of just how important—and challenging—communication can be when conducting business across cultural boundaries.

Discussion Questions
1. Explain what the video means when it says that your own culture can "sneak up on you."
2. How is business influencing the economic gulf between urban and rural populations in Latin America?
3. How have imperial conquests and slavery affected the populations and cultures of Latin America?
4. How do many outsiders view the issue of business and government corruption in Latin America?
5. Is business etiquette in most of Latin America considered relatively formal or relatively informal?

Follow-Up Assignment
The World Bank plays an important role in today's fast-changing, closely meshed global economy. Visit the bank's website, at www.worldbank.org, and explore the programs and initiatives under way in the Latin American region. How is the bank using this website to foster better communication between Latin America and the rest of the world?

For Further Research
In today's global marketplace, knowing as much as possible about your international customers' business practices and customs could give you a strategic advantage. To help you successfully conduct business around the globe, visit www.buyusainfo.net and select any country from the drop-down menu. How can resources such as this website help U.S. businesses communicate more successfully with customers, employees, and other groups in Latin America?

EFFECTIVE ORAL PRESENTATIONS
Learning Objectives
After viewing this video, you will be able to

1. Reiterate the importance of knowing your audience before creating and delivering oral presentations
2. Discuss the role of teamwork in preparing and delivering complex presentations
3. Explain the importance of anticipating objections likely to be raised during a presentation

Background Information

Oral presentations are a vital communication medium in most companies. In particular, important decisions often involve one or more presentations, either in person or online, in which people advocating a specific choice present their case to the people responsible for making the decision. Such presentations usually combine informational and analytical reporting, along with the persuasive aspects of a proposal. Beyond the mere delivery of information, however, presentations also involve an element of performance. Audiences search for both verbal and nonverbal clues to help them assess presenters' knowledge, confidence, and credibility.

The Video

This video follows three colleagues as they create and deliver a presentation that seeks to convince the audience to approve the purchase of a particular software system that will be used to manage the company's sales force. The presenters explain the importance of understanding the expectations of their audience, from the types of visuals they prefer to the objections they are likely to raise. The team also explains how they took advantage of each member's individual strengths to create a more effective presentation.

Discussion Questions

1. How did the presenters demonstrate their knowledge of the audience?
2. Why did one presenter use a $100 bill as a prop?
3. What are the risks of using props such as the $100 bill?
4. How did the presenters prepare for objections raised by the audience?
5. How would the team need to modify its presentation for an online webcast instead of an in-person oral presentation?

Follow-Up Assignment

Podcasts (audio only) and vidcasts (podcasts with video) are quickly catching on as a medium for business presentations. Visit www.technorati.com and click on the Business channel. Select any three podcasts. Listen to them, taking careful notes so that you can compare the three selections in terms of grabbing your attention, keeping your attention, and effectively communicating the podcast's information. Which of the three podcasts is the most effective? Why?

For Further Research

Musicians, actors, jugglers—virtually everyone who performs in public experiences *performance anxiety*, or *stage fright*, as it is commonly known. This anxiety is simply the natural outcome of caring about how well you do. After all, if you didn't care, you wouldn't feel anxious. Seasoned performers not only recognize that anxiety is natural but they also have learned how to use this emotion to their advantage by giving them extra energy. Search online for advice on dealing with stage fright to see how accomplished performers handle the anxiety of performing in public. How can you adapt their techniques to business presentations?

INTERVIEWING SKILLS

Learning Objectives

After viewing this video, you will be able to

1. Explain how the AIDA approach helps create effective application letters

2. Identify mistakes that can cause an otherwise qualified candidate to lose out on a job opportunity
3. Explain why planning for tough questions is such an important part of your interviewing strategy

Background Information

Most companies would admit that an employment interview is an imperfect test of a candidate's skills and personality fit with the organization. In response, some are beginning to add testing, job simulations, and other evaluation tools to the selection process. However, the classic face-to-face interview remains the dominant decision-making tool in the hiring process, so developing your interviewing skills will be vital to your success at every stage in your career.

The Video

This video follows the progress of two candidates applying and interviewing for a technical writing position. One candidate has more experience in this area, but his approach to the interview process ends up costing him the job opportunity. In contrast, a candidate with less experience takes a confident and creative approach that nets her the job.

Discussion Questions

1. Why are multiple StayCom managers involved in this interviewing process? Couldn't one manager handle it?
2. Why does one of the managers compare an application letter to a news story?
3. What steps did Cheryl Yung take to overcome a potential shortcoming in her qualifications?
4. What mistakes did candidate Buddy McCoy make in his interview?
5. Why would the interviewers care about the interpersonal skills of someone who will be writing for a living?

Follow-Up Assignment

Nonverbal cues are important in every communication scenario, but they are perhaps never more important than in job interviews. Not only are interviewers looking for any clues they can find that will guide their decisions but they tend to make up their minds quickly—perhaps even before the candidate has said anything at all. Use the Web Search feature at http://businesscommunicationblog.com/websearch to find advice on nonverbal communication in interviews. Distill this information down to a half dozen or so key points that you can write on a note card to study before you step into your next job interview.

For Further Research

You look great in your new interview outfit, your hair is perfect but not too perfect, your smile radiates positive energy, and you're ready to dazzle the interviewer. Then, oops—you discover that your first interview will be held over the telephone, so none of your visual cues will help you at this stage. Don't fret; read the telephone interviewing advice at www.collegegrad.com/jobsearch/phone-Interviewing-Success/, and you'll be ready to dazzle the interviewer long distance.

Handbook of Grammar, Mechanics, and Usage

The rules of grammar, mechanics, and usage provide the guidance every professional needs in order to communicate successfully with colleagues, customers, and other audiences. Understanding and following these rules helps you in two important ways. First, the rules determine how meaning is encoded and decoded in the communication process. If you don't encode your messages using the same rules your readers or listeners use to decode them, chances are your audiences will not extract your intended meaning from your messages. Without a firm grasp of the basics of grammar, mechanics, and usage, you risk being misunderstood, damaging your company's image, losing money for your company, and possibly even losing your job. In other words, if you want to get your point across, you need to follow the rules of grammar, mechanics, and usage. Second, apart from transferring meaning successfully, following the rules tells your audience that you respect the conventions and expectations of the business community.

You can think of *grammar* as the agreed-upon structure of a language, the way that individual words are formed and the manner in which those words are then combined to form meaningful sentences. *Mechanics* are style and formatting issues such as capitalization, spelling, and the use of numbers and symbols. *Usage* involves the accepted and expected way in which specific words are used by a particular community of people—in this case, the community of businesspeople who use English. This handbook can help you improve your knowledge and awareness in all three areas. It is divided into the following sections:

- **Diagnostic Test of English Skills.** Testing your current knowledge of grammar, mechanics, and usage helps you find out where your strengths and weaknesses lie. This test offers 50 items taken from the topics included in this handbook.

- **Assessment of English Skills.** After completing the diagnostic test, use the assessment form to highlight the areas you most need to review.

- **Essentials of Grammar, Mechanics, and Usage with Practice Sessions.** This section helps you quickly review the basics. You can study the things you've probably already learned but may have forgotten about grammar, punctuation, mechanics (including capitalization, abbreviation, number style, and word division), and vocabulary (including frequently confused words, frequently misused words, frequently misspelled words, and transitional words and phrases). Practice sessions throughout this section help you test yourself and reinforce what you learn. Use this essential review not only to study and improve your English skills but also as a reference for any questions you may have during this course.

DIAGNOSTIC TEST OF ENGLISH SKILLS

Use this test to determine whether you need more practice with grammar, punctuation, mechanics, or vocabulary. When you've answered all the questions, ask your instructor for an answer sheet so that you can score the test. On the Assessment of English Skills form (page 469), record the number of questions you answered incorrectly in each section.

The following choices apply to items 1–5. Write in each blank the letter of the choice that best describes the part of speech that is underlined.

A. noun
B. pronoun
C. verb
D. adjective
E. adverb
F. preposition
G. conjunction
H. article

_____ 1. The new branch location will be decided <u>by</u> next week.
_____ 2. We must hire only <u>qualified</u>, ambitious graduates.
_____ 3. After their <u>presentation</u>, I was still undecided.
_____ 4. See <u>me</u> after the meeting.
_____ 5. Margaret, pressed for time, turned in <u>unusually</u> sloppy work.

In the blanks for items 6–15, write the letter of the word or phrase that best completes each sentence.

_____ 6. (A. Russ's, B. Russ') laptop was stolen last week.
_____ 7. Speaking only for (A. me, B. myself), I think the new policy is discriminatory.
_____ 8. Of the five candidates we interviewed yesterday, (A. who, B. whom) do you believe is the best choice?
_____ 9. India has increased (A. it's, B. its) imports of corn and rice.
_____ 10. Anyone who wants to be (A. their, B. his or her) own boss should think about owning a franchise.
_____ 11. If the IT department can't (A. lie, B. lay) the fiber-optic cable by March 1, the plant will not open on schedule.
_____ 12. Starbucks (A. is, B. are) opening five new stores in San Diego in the next year.
_____ 13. The number of women-owned small businesses (A. has, B. have) increased sharply in the past two decades.
_____ 14. Greg and Bernyce worked (A. good, B. well) together.
_____ 15. They distributed the supplies (A. among, B. between) the six staff members.

The following choices apply to items 16–20. Write in each blank the letter of the choice that best describes the sentence structure problem with each item.

A. sentence fragment
B. comma splice
C. misplaced modifier

467

D. fused sentence
E. lack of parallelism
F. unclear antecedent

_____ 16. The number of employees who took the buyout offer was much higher than expected, now the entire company is understaffed.

_____ 17. The leader in Internet-only banking.

_____ 18. Diamond doesn't actually sell financial products rather it acts as an intermediary.

_____ 19. Helen's proposal is for not only the present but also for the future.

_____ 20. When purchasing luxury products, quality is more important than price for consumers.

For items 21–30, circle the letter of the preferred choice in each of the following groups of sentences.

21. A. What do you think of the ad slogan "Have it your way?"
    B. What do you think of the ad slogan "Have it your way"?

22. A. Send copies to Jackie Cross, Uniline, Brad Nardi, Peale & Associates, and Tom Griesbaum, MatchMakers.
    B. Send copies to Jackie Cross, Uniline; Brad Nardi, Peale & Associates; and Tom Griesbaum, MatchMakers.

23. A. They've recorded 22 complaints since yesterday, all of them from long-time employees.
    B. They've recorded 22 complaints since yesterday; all of them from long-time employees.

24. A. We are looking for two qualities in applicants: experience with computers and an interest in people.
    B. We are looking for two qualities in applicants; experience with computers and an interest in people.

25. A. At the Center for the Blind the clients we serve have lost vision, due to a wide variety of causes.
    B. At the Center for the Blind, the clients we serve have lost vision due to a wide variety of causes.

26. A. Replace your standard light bulbs with new, compact fluorescent bulbs.
    B. Replace your standard light bulbs with new, compact, fluorescent bulbs.
    C. Replace your standard light bulbs with new compact fluorescent bulbs.

27. A. Blue Cross of California may have changed its name to Anthem Blue Cross but the company still has the same commitment to California.
    B. Blue Cross of California may have changed its name to Anthem Blue Cross, but the company still has the same commitment to California.

28. A. Only eight banks in this country—maybe nine can handle transactions of this magnitude.
    B. Only eight banks in this country—maybe nine—can handle transactions of this magnitude.

29. A. Instead of focusing on high-growth companies, we targeted mature businesses with only one or two people handling the decision making.
    B. Instead of focusing on high growth companies, we targeted mature businesses with only one or two people handling the decision-making.

30. A. According to board president Damian Cabaza "having a crisis communication plan is a high priority."
    B. According to board president Damian Cabaza, "Having a crisis communication plan is a high priority."

For items 31–40, select the best choice from among those provided.

31. A. At her previous employer, Mary-Anne worked in Marketing Communications and Human Resources.
    B. At her previous employer, Mary-Anne worked in marketing communications and human resources.

32. A. By fall, we'll have a dozen locations between the Mississippi and Missouri rivers.
    B. By Fall, we'll have a dozen locations between the Mississippi and Missouri Rivers.

33. A. The Board applauded President Donlan upon her reelection for a fifth term.
    B. The board applauded president Donlan upon her reelection for a fifth term.
    C. The board applauded President Donlan upon her reelection for a fifth term.

34. A. If you want to travel to France, you need to be au courant with the business practices.
    B. If you want to travel to France, you need to be "au courant" with the business practices.

35. A. As the company's CEO, Thomas Spurgeon handles all dealings with the FDA.
    B. As the company's C.E.O., Thomas Spurgeon handles all dealings with the F.D.A.

36. A. The maximum speed limit in most states is 65 mph.
    B. The maximum speed limit in most states is 65 m.p.h.

37. A. Sales of graphic novels increased nine percent between 2008 and 2009.
    B. Sales of graphic novels increased 9 percent between 2008 and 2009.

38. A. Our store is open daily from nine a.m. to seven p.m.
    B. Our store is open daily from 9:00 a.m. to 7:00 p.m.

39. A. The organizing meeting is scheduled for July 27, and the event will be held in January 2010.
    B. The organizing meeting is scheduled for July 27th, and the event will be held in January, 2010.

40. A. We need six desks, eight file cabinets, and 12 trashcans.
    B. We need 6 desks, 8 file cabinets, and 12 trashcans.

For items 41–50, write in each blank the letter of the word that best completes each sentence.

_____ **41.** Will having a degree (A. affect, B. effect) my chances for promotion?

_____ **42.** Try not to (A. loose, B. lose) this key; we will charge you a fee to replace it.

_____ **43.** I don't want to discuss my (A. personal, B. personnel) problems in front of anyone.

_____ **44.** Let us help you choose the right tie to (A. complement, B. compliment) your look.

_____ **45.** The repairman's whistling (A. aggravated, B. irritated) all of us in accounting.

_____ **46.** The bank agreed to (A. loan, B. lend) the Smiths $20,000 for their start-up.

_____ **47.** The credit card company is (A. liable, B. likely) to increase your interest rate if you miss a payment.

_____ **48.** The airline tries to (A. accommodate, B. accomodate) disabled passengers.

_____ **49.** Every company needs a policy regarding sexual (A. harrassment, B. harassment).

_____ **50.** Use your best (A. judgment, B. judgement) in selecting a service provider.

ASSESSMENT OF ENGLISH SKILLS

In the space provided, record the number of questions you answered incorrectly.

Questions	Skills Area	Number of Incorrect Answers
1–5	Parts of speech	_____
6–15	Usage	_____
16–20	Sentence structure	_____
21–30	Punctuation	_____
31–40	Mechanics	_____
41–50	Vocabulary	_____

If you had more than two incorrect answers in any of the skills areas, focus on those areas in the appropriate sections of this handbook.

ESSENTIALS OF GRAMMAR, MECHANICS, AND USAGE

The following sentence looks innocent, but is it really?

We sell tuxedos as well as rent.

You sell tuxedos, but it's highly unlikely that you sell rent—which is what this sentence says. Whatever you're selling, some people will ignore your message because of a blunder like this. The following sentence has a similar problem:

Vice President Eldon Neale told his chief engineer that he would no longer be with Avix, Inc., as of June 30.

Is Eldon or the engineer leaving? No matter which side the facts are on, the sentence can be read the other way. Now look at this sentence:

The year before we budgeted more for advertising sales were up.

Confused? Perhaps this is what the writer meant:

The year before, we budgeted more for advertising. Sales were up.

Or maybe the writer meant this:

The year before we budgeted more for advertising, sales were up.

These examples show that even short, simple sentences can be misunderstood because of errors on the part of the writer. As you've learned in numerous courses over your schooling, an English sentence consists of the parts of speech being combined with punctuation, mechanics, and vocabulary to convey meaning. Making a point of brushing up on your grammar, punctuation, mechanics, and vocabulary skills will help ensure that you create clear, effective business messages.

1.0 GRAMMAR

Grammar is the study of how words come together to form sentences. Categorized by meaning, form, and function, English words fall into various parts of speech: nouns, pronouns, verbs, adjectives, adverbs, prepositions, conjunctions, articles, and interjections. You will communicate more clearly if you understand how each of these parts of speech operates in a sentence.

1.1 Nouns

A **noun** names a person, a place, a thing, or an idea. Anything you can see or detect with one of your senses has a noun to name it. Some things you can't see or sense are also nouns—ions, for example, or space. So are things that exist as ideas, such as accuracy and height. (You can see that something is accurate or that a building is tall, but you can't see the idea of accuracy or the idea of height.) These names for ideas are known as **abstract nouns**. The simplest nouns are the names of things you can see or touch: *car, building, cloud, brick*; these are termed **concrete nouns**. A few nouns, such as *algorithm, software,* and *code,* are difficult to categorize as either abstract or concrete but can reasonably be considered concrete even though they don't have a physical presence.

1.1.1 Proper Nouns and Common Nouns

So far, all the examples of nouns have been **common nouns**, referring to general classes of things. The word *building* refers to a whole class of structures. Common nouns such as *building* are not capitalized.

If you want to talk about one particular building, however, you might refer to the Glazier Building. The name is capitalized, indicating that *Glazier Building* is a **proper noun**.

Here are three sets of common and proper nouns for comparison:

Common	Proper
city	Kansas City
company	Blaisden Company
store	Books Galore

1.1.2 Nouns as Subject and Object

Nouns may be used in sentences as subjects or objects. That is, the person, place, thing, or idea that is being or doing (subject) is represented by a noun. So is the person, place, idea, or thing that is being acted on (object). In the following sentence, the nouns are underlined:

The <u>web designer</u> created the <u>homepage</u>.

The web designer (subject) is acting in a way that affects the home page (object). The following sentence is more complicated:

The <u>installer</u> delivered the <u>carpet</u> to the <u>customer</u>.

Installer is the subject. *Carpet* is the object of the main part of the sentence (acted on by the installer), and *customer* is the object of the phrase *to the customer*. Nevertheless, both *carpet* and *customer* are objects.

1.1.3 Plural Nouns

Nouns can be either singular or plural. The usual way to make a plural noun is to add *s* or *es* to the singular form of the word:

Singular	Plural
file	files
tax	taxes
cargo	cargoes

Many nouns have other ways of forming the plural. Some plurals involve a change in a vowel (*mouse/mice, goose/geese, woman/women*), the addition of *en* or *ren* (*ox/oxen, child/children*), the change from *y* to *ies* (*city/cities, specialty/specialties*), or the change from *f* to *v* (*knife/knives, half/halves;* some exceptions: *fifes, roofs*). Some words of Latin origin offer a choice of plurals (*phenomena/phenomenons, indexes/indices, appendixes/appendices*). It's always a good idea to consult a dictionary if you are unsure of the correct or preferred plural spelling of a word.

The plurals of compound nouns are usually formed by adding *s* or *es* to the main word of the compound (*fathers-in-law, editors-in-chief, attorneys-at-law*).

Some nouns are the same whether singular or plural (*sleep, deer, moose*). Some nouns are plural in form but singular in use (*ethics, measles*). Some nouns are used in the plural only (*scissors, trousers*).

Letters, numbers, and words used as words are sometimes made plural by adding an apostrophe and an *s* (*A's, Ph.D.'s, I's*). However, if no confusion would be created by leaving off the apostrophe, it is common practice to just add the *s* (*1990s, RFPs, DVDs*).

1.1.4 Possessive Nouns

A noun becomes possessive when it's used to show the ownership of something. Then you add *'s* to the word:

the man's car   the woman's apartment

However, ownership does not need to be legal:

the secretary's desk   the company's assets

Also, ownership may be nothing more than an automatic association:

a day's work   the job's prestige

An exception to the rule about adding *'s* to make a noun possessive occurs when the word is singular and already has two "s" sounds at the end. In cases like the following, an apostrophe is all that's needed:

crisis' dimensions   Mr. Moses' application

When the noun has only one "s" sound at the end, however, retain the *'s*:

Chris's book   Carolyn Nuss's office

With compound (hyphenated) nouns, add *'s* to the last word:

Compound Noun	Possessive Noun
mother-in-law	mother-in-law's
mayor-elect	mayor-elect's

To form the possessive of plural nouns, just begin by following the same rule as with singular nouns: add *'s*. However, if the plural noun already ends in an *s* (as most do), drop the one you've added, leaving only the apostrophe:

the clients' complaints   employees' benefits

To denote joint possession by two or more proper nouns, add the *'s* to the last name only (*Moody, Nation, and Smith's* ad agency). To denote individual possession by two or more persons, add an *'s* to each proper noun (*Moody's, Nation's, and Smith's* ad agencies).

1.1.5 Collective Nouns

Collective nouns encompass a group of people or objects: *crowd, jury, committee, team, audience, family, couple, herd, class.* They are often treated as singular nouns. (For more on collective nouns, see Section 1.3.4, Subject–Verb Agreement.)

Practice Session: Nouns

Underline the preferred choice within each set of parentheses in the following sentences.

1. We are moving company headquarters to New York (*City, city*).
2. The historic Bradbury (*Building, building*) is the site of the press conference; the (*Building, building*) is located in downtown Los Angeles.
3. During the conference, our staff will be staying at the Hyatt, Hilton, and Marriott (*hotels', hotels*).

4. Accuracy requires that you cross your (*ts, t's*) and dot your (*is, i's*).
5. The industry has been on a downward spiral since the early (*1990's, 1990s*).
6. The new (*shelfs, shelves*) will be installed on Friday.
7. Our (*specialtys, specialties*) are unparalleled service and premium brands.
8. As a result of several Internet-related (*cases, case's*), the copyright laws are under scrutiny.
9. Before a job interview, you should learn about the (*company's, companies'*) mission statement.
10. Sending the newsletter to the printer is the (*editor's-in-chief, editor-in-chief 's*) responsibility.
11. All the downtown (*business', businesses', businesses's*) signs must be repainted.
12. Because the (*passenger's, passengers'*) luggage had been damaged, they had to file claims with the airline.
13. Dealing with angry customers is all in a (*days, day's, days'*) work for Mr. Jemas.
14. Its large airport is one of (*Dallases, Dallas', Dallas's*) main appeals for industrial firms.
15. We were skeptical of (*Jone's, Jones', Jones's*) plan.

1.2 Pronouns

A **pronoun** is a word that stands for a noun; it saves repeating the noun:

> Employees have some choice of weeks for vacation, but *they* must notify the HR office of *their* preference by March 1.

The pronouns *they* and *their* stand in for the noun *employees*. The noun that a pronoun stands for is called the **antecedent** of the pronoun; *employees* is the antecedent of *they* and *their*.

When the antecedent is plural, the pronoun that stands in for it has to be plural; *they* and *their* are plural pronouns because *employees* is plural. Likewise, when the antecedent is singular, the pronoun has to be singular:

> We thought the contract had expired, but we soon learned that *it* had not.

1.2.1 Multiple Antecedents

Sometimes a pronoun has a double (or even a triple) antecedent:

> Kathryn Boettcher and Luis Gutierrez went beyond *their* sales quotas for January.

If taken alone, *Kathryn Boettcher* is a singular antecedent. So is *Luis Gutierrez*. However, when together they are the plural antecedent of a pronoun, so the pronoun has to be plural. Thus the pronoun is *their* instead of *her* or *his*.

1.2.2 Unclear Antecedents

In some sentences the pronoun's antecedent is unclear:

> Sandy Wright sent Jane Brougham *her* production figures for the previous year. *She* thought they were too low.

To which person does the pronoun *her* refer? Someone who knew Sandy and Jane and knew their business relationship might be able to figure out the antecedent for *her*. Even with such an advantage, however, a reader might receive the wrong

meaning. Also, it would be nearly impossible for any reader to know which name is the antecedent of *she*.

The best way to clarify an ambiguous pronoun is usually to rewrite the sentence, repeating nouns when needed for clarity:

> Sandy Wright sent her production figures for the previous year to Jane Brougham. Jane thought they were too low.

The noun needs to be repeated only when the antecedent is unclear.

1.2.3 Pronoun Classes

Personal pronouns consist of *I, you, we/us, he/him, she/her, it,* and *they/them*.

Compound personal pronouns are created by adding *self* or *selves* to simple personal pronouns: *myself, ourselves, yourself, yourselves, himself, herself, itself, themselves*. Compound personal pronouns are used either *intensively*, to emphasize the identity of the noun or pronoun (I *myself* have seen the demonstration), or *reflexively*, to indicate that the subject is the receiver of his or her own action (I promised *myself* I'd finish by noon). Compound personal pronouns are used incorrectly if they appear in a sentence without their antecedent:

> Walter, Virginia, and *I* (not *myself*) are the top salespeople.
> You need to tell *her* (not *herself*) about the mixup.

Relative pronouns refer to nouns (or groups of words used as nouns) in the main clause and are used to introduce clauses:

> Purina is the brand *that* most dog owners purchase.

The relative pronouns are *which, who, whom, whose,* and *what*. Other words used as relative pronouns include *that, whoever, whomever, whatever,* and *whichever*.

Interrogative pronouns are those used for asking questions: *who, whom, whose, which,* and *what*.

Demonstrative pronouns point out particular persons, places, or things:

> *That* is my desk.   *This* can't be correct.

The demonstrative pronouns are *this, these, that,* and *those*.

Indefinite pronouns refer to persons or things not specifically identified. They include *anyone, someone, everyone, everybody, somebody, either, neither, one, none, all, both, each, another, any, many,* and similar words.

1.2.4 Case of Pronouns

The case of a pronoun tells whether it's acting or acted upon:

> *She* sells an average of five packages each week.

In this sentence, *she* is doing the selling. Because *she* is acting, *she* is said to be in the **nominative case**. Now consider what happens when the pronoun is acted upon:

> After six months, Ms. Browning promoted *her*.

In this sentence, the pronoun *her* is acted upon and is thus said to be in the **objective case**.

Contrast the nominative and objective pronouns in this list:

Nominative	Objective
I	me
we	us
he	him
she	her
they	them
who	whom
whoever	whomever

Objective pronouns may be used as either the object of a verb (such as *promoted*) or the object of a preposition (such as *with*):

Rob worked with *them* until the order was filled.

In this example, *them* is the object of the preposition *with* because Rob acted upon—worked with—them. Here's a sentence with three pronouns, the first one nominative, the second the object of a verb, and the third the object of a preposition:

He paid *us* as soon as the check came from *them.*

He is nominative; *us* is objective because it's the object of the verb *paid*; *them* is objective because it's the object of the preposition *from.*

Every writer sometimes wonders whether to use *who* or *whom:*

(*Who, Whom*) will you hire?

Because this sentence is a question, it's difficult to see that *whom* is the object of the verb *hire.* You can figure out which pronoun to use if you rearrange the question and temporarily try *she* and *her* in place of *who* and *whom:* "Will you hire *she*?" or "Will you hire *her*?" *Her* and *whom* are both objective, so the correct choice is "Whom will you hire?" Here's a different example:

(*Who, Whom*) logged so much travel time?

Turning the question into a statement, you get:

He logged so much travel time.

Therefore, the correct statement is:

Who logged so much travel time?

1.2.5 Possessive Pronouns

Possessive pronouns work like possessive nouns—they show ownership or automatic association:

her job	their preferences
his account	its equipment

However, possessive pronouns are different from possessive nouns in the way they are written. Possessive pronouns never have an apostrophe:

Possessive Noun	Possessive Pronoun
the woman's estate	her estate
Roger Franklin's plans	his plans
the shareholders' feelings	their feelings
the vacuum cleaner's attachments	its attachments

The word *its* is the possessive of *it.* Like all other possessive pronouns, *its* has no apostrophe. Some people confuse *its* with *it's*, the contraction of *it is.* (Contractions are discussed in Section 2.9, Apostrophes.)

1.2.6 Pronoun–Antecedent Agreement

Like nouns, pronouns can be singular or plural. Pronouns must agree in number with their antecedents—a singular antecedent requires a singular pronoun:

The president of the board tendered *his* resignation.

Multiple antecedents require a plural pronoun:

The members of the board tendered *their* resignations.

A pronoun referring to singular antecedents connected by *or* or *nor* should be singular:

Neither Sean nor Terry made his quota.

But a pronoun referring to a plural and a singular antecedent connected by *or* or *nor* should be plural:

Neither Sean nor the twins made *their* quotas.

Formal English prefers the nominative case after the linking verb *to be:*

It is *I.*   That is *he.*

However, for general usage it's perfectly acceptable to use the more natural "It's me" and "That's him."

Practice Session: Pronouns

Underline the preferred choice within each set of parentheses in the following sentences.

1. Just between you and (*I, me*), I don't think we will make the deadline.
2. The final speaker at the luncheon was (*she, her*).
3. When you are finished, give the report to (*he, him*).
4. (*We, Us*) telemarketers have a tarnished reputation.
5. The company is sending the marketing communications staff—Mary-Ann, Alan, and (*I, me, myself*)—to the conference.
6. The company will issue (*their, its*) annual report next month.
7. Anyone who hasn't yet turned in (*their, his or her*) questionnaire should do so by tomorrow.
8. (*Who, Whom*) shall I say called?
9. To (*who, whom*) should I address the letter?
10. (*Who, Whom*) will they hire?
11. We need more people in our department like (*she, her*).
12. When dealing with an angry customer, try to calm (*him, him or her, them*) down.

13. It was either Sarah or Charlene who left (*her, their*) briefcase on the train.
14. The company needs to update (*its, it's*) website.
15. (*Who, Whom*) do you think will be given the promotion?
16. Be sure to include (*your, you're*) e-mail address on the form.
17. Each brand should have (*its, their*) own trademark.
18. The "dynamic duo"—Bruce and (*I, me*)—are in charge of next week's office party.
19. The supervisor thanked the team members for (*their, they're*) support.
20. The pharmaceutical giant agreed to take (*their, its*) diet drug off the market.

1.3 Verbs

A **verb** describes an action or acts as a link between a subject and words that define or describe that subject:

> They all *quit* in disgust.
>
> Working conditions *were* substandard.

The English language is full of **action verbs**. Here are a few you'll often run across in the business world:

verify	perform	fulfill
hire	succeed	send
leave	improve	receive
accept	develop	pay

You could undoubtedly list many more.

The most common linking verbs are all the forms of *to be*: I *am, was,* or *will be*; you *are, were,* or *will be*. Other words that can serve as linking verbs include *seem, become, appear, prove, look, remain, feel, taste, smell, sound, resemble, turn,* and *grow*:

> It *seemed* a good plan at the time.
>
> She *sounds* impressive at a meeting.
>
> The time *grows* near for us to make a decision.

These verbs link what comes before them in the sentence with what comes after; no action is involved. (See Section 1.7.5 for a fuller discussion of linking verbs.)

An **auxiliary verb** is one that helps another verb and is used for showing tense, voice, and so on. A verb with its helpers is called a **verb phrase**. Verbs used as auxiliaries include *do, did, have, may, can, must, shall, might, could, would,* and *should*.

1.3.1 Verb Tenses

English has three simple verb tenses: present, past, and future.

Present:	Our branches in Hawaii *stock* other items.
Past:	We *stocked* Purquil pens for a short time.
Future:	Rotex Tire Stores *will stock* your line of tires when you begin a program of effective national advertising.

With most verbs (the regular ones), the past tense ends in *ed*, and the future tense always has *will* or *shall* in front of it. But the present tense is more complex, depending on the subject:

	First Person	Second Person	Third Person
Singular	I stock	you stock	he/she/it stocks
Plural	we stock	you stock	they stock

The basic form, *stock*, takes an additional *s* when *he, she,* or *it* precedes it. (See Section 1.3.4 for more on subject–verb agreement.)

In addition to the three simple tenses, the three **perfect tenses** are created by adding forms of the auxiliary verb *have*. The present perfect tense uses the past participle (regularly the past tense) of the main verb, *stocked*, and adds the present-tense *have* or *has* to the front of it:

> (I, we, you, they) *have stocked*.
>
> (He, she, it) *has stocked*.

The past perfect tense uses the past participle of the main verb, *stocked*, and adds the past-tense *had* to the front of it:

> (I, you, he, she, it, we, they) *had stocked*.

The future perfect tense also uses the past participle of the main verb, *stocked*, but adds the future-tense *will have*:

> (I, you, he, she, it, we, they) *will have stocked*.

Verbs should be kept in the same tense when the actions occur at the same time:

> When the payroll checks *came in*, everyone *showed up* for work.
>
> We *have found* that everyone *has pitched* in to help.

When the actions occur at different times, you may change tense accordingly:

> The shipment *came* last Wednesday, so if another one *comes* in today, please return it.
>
> The new employee *had been* ill at ease, but now she *has become* a full-fledged member of the team.

1.3.2 Irregular Verbs

Many verbs don't follow some of the standard patterns for verb tenses. The most irregular of these verbs is *to be*:

Tense	Singular	Plural
Present:	I *am* you *are* he, she, it *is*	we *are* you *are* they *are*
Past:	I *was* you *were* he, she, it *was*	we *were* you *were* they *were*

The future tense of *to be* is formed in the same way that the future tense of a regular verb is formed.

The perfect tenses of *to be* are also formed as they would be for a regular verb, except that the past participle is a special form, *been*, instead of just the past tense:

Present perfect:	you have been
Past perfect:	you had been
Future perfect:	you will have been

Here's a sampling of other irregular verbs:

Present	Past	Past Participle
begin	began	begun
shrink	shrank	shrunk
know	knew	known
rise	rose	risen
become	became	become
go	went	gone
do	did	done

Dictionaries list the various forms of other irregular verbs.

1.3.3 Transitive and Intransitive Verbs

Many people are confused by three particular sets of verbs:

lie/lay	sit/set	rise/raise

Using these verbs correctly is much easier when you learn the difference between transitive and intransitive verbs.

Transitive verbs require a receiver; they "transfer" their action to an object. Intransitive verbs do not have a receiver for their action. Some intransitive verbs are complete in themselves and need no help from other words (prices *dropped*; we *won*). Other intransitive words must be "completed" by a noun or adjective called a **complement**. Complements occur with linking verbs.

Here are some sample uses of transitive and intransitive verbs:

Intransitive	Transitive
We should include in our new offices a place to *lie* down for a nap.	The workers will be here on Monday to *lay* new carpeting.
Even the way an interviewee *sits* is important.	That crate is full of stemware, so *set* it down carefully.
Salaries at Compu-Link, Inc., *rise* swiftly.	They *raise* their level of production every year.

The workers *lay* carpeting, you *set down* the crate, they *raise* production; each action is transferred to something. In the intransitive sentences, a person *lies down*, an interviewee *sits*, and salaries *rise* without affecting anything else. Intransitive sentences are complete with only a subject and a verb; transitive sentences are not complete unless they also include an object; or something to transfer the action to.

Tenses are a confusing element of the lie/lay problem:

Present	Past	Past Participle
I *lie*	I *lay*	I *have lain*
I *lay* (something down)	I *laid* (something down)	I *have laid* (something down)

The past tense of *lie* and the present tense of *lay* look and sound alike, even though they're different verbs.

1.3.4 Subject–Verb Agreement

Whether regular or irregular, every verb must agree with its subject, both in person (first, second, or third) and in number (single or plural).

	First Person	Second Person	Third Person
Singular	I *am* I *write*	you *are* you *write*	he/she/it *is* he/she/it *writes*
Plural	we *are* we *write*	you *are* you *write*	they *are* they *write*

In a simple sentence, making a verb agree with its subject is a straightforward task:

Hector Ruiz *is* a strong competitor. (third-person singular)

We *write* to you every month. (first-person plural)

Confusion sometimes arises when sentences are a bit more complicated. For example, be sure to avoid agreement problems when words come between the subject and verb. In the following examples, the verb appears in italics, and its subject is underlined:

The <u>analysis</u> of existing documents *takes* a full week.

Even though *documents* is a plural, the verb is in the singular form. That's because the subject of the sentence is *analysis*, a singular noun. The phrase *of existing documents* can be disregarded. Here is another example:

The <u>answers</u> for this exercise *are* in the study guide.

Take away the phrase *for this exercise* and you are left with the plural subject *answers*. Therefore, the verb takes the plural form.

Verb agreement is also complicated when the subject is a collective noun or pronoun or when the subject may be considered either singular or plural. In such cases, you often have to analyze the surrounding sentence to determine which verb form to use:

The <u>staff</u> *is* quartered in the warehouse.

The <u>staff</u> *are* at their desks in the warehouse.

The <u>computers</u> and the <u>staff</u> *are* in the warehouse.

Neither the staff nor the <u>computers</u> *are* in the warehouse.

<u>Every</u> computer *is* in the warehouse.

Many a <u>computer</u> *is* in the warehouse.

Did you notice that words such as *every* use the singular verb form? In addition, when an *either/or* or a *neither/nor* phrase combines singular and plural nouns, the verb takes the form that matches the noun closest to it.

In the business world, some subjects require extra attention. Company names, for example, are considered singular and therefore take a singular verb in most cases—even if they contain plural words:

Stater Brothers *offers* convenient grocery shopping.

In addition, quantities are sometimes considered singular and sometimes plural. If a quantity refers to a total amount, it takes a singular verb; if a quantity refers to individual, countable units, it takes a plural verb:

> Three hours *is* a long time.
>
> The eight dollars we collected for the fund *are* tacked on the bulletin board.

Fractions may also be singular or plural, depending on the noun that accompanies them:

> One-third of the warehouse *is* devoted to this product line.
>
> One-third of the products *are* defective.

To decide whether to use a singular or plural verb with subjects such as *number* and *variety*, follow this simple rule: If the subject is preceded by *a*, use a plural verb:

> *A* number of products *are* being displayed at the trade show.

If the subject is preceded by *the*, use a singular verb:

> *The* variety of products on display *is* mind-boggling.

For a related discussion, see Section 1.7.1, Longer Sentences.

1.3.5 Voice of Verbs

Verbs have two voices, active and passive. When the subject comes first, the verb is in **active voice**; when the object comes first, the verb is in **passive voice**:

> **Active:** The buyer *paid* a large amount.
> **Passive:** A large amount *was paid* by the buyer.

The passive voice uses a form of the verb *to be*, which adds words to a sentence. In the example, the passive-voice sentence uses eight words, whereas the active-voice sentence uses only six to say the same thing. The words *was* and *by* are unnecessary to convey the meaning of the sentence. In fact, extra words usually clog meaning. So be sure to opt for the active voice when you have a choice.

At times, however, you have no choice:

> Several items *have been taken*, but so far we don't know who took them.

The passive voice becomes necessary when you don't know (or don't want to say) who performed the action; the active voice is bolder and more direct.

1.3.6 Mood of Verbs

Verbs can express one of three moods: indicative, imperative, or subjunctive. The **indicative mood** is used to make a statement or to ask a question:

> The secretary mailed a letter to each supplier.
>
> Did the secretary mail a letter to each supplier?

Use the **imperative mood** when you wish to command or request:

> Please mail a letter to each supplier.

With the imperative mood, the subject is the understood *you*.

The **subjunctive mood** is used to express doubt or a wish or a condition contrary to fact:

> If I *were* you, I wouldn't send that e-mail.

The subjunctive is also used to express a suggestion or a request:

> I asked that Rosario *be* [not *is*] present at the meeting.

1.3.7 Verbals

Verbals are verbs that are modified to function as other parts of speech. They include infinitives, gerunds, and participles.

Infinitives are formed by placing a *to* in front of the verb (*to go, to purchase, to work*). They function as nouns. Although many of us were taught that it is "incorrect" to split an infinitive—that is, to place an adverb between the *to* and the verb—that rule is not a hard and fast one. In some cases, the adverb is best placed in the middle of the infinitive to avoid awkward constructions or ambiguous meaning:

> Production of steel is expected to *moderately exceed* domestic use.

Gerunds are verbals formed by adding *ing* to a verb (*going, having, working*). Like infinitives, they function as nouns. Gerunds and gerund phrases take a singular verb:

> *Borrowing* from banks *is* preferable to getting venture capital.

Participles are verb forms used as adjectives. The present participle ends in *ing* and generally describes action going on at the same time as other action:

> *Checking* the schedule, the contractor was pleased with progress on the project.

The past participle is usually the same form as the past tense and generally indicates completed action:

> When *completed*, the project will occupy six city blocks.

The **perfect participle** is formed by adding *having* to the past participle:

> *Having completed* the project, the contractor submitted his last invoice.

Practice Session: Verbs

Underline the preferred choice within each set of parentheses in the following sentences.

1. When Hastings (*come, comes, came*) in, tell him I (*want, wanted*) to see him.
2. Even though Sheila (*knowed, knew*) the right password, she typed it incorrectly.
3. The presentation had not yet (*began, begun*) when Charles arrived.
4. What I always say is, let sleeping dogs (*lay, lie*).
5. The workers (*lay, laid*) the tile in the executive bathroom yesterday.
6. This is where the president of the board (*sits, sets*) during meetings.
7. Just (*sit, set*) the boxes down over there.
8. Do you think management will (*raise, rise*) prices across the board next week?
9. A list of promotions (*was, were*) posted on the company intranet.

10. The supervisor of the assembly-line workers (*is, are*) being replaced.
11. The committee (*is, are*) considering the proposal today.
12. The board and the committee (*is, are*) having a joint meeting on June 25.
13. Neither the board nor the committee (*is, are*) expected to approve the proposal.
14. Every member of the board (*is, are*) going to make a statement.
15. Katten and Associates (*represent, represents*) clients in the entertainment industry.
16. Five hours (*is, are*) all I can give you to get the project done.
17. Half of the vacant lots (*is, are*) already sold.
18. Half of the hall (*is, are*) reserved for the luncheon.
19. Mario suggested that the public relations department (*send, sends*) out a news release about the merger.
20. If I (*was, were*) CEO, I'd fire the whole accounting staff.

1.4 Adjectives

An **adjective** modifies (tells something about) a noun or pronoun. Each of the following phrases says more about the noun or pronoun than the noun or pronoun would say alone:

an *efficient* staff	a *heavy* price
brisk trade	*light* web traffic

Adjectives modify nouns more often than they modify pronouns. When adjectives do modify pronouns, however, the sentence usually has a linking verb:

They were *attentive*.	It looked *appropriate*.
He seems *interested*.	You are *skillful*.

1.4.1 Types of Adjectives

Adjectives serve a variety of purposes. **Descriptive adjectives** express some quality belonging to the modified item (*tall, successful, green*). **Limiting** or **definitive adjectives**, on the other hand, point out the modified item or limit its meaning without expressing a quality. Types include:

- Numeral adjectives (*one, fifty, second*)
- Articles (*a, an, the*)
- Pronominal adjectives: pronouns used as adjectives (*his* desk, *each* employee)
- Demonstrative adjectives: *this, these, that, those* (*these* tires, *that* invoice)

Proper adjectives are derived from proper nouns:

Chinese customs	*Orwellian* overtones

Predicate adjectives complete the meaning of the predicate and are introduced by linking verbs:

The location is *perfect*.	Prices are *high*.

1.4.2 Comparative Degree

Most adjectives can take three forms: simple, comparative, and superlative. The simple form modifies a single noun or pronoun. Use the comparative form when comparing two items. When comparing three or more items, use the superlative form:

Simple	Comparative	Superlative
hard	harder	hardest
safe	safer	safest
dry	drier	driest

The comparative form adds *er* to the simple form, and the superlative form adds *est*. (The *y* at the end of a word changes to *i* before the *er* or *est* is added.)

A small number of adjectives are irregular, including these:

Simple	Comparative	Superlative
good	better	best
bad	worse	worst
little	less	least

When the simple form of an adjective has two or more syllables, you usually add *more* to form the comparative and *most* to form the superlative:

Simple	Comparative	Superlative
useful	more useful	most useful
exhausting	more exhausting	most exhausting
expensive	more expensive	most expensive

The most common exceptions are two-syllable adjectives that end in *y*:

Simple	Comparative	Superlative
happy	happier	happiest
costly	costlier	costliest

If you choose this option, change the *y* to *i* and tack *er* or *est* onto the end.

Some adjectives cannot be used to make comparisons because they themselves indicate the extreme. For example, if something is perfect, nothing can be more perfect. If something is unique or ultimate, nothing can be more unique or more ultimate.

1.4.3 Hyphenated Adjectives

Many adjectives used in the business world are actually combinations of words: *up-to-date* report, *last-minute* effort, *fifth-floor* suite, *well-built* engine. As you can see, they are hyphenated when they come before the noun they modify. However, when such word combinations come after the noun they modify, they are not hyphenated. In the following example, the adjectives appear in italics and the nouns they modify are underlined:

The <u>report</u> is *up to date* because of our team's *last-minute* <u>efforts</u>.

Hyphens are not used when part of the combination is a word ending in *ly* (because that word is usually not an adjective). Hyphens are also omitted from word combinations that are used so frequently that readers are used to seeing the words together:

We live in a *rapidly shrinking* world.

Our *highly motivated* employees will be well paid.

Please consider renewing your *credit card* account.

Send those figures to our *data processing* department.

Our new intern is a *high school* student.

1.5 Adverbs

An **adverb** modifies a verb, an adjective, or another adverb:

Modifying a verb: Our marketing department works *efficiently*.

Modifying an adjective: She was not dependable, although she was *highly* intelligent.

Modifying another adverb: When signing new clients, he moved *extremely* cautiously.

An adverb can be a single word (*clearly*), a phrase (*very clearly*), or a clause (*because it was clear*).

1.5.1 Types of Adverbs

Simple adverbs are simple modifiers:

The door opened *automatically*.

The order arrived *yesterday*.

Top companies were *there*.

Interrogative adverbs ask a question:

Where have you been?

Conjunctive adverbs connect clauses:

We can't start *until* Maria gets here.

Jorge tried to explain *how* the new software works.

Words frequently used as conjunctive adverbs include *where, wherever, when, whenever, while, as, how, why, before, after, until,* and *since*.

Negative adverbs include *not, never, seldom, rarely, scarcely, hardly,* and similar words. Negative adverbs are powerful words and therefore do not need any help in conveying a negative thought. Avoid using double negatives like these:

I don't want no mistakes.
(Correct: "I don't want any mistakes," or "I want no mistakes.")

They couldn't hardly read the report.
(Correct: "They could hardly read the report," or "They couldn't read the report.")

They scarcely noticed neither one.
(Correct: "They scarcely noticed either one," or "They noticed neither one.")

1.5.2 Adverb–Adjective Confusion

Many adverbs are adjectives turned into adverbs by adding *ly: highly, extremely, officially, closely, really*. In addition, many words can be adjectives or adverbs, depending on their usage in a particular sentence:

The *early* bird gets the worm.
[adjective]

We arrived *early*.
[adverb]

It was a *hard* decision.
[adjective]

He hit the wall *hard*.
[adverb]

Because of this situation, some adverbs are difficult to distinguish from adjectives. For example, in the following sentences, is the underlined word an adverb or an adjective?

They worked <u>well</u>.

The baby is <u>well</u>.

In the first sentence, *well* is an adverb modifying the verb *worked*. In the second sentence, *well* is an adjective modifying the noun *baby*. You may find it helpful to remember that a *linking verb* (such as *is* in "The baby is well") connects an adjective to the noun it modifies. In contrast, an *action verb* is modified by an adverb:

Adjective	Adverb
He is a *good* worker. (What kind of worker is he?)	He works *well*. (How does he work?)
It is a *real* computer. (What kind of computer is it?)	It *really* is a computer. (To what extent is it a computer?)
The traffic is *slow*. (What quality does the traffic have?)	The traffic moves *slowly*. (How does the traffic move?)
This food tastes *bad* without salt. (What quality does the food have?)	This food *badly* needs salt. (How much is it needed?)

1.5.3 Comparative Degree

Like adjectives, adverbs can be used to compare items. Generally, the basic adverb is combined with *more* or *most*, just as long adjectives are. However, some adverbs have one-word comparative forms:

One Item	Two Items	Three Items
quickly	more quickly	most quickly
sincerely	less sincerely	least sincerely
fast	faster	fastest
well	better	best

Practice Session: Adjectives and Adverbs

Underline the preferred choice within each set of parentheses in the following sentences.

1. I always choose the (*less, least*) expensive brand.
2. Which would be (*better, best*), the store brand or the generic brand?
3. This audit couldn't have come at a (*worse, worst*) time.
4. When it comes to data analysis, Claire is (*more competent, competenter*) than Alexander.
5. The ad agency's campaign for our new vitamin supplement is (*unique, very unique, most unique*), to say the least.
6. A corporation can benefit from a (*well written, well-written*) annual report.
7. The chairman's introductory message to the annual report was (*well written, well-written*).

8. Even a (*beautifully written, beautifully-written*) report can be hampered by poor design and production.
9. According to Bank of America, the number of mortgage applications from (lower-income, lower income) consumers has tripled in the past year.
10. Angela wasn't feeling (*good, well*), so she went home early.
11. Harrison and Martinez work (*good, well*) together.
12. We are (*real, really*) excited about next week's product launch.
13. Could this project be moving any more (*slow, slowly*) through the bureaucratic system?
14. We (*could hardly, couldn't hardly*) wait to see how the brochure had turned out.
15. Today TeKTech is (*more heavy, more heavily, most heavily*) involved in nanotechnology, compared to five years ago.

1.6 Other Parts of Speech

Nouns, pronouns, verbs, adjectives, and adverbs carry most of the meaning in a sentence. Four other parts of speech link them together in sentences: prepositions, conjunctions, articles, and interjections.

1.6.1 Prepositions

A **preposition** is a word or group of words that describes a relationship between other words in a sentence. A simple preposition is made up of one word: *of, in, by, above, below*. A *compound preposition* is made up of two prepositions: *out of, from among, except for, because of*.

A **prepositional phrase** is a group of words introduced by a preposition that functions as an adjective (an adjectival phrase) or as an adverb (adverbial phrase) by telling more about a pronoun, noun, or verb:

> The shipment will be here *by next Friday*.
>
> Put the mail *in the out-bin*.

Prepositional phrases should be placed as close as possible to the element they are modifying:

> Shopping *on the Internet* can be confusing for the uninitiated. (*not* Shopping can be confusing for the uninitiated *on the Internet*.)

Some prepositions are closely linked with a verb. When using phrases such as *look up* and *wipe out*, keep them intact and do not insert anything between the verb and the preposition.

You may have been told that it is unacceptable to put a preposition at the end of a sentence. However, that is not a hard-and-fast rule, and trying to follow it can sometimes be a challenge. You can end a sentence with a preposition as along as the sentence sounds natural and as long as rewording the sentence would create awkward wording:

> I couldn't tell what they were interested in.
>
> What did she attribute it to?
>
> What are you looking for?

Avoid using unnecessary prepositions. In the following examples, the prepositions in parentheses should be omitted:

> All (of) the staff members were present.
>
> I almost fell off (of) my chair with surprise.

> Where was Mr. Steuben going (to)?
>
> They couldn't help (from) wondering.

The opposite problem is failing to include a preposition when you should. Consider these two sentences:

> Sales were over $100,000 for Linda and Bill.
>
> Sales were over $100,000 for Linda and for Bill.

The first sentence indicates that Linda and Bill had combined sales over $100,000; the second, that Linda and Bill each had sales over $100,000, for a combined total in excess of $200,000. The preposition *for* is critical here.

When the same preposition can be used for two or more words in a sentence without affecting the meaning, only the last preposition is required:

> We are familiar (with) and satisfied with your company's products.

But when different prepositions are normally used with the words, all the prepositions must be included:

> We are familiar with and interested in your company's products.

Some prepositions have come to be used in a particular way with certain other parts of speech. Here is a partial list of some prepositions that have come to be used with certain words:

according to	independent of
agree to (a proposal)	inferior to
agree with (a person)	plan to
buy from	prefer to
capable of	prior to
comply with	reason with
conform to	responsible for
differ from (things)	similar to
differ with (person)	talk to (without interaction)
different from	talk with (with interaction)
get from (receive)	wait for (person or thing)
get off (dismount)	wait on (like a waiter)

If you are unsure of the correct idiomatic expression, check a dictionary.

Some verb-preposition idioms vary depending on the situation: You agree *to* a proposal but *with* a person, *on* a price, or *in* principle. You argue *about* something, *with* a person, and *for* or *against* a proposition. You compare one item *to* another to show their similarities; you compare one item *with* another to show differences.

Here are some other examples of preposition usage that have given writers trouble:

> **among/between:** *Among* is used to refer to three or more (Circulate the memo *among* the staff); *between* is used to refer to two (Put the copy machine *between* Judy and Dan).
>
> **as if/like:** *As if* is used before a clause (It seems *as if* we should be doing something); *like* is used before a noun or pronoun (He seems *like* a nice guy).

have/of: *Have* is a verb used in verb phrases (They should *have* checked first); *of* is a preposition and is never used in such cases.

in/into: *In* is used to refer to a static position (The file is *in* the cabinet); *into* is used to refer to movement toward a position (Put the file *into* the cabinet).

1.6.2 Conjunctions

Conjunctions connect the parts of a sentence: words, phrases, and clauses. A **coordinating conjunction** connects two words, phrases, or clauses of equal rank. The simple coordinating conjunctions include *and, but, or, nor, for, yet,* and *so.* **Correlative conjunctions** are coordinating conjunctions used in pairs: *both/and, either/or, neither/nor, not only/but also.* Constructions with correlative conjunctions should be parallel, with the same part of speech following each element of the conjunction:

> The purchase was *not only* expensive *but also* unnecessary.
>
> The purchase *not only was* expensive *but also was* unnecessary.

Conjunctive adverbs are adverbs used to connect or show relationships between clauses. They include *however, nevertheless, consequently, moreover,* and *as a result.*

A **subordinate conjunction** connects two clauses of unequal rank; it joins a dependent (subordinate) clause to the independent clause on which it depends (for more on dependent and independent clauses, see Section 1.7.1). Subordinate conjunctions include *as, if, because, although, while, before, since, that, until, unless, when, where,* and *whether.*

1.6.3 Articles and Interjections

Only three **articles** exist in English: *the, a,* and *an.* These words are used, like adjectives, to specify which item you are talking about. *The* is called the *definite article* because it indicates a specific noun; *a* and *an* are called the *indefinite articles* because they are less specific about what they are referring to.

If a word begins with a vowel (soft) sound, use *an;* otherwise, use *a.* It's *a history,* not *an history, a hypothesis,* not *an hypothesis.* Use *an* with an "h" word only if it is a soft "h," as in *honor* and *hour.* Use *an* with words that are pronounced with a soft vowel sound even if they are spelled beginning with a consonant (usually in the case of abbreviations): *an SEC application, an MP3 file.* Use *a* with words that begin with vowels if they are pronounced with a hard sound: *a university, a Usenet account.*

Repeat an article if adjectives modify different nouns: *The red house and the white house are mine.* Do not repeat an article if all adjectives modify the same noun: *The red and white house is mine.*

Interjections are words that express no solid information, only emotion:

> Wow!   Well, well!
> Oh, no!   Good!

Such purely emotional language has its place in private life and advertising copy, but it only weakens the effect of most business writing.

Practice Session: Prepositions, Conjunctions, Articles, and Interjections

Circle the letter of the preferred choice in each pair of sentences.

1. **A.** If we want to have the project done next week, we'll need those balance sheets by Wednesday.
   B. If we want to have the project done next week, by Wednesday we'll need those balance sheets.

2. **A.** From where did that information come?
   B. Where did that information come from?

3. **A.** Please look up the shipping rates for packages to France.
   B. Please look the shipping rates up for packages to France.

4. **A.** You need to indicate the type job you're seeking.
   B. You need to indicate the type of job you're seeking.

5. **A.** Michael got the actuarial data off of the Internet.
   B. Michael got the actuarial data off the Internet.

6. **A.** When the meeting is over, Michelle will prepare the minutes.
   B. When the meeting is over with, Michelle will prepare the minutes.

7. **A.** Sharon is familiar and knowledgeable about HTML coding.
   B. Sharon is familiar with and knowledgeable about HTML coding.

8. **A.** We'll be deciding among the four applicants this afternoon.
   B. We'll be deciding between the four applicants this afternoon.

9. **A.** Because Marshall isn't here, it looks like the conference call will have to be canceled.
   B. Because Marshall isn't here, it looks as if the conference call will have to be canceled.

10. **A.** I would have had the memo done sooner, but my computer crashed.
    B. I would of had the memo done sooner, but my computer crashed.

11. **A.** When we have the survey results, we can put them in the report.
    B. When we have the survey results, we can put them into the report.

12. **A.** If you agree with the settlement, I can prepare the final papers.
    B. If you agree to the settlement, I can prepare the final papers.

13. **A.** It is important that you provide not only your name but also your address and telephone number.
    B. It is important that you provide not only your name but also address and telephone number.

14. A. The conference will be held in either March or July.
  B. The conference will be held either in March or July.

15. A. Please prepare an RFP for the construction job.
  B. Please prepare a RFP for the construction job.

1.7 Sentences

Sentences are constructed with the major building blocks, the parts of speech. Take, for example, this simple two-word sentence:

> Money talks.

It consists of a noun (*money*) and a verb (*talks*). When used in this way, the noun works as the first requirement for a sentence, the **subject**, and the verb works as the second requirement, the **predicate**. Without a subject (who or what does something) and a predicate (the doing of it), you have merely a collection of words, not a sentence.

1.7.1 Longer Sentences

More complicated sentences have more complicated subjects and predicates, but they still have a simple subject and a predicate verb. In the following examples, the subject is underlined once, the predicate verb twice:

> <u>Marex</u> and <u>Contron</u> <u><u>enjoy</u></u> higher earnings each quarter.

Marex [and] *Contron* do something; *enjoy* is what they do.

> My <u>interview</u>, coming minutes after my freeway accident, <u><u>did</u></u> not <u><u>impress</u></u> or <u><u>move</u></u> anyone.

Interview is what did something. What did it do? It *did* [not] *impress* [or] *move*.

> In terms of usable space, a steel <u>warehouse</u>, with its extremely long span of roof unsupported by pillars, <u><u>makes</u></u> more sense.

Warehouse is what *makes*.

These three sentences demonstrate several things. First, in all three sentences, the simple subject and predicate verb are the "bare bones" of the sentence, the parts that carry the core idea of the sentence. When trying to find the subject and predicate verb, disregard all prepositional phrases, modifiers, conjunctions, and articles.

Second, in the third sentence, the verb is singular (*makes*) because the subject is singular (*warehouse*). Even though the plural noun *pillars* is closer to the verb, *warehouse* is the subject. So *warehouse* determines whether the verb is singular or plural. Subject and predicate must agree.

Third, the subject in the first sentence is compound (*Marex* [and] *Contron*). A compound subject, when connected by *and*, requires a plural verb (*enjoy*). Also, the second sentence shows how compound predicates can occur (*did* [not] *impress* [or] *move*).

Fourth, the second sentence incorporates a group of words—*coming minutes after my freeway accident*—containing a form of a verb (*coming*) and a noun (*accident*). Yet, this group of words is not a complete sentence for two reasons:

- Not all nouns are subjects: *Accident* is not the subject of *coming*.
- Not all verbs are predicates: A verb that ends in *ing* can never be the predicate of a sentence (unless preceded by a form of *to be*, as in *was coming*).

Because they don't contain a subject and a predicate, the words *coming minutes after my freeway accident* (called a **phrase**) can't be written as a sentence. That is, the phrase cannot stand alone; it cannot begin with a capital letter and end with a period. So a phrase must always be just one part of a sentence.

Sometimes a sentence incorporates two or more groups of words that do contain a subject and a predicate; these word groups are called **clauses**:

> My <u>interview</u>, because it <u>came</u> minutes after my freeway accident, <u>did</u> not <u>impress</u> or <u>move</u> anyone.

The **independent clause** is the portion of the sentence that could stand alone without revision:

> My *interview* <u>did</u> not <u>impress</u> or <u>move</u> anyone.

The other part of the sentence could stand alone only by removing *because*:

> (because) It <u>came</u> minutes after my freeway accident.

This part of the sentence is known as a **dependent clause**; although it has a subject and a predicate (just as an independent clause does), it's linked to the main part of the sentence by a word (*because*) showing its dependence.

In summary, the two types of clauses—dependent and independent—both have a subject and a predicate. Dependent clauses, however, do not bear the main meaning of the sentence and are therefore linked to an independent clause. Nor can phrases stand alone, because they lack both a subject and a predicate. Only independent clauses can be written as sentences without revision.

1.7.2 Types of Sentences

Sentences come in four main types, depending on the extent to which they contain clauses. A **simple sentence** has one subject and one predicate; in short, it has one main independent clause:

> Boeing is the world's largest aerospace company.

A **compound sentence** consists of two independent clauses connected by a coordinating conjunction (*and, or, but*, etc.) or a semicolon:

> Airbus outsold Boeing for several years, but Boeing has recently regained the lead.

A **complex sentence** consists of an independent clause and one or more dependent clauses:

> Boeing is betting [independent clause] that airlines will begin using moderately smaller planes to fly passengers between smaller cities [dependent clause introduced by *that*].

A **compound-complex sentence** has two main clauses, at least one of which contains a subordinate (dependent clause):

> Boeing is betting [independent clause] that airlines will begin using moderately smaller planes to fly passengers between smaller cities [dependent clause], and it anticipates that new airports will be developed to meet passenger needs [independent clause].

1.7.3 Sentence Fragments

An incomplete sentence (a phrase or a dependent clause) that is written as though it were a complete sentence is called a **fragment**. Consider the following sentence fragments:

> Marilyn Sanders, having had pilferage problems in her store for the past year. Refuses to accept the results of our investigation.

This serious error can easily be corrected by putting the two fragments together:

> Marilyn Sanders, having had pilferage problems in her store for the past year, refuses to accept the results of our investigation.

The actual details of a situation will determine the best way for you to remedy a fragment problem.

The ban on fragments has one exception. Some advertising copy contains sentence fragments, written knowingly to convey a certain rhythm. However, advertising is the only area of business in which fragments are acceptable.

1.7.4 Fused Sentences and Comma Splices

Just as there can be too little in a group of words to make it a sentence, there can also be too much:

> All our mail is run through a postage meter every afternoon someone picks it up.

This example contains two sentences, not one, but the two have been blended so that it's hard to tell where one ends and the next begins. Is the mail run through a meter every afternoon? If so, the sentences should read:

> All our mail is run through a postage meter every afternoon. Someone picks it up.

Perhaps the mail is run through a meter at some other time (morning, for example) and is picked up every afternoon:

> All our mail is run through a postage meter. Every afternoon someone picks it up.

The order of words is the same in all three cases; sentence division makes all the difference. Either of the last two cases is grammatically correct. The choice depends on the facts of the situation.

Sometimes these so-called **fused sentences** have a more obvious point of separation:

> Several large orders arrived within a few days of one another, too many came in for us to process by the end of the month.

Here, the comma has been put between two independent clauses in an attempt to link them. When a lowly comma separates two complete sentences, the result is called a **comma splice**. A comma splice can be remedied in one of three ways:

- Replace the comma with a period and capitalize the next word: "... one another. Too many "..."
- Replace the comma with a semicolon and do not capitalize the next word: "... one another; too many ..." This remedy works only when the two sentences have closely related meanings.

- Change one of the sentences so that it becomes a phrase or a dependent clause. This remedy often produces the best writing, but it takes more work.

The third alternative can be carried out in several ways. One is to begin the sentence with a subordinating conjunction:

> Whenever several large orders arrived within a few days of one another, too many came in for us to process by the end of the month.

Another way is to remove part of the subject or the predicate verb from one of the independent clauses, thereby creating a phrase:

> Several large orders arrived within a few days of one another, too many for us to process by the end of the month.

Finally, you can change one of the predicate verbs to its *ing* form:

> Several large orders arrived within a few days of one another, too many coming in for us to process by the end of the month.

In many cases, simply adding a coordinating conjunction can separate fused sentences or remedy a comma splice:

> You can fire them, or you can make better use of their abilities.

> Margaret drew up the designs, and Matt carried them out.

> We will have three strong months, but after that sales will taper off.

Be careful with coordinating conjunctions: Use them only to join simple sentences that express similar ideas.

Also, because they say relatively little about the relationship between the two clauses they join, avoid using coordinating conjunctions too often: *and* is merely an addition sign; *but* is just a turn signal; *or* only points to an alternative. Subordinating conjunctions such as *because* and *whenever* tell the reader a lot more.

1.7.5 Sentences with Linking Verbs

Linking verbs were discussed briefly in the section on verbs (Section 1.3). Here, you can see more fully the way they function in a sentence. The following is a model of any sentence with a linking verb:

> A *(verb)* B.

Although words such as *seems* and *feels* can also be linking verbs, let's assume that the verb is a form of *to be*:

> A *is* B.

In such a sentence, A and B are always nouns, pronouns, or adjectives. When one is a noun and the other is a pronoun, or when both are nouns, the sentence says that one is the same as the other:

> She is president.

> Rachel is president.

> She is forceful.

Recall from Section 1.3.3 that the noun or adjective that follows the linking verb is called a *complement*. When it is a noun or noun phrase, the complement is called a *predicate nominative*, when the complement is an adjective, it is referred to as a *predicate adjective*.

1.7.6 Misplaced Modifiers

The position of a modifier in a sentence is important. The movement of *only* changes the meaning in the following sentences:

> Only we are obliged to supply those items specified in your contract.

> We are obliged only to supply those items specified in your contract.

> We are obliged to supply only those items specified in your contract.

> We are obliged to supply those items specified only in your contract.

In any particular set of circumstances, only one of those sentences would be accurate. The others would very likely cause problems. To prevent misunderstanding, place such modifiers as close as possible to the noun or verb they modify.

For similar reasons, whole phrases that are modifiers must be placed near the right noun or verb. Mistakes in placement create ludicrous meanings:

> Antia Information Systems bought new computer chairs for the programmers with more comfortable seats.

The anatomy of programmers is not normally a concern of business writers. Obviously, the comfort of the chairs was the issue:

> Antia Information Systems bought programmers the new computer chairs with more comfortable seats.

Here is another example:

> I asked him to file all the letters in the cabinet that had been answered.

In this ridiculous sentence, the cabinet has been answered, even though no cabinet in history is known to have asked a question. *That had been answered* is too far from *letters* and too close to *cabinet*. Here's an improvement:

> I asked him to file in the cabinet all the letters that had been answered.

The term **dangling modifier** is often used to refer to a clause or phrase that because of its position in the sentence seems to modify a word that it is not meant to modify. For instance:

> Lying motionless, co-workers rushed to Barry's aid.

Readers expect an introductory phrase to modify the subject of the main clause. But in this case it wasn't the *co-workers* who were lying motionless but rather *Barry* who was in this situation. Like this example, most instances of dangling modifiers occur at the beginning of sentences. The source of some danglers is a passive construction:

> To find the needed information, the whole book had to be read.

In such cases, switching to the active voice can usually remedy the problem:

> To find the needed information, you will need to read the whole book.

1.7.7 Parallelism

Two or more sentence elements that have the same relation to another element should be in the same form. Otherwise, the reader is forced to work harder to understand the meaning of the sentence. When a series consists of phrases or clauses, the same part of speech (preposition, gerund, etc.) should introduce them. Do not mix infinitives with participles or adjectives with nouns. Here are some examples of nonparallel elements:

> Andersen is hiring managers, programmers, and people who work in accounting. [nouns not parallel]

> Andersen earns income by auditing, consulting, and by bookkeeping. [prepositional phrases not parallel]

> Andersen's goals are to win new clients, keeping old clients happy, and finding new enterprises. [infinitive mixed with gerunds]

Practice Session: Sentences

Circle the letter of the preferred choice in each group of sentences.

1. **A.** Cyberterrorism—orchestrated attacks on a company's information systems for political or economic purposes—is a very real threat.
   B. Cyberterrorism—orchestrated attacks on a company's information systems for political or economic purposes—are a very real threat.

2. **A.** E-mail, phone calls, and IM messages, each one a distraction, interrupts employees when they work.
   B. E-mail, phone calls, and IM messages, each one a distraction, interrupt employees when they work.

3. **A.** About 35 percent of major U.S. companies keep tabs on workers. Because they want to protect valuable company information.
   B. About 35 percent of major U.S. companies keep tabs on workers because they want to protect valuable company information.
   C. About 35 percent of major U.S. companies keep tabs on workers; because they want to protect valuable company information.

4. **A.** Despite its small size and relative isolation in the Arctic Circle. Finland leads the pack in mobile phone technology and its applications.
   B. Despite its small size and relative isolation in the Arctic Circle; Finland leads the pack in mobile phone technology and its applications.

C. Despite its small size and relative isolation in the Arctic Circle, Finland leads the pack in mobile phone technology and its applications.

5. A. Many employees erroneously believe that their e-mail and voice mail messages are private they're surprised when e-mail ends up in places where they did not intend it to go.
   B. Many employees erroneously believe that their e-mail and voice mail messages are private, they're surprised when e-mail ends up in places where they did not intend it to go.
   C. Many employees erroneously believe that their e-mail and voice mail messages are private, so they're surprised when e-mail ends up in places where they did not intend it to go.

6. A. Each day people in the United States treat themselves to more than 3 million Krispy Kreme doughnuts, they buy more than 11,000 dozen of those doughnuts every hour.
   B. Each day people in the United States treat themselves to more than 3 million Krispy Kreme doughnuts, buying more than 11,000 dozen of those doughnuts every hour.

7. A. The procedure for making Krispy Kreme doughnuts takes about an hour, the manufacturing process begins long before local stores crank up their production lines.
   B. The procedure for making Krispy Kreme doughnuts takes about an hour; the manufacturing process begins long before local stores crank up their production lines.
   C. The procedure for making Krispy Kreme doughnuts takes about an hour. But the manufacturing process begins long before local stores crank up their production lines.

8. A. After blending the ingredients, the doughnut mix is stored in Krispy Kreme's warehouse for a week.
   B. After blending the ingredients, Krispy Kreme's warehouse is used to store the doughnut mix for a week.
   C. After the ingredients have been blended, the doughnut mix is stored in Krispy Kreme's warehouse for a week.

9. A. Using computer-aided design, our engineers customize every bike to meet the rider's size and component preferences.
   B. Our engineers customize every bike with computer-aided design to meet the rider's size and component preferences

10. A. Catering to its customers, about 2,000 bikes are built annually by Green Gear Cycling.
    B. Catering to its customers, about 2,000 bikes are built by Green Gear Cycling annually.
    C. Catering to its customers, Green Gear Cycling builds about 2,000 bikes annually.

2.0 PUNCTUATION

On the highway, signs tell you when to slow down or stop, where to turn, and when to merge. In similar fashion, punctuation helps readers negotiate your prose. The proper use of punctuation keeps readers from losing track of your meaning.

2.1 Periods

Use a period (1) to end any sentence that is not a question, (2) with certain abbreviations, and (3) between dollars and cents in an amount of money.

2.2 Question Marks

Use a question mark after any direct question that requests an answer:

> Are you planning to enclose a check, or shall we bill you?

Don't use a question mark with commands phrased as questions for the sake of politeness:

> Will you send us a check today.

A question mark should precede quotation marks, parentheses, and brackets if it is part of the quoted or parenthetical material; otherwise, it should follow:

> This issue of *Inc.* has an article titled "What's Your Entrepreneurial IQ?"

> Have you read the article "Five Principles of Guerrilla Marketing"?

Do not use the question mark with indirect questions or with requests:

> Mr. Antonelli asked whether anyone had seen Nathalia lately.

Do not use a comma or a period with a question mark; the question mark takes the place of these punctuation marks.

2.3 Exclamation Points

Use exclamation points after highly emotional language. Because business writing almost never calls for emotional language, you will seldom use exclamation points.

2.4 Semicolons

Semicolons have three main uses. One is to separate two closely related independent clauses:

> The outline for the report is due within a week; the report itself is due at the end of the month.

A semicolon should also be used instead of a comma when the items in a series have commas within them:

> Our previous meetings were on November 11, 2004; February 20, 2005; and April 28, 2006.

Finally, a semicolon should be used to separate independent clauses when the second one begins with a conjunctive adverb such as *however, therefore,* or *nevertheless* or a phrase such as *for example* or *in that case:*

> Our supplier has been out of part D712 for 10 weeks; however, we have found another source that can ship the part right away.

> His test scores were quite low; on the other hand, he has a lot of relevant experience.

Section 4.4 provides more information on using transitional words and phrases.

Semicolons should always be placed outside parentheses:

> Events Northwest has the contract for this year's convention (August 23–28); we haven't awarded the contract for next year yet.

2.5 Colons

Use a colon after the salutation in a business letter. You should also use a colon at the end of a sentence or phrase introducing a list or (sometimes) a quotation:

> Our study included the three most critical problems: insufficient capital, incompetent management, and inappropriate location.

A colon should not be used when the list, quotation, or idea is a direct object of the verb or preposition. This rule applies whether the list is set off or run in:

> We are able to supply
>
> staples
>
> wood screws
>
> nails
>
> toggle bolts
>
> This shipment includes 9 DVDs, 12 CDs, and 4 USB flash drives.

Another way you can use a colon is to separate the main clause and another sentence element when the second explains, illustrates, or amplifies the first:

> Management was unprepared for the union representatives' demands: this fact alone accounts for their arguing well into the night.

However, in contemporary usage, such clauses are frequently separated by a semicolon.

Like semicolons, colons should always be placed outside parentheses:

> He has an expensive list of new demands (none of which is covered in the purchase agreement): new carpeting, network cabling, and a new security system.

Practice Session: Punctuation 1

Circle the letter of the preferred choice in the following groups of sentences.

1. **A.** She asked me whether we should increase our insurance coverage?
   B. She asked me whether we should increase our insurance coverage.

2. **A.** Would you please let me know when the copier is free.
   B. Would you please let me know when the copier is free?

3. **A.** You won't want to miss this exciting seminar!
   B. You won't want to miss this exciting seminar.

4. **A.** The officers of the board of directors are John Rogers, president, Robin Doug Donlan, vice president for programming, Bill Pittman, vice president for operations, and Mary Sturhann, secretary.
   B. The officers of the board of directors are John Rogers, president; Robin Doug Donlan, vice president for programming; Bill Pittman, vice president for operations; and Mary Sturhann, secretary.

   C. The officers of the board of directors are John Rogers, president; Robin Doug Donlan, vice president for programming; Bill Pittman, vice president for operations, and Mary Sturhann, secretary.

5. **A.** Edward Jones is the best brokerage house in America; it has more offices than any other brokerage house.
   B. Edward Jones is the best brokerage house in America, it has more offices than any other brokerage house.

6. **A.** One of the SEC's top priorities is to crack down on insider trading, however it readily admits that it has not been very successful to date.
   B. One of the SEC's top priorities is to crack down on insider trading; however, it readily admits that it has not been very successful to date.

7. **A.** To keep on top of financial news, you should consult three newspapers aimed specifically at investors: *The Wall Street Journal, Investor's Business Daily,* and *Barron's.*
   B. To keep on top of financial news, you should consult three newspapers aimed specifically at investors; such as, *The Wall Street Journal, Investor's Business Daily,* and *Barron's.*
   C. To keep on top of financial news, you should consult three newspapers aimed specifically at investors; such as *The Wall Street Journal, Investor's Business Daily,* and *Barron's.*

8. **A.** I wonder if it is appropriate to call John's clients while he is on vacation.
   B. I wonder if it is appropriate to call John's clients while he is on vacation?

9. **A.** The three basic concepts that guide accountants are: the fundamental accounting equation, double-entry bookkeeping, and the matching principle.
   B. The three basic concepts that guide accountants are the fundamental accounting equation, double-entry bookkeeping, and the matching principle.
   C. The three basic concepts that guide accountants are the fundamental accounting equation; double-entry bookkeeping; and the matching principle.

10. **A.** Accountants are guided by three basic concepts, the fundamental accounting equation, double-entry bookkeeping, and the matching principle.
    B. Accountants are guided by three basic concepts: the fundamental accounting equation; double-entry bookkeeping; and the matching principle.
    C. Accountants are guided by three basic concepts: the fundamental accounting equation, double-entry bookkeeping, and the matching principle.

2.6 Commas

Commas have many uses; the most common is to separate items in a series:

> He took the job, learned it well, worked hard, and succeeded.
>
> Put paper, pencils, and paper clips on the requisition list.

Company style may dictate omitting the final comma in a series. However, if you have a choice, use the final comma; it's often necessary to prevent misunderstanding.

A second place to use a comma is between independent clauses that are joined by a coordinating conjunction (*and*, *but*, or *or*):

> She spoke to the sales staff, and he spoke to the production staff.

> I was advised to proceed, and I did.

A third use for the comma is to separate a dependent clause at the beginning of a sentence from an independent clause:

> Because of our lead in the market, we may be able to risk introducing a new product.

However, a dependent clause at the end of a sentence is separated from the independent clause by a comma only when the dependent clause is unnecessary to the main meaning of the sentence:

> We may be able to introduce a new product, although it may involve some risk.

A fourth use for the comma is after an introductory phrase or word:

> Starting with this amount of capital, we can survive in the red for one year.

> Through more careful planning, we may be able to serve more people.

> Yes, you may proceed as originally planned.

However, with short introductory prepositional phrases and some one-syllable words (such as *hence* and *thus*), the comma is often omitted:

> Before January 1 we must complete the inventory.

> Thus we may not need to hire anyone.

> In July we will complete the move to Tulsa.

Fifth, paired commas are used to set off nonrestrictive clauses and phrases. A **restrictive clause** is one that cannot be omitted without altering the meaning of the main clause, whereas a **nonrestrictive clause** can be:

> The *Time* magazine website, which is produced by Steve Conley, has won several design awards. [nonrestrictive: the material set off by commas could be omitted]

> The website that is produced by Steve Conley has won several design awards. [restrictive: no commas are used before and after *that is produced by Steve Conley* because this information is necessary to the meaning of the sentence—it specifies which website]

A sixth use for commas is to set off appositive words and phrases. (An **appositive** has the same meaning as the word it is in apposition to.) Like nonrestrictive clauses, appositives can be dropped without changing or obscuring the meaning of the sentence:

> Conley, a freelance designer, also produces the websites for several nonprofit corporations.

Seventh, commas are used between adjectives modifying the same noun (coordinate adjectives):

> She left Monday for a long, difficult recruiting trip.

To test the appropriateness of such a comma, try reversing the order of the adjectives: *a difficult, long recruiting trip*. If the order cannot be reversed, leave out the comma (a *good old friend* isn't the same as an *old good friend*). A comma should not be used when one of the adjectives is part of the noun. Compare these two phrases:

> a distinguished, well-known figure

> a distinguished public figure

The adjective–noun combination of *public* and *figure* has been used together so often that it has come to be considered a single thing: *public figure*. So no comma is required.

Eighth, commas are used both before and after the year in sentences that include month, day, and year:

> It will be sent by December 15, 2007, from our Cincinnati plant.

Some companies write dates in another form: 15 December 2007. No commas should be used in that case. Nor is a comma needed when only the month and year are present (December 2007).

Ninth, commas are used to set off a variety of parenthetical words and phrases within sentences, including state names, dates, abbreviations, transitional expressions, and contrasted elements:

> They were, in fact, prepared to submit a bid.

> Habermacher, Inc., went public in 1999.

> Our goal was increased profits, not increased market share.

> Service, then, is our main concern.

> The factory was completed in Chattanooga, Tennessee, just three weeks ago.

> Joanne Dubiik, M.D., has applied for a loan from First Savings.

> I started work here on March 1, 2003, and soon received my first promotion.

Tenth, a comma is used to separate a quotation from the rest of the sentence:

> Your warranty reads, "These conditions remain in effect for one year from date of purchase."

However, the comma is left out when the quotation as a whole is built into the structure of the sentence:

> He hurried off with an angry "Look where you're going."

Finally, a comma should be used whenever it's needed to avoid confusion or an unintended meaning. Compare the following:

> Ever since they have planned new ventures more carefully.

> Ever since, they have planned new ventures more carefully.

2.7 Dashes

Use dashes to surround a comment that is a sudden turn in thought:

> Membership in the IBSA—it's expensive but worth it—may be obtained by applying to our New York office.

A dash can also be used to emphasize a parenthetical word or phrase:

> Third-quarter profits—in excess of $2 million—are up sharply.

Finally, use dashes to set off a phrase that contains commas:

> All our offices—Milwaukee, New Orleans, and Phoenix—have sent representatives.

Don't confuse a dash with a hyphen. A dash separates and emphasizes words, phrases, and clauses more strongly than commas or parentheses can; a hyphen ties two words so tightly that they almost become one word.

When using a computer, use the em dash symbol. When typing a dash in e-mail, type two hyphens with no space before, between, or after.

A second type of dash, the en dash, can be produced with computer word processing and page-layout programs. This kind of dash is shorter than the regular dash and longer than a hyphen. It is reserved almost exclusively for indicating "to" or "through" with numbers such as dates and pages: *2001–2002, pages 30–44.*

2.8 Hyphens

Hyphens are mainly used in three ways. The first is to separate the parts of compound words beginning with such prefixes as *self-, ex-, quasi-,* and *all-*:

self-assured	quasi-official
ex-wife	all-important

However, do not use hyphens in words that have prefixes such as *pro, anti, non, re, pre, un, inter,* and *extra*:

prolabor	nonunion
antifascist	interdepartmental

Exceptions occur when (1) the prefix occurs before a proper noun or (2) the vowel at the end of the prefix is the same as the first letter of the root word:

pro-Republican	anti-American
anti-inflammatory	extra-atmospheric

When in doubt, consult your dictionary.

Hyphens are used in some types of spelled-out numbers. For instance, they are used to separate the parts of a spelled-out number from *twenty-one* to *ninety-nine* and for spelled-out fractions: *two-thirds, one-sixth* (although some style guides say not to hyphenate fractions used as nouns).

Certain compound nouns are formed by using hyphens: *secretary-treasurer, city-state.* Check your dictionary for compounds you're unsure about.

Hyphens are also used in some compound adjectives, which are adjectives made up of two or more words. Specifically, you should use hyphens in compound adjectives that come before the noun:

an interest-bearing account	well-informed executives

However, you need not hyphenate when the adjective follows a linking verb:

> This account is interest bearing.
>
> Their executives are well informed.

You can shorten sentences that list similar hyphenated words by dropping the common part from all but the last word:

> Check the costs of first-, second-, and third-class postage.

Finally, hyphens may be used to divide words at the end of a typed line. Such hyphenation is best avoided, but when you have to divide words at the end of a line, do so correctly (see Section 3.5). Dictionaries show how words are divided into syllables.

2.9 Apostrophes

Use an apostrophe in the possessive form of noun (but not in a pronoun):

> On his desk was a reply to Bette *Ainsley's* application for the *manager's* position.

Apostrophes are also used in place of the missing letter(s) of a contraction:

Whole Words	Contraction
we will	we'll
do not	don't
they are	they're

2.10 Quotation Marks

Use quotation marks to surround words that are repeated exactly as they were said or written:

> The collection letter ended by saying, "This is your third and final notice."

Remember: (1) When the quoted material is a complete sentence, the first word is capitalized. (2) The final comma or period goes inside the closing quotation marks.

Quotation marks are also used to set off the title of a newspaper story, magazine article, or book chapter:

> You should read "Legal Aspects of the Collection Letter" in *Today's Credit.*

Quotation marks may also be used to indicate special treatment for words or phrases, such as terms that you're using in an unusual or ironic way:

> Our management "team" spends more time squabbling than working to solve company problems.

When you are defining a word, put the definition in quotation marks:

> The abbreviation *etc.* means "and so forth."

When using quotation marks, take care to insert the closing marks as well as the opening ones.

Although periods and commas go inside any quotation marks, colons and semicolons generally go outside them.

A question mark goes inside the quotation marks only if the quotation is a question:

> All that day we wondered, "Is he with us?"

If the quotation is not a question but the entire sentence is, the question mark goes outside:

> What did she mean by "You will hear from me"?

For quotes within quotes, use single quotation marks within double:

> As David Pottruck, former co-CEO of Charles Schwab, told it, "I assembled about 100 managers at the base of the Golden Gate Bridge and gave them jackets emblazoned with the phrase 'Crossing the Chasm' and then led them across the bridge."

Otherwise, do not use single quotation marks for anything, including titles of works—that's British style.

2.11 Parentheses and Brackets

Use parentheses to surround comments that are entirely incidental or to supply additional information:

> Our figures do not match yours, although (if my calculations are correct) they are closer than we thought.
>
> These kinds of supplements do not require FDA (Food and Drug Administration) approval.

Parentheses are used in legal documents to surround figures in arabic numerals that follow the same amount in words:

> Remittance will be One Thousand Two Hundred Dollars ($1,200).

Be careful to put punctuation marks (period, comma, and so on) outside the parentheses unless they are part of the statement in parentheses. And keep in mind that parentheses have both an opening and a closing mark; both should always be used, even when setting off listed items within text: *(1)*, not *1)*.

Brackets are used for notation, comment, explanation, or correction within quoted material:

> In the interview, multimillionaire Bob Buford said, "One of my major influences was Peter [Drucker], who encourages people and helps them believe in themselves."

Brackets are also used for parenthetical material that falls within parentheses:

> Drucker's magnum opus (*Management: Tasks, Responsibilities, Practices* [Harper & Row, 1979]) has influenced generations of entrepreneurs.

2.12 Ellipses

Use ellipsis points, or three evenly spaced periods, to indicate that material has been left out of a direct quotation. Use them only in direct quotations and only at the point where material was left out. In the following example, the first sentence is quoted in the second:

> The Dow Jones Industrial Average fell 276.39 points, or 2.6%, during the week to 10292.31.

> According to the *Wall Street Journal*, "The Dow Jones Industrial Average fell 276.39 points . . . to 10,292.31."

The number of dots in ellipses is not optional; always use three. Occasionally, the points of an ellipsis come at the end of a sentence, where they seem to grow a fourth dot. Don't be fooled: One of the dots is a period. Ellipsis points should always be preceded and followed by a space.

Avoid using ellipses to represent a pause in your writing; use a dash for that purpose:

> At first we had planned to leave for the conference on Wednesday—but then we changed our minds. [not *on Wednesday . . . but then*]

2.12.1 Practice Session: Punctuation 2

Circle the letter of the preferred choice in each group of sentences.

1. **A.** Capital One uses data mining to predict what customers might buy, and how the company can sell those products to them.
   B. Capital One uses data mining to predict what customers might buy and how the company can sell those products to them.

2. **A.** During the three-year lawsuit, pressure built to settle out of court.
   B. During the three-year lawsuit pressure built to settle out of court.

3. **A.** The music store, which had been in the Harper family for three generations, was finally sold to a conglomerate.
   B. The music store which had been in the Harper family for three generations was finally sold to a conglomerate.

4. **A.** After the fire, Hanson resolved to build a bigger better bottling plant.
   B. After the fire, Hanson resolved to build a bigger, better bottling plant.

5. **A.** Wild Oats, a chain of natural food grocery stores, uses kiosks to deliver nutrition information to customers.
   B. Wild Oats; a chain of natural food grocery stores; uses kiosks to deliver nutrition information to customers.

6. **A.** Management consultant Peter Drucker said "The aim of marketing is to know the customer so well that the product or service sells itself.
   B. Management consultant Peter Drucker said, "The aim of marketing is to know the customer so well that the product or service sells itself."

7. **A.** Companies use a wide variety of techniques-contests, displays, and giveaways, to name a few-to sell you things.
   B. Companies use a wide variety of techniques—contests, displays, and giveaways, to name a few—to sell you things.
   C. Companies use a wide variety of techniques—contests, displays, and giveaways to name a few—to sell you things.

8. A. Self-insurance plans are not subject to state regulation or premium taxes.
   B. Self insurance plans are not subject to state regulation or premium taxes.
   C. Selfinsurance plans are not subject to state regulation or premium taxes.

9. A. Because ours is a non-profit corporation, we don't pay federal taxes.
   B. Because ours is a nonprofit corporation, we don't pay federal taxes.

10. A. The decision-making process depends on a buyer's culture, social class, and self-image.
    B. The decision-making process depends on a buyer's culture, social class, and self image.
    C. The decision making process depends on a buyer's culture, social class, and self-image.

11. A. Situation factors also play a role in consumer decision-making.
    B. Situation factors also play a role in consumer decision making.

12. A. Did you read the article "Citi Will Return $7 Billion to Investors"?
    B. Did you read the article "Citi Will Return $7 Billion to Investors?"
    C. Did you read the article "Citi Will Return $7 Billion to Investors?".

13. A. An insider at Arthur Andersen said that "the fall of the accounting giant stemmed from a series of poor management decisions made over decades."
    B. An insider at Arthur Andersen said that, "The fall of the accounting giant stemmed from a series of poor management decisions made over decades."

14. A. Have you read Jason Zein's article "Measuring the Internet?"
    B. Have you read Jason Zein's article "Measuring the Internet"?

15. A. According to Jamba Juice founder Kirk Peron, "jamba" is a West African word meaning *to celebrate*.
    B. According to Jamba Juice founder Kirk Peron, *jamba* is a West African word meaning "to celebrate."
    C. According to Jamba Juice founder Kirk Peron, "jamba" is a West African word meaning to celebrate.

3.0 MECHANICS

The most obvious and least tolerable mistakes that a business writer makes are probably those related to grammar and punctuation. However, a number of small details, known as writing mechanics, demonstrate the writer's polish and reflect on the company's professionalism.

When it comes to mechanics, also called *style*, many of the "rules" are not hard and fast. Publications and organizations vary in their preferred styles for capitalization, abbreviations, numbers, italics, and so on. Here, we'll try to differentiate between practices that are generally accepted and those that can vary. When you are writing materials for a specific company or organization, find out the preferred style (such as *The Chicago Manual of Style* or Webster's *Style Manual*). Otherwise, choose a respected style guide. The key to style is consistency: If you spell out the word *percent* in one part of a document, don't use the percent sign in a similar context elsewhere in the same document.

3.1 Capitalization

With capitalization, you can follow either an "up" style (when in doubt, capitalize: *Federal Government, Board of Directors*) or a "down" style (when in doubt, use lowercase: *federal government, board of directors*). The trend over the last few decades has been toward the down style. Your best bet is to get a good style manual and consult it when you have a capitalization question. Following are some rules that most style guides agree on.

Capital letters are used at the beginning of certain word groups:

- **Complete sentence:** Before hanging up, he said, "We'll meet here on Wednesday at noon."
- **Formal statement following a colon:** She has a favorite motto: Where there's a will, there's a way.
- **Phrase used as sentence:** Absolutely not!
- **Quoted sentence embedded in another sentence:** Scott said, "Nobody was here during lunch hour except me."
- **List of items set off from text:** Three preliminary steps are involved:
  Design review
  Budgeting
  Scheduling

Capitalize proper adjectives and proper nouns (the names of particular persons, places, and things):

Darrell Greene lived in a Victorian mansion.

We sent Ms. Larson an application form, informing her that not all applicants are interviewed.

Let's consider opening a branch in the West, perhaps at the west end of Tucson, Arizona.

As office buildings go, the Kinney Building is a pleasant setting for TDG Office Equipment.

We are going to have to cancel our plans for hiring French and German sales reps.

Larson's name is capitalized because she is a particular applicant, whereas the general term *applicant* is left uncapitalized. Likewise, *West* is capitalized when it refers to a particular place but not when it means a direction. In the same way, *office* and *building* are not capitalized when they are general terms (common nouns), but they are capitalized when they are part of the title of a particular office or building (proper nouns). Some proper adjectives are lowercased when they are part of terms that have come into common use, such as *french fries* and *roman numerals*.

Titles within families or companies as well as professional titles may also be capitalized:

I turned down Uncle David when he offered me a job.

I wouldn't be comfortable working for one of my relatives.

We've never had a president quite like President Sweeney.

People's titles are capitalized when they are used in addressing a person, especially in a formal context. They are not usually capitalized, however, when they are used merely to identify the person:

> Address the letter to Chairperson Anna Palmer.
>
> I wish to thank Chairperson Anna Palmer for her assistance.
>
> Anna Palmer, chairperson of the board, took the podium.

Also capitalize titles if they are used by themselves in addressing a person:

> Thank you, Doctor, for your donation.

Always capitalize the first word of the salutation and complimentary close of a letter:

> *Dear* Mr. Andrews: *Yours* very truly,

The names of organizations are capitalized, of course; so are the official names of their departments and divisions. However, do not use capitals when referring in general terms to a department or division, especially one in another organization:

> Route this memo to Personnel.
>
> Larry Tien was transferred to the Microchip Division.
>
> Will you be enrolled in the Psychology Department?
>
> Someone from the personnel department at EnerTech stopped by the booth.

Capitalization is unnecessary when using a word like *company*, *corporation*, or *university* alone:

> The corporation plans to issue 50,000 shares of common stock.

Likewise, the names of specific products are capitalized, although the names of general product types are not:

> Apple Inc.   Xerox machine
> Tide laundry detergent

When it comes to government terminology, here are some guides to capitalization: (1) Lowercase *federal* unless it is part of an agency name; (2) capitalize names of courts, departments, bureaus, offices, and agencies but lowercase such references as *the bureau* and *the department* when the full name is not used; (3) lowercase the titles of government officers unless they precede a specific person's name: *the secretary of state, the senator, the ambassador, the governor, and the mayor* but *Mayor Gonzalez* (Note: style guides vary on whether to capitalize *president* when referring to the president of the United States without including the person's name); (4) capitalize the names of laws and acts: *the Sherman Antitrust Act, the Civil Rights Act*; (5) capitalize the names of political parties but lowercase the word *party: Democratic party, Libertarian party*.

When writing about two or more geographic features of the same type, it is now accepted practice to capitalize the common noun in addition to the proper nouns, regardless of word order:

> Lakes Ontario and Huron
>
> Allegheny and Monongahela Rivers
>
> Corson and Ravenna Avenues

The names of languages, races, and ethnic groups are capitalized: Japanese, Caucasian, Hispanic. But racial terms that denote only skin color are not capitalized: black, white.

When referring to the titles of books, articles, magazines, newspapers, reports, movies, and so on, you should capitalize the first and last words and all nouns, pronouns, adjectives, verbs, and adverbs, and capitalize prepositions and conjunctions with five letters or more. Except for the first and last words, do not capitalize articles:

> *Economics During the Great War*
>
> "An Investigation into the Market for Long-Distance Services"
>
> "What Successes Are Made Of"

When *the* is part of the official name of a newspaper or magazine, it should be treated this way too:

> *The Wall Street Journal*

Style guides vary in their recommendations regarding capitalization of hyphenated words in titles. A general guide is to capitalize the second word in a temporary compound (a compound that is hyphenated for grammatical reasons and not spelling reasons), such as *Law-Abiding Citizen*, but to lowercase the word if the term is always hyphenated, such as *Son-in-law*).

References to specific pages, paragraphs, lines, and the like are not capitalized: *page 73, line 3*. However, in most other numbered or lettered references, the identifying term is capitalized:

> Chapter 4   Serial No. 382-2203   Item B-11

Finally, the names of academic degrees are capitalized when they follow a person's name but are not capitalized when used in a general sense:

> I received a bachelor of science degree.
>
> Thomas Whitelaw, Doctor of Philosophy, will attend.

Similarly, general courses of study are not capitalized, but the names of specific classes are:

> She studied accounting as an undergraduate.
>
> She is enrolled in Accounting 201.

3.2 Underscores and Italics

Usually a line typed underneath a word or phrase either provides emphasis or indicates the title of a book, magazine, or newspaper. If possible, use italics instead of an underscore. Italics (or underlining) should also be used for defining terms and for discussing words as words:

> In this report, *net sales* refers to after-tax sales dollars.
>
> The word *building* is a common noun and should not be capitalized.

Also use italics to set off foreign words, unless the words have become a common part of English:

> Top Shelf is considered the *sine qua non* of comic book publishers.
>
> Chris uses a laissez-faire [no italic] management style.

3.3 Abbreviations

Abbreviations are used heavily in tables, charts, lists, and forms. They're used sparingly in prose. Here are some abbreviation situations to watch for:

- In most cases do not use periods with acronyms (words formed from the initial letter or letters of parts of a term): *CEO, CD-ROM, DOS, YWCA, FDA;* but *Ph.D., M.A., M. D.*
- Use periods with abbreviations such as *Mr., Ms., Sr., Jr., a.m., p.m., B.C.,* and *A.D.*
- The trend is away from using periods with such units of measure as *mph, mm,* and *lb.*
- Use periods with such Latin abbreviations as *e.g., i.e., et al.,* and *etc.* However, style guides recommend that you avoid using these Latin forms and instead use their English equivalents (*for example, that is, and others,* and *and so on,* respectively). If you must use these abbreviations, such as in parenthetical expressions or footnotes, do not put them in italics.
- Some companies have abbreviations as part of their names (*&, Co., Inc., Ltd.*). When you refer to such firms by name, be sure to double-check the preferred spelling, including spacing: *AT&T; Barnes & Noble; Carson Pirie Scott & Company; PepsiCo; Kate Spade, Inc.; National Data Corporation; Siemens Corp.; Glaxo Wellcome PLC; US Airways; U.S. Business Reporter.*
- Most style guides recommend that you spell out *United States* as a noun and reserve *U.S.* as an adjective preceding the noun modified.

One way to handle an abbreviation that you want to use throughout a document is to spell it out the first time you use it, follow it with the abbreviation in parentheses, and then use the abbreviation in the remainder of the document.

3.4 Numbers

Numbers may be correctly handled many ways in business writing, so follow company style. In the absence of a set style, however, generally spell out all numbers from one to nine and use arabic numerals for the rest.

There are some exceptions to this general rule. For example, never begin a sentence with a numeral:

> Twenty of us produced 641 units per week in the first 12 weeks of the year.

Use numerals for the numbers one through nine if they're in the same list as larger numbers:

> Our weekly quota rose from 9 to 15 to 27.

Use numerals for percentages, time of day (except with o'clock), dates, and (in general) dollar amounts:

> Our division is responsible for 7 percent of total sales.
>
> The meeting is scheduled for 8:30 a.m. on August 2.
>
> Add $3 for postage and handling.

When using numerals for time, be consistent: It should be *between 10:00 a.m. and 4:30 p.m.,* not *between 10 a.m. and 4:30 p.m.* Expressions such as *4:00 o'clock* and *7 a.m. in the morning* are redundant.

Use a comma in numbers expressing thousands (1,257), unless your company specifies another style. When dealing with numbers in the millions and billions, combine words and figures: 7.3 million, 2 billion.

When writing dollar amounts, use a decimal point only if cents are included. In lists of two or more dollar amounts, use the decimal point either for all or for none:

> He sent two checks, one for $67.92 and one for $90.00.

When two numbers fall next to each other in a sentence, use figures for the number that is largest, most difficult to spell, or part of a physical measurement; use words for the other:

> I have learned to manage a classroom of 30 twelve-year-olds.
>
> She won a bonus for selling 24 thirty-volume sets.
>
> You'll need twenty 3-inch bolts.

In addresses, all street numbers except One are in numerals. So are suite and room numbers and zip codes. For street names that are numbered, practice varies so widely that you should use the form specified on an organization's letterhead or in a reliable directory. All the following examples are correct:

One Fifth Avenue	297 Ninth Street
1839 44th Street	11026 West 78 Place

Telephone numbers are always expressed in numerals. Parentheses may separate the area code from the rest of the number, but a slash or a hyphen may be used instead, especially if the entire phone number is enclosed in parentheses:

382-8329	(602/382-8329)	602-382-8329

Percentages are always expressed in numerals. The word *percent* is used in most cases, but % may be used in tables, forms, and statistical writing.

Ages are usually expressed in words—except when a parenthetical reference to age follows someone's name:

> Mrs. Margaret Sanderson is seventy-two.
>
> Mrs. Margaret Sanderson, 72, swims daily.

Also, ages expressed in years and months are treated like physical measurements that combine two units of measure: *5 years, 6 months.*

Physical measurements such as distance, weight, and volume are also often expressed in numerals: *9 kilometers, 5 feet 3 inches, 7 pounds 10 ounces.*

Decimal numbers are always written in numerals. In most cases, add a zero to the left of the decimal point if the number is less than one and does not already start with a zero:

1.38	.07	0.2

In a series of related decimal numbers with at least one number greater than one, make sure that all numbers smaller than one have a zero to the left of the decimal point: 1.20, 0.21, 0.09.

Simple fractions are written in words, but more complicated fractions are expressed in figures or, if easier to read, in figures and words:

two-thirds	9/32	2 hundredths

Most style guides recommend that you use a comma with numbers consisting of four digits: *2,345,* not *2345.*

When typing ordinal numbers, such as *3rd edition* or *21st century,* your word processing program may automatically make the letters *rd* (or *st, th,* or *nd*) into a superscript. Do yourself a favor and turn that formatting function off in your "Preferences," as superscripts should not be used in regular prose or even in bibliographies.

3.5 Word Division

In general, avoid dividing words at the end of lines. When you must do so, follow these rules:

- Don't divide one-syllable words (such as *since, walked,* and *thought*), abbreviations (*mgr.*), contractions (*isn't*), or numbers expressed in numerals (*117,500*).

- Divide words between syllables, as specified in a dictionary or word-division manual.

- Make sure that at least three letters of the divided words are moved to the second line: *sin-cerely* instead of *sincere-ly.*

- Do not end a page or more than three consecutive lines with hyphens.

- Leave syllables consisting of a single vowel at the end of the first line (*impedi-ment* instead of *imped-iment*), except when the single vowel is part of a suffix such as *-able, -ible, -ical,* or *-ity (re-spons-ible* instead of *re-sponsi-ble).*

- Divide between double letters (*tomor-row*), except when the root word ends in double letters (*call-ing* instead of *cal-ling*).

- Wherever possible, divide hyphenated words at the hyphen only: instead of *anti-inde-pendence,* use *anti-independence.*

- Whenever possible, do not break URLs or e-mail addresses. If you have to break a long URL or e-mail address, do not insert a hyphen at the end of the first line.

Practice Session: Mechanics

Circle the letter of the preferred choice in each of the following groups of sentences.

1. **A.** When you are in New York City for the sales meeting, be sure to visit the art deco Chrysler Building.
   B. When you are in New York city for the sales meeting, be sure to visit the Art Deco Chrysler building.
   C. When you are in New York City for the sales meeting, be sure to visit the Art Deco Chrysler Building.

2. **A.** We plan to expand our national operations to the west as well as the south.
   B. We plan to expand our national operations to the West as well as the South.
   C. We plan to expand our national operations to the west as well as the South.

3. **A.** Lee Marrs, who is President of Lee Marrs Designs, has been chosen to revamp our website.
   B. Lee Marrs, who is president of Lee Marrs Designs, has been chosen to revamp our website.
   C. Lee Marrs, who is President of Lee Marrs Designs, has been chosen to revamp our Website.

4. **A.** There's one thing we know for sure: Having a good idea doesn't guarantee success.
   B. There's one thing we know for sure: having a good idea doesn't guarantee success.

5. **A.** Be sure to order manila envelopes in all sizes: 9", 12", 11", 14", etc.
   B. Be sure to order manila envelopes in all sizes: 9", 12", 11", 14" and etc.

6. **A.** The traditional trading period for U.S. stock exchanges is 9:30 a.m. to 4 o'clock p.m.

B. The traditional trading period for U.S. stock exchanges is 9:30 a.m. to 4 p.m.
   C. The traditional trading period for U.S. stock exchanges is 9:30 a.m to 4:00 p.m.

7. **A.** The number of members on the board of directors has been reduced from 13 to nine.
   B. The number of members on the board of directors has been reduced from 13 to 9.

8. **A.** The CDs are priced at $15, $12.95, and $11.00.
   B. The CDs are priced at $15.00, $12.95, and $11.00.
   C. The CDs are priced at $15, $12.95, and $11.

9. **A.** Twenty people have signed up for the spreadsheet software class, but there is room for 25.
   B. 20 people have signed up for the spreadsheet software class, but there is room for 25.

10. **A.** The best way to divide the word *sincerely* is "sin-cerely."
    B. The best way to divide the word *sincerely* is "sincere-ly."

4.0 VOCABULARY

Using the right word in the right place is a crucial skill in business communication. However, many pitfalls await the unwary.

4.1 Frequently Confused Words

Because the following sets of words sound similar, be careful not to use one when you mean to use the other:

Word	Meaning
accede	to comply with
exceed	to go beyond
accept	to take
except	to exclude
access	admittance
excess	too much
advice	suggestion
advise	to suggest
affect	to influence
effect	the result
allot	to distribute
a lot	much or many
all ready	completely prepared
already	completed earlier
born	given birth to
borne	carried
capital	money; chief city
capitol	a government building
cite	to quote
sight	a view
site	a location
complement	complete amount; to go well with
compliment	expression of esteem; to flatter
corespondent	party in a divorce suit
correspondent	letter writer

Word	Meaning
council	a panel of people
counsel	advice; a lawyer
defer	to put off until later
differ	to be different
device	a mechanism
devise	to plan
die	to stop living; a tool
dye	to color
discreet	careful
discrete	separate
envelop	to surround
envelope	a covering for a letter
forth	forward
fourth	number four
holey	full of holes
holy	sacred
wholly	completely
human	of people
humane	kindly
incidence	frequency
incidents	events
instance	example
instants	moments
interstate	between states
intrastate	within a state
later	afterward
latter	the second of two
lead	a metal; to guide
led	guided
lean	to rest at an angle
lien	a claim
levee	embankment
levy	tax
loath	reluctant
loathe	to hate
loose	free; not tight
lose	to mislay
material	substance
materiel	equipment
miner	mineworker
minor	underage person
moral	virtuous; a lesson
morale	sense of well-being
ordinance	law
ordnance	weapons
overdo	to do in excess
overdue	past due

Word	Meaning
peace	lack of conflict
piece	a fragment
pedal	a foot lever
peddle	to sell
persecute	to torment
prosecute	to sue
personal	private
personnel	employees
precedence	priority
precedents	previous events
principal	sum of money; chief; main
principle	general rule
rap	to knock
wrap	to cover
residence	home
residents	inhabitants
right	correct
rite	ceremony
write	to form words on a surface
role	a part to play
roll	to tumble; a list
root	part of a plant
rout	to defeat
route	a traveler's way
shear	to cut
sheer	thin, steep
stationary	immovable
stationery	paper
than	as compared with
then	at that time
their	belonging to them
there	in that place
they're	they are
to	a preposition
too	excessively; also
two	the number
waive	to set aside
wave	a swell of water; a gesture
weather	atmospheric conditions
whether	if
who's	contraction of "who is" or "who has"
whose	possessive form of who

In the preceding list, only enough of each word's meaning is given to help you distinguish between the words in each group. Several meanings are left out entirely. For more complete definitions, consult a dictionary.

Practice Session: Confused Words

In the following sentences, underline the preferred choice within each set of parentheses.

1. If our bid is (*accepted, excepted*), we will begin the project in November.
2. This website offers some great (*advice, advise*) on setting up a new business.
3. How will the accounting scandal (*affect, effect*) Arthur Andersen's future?
4. Most of the costs of the project will be (*born, borne*) by the contractor.
5. In preparing the budget, we have to decide where best to invest our (*capital, capitol*).
6. Be sure to (*cite, site*) the sources for your data when you prepare your report.
7. The acquisition of LPC Group should (*compliment/complement*) our other holdings.
8. Leo sought the (*council, counsel*) of his attorney before signing the contract.
9. I didn't have to be told to be (*discrete, discreet*) about the sexual harassment case.
10. When Jennings Hardware got behind in its debts, one of the creditors placed a (*lean, lien*) on its building.
11. Mr. Hathaway was (*loath, loathe*) to fire Elizabeth, but he had no choice.
12. To comply with local zoning (*ordinances, ordnances*), we had to replace our sign.
13. As a teenager, Gary Sassaman used to (*pedal, peddle*) newspapers in downtown Pittsburgh.
14. Business owners along El Cajon Boulevard have vowed to (*persecute, prosecute*) anyone caught painting graffiti on their buildings.
15. We don't know of any (*precedence, precedents*) for the exponential growth of sales for this kind of product.
16. The (*principle, principal*) reason for closing down operations was obsolete production equipment that was too expensive to replace.
17. It's hard to say what (*role, roll*) the downturn in the economy played in the failure of Seven Hills Distribution.
18. Sunbeam employees were shocked by new CEO Al Dunlap's (*shear, sheer*) ruthlessness in axing jobs and slashing costs.
19. Now that our area code has changed, we will need to order new (*stationary, stationery*).
20. The Rodriguez brothers couldn't decide (*weather, whether*) to form a partnership or establish a corporation.

4.2 Frequently Misused Words

The following words tend to be misused for reasons other than their sound. Reference books (including the *Random House College Dictionary*, revised edition; Follett's *Modern American Usage*; and Fowler's *Modern English Usage*) can help you with similar questions of usage:

a lot: When the writer means "many," *a lot* is always two separate words, never one.

aggravate/irritate: *Aggravate* means "to make things worse." Sitting in the smoke-filled room *aggravated* his sinus condition. *Irritate* means "to annoy." Her constant questions *irritated* [not *aggravated*] me.

anticipate/expect: *Anticipate* means "to prepare for": Macy's *anticipated* increased demand for athletic shoes in spring by ordering in November. In formal usage, it is incorrect to use *anticipate* for *expect*: I *expected* (not *anticipated*) a better response to our presentation than we actually got.

compose/comprise: The whole comprises the parts:

The company's distribution division *comprises* four departments.

The following usage is incorrect:

The company's distribution division *is comprised of* four departments.

In that construction, *is composed of* or *consists of* would be preferable. It might be helpful to think of *comprise* as meaning "encompasses" or "contains."

continual/continuous: *Continual* refers to ongoing actions that have breaks:

Her *continual* complaining will accomplish little in the long run.

Continuous refers to ongoing actions without interruptions or breaks:

A *continuous* stream of paper came out of the fax machine.

convince/persuade: One is *convinced* of a fact or that something is true; one is *persuaded* by someone else to do something. The use of *to* with *convince* is unidiomatic—you don't convince someone to do something, you persuade them to do it.

correspond with: Use this phrase when you are talking about exchanging letters. Use *correspond to* when you mean "similar to." Use either *correspond with* or *correspond to* when you mean "relate to."

dilemma/problem: Technically, a *dilemma* is a situation in which one must choose between two undesirable alternatives. It shouldn't be used when no choice is actually involved.

disinterested: This word means "fair, unbiased, having no favorites, impartial." If you mean "bored" or "not interested," use *uninterested*.

etc.: This abbreviated form of the Latin phrase *et cetera* means "and so on" or "and so forth," so it is never correct to write *and etc*. The current tendency among business writers is to use English rather than Latin.

flaunt/flout: To *flaunt* is to be ostentatious or boastful; to *flout* is to mock or scoff at.

impact: Avoid using *impact* as a verb when *influence* or *affect* is meant.

imply/infer: Both refer to hints. Their great difference lies in who is acting. The writer *implies*, the reader *infers*, sees between the lines.

lay: This word is a transitive verb. Never use it for the intransitive *lie*. (See Section 1.3.3.)

lend/loan: *Lend* is a verb; *loan* is a noun. Usage such as "Can you loan me $5?" is therefore incorrect.

less/fewer: Use *less* for uncountable quantities (such as amounts of water, air, sugar, and oil). Use *fewer* for countable quantities (such as numbers of jars, saws, words, page, and humans). The same distinction applies to *much* and *little* (uncountable) versus *many* and *few* (countable).

494 Handbook of Grammar, Mechanics, and Usage

liable/likely: *Liable* means "responsible for": I will hold you *liable* if this deal doesn't go through. It is incorrect to use *liable* for "possible": Anything is *likely* (not *liable*) to happen.

literally: *Literally* means "actually" or "precisely"; it is often misused to mean "almost" or "virtually." It is usually best left out entirely or replaced with *figuratively*.

many/much: See *less/fewer*.

regardless: The *less* suffix is the negative part. No word needs two negative parts, so don't add *ir* (a negative prefix) to the beginning. There is no such word as *irregardless*.

try: Always follow with *to*, never *and*.

verbal: People in the business community who are careful with language frown on those who use *verbal* to mean "spoken" or "*oral*." Many others do say "verbal agreement." Strictly speaking, *verbal* means "of words" and therefore includes both spoken and written words. Follow company usage in this matter.

Practice Session: Misused Words

In the following sentences, underline the preferred choice within each set of parentheses.

1. My boss told me that I still have (*a lot, alot*) to learn.
2. The U.S. Congress corresponds (*to, with*) the British Parliament.
3. I tried to convince my co-workers to sign up for the stress reduction program, but they all seemed (*uninterested, disinterested*).
4. When you say that the books have some discrepancies, are you (*inferring, implying*) that our accountant is embezzling from us?
5. From the auditor's silent stare, Margaret (*implied, inferred*) that the man was not amused by her jokes.
6. The report came out to (*less, fewer*) pages than we had originally anticipated.
7. Mr. Martens was treating Heather (*like, as if*) she had done something wrong.
8. You have to finish the job, (*irregardless, regardless*) of your loathing for it.
9. When talking to customers on the phone, try (*and, to*) be as pleasant as possible.
10. When making (*an oral, a verbal*) presentation, it's a good idea to make eye contact with your audience.

4.3 Frequently Misspelled Words

All of us, even the world's best spellers, sometimes have to check a dictionary for the spelling of some words. People who have never memorized the spelling of commonly used words must look up so many that they grow exasperated and give up on spelling words correctly.

Don't expect perfection and don't surrender. If you can memorize the spelling of just the words listed here, you'll need the dictionary far less often and you'll write with more confidence:

absence	achieve	aluminum	gesture
absorption	advantageous	ambience	grievous
accessible	affiliated	analyze	
accommodate	aggressive	apparent	haphazard
accumulate	alignment	appropriate	harassment
		argument	holiday
		asphalt	
		assistant	illegible
		asterisk	immigrant
		auditor	incidentally
			indelible
		bankruptcy	independent
		believable	indispensable
		brilliant	insistent
		bulletin	intermediary
			irresistible
		calendar	
		campaign	jewelry
		category	judgment
		ceiling	judicial
		changeable	
		clientele	labeling
		collateral	legitimate
		committee	leisure
		comparative	license
		competitor	litigation
		concede	
		congratulations	maintenance
		connoisseur	mathematics
		consensus	mediocre
		convenient	minimum
		convertible	
		corroborate	necessary
		criticism	negligence
			negotiable
		definitely	newsstand
		description	noticeable
		desirable	
		dilemma	occurrence
		disappear	omission
		disappoint	
		disbursement	parallel
		discrepancy	pastime
		dissatisfied	peaceable
		dissipate	permanent
			perseverance
		eligible	persistent
		embarrassing	personnel
		endorsement	persuade
		exaggerate	possesses
		exceed	precede
		exhaust	predictable
		existence	preferred
		extraordinary	privilege
			procedure
		fallacy	proceed
		familiar	pronunciation
		flexible	psychology
		fluctuation	pursue
		forty	

questionnaire

receive

recommend

repetition

rescind

rhythmical

ridiculous

salable

secretary

seize

separate

sincerely

succeed

suddenness

superintendent

supersede

surprise

tangible

tariff

technique

tenant

truly

unanimous

until

vacillate

vacuum

vicious

Practice Session: Misspelled Words

In the following sentences, underline the preferred choice within each set of parentheses.

1. We try to (*accomodate, accommodate*) any reasonable request from our customers.
2. You will need to (*analyse, analyze*) the sales data to determine which products to phase out.
3. Because the weather in Chicago is so (*changable, changeable*), the conference reception has a backup indoor venue.
4. The board reached a (*concensus, consensus*) on the new CEO.
5. It will be (*embarassing, embarrassing*) for the company if this information leaks out.
6. The auditors discovered the (*existance, existence*) of hidden accounts in foreign banks.
7. Every company should have a written sexual (*harassment, harrassment*) policy.
8. In today's book business, (*independant, independent*) publishers are having a tough time finding distribution.
9. Use your best (*judgment, judgement*) when choosing the paper for our new stationery.
10. The cost of a business (*licence, license, liscence*) varies from city to city.
11. With all the turmoil (*occuring, occurring*) in the stock market, we've decided to shift our investments toward real estate.
12. The marketing survey found that consumers (*prefered, preferred*) brand-name dog food over generic brands.
13. Because her cost-cutting measures saved the company millions of dollars, Carolyn Kelly (*received, recieved*) a raise and a promotion.
14. Please send (*separate, seperate*) invoices for the two projects.
15. My supervisor didn't need to be so (*vicious, viscious*) in his critique of my performance.

4.4 Transitional Words and Phrases

The following sentences don't communicate as well as they could because they lack a transitional word or phrase:

> Production delays are inevitable. Our current lag time in filling orders is one month.

A semicolon between the two sentences would signal a close relationship between their meanings, but it wouldn't even hint at what that relationship is. Here are the sentences again, now linked by means of a semicolon, with a space for a transitional word or phrase:

> Production delays are inevitable; _____, our current lag time in filling orders is one month.

Now read the sentence with *nevertheless* in the blank space. Then try *therefore, incidentally, in fact*, and *at any rate* in the blank. Each substitution changes the meaning of the sentence.

Here are some transitional words (conjunctive adverbs) that will help you write more clearly:

accordingly	furthermore	moreover
anyway	however	otherwise
besides	incidentally	still
consequently	likewise	therefore
finally	meanwhile	

The following transitional phrases are used in the same way:

as a result	in other words
at any rate	in the second place
for example	on the other hand
in fact	to the contrary

When one of these words or phrases joins two independent clauses, it should be preceded by a semicolon and followed by a comma:

> The consultant recommended a complete reorganization; moreover, she suggested that we drop several products.

PRACTICE SESSION ANSWERS

Answers for Nouns: 1. City 2. Building / building 3. hotels 4. *t*'s / *i*'s 5. 1990s 6. shelves 7. specialties 8. cases 9. company's 10. editor-in-chief's 11. businesses' 12. passengers' 13. day's 14. Dallas's 15. Jones's

Answers for Pronouns: 1. me 2. she 3. him 4. We 5. me 6. its 7. his or her 8. Who 9. whom 10. Whom 11. her 12. him or her 13. her 14. its 15. Who 16. your 17. its 18. I 19. their 20. its

Answers for Verbs: 1. comes, want 2. knew 3. begun 4. lie 5. laid 6. sits 7. set 8. raise 9. was 10. is 11. is 12. are 13. is 14. is 15. represents 16. is 17. are 18. is 19. send 20. were

Answers for Adjectives and Adverbs: 1. least 2. better 3. worse 4. more competent 5. unique 6. well-written 7. well written 8. beautifully written 9. lower-income 10. well 11. well 12. really 13. slowly 14. could hardly 15. more heavily

Answers for Prepositions, Conjunctions, Articles, and Interjections: 1. a 2. b 3. a 4. b 5. b 6. a 7. b 8. a 9. b 10. a 11. b 12. b 13. a 14. a 15. a

Answers for Sentences: 1. a 2. b 3. b 4. c 5. c 6. b 7. c 8. c 9. a 10. c

Answers for Punctuation 1: 1. b 2. a 3. b 4. b 5. a 6. b 7. a 8. a 9. b 10. c

Answers for Punctuation 2: 1. b 2. a 3. a 4. b 5. a 6. b 7. b 8. a 9. b 10. a 11. b 12. a 13. a 14. b 15. b

Answers for Mechanics: 1. c 2. b 3. b 4. a 5. a 6. c 7. b 8. b 9. a 10. a

Answers for Confused Words: 1. accepted 2. advice 3. affect 4. borne 5. capital 6. cite 7. complement 8. counsel

9. discreet 10. lien 11. loath 12. ordinances 13. peddle 14. prosecute 15. precedents 16. principal 17. role 18. sheer 19. stationery 20. whether

Answers for Misused Words: 1. a lot 2. to 3. uninterested 4. implying 5. inferred 6. fewer 7. as if 8. regardless 9. to 10. an oral

Answers for Misspelled Words: 1. accommodate 2. analyze 3. changeable 4. consensus 5. embarrassing 6. existence 7. harassment 8. independent 9. judgment 10. license 11. occurring 12. preferred 13. received 14. separate 15. vicious

Answer Key

ANSWER KEY TO THE LEVEL 1 SELF-ASSESSMENT EXERCISES

Chapter 1: Self-Assessment—Nouns

For 1–5, common nouns are underlined, and proper nouns are boxed.

1. Give the balance sheet to Melissa. (1.1.1)
2. After three years of declining sales, the board fired the CEO and hired a replacement from Google. (1.1.1)
3. Tarnower Corporation donates a portion of its profits to charity every year. (1.1.1)
4. Which aluminum bolts are packaged? (1.1.1)
5. Please send the Joneses a dozen of the following: stopwatches, canteens, headbands, and wristbands. (1.1.1)

For 6–10, subjects are underlined, and objects are boxed.

6. The technician has already repaired the machine for the client. (1.1.2)
7. An attorney will talk to the group about incorporation. (1.1.2)
8. After her vacation, the buyer prepared a third-quarter budget. (1.1.2)
9. More than 90 percent of the research staff has contributed to the new wiki. (1.1.2)
10. Accuracy overrides speed in importance. (1.1.2)

For 11–15, incorrect plurals and possessives are underlined, and the correct forms are shown in bold.

11. Make sure that all copys **copies** include the new addresses. (1.1.2)
12. Ask Jennings to collect all employee's **employees'** donations for the Red Cross drive. (1.1.4)
13. Charlie now has two son-in-laws **sons-in-law** to help him with his two online business's **businesses**. (1.1.3, 1.1.4)
14. Avoid using too many parenthesises **parentheses** when writing your reports. (1.1.3)
15. Follow President Nesses **Ness's** rules about what constitutes a weeks **week's** work. (1.1.4)

Chapter 2: Self-Assessment—Pronouns

For 1–5, the correct pronouns are shown in bold.

1. To **whom** will you send your merchandise? (1.2)
2. Have you given **them** a list of parts? (1.2)
3. The main office sent the invoice to **them** on December 5. (1.2)
4. The company settled **its** accounts before the end of the year. (1.2)
5. **Whose** umbrella is this? (1.2)

For 6–15, the correct pronouns are boxed.

6. The sales staff is preparing guidelines for (*their*, *its*) clients. (1.2.5)
7. Few of the sales representatives turn in (*their*, *its*) reports on time. (1.2.5)
8. The board of directors has chosen (*their*, *its*) officers. (1.2.5)
9. Gomez and Archer have told (*his*, *their*) clients about the new program. (1.2.1)
10. Each manager plans to expand (*his*, *their*, *his or her*) sphere of control next year. (1.2.3)
11. Has everyone supplied (*his*, *their*, *his or her*) Social Security number? (1.2.3)
12. After giving every employee (*his*, *their*, *a*) raise, George told (*them*, *they*, *all*) about the increased workload. (1.2.3, 1.2.4)
13. Bob and Tim have opposite ideas about how to achieve company goals. (*Who*, *Whom*) do you think will win the debate? (1.2.4)
14. City Securities has just announced (*who*, *whom*) it will hire as CEO. (1.2.4)
15. Either of the new products would readily find (*their*, *its*) niche in the marketplace. (1.2.5)

Chapter 3: Self-Assessment—Verbs

1. have become (1.3.1)
2. knew (1.3.1)
3. has moved (1.3.1)
4. will do (1.3.1)
5. will have returned (1.3.1)
6. Leslie Cartwright will write the report. (1.3.5)
7. I failed to record the transaction. (1.3.5)
8. Has the claims department notified you of your rights? (1.3.5)
9. We depend on their services for our operation. (1.3.5)
10. The customer returned the damaged equipment before we even located a repair facility. (1.3.5)
11. Everyone upstairs (*receive*/ *receives*) mail before we do. (1.3.4)
12. Neither the main office nor the branches (*is*/ *are*) blameless. (1.3.4)
13. C&B Sales (*is* /*are*) listed in the directory. (1.3.4)
14. When measuring shelves, 7 inches (*is* /*are*) significant. (1.3.4)
15. About 90 percent of the employees (*plan* /*plans*) to come to the company picnic. (1.3.4)

Chapter 4: Self-Assessment—Adjectives

1. greater (1.4.1)
2. perfect (1.4.1)
3. most interesting (1.4.1)
4. better (1.4.1)
5. hardest (1.4.1)
6. A highly placed source revealed Dotson's last-ditch efforts to cover up the mistake. (1.4.2)
7. Please send an extra-large dust cover for my photocopier. (1.4.2)

8. A top-secret document was taken from the president's office last night. (1.4.2)
9. A 30-year-old person should know better. (1.4.2)
10. If I write a large-scale report, I want to know that it will be read by upper-level management. (1.4.2)
11. The two companies are engaged in an all-out, no-holds-barred struggle for dominance. (1.4)
12. A tiny metal shaving is responsible for the problem. (1.4)
13. She came to the office with a bruised, swollen knee. (1.4)
14. A chipped, cracked sheet of glass is useless to us. (1.4)
15. You'll receive our usual cheerful, prompt service. (1.4)

Chapter 5: Self-Assessment—Adverbs

1. good (1.5)
2. surely (1.5)
3. sick (1.5)
4. well (1.5)
5. good (1.5)
6. faster (1.5.2)
7. most recently (1.5.2)
8. more happily (1.5.2)
9. better (1.5.2)
10. most logically (1.5.2)
11. He doesn't seem to have any. *OR* He seems to have none. (1.5.1)
12. That machine is scarcely ever used. *OR* That machine is never used. (1.5.1)
13. They can't get any replacement parts until Thursday. *OR* They can get no replacement parts until Thursday. (1.5.1)
14. It wasn't any different from the first event we promoted. *OR* It was no different from the first event we promoted. (1.5.1)
15. We've looked for it, and it doesn't seem to be anywhere. *OR* It seems to be nowhere. (1.5.1)

Chapter 6: Self-Assessment—Prepositions and Conjunctions

1. Where was your argument leading ~~to~~? (1.6.1)
2. I wish he would get off ~~of~~ the phone. (1.6.1)
3. This is a project ~~into which~~ you can sink your teeth into. (1.6.1)
4. U.S. Mercantile must become aware of and sensitive to its customers' concerns. (1.6.1)
5. We are responsible for aircraft safety in the air, in the hangars, and on the runways. (1.6.1)
6. to (1.6.1)
7. among (1.6.1)
8. for (1.6.1)
9. to (1.6.1)
10. from (1.6.1)
11. She is active ~~in~~ not only in a civic group but also in an athletic organization. *OR* She is active in not only a civic group but ~~in~~ also an athletic organization. (1.6.2)
12. That is either a mistake or ~~was~~ an intentional omission. (1.6.2)
13. The question is whether to set up a booth at the convention or ~~be~~ to host a hospitality suite. (1.6.2)
14. We are doing better ~~in~~ both in overall sales and in profits. *OR* in both overall sales and ~~in~~ profits. (1.6.2)
15. She had neither the preferred educational background, nor ~~did she have~~ the suitable experience. (1.6.2)

Chapter 7: Self-Assessment—Periods, Question Marks, and Exclamation Points

1. Dr. Eleanor H. Hutton has requested information on TaskMasters, Inc. (2.1)
2. That qualifies us as a rapidly growing new company, don't you think? (2.2)
3. Our president, Daniel Gruber, is a CPA. On your behalf, I asked him why he started the company. (2.1)
4. In the past three years, we have experienced phenomenal growth of 800 percent. *OR* ! (2.1, 2.3)
5. Contact me at 1358 N. Parsons Avenue, Tulsa, OK 74204. (2.1)
6. Jack asked, "Why does he want to know? Maybe he plans to become a competitor." *OR* ! (2.1, 2.2, 2.3)
7. The debt load fluctuates with the movement of the U.S. prime rate. (2.1)
8. I can't believe we could have missed such a promising opportunity! (2.3)
9. Is consumer loyalty extinct? Yes and No. (2.2, 2.1)
10. Johnson and Kane, Inc., has gone out of business. What a surprise. *OR* ! (2.1, 2.3)
11. Will you please send us a check today so that we can settle your account. (2.1)
12. Mr. James R. Capp will be our new CEO, beginning January 20, 2009. (2.1)
13. The rag doll originally sold for $1,098, but we have lowered the price to a mere $599. (2.1)
14. Will you be able to make the presentation at the conference, or should we find someone else? (2.2)
15. So I ask you, "When will we admit defeat?" Never! (2.2, 2.3)

Chapter 8: Self-Assessment—Semicolons, Colons, and Commas

1. This letter looks good; that one doesn't. (2.4)
2. I want to make one thing perfectly clear: neither of you will be promoted if sales figures don't improve. (2.5)
3. The Zurich airport has been snowed in; therefore, I won't be able to meet with you before January 4. (2.4)
4. His motivation was obvious: to get Meg fired. (2.5)
5. Only two firms have responded to our survey: J. J. Perkins and Tucker & Tucker. (2.5)
6. Send a copy to Mary Kent, Marketing Director; Robert Bache, Comptroller; and Dennis Mann, Sales Director. (2.4)
7. Please be sure to interview these employees next week: Henry Gold, Doris Hatch, and George Iosupovich. (2.5)
8. We have observed your hard work; because of it, we are promoting you to manager of your department. (2.4)
9. You shipped three items on June 7; however, we received only one of them. (2.4)
10. The convention kit includes the following response cards: giveaways, brochures, and a display rack. (2.5)
11. The workers wanted an immediate wage increase; they had not had a raise in nearly two years. (2.4)
12. This, then, is our goal for 2009: increase sales 35 percent. (2.5)
13. His writing skills are excellent; however, he still needs to polish his management style. (2.4)

14. We would like to address three issues: efficiency, profitability, and market penetration. (2.5)
15. Remember this rule: When in doubt, leave it out. (2.5)

Chapter 9: Self-Assessment—Commas

1. Please send us four cases of filters, two cases of wing nuts, and a bale of rags. (2.6)
2. Your analysis, however, does not account for returns. (2.6)
3. As a matter of fact, she has seen the figures. (2.6)
4. Before May 7, 1999, they wouldn't have minded either. (2.6)
5. After Martha has gone, talk to me about promoting her. (2.6)
6. Stoneridge, Inc., went public on September 9, 2012. (2.6)
7. We want the new copier, not the old model. (2.6)
8. "Talk to me," Sandra said, "before you change a thing." (2.6)
9. Because of a previous engagement, Dr. Stoeve will not be able to attend. (2.6)
10. The company started attracting attention during the long, hard recession of the mid-1970s. (2.6)
11. You can reach me at this address: 717 Darby Place, Scottsdale, Arizona 85251. (2.6)
12. Transfer the documents from Fargo, North Dakota, to Boise, Idaho. (2.6)
13. Sam O'Neill, the designated representative, is gone today. (2.6)
14. With your help, we will soon begin. (2.6)
15. She may hire two new representatives, or she may postpone filling those territories until spring. (2.6)

Chapter 10: Self-Assessment—Dashes and Hyphens

1. Three qualities—speed, accuracy, and reliability—are desirable in any applicant to the data entry department. (2.7)
2. A highly placed source explained the top-secret negotiations. (2.8)
3. The file on Marian Gephardt—yes, we finally found it—reveals a history of late payments. (2.7)
4. They're selling a well-designed machine. (2.8)
5. A bottle-green sports jacket is hard to find. (2.8)
6. Argentina, Brazil, Mexico—these are the countries we hope to concentrate on. (2.7)
7. Only two sites—maybe three—offer the things we need. (2.7)
8. How many owner-operators are in the industry? (2.8)
9. Your ever-faithful assistant deserves—without a doubt—a substantial raise. (2.8, 2.7)
10. Myrna Talefiero is this organization's president-elect. (2.8)
11. Stealth, secrecy, and surprise—those are the elements that will give us a competitive edge. (2.7)
12. The charts are well-placed on each page—unlike the running heads and footers. (2.8, 2.7)
13. We got our small-business loan—an enormous advantage. (2.8, 2.7)
14. Ron Franklin—do you remember him?—will be in town Monday. (2.7)
15. Your devil-may-care attitude affects everyone involved in the decision-making process. (2.8)

Chapter 11: Self-Assessment—Quotation Marks, Parentheses, Ellipses, Underscores, and Italics

1. Be sure to read "How to Sell by Listening" in this month's issue of *Fortune*. (2.10, 3.2)
2. Her response (see the attached memo) is disturbing. (2.11)
3. *Contact* is an overused word. (3.2)
4. We will operate with a skeleton staff during the holiday break (December 21 through January 2). (2.11)
5. "The SBP's next conference," the bulletin noted, "will be held in Minneapolis." (2.10)
6. Sara O'Rourke (a reporter from *The Wall Street Journal*) will be here on Thursday. (2.11, 3.2)
7. I don't care *why* you didn't fill my order; I want to know *when* you'll fill it. (3.2)
8. The term *up in the air* means "undecided." (2.10, 3.2)
9. Her assistant (the one who just had the baby) won't be back for four weeks. (2.11)
10. "Ask not what your country can do for you . . ." is the beginning of a famous quotation from John F. Kennedy. (2.10, 2.12)
11. Whom do you think *Time* magazine will select as its Person of the Year? (3.2)
12. Do you remember who said "And away we go"? (2.10)
13. Refinements in robotics may prove profitable. (More detail about this technology appears in Appendix A.) (2.11)
14. The resignation letter begins, "Since I'll never regain your respect . . ." and goes on to explain why that's true. (2.10, 2.12)
15. You must help her distinguish between *i.e.* (which means "that is") and *e.g.* (which means "for example"). (2.10, 3.2)

Chapter 12: Self-Assessment—Capitals and Abbreviations

1. Dr. Paul Hansen is joining our staff. (3.1)
2. New Caressa skin cream should be in a position to dominate that market. (3.1)
3. Send this report to ~~Mister~~ Mr. H. K. Danforth, ~~rural route~~RR 1, Warrensburg, ~~new york~~NY 12885. (3.1, 3.3)
4. You are responsible for training my new assistant to operate the Xerox machine. (3.1)
5. She received her ~~master of business administration~~MBA degree from the University of Michigan. (3.1, 3.3)
6. The building is located on the corner of Madison and Center Streets. (3.1)
7. Call me tomorrow at 8 a.m. ~~morning, pacific standard time~~PST, and I'll have the information you need. (3.3)
8. When Jones becomes CEO next month, we'll need your input ASAP. (3.1, 3.3)
9. Address it to Art Bowers, Chief of Production. (3.1)
10. Please RSVP to Sony ~~corp.~~Corporation just as soon as you know your schedule. (3.1, 3.3)
11. The data-processing department will begin work on ~~feb.~~February 2, just one ~~wk.~~week from today. (3.3)
12. You are to meet him on Friday at the UN building in NYC. (3.3)
13. Whenever you can come, Professor, our employees will greatly enjoy your presentation. (3.1)

14. At 50 per box, our ~~std.~~standard contract forms are $9 a box, and our warranty forms are $7.95 a box. (3.3)
15. We plan to establish a sales office on the West Coast. (3.1)

Chapter 13: Self-Assessment—Numbers

1. We need to hire ~~one~~1 office manager, ~~four~~4 bookkeepers, and ~~twelve~~12 clerk-typists. (3.4)
2. The market for this product is nearly ~~six~~6 million people in our region alone. (3.4)
3. Make sure that all 1,835 pages are on my desk no later than ~~nine o'clock~~9:00 a.m. (*OR* nine o'clock in the morning.) (3.4)
4. In 2004, ~~was the year that~~José Guiterez sold more than $50,000 ~~thousand dollars~~ worth of stock. (3.4)
5. Our deadline is ~~4/7~~April 7, but we won't be ready before ~~4/11~~April 11. (3.4)
6. ~~95~~Ninety-five percent of our customers are men. (*OR* Of our customers, 95 percent are men.) (3.4)
7. More than ~~1/2~~ half the U.S. population is female. (3.4)
8. Cecile Simmons, ~~thirty-eight~~38, is the first woman in this company to be promoted to management. (3.4)
9. Last year, I wrote 20 ~~15~~-fifteen-page reports, and Michelle wrote 24 three-page reports. (3.4)
10. Of the 15 applicants, ~~seven~~7 are qualified. (3.4)
11. Our blinds should measure 38 inches wide by 64-1/2 ~~and one half~~ inches long by 7/16 inches deep. (3.4)
12. Deliver the couch to ~~seven eighty-three~~783 Fountain Road, Suite ~~three~~3, Procter Valley, CA 92074. (3.4)
13. Here are the corrected figures: 42.70% agree, 23.25% disagree, 34.00% are undecided, and the error is 0.05%. (3.4)
14. You have to agree that 50,~~000,000~~ million U.S. citizens cannot be wrong. (3.4)
15. We need a set of shelves 10 feet, ~~eight~~8 inches long. (3.4)

Chapter 14: Self-Assessment—Vocabulary

1. except (4.1)
2. device (4.1)
3. loath (4.1)
4. ordinance (4.1)
5. precedence (4.1)
6. than (4.1)
7. who's (4.1)
8. In this department, we see **a lot** of mistakes like that. (4.2)
9. In my **judgment**, you'll need to redo the cover. (4.3)
10. He decided to reveal the information **regardless** of the consequences. (4.2)
11. Why not go along when it is so easy to **accommodate** his demands? (4.3)
12. When you say that, do you mean to **imply** that I'm being unfair? (4.2)
13. She says that she finds this sort of ceremony **embarrassing**. (4.3)
14. All we have to do is try **to** get along with him for a few more days. (4.2)
15. A friendly handshake should always **precede** negotiations. (4.3)

References

PROLOGUE

1. Jeanne C. Meister and Karie Willyerd, "Leading Virtual Teams to Real Results," *Harvard Business Review* blogs, 30 June 2010 [accessed 16 August 2010] http://blogs.hbr.org; *The Small Business Economy, 2009*, U.S. Small Business Administration website [accessed 16 August 2010] www.sba.gov; Malik Singleton, "Same Markets, New Marketplaces," *Black Enterprise*, September 2004, 34; Edmund L. Andrews, "Where Do the Jobs Come From?" *New York Times*, 21 September 2004, E1, E11; Maureen Jenkins, "Yours for the Taking," *Boeing Frontiers Online*, June 2004 [accessed 25 September 2005] www.boeing.com; "Firm Predicts Top 10 Workforce/Workplace Trends for 2004," *Enterprise*, 8–14 December 2003, 1–2; Ricky W. Griffin and Michael W. Pustay, *International Business*, 6th ed. (Upper Saddle River, N.J.: Pearson Prentice Hall, 2010), 21.

2. Vivian Yeo, "India Still Top Choice for Offshoring," *BusinessWeek*, 27 June 2008 [accessed 7 July 2008] www.businessweek.com; Jim Puzzanghera, "Coalition of High-Tech Firms to Urge Officials to Help Keep U.S. Competitive," *San Jose Mercury News*, 8 January 2004 [accessed 14 February 2004] www.ebscohost.com.

3. Courtland L. Bovée and John V. Thill, *Business in Action*, 5th ed. (Upper Saddle River, N.J.: Pearson Prentice Hall, 2010), 18–21; Randall S. Hansen and Katharine Hansen, "What Do Employers Really Want? Top Skills and Values Employers Seek from Job-Seekers," QuintCareers.com [accessed 17 August 2010] www.quintcareers.com.

4. Nancy M. Somerick, "Managing a Communication Internship Program," *Bulletin of the Association for Business Communication* 56, no. 3 (1993): 10–20.

5. Fellowforce website [accessed 17 August 2010] www.fellowforce.com.

6. Jeffrey R. Young, "'E-Portfolios' Could Give Students a New Sense of Their Accomplishments," *The Chronicle of Higher Education*, 8 March 2002, A31.

7. Brian Carcione, e-portfolio [accessed 20 December 2006] http://eportfolio.psu.edu.

8. Mohammed Al-Taee, "Personal Branding," Al-Taee blog [accessed 17 August 2010] http://altaeeblog.com.

9. Pete Kistler, "Seth Godin's 7-Point Guide to Bootstrap Your Personal Brand," Personal Branding blog, 28 July 2010 [accessed 17 August 2010] www.personalbrandingblog; Kyle Lacy, "10 Ways to Building Your Personal Brand Story," Personal Branding blog, 5 August 2010 [accessed 17 August 2010] www.personalbrandingblog; Al-Taee, "Personal Branding"; Scot Herrick, "30 Career Management Tips— Marketing AND Delivery Support Our Personal Brand," Cube Rules blog, 8 September 2007 [accessed 17 August 2010] http://cuberules.com; Alina Tugend, "Putting Yourself Out There on a Shelf to Buy," *New York Times*, 27 March 2009 [accessed 9 August 2009] www.nytimes.com.

CHAPTER 1

1. Chris O'Brien, "Facebook Needs to Break Its Cycle of Backlash," *Mercury News* (San Jose, Calif.), 17 May 2010 [accessed 28 May 2010] www.mercurynews.com.

2. Richard L. Daft, *Management*, 6th ed. (Cincinnati: Cengage South-Western, 2003), 580.

3. Julie Connelly, "Youthful Attitudes, Sobering Realities," *New York Times*, 28 October 2003, E1, E6; Nigel Andrews and Laura D'Andrea Tyson, "The Upwardly Global MBA," *Strategy + Business* 36: 60–69; Jim McKay, "Communication Skills Found Lacking," *Pittsburgh Post-Gazette*, 28 February 2005 [accessed 28 February 2005] www.delawareonline.com.

4. Brian Solis, *Engage!* (Hoboken: John Wiley & Sons, 2010), 11–12; "Majority of Global Companies Face an Engagement Gap," Internal Comms Hub website, 23 October 2007 [accessed 5 July 2008] www.internalcommshub.com; Gary L. Neilson, Karla L. Martin, and Elizabeth Powers, "The Secrets to Successful Strategy Execution," *Harvard Business Review*, June 2008, 61–70; Nicholas Carr, "Lessons in Corporate Blogging," *BusinessWeek*, 18 July 2006, 9; Susan Meisinger, "To Keep Employees, Talk—and Listen—to Them!" *HR Magazine*, August 2006, 10.

5. "Watson Wyatt Study Reveals Six Communication 'Secrets' of Top-Performing Employers," CNNMoney.com, 4 December 2007 [accessed 26 January 2008] www.money.cnn.com.

6. Daft, *Management*, 147.

7. Richard Edelman, "Teaching Social Media: What Skills Do Communicators Need?" in *Engaging the New Influencers; Third Annual Social Media Academic Summit* (white paper) [accessed 7 June 2010] www.newmediaacademicsummit.com; "CEOs to Communicators: 'Stick to Common Sense,'" Internal Comms Hub website, 23 October 2007 [accessed 11 July 2008] www.internalcommshub.com; "A Writing Competency Model for Business," BizCom 101.com, 14 December 2007 [accessed 11 July 2008] www.businesswriting-courses.com; Sue Dewhurst and Liam FitzPatrick, "What Should Be the Competency of Your IC Team?" white paper, 2007 [accessed 11 July 2008] http://competent communicators.com.

8. Paul Martin Lester, *Visual Communication: Images with Messages* (Belmont, Calif.: Cengage South-Western, 2006), 6–8.

9. Anne Field, "What You Say, What They Hear," *Harvard Management Communication Letter*, Winter 2005, 3–5.

10. Ben Hanna, *2009 Business Social Media Benchmarking Study* (published by Business.com), 2 November 2009, 11.

11. Michael Killian, "The Communication Revolution—'Deep Impact' About to Strike," Avaya Insights blog, 4 December 2009 [accessed 2 June 2010] www.avayablog.com.

12. Thomas Young, "Ethics in Business: Business of Ethics," *Vital Speeches*, 15 September 1992, 725–730.

13. Philip C. Kolin, *Successful Writing at Work*, 6th ed. (Boston: Houghton Mifflin, 2001), 17–23.

14. Nancy K. Kubasek, Bartley A. Brennan, and M. Neil Browne, *The Legal Environment of Business*, 3rd ed. (Upper Saddle River, N.J.: Prentice Hall, 2003), 172.

15. Henry R. Cheeseman, *Contemporary Business and E-Commerce Law*, 4th ed. (Upper Saddle River, N.J.: Prentice Hall, 2003), 325.

16. Linda Pophal, "Tweet Ethics: Trust and Transparency in a Web 2.0 World," *CW Bulletin*, September 2009 [accessed 3 June 2010] www.iabc.com.

17. Robert Plummer, "Will Fake Business Blogs Crash and Burn?" BBC News, 22 May 2008 [accessed 3 June 2010] http://news.bbc.co.uk.

18. Word of Mouth Marketing Association, "WOM 101" [accessed 2 June 2010] http://womma.org; Nate Anderson, "FTC Says Stealth Marketing Unethical," Ars Technica, 13 December 2006 [accessed 27 January 2008] http:// arstechnica.com; "Undercover Marketing Uncovered," CBSnews.com, 25 July 2004 [accessed 11 April 2005] www.cbsnews.com; Stephanie Dunnewind, "Teen Recruits Create Word-of-Mouth 'Buzz' to Hook Peers on Products," *Seattle Times*, 20 November 2004 [accessed 11 April 2005] www.seattletimes.com.

19. Tim Arango, "Soon, Bloggers Must Give Full Disclosure," *New York Times*, 5 October 2009 [accessed 7 June 2010] www.nytimes.com.

20. Pophal, "Tweet Ethics: Trust and Transparency in a Web 2.0 World."

21. Rich Phillips and John Zarrella, "Live Bombs Haunt Orlando Neighborhood," CNN.com, 1 July 2008 [accessed 24 July 2008] www.cnn.com.

22. Daft, *Management*, 155.

23. "Work–Life Balance Affects Ethics, Survey Says," Internal Comms Hub, 23 April 2007 [accessed 25 January 2008] www.internalcommshub.com.

24. Based in part on Robert Kreitner, *Management*, 9th ed. (Boston: Houghton Mifflin, 2004), 163.

25. Podcast interview with Ron Glover, IBM website [accessed 17 August 2008] www.ibm.com.

26. "Culture Influences Brain Function, Study Shows," *Science Daily*, 13 January 2008 [accessed 5 June 2010] www.sciencedaily.com;" Tracy Novinger, *Intercultural Communication, A Practical Guide* (Austin, Tex.: University of Texas Press, 2001), 15.

27. Lillian H. Chaney and Jeanette S. Martin, *Intercultural Business Communication*, 4th ed. (Upper Saddle River, N.J.: Pearson Prentice Hall, 2007), 53.

28. Geneviève Hilton, "Becoming Culturally Fluent," *Communication World*, November/December 2007, 34–35.

29. Mary O'Hara-Devereaux and Robert Johansen, *Global Work: Bridging Distance, Culture, and Time* (San Francisco: Jossey-Bass, 1994), 55, 59.

30. Edward T. Hall, "Context and Meaning," in *Intercultural Communication: A Reader*, 6th ed., edited by Larry A. Samovar and Richard E. Porter (Belmont, Calif: Wadsworth, 1991), 34–42.

31. Daft, *Management*, 459.

32. Shital Kakkar Mehra, "Understanding Cultures," *The Economic Times* (India), 21 September 2007 [accessed 27 January 2008] http://economictimes.indiatimes.com.

33. O'Hara-Devereaux and Johansen, *Global Work: Bridging Distance, Culture, and Time*, 55, 59.

34. Linda Beamer, "Teaching English Business Writing to Chinese-Speaking Business Students," *Bulletin of the Association for Business Communication* 57, no. 1 (1994): 12–18.

35. Charley H. Dodd, *Dynamics of Intercultural Communication*, 3rd ed. (Dubuque, Iowa: Brown, 1991), 69–70.

36. Daft, *Management*, 459.

37. "Different Personalities Can Create Culture Clashes, Study Warns," Internal Comms Hub 27 February 2007 [accessed 25 January 2008] www.internalcommshub.com.

38. Hannah Seligson, "For American Workers in China, a Culture Clash," *New York Times*, 23 December 2009 [accessed 5 June 2010] www.nytimes.com.

39. James Wilfong and Toni Seger, *Taking Your Business Global* (Franklin Lakes, N.J.: Career Press, 1997), 277–278.

40. Guo-Ming Chen and William J. Starosta, *Foundations of Intercultural Communication* (Boston: Allyn & Bacon, 1998), 288–289.

41. Peter Coy, "Old. Smart. Productive." *BusinessWeek*, 27 June 2005 [accessed 24 August 2006] www.businessweek.com; Linda Beamer and Iris Varner, *Intercultural Communication in the Workplace*, 2nd ed. (New York: McGraw-Hill Irwin, 2001), 107–108.

42. Tonya Vinas, "A Place at the Table," *IndustryWeek*, 1 July 2003, 22.

43. John Gray, *Mars and Venus in the Workplace* (New York: HarperCollins, 2002), 10, 25–27, 61–63.

44. Mark D. Downey, "Keeping the Faith," *HR Magazine*, January 2008, 85–88.

45. Jensen J. Zhao and Calvin Parks, "Self-Assessment of Communication Behavior: An Experiential Learning Exercise for Intercultural Business Success," *Business Communication Quarterly* 58, no. 1 (1995): 20–26; Dodd, *Dynamics of Intercultural Communication*, 142–143, 297–299; Stephen P. Robbins, *Organizational Behavior*, 6th ed. (Paramus, N.J.: Prentice Hall, 1993), 345.

46. Chaney and Martin, *Intercultural Business Communication*, 9.

47. Mona Casady and Lynn Wasson, "Written Communication Skills of International Business Persons," *Bulletin of the Association for Business Communication* 57, no. 4 (1994): 36–40.

48. "Brain Overload Causing Loss of Deep Thinking: Study," ZeeNews, 14 December 2009 [accessed 5 June 2010] www.zeenews.com; Tara Craig, "How to Avoid Information Overload," *Personnel Today*, 10 June 2008, 31; Jeff Davidson, "Fighting Information Overload," *Canadian Manager*, Spring 2005, 16+.

49. Ker Than, "Workers Should Turn Off Visual Alerts, Study Finds," *LiveScience*, 7 December 2009 [accessed 5 June 2010] www.livescience.com.

50. Robert X. Cringely, "Let's Get Small," I, Cringely blog, 26 May 2010 [accessed 5 June 2010] www.cringely.com.

51. "Many Senior Managers Communicate Badly, Survey Says," Internal Comms Hub, 6 August 2007 [accessed 25 January 2008] www.internalcommshub.com.

52. Mike Schaffner, "Step Away from the Computer," *Forbes*, 7 August 2009 [accessed 5 June 2010] www.forbes.com.

53. Steve Lohr, "As Travel Costs Rise, More Meetings Go Virtual," *New York Times*, 22 July 2008 [accessed 23 July 2008] www.nytimes.com.

54. The concept of a four-tweet summary is adapted from Cliff Atkinson, *The Backchannel* (Berkeley, Calif.: New Riders, 2010), 120–121.

CHAPTER 2

1. Evelyn Nussenbaum, "Boosting Teamwork with Wikis," Fortune Small Business, 12 February 2008 [accessed 12 June 2010] http://money.cnn.com; Doug Cornelius, "Wikis at the Rosen Law Firm," KM Space blog, 28 February 2008 [accessed 15 August 2008] http:// kmspace.blogspot.com; Rosen Law Firm website [accessed 12 June 2010] www.rosen.com.

2. Courtland L. Bovée and John V. Thill, *Business in Action*, 3rd ed. (Upper Saddle River, N.J.: Pearson Prentice Hall, 2005), 175.

3. "Five Case Studies on Successful Teams," *HR Focus*, April 2002, 18+.

4. Stephen R. Robbins, *Essentials of Organizational Behavior*, 6th ed. (Upper Saddle River, N.J.: Prentice Hall, 2000), 98.

5. Max Landsberg and Madeline Pfau, "Developing Diversity: Lessons from Top Teams," *Strategy + Business*, Winter 2005, 10–12.

6. "Groups Best at Complex Problems," *Industrial Engineer*, June 2006, 14.

7. Nicola A. Nelson, "Leading Teams," *Defense AT&L*, July–August 2006, 26–29; Larry Cole and Michael Cole, "Why Is the Teamwork Buzz Word Not Working?" *Communication World*, February–March 1999, 29; Patricia Buhler, "Managing in the 90s: Creating Flexibility in Today's Workplace," *Supervision*, January 1997, 241; Allison W. Amason, Allen C. Hochwarter, Wayne A. Thompson, and Kenneth R. Harrison, "Conflict: An Important Dimension in Successful Management Teams," *Organizational Dynamics*, Autumn 1995, 201.

8. Richard L. Daft, *Management*, 6th ed. (Cincinnati: Cengage South-Western, 2003), 614.

9. Geoffrey Colvin, "Why Dream Teams Fail," *Fortune*, 12 June 2006, 87–92.

10. Vijay Govindarajan and Anil K. Gupta, "Building an Effective Global Business Team," *MIT Sloan Management Review*, Summer 2001, 631.

11. Louise Rehling, "Improving Teamwork Through Awareness of Conversational Styles," *Business Communication Quarterly*, December 2004, 475–482.

12. Andy Boynton and Bill Fischer, *Virtuoso Teams: Lessons from Teams That Changed Their Worlds* (Harrow, UK: FT Prentice Hall, 2005), 10.

13. Jon Hanke, "Presenting as a Team," *Presentations*, January 1998, 74–82.

14. William P. Galle, Jr., Beverly H. Nelson, Donna W. Luse, and Maurice F. Villere, *Business Communication: A Technology-Based Approach* (Chicago: Irwin, 1996), 260.

15. Mary Beth Debs, "Recent Research on Collaborative Writing in Industry," *Technical Communication*, November 1991, 476–484.

16. Mark Choate, "What Makes an Enterprise Wiki?" CMS Watch website, 28 April 2006 [accessed 18 August 2006] www.cmswatch.com.

17. Rob Koplowitz, "Building a Collaboration Strategy," *KM World*, November/December 2009, 14–15.

18. Eric Knorr and Galen Gruman, "What Cloud Computing Really Means," *InfoWorld* [accessed 11 June 2010] www.infoworld.com; Lamont Wood, "Cloud Computing Poised to Transform Communication," LiveScience, 8 December 2009 [accessed 11 June 2010] www.livescience.com.

19. Christopher Carfi and Leif Chastaine, "Social Networking for Businesses & Organizations," white paper, Cerado website [accessed 13 August 2008] www.cerado.com.

20. Richard McDermott and Douglas Archibald, "Harnessing Your Staff's Informal Networks," *Harvard Business Review*, March 2010, 89–89.

21. Tony Hsieh, "Why I Sold Zappos," *Inc.*, 1 June 2010 [accessed 11 June 2010] www.inc.com.

22. Chuck Williams, *Management*, 2nd ed. (Cincinnati: Cengage South-Western, 2002), 706–707.

23. Douglas Kimberly, "Ten Pitfalls of Pitiful Meetings," Payroll Manager's Report, January 2010, 1, 11; "Making the Most of Meetings," *Journal of Accountancy*, March 2009, 22.

24. Roger O. Crockett, "The 21st Century Meeting," *BusinessWeek*, 26 February 2007, 72–79.

25. Steve Lohr, "As Travel Costs Rise, More Meetings Go Virtual," *New York Times*, 22 July 2008 [accessed 23 July 2008] www.nytimes.com.

26. "Unlock the Full Power of the Web Conferencing," CEOworld.biz, 20 November 2007 [accessed 30 January 2008] www.ceoworld.biz.

27. IBM Jam Events website [accessed 10 June 2010] www.collaborationjam.com; "Big Blue Brainstorm," *BusinessWeek*, 7 August 2006 [accessed 15 August 2006] www.businessweek.com.

28. "17 Tips for More Productive Conference Calls," AccuConference [accessed 30 January 2008] www.accuconference.com.

29. Judi Brownell, *Listening*, 2nd ed. (Boston: Allyn & Bacon, 2002), 9, 10.

30. Carmine Gallo, "Why Leadership Means Listening," *BusinessWeek*, 31 January 2007 [accessed 29 January 2008] www.businessweek.com.

31. Augusta M. Simon, "Effective Listening: Barriers to Listening in a Diverse Business Environment," *Bulletin of the Association for Business Communication* 54, no. 3 (September 1991): 73–74.

32. Robyn D. Clarke, "Do You Hear What I Hear?" *Black Enterprise*, May 1998, 129.

33. John Boe, "Listen While You Work," *American Salesman*, April 2010, 15–16.

34. Dennis M. Kratz and Abby Robinson Kratz, *Effective Listening Skills* (New York: McGraw-Hill, 1995), 45–53; J. Michael Sproule, *Communication Today* (Glenview, Ill.: Scott Foresman, 1981), 69.

35. Brownell, *Listening*, 230–231.

36. Kratz and Kratz, *Effective Listening Skills*, 78–79; Sproule, *Communication Today*.

37. Tyner Blaine, "Ten Supercharged Active Listening Skills to Make You More Successful," Tyner Blain blog, 15 March 2007 [accessed 16 April 2007] http://tynerblain.com/blog; Bill Brooks, "The Power of Active Listening," *American Salesman*, June 2003, 12; "Active Listening," Study Guides and Strategies [accessed 5 February 2005] www.studygs.net.

38. Bob Lamons, "Good Listeners Are Better Communicators," *Marketing News*, 11 September 1995, 13+; Phillip Morgan and

H. Kent Baker, "Building a Professional Image: Improving Listening Behavior," *Supervisory Management*, November 1985, 35–36.

39. Clarke, "Do You Hear What I Hear?"; Dot Yandle, "Listening to Understand," *Pryor Report Management Newsletter Supplement* 15, no. 8 (August 1998): 13.

40. Brownell, *Listening*, 14; Kratz and Kratz, *Effective Listening Skills*, 8–9; Sherwyn P. Morreale and Courtland L. Bovée, *Excellence in Public Speaking* (Orlando, Fla.: Harcourt Brace, 1998), 72–76; Lyman K. Steil, Larry L. Barker, and Kittie W. Watson, *Effective Listening: Key to Your Success* (Reading, Mass.: Addison-Wesley, 1983), 21–22.

41. Patrick J. Collins, *Say It with Power and Confidence* (Upper Saddle River, N.J.: Prentice Hall, 1997), 40–45.

42. Morreale and Bovée, *Excellence in Public Speaking*, 296.

43. Dale G. Leathers, *Successful Nonverbal Communication: Principles and Applications* (New York: Macmillan, 1986), 19.

44. Gerald H. Graham, Jeanne Unrue, and Paul Jennings, "The Impact of Nonverbal Communication in Organizations: A Survey of Perceptions," *Journal of Business Communication* 28, no. 1 (Winter 1991): 45–62.

45. Bremer Communications website [accessed 28 January 2008] www.bremercommunications.com.

46. Danielle S. Urban, "What to Do About 'Body Art' at Work," *Workforce Management*, March 2010 [accessed 11 June 2010] www.workforce.com.

47. Virginia P. Richmond and James C. McCroskey, *Nonverbal Behavior in Interpersonal Relations* (Boston: Allyn & Bacon, 2000), 153–157.

48. Joe Navarro, "Body Language Myths," *Psychology Today*, 25 October 2009 [accessed 11 June 2010] www.psychologytoday.com; Richmond and McCroskey, *Nonverbal Behavior in Interpersonal Relations*, 2–3.

49. John Hollon, "No Tolerance for Jerks," *Workforce Management*, 12 February 2007, 34.

50. "Use Proper Cell Phone Etiquette at Work," Kelly Services website [accessed 11 June 2010] www.kellyservices.us.

51. J. J. McCorvey, "How to Create a Cell Phone Policy," *Inc.*, 10 February 2010 [accessed 11 June 2010] www.inc.com; "Use Proper Cell Phone Etiquette at Work."

52. Dana May Casperson, *Power Etiquette: What You Don't Know Can Kill Your Career* (New York: AMACOM, 1999), 10–14; Ellyn Spragins, "Introducing Politeness," *Fortune Small Business*, November 2001, 30.

53. Tanya Mohn, "The Social Graces as a Business Tool," *New York Times*, 10 November 2002, sec. 3, 12.

54. Casperson, *Power Etiquette*, 44–46.

55. Casperson, *Power Etiquette*, 109–110.

56. "Are You Practicing Proper Social Networking Etiquette?" *Forbes*, 9 October 2009 [accessed 11 June 2010] www.forbes.com; Pete Babb, "The Ten Commandments of Blog and Wiki Etiquette," *InfoWorld*, 28 May 2007 [accessed 3 August 2008] www.infoworld.com; Judith Kallos, "Instant Messaging Etiquette," NetM@nners blog [accessed 3 August 2008] www.netmanners.com; Michael S. Hyatt, "E-Mail Etiquette 101," From Where I Sit blog, 1 July 2007 [accessed 3 August 2008] www.michaelhyatt.com.

57. Dan Schawbel, "5 Lessons Celebrities Can Teach Us About Facebook Pages," Mashable, 15 May 2009 [accessed 13 June 2010] http://mashable.com.

CHAPTER 3

1. Chip Heath and Dan Heath, *Made to Stick: Why Some Ideas Survive and Others Die* (New York: Random House: 2008), 214.

2. Sanford Kaye, "Writing Under Pressure," *Soundview Executive Book Summaries* 10, no. 12, part 2, December 1988, 1–8.

3. Laurey Berk and Phillip G. Clampitt, "Finding the Right Path in the Communication Maze," *IABC Communication World*, October 1991, 28–32.

4. Linda Duyle, "Get Out of Your Office," *HR Magazine*, July 2006, 99–101.

5. Caroline McCarthy, "The Future of Web Apps Will See the Death of E-Mail," Webware blog, 29 February 2008 [accessed 25 August 2008] http://news.cnet.com; Kris Maher, "The Jungle," *Wall Street Journal*, 5 October 2004, B10; Kevin Maney, "Surge in Text Messaging Makes Cell Operators :-)," *USA Today*, 28 July 2005, B1–B2.

6. David Kirkpatrick, "It's Hard to Manage if You Don't Blog," *Fortune*, 4 October 2004, 46; Lee Gomes, "How the Next Big Thing in Technology Morphed into a Really Big Thing," *Wall Street Journal*, 4 October 2004, B1; Jeff Meisner, "Cutting Through the Blah, Blah, Blah," *Puget Sound Business Journal*, 19–25 November 2004, 27–28; Lauren Gard, "The Business of Blogging," *BusinessWeek*, 13 December 2004, 117–119; Heather Green, "Online Video: The Sequel," *BusinessWeek*, 10 January 2005, 40; Michelle Conlin and Andrew Park, "Blogging with the Boss's Blessing," *BusinessWeek*, 28 June 2004, 100–102.

7. Presslite website [accessed 28 June 2010] www.presselite.com; Neville Hobson, "Augmented Reality: Overlay Your World," Neville Hobson blog, 27 July 2009 [accessed 28 June 2010] www.nevillehobson.com.

8. Berk and Clampitt, "Finding the Right Path in the Communication Maze."

9. Samantha R. Murray and Joseph Peyrefitte, "Knowledge Type and Communication Media Choice in the Knowledge Transfer Process," *Journal of Managerial Issues*, Spring 2007, 111–133.

10. Raymond M. Olderman, *10 Minute Guide to Business Communication* (New York: Alpha Books, 1997), 19–20.

11. Mohan R. Limaye and David A. Victor, "Cross-Cultural Business Communication Research: State of the Art and Hypotheses for the 1990s," *Journal of Business Communication*, Summer 1991, 277–299.

12. Heath and Heath, *Made to Stick: Why Some Ideas Survive and Others Die*, 206.

CHAPTER 4

1. ING Direct website [accessed 25 June 2010] http://home.ingdirect.com; Arkadi Kuhlmann quotation from Irene Etzkorn, "Amazingly Simple Stuff," presentation, Plain English Symposium 2008.

2. Annette N. Shelby and N. Lamar Reinsch, Jr., "Positive Emphasis and You Attitude: An Empirical Study," *Journal of Business Communication* 32, no. 4 (1995): 303–322.

3. Sherryl Kleinman, "Why Sexist Language Matters," *Qualitative Sociology* 25, no. 2 (Summer 2002): 299–304.

4. Judy E. Pickens, "Terms of Equality: A Guide to Bias-Free Language," *Personnel Journal*, August 1985, 24.

5. Biography of Ursula M. Burns, Xerox website [accessed 25 June 2010] www.xerox.com; biography of Shelly Lazarus, Ogilvy & Mather website [accessed 25 June 2010] www.ogilvy.com; biography of Andrea Jung, Avon website [accessed 25 June 2010] www.avoncompany.com.

6. Lisa Taylor, "Communicating About People with Disabilities: Does the Language We Use Make a Difference?" *Bulletin of the Association for Business Communication* 53, no. 3 (September 1990): 65–67.

7. Susan Benjamin, *Words at Work* (Reading, Mass.: Addison-Wesley, 1997), 136–137.

8. Stuart Crainer and Des Dearlove, "Making Yourself Understood," *Across the Board*, May/June 2004, 23–27.

9. Plain Language.gov website [accessed 28 June 2010] www.plainlanguage.gov.

10. Plain English Campaign website [accessed 28 June 2010] www.plainenglish.co.uk.

11. Plain Language website; Etzkorn, "Amazingly Simple Stuff."

12. Susan Jaderstrom and Joanne Miller, "Active Writing," *Office Pro*, November/December 2003, 29.

13. Portions of this section are adapted from Courtland L. Bovée, *Techniques of Writing Business Letters, Memos, and Reports* (Sherman Oaks, Calif.: Banner Books International, 1978), 13–90.

14. Catherine Quinn, "Lose the Office Jargon; It May Sunset Your Career," *The Age* (Australia), 1 September 2007 [accessed 5 February 2008] www.theage.com.au.

15. Visuwords website [accessed 26 June 2010] www.visuwords.com.

16. Food Allergy Initiative website [accessed 23 September 2006] www.foodallergyinitiative.org; Diana Keough, "Snacks That Can Kill; Schools Take Steps to Protect Kids Who Have Severe Allergies to Nuts," *Plain Dealer*, 15 July 2003, E1; "Dawdling Over Food Labels," *New York Times*, 2 June 2003, A16; Sheila McNulty, "A Matter of Life and Death," *Financial Times*, 10 September 2003, 14.

17. Inspired by Inglesina website [accessed 14 March 2008] www.inglesina.com and BestBabyGear website [accessed 14 March 2008] www.bestbabygear.com. (The text contained in the sample message does not appear on either website.)

18. Adapted from a mailer received from Evolution Benefits, 10 January 2008. (None of the errors shown in this exercise exist in the original.)

CHAPTER 5

1. Leo Babauta, "Edit to Done: Revision and the Art of Being Concise," Write to Done blog, 1 January 2008 [accessed 29 June 2010] www.writetodone.com.

2. Natalie Canavor and Claire Meirowitz, "Good Corporate Writing: Why It Matters, and What to Do," *Communication World*, July–August 2005, 30–33.

3. "Revision in Business Writing," Purdue OWL website [accessed 8 February 2008] http://owl.english.purdue.edu.

4. Holly Weeks, "The Best Memo You'll Ever Write," *Harvard Management Communication Letter*, Spring 2005, 3–5.

5. Lynn Gaertner-Johnston, "Best Practices for Bullet Points," Business Writing blog, 17 December 2005 [accessed 8 February 2008] www.businesswritingblog.com.

6. Mary A. DeVries, *Internationally Yours* (Boston: Houghton Mifflin, 1994), 160.

7. William Zinsser, *On Writing Well*, 5th ed. (New York: HarperCollins, 1994), 126.

8. Deborah Gunn, "Looking Good on Paper," *Office Pro*, March 2004, 10–11.

9. Jacci Howard Bear, "Desktop Publishing Rules of Page Layout," About.com [accessed 22 August 2005] www.about.com.

10. Jacci Howard Bear, "Desktop Publishing Rules for How Many Fonts to Use," About.com [accessed 22 August 2005] www.about.com.

11. The writing sample in this exercise was adapted from material on the Marsh Risk Consulting website [accessed 2 October 2006] www.marshriskconsulting.com.

CHAPTER 6

1. "Welcome to the 'New and Improved' Nuts About Southwest—A User's Guide," Nuts About Southwest blog [accessed 21 July 2010] www.blogsouthwest.com; Bill Owens, "Why Can't I Make Reservations Further in Advance?" Nuts About Southwest blog, 24 January 2007 [accessed 15 May 2007] www.blogsouthwest.com; Bill Owens, "I Blogged. You Flamed. We Changed," Nuts About Southwest blog, 18 April 2007 [accessed 10 May 2007] www.blogsouthwest.com; "Southwest Airlines Is Nuts About Blogging," Southwest Airlines press release, 27 April 2007 [accessed 15 May 2007] www.prnewswire.com.

2. "Southwest Airlines Is Nuts About Blogging."

3. Angelo Fernando, "Social Media Change the Rules," *Communication World*, January February 2007, 9–10; Geoff Livingston and Brian Solis, *Now Is Gone: A Primer on New Media for Executives and Entrepreneurs* (Laurel, Md.: Bartleby Press, 2007), 60.

4. Don Tapscott and Anthony D. Williams, *Wikinomics: How Mass Collaboration Changes Everything* (London: Portfolio, 2006), 216–217; Dan Schawbel, "Why Social Media Makes It Possible for Gen-Y to Succeed," Personal Branding Blog, 12 December 2007 [accessed 14 February 2008] http://personalbrandingblog.wordpress.com.

5. "Ten Ways to Use Texting for Business," *Inc.* [accessed 21 July 2010] www.inc.com; Kate Maddox, "Warrillow Finds 39% of Small-Business Owners Use Text Messaging," BtoB, 1 August 2008 [accessed 15 September 2008] www.btobonline.com; Dave Carpenter, "Companies Discover Marketing Power of Text Messaging," *Seattle Times*, 25 September 2006 [accessed 25 September 2006] www.seattletimes.com.

6. Adam Ostrow, "A Look Back at the Last 5 Years in Social Media," Mashable, 20 July 2010 [accessed 21 July 2010] www.mashable.com.

7. Daniel Goleman, "E-Mail Is Easy to Write (and to Misread)," *New York Times*, 7 October 2007 [accessed 14 February 2008] www.nytimes.com.

8. Dana Mattioli, "Leaks Grow in World of Blogs," *Wall Street Journal*, 20 July 2009 [accessed 20 July 2009] http://online.wsj.com.

9. Richard Edelman, "Teaching Social Media: What Skills Do Communicators Need?" in *Engaging the New Influencers; Third Annual Social Media Academic Summit* (white paper) [accessed 7 June 2010] www.newmediaacademicsummit.com.

10. "Facebook Analytics: Full-on Facebook Tracking and Measurement," Webtrends [accessed 10 July 2010] www.webtrends.com; Facebook statistics page, Facebook.com[accessed 10 July 2010] www.facebook.com; Facebook pages of Adidas, Red Bull, and Starbucks [accessed 11 July 2010] www.facebook.com.

11. Todd Henneman, "At Lockheed Martin, Social Networking Fills Key Workforce Needs While Improving Efficiency and Lowering Costs," *Workforce Management*, March 2010 [accessed 14 July 2010] www.workforce.com.

12. Sharon Gaudin, "Companies Not Using Social Nets at Risk, Report Says," *Computerworld*, 15 July 2010 [accessed 21 July 2010] www.computerworld.com.

13. Alex Wright, "Mining the Web for Feelings, Not Facts," *New York Times*, 23 August 2009 [accessed 9 September 2009] www.nytimes.com.

14. Erica Swallow, "How to Use Social Media for Lead Generation," Mashable, 24 June 2010 [accessed 11 July 2010] http://mashable.com.

15. Susan Fournier and Lara Lee, "Getting Brand Communities Right," *Harvard Business Review*, April 2009, 105–111.

16. Patrick Hanlon and Josh Hawkins, "Expand Your Brand Community Online," *Advertising Age*, 7 January 2008, 14–15.

17. Josh Bernoff, "Social Strategy for Exciting (and Not So Exciting) Brands," *Marketing News*, 15 May 2009, 18; Larry Weber, *Marketing to the Social Web* (Hoboken, N.J.: Wiley, 2007), 12–14; David Meerman Scott, *The New Rules of Marketing and PR* (Hoboken, N.J.: Wiley, 2007), 62; Paul Gillin, *The New Influencers* (Sanger, Calif.: Quill Driver Books, 2007), 34–35; Jeremy Wright, *Blog Marketing: The Revolutionary Way to Increase Sales, Build Your Brand, and Get Exceptional Results* (New York: McGraw-Hill, 2006), 263–365.

18. Matt Rhodes, "Build Your Own Community or Go Where People Are? Do Both," FreshNetworks blog, 12 May 2009 [accessed 21 July 2010] www.freshnetworks.com.

19. Brian Solis, *Engage!* (Hoboken, N.J.: Wiley, 2010), 13.

20. Zachary Sniderman, "5 Ways to Clean Up Your Social Media Identity," 7 July 2010, Mashable [accessed 10 July 2010] http://mashable.com.

21. HP company profiles on LinkedIn and Facebook [accessed 21 July 2010] www.facebook.com/hp and www.linkedin.com/hp.

22. Ben Hanna, *2009 Business Social Media Benchmarking Study* (published by Business.com), 2 November 2009, 22.

23. Vanessa Pappas, "5 Ways to Build a Loyal Audience on YouTube," Mashable, 15 June 2010 [accessed 21 July 2010] www.mashable.com.

24. Tamar Weinberg, *The New Community Rules: Marketing on the Social Web* (Sebastapol, Calif.: O'Reilly Media, 2009), 288.

25. Reid Goldborough, "More Trends for 2009: What to Expect with Personal Technology," *Public Relations Tactics*, February 2009, 9.

26. Jessica E. Vascellaro, "Why Email No Longer Rules . . ." *Wall Street Journal*, 12 October 2008 [accessed 21 July 2010] http://online.wsj.com.

27. Matt Cain, "Managing E-Mail Hygiene," ZD Net Tech Update, 5 February 2004 [accessed 19 March 2004] www.techupdate.zdnet.com.

28. Hilary Potkewitz and Rachel Brown, "Spread of E-Mail Has Altered Communication Habits at Work," *Los Angeles Business Journal*, 18 April 2005 [accessed 30 April 2006] www.findarticles.com; Nancy Flynn, *Instant Messaging Rules* (New York: AMACOM, 2004), 47–54.

29. Mary Munter, Priscilla S. Rogers, and Jone Rymer, "Business E-Mail: Guidelines for Users," *Business Communication Quarterly*, March 2003, 26+; Renee B. Horowitz and Marian G. Barchilon, "Stylistic Guidelines for E-Mail," *IEEE Transactions on Professional Communication* 37, no. 4 (December 1994): 207–212.

30. Steve Rubel, "Tip: Tweetify the Lead of Your Emails," The Steve Rubel Stream blog, 20 July 2010 [accessed 22 July 2010] www.steverubel.com.

31. Robert J. Holland, "Connected—More or Less," Richmond.com, 8 August 2006 [accessed 5 October 2006] www.richmond.com.

32. Douglas MacMillan, "The End of Instant Messaging (As We Know It)," *BusinessWeek*, 16 November 2008 [accessed 16 December 2008] www.businessweek.com.

33. Vayusphere website [accessed 22 January 2006] www.vayusphere.com; Christa C. Ayer, "Presence Awareness: Instant Messaging's Killer App," *Mobile Business Advisor*, 1 July 2004 [accessed 22 January 2006] www.highbeam.com; Jefferson Graham, "Instant Messaging Programs Are No Longer Just for Messages," *USA Today*, 20 October 2003, 5D; Todd R. Weiss, "Microsoft Targets Corporate Instant Messaging Customers," *Computerworld*, 18 November 2002, 12; "Banks Adopt Instant Messaging to Create a Global Business Network," *Computer Weekly*, 25 April 2002, 40; Michael D. Osterman, "Instant Messaging in the Enterprise," *Business Communications Review*, January 2003, 59–62; John Pallato, "Instant Messaging Unites Work Groups and Inspires Collaboration," *Internet World*, December 2002, 14+.

34. Paul Mah, "Using Text Messaging in Business," Mobile Enterprise blog, 4 February 2008 [accessed 16 September 2008] http://blogs.techrepublic.com.com/wireless; Paul Kedrosky, "Why We Don't Get the (Text) Message," *Business 2.0*, 2 October 2006 [accessed 4 October 2006] www.business2.com; Carpenter, "Companies Discover Marketing Power of Text Messaging."

35. Mark Gibbs, "Racing to Instant Messaging," *NetworkWorld*, 17 February 2003, 74.

36. "E-Mail Is So Five Minutes Ago," *BusinessWeek*, 28 November 2005 [accessed 31 July 2009] www.businessweek.com.

37. *SANS Top-20 2007 Security Risks*, SANS Institute [accessed 16 September 2008] www.sans.org; Tom Espiner, "Spim, Splog on the Rise," CNET News, 6 July 2006 [accessed 16 September 2008] http://news.cnet.com; Anita Hamilton, "You've Got Spim!" *Time*, 2 February 2004 [accessed 1 March 2004] www.time.com; Elizabeth Millard, "Instant Messaging Threats Still Rising," Newsfactor.com, 6 July 2005 [accessed 5 October 2006] www.newsfactor.com.

38. Clint Boulton, "IDC: IM Use Is Booming in Business," InstantMessagingPlanet.com, 5 October 2005 [accessed 22 January 2006] www.instantmessagingplanet.com; Jenny Goodbody, "Critical Success Factors for Global Virtual Teams," *Strategic Communication Management*, February/March 2005, 18–21; Ann Majchrzak, Arvind Malhotra, Jeffrey Stamps, and Jessica Lipnack, "Can Absence Make a Team Grow Stronger?" *Harvard Business Review*, May 2004, 131–137; Christine Y. Chen, "The IM Invasion,"

Fortune, 26 May 2003, 135–138; Yudhijit Bhattacharjee, "A Swarm of Little Notes," *Time*, September 2002, A3–A8; Mark Bruno, "Taming the Wild Frontiers of Instant Messaging," *Bank Technology News*, December 2002, 30–31; Richard Grigonis, "Enterprise-Strength Instant Messaging," Convergence.com, 10–15 [accessed March 2003] www.convergence.com.

39. Leo Babauta, "17 Tips to Be Productive with Instant Messaging," Web Worker Daily, 14 November 2007 [accessed 14 February 2008] http://webworkerdaily.com; Pallato, "Instant Messaging Unites Work Groups and Inspires Collaboration."

40. GM FastLane blog [accessed 22 July 2010] http://fastlane.gmblogs.com.

41. Fredrik Wackå, "Six Types of Blogs—A Classification," CorporateBloggingInfo website, 10 August 2004 [accessed 5 October 2006] www.corporateblogginginfo.com; Stephen Baker, "The Inside Story on Company Blogs," *BusinessWeek* 14 February 2006 [accessed 15 February 2006] www.businessweek.com; Jeremy Wright, *Blog Marketing* (New York: McGraw-Hill, 2006), 45–56; Paul Chaney, "Blogs: Beyond the Hype!" 26 May 2005 [accessed 4 May 2006] http://radiantmarketinggroup.com.

42. Solis, *Engage!*, 314.

43. Michael Barbaro, "Wal-Mart Tastemakers Write Unfiltered Blog," *New York Times*, 3 March 2008 [accessed 1 June 2008] www.nytimes.com.

44. Jake Swearingen, "Four Ways Social Networking Can Build Business," Bnet.com [accessed 11 July 2010] www.bnet.com.

45. Evolve24 website [accessed 22 July 2010] http://evolve24.com.

46. Dianne Culhane, "Blog Logs a Culture Change," *Communication World*, January/February 2008, 40–41.

47. Weinberg, *The New Community Rules: Marketing on the Social Web*, 89.

48. Stephen Baker and Heather Green, "Blogs Will Change Your Business," *BusinessWeek*, 2 May 2005, 57–67.

49. Joel Falconer, "Six Rules for Writing Great Web Content," Blog News Watch, 9 November 2007 [accessed 14 February 2008] www.blognewswatch.com.

50. Dion Hinchcliffe, "Twitter on Your Intranet: 17 Microblogging Tools for Business," ZDNet, 1 June 2009 [accessed 22 July 2010] www.zdnet.com.

51. "The Library of Congress Is Archiving Your Tweets," NPR, 19 July 2010 [accessed 19 July 2010] www.npr.org.

52. Hinchcliffe, "Twitter on Your Intranet: 17 Microblogging Tools for Business."

53. "Warner Brothers Television Group Social Media Contacts," The WB website [accessed 9 August 2010] www.thewb.com.

54. "Turn Your Feed into a Podcast," Lifehacker blog, 12 January 2006 [accessed 6 May 2006] www.lifehacker.com.

55. "Set Up Your Podcast for Success," FeedForAll website [accessed 4 October 2006] www.feedforall.com.

56. Shel Holtz, "Ten Guidelines for B2B Podcasts," Webpronews.com, 12 October 2005 [accessed 9 March 2006] www.webpronews.com.

57. Adapted from *Logan* website [accessed 19 July 2010] www.loganmagazine.com.

58. Adapted from "Side Impact Protection Revealed," Britax website [accessed 19 July 2010] www.britaxusa.com.

59. Adapted from Lisa Marsh, "Why Fashion Loves Skinny," MSN Lifestyle [accessed 17 September 2008] http://lifestyle.msn.com.

60. Adapted from Seymour Powell website [accessed 20 July 2010] www.seymourpowell.com; Sam Roberts, "51% of Women Now Living Without a Spouse," *New York Times*, 16 January 2007 [accessed 16 January 2007] www.nytimes.com.

61. Adapted from Crutchfield website [accessed 20 July 2010] www.crutchfield.com.

62. Adapted from "Major New Study Shatters Stereotypes About Teens and Video Games," MacArthur Foundation, 16 September 2008 [accessed 18 September 2008] www.macfound.org.

63. JetBlue Twitter website [accessed 20 July 2010] http://twitter.com/JetBlue; "JetBlue Lands on eBay," JetBlue website [accessed 18 September 2008] http://jetblue.com/ebay.

64. Adapted from Comic-Con website [accessed 19 July 2010] www.comic-con.org; Tom Spurgeon, "Welcome to Nerd Vegas: A Guide to Visiting and Enjoying Comic-Con International in San Diego, 2006!" The Comics Reporter.com, 11 July 2006 [accessed 16 January 2007] www.comicsreporter.com; Rebecca Winters Keegan, "Boys Who Like Toys," *Time*, 19 April 2007 [accessed 15 May 2007] www.time.com.

CHAPTER 7

1. Warren E. Buffett, *Preface* to *A Plain English Handbook*, U.S. Securities and Exchange Commission website [accessed 4 July 2010] www.sec.gov.

2. "How to Write Reference Letters," National Association of Colleges and Employers website [accessed 5 July 2010] www.naceweb.org; "Five (or More) Ways You Can Be Sued for Writing (or Not Writing) Reference Letters," *Fair Employment Practices Guidelines*, July 2006, 1, 3.

3. Fraser P. Seitel, *The Practice of Public Relations*, 9th ed. (Upper Saddle River, N.J.: Prentice Hall, 2004), 402–411; *Techniques for Communicators* (Chicago: Lawrence Ragan Communication, 1995), 34, 36.

4. David Meerman Scott, *The New Rules of Marketing and PR* (Hoboken, N.J.: Wiley, 2007), 62.

5. Shel Holz, "Next-Generation Press Releases," CW Bulletin, September 2009 [accessed 9 August 2010] www.iabc.com; Steph Gray, "Baby Steps in Social Media News Releases," Helpful Technology blog, 15 May 2009 [accessed 9 August 2010] http://blog.helpfultechnology.com.

6. Pat Cataldo, "Op-Ed: Saying 'Thank You' Can Open More Doors Than You Think," Penn State University Smeal College of Business website [accessed 19 February 2008] www.smeal.psu.edu.

7. Jackie Huba, "Five Must-Haves for Thank-You Notes," Church of the Customer Blog, 16 November 2007 [accessed 19 February 2008] www.churchofthecustomer.com.

8. Mary Mitchell, "The Circle of Life—Condolence Letters," ULiveandLearn.com [accessed 18 July 2005] www.liveandlearn.com; Donna Larcen, "Authors Share the Words of Condolence," *Los Angeles Times*, 20 December 1991, E11.

9. Adapted from Keith H. Hammonds, "Difference Is Power," *Fast Company*, 36, 258 [accessed 11 July 2000] www.fastcompany.com; Terri Morrison, Wayne Conaway, and

George A. Borden, *Kiss, Bow, or Shake Hands* (Avon, Mass.: Adams Media Corp., 1994), 1–5.

10. Adapted from Tom Abate, "Need to Preserve Cash Generates Wave of Layoffs in Biotech Industry," *San Francisco Chronicle*, 10 February 2003 [accessed 18 July 2005] www.sfgate.com.

11. Adapted from Lisa DiCarlo, "IBM Gets the Message—Instantly," Forbes.com, 7 July 2002 [accessed 22 July 2003] www.forbes.com; "IBM Introduces Breakthrough Messaging Technology for Customers and Business Partners," *M2 Presswire*, 19 February 2003 [accessed 24 July 2003] www.proquest.com; "IBM and America Online Team for Instant Messaging Pilot," *M2 Presswire*, 4 February 2003 [accessed 24 July 2003] www.proquest.com.

12. Adapted from CES website [accessed 7 July 2010] www.cesweb.org.

13. Adapted from Public Relations Society of America website [accessed 18 June 2005] www.prsa.org.

14. Adapted from Mitchell, "The Circle of Life—Condolence Letters"; Larcen, "Authors Share the Words of Condolence."

15. Adapted from GSD&M Idea City website [accessed 7 July 2010] www.ideacity.com; Burt Helm, "Wal-Mart, Please Don't Leave Me," *BusinessWeek*, 9 October 2006, 84–89.

16. Adapted from SolarCity website [accessed 7 July 2010] www.solarcity.com.

CHAPTER 8

1. Matt Rhodes, "Social Media as a Crisis Management Tool," Social Media Today blog, 21 December 2009 [accessed 8 July 2010] www.socialmediatoday.com.

2. Katie Grasso, "Deliver Bad News to Workers Face-to-Face, with Empathy," *(Camden, New Jersey) Courier-Post*, 8 February 2006 [accessed 14 May 2006] www.courierpostonline.com.

3. Ian McDonald, "Marsh Can Do $600 Million, but Apologize?" *Wall Street Journal*, 14 January 2005, C1, C3; Adrienne Carter and Amy Borrus, "What if Companies Fessed Up?" *BusinessWeek*, 24 January 2005, 59–60; Patrick J. Kiger, "The Art of the Apology," *Workforce Management*, October 2004, 57–62.

4. "The Power of Apology: Removing the Legal Barriers," A Special Report by the Ombudsman of the Province of British Columbia, February 2006 [accessed 14 May 2006] www.ombud.gov.bc.ca; Ameeta Patel and Lamar Reinsch, "Companies Can Apologize: Corporate Apologies and Legal Liability," *Business Communication Quarterly*, March 2003 [accessed 1 December 2003] www.elibrary.com.

5. John Guiniven, "Sorry! An Apology as a Strategic PR Tool," *Public Relations Tactics*, December 2007, 6.

6. Deven Sharma, "Standard & Poor's Commitment to Reform: Restoring Confidence in the Credit Markets," Standard & Poor's [accessed 13 July 2010] www.standardandpoors.com.

7. Jessica Marquez, "Breaking the Bad News on 401(k)s," *Workforce Management*, 22 June 2009, 30–32.

8. "HR Manners," *Workforce Week Management*, January 29–February 4, 2006.

9. Dawn Wolf, "Job Applicant Rejection Letter Dos and Donts—Writing an Appropriate 'Dear John' Letter to an Unsuccessful Applicant," 31 May 2009, Employment Blawg.com [accessed 14 July 2010] www.employmentblawg.com.

10. Wolf, "Job Applicant Rejection Letter Dos and Donts—Writing an Appropriate 'Dear John' Letter to an Unsuccessful Applicant"; "Prohibited Employment Policies/Practices," U.S. Equal Employment Opportunity Commission [accessed 14 July 2010] www.eeoc.gov; Susan M. Heathfield, "Candidate Rejection Letter," About.com [accessed 14 July 2010] http://humanresources.about.com; "Rejection Letters Under Scrutiny: 7 Do's & Don'ts," *Business Management Daily*, 1 April 2009 [accessed 14 July 2010] www.businessmanagementdaily.com.

11. Kelly Spors, "Why Performance Reviews Don't Work—And What You Can Do About It," Independent Street blog, *Wall Street Journal*, 21 October 2008 [accessed 14 July 2010] http://blogs.wsj.com.

12. Carrie Brodzinski, "Avoiding Wrongful Termination Suits," *National Underwriter Property & Casualty—Risk & Benefits Management*, 13 October 2003 [accessed 2 December 2003] www.elibrary.com.

13. Susan Friedfel, "Protecting Yourself in the Performance Review Process," *Workforce Management*, April 2009 [accessed 14 July 2010] www.workforce.com.

14. Friedfel, "Protecting Yourself in the Performance Review Process."

15. E. Michelle Bohreer and Todd J. Zucker, "Five Mistakes Managers Make When Terminating Employees," *Texas Lawyer*, 2 May 2006 [accessed 14 July 2010] www.law.com; Deborah Muller, "The Right Things to Do to Avoid Wrongful Termination Claims," *Workforce Management*, October 2008 [accessed 14 July 2010] www.workforce.com; Maria Greco Danaher, "Termination: Telling an Employee," *Workforce Management* [accessed 14 July 2010] www.workforce.com.

16. Matt Rhodes, "Build Your Own Community or Go Where People Are? Do Both," FreshNetworks blog, 12 May 2009 [accessed 14 July 2010] www.freshnetworks.com.

17. "Gulf of Mexico Response," BP website [accessed 14 July 2010] www.bp.com.

18. David Meerman Scott, "The US Air Force: Armed with Social Media," WebInkNow blog, 15 December 2008 [accessed 14 July 2010] www.webinknow.com; Matt Rhodes, "How to React If Somebody Writes About Your Brand Online," FreshNetworks blog, 9 January 2009 [accessed 14 July 2010] www.freshnetworks.com; Rhodes, "Social Media as a Crisis Management Tool."

19. Adapted from Pui-Wing Tam, Erin White, Nick Wingfield, and Kris Maher, "Snooping E-Mail by Software Is Now a Workplace Norm," *Wall Street Journal*, 9 March 2005, B1+.

20. Adapted from "Bathtub Curve," *Engineering Statistics Handbook*, National Institute of Standards and Technology website [accessed 16 April 2005] www.nist.gov; Robert Berner, "The Warranty Windfall," *BusinessWeek*, 20 December 2004, 84–86; Larry Armstrong, "When Service Contracts Make Sense," *BusinessWeek*, 20 December 2004, 86.

21. Adapted from Twitter/JetBlue website [accessed 15 July 2010] http://twitter.com/JetBlue.

22. Adapted from Fookes Software website [accessed 28 October 2008] www.fookes.com.

23. Adapted from Lee Valley website [accessed 29 October 2008] www.leevalley.com.

24. Adapted from "FDA Notifies Public That Vail Products, Inc., Issues Nationwide Recall of Enclosed Bed Systems," FDA press release, 30 June 2005 [accessed 18 August 2005] www.fda.gov.

25. "Viral Effect of Email Promotion," Alka Dwivedi blog [accessed 19 October 2006] www.alkadwivedi.net; Teresa Valdez Klein, "Starbucks Makes a Viral Marketing Misstep," Blog Business Summit website [accessed 19 October 2006] www.blogbusinesssummit.com.

26. Adapted from EQ Company press releases [accessed 27 October 2006] www.eqonline.com; "N.C. Residents to Return After Fire," *ScienceDaily*, 6 October 2006 [accessed 27 October 2006] www.sciencedaily.com; "Hazardous Waste Plant Fire in N.C. Forces 17,000 to Evacuate," FOXNews.com, 6 October 2006 [accessed 27 October 2006] www.foxnews.com.

27. Adapted from Rodney Manley, "Milledgeville Plan to Close; 150 to Lose Jobs," Macon.com, 28 January 2009 [accessed 1 February 2009] www.macon.com; Jamie Jones, "Shaw Plant Closing in Milledgeville," *The Daily Citizen* (Dalton, Georgia), 29 January 2009 [accessed 1 February 2009] www.northwestgeorgia.com.

28. Adapted from "Recall Safety Notice," Bombardier Recreational Products website, 10 September 2008 [accessed 30 October 2008] www.brp.com; Bombardier Recreational Products website [accessed 30 October 2008] www.brp.com.

CHAPTER 9

1. Brian Clark, "The Two Most Important Words in Blogging," Copyblogger blog [accessed 1 March 2008] www.copyblogger.com.

2. Jay A. Conger, "The Necessary Art of Persuasion," *Harvard Business Review*, May–June 1998, 84–95; Jeanette W. Gilsdorf, "Write Me Your Best Case for . . ." *Bulletin of the Association for Business Communication* 54, no. 1 (March 1991): 7–12.

3. "Vital Skill for Today's Managers: Persuading, Not Ordering, Others," *Soundview Executive Book Summaries*, September 1998, 1.

4. Mary Cross, "Aristotle and Business Writing: Why We Need to Teach Persuasion," *Bulletin of the Association for Business Communication* 54, no. 1 (March 1991): 3–6.

5. Stephen Bayley and Roger Mavity, "How to Pitch," *Management Today*, March 2007, 48–53.

6. Robert B. Cialdini, "Harnessing the Science of Persuasion," *BusinessWeek*, 4 December 2007 [accessed 4 March 2008] www.businessweek.com.

7. Wesley Clark, "The Potency of Persuasion," *Fortune*, 12 November 2007, 48; W. H. Weiss, "Using Persuasion Successfully," *Supervision*, October 2006, 13–16.

8. Tom Chandler, "The Copywriter's Best Friend," The Copywriter Underground blog, 20 December 2006 [accessed 4 March 2008] http://copywriterunderground.com.

9. John D. Ramage and John C. Bean, *Writing Arguments: A Rhetoric with Readings*, 3rd ed. (Boston: Allyn & Bacon, 1995), 430–442.

10. Philip Vassallo, "Persuading Powerfully: Tips for Writing Persuasive Documents," *et Cetera*, Spring 2002, 65–71.

11. Dianna Booher, *Communicate with Confidence* (New York: McGraw-Hill, 1994), 102.

12. Conger, "The Necessary Art of Persuasion."

13. "Social Factors in Developing a Web Accessibility Business Case for Your Organization," W3C website [accessed 17 July 2010] www.w3.org.

14. Paul Endress, "The Art of Persuasion: Get the Edge You Need to Reach Your Goals," *American Salesman*, April 2007, 7–10.

15. iPod main product page, Apple website [accessed 17 July 2010] www.apple.com/ipod.

16. "HealthGrades Reveals America's Best Hospitals," 27 February 2008 [accessed 4 March 2008] www.ivanhoe.com.

17. Biokleen home page [accessed 17 July 2010] http://biokleenhome.com.

18. Ford Focus product page, Ford website [accessed 17 July 2010] www.fordvehicles.com.

19. *Living in France* product page, Insider Paris Guides website [accessed 4 March 2008] www.insiderparisguides.com.

20. Barnes & Noble website [accessed 17 July 2010] www.barnesandnoble.com.

21. Mint.com website [accessed 17 July 2010] www.mint.com.

22. FlightWise Carry-on Backpack product page, Lands End website [accessed 17 July 2010] www.landsend.com.

23. iPod touch product page, Apple website [accessed 17 July 2010] www.apple.com/ipodtouch/what-is/gaming-device.html.

24. iPod touch product page.

25. Tamar Weinberg, *The New Community Rules: Marketing on the Social Web* (Sebastapol, Calif.: O'Reilly Media, 2009), 325.

26. Weinberg, *The New Community Rules: Marketing on the Social Web*, 22; 23–24; 187–191; Larry Weber, *Marketing to the Social Web* (Hoboken, N.J.: Wiley, 2007), 12–14; David Meerman Scott, *The New Rules of Marketing and PR* (Hoboken, N.J.: Wiley, 2007), 62; Paul Gillin, *The New Influencers* (Sanger, Calif.: Quill Driver Books, 2007), 34–35; Jeremy Wright, *Blog Marketing: The Revolutionary Way to Increase Sales, Build Your Brand, and Get Exceptional Results* (New York: McGraw-Hill, 2006), 263–365.

27. Michael Zeisser, "Unlocking the Elusive Potential of Social Networks," *McKinsey Quarterly*, June 2010 [accessed 17 July 2010] www.mckinseyquarterly.com.

28. Gilsdorf, "Write Me Your Best Case for . . ."

29. "How to Comply With the Children's Online Privacy Protection Rule," U.S. Federal Trade Commission website [accessed 17 July 2010] www.ftc.gov; "Frequently Asked Advertising Questions: A Guide for Small Business," U.S. Federal Trade Commission website [accessed 17 July 2010] www.ftc.gov.

30. Adapted from Samsung website [accessed 22 October 2006] www.samsung.com.

31. Adapted from Whole Foods Market website [accessed 19 July 2010] www.wholefoodsmarket.com.

32. Adapted from Web Accessibility Initiative website [accessed 19 July 2010] www.w3.org/wai.

33. Adapted from Podcast Bunker website [accessed 19 July 2010] www.podcastbunker.com.

34. Kentucky Cabinet for Economic Development website [accessed 19 July 2010] www.thinkkentucky.com.

35. Adapted from Time Inc. website [accessed 19 July 2010] www.timewarner.com.

36. Adapted from Kelly Services website [accessed 19 July 2010] www.kellyservices.com.

37. Adapted from American National Red Cross website [accessed 19 July 2010] www.redcrossblood.org; American Red Cross San Diego Chapter website [accessed 19 July 2010] www.sdarc.org.

38. Adapted from "Community Relations," IBM website [accessed 15 January 2004] www.ibm.com; "DAS Faces

an Assured Future with IBM," IBM website [accessed 16 January 2004] www.ibm.com; IBM website, "Sametime" [accessed 16 January 2004] www.ibm.com.

39. Adapted from Hangers Cleaners (Kansas City) website [accessed 19 July 2010] www.hangerskc.com; Charles Fishman, "The Greener Cleaners," Fast Company website [accessed 11 July 2000] http://fastcompany.com; Micell Technologies website [accessed 1 September 2000] www.micell.com; Cool Clean Technologies, Inc., website [accessed 9 January 2004] www.coolclean.com.

40. Adapted from Curves website [accessed 19 July 2010] www.curves.com.

CHAPTER 10

1. Molly Selvin, "No Gobbledygook; Company Handbook Is in Plain English," *Seattle Times*, 27 January 2008 [accessed 8 March 2008] www.seattletimes.com.

2. Courtland L. Bovée, Michael J. Houston, and John V. Thill, *Marketing*, 2d ed. (New York: McGraw-Hill, 1995), 194–196.

3. Legal-Definitions.com [accessed 17 December 2003] www.legal-definitions.com.

4. Lynn Quitman Troyka, *Simon & Schuster Handbook for Writers*, 6th ed. (Upper Saddle River, N.J.: Prentice Hall, 2002), 481.

5. "Mahalo," CrunchBase [accessed 25 July 2010] www.crunchbase.com.

6. AllTheWeb.com advanced search page [accessed 27 August 2005] www.alltheweb.com; Google advanced search page [accessed 27 August 2005] www.google.com; Yahoo! advanced search page [accessed 27 August 2005] www.yahoo.com.

7. Christina Warren, "Yolink Helps Web Researchers Search Behind Links," Mashable, 24 July 2010 [accessed 26 July 2010] http://mashable.com.

8. Naresh K. Malhotra, *Basic Marketing Research* (Upper Saddle River, N.J.: Prentice-Hall, 2002), 314–317; "How to Design and Conduct a Study," *Credit Union Magazine*, October 1983, 36–46.

9. Tesco website [accessed 25 July 2010] www.tesco.com.

10. Jakob Nielsen, "How Users Read on the Web" [accessed 11 November 2004] www.useit.com/alertbox/9710a.html.

11. Reid Goldsborough, "Words for the Wise," *Link-Up*, September–October 1999, 25–26.

12. Julie Rohovit, "Computer Eye Strain: The Dilbert Syndrome," Virtual Hospital website [accessed 9 November 2004] www.vh.org.

13. Nick Usborne, "Two Pillars of a Successful Site," *Excess Voice*, May 2004 [accessed 8 November 2004] www.excessvoice.com.

14. Shel Holtz, "Writing for the Wired World," *International Association of Business Communicators*, 1999, 6–9.

15. Holtz, "Writing for the Wired World," 28–29.

16. Adapted from SXSW website [accessed 27 July 2010] http://sxsw.com; Catherine Holahan and Spencer E. Ante, "SXSW: Where Tech Mingles with Music," *BusinessWeek*, 7 March 2008 [accessed 9 March 2008] www.businessweek.com.

17. Adapted from Air-Trak website [accessed 26 July 2010] www.air-trak.com.

CHAPTER 11

1. George Stenitzer, "New Challenges for Annual Reports," Presentation to National Investor Relations Institute, November 2005 [accessed 11 November 2006] www.niri-chicago.org.

2. Martin Couzins, "Expert's View: Tania Menegatti on How to Improve Your Communication Skills," *Personnel Today*, 30 August 2005 [accessed 22 May 2006] www.epnet.com.

3. A. S. C. Ehrenberg, "Report Writing—Six Simple Rules for Better Business Documents," *Admap*, June 1992, 39–42.

4. Michael Netzley and Craig Snow, *Guide to Report Writing* (Upper Saddle River, N.J.: Prentice Hall, 2001), 15.

5. Philip C. Kolin, *Successful Writing at Work*, 6th ed. (Boston: Houghton Mifflin, 2001), 552–555.

6. Martin James, "PDF Virus Spreads Without Exploiting any Flaw," IT Pro, 8 April 2010 [accessed 29 July 2010] www.itpro.co.uk.

7. Sant Corporation website [accessed 29 July 2010] www.santcorp.com.

8. "Web Writing: How to Avoid Pitfalls," *Investor Relations Business*, 1 November 1999, 15.

9. Patsi Krakoff, "Writing on the Web: Letting Go of the Words," Writing on the Web blog, 15 April 2010 [accessed 28 July 2010] http://writingontheweb.com.

10. Jakob Nielsen, "Writing Style for Print vs. Web," Useit.com, 9 June 2008 [accessed 28 July 2010] www.useit.com.

11. Paul Boag, "10 Harsh Truths About Corporate Websites," Smashing Magazine blog, 10 February 2009 [accessed 28 July 2010] www.smashingmagazine.com.

12. "Web Writing: The Good, Bad and Ugly," Webcopyplus! blog, 7 January 2009 [accessed 28 July 2010] http://blog.webcopyplus.com.

13. Mark Choate, "What Makes an Enterprise Wiki?" CMS Watch website, 28 April 2006 [accessed 18 August 2006] www.cmswatch.com.

14. "Codex: Guidelines," WordPress website [accessed 16 February 2008] http://wordpress.com; Michael Shanks, "Wiki Guidelines," Traumwerk website [accessed 18 August 2006] http://metamedia.stanford.edu/projects/traumwerk/home; Joe Moxley, MC Morgan, Matt Barton, and Donna Hanak, "For Teachers New to Wikis," Writing Wiki [accessed 18 August 2006] http://writingwiki.org; "Wiki Guidelines," PsiWiki [accessed 18 August 2006] http://psi-im.org.

15. Rachael King, "No Rest for the Wiki," *BusinessWeek*, 12 March 2007 [accessed 14 February 2008] www.businessweek.com.

16. "Codex: Guidelines," WordPress website [accessed 28 July 2010] http://wordpress.com.

17. Alexis Gerard and Bob Goldstein, *Going Visual* (Hoboken, N.J.: Wiley, 2005), 18.

18. Gerard and Goldstein, *Going Visual*, 103–106.

19. Edward R. Tufte, *Visual Explanations: Images and Quantities, Evidence and Narrative* (Cheshire, Conn.: Graphics Press, 1997), 82.

20. Joshua David McClurg-Genevese, "The Principles of Design," *Digital Web Magazine*, 13 June 2005 [accessed 23 November 2006] www.digital-web.com.

21. Charles Kostelnick and Michael Hassett, *Shaping Information: The Rhetoric of Visual Conventions* (Carbondale, Ill.: Southern Illinois University Press, 2003), 17.

22. Edward R. Tufte, *The Visual Display of Quantitative Information* (Cheshire, Conn.: Graphic Press, 1983), 113.

23. Stephen Few, "Oracle—Have You No Shame?" Visual Business Intelligence blog, 29 April 2010 [accessed 29 July 2010] www.perceptualedge.com.

24. "Pyramid Perversion—More Junk Charts," Stubborn Mule blog, 12 March 2010 [accessed 29 July 2010] www.stubbornmule.com.

25. Stephen Few, "Save the Pies for Dessert," *Visual Business Intelligence Newsletter*, August 2007 [accessed 29 July 2010] www.perceptualedge.com.

26. Maria Popova, "Data Visualization: Stories for the Information Age," *BusinessWeek*, 12 August 2009 [accessed 29 July 2010] www.businessweek.com.

27. "Data Visualization: Modern Approaches," Smashing Magazine website, 2 August 2007 [accessed 15 March 2008] www.smashingmagazine.com; "7 Things You Should Know About Data Visualization," Educause Learning Initiative [accessed 15 March 2008] www.educause.edu; TagCrowd website [accessed 15 March 2008] www.tagcrowd.com.

28. Eric Binfet, personal communication, 26 November 2008.

29. Based in part on Tufte, *Visual Explanations: Images and Quantities, Evidence and Narrative*, 29–37, 53; Paul Martin Lester, *Visual Communication: Images with Messages*, 4th ed. (Belmont, Calif.: Cengage Wadsworth, 2006), 95–105, 194–196.

30. John Morkes and Jakob Nielsen, "Concise, Scannable, and Objective: How to Write for the Web," UseIt.com [accessed 13 November 2006] www.useit.com.

31. Netzley and Snow, *Guide to Report Writing*, 57.

32. Toby B. Gooley, "Ocean Shipping: RFPs that Get Results," *Logistics Management*, July 2003, 47–52.

33. Adapted from Ieva M. Augstumes, "Buyers Take the Driver's Seat," *Dallas Morning News*, 20 February 2004 [accessed 30 June 2004] www.highbeam.com; Jill Amadio, "A Click Away: Automotive Web Sites Are Revved Up and Ready to Help You Buy," *Entrepreneur*, 1 August 2003 [accessed 30 June 2004] www.highbeam.com; Dawn C. Chmielewski, "Car Sites Lend Feel-Good Info for Haggling," *San Jose Mercury News*, 1 August 2003 [accessed 30 June 2004] www.highbeam.com; Cromwell Schubarth, "Autoheroes Handle Hassle of Haggling," *Boston Herald*, 24 July 2003 [accessed 30 June 2004] www.highbeam.com; Rick Popely, "Internet Doesn't Change Basic Shopping Rules," *Chicago Tribune*, 28 February 2004 [accessed 30 June 2004] www.highbeam.com; Matt Nauman, "Walnut Creek, Calif., Firm Prospers as Online Car Buying Becomes More Popular," *San Jose Mercury News*, 21 June 2004 [accessed 30 June 2004] www.highbeam.com; Cliff Banks, "e-Dealer 100," *Ward's Dealer Business*, 1 April 2004 [accessed 30 June 2004] www.highbeam.com; Cars.com website [accessed 30 June 2004] www.cars.com; CarsDirect.com website [accessed 30 June 2004] www.carsdirect.com.

CHAPTER 12

1. EZspeech website [accessed 19 March 2008] www.ez-speech.com; Marc S. Friedman, "Use Visual Aids, Not Visual Crutches," *Training*, 24 December 2007 [accessed 19 March 2008] www.presentations.com.

2. Nancy Duarte, *Slide:ology: The Art and Science of Creating Great Presentations* (Sebastopol, Calif.: O'Reilly Media, 2008), 13.

3. Amber Naslund, "Twebinar: GE's Tweetsquad," 4 August 2009 [accessed 3 August 2010] www.radian6.com/blog.

4. Carmine Gallo, "Loaded for Bore," *BusinessWeek* online, 5 August 2005 [accessed 19 September 2005] www.businessweek.com.

5. Carmine Gallo, "How to Deliver a Presentation Under Pressure," *BusinessWeek* online, 18 September 2008 [accessed 15 August 2009] www.businessweek.com.

6. Sarah Lary and Karen Pruente, "Powerless Point: Common PowerPoint Mistakes to Avoid," *Public Relations Tactics*, February 2004, 28.

7. Garr Reynolds, *Presentation Zen* (Berkeley, Calif.: New Riders, 2008), 66.

8. Reynolds, *Presentation Zen*, 39–42.

9. Sherwyn P. Morreale and Courtland L. Bovée, *Excellence in Public Speaking* (Fort Worth, Tex.: Harcourt Brace College Publishers, 1998), 234–237.

10. John Windsor, "Presenting Smart: Keeping the Goal in Sight," *Presentations*, 6 March 2008 [accessed 19 March 2008] www.presentations.com.

11. Morreale and Bovée, *Excellence in Public Speaking*, 241–243.

12. Adapted from Eric J. Adams, "Management Focus: User-Friendly Presentation Software," *World Trade*, March 1995, 92.

13. Carmine Gallo, "Grab Your Audience Fast," *BusinessWeek*, 13 September 2006, 19.

14. Walter Kiechel III, "How to Give a Speech," *Fortune*, 8 June 1987, 180.

15. *Communication and Leadership Program* (Santa Ana, Calif.: Toastmasters International, 1980), 44, 45.

16. Reynolds, *Presentation Zen: Simple Ideas on Presentation Design and Delivery*, 10.

17. An example of such a presentation is Dick Hardt's keynote presentation at OSCON 2005; the presentation can be viewed at www.identity20.com/media/OSCON2005.

18. Cliff Atkinson, "The Cognitive Load of PowerPoint: Q&A with Richard E. Mayer," Sociable Media [accessed 15 August 2009] http://www.sociablemedia.com/articles_mayer.htm.

19. "The Power of Color in Presentations," 3M Meeting Network [accessed 25 May 2007] www.3m.com/meetingnetwork/readingroom/meetingguide_power_color.html.

20. Duarte, *Slide:ology: The Art and Science of Creating Great Presentations*, 118.

21. Duarte, *Slide:ology: The Art and Science of Creating Great Presentations*, 152.

22. Sarah Lary and Karen Pruente, "Powerless Point: Common PowerPoint Mistakes to Avoid," *Public Relations Tactics*, February 2004, 28.

23. Reynolds, *Presentation Zen: Simple Ideas on Presentation Design and Delivery*, 85.

24. Jerry Weissman, *Presenting to Win: The Art of Telling Your Story* (Upper Saddle River, N.J.: Pearson Prentice Hall, 2006), 162–163.

25. Reynolds, *Presentation Zen: Simple Ideas on Presentation Design and Delivery*, 208

26. Reynolds, *Presentation Zen: Simple Ideas on Presentation Design and Delivery*, 37.

27. Richard Zeoli, "The Seven Things You Must Know About Public Speaking," *Forbes*, 3 June 2009 [accessed 2 August 2010] www.forbes.com; Morreale and Bovée, *Excellence in Public Speaking*, 24–25.

28. Jennifer Rotondo and Mike Rotondo, Jr., *Presentation Skills for Managers* (New York: McGraw-Hill, 2002), 9.

29. Rick Gilbert, "Presentation Advice for Boardroom Success," *Financial Executive*, September 2005, 12.

30. Rotondo and Rotondo, *Presentation Skills for Managers*, 151.

31. Teresa Brady, "Fielding Abrasive Questions During Presentations," *Supervisory Management*, February 1993, 6.

32. Robert L. Montgomery, "Listening on Your Feet," *The Toastmaster*, July 1987, 14–15.

33. Cliff Atkinson, *The Backchannel* (Berkeley, Calif.: New Riders, 2010), 17.

34. Atkinson, *The Backchannel*, 51, 68–73.

35. Olivia Mitchell, "10 Tools for Presenting with Twitter," Speaking About Presenting blog, 3 November 2009 [accessed 3 August 2010] www.speakingaboutpresenting .com; Atkinson, *The Backchannel*, 51, 68–73, 99.

36. SlideShare website [accessed 3 August 2010] www .slideshare.net.

37. Adapted from PechaKucha20x20 website [accessed 4 August 2010] www.pecha-kucha.org; Reynolds, *Presentation Zen: Simple Ideas on Presentation Design and Delivery*, 41.

38. Adapted from Foursquare website [accessed 4 August 2010] http://foursquare.com; Christina Warren, "Foursquare Reaches 100 Millions Checkins," Mashable, 20 July 2010 [accessed 4 August 2010] http://mashable.com.

CHAPTER 13

1. EMC, *100 Job Search Tips from FORTUNE 500 Recruiters*, ebook [accessed 10 August 2010] www.emc.com.

2. Courtland L. Bovée and John V. Thill, *Business in Action*, 5th ed. (Boston: Pearson Prentice Hall, 2011), 241–242.

3. Anne Fisher, "How to Get Hired by a 'Best' Company," *Fortune*, 4 February 2008, 96.

4. Jim Schaper, "Finding Your Future Talent Stars," *BusinessWeek*, 2 July 2010 [accessed 5 August 2010] www.businessweek.com.

5. Eve Tahmincioglu, "Revamping Your Job-Search Strategy," MSNBC.com, 28 February 2010 [accessed 5 August 2010] www.msnbc.com.

6. Tahmincioglu, "Revamping Your Job-Search Strategy."

7. Jessica Dickler, "The Hidden Job Market," CNNMoney.com, 10 June 2009 [accessed 6 August 2010] http:// money.cnn.com.

8. Tara Weiss, "Twitter to Find a Job," *Forbes*, 7 April 2009 [accessed 6 August 2010] www.forbes.com.

9. Miriam Saltpeter, "Using Facebook Groups for Job Hunting," Keppie Careers blog, 13 November 2008 [accessed 6 August 2010] www.keppiecareers.com.

10. Anne Fisher, "Greener Pastures in a New Field," *Fortune*, 26 January 2004, 48.

11. Liz Ryan, "Etiquette for Online Outreach," Yahoo! Hotjobs website [accessed 26 March 2008] http://hotjobs.yahoo.com.

12. Eve Tahmincioglu, "Employers Digging Deep on Prospective Workers," MSNBC.com, 26 October 2009 [accessed 10 August 2010] www.msnbc.com.

13. Career and Employment Services, Danville Area Community College website [accessed 23 March 2008] www.dacc.edu/ career; Career Counseling, Sarah Lawrence College website [accessed 23 March 2008] www.slc.edu/occ/index.php; Cheryl L. Noll, "Collaborating with the Career Planning and Placement Center in the Job-Search Project," *Business Communication Quarterly* 58, no. 3 (1995): 53–55.

14. Fay Hansen, "Recruiters Bear a Bigger Load as Hiring Takes Off," *Workforce Management*, May 2010 [accessed 5 August 2010] www.workforce.com.

15. Randall S. Hansen and Katharine Hansen, "What Résumé Format Is Best for You?" QuintCareers.com [accessed 7 August 2010] www.quintcareers.com.

16. Hansen and Hansen, "What Résumé Format Is Best for You?"

17. Katharine Hansen, "Should You Consider a Functional Format for Your Resume?" QuintCareers.com [accessed 7 August 2010] www.quintcareers.com.

18. Kim Isaacs, "Resume Dilemma: Criminal Record," Monster.com [accessed 23 May 2006] www.monster.com; Kim Isaacs, "Resume Dilemma: Employment Gaps and Job-Hopping," Monster.com [accessed 23 May 2006] www .monster.com; Susan Vaughn, "Answer the Hard Questions Before Asked," *Los Angeles Times*, 29 July 2001, W1–W2.

19. John Steven Niznik, "Landing a Job with a Criminal Record," About.com [accessed 12 December 2006] http://jobsearchtech.about.com.

20. "How to Ferret Out Instances of Résumé Padding and Fraud," *Compensation & Benefits for Law Offices*, June 2006, 1+.

21. "Resume Fraud Gets Slicker and Easier," CNN.com [accessed 11 March 2004] www.cnn.com.

22. Cari Tuna and Keith J. Winstein, "Economy Promises to Fuel Résumé Fraud," *Wall Street Journal*, 17 November 2008 [accessed 8 August 2010] http://online.wsj.com; Lisa Takeuchi Cullen, "Getting Wise to Lies," *Time*, 1 May 2006, 59; "Resume Fraud Gets Slicker and Easier"; Employment Research Services website [accessed 18 March 2004] www .erscheck.com.

23. "How to Ferret Out Instances of Résumé Padding and Fraud."

24. Jacqueline Durett, "Redoing Your Résumé? Leave Off the Lies," *Training*, December 2006, 9; "Employers Turn Their Fire on Untruthful CVs," *Supply Management*, 23 June 2005, 13.

25. Cynthia E. Conn, "Integrating Writing Skills and Ethics Training in Business Communication Pedagogy: A Résumé Case Study Exemplar," *Business Communication Quarterly*, June 2008, 138–151; Marilyn Moats Kennedy, "Don't Get Burned by Résumé Inflation," *Marketing News*, 15 April 2007, 37–38.

26. Rockport Institute, "How to Write a Masterpiece of a Résumé" [accessed 9 August 2010] www.rockportinstitute .com.

27. Lora Morsch, "25 Words That Hurt Your Resume," CNN.com, 20 January 2006 [accessed 20 January 2006] www.cnn.com.

28. Liz Ryan, "The Reengineered Résumé," *BusinessWeek*, 3 December 2007, SC12.

29. Katharine Hansen, "Tapping the Power of Keywords to Enhance Your Resume's Effectiveness," QuintCareers.com [accessed 7 August 2010] www.quintcareers.com.

30. Hansen, "Tapping the Power of Keywords to Enhance Your Resume's Effectiveness."

31. Anthony Balderrama, "Resume Blunders That Will Keep You from Getting Hired," CNN.com, 19 March 2008 [accessed 26 March 2008] www.cnn.com; Michelle Dumas, "5 Resume Writing Myths," Distinctive Documents blog, 17 July 2007 [accessed 26 March 2008] http://blog.distinctiveweb.com; Kim Isaacs, "Resume Dilemma: Recent Graduate," Monster.com [accessed 26 March 2008] http://career-advice.monster.com.

32. Karl L. Smart, "Articulating Skills in the Job Search," *Business Communication Quarterly* 67, no. 2 (June 2004): 198–205.

33. "When to Include Personal Data," ResumeEdge.com [accessed 25 March 2008] www.resumeedge.com.

34. "Résumé Length: What It Should Be and Why It Matters to Recruiters," *HR Focus*, June 2007, 9.

35. Rachel Zupek, "Seven Exceptions to Job Search Rules," CNN.com, 3 September 2008 [accessed 29 December 2008] www.cnn.com.

36. John Hazard, "Resume Tips: No Pictures, Please and No PDFs," Career-Line.com, 26 May 2009 [accessed 10 August 2010] www.career-line.com; "25 Things You Should Never Include on a Resume," HR World website 18 December 2007 [accessed 25 March 2008] www.hrworld.com.

37. John Sullivan, "Résumés: Paper, Please," *Workforce Management*, 22 October 2007, 50; "Video Résumés Offer Both Pros and Cons During Recruiting," *HR Focus*, July 2007, 8.

38. Nancy M. Schullery, Linda Ickes, and Stephen E. Schullery, "Employer Preferences for Résumés and Cover Letters," *Business Communication Quarterly*, June 2009, 163–176.

39. VisualCV website [accessed 10 August 2010] www.visualcv.com.

40. Elizabeth Garone, "Five Mistakes Online Job Hunters Make," *Wall Street Journal*, 28 July 2010 [accessed 10 August 2010] http://online.wsj.com.

41. "10 Reasons Why You Are Not Getting Any Interviews," *Miami Times*, 7–13 November 2007, 6D.

42. "Protect Yourself From Identity Theft When Hunting for a Job Online," *Office Pro*, May 2007, 6.

CHAPTER 14

1. Max Messmer, "Five Common Interview Mistakes and How to Avoid Them," *Strategic Finance*, April 2005, 12–14.

2. Matthew Rothenberg, "Manuscript vs. Machine," The Ladders, 15 December 2009 [accessed 13 August 2010] www.theladders.com; Joann Lublin, "Cover Letters Get You in the Door, So Be Sure Not to Dash Them Off," *Wall Street Journal*, 6 April 2004, B1.

3. Lisa Vaas, "How to Write a Great Cover Letter," The Ladders, 20 November 2009 [accessed 13 August 2010] www.theladders.com.

4. Allison Doyle, "Introduction to Cover Letters," About.com [accessed 13 August 2010] http://jobsearch.about.com.

5. Doyle, "Introduction to Cover Letters"; Vaas, "How to Write a Great Cover Letter"; Toni Logan, "The Perfect Cover Story," *Kinko's Impress* 2 (2000): 32, 34.

6. Lisa Vaas, "How to Follow Up a Résumé Submission," The Ladders, 9 August 2010 [accessed 12 August 2010] www.theladders.com.

7. Alison Doyle, "How to Follow Up After Submitting a Resume," About.com [accessed 13 August 2010] http:// job-search.about.com; Vaas, "How to Follow Up a Résumé Submission."

8. Anne Fisher, "How to Get Hired by a 'Best' Company," *Fortune*, 4 February 2008, 96.

9. Fisher, "How to Get Hired by a 'Best' Company."

10. Sarah E. Needleman, "Speed Interviewing Grows as Skills Shortage Looms; Strategy May Help Lock in Top Picks; Some Drawbacks," *Wall Street Journal*, 6 November 2007, B15.

11. Scott Beagrie, "How to Handle a Telephone Job Interview," *Personnel Today*, 26 June 2007, 29.

12. John Olmstead, "Predict Future Success with Structured Interviews," *Nursing Management*, March 2007, 52–53.

13. Fisher, "How to Get Hired by a 'Best' Company."

14. Erinn R. Johnson, "Pressure Sessions," *Black Enterprise*, October 2007, 72.

15. "What's a Group Interview?" About.com Tech Careers [accessed 5 April 2008] http://jobsearchtech.about.com.

16. Fisher, "How to Get Hired by a 'Best' Company."

17. Katherine Hansen, "Behavioral Job Interviewing Strategies for Job-Seekers," QuintCareers.com [accessed 13 August 2010] www.quintcareers.com.

18. Hansen, "Behavioral Job Interviewing Strategies for Job-Seekers."

19. Chris Pentilla, "Testing the Waters," *Entrepreneur*, January 2004 [accessed 27 May 2006] www.entrepreneur.com; Terry McKenna, "Behavior-Based Interviewing," *National Petroleum News*, January 2004, 16; Nancy K. Austin, "Goodbye Gimmicks," *Incentive*, May 1996, 241.

20. William Poundstone, "Beware the Interview Inquisition," *Harvard Business Review*, May 2003, 18+.

21. Peter Vogt, "Mastering the Phone Interview," Monster.com [accessed 13 December 2006] www.monster.com; Nina Segal, "The Global Interview: Tips for Successful, Unconventional Interview Techniques," Monster.com [accessed 13 December 2006] www.monster.com.

22. Segal, "The Global Interview: Tips for Successful, Unconventional Interview Techniques."

23. Barbara Kiviat, "How Skype Is Changing the Job Interview," *Time*, 20 October 2009 [accessed 13 August 2010] www.time.com.

24. HireVue website [accessed 4 April 2008] www.hirevue.com; in2View website [accessed 4 April 2008] www.in2view.biz; Victoria Reitz, "Interview Without Leaving Home," *Machine Design*, 1 April 2004, 66.

25. Gina Ruiz, "Job Candidate Assessment Tests Go Virtual," *Workforce Management*, January 2008 [accessed 14 August 2010] www.workforce.com; Connie Winkler, "Job Tryouts Go Virtual," *HR Magazine*, September 2006, 131–134.

26. Jonathan Katz, "Rethinking Drug Testing," *Industry Week*, March 2010, 16–18; Ashley Shadday, "Assessments 101: An Introduction to Candidate Testing," *Workforce Management*, January 2010 [accessed 14 August 2010] www.workforce.com; Dino di Mattia, "Testing Methods and Effectiveness of Tests," *Supervision*, August 2005, 4–5; David

W. Arnold and John W. Jones, "Who the Devil's Applying Now?" *Security Management*, March 2002, 85–88; Matthew J. Heller, "Digging Deeper," *Workforce Management*, 3 March 2008, 35–39.

27. Frederick P. Morgeson, Michael A. Campion, Robert L. Dipboye, John R. Hollenbeck, Kevin Murphy, and Neil Schmitt, "Are We Getting Fooled Again? Coming to Terms with Limitations in the Use of Personality Tests in Personnel Selection," *Personnel Psychology* 60, no. 4 (Winter 2007): 1029–1049.

28. Austin, "Goodbye Gimmicks."

29. Rachel Zupek, "How to Answer 10 Tough Interview Questions," CNN.com, 4 march 2009 [accessed 13 August 2010] www.cnn.com; Barbara Safani, "How to Answer Tough Interview Questions Authentically," The Ladders, 5 December 2009 [accessed 13 August 2010] www.theladders.com.

30. Nick Corcodilos, "How to Answer a Misguided Interview Question," *Seattle Times*, 30 March 2008 [accessed 5 April 2008] www.seattletimes.com.

31. Katherine Spencer Lee, "Tackling Tough Interview Questions," *Certification Magazine*, May 2005, 35.

32. Scott Ginsberg, "10 Good Ways to 'Tell Me About Yourself,'" The Ladders, 26 June 2010 [accessed 13 August 2010] www.theladders.com.

33. InterviewUp website [accessed 13 August 2010] www.interviewup.com.

34. Joe Turner, "An Interview Strategy: Telling Stories," Yahoo! HotJobs [accessed 5 April 2008] http://hotjobs.yahoo.com.

35. "A Word of Caution for Chatty Job Candidates," *Public Relations Tactics*, January 2008, 4.

36. Randall S. Hansen, "When Job-Hunting: Dress for Success," QuintCareers.com [accessed 5 April 2008] www.quintcareers.com; Alison Doyle, "Dressing for Success," About.com [accessed 5 April 2008] http://jobsearch.about.com.

37. William S. Frank, "Job Interview: Pre-Flight Checklist," *The Career Advisor* [accessed 28 September 2005] http:// career-planning.about.com.

38. T. Shawn Taylor, "Most Managers Have No Idea How to Hire the Right Person for the Job," *Chicago Tribune*, 23 July 2002 [accessed 29 September 2005] www.ebsco.com.

39. "10 Minutes to Impress," *Journal of Accountancy*, July 2007, 13.

40. Steven Mitchell Sack, "The Working Woman's Legal Survival Guide: Testing," FindLaw.com [accessed 22 February 2004] www.findlaw.com.

41. Todd Anten, "How to Handle Illegal Interview Questions," Yahoo! HotJobs [accessed 7 August 2009] http://hotjobs.yahoo.com.

42. "Negotiating Salary: An Introduction," *InformationWeek* online [accessed 22 February 2004] www.informationweek.com.

43. "Negotiating Salary: An Introduction."

44. Lisa Vaas, "Resume, Meet Technology: Making Your Resume Format Machine-Friendly," The Ladders [accessed 13 August 2010] www.theladders.com.

45. Joan S. Lublin, "Notes to Interviewers Should Go Beyond a Simple Thank You," *Wall Street Journal*, 5 February 2008, B1.

46. Adapted from Google Earth website [accessed 15 August 2010] http://earth.google.com.

APPENDIX A

1. Mary A. De Vries, *Internationally Yours* (Boston: Houghton Mifflin, 1194), 9.

2. Patricia A. Dreyfus, "Paper That's Letter Perfect," *Money*, May 1985, 184.

3. Linda Driskill, *Business and Managerial Communication: New Perspectives* (Orlando, Fla.: Harcourt Brace Jovanovich, 1992), 470.

4. Lennie Copeland and Lewis Griggs, *Going International: How to Make Friends and Deal Effectively in the Global Marketplace*, 2d ed. (New York: Random House, 1985), 24–27.

5. De Vries, *Internationally Yours*, 8.

6. U.S. Postal Service, *International Mail Manual*, Issue 34, 14 May 2007 [accessed 23 October 2007] www.usps.gov.

Acknowledgments

(Unit 1) Marco Cappalunga, Shutterstock; (Chapter 1 Opener) AP Wide World Photos; (Figure 1.2) Used with permission of FreshBooks; (Chapter 1: Photo Essay, pp. 48–51) Cranial Tap, Inc.; EMC Documentation; Getty Images–Digital Vision; Ethan Hill Photography; Belkin International, Inc.; WordPress, Automatic Inc.; InstantPresenter; Ethan Hill Photography; Connie French, Innocentive; Biznik, Inc.; del.icio.us/Ross_Pennick; info@touchgraph.com; Masterfile Corporation; Autodesk Inc.; CustomerReach; Segway, Inc.; Christine Winter, Xerox; Patagonia Twitter; AP Wide World Photos; (Chapter 2 Opener) Rosen Law Firm; (Figure 2.1) Used with permission of Wikia; Inc.; (Figure 2.4) Peter Wynn Thompson/The New York Times, Redux Pictures. (Figure 2.5) Courtesy of Cranial Tap; (Table 2.2) Madelyn Burley-Allen, *Listening: The Forgotten Skill* (New York: Wiley, 1995), 70–71, 119–120; Judi Brownell, *Listening: Attitudes, Principles, and Skills* (Boston: Allyn and Bacon, 2002), 3, 9, 83, 89, 125; Larry Barker and Kittie Watson, *Listen Up* (New York: St. Martin's Press, 2000), 8, 9, 64; (Table 2.3) Alf Nucifora, "Voice Mail Demands Good Etiquette from Both Sides," *Puget Sound Business Journal*, 5–11 September 2003, 24; Ruth Davidhizar and Ruth Shearer, "The Effective Voice Mail Message," *Hospital Material Management Quarterly*, 45–49; "How to Get the Most Out of Voice Mail," *The CPA Journal*, February 2000, 11; Jo Ind, "Hanging on the Telephone," *Birmingham Post*, 28 July 1999, PS10; Larry Barker and Kittie Watson, *Listen Up* (New York: St. Martin's Press, 2000), 64–65; Lin Walker, *Telephone Techniques* (New York: AMACOM, 1998), 46–47; Dorothy Neal, *Telephone Techniques*, 2d ed. (New York: Glencoe McGraw-Hill, 1998), 31; Jeannie Davis, *Beyond "Hello"* (Aurora, Col.: Now Hear This, Inc., 2000), 2–3; "Ten Steps to Caller-Friendly Voice Mail," *Managing Office Technology*, January 1995, 25; Rhonda Finniss, "Voice Mail: Tips for a Positive Impression," *Administrative Assistant's Update*, August 2001, 5; (Unit 2) Asia Images Group, Getty Images, Inc. Asia Images Group—Royalty Free; (Chapter 3 Opener) Amy Surducki, Surdacki Photo Projects (Figure 3.1) Adapted from Kevin J. Harty and John Keenan, *Writing for Business and Industry: Process and Product* (New York: Macmillan Publishing Company, 1987), 3–4; Richard Hatch, *Business Writing* (Chicago, Ill.: Science Research Associates, 1983), 88–89; Richard Hatch, *Business Communication Theory and Technique* (Chicago, Ill.: Science Research Associates, 1983), 74–75; Center for Humanities, *Writing as a Process: A Step-by-Step Guide, Four Filmstrips and Cassettes* (Mount Kisco, N.Y.: Center for Humanities, 1987); Michael L. Keene, *Effective Professional Writing* (New York: D. C. Heath, 1987), 28–34; (Figure 3.4) Used with permission of World Voyager Vacations. (Figure 3.8) Courtesy of Patagonia, Inc.; (Chapter 4 Opener) Getty Images Editorial; (Chapter 5 Opener) Max Messmer, Chairman and CEO, Robert Half International; (Figure 5.4) Photo by Ryan Lackey. Adobe product screen shot(s) reprinted with permission from Adobe Systems Incorporated; (Unit 3) Stockbyte, Getty Images, Inc.—Stockbyte Royalty Free; (Chapter 6 Opener) Southwest Airlines Co; (Figure 6.1)

©2010 Linden Research, Inc.; (Figure 6.2) Red Bull Communications; (Figure 6.5) Used with permission of chick-downtown.com; (Figure 6.6) Courtesy of Patagonia, Inc.; (Table 6.1) Adapted from Christopher Carfi and Leif Chastaine, "Social Networking for Businesses & Organizations," white paper, Cerado website [accessed 13 August 2008] www.cerado.com; Anusorn Kansap, "Social Networking," PowerPoint presentation, Silpakorn University [accessed 14 August 2008] http://real-timeupdates.com; "Social Network Websites: Best Practices from Leading Services," white paper, 28 November 2007, FaberNovel Consulting [accessed 14 August 2008] www.fabernovel.com; (Table 6.3) Robert Scoble and Shel Israel, *Naked Conversations* (Hoboken, N.J.: John Wiley & Sons, 2006), 78–81, 190–194; Paul McFedries, *The Complete Idiot's Guide to Creating a Web Page & Blog*, 6th ed. (New York: Alpha, 2004), 206–208; 272–276; Shel Holtz and Ted Demopoulos, *Blogging for Business* (Chicago: Kaplan, 2006), 54–59, 113–114; Denise Wakeman, "Top 10 Blog Writing Tips," Blogarooni.com [accessed 1 February 2006] www.blogarooni.com; Dennis A. Mahoney, "How to Write a Better Weblog," 22 February 2002, A List Apart [accessed 1 February 2006] www.alistapart.com. (Chapter 6: Social Media, pp. 160–161) Text: Adapted from Andrew Lippert, Chief Technology Officer, Biznik, personal communication, 29 June 2010; Specialized Bicycle Components website [accessed 21 July 2010] www.specialized.com; Specialized Riders Club website [accessed 21 July 2010] www.specializedriders.com; Steven Outing, "Enabling the Social Company," white paper, September 2007 [accessed 14 September 2008] www.enthusiastgroup.com; Get Satisfaction pages of Mint.com and Zappos [accessed 22 July 2010] http://getsatisfaction.com; Experts Exchange [accessed 22 July 2010] www.experts-exchange.com; Lie-Nielsen Toolworks YouTube Channel [accessed 22 July 2010] www.youtube.com/user/lienielsen; Gil Carlson, *Social Media Marketing Results* ebook; My Starbucks Idea website [accessed 22 July 2010] http://mystarbucksidea.force.com. Photos: ©2010 Biznik, Inc. Used with permission of Segway, Inc.; Used with permission of Quizzle, www.quizzle.com; ©2010 Quizzle LLC, All rights reserved. Used with permission of Lie-Nielsen Toolworks, Inc.; Used with permission of Kelly Services, Inc.; (Chapter 7 Opener) AP Wide World Photos. (Figure 7.1) Copyright © 2008 Google Inc. All rights reserved; (Figure 7.6) Courtesy Herman Miller; (Chapter 8 Opener) Used with permission of Freshbooks; (Figure 8.2) Used with permission of Spherion Corporation; (Chapter 9 Opener) www.copyblogger.com/copywriter; (Figure 9.3) BlackBerry®, RIM®, Research in Motion®, SureType®, SurePress™, and related trademarks, names, and logos are the property of Research in Motion Limited and are registered and/or used in the U.S. and countries around the world; (Figure 9.4) Used with permission of R.C. Bigelow, Inc.; (Figure 9.5) Courtesy of Conversation Marketing, http://www.conversationmarketing.com; (Table 9.1) Adapted from Saundra K. Ciccarelli and Glenn E. Meyer, *Psychology* (Upper Saddle

River, N.J.: Prentice Hall, 2006), 336–346; Courtland L. Bovée, John V. Thill, and Michael H. Mescon, *Excellence in Business*, 3rd ed. (Upper Saddle River, N.J.: Prentice Hall, 2006), 327–333; Abraham H. Maslow, "A Theory of Human Motivation," *Psychological Review* 50 (1943): 370–396; (Table 9.2) Adapted in part from "What Is the HYBRID HEAT Dual Fuel System by Carrier?" Carrier website [accessed 5 November 2008] www .residential.carrier.com; (Unit 4) Image Source, Getty Images Inc.— Image Source Royalty Free; (Chapter 10 Opener) Robert Seale, Tellabs; (Figure 10.6) Used with permission of the American Coatings Association, Inc.; (Chapter 11 Opener) Robert Seale, Tellabs; (Figure 11.2) Alan Gough/Alan Gough Photography; (Figure 11.3) Reprint Courtesy of International Business Machines Corporation, © International Business Machines Corporation; (Figure 11.10a) Used with permission of TouchGraph; (Figure 11.10b) Used with permission of Barry Graubart. (Figure 11.10d) Copyright 2005–2009 Mozilla. All Rights Reserved. All rights in the names, trademarks, and logos of the Mozilla Foundation, including without limitation, Firefox®, as well as the Firefox logo are owned exclusively by the Mozilla Foundation; (Chapter 12 Opener) Getty Images/Thinkstock (Table 12.2) Adapted from Claudyne Wilder and David Fine, *Point, Click & Wow* (San Francisco: Jossey-Bass Pfeiffer, 1996), 63, 527; (Unit 5) Matt Carr, Getty Images; (Chapter 13 Opener) Stephen Coburn/Shutterstock; (Figure 13.6) VisualCV, Reinaldo; (Table 13.1) TweetMyJob.com [accessed 10 August 2010] http://tweetmyjob.com; The Riley Guide [accessed 10 August 2010] www.rileyguide.com; SimplyHired website [accessed 10 August 2010] www.simply-hired.com; Indeed website [accessed 10 August 2010] www .indeed.com; CollegeRecruiter .com [accessed 10 August 2010] www.collegerecruiter.com; Jobster website [accessed 10 August 2010] www.jobster.com; InternshipPrograms.com [accessed 10 August 2010] http://internshipprograms.com; (Chapter 14 Opener) Leo Babauta, blogger, journalist, and author of *The Power of Less*; (Figure 14.3) Used with permission of Working Worlds. (Figure 14.4) Job Task Simulations Shaker Consulting Group at www.shakercg.com/clients-and-case-studies/case-studies. (Table 14.3) Adapted from Alison Doyle, "Interview Questions and Answers," About.com [accessed 14 August 2010] http://jobsearch.about.com; InterviewUp website [accessed 14 August 2010] www.interviewup.com; *The Northwestern Endicott Report* (Evanston, Ill.: Northwestern University Placement Center); (Figure 14.5) courtesy of Perfect Interview.com/contexxa corporation; (Figure 14.6) Jon Feingersh/Zefa; (Table 14.4) Adapted from Joe Conklin, "Turning the Tables: Six Questions to Ask Your Interviewer," *Quality Progress*, November 2007, 55; Andrea N. Browne, "Keeping the Momentum at the Interview; Ask Questions, Do Your Research, and Be a Team Player," *Washington Post*, 29 July 2007, K1; Marilyn Sherman, "Questions R Us: What to Ask at a Job Interview," *Career World*, January 2004, 20; H. Lee Rust, *Job Search: The Complete Manual for Jobseekers* (New York: American Management Association, 1979), 56. (Table 14.5) Adapted from *The Northwestern Endicott Report* (Evanston, Ill.: Northwestern University Placement Center); (Table 14.6) Adapted from Deanna G. Kucler, "Interview Questions: Legal or Illegal?" *Workforce Management* [accessed 14 August 2010] www.workforce.com; "Illegal Interview Questions," *USA Today*, 29 January 2001 [accessed 28 September 2005] www.usatoday.com; "Dangerous Questions," *Nation's Business*, May 1999, 22; (Figure A.9) Used with permission of Carnival Corporation.

Index